CIVIL LITIGATION

FOURTH EDITION

The West Legal Studies Series

Your options keep growing with West Legal Studies

Each year our list continues to offer you more options for every area of the law to meet your course or on-the-job reference requirements. We now have over 140 titles from which to choose in the following areas:

Accounting and Financials for the Law Office	Family Law
Administrative Law	Intellectual Property
Alternative Dispute Resolution	Interviewing and Investigation
Bankruptcy	Introduction to Law
Business Organizations/Corporations	Introduction to Paralegalism
Careers and Employment	Law Office Management
Civil Litigation and Procedure	Law Office Procedures
CLA Exam Preparation	Legal Nurse Consulting
Computer Applications in the Law Office	Legal Research, Writing, and Analysis
Contract Law	Legal Terminology
Court Reporting	Paralegal Internships
Criminal Law and Procedure	Product Liability
Document Preparation	Real Estate Law
Elder Law	Reference Materials
Employment Law	Social Security
Environmental Law	Sports Law
Ethics	Torts and Personal Injury Law
Evidence Law	Wills, Trusts, and Estate Administration

You will find unparalleled, practical support

Each book is augmented by instructor and student supplements to ensure the best learning experience possible. We also offer custom publishing and other benefits such as West's Student Achievement Award. In addition, our sales representatives are ready to provide you with dependable service.

We want to hear from you

Our best contributions for improving the quality of our books and instructional materials is feedback from the people who use them. If you have a question, concern, or observation about any of our materials, or you have a product proposal or manuscript, we want to hear from you. Please contact your local representative or write us at the following address:

West Legal Studies, 5 Maxwell Drive, Clifton Park, NY 12065-2919

For additional information point your browser at

www.westlegalstudies.com

THOMSON

DELMAR LEARNING

CIVIL LITIGATION

FOURTH EDITION

Peggy N. Kerley
Joanne Banker Hames
Paul A. Sukys

THOMSON
DELMAR LEARNING

Australia Canada Mexico Singapore Spain United Kingdom United States

THOMSON

™

DELMAR LEARNING

Civil Litigation, Fourth Edition
by Peggy N. Kerley, Joanne Banker Hames, Paul A. Sukys

Vice President, Career Education Strategic Busines Unit: Dawn Gerrain	**Director of Production:** Wendy A. Troeger	**Director of Marketing:** Wendy E. Mapstone
Director of Editorial: Sherry Gomoll	**Production Manager:** Carolyn Miller	**Cover Design:** Joe Villanova
Senior Developmental Editor: Melissa Riveglia	**Production Editor:** Matthew J. Williams	

For permission to use material from this text or product, contact us by
Tel   (800) 730-2214
Fax   (800) 730-2215
www.thomsonrights.com

Library of Congress Cataloging-in-Publication Data
Kerley, Peggy N.
   Civil litigation / Peggy N. Kerley, Joanne Banker Hames, Paul A. Sukys.—4th ed.
      p.   cm.
   Includes index.
   ISBN 1-4018-4829-X
   1. Civil procedure—United States. 2. Legal assistants—United States—Handbooks, manuals, etc. I. Hames, Joanne Banker. II. Sukys, Paul. III. Title.

   KF8841.K47 2004
   347.73'5—dc22   2004049386

NOTICE TO THE READER

Publisher does not warrant or guarantee any of the products described herein or perform any independent analysis in connection with any of the product information contained herein. Publisher does not assume, and expressly disclaims, any obligation to obtain and include information other than that provided to it by the manufacturer.

The reader is notified that this text is an educational tool, not a practice book. Since the law is in constant change, no rule or statement of law in this book should be relied upon for any service to any client. The reader should always refer to standard legal sources for the current rule or law. If legal advice or other expert assistance is required, the services of the appropriate professional should be sought.

The Publisher makes no representation or warranties of any kind, including but not limited to, the warranties of fitness for particular purpose or merchantability, nor are any such representations implied with respect to the material set forth herein, and the publisher takes no responsibility with respect to such material. The publisher shall not be liable for any special, consequential, or exemplary damages resulting, in whole or part, from the readers use of, or reliance upon, this material.

CONTENTS

**PART III
DISCOVERY**

**PART IV
PRETRIAL, TRIAL, AND POSTTRIAL**

PREFACE

The paralegal profession remains one of the fastest growing professions in the United States. One reason for the phenomenal growth of this relatively young profession is the unique role that the paralegal plays within the legal system. The paralegal bridges the gap between the attorney and the legal secretary by bringing to the law office a body of knowledge and a set of skills developed specifically for the day-to-day practical realities of the practice of law.

The Reason for the Development of *Civil Litigation*

Paralegal education requires a skillful blend of the principles of the law with its practical application. Nowhere in the law is that skillful blend of theory and practice more imperative than in the study of litigation. The litigation paralegal meets new and different challenges each day on the job. These daily challenges mean that, from the very first hour on the job, the paralegal must be prepared to understand not only what must be done in a specific situation but also why it must be done. The paralegal must also know the most efficient, the most effective, and the most economical way to accomplish the task at hand. In recent years this often involves the use of technology. Familiarity with the many uses of technology, including the Internet, is essential to a litigation paralegal. *Civil Litigation* was planned and written with these specific goals in mind.

While paralegal educators have recognized the requirements of proper paralegal training, many of the available textbooks have not satisfied those requirements, either concentrating too heavily on legal theory, or containing one form after another with little or no discussion of the relevant law. Too many times paralegal instructors have had to supplement texts by creating their own practical assignments or by filling in all the legal blanks. This textbook combines theory and practice and includes several practical assignments for students. Also, although this is not a computer text, each chapter addresses the use of technology, including the Internet, in litigation.

Additional factors also prompted our development of this text. Civil litigation instructors know that one of the most difficult tasks is covering both federal and state law and doing it in a way that does not confuse students. Although the text emphasizes federal litigation practice and forms, it also incorporates common state practice and forms. Furthermore, several individual state supplements for this text have been prepared and are available for students.

To successfully acquaint the fledgling paralegal student with this intricate mix of legal theory and practical legal skills, we have remained attuned to the fact that, for many students, civil litigation will be their first legal studies course. Consequently, we have been careful to present the study of litigation in a straightforward, yet lively, fashion that should not only inform but also challenge both student and instructor. All legal terms are in bold type and defined in the text, a necessity for beginning paralegal students. We also begin each chapter with a hypothetical case that is fully developed as the chapter unfolds. Our objective in doing this is to show students that the law deals not only with books and documents but also with people—usually people in trouble, often people who have been hurt or unfairly treated and who have turned to the law and to legal professionals for help. The hypothetical cases, found in the chapter-opening case commentaries, deal with a variety of factual and legal problems illustrating the breadth of civil litigation in the legal system. In addition, so that students can follow the progression of a single case, we have included assignments in each chapter that refer back to the case introduced in the Chapter 1 commentary. It is our belief that this approach will give a realistic and energetic flavor to the study of litigation.

The Organization of *Civil Litigation*

For clarity and ease of understanding, we have chosen to use chronological order throughout the text. The book has been divided into four parts representing the four major stages in the litigation process. In Part I we introduce the student to the role of the paralegal in the litigation process. The two chapters in this section also provide an overview of the court system and the litigation process, along with a discussion of the concepts of jurisdiction and venue.

In Part II we begin the study of litigation in earnest by walking the student through the opening stages of a lawsuit. Naturally, this means concentrating on the preliminary legal and practical concerns that must be taken into consideration at the onset of a lawsuit. Consequently, these early chapters focus on such things as interviewing and investigation skills, the role of evidence in litigation, the writing and filing of initial and responsive pleadings, and an understanding of motion practice. To accomplish our objective of making the text a practical guide for students, we have explained the requirements for pleadings and motions found in the Federal Rules of Civil Procedure and have included many examples and sample documents. We have also provided detailed explanations and guidelines for the drafting of various legal documents.

Following our chronological plan, Part III explores the discovery process. Because the paralegal has an extensive role in discovery, we have devoted one of the six chapters in this section to an overview of the process, including a lengthy discussion of the most recent changes to the Federal Rules of Civil Procedure relating to discovery. The remaining five chapters discuss specific discovery techniques. Separate chapters cover depositions, interrogatories, requests for physical and mental examinations, requests for the production of documents, and requests for admissions. Again, . . . in keeping with our objective of providing students with a practical guide, we have explained in great detail the day-to-day role of the paralegal during each stage of the discovery process. These chapters also combine theory with practice, covering the discovery rules in the Federal Rules of Civil Procedure. We have also included an extensive array of sample documents, including requests for physical and mental examinations, requests for the production of documents, and requests for admissions. As a supplement to Part III, Appendix A provides a sample deposition based on the case scenario that serves as the basis for the examples and samples in Chapter 9.

Part IV provides the student with an in-depth view of the final stages in the litigation process. We have devoted one chapter to pretrial settlements, dismissals, and alternative dispute resolution; one to the trial itself; and one to posttrial procedures. Again in keeping with our goal of making *Civil Litigation* a practical guide, we have provided students with a wide variety of suggestions for making the trial process run as smoothly as possible. Some of these tips include how to prepare a trial notebook, how to arrange for accommodations during the trial, how to contact court personnel, how to prepare a jury profile, how to use shadow juries, and how to prepare a trial box, among many others. We have also been careful to include a wide variety of practical illustrations and sample documents, including releases and dismissals, a settlement summary, a settlement letter, a detailed settlement agreement, a notice of appeal, and a motion for enlargement of time, among others. Sample letters, charts, and diagrams are also included, as are appropriate references to the Federal Rules of Civil Procedure and the Federal Rules of Appellate Procedure.

Chapter Organization

Each chapter follows the same organizational pattern. Chapters begin with a case commentary, establishing a realistic setting for the material to be covered in the chapter. This is followed by a statement of the chapter objectives. The student immediately identifies the learning goals of the specific chapter. Text material is presented along with multiple charts, diagrams, and sample forms. Where applicable, reference is made to the facts described in the commentary. All legal terms are bold and defined. Special features in each chapter address the application of technology and the Internet to litigation practice. Each chapter ends with a chapter summary, questions for review, chapter exercises, and a major chapter project. At the end of each chapter is an exercise relating to the fictional *Bennet* case which is introduced in Chapter 1.

Teaching and Learning Features

The practical nature of *Civil Litigation* makes it an ideal text for use in and beyond the classroom. Because of its many forms, letters, memos, charts, and diagrams, it can easily serve as a reference manual for the paralegal in the litigation section of a law firm. Nevertheless, the primary objective of the book is to serve as a textbook for a basic civil litigation course for paralegal students. Consequently, we have included several important features to enhance this objective and to make the book the best in its market. Those features include:

■ case commentaries at the beginning of each chapter that illustrate the varied nature of civil litigation, demonstrate the practical application of the matters contained within the chapter, and give a realistic color to the study of litigation
■ an outline at the beginning of each chapter pointing out the major topics to be covered in the chapter
■ a list of learning objectives at the beginning of each chapter to provide the student with a sense of direction

- a set of review questions at the end of each chapter to provide students with a sense of continuity with the learning objectives and to guarantee that students understand the chapter material
- definitions of all legal terms in the chapter material (all terms are bold), in a running glossary and in a full glossary at the end of the text
- chapter exercises at the end of each chapter that include questions for analysis and practical assignments, including those that require students to investigate specific state statutes and apply them to the topics covered in the chapter
- a chapter project that offers a chance for the student to undertake a major paralegal task related to the matter in the chapter, including such activities as writing letters and memos, drafting pleadings, motions, and affidavits, and preparing discovery devices
- a case assignment in each chapter based on the same case to give students the opportunity to work one case from start to finish
- a computerized law firm feature in each chapter that relates the effective use of technology to the material in the chapter
- Finding It On the Internet, a feature in each chapter that describes Internet applications to the material in the chapter and includes several Web sites as well as Internet assignments
- an appendix containing the transcript of a deposition.
- an appendix containing research material and forms to enable students to complete the case assignments based on the Chapter 1 hypothetical case
- state-specific supplements for Florida, New York, Texas, California, Ohio, and Pennsylvania that are downloadable through the book's Web page at <http://www.westlegalstudies.com> at no cost.

The Fourth Edition of Civil Litigation

When we first wrote this text our basic plan was to present the litigation process in a chronological order, emphasizing the practical aspects of litigation and the role of the paralegal in the process. Comments from instructors and students who have used the book convince us that this is the correct approach. However, nothing in the law, including litigation, remains static. Of course, there have been changes in the law. But more importantly, the development and use of technology, including the Internet, have resulted in tremendous changes in the way that litigation is practiced. The increased utilization of paralegals in law firms, especially in the area of litigation, has also affected litigation practice. Attorneys have come to recognize the full potential of paralegals and are now giving them more and more responsibility. We have revised this text with these thoughts in mind. Accordingly, the following matters have been revised.

- Where applicable, legal concepts have been updated to reflect revisions of the United States Code and Federal Rules.

- Each chapter contains an updated feature illustrating the ways that technology plays a role in the litigation process.
- Each chapter contains Internet sites to allow students to avail themselves of the wealth of information related to litigation. Of primary importance are sites containing the United States Code, the Federal Rules of Civil Procedure, and the Federal Rules of Evidence. Accessing these rules through the Internet assures that students will be reading the latest version of the law, something that would not happen if the rules were included as an appendix to the text.
- Each chapter contains an Internet assignment.
- Each chapter contains questions for analysis in order to more completely address the use and development of analytic skills by paralegals.
- Each chapter contains a list of Terms to Remember at the end of the chapter so that students can review their comprehension of terminology.
- More forms, charts, and checklists have been added to the text.
- Treatment of certain substantive subjects such as jurisdiction and electronic filing have been revised.

How to Use This Text

This text was designed to follow the litigation process from beginning to end. Following this pattern, we believe, gives the student a realistic and complete picture of the litigation process and the role of the paralegal at the various stages of litigation. We do offer some suggestions about the various chapter features.

- Students can be required to answer the questions for review in writing. Alternatively, they can be used for discussion in class either with the entire class or in small groups.
- The chapter exercises provide opportunities for students to explore state law and to engage in factual analysis. Students can, of course, be assigned all of the exercises. Alternatively, with exercises requiring outside research, small groups in the class can each be assigned a different exercise and asked to report their findings to the class. The exercises requiring analysis can be assigned for writing or for discussion.
- The chapter project provides an important opportunity for students to engage in realistic litigation tasks. For the most part, the projects at the end of each chapter relate to the case commentary. Students are given the experience of working on different cases, just as litigation paralegals commonly do. Additionally students can work on one case from start to finish by completing the assignments found at the end of each chapter relating to the *Bennett* case.
- Internet access gives students the opportunity to read actual code sections (both federal and state) and case law. Relevant Web sites are included in the chapters.
- The chapters in the state-specific supplements relate state law to the material in the corresponding chapter in the text. In those states for which there is a state-specific supplemental, reading assignments should include both the text and the corresponding chapter in the supplement.

Supplements to the Textbook

State-Specific Supplements

One of the features that makes *Civil Litigation* the most innovative and unique textbook of its kind on the market today is the availability of state-specific supplements. These supplements are available on line and can be downloaded. For uniformity and consistency, we wrote *Civil Litigation* with the Federal Rules of Civil Procedure and the Federal Rules of Appellate Procedure in mind. Whenever possible, we make appropriate references to possible differences in state and local procedures. Moreover, as noted earlier, we provide the exercises at the end of each chapter to encourage instructors to include state and local procedural variations. Often, however, this is not enough. Many instructors, ourselves included, would like a textbook written specifically with our home states in mind. We believe that our state-specific pocket-part supplements provide the next-best alternative. We chose several key states, including California, Florida, New York, Ohio, Pennsylvania, and Texas, and developed supplements that present the procedural variations in the courts of each of these states. The supplements are intended to familiarize the students with the rules of procedure in each of these states. Instructors may wish to use the supplement of their own state, if that is possible, or to choose the supplement of the state whose rules are similar to the rules in their home state. Supplements can be found on this book's Web page at <http://www.westlegalstudies.com> at no cost.

Instructor's Manual

Because each of us has been deeply involved in legal education for many years, we recognize the crucial need for a well-written and highly accurate instructor's manual. The manual that we have developed for *Civil Litigation* provides the instructor with an excellent supplemental for the text. It provides a key to all end-of-chapter questions, activities, and projects found in the book. Whenever possible, we have provided the complete text for any memos, letters, pleadings, and the like that are called for by the chapter projects. If, because of the individualized nature of the project, we could not provide the complete text, then we have included guidelines to show the instructor what to look for in the evaluation of each student's work. The Instructor's Manual includes a Test Bank and transparency masters.

Online Companion

Visit the Student Center at <www.westlegalstudies.com> for access to additional online study materials. Written by the authors of the text, the supplemental material includes Study Tips and Key Points, chapter outlines, Web links, chapter quizzes, and learning exercises.

Web Page

Come visit this book's Web page at <http://www.westlegalstudies.com> where you will find sample materials, hotlinks, state-specific materials for Florida, New York, Texas, California, Ohio, and Pennsylvania, and updates to this text.

Westlaw®

West's online computerized legal research system offers students hands-on experience with a system commonly used in law offices. Qualified adopters can receive 10 free hours of WESTLAW®. WESTLAW® can be accessed with Macintosh, IBM, and PC compatibles. A modem is required.

Supplemental Teaching Materials

■ **Survival Guide for Paralegal Students,** a pamphlet by Kathleen Mercer Reed and Bradene Moore covers practical and basic information to help students make the most of their paralegal courses. Topics covered include choosing courses of study and note-taking skills.

■ **West's Paralegal Video Library**—West Legal Studies is pleased to offer the following videos at no charge to qualified adopters:

　■ *The Drama of the Law II: Paralegal Issues Video*
　　ISBN: 0-314-07088-5

　■ *The Making of a Case Video*
　　ISBN: 0-314-07300-0

　■ *ABA Mock Trial Video-Product Liability*
　　ISBN: 0-314-07342-6

　■ *Arguments to the United States Supreme Court Video*
　　ISBN: 0-314-07070-2

Please note the Internet resources are of a time-sensitive nature and URL addresses may often change or be deleted.

Contact us at westlegalstudies@delmar.com

ACKNOWLEDGMENTS

Civil Litigation is the result of the planning and input of many individuals and entities. With grateful appreciation, we would like to acknowledge and give our thanks to the editors of West Legal Studies; to Bob Nirkind, who supported the authors in the original ideas for the book; to the Southeastern Paralegal Institute, which initially introduced Peggy Kerley to the exciting field of paralegal textbook publishing; to our former and present students for the positive comments about the text. To Mark Hames, for his support, encouragement and especially his assistance with technology questions and issues; to Terry Ellis, Director of the Administration of Justice program at DeAnza College for his support and flexibility and to all of the paralegal students at DeAnza College who have helped in the development of this fourth edition; to Addie Tackett, director of the Radiologic Technology Department of North Central State College, and Dale Maurer, a registered radiologic technologist, who provided the medical details for the sample deposition; to Jane Skaluba, staff attorney for the Richland County Legal Services Department in Mansfield, Ohio, for her help in ensuring the accuracy of the text; to L. Dan Richards, John Falls, and Diane Hipsher of North Central State College for their support of the paralegal program at the college; to the spring quarter 1991 advanced business law students at North Central State College for their enthusiastic willingness to test several of the cases in the text; to John and Louise Sukys, Jennifer Ann Sukys, and Susan Sukys for their patient understanding and loyal encouragement; and to the many paralegal students whose enthusiasm and intelligence continually motivate us. The authors gratefully acknowledge the encouragement and support and extend their sincere appreciation to these individuals and entities.

In addition, we acknowledge the contributions of the following reviewers, whose suggestions and insights have helped us enormously:

Stacey Barone
Hofstra University
Hempstead, New York

Ana Otero
Center for Advanced Legal Studies
Houston, Texas

Joellyn Champagne
Center for Advanced Legal Studies
Houston, Texas

Jill Bush Raines
Oklahoma University College of Law
Norman, Oklahoma

Luci Hoover
Rockford Business College
Rockford, Illinois

Brian Wilson
Springfield College
Springfield, Missouri

Peggy Kerley
Joanne Hames
Paul Sukys

ABOUT THE AUTHORS

Peggy N. Kerley is a litigation paralegal, working with the law firm of Weil, Gotshal & Manges, and a former paralegal instructor at Southeastern Paralegal Institute, in Dallas, Texas. She has more than 40 years of legal experience. Ms. Kerley received her undergraduate degree in political economy from the University of Texas at Dallas, and her paralegal certificate from the University of Oklahoma. She is also the author of another paralegal text, *Employment Law for the Paralegal.*

Joanne Banker Hames is currently an instructor for and the coordinator of the paralegal program at DeAnza Community College, located in Cupertino, California. She earned her J. D. degree from Santa Clara University School of Law and was admitted to the California Bar in January 1972. She has been an active member since that time. For several years Ms. Hames was employed as an attorney in a busy litigation law firm. During that time she was involved in all aspects of civil litigation, including pretrial preparation, jury trials, and appeals. For the past several years, she has been involved primarily in paralegal education, teaching at DeAnza Community College and previously at Santa Clara University Paralegal Institute. Civil litigation is among the classes she has taught. She is also a co-author of two other paralegal texts, *Introduction to Law,* and *Legal Research, Analysis and Writing, an Integrated Approach.*

Paul A. Sukys is a professor of law and legal studies at North Central State College in Mansfield, Ohio. He is co-author of *Understanding Business and Personal Law* and *Business Law with UCC Applications.* Mr. Sukys is also a charter member of the advisory committee for the paralegal program at North Central State College, and was instrumental in designing the curriculum for that program. He received his bachelor's and master's degrees from John Carroll University in Cleveland. Mr. Sukys received his law degree from Cleveland State University. In the past he has served as an adjunct professor at Cuyahoga Community College in Cleveland. He is a member of the Ohio Bar.

PART I
INTRODUCTION
TO CIVIL LITIGATION

Chapter 1

Litigation and the Paralegal

CHAPTER OUTLINE

COMMENTARY—YOUR FIRST JOB AS A LITIGATION PARALEGAL

You have just finished your first day as a litigation paralegal, and what a day it has been. After meeting coworkers and supervisors, you were asked to attend a meeting with a new client. The purpose of the meeting is to obtain detailed information about the case, an employment matter based on sex discrimination. The client, Alice Bennett, claims that she was denied a promotion and eventually fired because of sex discrimination. Your supervisor told you that you would be working on this case throughout the entire litigation process. However, your supervisor made it clear that you work in a very busy litigation firm and this is not the only case in the office—you will also be required to work on several other pending cases. You can't wait to get started.

OBJECTIVES

In this chapter we will see, in general, what civil litigation is, what it is not, and the role of the paralegal in the civil litigation process. Subsequent chapters analyze each step in the process, explaining the role of the paralegal in each. After reading this chapter, you should be able to:

- Differentiate between civil and criminal procedure.
- Outline the basic litigation process.
- Explain why the basic litigation process is similar for all cases.
- List alternatives to litigation.
- Know where to locate recent developments in litigation.
- Explain the relationship of substantive law to procedural rules.
- Know where to find the laws relating to litigation.
- List tasks performed by litigation paralegals.
- Identify skills required of litigation paralegals.

civil litigation
The process of resolving private disputes through the court system.

trial
The process of deciding a case (giving evidence, making arguments, deciding by a judge and jury, etc.). It occurs if the dispute is not resolved by pleadings, pretrial motions, or settlement. A trial usually takes place in open court, and may be followed by a judgment, an appeal, and so on.

What Civil Litigation Is

Civil litigation is the process of resolving private disputes through the court system. Unless the parties are able to resolve their dispute, the litigation process usually results in a **trial,** or hearing, where the parties present their evidence to a judge or jury. The judge or jury then decides the dispute. Before this happens, however, a great deal of investigation, research, and preparation takes place. Although most of this occurs outside of the courtroom, it is an important part of the litigation process. Litigation attorneys and their paralegals often spend considerable time gathering and analyzing the facts as well as researching the law. Formal legal documents must be prepared and filed with the court, witnesses must be interviewed, and other evidence must be identified and located.

Civil Law versus Criminal Law

Not all disputes that end in litigation are civil in nature, for our court system handles both civil and criminal cases. However, the litigation procedures for civil cases vary considerably from the litigation procedures employed in a criminal case. Being able to distinguish a civil case from a criminal one is therefore very important.

The rules of civil litigation, sometimes referred to as **civil procedure,** apply only if a civil law is involved. **Civil laws** are those that deal with private disputes between parties. If a lawsuit results, it is between the disputing parties. The parties may be individuals, organizations, or governmental entities. Civil law includes such areas as contracts, real estate, commercial and business transactions, and torts (civil wrongs or injuries not stemming from a contract). A typical civil case is illustrated by the following situation. While shopping at Dave's Department Store, Kirkland trips on torn carpeting, seriously injuring himself. The carpeting had been torn for several weeks, but the store ignored the condition. Kirkland requests that the department store pay for his injuries, but the store refuses. Kirkland could sue the department store, asking the court to order the store to pay for his medical bills, for his lost wages, and for any pain and suffering he may have experienced. The basis for such a lawsuit is found in the law of torts, in particular, negligence. The Bennett situation described in the commentary at the beginning of this chapter is another example of a civil case. If Alice Bennett proves that she was the victim of sex discrimination and wrongfully terminated she is probably entitled to recover money damages from her employer. The basis for this type of lawsuit may be found in several areas of civil law, including tort law, contract law, and employment law. The procedures and rules that would govern these lawsuits are known as the rules of civil procedure.

Criminal law, in contrast, deals with acts that are offenses against society as a whole, and includes such acts as murder, robbery, and drunk driving. If a criminal action results, it is usually between the government and the accused. The procedures and rules that apply when an individual is accused of committing a crime are known as the rules of **criminal procedure.** To a large extent, the Bill of Rights found in the United States Constitution governs the rules of criminal procedure. In a criminal case the defendant enjoys various rights, such as the right not to testify against himself. The defendant also has the right to a court-appointed counsel if he is indigent, and is entitled to a speedy trial, all rights found in the Constitution. None of these rights exist in civil cases.

Sometimes the same act results in both a civil dispute and a criminal action. For example, suppose that Rader drives his car while under the influence of alcohol. As a result he crashes into another vehicle and injures the driver of that car, Horowitz. Rader would be arrested for the crime of drunk driving, but Horowitz might also sue civilly. The civil case *(Horowitz v. Rader)* will be conducted according to the rules of civil procedure. The criminal case *(People v. Rader)* will be conducted according to the rules of criminal procedure. In the criminal case, the government (in this case the state) would file an action against Rader for the crime of drunk driving. If he is found guilty, the

civil procedure
The laws and rules that govern how noncriminal lawsuits are handled by the individuals involved and by the court.

civil laws
Laws dealing with private disputes between parties.

criminal law
Having to do with the law of crimes and illegal conduct.

criminal procedure (criminal action)
The procedure by which a person accused of a crime is brought to trial and given punishment.

court could sentence him to jail or impose a fine payable to the state. In the civil case, Horowitz would sue Rader for money to compensate him for his medical bills, his lost wages, and his pain and suffering. When the same act results in both a civil action and a criminal case, the two legal cases are always kept separate. They will never be tried together. In part, this is because a different standard or burden of proof is required in the criminal case. The standard of evidence used to judge the criminal case is higher than the standard applied in civil cases.

Considerable differences between civil and criminal cases also exist in the documents that are filed in court, the proceedings that occur before trial, the hearings that take place in court, and the kinds of relief or remedies that the court can order. The documents, proceedings, and kinds of remedies discussed in this and subsequent chapters apply only in civil cases.

An Overview of Civil Litigation

The rules and procedures followed in the litigation process vary, depending on the court in which the action is filed. Rules or procedures applicable in one state may not apply in another state, and they may not apply if the action is in federal court. However, the general litigation process is similar from one court to another. The process of civil litigation formally begins when one party, the **plaintiff,** files a written document in court. This document is generally called a **complaint,** although in some states it is referred to as a **petition.** In the complaint, or petition, the plaintiff alleges or claims that the party who is being sued, the **defendant,** has done something, or has failed to do something, which entitles the plaintiff to some sort of relief. As noted earlier, the relief is frequently money, but may involve nonmonetary matters, such as determining the validity of a will, issuing an injunction (an order requiring the defendant to do something or to stop doing something), or ordering specific performance of a contract (an order requiring the defendant to comply with the terms of an agreement). For example, suppose that two individuals, Ford and Fraser, enter into a contract in which Fraser agrees to sell Ford her house. Before the transfer is completed, Fraser changes her mind about selling and refuses to comply with the terms of the contract. On the one hand, Ford might sue for any money she has lost. On the other hand, she could sue for specific performance of the contract. This means she is asking the court to force Fraser to fulfill the terms of their agreement.

After the complaint or petition is filed, the defendant is served with a copy of the complaint and is given the opportunity to contest the lawsuit. This is done by filing a document called an **answer** in court. In an answer, the defendant states why the plaintiff is not entitled to any relief. A defendant can also challenge a lawsuit by raising certain legal issues. (This method of responding to a complaint is discussed in detail in Chapter 6.) At this point, the defendant also has the option of doing nothing and ignoring the complaint. However, if this is done, the defendant is said to **default.** In most cases the plaintiff will then obtain a **judgment,** an award of money damages, or other relief.

If both the plaintiff and defendant have filed appropriate documents with the court, litigation proceeds with the parties trying to find out as much as they can about the other side's case. This is known as **discovery.** Sometimes, prior to the time for trial, the par-

---

plaintiff

A person who brings (starts) a lawsuit against another person.

complaint

The first main paper filed in a civil lawsuit. It includes, among other things, a statement of the wrong or harm done to the plaintiff by the defendant, a request for specific help from the court, and an explanation of why the court has the power to do what the plaintiff wants.

petition

A written request to a court asking that it take a particular action. In some states the word is limited to written requests made when there is no other side in a case; in some states, *"petition"* is used in place of *"complaint"* (the first pleading in a lawsuit).

defendant

The person against whom a legal action is brought. This legal action may be civil or criminal.

answer

The first pleading by the defendant in a lawsuit. This pleading responds to the charges and demands of the plaintiff's complaint. The defendant may deny the plaintiff's charges, may present new facts to defeat them, or may show why the plaintiff's facts are legally invalid.

ties request various orders from the court dealing with the case. These requests range from very simple procedural issues, such as requests for more time in which to file a pleading, to more complicated legal issues, such as a request to dismiss the case. These requests are known as **motions.** Some motions, if granted, dispose of the case before any trial takes place. For example, if one party makes a motion to dismiss the case and that motion is granted, there is no trial. The matter was decided without any need for a trial (however, an appeal may result from this kind of order). Motions can also occur during or after a trial.

If the parties are unable to settle their dispute, and the case is not disposed of by a motion, then normally the parties will eventually go to court and present evidence to support their claims. This occurs at a trial, where a judge or jury will decide the case. The litigation process does not necessarily end at trial because, in a civil case, both sides have the right to appeal the decision to a higher court if they feel that a substantial legal error has been committed (see Exhibit 1–1). Even if no appeal is filed, if the plaintiff wins the

default

Failure to take a required step in a lawsuit; for example, to file a paper on time. Such default can sometimes lead to a *"default* judgment" against the side failing to file the paper.

judgment

The official decision of a court about the rights and claims of each side in a lawsuit. *"Judgment"* usually refers to a final decision that is based on the facts of the case and made at the end of a trial. It is called a *judgment on the merits.*

discovery

The formal and informal exchange of information between two sides in a lawsuit. Two types of *discovery* are interrogatories and depositions.

motion

A request that a judge make a ruling or take some other action. Motions are either *granted* or *denied* by the judge.

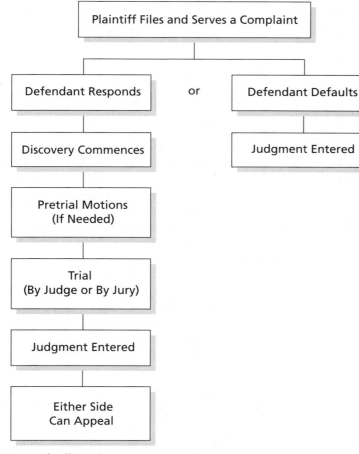

EXHIBIT 1–1 The litigation process

writ
A judge's order requiring that something be done outside the courtroom or authorizing it to be done.

execution
An official carrying out of a court's order or judgment. For example, a writ of execution orders a court official to take a debtor's property to pay court-decided debt, usually by holding an execution sale.

case, collecting or enforcing the judgment sometimes requires further court action. At times, the plaintiff needs to obtain a **writ of execution,** a document that allows the plaintiff to seize and sell the defendant's property and use the proceeds to satisfy the judgment.

Different Types of Civil Lawsuits

Civil lawsuits can range from very simple procedures to very complex court proceedings. Consider the following. Lombardi loans McNair $1,000. McNair signs a promissory note for that amount, promising to pay the money back in three months. At the end of four months McNair has still not paid back the money. Lombardi asks for the money, but McNair refuses to pay. The dispute between Lombardi and McNair is obviously very simple, as are the legal issues involved in the case. Nonetheless, if McNair refuses to pay, Lombardi could file a lawsuit against McNair. In such a lawsuit, there will be one plaintiff, Lombardi, and one defendant, McNair. The complaint itself will be short and straightforward.

Some cases, however, are more complex. This is illustrated by the following factual situation. Woo buys a new automobile. While she is driving the car home from the dealership, the brakes fail, the car crashes, and Woo is seriously injured. Although this seems to be a simple case, it may become quite complex. In such a case, the plaintiff (or her attorney) would have to decide whom to sue. Is the dealership the only potential defendant, or does Woo also name the car manufacturer as a defendant? Was the car manufacturer negligent in making the brakes, or did it buy a defective part from some other business? If so, from whom was it purchased? If Woo plans to sue parties other than the dealership, and they are out of state, where can they be sued? If Woo brings all of these parties into the lawsuit as defendants, they will probably try to sue one another. The case could be further complicated if it turns out that several people have been injured in similar accidents involving the same type of vehicle. Complex cases like this present many practical problems. Many legal and procedural questions also arise, as does the need for extensive pretrial preparation. Often voluminous documents must be organized, analyzed, and indexed. Many courts have developed special procedures and rules for complex litigation. The Federal Judicial Center, an education and research agency for the federal courts, publishes a *Manual for Complex Litigation,* describing approaches that trial judges have found useful for complex cases in federal court. (The *Manual* can be found on the Web site for the Federal Judicial Center, http://www.fjc.gov/) However, whether Lombardi is suing McNair for $1,000 or whether Woo is suing the car dealership and manufacturer for $100,000,000, the basic litigation procedures outlined in this section apply.

Alternatives and Limitations to Litigation

Not all civil disputes are resolved through litigation. In fact, most disputes are not litigated. Several other methods of resolving disputes exist.

Alternative Dispute Resolution

The term **alternative dispute resolution (ADR)** applies to many of the procedures utilized by parties in an attempt to avoid litigation. Three common forms of ADR are negotiation, mediation, and arbitration. **Negotiation** involves the disputing parties discussing their problems with one another and—it is hoped—reaching an agreement or **settlement** of those problems. **Mediation** is a form of settlement that uses a third person, known as a **mediator,** to help the parties come to an agreement to settle their differences. **Arbitration** is an out-of-court process in which a neutral party, known as an **arbitrator,** hears both sides of the dispute and then makes a decision. Alternative dispute resolution is discussed in more detail in Chapter 14.

Administrative Agency Hearings

Some civil disputes cannot be resolved through litigation because the law does not allow it. For example, if an individual has a dispute with the government over his social security payments, that dispute must first be presented to a special board or agency that has been established to handle such disputes. Often, whether or not a case can be resolved through the courts is a question of state law. In some states, for example, absent special circumstances, employees cannot sue their employers if they are injured on the job. However, employees are entitled to compensation for their injuries. If disputes arise regarding the extent of the compensation, they are resolved by a special board or agency that exists separate from the court system.

Legislative Limitations

In recent years, a great deal of criticism has been directed to the area of tort litigation relating to personal injury claims. Critics point out that these types of cases often result in fraudulent practices and abuses of the legal system. They also claim that these cases contribute to the high cost of insurance premiums. Awards of punitive damages have also been highly criticized. As a result, various state and federal legislatures have recently considered legislation to control this area. In the past, several states adopted laws, known as "no-fault" insurance laws, that prevent or severely limit a person from filing a lawsuit stemming from an automobile accident. Although such laws have been considered by the United States Congress, they have never passed. More recently, legislatures are considering laws to regulate the areas of medical malpractice and the award of punitive damages. Laws have been passed that limit the amount of money that a plaintiff is allowed to recover for pain and suffering in a medical malpractice case and the amount recoverable as punitive damages. On the other hand, there are many who believe that the ability to maintain lawsuits against HMOs should be broadened.

Judicial Limitations

In several cases, the United States Supreme Court has considered the constitutionality of punitive damages. The Court has held that excessive punitive damages violate the Due Process Clauses of the Fifth and Fourteenth Amendments to the Constitution.

alternative dispute resolution (ADR)
Ways to resolve legal problems without a court decision; for example, arbitration, mediation, minitrial, rent-a-judge, summary jury trial, and so on.

negotiation (negotiate)
1. Discuss, arrange, or bargain about a business deal. 2. Discuss a compromise to a situation.

settlement (settle)
To come to an agreement about a price, debt, payment of a debt, or disposition of a lawsuit.

mediation
Outside help in settling a dispute. The person who does this is called a *mediator.* This is different from arbitration in that a mediator can only persuade, not force, people into a settlement.

mediator
The person who helps settle a dispute through mediation.

arbitration
Resolution of a dispute by a person (other than a judge) whose decision is binding. This person is called an *arbitrator.* Submission of the dispute for decision is often the result of an agreement (an *"arbitration clause"*) in a contract. If arbitration is required by law, it is called *"compulsory."*

arbitrator
The person who resolves a dispute in an arbitration hearing.

Procedural versus Substantive Law

procedural law

The rules of carrying on a civil lawsuit or a criminal case (how to enforce rights in court) as opposed to substantive law (the law of the rights and duties themselves).

As we have discussed, the law of civil litigation deals primarily with how a civil case is handled in the court system. It consists of rules of procedure, known as procedural law. **Procedural law** tells us the method to use to enforce our rights or to obtain redress for the violation of our rights. For example, recall the Bennett case described in the chapter commentary. In that situation, Bennett has the right to recover money if she was fired because of sex discrimination. The rules of procedural law dictate how Bennett must proceed to recover the money. Bennett would normally begin by filing a complaint in court. The rules of procedural law would govern such matters as how much time she has to file the complaint and in which court it should be filed, as well as the form and content of the complaint.

substantive law

The basic law of rights and duties (contract law, criminal law, accident law, law of wills, etc.) as opposed to procedural law (law of pleading, law of evidence, law of jurisdiction, etc.)

However, litigation is not an area of law that can be practiced by itself. Before attorneys litigate a case, they must determine that there is a case to be litigated. This is a question of substantive law. **Substantive law** is the area of law that creates, defines, or explains what our rights are. For example, suppose that Ortiz promises to marry Hanley but then later changes her mind. Hanley has no right to sue Ortiz for breaking that promise because no substantive law gives Hanley the right to sue for that kind of promise. Thus there is no basis for a civil lawsuit. In contrast, if Bennett is the victim of sex discrimination in her employment, various substantive laws give her the right to sue. The methods she would use to enforce that right are determined by the rules of civil procedure.

Areas of substantive law that frequently form the basis of civil lawsuits include torts, contracts, real estate, and corporate and employment law. The technology revolution has also resulted in numerous civil lawsuits based on the substantive law of intellectual property (patents, copyrights, etc.). This book concentrates on familiarizing you with the basics of procedural law. As your paralegal education continues, you will take specific courses in the various areas of substantive law.

Sources of the Law

primary sources

Books that contain the actual law (i.e., case reporters, codes, constitutions).

secondary sources

1. Persuasive authority.
2. Writings about the law, such as articles, treatises, and encyclopedias.

Answers to legal questions concerning civil litigation can be found in either **primary sources** (books that contain the actual law itself) or **secondary sources** (books that explain or describe the law). Form books are an important secondary source of the law.

Primary Sources

In the American legal system, laws are found in three sources: constitutions, statutes (laws adopted by legislative action), and cases (laws created by the courts). A *primary source* of the law is the place in which we find the law itself. Therefore, the primary sources of the law are found in the constitutions, code books (books containing statutes), and in case reporters (books containing opinions from the various courts).

These three primary sources exist for both the federal legal system and the various state legal systems.

The law of civil litigation is found in the same sources as are all our laws: constitutions, statutes, and case law. If a case is litigated in federal court, then the United States Constitution, United States Code, the Federal Rules of Civil Procedure, and cases from the federal courts usually control. If a case is brought in state court, the state constitution, state codes, and state case law are the primary sources of the law.

Constitutions provide some general guidelines that pertain to civil litigation. For example, the Seventh Amendment to the Constitution provides for the right to juries in common law cases exceeding $20. The Constitution also mandates that due process be followed in civil cases. Very briefly, this means that the procedures followed in a civil case must be fair to all parties, especially to the defendant. The authority and power of the various courts in the litigation process are also often found in constitutions.

More specific litigation matters are controlled by codes or statutes and rules of court. Rules of court are rules of procedure adopted by representatives of the federal and state courts under authority given by the respective legislatures. The Federal Rules of Civil Procedure are rules of practice that have been adopted for civil practice in the federal courts. They cover such matters as the content and filing of pleadings, descriptions of various motions, and types of discovery permitted. State codes contain comparable provisions. Individual federal and state trial and appellate courts also adopt rules for practice within their local courts. These are known as **local rules of court.** In the federal system, these rules can vary from district to district. In state systems, they can vary from one local area to another. In other words, within one state some rules of procedure may be different from one court to another. Local rules of a court should always be checked before initiating any litigation within that court.

local rules of court
Rules that are adopted by individual courts and apply only in those courts.

Case law, law that results from court decisions, is also a major source of rules regarding civil litigation. The courts have the power and the duty to interpret the constitutions and statutes. The Supreme Court has frequently done this with the constitutional phrase "due process." Moreover, even when a statute seems to be clear and explicit, case law cannot be ignored. For instance, California has the following statute relating to default judgments:

> The court may . . . relieve a party . . . from a judgment . . . taken against him . . . through his . . . mistake, inadvertence, surprise or excusable neglect. . . . Application for such relief . . . must be made within a reasonable time, in no case exceeding six months, after such judgment, order or proceeding was taken.

The phrase, "in no case more than six months" seems to be clear and without need of further interpretation. Nonetheless, the courts of the state have repeatedly decided that if fraud exists, a party may apply for relief after six months. Case law tells us that "in no case" does not mean never. It is therefore imperative that when you rely on a statute, you also check any case law relating to that statute.

Secondary Sources

When questions arise relating to litigation, the primary sources of the law are not the only reference materials that can be used. It is often quicker and easier to use a secondary source. A secondary source is a book in which an author explains or describes

FEDERAL PRACTICE AND PROCEDURE   **Form 1791**

Notes

Judgment following motion for summary judgment, generally. 73 Am Jur 2d SUMMARY JUDG-
MENTS §§ 37 et seq.
   Effect of summary judgment. 73 Am Jur 2d SUMMARY JUDGMENT § 40.
   Rules: FRCP 56.

D. DEFAULT JUDGMENTS

1. REQUESTS AND APPLICATIONS; ENTRY OF DEFAULT AND DEFAULT
JUDGMENTS

Governing Principles

When a party against whom a judgment for affirmative relief is sought has
failed to plead or to otherwise defend as provided by the Federal Rules of
Civil Procedure, and that fact is made to appear by affidavit or otherwise, the
clerk is required to enter the party's default. *(FRCP 55(a))*

Judgment by default may be entered as follows:

(1) When the plaintiff's claim against a defendant is for a sum certain or for
a sum that can by computation be made certain, the clerk upon request of the
plaintiff and upon affidavit of the amount due is to enter judgment for that
amount and costs against the defendant, if he or she has been defaulted for
failure to appear and if the defendant is not an infant or incompetent person.
(FRCP 55(b)(1))

(2) In all other cases, the party entitled to a judgment by default is to apply
to the court for recovery; but no judgment by default is to be entered against
an infant or incompetent person unless they are represented in the action by a
general guardian, committee, conservator, or other such representative who
has appeared in their behalf. If the party against whom judgment by default is
sought has appeared in the action, the party (or, if appearing by representative, his or her representative) is to be served with written notice of the
application for judgment at least three days prior to the hearing on such
application. If, in order to enable the court to enter judgment or to carry it
into effect, it is necessary to take an account or to determine the amount of
damages or to establish the truth of any averment by evidence or to make an
investigation of any other matter, the court may conduct such hearings or
order such references as it deems necessary and proper and is to accord a
right of trial by jury to the parties when and as required by any statute of the
United States. *(FRCP 55(b)(2).)*

ANNOTATIONS

   Granting relief not specifically demanded in pleading or notice in rendering default judgment in
divorce or separation action. 12 ALR2d 340.
   Necessity of notice of application or intention to correct error in judgment entry. 14 ALR2d
224.
   Setting aside default judgment for failure of statutory agent on whom process was served to
notify defendant. 20 ALR2d 1179.
   Effect, under Rule 55(b)(2) of the Federal Rules of Civil Procedure and similar state statutes
and rules, of failure, prior to taking default judgment against party who has appeared, to serve 3-
day written notice of application for judgment. 51 ALR2d 837.
   Soldiers' and Sailors' Civil Relief Act of 1940, as amended, as affecting matrimonial actions. 54
ALR2d 390.
   Soldiers' and Sailors' Civil Relief Act of 1940, as amended, as affecting negligence actions. 75
ALR2d 1062.
   Doctrine of res judicata as applied to default judgments. 77 ALR2d 1410.
   Necessity of taking proof as to liability against defaulting defendant. 8 ALR3d 1070.
   Appealability of order setting aside, or refusing to set aside, default judgment. 8 ALR3d 1272.

231

EXHIBIT 1–2   Sample pages from *Am. Jur.,* formally known as *American
Jurisprudence Pleading and Practice Forms Annotated.* Reprinted with permission
of West, a Thomson business.

Form 1791   11A AM JUR PL & PR FORMS (Rev)

Defaulting defendant's right to notice and hearing as to determination of amount of damages. 15 ALR3d 586.

Opening default or default judgment claimed to have been obtained because of attorney's mistake as to time or place of appearance, trial, or filing of necessary papers. 21 ALR3d 1255.

Liability insurer's right to open or set aside, or contest matters relating to merits of, judgment against insured, entered in action in which insurer did not appear or defend. 27 ALR3d 350.

What amounts to an "appearance" under Rule 55(b)(2) of the Federal Rules of Civil Procedure, providing that if the party against whom a judgment by default is sought has "appeared" in the action he shall be served with written notice of the application for judgment. 27 ALR Fed 620.

a. ENTRY OF DEFAULT

Form 1791   Affidavit—In support of entry of default—With request to clerk

[Caption, see Forms 1 et seq.]
[Venue]

[Title]

I, ___1___, being first duly sworn, depose and say:

I

I am the attorney for plaintiff in the above action.

II

A copy of the summons and complaint was served on defendant on ___2___, 19_3_, and the return of service of ___4___, United States Marshal, is on file in this action.

III

Defendant ___5___ [has not answered or otherwise appeared in this action, and the time within which defendant may appear has expired *or, if defendant has appeared, state facts showing default*].

[Jurat]
[Signature of attorney for plaintiff]

Request to Clerk To Enter Default

To: Clerk of the above-entitled court.

Defendant ___6___, having failed to ___7___ [answer or otherwise appear in the above-entitled action, and the time for appearance having expired *or, if defendant has appeared, state manner in which he or she is in default*], you are requested to enter ___8___ [his *or* her] default pursuant to Rule 55(a) of the Federal Rules of Civil Procedure.

Dated ___9___, 19_10_.

[Signature]

Notes

Clerk's entry of default. 47 Am Jur 2d JUDGMENTS §§ 1155 et seq.
Rules: FRCP 55(a).

Form 1792   Certificate—By clerk—Entry of default

[Caption, see Forms 1 et seq.]

[Title]

In this cause, the defendant ___1___ having been regularly served with process, as appears from the record and papers on file herein, and having

232

EXHIBIT 1–2   *(continued)*

form books

Books containing sample forms for legal professionals to follow in preparing pleadings and other documents.

the primary sources of the law. Many secondary sources exist for both state and federal procedure. Secondary sources include legal encyclopedias, practice manuals, textbooks, and various legal periodicals.

A secondary source that is heavily relied upon in the area of litigation is the **form book.** As the name suggests, form books contain sample forms for all aspects of litigation, from complaints to judgments. Better form books also contain explanations of the laws relating to the various forms, and as such are valuable research tools. One example is the *American Jurisprudence Pleading and Practice Forms Annotated,* published by the West Group. Exhibit 1–2 illustrates a sample page from this form book.

The Role of the Litigation Paralegal

When you become a paralegal employed to help in litigation, you will have numerous tasks and responsibilities. However, the job of the litigation paralegal does vary from firm to firm and from case to case. In a complex litigation case, you may be part of a litigation team along with attorneys, other paralegals, and legal secretaries. Your responsibilities may be limited to one aspect of the case. For example, you might be responsible for organizing and indexing documentary evidence in a case (i.e., contracts, purchase orders, letters between parties), while another paralegal in your firm is responsible for researching legal issues that arise. In smaller, less complex cases, you may be involved in all aspects of the case.

Litigation Paralegal Job Description

The following list contains some of the more common tasks that may be included in the job description of a litigation paralegal.

General Responsibilities
1. maintaining firm's calendaring system
2. organizing client files
3. assisting with computerization of litigation

Prelitigation Facts Investigation
1. interviewing clients
2. interviewing witnesses
3. obtaining statements from witnesses
4. gathering evidence (police reports, photographs, etc.)
5. organizing and indexing documentary evidence
6. researching factual and legal issues

Commencing Litigation
1. researching the substantive law of the case
2. drafting pleadings
3. coordinating service of process

4. reviewing pleadings from opposing party
5. drafting motions, including memoranda of points and authorities
6. preparing orders after motions
7. evaluating possible case-management software

Discovery
1. drafting written forms of discovery (interrogatories, requests to produce, requests for admissions)
2. assisting client in complying with discovery requests
3. reviewing discovery obtained from opposing parties
4. preparing client for deposition
5. setting up, reviewing, and summarizing depositions
6. organizing, analyzing, and coding documents for document production and, where appropriate, creating a document database

Trial
1. organizing file and evidence for trial
2. serving witnesses with subpoenas
3. interviewing witnesses
4. preparing the client
5. drafting jury instructions
6. drafting proposed judgments
7. assisting with research and preparation of trial brief
8. preparing and organizing trial exhibits
9. coordinating technology needs with the court
10. assisting the attorney during trial

Posttrial
1. researching possible posttrial motions
2. drafting possible posttrial motions
3. drafting notice of appeal and requests for transcripts
4. assisting with research and writing of appellate briefs
5. preparing documents associated with enforcing judgments

What a Litigation Paralegal Cannot Do

Obviously, as a litigation paralegal, you can perform many tasks in the course of a lawsuit and can play an important role in the litigation law firm. However, the litigation paralegal is not an attorney and therefore cannot practice law. In a litigation law firm, some important functions cannot be performed by the paralegal. With very limited exceptions, the paralegal cannot appear in court, cannot ask questions at a deposition, and cannot give legal advice to a client.

Skills Required of the Litigation Paralegal

As a litigation paralegal, you will need some very definite skills. You must be able to communicate both orally and in writing. You cannot conduct intelligent interviews with clients or prospective witnesses without the ability to communicate orally. Nor can you help draft witness statements or pleadings without the ability to communicate in writing. As a litigation paralegal you also must possess organizational and analytical skills. Reviewing and analyzing documentary evidence and pleadings is a task often given to paralegals. Likewise, as a paralegal you will sometimes be asked to organize documents, discovery information, and pleadings. The ability to do legal research, including familiarity with form books, is also important. Drafting court documents and preparing memoranda of points and authorities (discussion or analysis of legal questions) require this skill. In today's law office, as a litigation paralegal, you must be computer literate, possessing general knowledge of the computer, word processing, and database and spreadsheet programs as well as the Internet. This is particularly important if you become a paralegal in a firm that handles complex litigation.

Continuing Legal Education

As a litigation paralegal, you must keep current on changes that constantly occur in the area of litigation. Our laws are always subject to change. Codes and rules are often amended. New cases are frequently decided. In addition to changes in the law, technological advances, especially in computers and software packages, often affect the way litigation is practiced.

Local legal newspapers generally report national and state judicial and legislative developments. They also contain information related to practices adopted by the local courts. You should develop the habit of reading your local legal newspaper regularly. Local and state bar associations and paralegal associations often sponsor seminars on selected areas of law. Paralegal schools may also offer courses or seminars that would benefit working paralegals. In addition, you can often find continuing legal education opportunities on line. If you want to be a conscientious paralegal, you will take advantage of opportunities to attend these seminars and courses.

Professional Organizations

As a paralegal, you should continuously strive for professional improvement. One source for growth in the profession is affiliation with local, state, and national paralegal organizations. A partial list of national organizations includes:

National Association of Legal Assistants, Inc. (NALA)
1516 South Boston Avenue, Suite 200
Tulsa, OK 74119
(918) 587-6828
www.nala.org

THE COMPUTERIZED LAW FIRM
The Language of Computers

SCENARIO

Congratulations! You have been hired as a paralegal by a prestigious litigation law firm and it's your first day on the job. You have your own parking space, your own office, your own computer, and your own password. A senior paralegal who will be conducting your orientation tells you that the firm is on a network and uses the latest technology in "automated litigation support." Your training will include instruction in specific software applications that will make your job easier. The firm has programs that handle document generation, calendaring, billing, and conflicts checks, as well as software designed to summarize, retrieve, and integrate discovery documents. You are also told that most legal research is performed by using on-line services of LEXIS and Westlaw, the Internet, and the firm's intranet. You are overwhelmed!

PROBLEM

Your success as a litigation paralegal in any litigation law firm depends on your ability to adapt your knowledge of litigation rules and procedures to the use of technology. You are willing and even eager to do this. You have a basic understanding of computers. You do word processing and can access the Internet, but you are overwhelmed by the whole concept of automated litigation support. Where do you start?

SOLUTION

Adapting to the litigation law firm of the 21st century requires that you know how the office computer system is set up, that you have a good understanding of computers and related equipment, and that you become familiar with the various software programs that are utilized by the firm. Because technology changes so rapidly, it also requires that you keep continually updated in the newest developments.

In a smaller law firm, each worker usually has a self-contained computer. Software products must be loaded onto each computer. Larger firms, in contrast, are often set up on a network. Commonly used software is loaded onto the hard drive of one main computer, the server, and individual computers access this. Specific software can also be loaded onto the individual computer for use on that computer alone. Today, some firms also use Web-based software. This is software that is loaded onto a remote computer and is accessed through the Internet. This allows attorneys to access the software from any location. Thus, if a law firm has several geographical locations, attorneys and paralegals situated in different locations can all access the same software program. It also allows attorneys to access the software from any computer that has access to the Internet. Obviously, a fee is paid to use the software and a password is generally needed to access the program.

Fortunately, you do not have to know exactly how computers work. However, some knowledge of computers and legal software is essential. Most legal journals include articles on legal technology. Several books, magazines, and Web sites are dedicated to this topic. *Law Office Computing, Law Technology News,* and the American Bar Association's *Law Practice Management* are three popular magazines that cover this topic. Seminars on legal technology are conducted regularly. You should make every effort to take advantage of these resources. However, if you do not understand some basic terminology you will never learn how to effectively utilize the computer in litigation.

Some basic terms that you should know include the following:

hardware the machinery that makes up the computer system; includes the computer itself and items such as a printer, scanner, or modem

software programmed information that allows you to perform various tasks on the computer

hard drive the place within the computer where information is stored

zip drive high capacity external disk drive

USB (Universal Serial Bus) connection an external port on the computer allowing the user to connect and easily use various peripheral devices

peripheral any device connected to the computer (such as a monitor, external hard drive, or keyboard)

CD-ROM compact disc containing large amounts of information; contains general legal research material, forms, or factual information related to a case; information is accessed through the computer's CD-ROM drive

modem a hardware item that enables the computer to talk to other computers over a telephone line

DSL (Digital Subscriber Line) a high-speed way of accessing the Internet without having to "dial up" each time a user accesses the Internet; the computer is permanently connected to the Internet

scanner a hardware item that allows the user to take graphics, pictures, or written text and place them into the computer (a process known as imaging); with proper software, known as optical character reading software (OCR), the images can be accessed or edited

Internet system consisting of computers on a large network allowing computers to communicate with one another

intranet an internet system accessible only by a limited group, usually one business or company

extranet an internet system accessible only by selected limited groups, usually a business or company and its clients

portal a Web site that provides a gateway or links to other related sites on the Web

firewall a system that provides security against hackers; it prevents anyone from accessing the computer while it is connected to the Internet

PDF (Portable Document Format) a file format for viewing and creating documents that are used and transferred over the Internet

automated litigation support software packages designed to assist the litigation law firm

National Federation of Paralegal Associations
P.O. Box 33108
Kansas City, MO 64114-0108
(816) 941-4000
www.paralegals.org

American Bar Association
ABA Center
750 North Lake Shore Drive
Chicago, IL 60611
(312) 988-5000
www.abanet.org (search for "Legal Assistants")

Legal Assistant Management Association
P.O. Box 659
Avondale Estates, GA 30002-0659
(404) 292-2976
www.lamanet.org

Practical Tips for Success in the Law Firm

Forms File—Invaluable Aid

As mentioned earlier, litigation paralegals often need to use form books. However, finding the proper form and adapting it to your particular needs is sometimes a time-consuming task. To find a proper form, a paralegal generally must go through an extensive index of the form books, looking up several topics, and then review several possible forms. Revising or adapting sample forms to fit a particular need is often required. Not only is all of this a time-consuming task, but it is also a task that repeats itself. A litigation firm often finds itself dealing with similar kinds of cases and facing similar problems in different cases. Thus, a form needed for one case can easily be followed for another. One way to ease the task of finding proper forms is for the law firm, or for you as a litigation paralegal, to maintain your own forms file. When you start employment as a paralegal in a litigation law firm, you should always check to see if the firm maintains its own form files. Many do. If the firm has an intranet, be sure to check there for forms. Even if a form file is maintained for the firm, as an individual litigation paralegal you would be wise to keep your own form file, with an index, retaining copies of forms that you have prepared, as well as copies of forms prepared by others, that might be useful in the future. Forms that should be kept include pleadings, motions, memoranda of points and authorities, and briefs.

How to Build a Litigation Training Manual

Another invaluable aid to litigation paralegals is a litigation training manual, in which the various tasks performed by the paralegals are described and step-by-step directions are given. In such a training manual, consideration should be given to two distinct procedures. In describing any paralegal task—for example, preparing and filing a complaint—all of the legal requirements must be set out. Additionally, a training manual should detail office policy. A training manual might also include detailed instructions on preparing various legal forms. If a law firm has its own training manual, the new litigation paralegal should consult it. Experienced paralegals will also find it helpful when they are involved in new tasks or engaged in tasks that are infrequently performed. If a training manual does not exist, the litigation paralegals can work together to assemble one. An easy way to accomplish this is for you and the other paralegals in your firm to keep a checklist or step-by-step directions for each task that you and the others perform. These can be collated into a complete training manual. As a paralegal student, you can also begin keeping your own reference manual by making checklists for each matter covered in class. See Exhibit 1–3 for a sample.

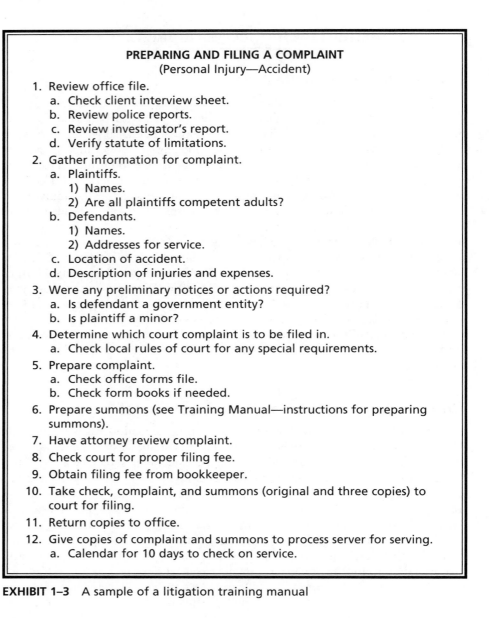

PREPARING AND FILING A COMPLAINT
(Personal Injury—Accident)

1. Review office file.
   a. Check client interview sheet.
   b. Review police reports.
   c. Review investigator's report.
   d. Verify statute of limitations.
2. Gather information for complaint.
   a. Plaintiffs.
      1) Names.
      2) Are all plaintiffs competent adults?
   b. Defendants.
      1) Names.
      2) Addresses for service.
   c. Location of accident.
   d. Description of injuries and expenses.
3. Were any preliminary notices or actions required?
   a. Is defendant a government entity?
   b. Is plaintiff a minor?
4. Determine which court complaint is to be filed in.
   a. Check local rules of court for any special requirements.
5. Prepare complaint.
   a. Check office forms file.
   b. Check form books if needed.
6. Prepare summons (see Training Manual—instructions for preparing summons).
7. Have attorney review complaint.
8. Check court for proper filing fee.
9. Obtain filing fee from bookkeeper.
10. Take check, complaint, and summons (original and three copies) to court for filing.
11. Return copies to office.
12. Give copies of complaint and summons to process server for serving.
    a. Calendar for 10 days to check on service.

EXHIBIT 1–3   A sample of a litigation training manual

FINDING IT ON THE INTERNET

An abundance of information about litigation, the courts, and the law in general can be found on the Internet. May legal sites contain a variety of types of legal information. One way to find specific information on a Web site is to use the "search" feature which is generally found on the home page of any Web site.

As explained in this chapter, litigation rules for the federal courts are found in the United States Code and Federal Rules of Civil Procedure. The following sites provide access to these:

<http://www.law.cornell.edu>

Click on "Constitutions and Codes" and follow the links to the United States Codes and the Federal Rules of Civil Procedure.

This site will also lead to state codes and rules.

<http://uscode.house.gov>

Both the United States Code and the Federal Rules of Civil Procedure can be accessed through this site.

<http://www.uscourts.gov>

Click on "Federal Rulemaking" and then "Rules and Forms in Effect" to access all of the Federal Rules of Civil Procedure.

a. Search the Internet for your state's code and rules and identify the specific Web site addresses for these.

b. Litigation practice requires more than knowledge of the law. Today's litigation paralegal must also be familiar with litigation technology. Two good sources for information on this topic are **<http://www.lawtechnews.com>** and **<http://www.abanet.org>** (search for "technology"). Access these sites and summarize one article from each dealing with litigation technology.

Summary

- Civil litigation is the process through which parties resolve their civil disputes in court. Civil cases deal with private disputes between individuals or parties. Civil litigation does not include the pursuit of any criminal case. Civil litigation usually begins with the plaintiff filing a complaint in court and having it served on the defendant. The defendant then responds by filing an answer or other appropriate pleading. While the parties are waiting to get to court for a trial, they try to find out as much about the other's case as possible by going through discovery. If problems with the case arise, they are often referred to the court in a proceeding known as a motion. After the trial has ended, either of the parties can appeal. Once the case is over, the prevailing party may use the court process to collect a judgment.

- Some civil lawsuits are very simple proceedings, whereas others are very complex. Regardless of the nature of the case, the basic litigation process remains the same. However, more complex cases can involve multiple parties, multiple pleadings, and voluminous documents. They might also require extensive legal research.

- Not all civil disputes are litigated. Other methods exist for resolving disputes. The term *alternative dispute resolution* applies to many of these methods, including such procedures as negotiation, mediation, and arbitration. Negotiation occurs when the parties discuss their problems in an effort to settle their dispute. Mediation resembles negotiation except that a neutral third party (the mediator) is brought in to help the parties settle their differences. Arbitration involves the parties submitting their dispute to a third, neutral party (the arbitrator) who decides the case. In addition to alternative dispute resolution methods, some disputes must be resolved by administrative agencies. In recent years various legislative action has begun to curb litigation, especially in the area of tort law.

- The substantive law of the case controls whether the parties have the right to sue. Procedural rules dictate how that case is to be handled in the court system. One cannot exist without the other.

- The laws of civil litigation are found primarily in constitutions, statutes, and cases. Cases brought in federal court are governed by the United States Constitution, federal statutes, and federal cases. Cases brought in state courts are controlled by state constitutions, statutes, and cases. In both federal and state courts, attention must also be paid to local rules of the various courts. In researching a question of civil litigation, the paralegal may use primary sources or secondary sources. Primary sources are constitutions, code books, or case reporters. Secondary sources include textbooks, legal encyclopedias, legal periodicals, and form books. It is important for the litigation paralegal to be aware of changes that occur in the law. Reading local legal newspapers and joining professional associations can help.

- Paralegals can perform a number of duties or jobs in the area of litigation. These include gathering evidence, interviewing clients and witnesses, preparing pleadings and motions, assisting with all aspects of discovery, and conducting factual and legal research.

- Litigation paralegals must be able to communicate orally and in writing. They must possess organizational and analytical skills. They must be able to do legal research. Familiarity with computers is also required.

- Litigation paralegals will find their jobs somewhat easier if personal form files and training manuals are available to them.

Key Terms

alternative dispute resolution (ADR)	default	negotiation
answer	defendant	petition
arbitration	discovery	plaintiff
arbitrator	execution	primary sources
civil law	form books	procedural law
civil litigation	judgment	secondary authority
civil procedure	local rules of court	settlement
complaint	mediation	substantive law
criminal law	mediator	trial
criminal procedure	motion	writ

Review Questions

1. What is the difference between civil procedure and criminal procedure?
2. What are the steps in the litigation process?
3. How are a simple case and a complex case alike? How do they differ?
4. What are some of the alternatives to litigating a case?
5. What is the importance of substantive laws to civil litigation?
6. What are the primary sources for finding the law of civil litigation?
7. What are the secondary sources for finding the law of civil litigation?
8. What are five tasks performed by litigation paralegals?
9. Why is it important for all litigation paralegals to know how to do legal research?
10. What skills must a litigation paralegal have? Why are these skills needed?

Chapter Exercises

Where necessary, check with your instructor prior to starting any of these exercises.

1. Check the classified sections of local newspapers and legal newspapers. (You can also check on the Internet.) Are there any ads for litigation paralegals? If so, what are the job requirements? Are any particular skills described?
2. Contact your local courts and find out if they have their own rules of court. If so, how do you get a copy of them?
3. Find out if there are any local paralegal associations. If so, how do you join? Do they ever sponsor seminars in the area of litigation?
4. Get a three-ring, loose-leaf binder and start your own training manual. As you go through each chapter in this book, prepare step-by-step directions or a checklist for each task described therein. As part of your training manual, include a glossary of terms and their definitions.
5. Review the advertisements in a local bar journal or legal newspaper that deal with computer software advertised as "automated litigation support." Make a list of the products and give a brief description of what the software does. Send for information or demonstration disks on relevant software.
6. Analyze the following factual disputes. Would these disputes result in a civil case, a criminal case, or both? Explain your answer. If a civil case would result, who would be the plaintiff and who would be the defendant?
   a. Baron and Finkle sign a written contract in which Baron agrees to build a room addition to Finkle's house. When the contract was signed, Finkle gave Baron a $1,000 deposit. Before construction was to begin, Baron called Finkle and told him he would not be able to do the work. Baron has not returned the $1,000 deposit.
   b. Martin sets fire to a building he owns in order to collect insurance.
   c. Reese works as a software engineer for DATA Corp. and has been involved in the design of a new computer chip. He has signed a confidentiality agreement with DATA Corp. and has agreed that all products developed by him while working for DATA belong to DATA. Reese has a dispute with DATA over salary and leaves. He sells the design for the computer chip to DISK Corp., his new employer. DISK knows that the chip design was developed while Reese was working for DATA.

    d. Bates, in a fit of anger, kills his wife. The couple has two minor children.

    e. Rosemond Corporation is engaged in a business that produces by-products that pollute water. It illegally dumps the by-products. Children in a nearby area develop a high incidence of cancer.

Chapter Project

Get a three-ring, loose-leaf binder and start your own forms file. From the table of contents of this book, set up a general index to the file. As you proceed through the course on Civil Litigation, add copies of all forms that you see or prepare.

The *Bennett* Case
Assignment 1: Preliminary Research

Your supervising attorney wants to prepare for the meeting with Alice Bennett. To help the attorney you have been asked to review the Web site for the Equal Employment Opportunity Commission (EEOC) (<http://www.eeoc.gov>). Write a memo summarizing information about sex discrimination found on the Web site.

In summarizing the material on the Web site include the following information:

1. A list and brief description of laws that might apply to Bennett
2. A discussion of what constitutes sex discrimination and sexual harassment
3. The procedures for filing a claim with the EEOC
4. Requirements for filing a lawsuit
5. Any other information you think is relevant

Chapter 2

The Courts and Jurisdiction

CHAPTER OUTLINE

COMMENTARY—THE "WEIGH TO GO" CASE

Your law firm has recently been retained by "Weigh To Go," a corporation that operates a chain of low-calorie, fast-food restaurants. The corporation was formed 10 years ago under the laws of the state of Texas and met with such success that it now has restaurants in Texas, Nevada, and Oregon. It plans to open restaurants in California. Weigh To Go currently maintains a Web site on the Internet containing information about the company. Local customers can place on-line orders but the company does not deliver. Weigh To Go has just learned that a few months ago another company started a similar business. This company calls itself "Go A Weigh" and does business solely within the state of California. Go A Weigh also maintains a Web site on the Internet. Your attorney tells you that the firm will be filing a lawsuit based on trade name infringement and asks you to research the following questions. Should the complaint be filed in federal or state court, or does it matter? If the complaint is to be filed in federal court, which district is the proper one? If the complaint is to be filed in state court, which state or states could hear the case?

OBJECTIVES

Chapter 1 introduced you to the general litigation process. Choosing the proper court in which to initiate a lawsuit is an important step in that process. After reading this chapter, you should be able to:

- Describe the functions of the various courts in the civil litigation process.
- Describe the various courts within the federal court system.
- Describe the various courts in state court systems.
- Define subject matter jurisdiction.
- List the types of cases that must be brought in federal court.
- Distinguish exclusive jurisdiction from concurrent jurisdiction.
- Determine if a court can obtain personal jurisdiction.
- Explain the relevance of long-arm statutes.
- Contrast personal jurisdiction with in rem jurisdiction.
- Identify how venue affects the location of the trial court.

The Courts and Litigation

Because civil litigation revolves around the courts, one of the first considerations in the litigation process is selection of the proper court in which to proceed. Numerous courts exist within the United States. Different court systems exist for each of the states and for the federal government. Furthermore, each court system contains many different courts. Although these court systems differ from one another in many ways, they do have some characteristics in common. All court systems have trial courts and courts of appeal or review. Many court systems have two levels of review courts, intermediate courts of appeals (in some jurisdictions called courts of appeal), and highest courts of appeal or courts of last resort (sometimes referred to as supreme courts). The function of all trial courts is similar, as are the functions of courts of appeals and courts of last resort.

Trial Courts

The civil litigation process usually begins in a **trial court.** This is where the parties to a lawsuit file their pleadings and present evidence to a judge or jury. Trial courts are also called **lower courts.** The primary function of any trial court in civil cases is to resolve disputes between parties by first determining the true facts and then applying appropriate legal principles. For instance, in a civil action, Stevens might sue Jackson for injuries he received in an automobile accident, claiming Jackson was at fault by failing to stop at a stop sign. Jackson might claim he owes Stevens nothing because it was Stevens who ran the stop sign. At trial, the judge or jury must decide what the facts are (that is, who did run the stop sign).

Once a factual dispute has been resolved, appropriate legal principles are applied to those facts—principles that for the most part have been established by the legislature and by higher courts. In the preceding factual situation, once a trial court judge or jury has determined that Jackson did in fact run a stop sign, causing injuries to Stevens, they would then apply the legal principles of negligence and could award Stevens money damages. Because litigation usually begins in a trial court, this court is referred to as a court of original jurisdiction. **Jurisdiction** refers to the power or authority of a court to hear a particular case. A court of **original jurisdiction** is a court where the case begins and is tried.

Courts of Appeals

Courts of appeals are primarily courts of review. These courts examine what happened in the trial court to guarantee that the parties received a fair trial. A case is not retried in an appellate court. The appellate courts review the trial court's actions by reviewing a written, verbatim transcript or record of the lower court proceedings. Along with this transcript, the attorneys for the parties (or the parties themselves if they have no attorney) submit **briefs,** written documents in which the attorneys discuss and analyze possible legal errors committed at trial, giving references to legal authorities in support of their claims. Attorneys (or, again, the parties themselves, if they are not represented) are also normally allowed to argue orally.

The appellate court's role is to determine if any legal errors occurred in the trial court. A **legal error** is an error in the way the law is interpreted or applied to a situation. Examples of legal errors include a judge's misstating the law when instructing the jury, or allowing attorneys to introduce evidence that is not relevant to the case or that has been improperly obtained. The appellate court is not allowed to substitute its judgment for that of the trial court when it comes to factual questions. If there is any reasonable basis for the trier of fact to have found as it did, the appellate court is not empowered to reverse the decision simply because it does not believe the evidence. In the case of *Stevens v. Jackson,* described earlier, suppose the evidence in the case

trial court
A court where the parties to a lawsuit file their pleadings and present evidence to a judge or jury.

lower court
Another term for a trial court.

jurisdiction
1. The geographical area within which a court (or a public official) has the right and power to operate. 2. The persons about whom and the subject matters about which a court has the right and power to make decisions that are legally binding.

original jurisdiction
The power of a court to take a case, try it, and decide it (as opposed to *appellate jurisdiction,* the power of a court to hear and decide an appeal).

court of appeals
A court that decides appeals from a trial court. In most states it is a middle-level court (similar to a United States Court of Appeals) but in some states it is the highest court.

brief
A written statement prepared by one side in a lawsuit to explain its case to the judge. It usually contains a fact summary, a law summary, and an argument about how the law applies to the facts. Most such "briefs" are not brief.

legal error
A mistake in the way the law is interpreted or applied to a situation.

appellate jurisdiction
The power and authority of a higher court to take up cases that have already been in a lower court and the power to make decisions about these cases. The process is called appellate review. Also, a trial court may have *appellate jurisdiction* over cases from an administrative agency.

higher court
Court of appeals.

supreme court
The highest of the United States courts and the highest court of most, but not all, of the states.

consisted of the following: Stevens, a 19-year-old college student, testified that Jackson ran the stop sign. Jackson, a police officer who was off-duty at the time of the accident, testified that Stevens ran the stop sign. There are no other witnesses. If the trial court found in favor of Stevens, an appellate court could not reverse just because an off-duty policeman seems more credible to it than a 19-year-old college student. The trial court already resolved this factual question, and the appellate court is bound by it.

The appellate review is usually conducted by a three-judge panel. To prevail, a party must have a majority (two of the three) on her side. Because the authority of the courts of appeals is to review a trial court's actions rather than to resolve factual disputes, courts of appeals are sometimes called courts of **appellate jurisdiction.** They may also be referred to as **higher courts.**

Courts of Last Resort

Many court systems have two levels of courts with appellate jurisdiction, intermediate courts of appeals and one court of last resort. The court of last resort is often referred to as a **supreme court.** Intermediate courts of appeals and the court of last resort are primarily courts of appellate jurisdiction. They review the proceedings at the trial level. However, one basic difference exists between intermediate courts of appeal and a court of last resort. Generally, intermediate courts of appeal must review cases in which the parties request a review. In contrast, in most civil cases a court of last resort has a discretionary right to review the cases. In other words, this court hears only those appeals that it wants to hear. The parties do not have the right to have their appeal heard in that court.

Federal Court System

The federal court system was established in the United States Constitution, Article III, which created the Supreme Court and such inferior courts as Congress may establish. Today those inferior courts include trial courts and appellate courts. The trial courts are most commonly known as the United States district courts (or federal district courts), but also include various specialized courts such as the United States Claims Court and the United States Court of International Trade. The appellate courts are known as United States courts of appeals (or federal courts of appeals). See Exhibit 2–1.

United States District Courts

The United States and its territories are divided into 94 different districts, each one having a federal district court. Some larger districts are further subdivided into different divisions. Each state has at least one federal district court in its boundaries and, depending on population, a state may have more. The number of judges assigned to each district varies according to need. District courts are trial courts. Thus, in the *Weigh To Go* case mentioned in this chapter's commentary, if a lawsuit were pursued in the federal court system, it would be started in a district court. The complaint and answer would be filed in that court, and any trial would take place there.

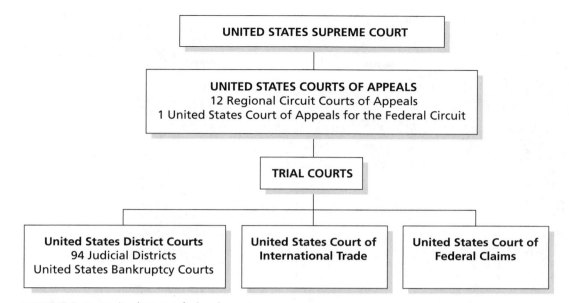

EXHIBIT 2–1   United States federal courts

Miscellaneous Federal Trial Courts

In addition to the United States district courts, the federal court system contains various specialized trial courts, including bankruptcy courts, the United States Court of International Trade, and the United States Claims Court. The bankruptcy courts are an "adjunct" to each district court. All bankruptcy proceedings originate there. The United States Court of International Trade deals with cases involving international trade and custom duties. The United States Claims Court handles suits against the federal government for money damages in numerous civil matters (except for tort claims, which must be brought in district court).

United States Courts of Appeals

The United States is divided into 12 appellate circuits, each one having jurisdiction over three or more states. These courts hear appeals from district courts within their boundaries. The United States courts of appeals are primarily courts of review, having appellate jurisdiction. These courts review the proceedings that took place in a district court and determine if any substantial legal error was committed. In addition to the courts of appeals for each of the 12 appellate districts, a 13th federal court of appeals with national jurisdiction has been established. This court hears appeals in patent, copyright, and trademark cases from any district court and all appeals from the United States Claims Court and the United States Court of International Trade. Generally, when any of the courts of appeals reviews a lower court decision, that decision is reviewed by a three-judge panel, and the majority decision prevails. However, similar to the district courts, the total number of justices in each appellate court varies according to need. See Exhibit 2–2 for a map showing the federal circuits and districts.

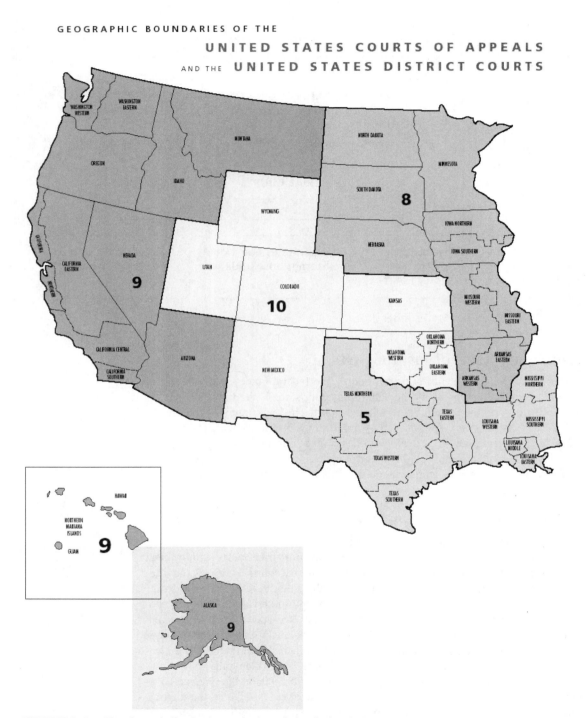

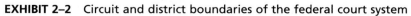

EXHIBIT 2–2 Circuit and district boundaries of the federal court system

LEGEND

CIRCUIT BOUNDARIES

STATE BOUNDARIES

DISTRICT BOUNDARIES

EXHIBIT 2–2   *(continued)*

United States Supreme Court

The United States has only one Supreme Court, consisting of nine Justices. The Court is located in Washington, D.C., and holds its sessions from October through June. Primarily, the Supreme Court exercises appellate jurisdiction. In most cases, the exercise of that appellate jurisdiction is discretionary. With limited exceptions, the Supreme

Court is not required to hear all cases in which a party requests review. In other words, the Supreme Court hears only those appeals that it wants to hear. In determining whether to grant a hearing in a case, the Court obviously considers the importance of the decision not only to the aggrieved parties, but also to society as a whole.

certiorari

(Latin) "To make sure." A request for certiorari (or "cert." for short) is like an appeal, but one which the higher court is not required to take for decision. It is literally a writ from the higher court asking the lower court for the record of the case. (pronunciation: sir-sho-rare-ee)

To request a hearing in the Supreme Court, a party files with the Court a document called a *petition for a writ of* ***certiorari.*** In this petition the party explains to the court why the case is important enough for the Supreme Court to consider. The Justices then consider each petition for writ of certiorari and vote on whether to grant it. In order for a petition to be granted, four of the nine Justices must agree. If the petition for the writ of certiorari is not granted, then the decision of the court of appeals stands. If a petition for writ of certiorari is granted, however, it does not mean that the party has won the case. The party has only managed to get a full hearing (review) by the Supreme Court. After the petition has been granted and the writ has been issued, the case proceeds much like an appeal in the appellate courts. The Justices consider the lower court transcripts. The attorneys submit legal briefs and are allowed to orally argue the case in front of the Court. Oral arguments before the Supreme Court, however, are very limited. By the time a case has reached the oral argument stage, the Justices know the legal arguments for both sides. Thus, the oral argument stage often serves as a chance for the Justices to ask questions about any legal arguments they want clarified. To prevail before the Supreme Court, a party must have the vote of five out of the nine Justices, or a simple majority. (In the event that fewer than nine Justices are hearing the case, it takes a majority to win. Should there be a tie vote, the decision of the court of appeals stands.)

The power of review by the Supreme Court differs from that of the federal courts of appeals in another way. Normally the federal courts of appeals hear appeals from cases tried in federal district courts. The Supreme Court, however, can and does review cases originally tried in state courts, as long as some federal or constitutional issue exists. Again, there is usually no right to have such cases heard by the Supreme Court. As with appeals from federal court, the Supreme Court generally hears only those cases from state courts that it wishes to review.

Although the Supreme Court is primarily a court of review, in certain cases it does have original jurisdiction. Article III, Section 2 of the United States Constitution provides:

> In all cases affecting ambassadors, other public ministers and consuls, and those in which a state shall be a party, the Supreme Court shall have original jurisdiction. In all other cases before mentioned (Art. III, § 2.1) the Supreme Court shall have appellate jurisdiction, both as to law and fact, with such exception, and under such regulations as the Congress shall make.

State Court Systems

Each state has its own court system, established pursuant to the laws of the state. For the most part, however, the individual states have patterned their court structures after the federal system. All states have some sort of trial courts and some sort of appellate, or review, courts. Most states also have a state supreme court or a court of last resort. The role of each of these courts is also comparable to their equivalents in the federal system. The names, however, differ from state to state. For example, general trial courts in California are called superior courts. In New York, trial courts are called supreme courts. In other states, trial courts are known as circuit courts, city courts, county courts, surrogate courts, and courts of common pleas. Many states have additional specialty trial courts such as probate court, juvenile court, and family court. In some states trial courts are broken down into different levels.

In addition, many state court systems today have something referred to as a *small claims court* (the people's court). In these courts, parties who are suing for small amounts of money go through a simplified litigation process. Attorneys are usually not involved, and all pleadings are extremely simple. These courts are intended to afford speedy legal relief in small cases where normal litigation costs would preclude other actions.

Jurisdiction

Before filing any lawsuit, an attorney must decide which of the many courts is the proper one for that lawsuit. This is a question of jurisdiction. *Jurisdiction* is the power or authority that a court has to hear a particular case.

In many cases the question of jurisdiction is a relatively simple one to answer. If a lawsuit arises under a state law and all of the parties are residents of that state, then jurisdiction is in the state courts. If a lawsuit arises under a federal law and all parties are residents of the same state, then jurisdiction is usually in the federal court located in the state of residence of the parties. However, in some instances jurisdiction becomes an extremely complicated issue. Where parties are not residents of the same state or where one party, especially a business, has a presence in several states determining proper jurisdiction is more involved. The use of the Internet by businesses raises several jurisdiction questions. In many cases several different state or federal courts may all have jurisdiction. The ultimate determination of which court hears a case is often based on practical rather than legal reasons. Location, judges' reputations, and the characteristics of the local community are often influencing factors in choosing a particular jurisdiction, assuming, of course, that the court meets the legal requirements for jurisdiction.

A court meets the legal requirements for jurisdiction if

1. it has **subject matter jurisdiction** and
2. it has **personal jurisdicition,** in rem jurisdiction or quasi in rem jurisdiction.

Subject matter jurisdiction refers to jurisdiction or authority to hear the type of case before the court, whereas personal jurisdiction (sometimes called *in personam* jurisdiction) refers to authority or power over the parties, especially the defendant.

At times, a court can hear a case if it lacks personal jurisdiction as long as it has in rem jurisdiction or quasi in rem jurisdiction. **In rem jurisdiction** means that property that is the subject of a lawsuit is located within the state. **Quasi in rem jurisdiction** sometimes exists when the defendant owns any property that is located within the state, even though that property is not the subject of the lawsuit. However, any judgment must be satisfied or collected from that property. To decide a case, a court must have subject matter and either personal jurisdiction, in rem jurisdiction, or quasi in rem jurisdiction (see Exhibit 2–3).

subject matter jurisdiction
The authority that a court has to hear a particular type of case.

personal jurisdiction
The power or authority of the court to make a ruling affecting the parties before the court.

in rem jurisdiction
The authority of a court to hear a case based on the fact that property, which is the subject of a lawsuit, is located within the state in which the court is situated.

quasi in rem jurisdiction
Authority of a court to hear a case based on the fact that the defendant owns property that is located within the state, even though that property is not the subject of the lawsuit.

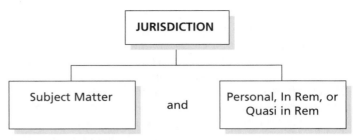

EXHIBIT 2–3   Jurisdiction

Subject Matter Jurisdiction

Subject matter jurisdiction determines whether a court has the power to hear a particular type of case. For example, consider the *Weigh To Go* case. The plaintiff must file this lawsuit in a trial court that has the power to hear a case based on trade name infringement. This lawsuit could not be filed in a court that was authorized to hear only juvenile matters. Nor could it be filed in an appellate court, which does not have the power to try any cases. If a court does not have proper subject matter jurisdiction, that court does not have the power to resolve the dispute, and any judgment rendered by the court is void. A void judgment is not enforceable and can be challenged at any time.

Because different court systems exist (federal and state), an individual initiating a lawsuit must first choose the proper court system. This is not a matter within the sole discretion of the plaintiff. Various laws dictate the kinds of cases that can be brought in federal courts and the kinds that can be brought in state courts.

Subject Matter Jurisdiction of the Federal Courts   The federal courts have limited subject matter jurisdiction. They can hear cases only when the Constitution, treaties, or some federal law specifically confers jurisdiction on those courts. Generally, in criminal cases the federal courts have jurisdiction when the offense is a crime under federal law. In civil cases, the federal courts have subject matter jurisdiction in the following circumstances:

diversity of citizenship
The situation that occurs when persons on one side of a case in federal court come from a different state than persons on the other side. *Complete diversity* (all of the plaintiffs are from a different state than all of the defendants) allows the court to accept and decide the case based on the court's *diversity* jurisdiction, provided that certain other criteria are met. *Diversity of citizenship* also applies to suits between citizens and foreign nationals.

1. the case involves a constitutional issue
2. the case involves a treaty
3. the case involves a federal law, such as those that regulate bankruptcy, patent and copyright, discrimination, or maritime issues
4. the United States government is a plaintiff or defendant in the lawsuit
5. the plaintiff and defendant are not citizens of the same state (**diversity of citizenship**)

Diversity of Citizenship   Federal courts have subject matter jurisdiction if diversity of citizenship exists (28 U.S.C. §1332). Jurisdiction based on diversity of citizenship has two requirements:

1. the plaintiff and defendant are not residents of the same state, and
2. if the case is a claim for money damages, the damages claimed must exceed $75,000.

Recall the automobile accident case of *Stevens v. Jackson* described earlier in this chapter. Assume the following situations at the time of the accident and assume that in all cases the amount of damages exceeds $75,000:

1. Stevens is a citizen of Oklahoma and Jackson is a citizen of Alabama, visiting a friend in Oklahoma.

Complete Diversity Exists

Stevens   *v.*   *Jackson*
(citizen of Oklahoma)   (citizen of Alabama)

2. Stevens is a citizen of Oklahoma and has a passenger, Deese, also a citizen of Oklahoma. Jackson is a citizen of Alabama.

Complete Diversity Exists

Stevens and Deese   *v.*   *Jackson*
(both citizens of Oklahoma)   (citizen of Alabama)

3. Stevens is a citizen of Oklahoma and Jackson is a citizen of Alabama driving a vehicle owned by his friend, Pearlman, a citizen of Oklahoma.

Complete Diversity Does Not Exist

Stevens   *v.*   *Jackson*   *and Pearlman*
(citizen of Oklahoma)   (citizen of Alabama)   (citizen of Oklahoma)

EXHIBIT 2–4 Determining diversity of citizenship

Most cases require complete diversity before the federal court can hear a case. This means that no plaintiff and no defendant can be citizens of the same state. Diversity also exists when a dispute is between citizens of a state and citizens or subjects of a foreign state. For examples of how diversity is determined, see Exhibit 2–4. However, complete diversity is not required in cases involving a single accident resulting in the death of at least 75 people. With some exceptions, the federal court can hear these multiparty cases if "minimal" diversity exists. Minimal diversity exists if any plaintiff is a citizen of a state and any defendant is a citizen of another state, a citizen or subject of a foreign state, or a foreign state (nation) itself.

One question that sometimes arises in connection with the monetary limit required for diversity jurisdiction is whether several small claims can be aggregated to achieve the minimum requirement. Unfortunately, the answer to this question is not a simple one and depends on the nature of the claims to be aggregated. In general, however, claims cannot be added together to meet the $75,000 requirement if the claims are separate and distinct. For example, if several people are injured in an automobile accident and individually each claim is under $75,000, but added together they exceed that amount, the federal court would not have diversity jurisdiction. Each person has a separate and distinct claim, even though they are related, and even though they could join in the same lawsuit.

When plaintiffs and defendants in a case are individuals, state citizenship is normally determined by the individuals' primary residence. In contrast, corporate parties are considered citizens of both the state in which they are incorporated and the state in which they maintain their principal place of business. Corporations may thus be citizens of more than one state.

Choice of Law   When a federal court exercises jurisdiction based on diversity of citizenship, the substantive law controlling the dispute is not found in federal law. If it were, subject matter jurisdiction would be based on that federal law rather than on the diversity of citizenship. When hearing a diversity case, therefore, the federal court must apply some state law to the substantive issues in the case. Usually the federal court applies the substantive law of the state in which the federal court is situated. For example, if a product liability case is filed in a federal court because the parties are citizens of different states, the federal court would have to base its decision on the state law dealing with product liability.

Exclusive versus Concurrent Jurisdiction   Even if the federal courts have subject matter jurisdiction, this does not always mean that the case must be brought in that court. Sometimes the state court also has jurisdiction. Subject matter jurisdiction of the federal courts can be either exclusive or concurrent. **Exclusive jurisdiction** means that the action must be brought in federal court. **Concurrent jurisdiction** means that it can be brought either in federal court or in state court. Under federal law, certain subject matters must be handled in federal court. Examples of federal court exclusive jurisdiction include maritime cases, patent cases, and bankruptcy cases. However, other subject matters can be litigated in either federal or state court. Furthermore, when federal jurisdiction is based on diversity of citizenship, jurisdiction is almost always concurrent with a state. For example, consider the *Weigh To Go* case described in the commentary to this chapter. The facts indicate that this is a case of concurrent jurisdiction. (See Exhibit 2–5.)

Removal to Federal Court   In cases where concurrent jurisdiction exists, the plaintiff makes the initial determination regarding the court. However, if the plaintiff chooses to file in a state court, in most cases the defendant has the right to have the case transferred or removed to the federal court. The defendant accomplishes this by following the requirements described in the United States Code (28 U.S.C. §1446). After the plaintiff files a complaint in state court, removal occurs as follows:

1. Within 30 days of service or receipt of papers, the defendant files in federal court the following:
   a. a *notice of removal* (a document requesting that the case be transferred to the federal court) and
   b. copies of all process, pleadings, and orders that she has received.
2. The defendant files these documents in the federal district and division located in the state where the plaintiff originally filed the complaint.
3. The defendant gives written notice to all adverse parties and the clerk of state court that notice of removal has been filed.

exclusive jurisdiction (exclusive)
If a court has exclusive jurisdiction over a subject, no other court in the area can decide a lawsuit on that subject.

concurrent jurisdiction (concurrent)
"Running together," or having the same authority at the same time. For example, courts have concurrent jurisdiction when each one has the power to deal with the same case.

removal
The transfer of a case from one court to another (most commonly, from a state to a federal court, often for civil rights reasons).

Concurrent Jurisdiction

State Court Has Jurisdiction:

1. California statutory and case law provides protection to a trade name. This gives California subject matter jurisdiction.
2. Defendant Go A Weigh is a citizen of California. This gives California state court personal jurisdiction.
3. Since both subject matter and personal jurisdiction exist, state court in California has jurisdiction to hear case.

Federal Court Has Jurisdiction:

1. Plaintiff Weigh To Go is a citizen of Texas (state of incorporation) and Oregon (principal place of business). Defendant is a citizen of California. Diversity of citizenship exists, giving the federal court subject matter jurisdiction (assuming that damage minimums are requested).
2. Since the defendant is a citizen of California, the federal court in California has personal jurisdiction.
3. Since both subject matter and personal jurisdiction exist, the federal court located in California has jurisdiction to hear the case.

Conclusion

1. This is a case of concurrent jurisdiction. The plaintiff initially chooses the court. If the plaintiff chooses to file in state court, the defendant can remove the case to federal court. If the plaintiff files in federal court, the case remains there.

EXHIBIT 2–5 Concurrent jurisdiction for *Weigh To Go v. Go A Weigh*

See Exhibit 2–6 for an example of a notice of removal.

Concurrent jurisdiction can also exist between two or more states. That is, where a case belongs in a state court system, more than one state may have subject matter jurisdiction. This would be determined by the facts of the case and the appropriate state laws.

Supplemental Jurisdiction Even if a matter is not normally within the subject matter jurisdiction of the federal courts it may still be heard in federal court if it is in conjunction with a case that is within the subject matter jurisdiction of the court. This is known as **supplemental jurisdiction.** This is also known as *pendent or ancillary jurisdiction.* For instance, Wilson works for Chipp Inc. as an electrical engineer. In the course of his employment Wilson designs certain products, which are patented. Pursuant to a written agreement, the patent belongs to Chipp Inc. because it was developed as part of Wilson's job. Wilson leaves Chipp Inc. and starts his own company, manufacturing products that he designed at Chipp and for which Chipp holds the patent. This action on Wilson's part violates his written contract with Chipp as well as Chipp's

supplemental jurisdiction
A federal court's right to decide a claim based on a nonfederal issue if this claim depends on the same set of facts as does a federal claim in the case before the court.

To the Honorable Judges of the United States District Court for the Northern District of California:

Defendants, Go A Weigh, a corporation, through its attorney, respectfully shows the court:

1. The above-entitled action was commenced in the Superior Court of the State of California, County of San Francisco, on January 10, _____, and is now pending in that court.

2. The above-mentioned action is a civil action for damages and injunctive relief based on alleged infringement of the trade name laws of the state of California.

3. All defendants that are required to join in this notice have joined.

4. The action is one of which the United States District Courts are given original jurisdiction under 28 USC § 1332 by reason of the diversity of citizenship of the parties.

5. The amount is controversy in the action, exclusive of interest and costs, exceeds $75,000.

6. A copy of the complaint was served on defendant at San Francisco, County of San Francisco, State of California, on January 3, _____.

7. Thirty days have not yet expired since the action thereby became removable to this court.

8. At the time of the commencement of this action, plaintiff was and now is a citizen of the state of Texas; at the time of the commencement of this action, defendants and each of them were and now are citizens and residents of the State of California.

9. Copies of all pleadings, process, and orders, served on petitioner in this action are attached and marked Exhibit A.

10. Defendants present and file with this notice a bond with a good and sufficient surety, as required by law, conditioned that defendants will pay all costs and disbursements incurred by reason of these removal proceedings, should it be determined that this action was not removable or was improperly removed.

Wherefore, defendants request that the above-entitled action be removed from the Superior Court of the State of California to the United States District Court for the Northern District of California.

Date: January 10, _____   Respectfully Submitted,

_____

Roberta Rios,
Attorney for Defendant

EXHIBIT 2–6   Notice of removal

patents on the products. Chipp Inc. wishes to sue Wilson for breach of contract as well as patent infringement. A lawsuit for breach of an employment contract would not normally be within federal court subject matter unless the case involved diversity of citizenship. However, in this case, if a breach of contract action was brought along with an action based on the patent infringement, the federal court could hear the matter because of pendent jurisdiction. Because the federal court has jurisdiction over the patent case, it can also exercise jurisdiction over the related action based on breach of contract.

Subject Matter Jurisdiction in the State Courts Except for cases that must be brought in federal court, each state has the right to determine the subject matter jurisdiction of the courts within that state. Subject matter jurisdiction of state courts is usually determined by the laws of the state. If a dispute arises under those laws, the state courts generally have subject matter jurisdiction. Sometimes, a state court has subject matter jurisdiction over disputes arising under federal law. This is because the federal law allows it. See Exhibit 2–7 for examples of types of cases within the subject matter jurisdiction of the federal and state courts.

State court systems often have more than one level of trial court. Subject matter jurisdiction requires that a case be filed in the correct court. States usually have at least one trial court that has **general jurisdiction** in civil cases, that is, the power to hear any kind of case except those that must be brought in federal court. These are often known

general jurisdiction
The power of a court to hear and decide any of a wide range of cases that arise within its geographic area.

FEDERAL COURT	STATE COURT	FEDERAL OR STATE COURT
Cases involving federal laws ■ civil rights ■ discrimination ■ social security ■ broadcasting	Cases involving state constitutional or state law issues	State law disputes where diversity of citizenship exists
	Most personal injury cases	Certain civil rights cases
Cases against the United States government	■ automobile accidents ■ medical and other malpractice ■ product liability	Federal constitutional issues
Intellectual property cases such as patent and copyright disputes		Cases involving certain federal laws
Corporate securities cases	Real property disputes	
Admiralty cases (cases arising on the high seas)	Landlord/tenant disputes	
	Contract disputes	
Cases involving rights under treaties	Business disputes	
	Family law cases	
Disputes between states	Probate matters	

EXHIBIT 2–7 Examples of subject matter jurisdiction: federal versus state

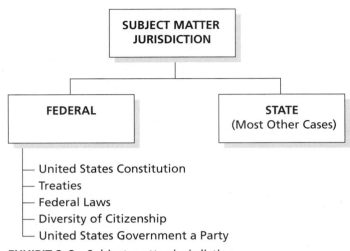

EXHIBIT 2–8   Subject matter jurisdiction

limited jurisdiction

Authority to hear only certain kinds of cases.

affirm

1. Make firm; repeat agreement; confirm. 2. When a higher court declares that a lower court's action was valid and right, it "*affirms*" the decision.

reverse

Set aside. For example, when a higher court reverses a lower court on appeal, it sets aside the judgment of the lower court and either substitutes its own judgment for it or sends the case back to the lower court with instructions on what to do with it.

remand

Send back. For example, a higher court may remand (send back) a case to the lower court, directing the lower court to take some action.

as county courts, circuit courts, superior courts, and courts of common pleas. However, unlike the federal system, where there is only one level of trial court, many states have created special trial courts that have limited subject matter jurisdiction. A court of **limited jurisdiction** has authority to hear only certain kinds of cases. For example, some courts have authority to hear limited types of cases, such as juvenile proceedings or family law matters; some courts with limited jurisdiction are only empowered to hear cases in which the amount of money in dispute is a limited amount. These courts are often known as municipal courts, district courts, or justice courts. See Exhibit 2–8 and Exhibit 2–9.

Original Jurisdiction   Determining whether a case belongs in federal court or state court is only one part of subject matter jurisdiction. After deciding which court system, federal or state, has subject matter jurisdiction, a party must file her lawsuit in the proper court within that system. All cases must be filed in a court that has original jurisdiction. *Original jurisdiction* is the power to first hear and resolve the dispute. In most civil cases, the court of original jurisdiction is the trial court (the federal district court or it state counterpart).

Appellate Jurisdiction   Appellate jurisdiction is the power of a court to review the decision of a court of original jurisdiction. In exercising appellate jurisdiction, a reviewing court has the power to **affirm** the decision (uphold the lower court), **reverse** the decision (change the lower court's decision), or reverse and **remand** the case (change the lower court's decision and send it back to the trial court to be retried). Appellate jurisdiction does not give a reviewing court power to retry a case. Generally the courts of appeals do not listen to witnesses, nor do they consider evidence that was not introduced in the trial court. Appellate jurisdiction lies in the federal and state courts of appeals, state supreme courts (sometimes referred to as courts of last resort), and the United States Supreme Court.

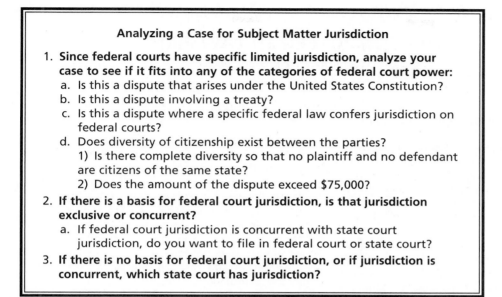

Analyzing a Case for Subject Matter Jurisdiction

1. **Since federal courts have specific limited jurisdiction, analyze your case to see if it fits into any of the categories of federal court power:**
   a. Is this a dispute that arises under the United States Constitution?
   b. Is this a dispute involving a treaty?
   c. Is this a dispute where a specific federal law confers jurisdiction on federal courts?
   d. Does diversity of citizenship exist between the parties?
      1) Is there complete diversity so that no plaintiff and no defendant are citizens of the same state?
      2) Does the amount of the dispute exceed $75,000?
2. **If there is a basis for federal court jurisdiction, is that jurisdiction exclusive or concurrent?**
   a. If federal court jurisdiction is concurrent with state court jurisdiction, do you want to file in federal court or state court?
3. **If there is no basis for federal court jurisdiction, or if jurisdiction is concurrent, which state court has jurisdiction?**

EXHIBIT 2–9 Analyzing subject matter jurisdiction

Challenging Subject Matter Jurisdiction A court that lacks subject matter jurisdiction has no power to decide a case. If it attempts to do so, that judgment is void and can be challenged at any time. Subject matter jurisdiction can be challenged in different ways, depending on where the lawsuit is filed. One common way to attack subject matter jurisdiction is by filing a motion to dismiss the case.

Personal Jurisdiction

In addition to having jurisdiction over the subject matter of the case, a court must also have jurisdiction over the parties. This authority, known as *personal jurisdiction,* means that the court has the power to render a judgment that affects the rights of the parties before the court.

Jurisdiction over Plaintiff Personal jurisdiction over the plaintiff seldom, if ever, presents any legal problems. The plaintiffs always file the lawsuit and select the trial court. Therefore they cannot complain that the court has no power over them. Having asked the court to make a decision concerning their rights, plaintiffs have no basis to challenge the court's right to do so.

Jurisdiction over Defendant Personal jurisdiction over the defendant exists when a court has the power to render a judgment that affects the rights of the defendant and when the defendant has been given proper notice of the lawsuit (that is, proper service of process). Because the defendant does not normally choose to be sued in a particular court, jurisdiction over the person of the defendant must be determined by other factors. Assuming that proper notice of the lawsuit is given, all state courts have personal

THE COMPUTERIZED LAW FIRM
The Internet

SCENARIO

Your supervising attorney, whose office is located in Texas, is anxious to file suit against Go A Weigh and has already determined that because of personal jurisdiction requirements the action must be maintained in California. Your attorney is also fairly certain that this case could be brought in federal court, under federal trademark laws. However, the attorney thinks that the case could also be brought in the state court of California under the laws of that state. Although your attorney is generally familiar with practice in the federal court, she knows nothing about practice within the state of California. She would like to be able to compare the substantive law and the procedures of the two jurisdictions before making any final decisions. The attorney has a meeting with the client tomorrow morning and would like to discuss the options with the client.

Your attorney asks you to research the California substantive law regarding infringement of trade names, along with the rules of procedure for that state. She tells you that if the matter is filed in state court it would be in San Francisco. She asks you to try to find out about the local rules of court for that area. She also tells you that one of her friends from law school is now practicing in the San Francisco area. She would like to give him a call and find out more about the courts in that area. However, she has not talked to him for several years and does not have his telephone number. She asks you to try to find it. The attorney needs this information by tomorrow morning. It is now late in the afternoon.

PROBLEM

Your law office has numerous resource materials for practice in the federal courts and for practice in your state, but has nothing for the substantive laws or rules of procedures for the courts of other states. Your local law library does have out-of-state materials, but is located several miles away, has very limited parking, and closes at 6 P.M. How can you research this case within your time frame? And how can you locate a specific attorney in California?

SOLUTION

The Internet provides extensive resources for litigation practitioners. Legal research materials, public documents, and factual information are readily available. You can find information on the Internet in two ways. If you know the Web site address (the URL) you can go directly to a specific site. On the other hand, if you are looking for information and do not know where it is located (or if it is locatable) on the Internet you can use one of many search engines to complete your search.

To use a search engine, you simply describe what you are looking for and the search engine searches for the material. Be aware, however, that not all search engines search the same way or the same sources. If your search is unsuccessful on one search engine, you should try another.

Some popular general search engines are:

<http://www.altavista.com>
<http://www.hotbot.com>
<http://www.google.com>
<http://www.askjeeves.com>

Some search engines that search only legal databases are:

<http://www.lawcrawler.com>
<http://www.lawguru.com>

Most law firms maintain law libraries containing statutory and case materials from their own state. However, generally there is little need for out-of-state references. Today, through the Internet, lawyers and paralegals can access several databases containing extensive federal, state, and international legal resources. The most popular legal databases are Westlaw or LEXIS which are fee-based. Attorneys must pay to use the service. Both of these services can be accessed through the Internet at **<http://www.westlaw.com>** and **<http://www. lexis.com>**. However, to use the databases and actually conduct research you need a special identification number and a password obtained by subscribing to the service. These services provide access to state and federal case law, and statutory law, as well as many secondary sources. They also contain public records such as corporate and real estate filings.

Other databases are available for free on the Internet. For example, on the Internet you can find most United States Supreme Court cases, many federal appellate court cases, many state court cases, the United States Codes, and the codes of many states. You can also find the local rules of court for a number of individual courts. The Internet also contains substantial factual information not available on LEXIS and Westlaw. For example, the Web site for the California Bar Association contains the business address and telephone number for all of its members. Lawyers can also be located at **<http://www.martindale.com>**.

Two popular Internet sites for extensive legal materials are:

<http://www.findlaw.com>
<http://www.law.cornell.edu>

Although the Internet contains a great deal of free legal information, most legal researchers find that using fee-based services is often easier and more efficient than the Internet, especially for difficult legal questions.

Whether one uses a fee-based service or the Internet, computerized research offers many advantages. The research can be done in the researcher's office or from a home computer, and it can be done at anytime.

jurisdiction over those who reside within the territorial limits of the court. According to Rule 4 of the Federal Rules of Civil Procedure, the federal courts have personal jurisdiction over residents of the state in which the federal district court is located. Rule 4 also sets out various circumstances under which a federal district court may acquire personal jurisdiction over a defendant who does not reside within the state in which the court is located. Primarily, the rule provides that if the state court is authorized to exercise personal jurisdiction over a nonresident, then the federal court is likewise authorized. If a defendant is not subject to the jurisdiction of any single state, jurisdiction in the federal courts is also proper if consistent with the Constitution and the claim arises under federal law.

No court has unlimited rights to exercise personal jurisdiction over nonresidents. Such a result would be basically unfair. For example, consider the *Weigh To Go* case described in the commentary. Weigh To Go wishes to sue Go A Weigh for using a deceptively similar name. Go A Weigh is incorporated in the state of California and does all of its business in that state. The plaintiff, however, is incorporated in the state of Texas. Should the plaintiff be allowed to file this action in a court in Texas, thus requiring that the California corporation appear in a Texas court to defend itself? Does a Texas court have power to render a judgment against a defendant that is incorporated in and does business solely in California?

Whether a court has jurisdiction over a nonresident defendant depends on two factors. First, the exercise of jurisdiction must be in accordance with the Fourteenth Amendment to the United States Constitution. Second, the exercise of jurisdiction must be in accordance with state law. See Exhibit 2–10.

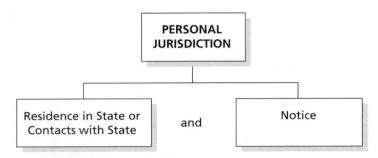

EXHIBIT 2–10   Personal jurisdiction

Constitutional Limitations   The Fourteenth Amendment to the United States Constitution requires that "due process of law" must be followed in civil as well as criminal cases. In the leading case of *International Shoe v. Washington,* printed on page 45, the United States Supreme Court held that a state cannot exercise personal jurisdiction over a nonresident defendant unless that defendant has sufficient contacts with the state to satisfy "traditional notions of fair play and substantial justice." The first factor a court often examines is whether a nonresident defendant (either an individual or a business entity) is doing business within the state. Courts can usually exercise personal jurisdiction over a nonresident defendant if that person or entity is doing business within the state and therefore has the opportunity to avail itself of the state's laws and state's courts. The courts refer to this as "purposeful availment." However, it is not necessary that a defendant is actually conducting an ongoing business within the state. Constitutional requirements are often satisfied with less. Circumstances in which personal jurisdiction has been found to exist include:

1. Doing an act in the state that causes injury
2. Causing an effect in the state by an act done elsewhere
3. Entering into a contract within the state
4. Ownership, use, or possession of a thing in the state

On the other hand, personal jurisdiction has been found to be lacking where defendants, an automobile wholesaler and a retailer, sold an automobile in New York. The buyers, claiming that the automobile was defective, sued the defendants in Oklahoma where they suffered an accident. Defendants had no other connection to Oklahoma.

In a series of recent cases, courts have been asked to determine questions of personal jurisdiction of parties who maintain Web sites for their businesses. In general, courts seem to find personal jurisdiction where there is some possibility of "interaction" with those visiting the Web site. That is, if a customer can order products through the site, personal jurisdiction probably exists. If the site is informational only, then personal jurisdiction probably will not exist.

State Long-Arm Statutes   Even though the exercise of jurisdiction may be constitutionally permissible, it must also be allowed by the laws of the state in question. State laws describing the circumstances under which the state may exercise jurisdiction over

INTERNATIONAL SHOE CO. v. WASHINGTON
326 U.S. 310 (1945)

Mr. Chief Justice STONE delivered the opinion of the Court.

The questions for decision are (1) whether, within the limitations of the due process clause of the Fourteenth Amendment, appellant, a Delaware corporation, has by its activities in the State of Washington rendered itself amenable to proceedings in the courts of that state to recover unpaid contributions to the state unemployment compensation fund exacted by state statutes, Washington Unemployment Compensation Act, Washington Revised Statutes, 9998-103a through 9998-123a, 1941 Supp., and (2) whether the state can exact those contributions consistently with the due process clause of the Fourteenth Amendment.

The facts as found by the appeal tribunal and accepted by the state Superior Court and Supreme Court, are not in dispute. Appellant is a Delaware corporation, having its principal place of business in St. Louis, Missouri, and is engaged in the manufacture and sale of shoes and other footwear. It maintains places of business in several states, other than Washington, at which its manufacturing is carried on and from which its merchandise is distributed interstate through several sales units or branches located outside the State of Washington.

Appellant has no office in Washington and makes no contracts either for sale or purchase of merchandise there. It maintains no stock of merchandise in that state and makes there no deliveries of goods in intrastate commerce. During the years from 1937 to 1940, now in question, appellant employed 11 to 13 salesmen under direct supervision and control of sales managers located in St. Louis. These salesmen resided in Washington; their principal activities were confined to that state; and they were compensated by commissions based upon the amount of their sales. The commissions for each year totaled more than $31,000. Appellant supplies its salesmen with a line of samples, each consisting of one shoe of a pair, which they display to prospective purchasers. On occasion they rent permanent sample rooms, for exhibiting samples, in business buildings, or rent rooms in hotels or business buildings temporarily for that purpose. The cost of such rentals is reimbursed by appellant.

The authority of the salesmen is limited to exhibiting their samples and soliciting orders from prospective buyers, at prices and on terms fixed by appellant. The salesmen transmit the orders to appellant's office in St. Louis for acceptance or rejection, and when accepted the merchandise for filling the orders is shipped f.o.b. from points outside Washington to the purchasers within the state. All the merchandise shipped into Washington is invoiced at the place of shipment from which collections are made. No salesman has authority to enter into contracts or to make collections.

The Supreme Court of Washington was of opinion that the regular and systematic solicitation of orders in the state by appellant's salesmen, resulting in a continuous flow of appellant's product into the state, was sufficient to constitute doing business in the state so as to make appellant amenable to suit in its courts. But it was also of opinion that there were sufficient additional activities shown to bring the case within the rule frequently stated, that solicitation within a state by the agents of a foreign corporation plus some additional activities there are sufficient to render the corporation amenable to suit brought in the courts of the state to enforce an obligation arising out of its activities there. [citations omitted] The court found such additional activities in the salesmen's display of samples sometimes in permanent display rooms, and the salesmen's residence within the state, continued over a period of years, all resulting in a substantial volume of merchandise regularly shipped by appellant to purchasers within the state.

* * *

Appellant also insists that its activities within the state were not sufficient to manifest its "presence" there and that in its absence the state courts were

(continued)

without jurisdiction, that consequently it was a denial of due process for the state to subject appellant to suit. It refers to those cases in which it was said that the mere solicitation of orders for the purchase of goods within a state, to be accepted without the state and filled by shipment of the purchased goods interstate, does not render the corporation seller amenable to suit within the state. And appellant further argues that since it was not present within the state, it is a denial of due process to subject it to taxation or other money exaction. It thus denies the power of the state to lay the tax or to subject appellant to a suit for its collection.

Historically the jurisdiction of courts to render judgment in personam is grounded on their de facto power over the defendant's person. Hence his presence within the territorial jurisdiction of court was prerequisite to its rendition of a judgment personally binding him. *Pennoyer v. Neff*, 95 U.S. 714, 733. But now that the capias ad respondendum has given way to personal service of summons or other form of notice, due process requires only that in order to subject a defendant to a judgment in personam, if he be not present within the territory of the forum, he have certain minimum contacts with it such that the maintenance of the suit does not offend "traditional notions of fair play and substantial justice."

Since the corporate personality is a fiction, although a fiction intended to be acted upon as though it were a fact, it is clear that unlike an individual its "presence" without, as well as within, the state of its origin can be manifested only by activities carried on in its behalf by those who are authorized to act for it. To say that the corporation is so far "present" there as to satisfy due process requirements, for purposes of taxation or the maintenance of suits against it in the courts of the state, is to beg the question to be decided. For the terms "present" or "presence" used merely to symbolize those activities of the corporation's agent within the state which courts will deem to be sufficient to satisfy the demands of due process. Those demands may be met by such contacts of the corporation with the state of the forum as make it reasonable,

in the context of our federal system of government, to require the corporation to defend the particular suit which is brought there. An "estimate of the inconveniences" which would result to the corporation from a trial away from its "home" or principal place of business is relevant in this connection. "Presence" in the state in this sense has never been doubted when the activities of the corporation there have not only been continuous and systematic, but also give rise to the liabilities sued on, even though no consent to be sued or authorization to an agent to accept service of process has been given. Conversely it has been generally recognized that the casual presence of the corporate agent or even his conduct of single or isolated items of activities in a state in the corporation's behalf are not enough to subject it to suit on causes of action unconnected with the activities there. To require the corporation in such circumstances to defend the suit away from its home or other jurisdiction where it carries on more substantial activities has been thought to lay too great and unreasonable a burden on the corporation to comport with due process. While it has been held in cases on which appellant relies that continuous activity of some sorts within a state is not enough to support the demand that the corporation be amenable to suits unrelated to that activity, there have been instances in which the continuous corporate operations within a state were thought so substantial and of such a nature as to justify suit against it on causes of action arising from dealings entirely distinct from those activities.

Finally, although the commission of some single or occasional acts of the corporate agent in a state sufficient to impose an obligation or liability on the corporation has not been thought to confer upon the state authority to enforce it, other such acts, because of their nature and quality and the circumstances of their commission, may be deemed sufficient to render the corporation liable to suit.

* * *

It is evident that the criteria by which we mark the boundary line between those activities which justify the subjection of a corporation to suit, and those which do not, cannot be simply mechanical or quantitative. The test is not merely, as has sometimes been suggested, whether the activity, which the corporation has seen fit to procure through its agents in another state, is a little more or a little less. Whether due process is satisfied must depend rather upon the quality and nature of the activity in relation to the fair and orderly administration of the laws which it was the purpose of the due process clause to insure. That clause does not contemplate that a state may make binding a judgment in personam against an individual or corporate defendant with which the state has no contacts, ties, or relations. But to the extent that a corporation exercises the privilege of conducting activities within a state, it enjoys the benefits and protection of the laws of that state. The exercise of that privilege may give rise to obligations; and, so far as those obligations arise out of or are connected with the activities within the state, a procedure which requires the corporation to respond to a suit brought to enforce them can, in most instances, hardly be said to be undue. Applying these standards, the activities carried on in behalf of appellant in the State of Washington were neither irregular nor casual. They were systematic and continuous throughout the years in question. They resulted in a large volume of interstate business, in the course of which appellant received the benefits and protection of the laws of the state, including the right to resort to the courts for the enforcement of its rights. The obligation which is here sued upon arose out of these very activities. It is evident that these operations establish sufficient contacts or ties with the state of the forum to make it reasonable and just according to our traditional conception of fair play and substantial justice to permit the state to enforce the obligations which appellant has incurred there. Hence we cannot say that the maintenance of the present suit in the State of Washington involves an unreasonable or undue procedure.

We are likewise unable to conclude that the service of the process within the state upon an agent whose activities establish appellant's "presence" there was not sufficient notice of the suit, or that the suit was so unrelated to those activities as to make the agent an inappropriate vehicle for communicating the notice. It is enough that appellant has established such contacts with the state that the particular form of substituted service adopted there gives reasonable assurance that the notice will be actual. Nor can we say that the mailing of the notice of suit to appellant by registered mail at its home office was not reasonably calculated to apprise appellant of the suit.

Only a word need be said of appellant's liability for the demanded contributions of the state unemployment fund. The Supreme Court of Washington, construing and applying the state, has held that it imposes a tax on the privilege of employing appellant's salesmen within the state measured by a percentage of the wages, here the commissions payable to the salesmen. This construction we accept for purposes of determining the constitutional validity of the statute. The right to employ labor has been deemed an appropriate subject of taxation in this country and England, both before and since the adoption of the *Constitution.* And such a tax imposed upon the employer for unemployment benefits is within the constitutional power of the states. Appellant having rendered itself amenable to suit upon obligations arising out of the activities of its salesmen in Washington, the state may maintain the present suit in personam to collect the tax laid upon the exercise of the privilege of employing appellant's salesmen within the state. For Washington has made one of those activities, which taken together establish appellant's "presence" there for purposes of suit, the taxable event by which the state brings appellant within the reach of its taxing power. The state thus has constitutional power to lay the tax and to subject appellant to a suit to recover it. The activities which establish its "presence" subject it alike to taxation by the state and to suit to recover the tax.

AFFIRMED.

long-arm statutes

A state law that allows the courts of that state to claim jurisdiction over (decide cases directly involving) persons outside the state who have allegedly committed torts or other wrongs inside the state. Even with a long-arm statute, the court will not have jurisdiction unless the person sued has certain minimum contacts with the state.

nonresident defendants are known as **long-arm statutes.** The following is an example of a such a long-arm statute:

> Any person . . . whether or not a citizen or resident of this state, who in person or through an agent does any of the following enumerated acts, submits himself, and if an individual, his personal representative, to the jurisdiction of the courts of this state as to any claim arising out of or related to:

1. the transaction of any business within this state;
2. contracting to supply services or goods in this state;
3. the causing of any injury within this state whether tortious or by breach of warranty;
4. the ownership, use, or possession of any real estate situated in this state;
5. contracting to insure any person, property, or risk located within this state at the time of contracting. . . .

Utah Code Ann. § 78-27-24 (2003).

Waiver by Appearance   As mentioned, if a court lacks subject matter jurisdiction, any judgment rendered by the court is void. To an extent, the same is true of personal jurisdiction. However, although the parties to a lawsuit cannot waive, or give up, the requirement of subject matter jurisdiction, a defendant can waive, or give up, the requirement of personal jurisdiction. A waiver of jurisdiction means that an individual voluntarily allows a court to hear a case against her even though the court does not have the power to do so. Furthermore, in some courts, if the defendant makes a general appearance in court and does not properly object to personal jurisdiction, she has automatically waived any defect in personal jurisdiction. A defendant makes a **general appearance** whenever she files a pleading or takes part in the proceedings by doing anything other than objecting to jurisdiction.

general appearance

Coming before a court and submitting to its jurisdiction in a case.

special appearance

Showing up in court for a limited purpose only, especially to argue that the court lacks jurisdiction over you or your client. *Special appearances* have been replaced in federal courts and many state courts by motions or pleadings for the same purpose.

motion to quash service of summons

A request that the court declare that service of the complaint and summons is invalid, either because the court lacks jurisdiction over the defendant or because of some procedural problem with the service itself.

Notice   Fairness demands that before a court can decide the rights of a defendant in a lawsuit, the defendant should be given proper notice of the action. This is known as *service of process.* How service can be accomplished is a matter determined by the laws of the jurisdiction in which the lawsuit is pending. The different methods of service of process are described in Chapter 5.

Challenging Personal Jurisdiction   A defendant must exercise care in challenging personal jurisdiction, because doing so in an improper manner may inadvertently confer personal jurisdiction on the court. Although federal courts allow defendants to challenge personal jurisdiction in the answer to the complaint, in some courts personal jurisdiction must be attacked by a **special appearance** (an appearance for the sole purpose of questioning the court's jurisdiction). This is normally done by filing a motion known as a motion to quash service of summons. A motion is simply a request to the court for a written order. A **motion to quash service of summons** is a request that the court not allow the complaint to be served, thereby preventing the plaintiff from pursuing her lawsuit. In federal court, a motion to quash service of summons is an alternative way of challenging personal jurisdiction.

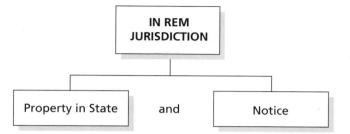

EXHIBIT 2–11 In rem jurisdiction

In Rem Jurisdiction

Sometimes, even though personal jurisdiction may be questionable or even non-existent, the court can still hear a case if it has jurisdiction over property that is the subject of a dispute. This is known as *in rem jurisdiction* and is a substitute in some cases for personal jurisdiction. See Exhibit 2–11. For example, Ryan Flynn, a resident of Pennsylvania, dies and leaves an estate consisting of real and personal property, all of which is located in Pennsylvania. He is survived by two sons, Martin, a Pennsylvania resident, and Michael, a resident of Georgia. In his will, Flynn leaves all of his property to Michael. Martin wishes to challenge this. Even though Michael may have no connection to the state of Pennsylvania, because the property that is the subject of this dispute is located in Pennsylvania the courts in Pennsylvania have jurisdiction to hear the matter. They have the right to determine ownership of property located within the state boundaries. This is in rem jurisdiction.

In exercising in rem jurisdiction, a court is limited to rendering judgments that affect only the property. The court cannot render personal judgments against the defendant that do not concern that property. For example, in the preceding case, suppose that Martin Flynn claimed that he was disinherited because of slanderous remarks made to his father by his brother. In addition to challenging the will, he might also wish to sue his brother for slander in the same action. In order for a court to hear this action, the Pennsylvania court would need to have personal jurisdiction over Michael.

Quasi In Rem Jurisdiction

Another substitute for personal jurisdiction is quasi in rem jurisdiction. For quasi in rem jurisdiction to exist, various requirements must be met. First, a defendant must own some property within the state, although the property need not be the subject of the lawsuit. Second, the plaintiff can use only that property that the court awards to satisfy a judgment. Third, that property is usually brought before the court at the beginning of the lawsuit through an attachment proceeding. In an **attachment** proceeding, the court usually orders that the property be seized and remain under the control of the court until the case is resolved.

If a court hears a case based on in rem or quasi in rem jurisdiction, due process still requires that the exercise of jurisdiction be fair and that the defendant be notified of the

attachment

Formally seizing property (or a person) in order to bring it under the control of the court. This is usually done by getting a court order to have a law enforcement officer take control of the property.

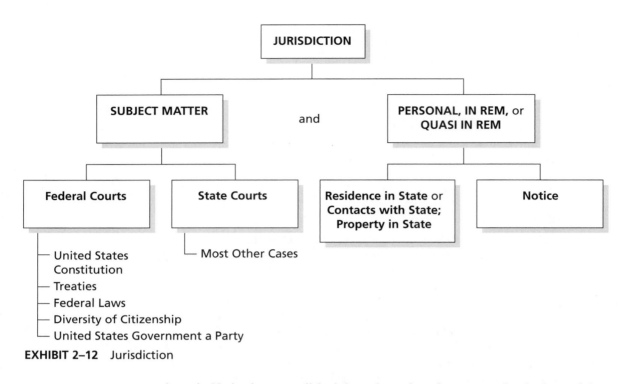

EXHIBIT 2–12 Jurisdiction

lawsuit. Notice is accomplished through service of process under the laws of the state in which the action is pending. See Exhibit 2–12.

Venue

An analysis of jurisdiction will tell a party whether to file an action in federal court or state court. If a case belongs in a state court, jurisdiction also determines in which state or states the action can be filed. However, within the federal court system and within each state court system there are a number of trial courts located in different geographical areas. Choosing the court in the proper geographical area is a question of **venue.**

Lawsuits should be filed and heard in a court that has proper venue. However, unlike jurisdiction, a court's lack of proper venue does not render a judgment void. If a defendant does not object to improper venue, she waives the right to object to the judgment rendered by the court.

Federal Court Venue

The general venue statute is 28 U.S.C. § 1391, but several different statutes control various situations. The general statute provides two locations for proper venue:

1. The judicial district where any defendant resides, as long as all of the defendants reside in the same state, or

venue
The local area where a case may be tried. Court systems may have jurisdiction (power) to take a case in a wide geographic area, but the proper *venue* for the case may be one place within that area for the convenience of the parties, or other reasons. Jurisdiction is the subject of fixed rules, but venue is often left up to the discretion (good judgment) of the judge.

2. The judicial district where the acts that form the basis of the lawsuit occurred.

If the action cannot be brought in any district meeting these criteria (i.e., if all defendants do not reside in the same state or if the lawsuit arose from acts that took place in a location that no longer has personal jurisdiction) an alternative venue is provided, depending on whether the action is based on diversity of citizenship or some other basis. If the action is based on diversity of citizenship, venue is proper in any judicial district having personal jurisdiction over any defendant. If the lawsuit is based on some other basis, venue is proper in any judicial district in which any defendant may be found. In determining the residence of a defendant, a corporation is considered to reside in any judicial district in which it is subject to personal jurisdiction at the time the lawsuit is filed.

In addition to the general venue statute, other sections of the code provide special venue rules. For example, lawsuits relating to copyrights or trademarks may be brought in the district in which the defendant or his agent resides or may be found, and patent infringement actions may be brought in the judicial district where the defendant resides or where the defendant has committed acts of infringement and has a regular and established place of business. (28 U.S.C. § 1400) Any civil action by a stockholder on behalf of his corporation may be brought in any judicial district where the corporation might have sued the same defendants. (28 U.S.C. § 1401) And generally, when the United States government is the defendant in a lawsuit, venue is proper in the judicial district where the plaintiff resides. (28 U.S.C. § 1402)

Sometimes, a statute that creates substantive rights also provides for venue. For example, the United States Code provides that employment discrimination lawsuits can be brought

> in any judicial district in the state in which the unlawful employment practice is alleged to have been committed, in the judicial district in which the employment records relevant to such practice are maintained and administered, or in the judicial district in which the aggrieved person would have worked but for the alleged unlawful employment practice, but if the respondent is not found within any such district, such an action may be brought within the judicial district in which the respondent has his principal office. [42 U.S.C. § 2000e-5 (f) (3)]

State Court Venue

Venue in state court actions is, of course, determined by state law. As a general rule, however, actions usually can be maintained in the county in which the defendant resides or where the cause of action arises. In different types of cases, other counties might also have proper venue. For example, in contract cases, actions can often be heard in the county in which the contract was made, was to be performed, or was breached. In lawsuits affecting title to real estate, the action is normally heard wherever the real estate is located.

Changing Venue

Because venue does not relate to the court's basic power to hear a case, under proper circumstances it can be changed. However, the place of trial can only be changed to another court that has jurisdiction. To change venue, a party makes a

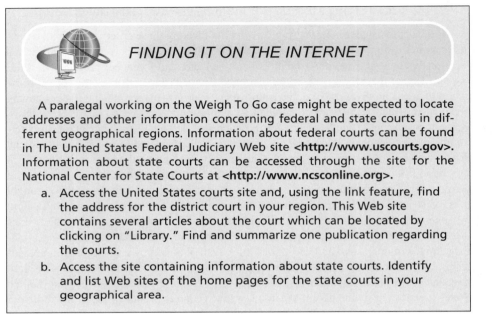

FINDING IT ON THE INTERNET

A paralegal working on the Weigh To Go case might be expected to locate addresses and other information concerning federal and state courts in different geographical regions. Information about federal courts can be found in The United States Federal Judiciary Web site **<http://www.uscourts.gov>**. Information about state courts can be accessed through the site for the National Center for State Courts at **<http://www.ncsconline.org>**.

a. Access the United States courts site and, using the link feature, find the address for the district court in your region. This Web site contains several articles about the court which can be located by clicking on "Library." Find and summarize one publication regarding the courts.

b. Access the site containing information about state courts. Identify and list Web sites of the home pages for the state courts in your geographical area.

formal written request of the court where the lawsuit was filed. This is done by making a *motion for change of venue.* Of course, there must be a good reason before a court will consider transferring the case to another location. Some of the more common reasons include the fact that in the original location the parties cannot get a fair trial, or the case was not filed in the proper court to begin with. A case might also be transferred to make the place of trial more convenient for the witnesses.

Summary

- The litigation process revolves around the courts. Because many different courts exist in the United States, plaintiffs must choose the proper court in which to pursue their case. The court chosen must have jurisdiction, or authority, to hear the case. In general, court systems are made up of trial courts, courts of appeals, and a court of last resort. In the litigation process, the function of trial courts is to determine the facts of the dispute and apply appropriate legal principles. The primary purpose of the courts of appeals is to review the proceedings in the trial court. A court of last resort, often called a supreme court, generally has discretionary right to review lower court proceedings.

- The federal court system consists of three levels of courts, United States district courts, United States Courts of Appeals, and the United States Supreme Court. The United States district courts are primarily trial courts. This is where a case is originally heard. The United States Courts of Appeals and the United States Supreme Court are primarily courts of review. They examine the proceedings that occurred in the trial courts.

- The structure of any state court system is determined by the laws of that state. Although some differences do exist from state to state, most state court systems are similar to the federal court system. All state court systems have some sort of trial courts and courts of appeals. Most states also have a state supreme court. The functions of the various state courts are similar to their counterparts in the federal court system.

■ Jurisdiction is the power or authority that a court has to hear a case. Proper jurisdiction requires that a court have the power to hear the kind of case before it (subject matter jurisdiction) and also power to make a decision binding the parties to the lawsuit (personal jurisdiction). The federal courts have subject matter jurisdiction in a case if the dispute arises under the Constitution, treaties, or federal laws. A federal court also has subject matter jurisdiction when there is diversity of citizenship and the amount in controversy exceeds $75,000. State law determines what kinds of cases can be brought in the state courts. If a court lacks subject matter jurisdiction, a judgment rendered is void. In addition to subject matter jurisdiction, a court must also have personal jurisdiction over the parties. A court (federal or state) has personal jurisdiction over those who voluntarily agree to submit to the court's jurisdiction or over those who reside within the state where the court is located. If a defendant resides outside of the state, then a court has personal jurisdiction only if the defendant has some substantial contacts with the state and state law authorizes the exercise of that jurisdiction. State laws that deal with the exercise of personal jurisdiction over nonresident defendants are known as long-arm statutes. Personal jurisdiction also requires that the defendant receive proper notice of the lawsuit. In rem jurisdiction and quasi in rem jurisdiction can sometimes substitute for personal jurisdiction. In rem jurisdiction exists when the subject matter of the lawsuit involves property that is located in a state. Quasi in rem jurisdiction can exist when the defendant owns any property within the state, but the plaintiff must satisfy any judgment from that property. In rem and quasi in rem jurisdiction also require that the exercise of jurisdiction be basically fair and that the defendant receive proper notice of the lawsuit.

■ In choosing the proper court in which to initiate a lawsuit, an attorney must consider not only the question of jurisdiction, but also the question of venue. Venue relates to selection of the court in the proper geographical area. In the federal courts, venue is usually proper where the cause of action arose or in the district in which the defendant resides. If the defendant is the United States government or if jurisdiction is based on diversity, it is also proper where the plaintiff resides. In the interest of justice, venue can be changed to another court of proper jurisdiction.

Key Terms

affirm	higher court	quasi in rem jurisdiction
appellate jurisdiction	in rem jurisdiction	remand
attachment	jurisdiction	removal
brief	legal error	reverse
certiorari	limited jurisdiction	special appearance
concurrent jurisdiction	long-arm statutes	subject matter jurisdiction
court of appeals	lower court	supplemental jurisdiction
diversity of citizenship	motion to quash service of	supreme court
exclusive jurisdiction	summons	trial court
general appearance	original jurisdiction	venue
general jurisdiction	personal jurisdiction	

Review Questions

1. What are the functions of trial courts and courts of appeals in the litigation process?
2. How is the federal court system structured?
3. What are some of the different courts in state court systems?
4. What is subject matter jurisdiction?
5. What are three types of cases that can be brought in federal court?
6. What is the difference between exclusive jurisdiction and concurrent jurisdiction?
7. When does a court have personal jurisdiction over a party to a lawsuit?
8. Why do states have long-arm statutes?
9. What is the difference between personal jurisdiction and in rem jurisdiction?
10. What is venue?

Chapter Exercises

Where necessary, check with your instructor prior to starting any of these exercises.

1. Find out about the court structure in your state. List the various courts and the functions of each.
2. Check the laws of your state to see if a long-arm statute exists. If it does, what does it provide?
3. Check the laws of your state to see how to do the following:
    a. Challenge subject matter jurisdiction.
    b. Challenge personal jurisdiction.
    c. Change venue from one court to another.
    Also check form books for your state to find proper forms to accomplish (a), (b), and (c).
4. Review the factual situation in the commentary to this chapter. Assume that Go A Weigh is operating within your state instead of California. In which court or courts could an action by Weigh To Go against Go A Weigh be filed? Check the United States Codes and the laws of your state, and give some authority for your answer.
5. Analyze the following situations and determine if the federal court has jurisdiction under diversity of citizenship.
    a. Brady and Jeffers, both citizens of North Dakota, wish to sue as a result of an automobile accident caused by the negligence of Crane, a citizen of Montana. The damages for each of them exceeds $75,000.
    b. Same facts as (a) except that Brady and Jeffers also want to name as a defendant, Dowd, the owner of the vehicle driven by Crane. Dowd is a citizen of North Dakota.
    c. Same as in (a) except that Brady is claiming damages of $50,000 and Jeffers is claiming damages of $40,000.
    d. Digicam, Inc., a manufacturer of digital cameras, is a corporation incorporated in the state of Delaware with its principle place of business in California. It distributes its product through several national retailers who do business in several states, including Washington state. Reider, a citizen of the state of Washington, buys a defective camera that "explodes" while Reider is holding it, injuring Reider. The retailer who sold Reider the camera has declared bankruptcy. Reider wishes to sue Digicam for his injuries. Reider is claiming that his damages exceed $75,000.

6. Analyze the following situations and determine if the forum state has personal jurisdiction.

   a. Review the Digicam situation described in (d) of question 5. Based on the facts given, would the state of Washington have personal jurisdiction over Digicam?

   b. Weigh To Go, the corporation mentioned at the beginning of this chapter, recently began to manufacture exercise equipment. It also maintains a Web site, **<http://www.weightogo.com>.** The Web site contains a description and pictures of its equipment; a feature entitled "Frequently Asked Questions"; a list of names, addresses, and telephone numbers of vendors who sell the exercise equipment; and an e-mail address to contact the company for more information. You cannot order any equipment through the Web site. Marley is a resident of the state of Maine. Marley sees its Web site and wants to order equipment. Unfortunately, Weigh To Go does not distribute exercise equipment through any vendors in Maine. However, Marley calls a vendor (listed on the Web site) in New York. The vendor agrees to ship Marley equipment. Marley is seriously injured using the equipment and claims his injury is a result of a defectively designed product. Can Marley sue Weigh To Go in Maine? Business records show that the equipment manufactured by Weigh To Go is occasionally sold to Maine residents but that its total revenue for the state of Maine is less than 1%.

7. Answer the following questions regarding the case of *International Shoe v. Washington* found in this chapter.

   a. Describe the contacts that International Shoe had with the state of Washington.

   b. Did the Court feel that these contacts were sufficient to give Washington personal jurisdiction over International Shoe?

   c. What was the reason for the Court's decision?

Chapter Project

Review the case of *Stevens v. Jackson* presented earlier in this chapter. Assume that the facts described occurred in your city and that both Stevens and Jackson are residents of your state. Determine which court has original jurisdiction over the matter. Give the address of that court, as well as a reference to your state laws that determine jurisdiction and venue. If the case were to be appealed, which court in your state would hear the matter? Does this court have a Web site? If so, what is the URL?

The *Bennett* Case
Assignment 2: Determining Jurisdiction

You have been given additional facts regarding the *Bennett* case (from Chapter 1 *Commentary*). Her employer, Rikards-Hayley, an investment banking firm, is a corporation incorporated in Delaware with its principal place of business in San Francisco, California. It has offices in several states. Bennett is employed in the New York office, located in Manhattan. Your supervising attorney does not believe that this case will settle. It will probably go to trial. Preliminary research indicates that both state and federal laws exist regarding employment discrimination based on sex. Your supervisor asked you to review the Bennett research file (see Appendix B) and to write a memo addressing the following questions:

1. If the action is based on New York state law, does the New York trial court have both subject and personal jurisdiction over the defendant?

2. If the action is filed in a New York state court, locate the address for the court or courts that would have venue.

3. If the action is based on federal law (Title VII—42 U.S.C. §2000e), which courts would have subject matter jurisdiction, personal jurisdiction and proper venue?

4. If the action is filed in federal court under 42 U.S.C. §2000e, can the federal court also hear a claim for infliction of emotional distress (based entirely on state law) suffered by Bennett as a result of the discrimination?

PART II
INITIATING LITIGATION

Chapter 3

Preliminary Considerations

CHAPTER OUTLINE

Determining the Existence of a Cause of Action
Time Limitations
Feasibility of the Lawsuit
Turning Down a Case
Ethical Considerations in Accepting a Case
Ethical Considerations after Accepting a Case

COMMENTARY—THE KELSEY CASE

Seven months ago Janet Kelsey was injured in an automobile-bus collision. The accident occurred when the brakes on the bus failed, resulting in the driver's inability to stop for a red light. The bus, in which Kelsey was a passenger, was hit broadside by a car entering the intersection at the green light. The bus was owned and operated by the city. However, all maintenance on the bus was performed by Allied Auto Repair, a private company under contract with the city to maintain and repair all city buses. Kelsey has requested that your firm represent her in a personal injury lawsuit for the injuries she sustained in the accident. Your attorney has requested that you do some preliminary research to determine whether this lawsuit should be accepted and, if so, whether any immediate action must be undertaken.

OBJECTIVES

Chapter 2 covered the factors that determine the appropriate court for filing any lawsuit. However, before any action is filed in court, certain preliminary aspects of litigation must be considered and reviewed. After reading this chapter, you should be able to:

- Explain the importance of a cause of action to the litigation process.
- List the reasons that a paralegal must be familiar with the elements of a cause of action.
- Define the various types of time limitations on filing a lawsuit.
- Explain the importance of tickler systems.
- List the practical considerations that affect the decision to accept a case.
- Explain the procedure for turning down a case.
- Identify the ethical standards an attorney must consider before accepting a case.
- Describe the responsibilities of a litigation paralegal in seeing that ethical standards are followed.
- Identify the ethical requirements for an attorney during the course of litigation.
- Describe special ethical concerns for litigation paralegals.

Determining the Existence of a Cause of Action

cause of action
1. Facts sufficient to support a valid lawsuit. 2. The legal theory upon which a lawsuit ("action") is based.

Not all damages suffered by individuals are recoverable through the litigation process. The mere fact that a party has been injured or has sustained some monetary loss does not in itself give that person the right to sue. A legal right to recover damages must exist. This legally recognized right to relief is known as a **cause of action.** For example, suppose that Bricker drives his motorcycle negligently and fails to stop at a stop sign. He is hit by Steinman, who is driving in accordance with all traffic laws, in a careful and prudent manner. Bricker is the only one injured in the accident. Can Bricker recover his damages from Steinman? Obviously not. In this kind of case, where the defendant has done nothing wrong, there is no cause of action, or right to sue.

In determining whether a cause of action exists, you, as a paralegal, must examine both the law and the facts in the case. First, you must determine what general area of substantive law applies to the case. For example, is it a contract case or a tort case? Or is it both? Second, the general substantive area of law must be narrowed and a more specific topic identified. Then you can examine that specific area and determine what factors or elements must be present before a cause of action is created. For example, the *Kelsey* case described in the commentary to this chapter is controlled by the substantive law of torts. More specifically, it is covered by the tort of negligence. A review of the law of negligence reveals that for Kelsey to have a cause of action, the following elements must be shown:

1. the defendant must have a duty of due care toward the victim,
2. that duty must have been breached (a careless act),
3. the defendant's careless act must be the actual cause of the damages,
4. the defendant's careless act must be the proximate cause of the damages (i.e., the damages must be foreseeable), and
5. damages must have been sustained.

Once the elements of a cause of action have been ascertained, the final step in determining whether a cause of action exists in a particular case is to review the case itself to see if facts exist that support each of the elements. In determining whether Kelsey has a cause of action in negligence against Allied Auto Repair, the analysis might go as follows:

1. An auto repair company owes a duty of care to all users of vehicles that it maintains or repairs. Because Kelsey was a passenger on the bus, Allied owed her a duty of due care.
2. If the bus had been properly maintained, the brakes would not have failed. Thus, there is some evidence of a breach of the duty owed to the users of that bus.
3. If the brakes had not failed, the accident would not have happened. Allied's failure to properly maintain the brakes is, therefore, the actual cause of Kelsey's injuries.
4. Kelsey's injuries were a foreseeable consequence of Allied's actions. This establishes proximate or legal causation.
5. Kelsey has sustained injuries and incurred expenses, thus establishing damages.

Because each of the elements of the cause of action is supported by facts, the conclusion is that Kelsey does have a cause of action against Allied Auto Repair for negligence. See Exhibit 3–1 for examples of the elements of some common causes of action.

Identifying the elements of a cause of action is important in the litigation process for various reasons. Probably most important is that each of the elements must be proven at trial for the plaintiff to prevail. In other words, to win the case the attorney must present evidence that supports each element of the cause of action. Also, in some state jurisdictions, the initial pleading must allege facts that support each element of the cause of action.

Knowing the elements of the cause of action in a particular case is essential to any litigation paralegal assisting the attorney in pretrial preparation. Understanding what the attorney must prove at trial enables you to gather appropriate evidence and conduct relevant discovery. It also equips you to prepare pleadings that comply with legal requirements and to review opposing pleadings for legal deficiencies.

Identifying the elements of a cause of action in a particular case may take some research. Case law and statutes might need to be reviewed. Secondary source books, such as encyclopedias and practice manuals, are valuable references. Form books, which often contain explanations and legal analysis of the forms, are also helpful.

Fraud

1. The defendant misrepresented, concealed, or failed to disclose a fact.
2. The defendant knew of the falsity of the statement.
3. The defendant intended to defraud.
4. The plaintiff justifiably relied on the statement.
5. Damages resulted.

Breach of Contract

1. Existence of a contract.
2. Plaintiff's performance or excuse of performance of his duties under the contract.
3. Defendant's breach or failure to perform.
4. Resulting damages.

Strict Liability—Products Liability

1. Defendant manufactured or distributed a product.
2. The product was defective.
3. The product was used in a foreseeable manner.
4. The defective product caused an injury
5. Damages resulted.

EXHIBIT 3–1   Elements of a cause of action

Time Limitations

Even though all of the elements of a cause of action exist in a particular case, parties have time limits in which to initiate their lawsuits. As a paralegal, you must be aware of these time limits in every case.

Statute of Limitations

The basic time limit is known as a **statute of limitations.** Unless a case is filed within the appropriate statute of limitations, it will be dismissed, regardless of the merits of the case. Statutes of limitations are found in state and federal codes and vary from one jurisdiction to another (see Exhibit 3–2 and Exhibit 3–3). Statutes of limitations also differ depending on the type of case.

Commonly, statutes of limitations set definite and exact times for filing suit, and are easily determined and calculated. For example, a plaintiff might have one year from the date of an accident in which to file an action for personal injuries. Because the date of the accident is easily determined from police reports and witnesses, the statute of limitations is calculated with no difficulty.

In some cases, however, time limitations are not as easily determined. For example, in professional malpractice cases or in fraud cases, the statute of limitations might start to run not from the date of the malpractice or fraudulent act, but from the date that the plaintiff discovers or should have discovered the malpractice or fraud. Sometimes this is years after the defendant's wrongdoing. This kind of statute of limitations often presents numerous legal and factual questions, and proving the date on which the plaintiff discovered or should have discovered the wrongdoing becomes an important part of the trial process.

statute of limitations (limitation)

A time limit. For example, a statute of limitations is a law that sets a maximum amount of time after something happens for it to be taken to court.

Calculating the Statute of Limitations   In calculating the statute of limitations you do not count the first day, but you do count the last day. However, if that day is a weekend or court holiday, you would have until the next court day to file your complaint. Consider the following examples:

1. Assume that Jeffers is in an automobile accident on July 1, 2004, and assume that this type of case has a one-year statute of limitations. The statute of limitations expires on July 1, 2005. This means that a lawsuit must be filed on or before July 1, 2005 unless July 1 falls on a Saturday or Sunday. In such a case the lawsuit would have to be filed on the following Monday.

2. Assume that Jeffers is in an automobile accident on July 4, 2004 and that this type of case has a one-year statute of limitations. The statute of limitations expires on July 4, 2005, but since this is a court holiday, Jeffers has until the next court day to file a lawsuit.

Tolling the Statute of Limitations   Certain events will sometimes toll or extend the statute of limitations. When a statute of limitations is tolled, the time stops running. The most common reason that a statute of limitations is tolled is that the plaintiff is a minor. The statute is tolled during the minority of the plaintiff and begins to run once

---

(Federal Statute—Actions Arising Under Acts of Congress)

Time limitations on the commencement of civil actions arising under Acts of Congress:

(a) Except as otherwise provided by law, a civil action arising under an Act of Congress enacted after the date of the enactment of this section may not be commenced later than four years after the cause of action accrues.

(b) Notwithstanding subsection (a), a private right of action that involves a claim of fraud, deceit, manipulation, or contrivance in contravention of a regulatory requirement concerning the securities laws, as defined in section 3(a)(47) of the Securities Exchange Act of 1934 (a)(47), may be brought not later than the earlier of—

    (1) Two years after the discovery of the facts constituting the violation; or
    (2) Five years after such violation.

28 U.S.C. § 1658

(Federal Statute—Time for Commencing Action Against United States)

Time for commencing action against United States:

(a) Except as provided by the Contract Disputes Act of 1978, every civil action commenced against the United States shall be barred unless the complaint is filed within six years after the right of action first accrues. The action of any person under legal disability or beyond the seas at the time the claim accrues may be commenced within three years after the disability ceases.

(b) A tort claim against the United States shall be forever barred unless it is presented in writing to the appropriate Federal agency within two years after such claim accrues or unless action is begun within six months after the date of mailing, by certified or registered mail, of notice of final denial of the claim by the agency to which it was presented.

28 U.S.C. § 2401

(State of California Statute—Oral Contract Action)

The periods prescribed for the commencement of actions other than for the recovery of real property, are as follows:

Two years; Oral obligations . . .

Within two years: 1. An action upon a contract, obligation or liability not founded upon an instrument of writing . . .

Cal. Civ. Proc. Code §§ 335 and 339

EXHIBIT 3–2 Statutes of limitations

Date of Discovery

(State of California Statute—Legal Malpractice)

. . . An action against an attorney for a wrongful act or omission, other than for actual fraud, arising in the performance of professional services, shall be commenced within one year after the plaintiff discovers, or through the use of reasonable diligence should have discovered, the facts constituting the wrongful act or omission, or four years from the date of the wrongful act or omission, whichever occurs first. . . .

Cal. Civ. Proc. Code § 340.6

EXHIBIT 3–3 Statutes of limitations

the minor reaches the age of majority. Thus if a 10-year-old child is injured in an automobile accident and the statute of limitations is normally one year, that one year does not begin to run until the child reaches the age of majority. The statute would expire on the child's 19th birthday (one year after reaching the age of majority). Do not assume, however, that the statute of limitations is always tolled during a child's minority. You must check the appropriate statutory law. For an example of a statute that incorporates a tolling period, refer back to Exhibit 3–2 and read 28 U.S.C. § 2401. This statute is tolled during a person's legal disability or during any time the person is "beyond the seas."

Claim Statutes

In lieu of statutes of limitations, some types of cases are governed by special statutes known as **claim statutes.** This kind of statute requires that a written claim be presented to the defendant before a lawsuit can be filed. These statutes are common when a governmental entity is being sued or when the defendant is deceased and a probate is pending. Naturally, there are time limits for presenting the claim, time limits that are often shorter than the statute of limitations for similar cases. For an example of a claim statute see Exhibit 3–4.

Time limits for filing claims are often *not* tolled during minority or other legal disabilities. For example, the court has held that the tort claim statute found in Exhibit 3–4 is not tolled during a person's minority. You must be careful to check specific laws to determine this. Claim statutes usually contain a provision dictating when a lawsuit must be filed if the claim is denied. These time limits must be followed just as any statute of limitations. Read 28 U.S.C. §2401 (b), found in Exhibit 3–4. This claim statute requires that a lawsuit must be filed within six months after the claim is denied.

The written claims that must be presented are usually much less formal than a complaint or petition. Basically, they require that the prospective defendant be notified that a claim is pending, who is making the claim, what the claim is for, and the amount of the claim. The party then has the opportunity to pay the claim before any lawsuit is filed. See Exhibit 3–5 for an example.

claim statute

A type of law that requires a written notice describing a claim to be presented to the defendant before a lawsuit can be filed.

> ### Federal Statutes—Claims Against United States
>
> . . . An action shall not be instituted upon a claim against the United States for money damages for injury or loss of property or personal injury or death caused by the negligent or wrongful act or omission of any employee of the Government while acting within the scope of his office or employment, unless the claimant shall have first presented the claim to the appropriate Federal agency and his claim shall have been finally denied by the agency in writing and sent by certified or registered mail. The failure of an agency to make final disposition of a claim within six months after it is filed shall, at the option of the claimant any time thereafter, be deemed a final denial of the claim for purposes of this section. . . . 28 U.S.C. § 2675(a)
>
> A tort claim against the United State shall be forever barred unless it is presented in wiring to the appropriate Federal agency within two years after such claim accrues or unless action is begun within six months after the date of mailing, by certified or registered mail, or notice of final denial of the claim by the agency to which it was presented. 28 U.S.C. § 2401(b)

EXHIBIT 3–4 Claim statutes

Laches

laches

The legal doctrine that a delay (in pursuing or enforcing a claim or right) can be so long that the person against whom you are proceeding is unfairly hurt or prejudiced by the delay itself. Laches is an equitable defense, used when a plaintiff delays unfairly in starting a lawsuit.

In addition to the statute of limitations, equitable cases (cases in which the plaintiff is asking for something other than money damages) are governed by another time limitation known as **laches.** Laches is an equitable principle that prevents lawsuits from being filed when, in fairness to the defendant, too much time has elapsed, even though the statute of limitations may not have expired. For example, suppose Jensen and Wilson sign a written contract in which Wilson agrees to sell his house to Jensen for $100,000. For various reasons, Wilson changes his mind and refuses to complete the sale. Rather than sue on the contract, Jensen finds another house for the same price and takes no immediate legal action against Wilson. Three years later, however, after a surge in the real estate market, Jensen decides to do something. Wilson's house is now worth $200,000, and Jensen assumes that if he can purchase the house for the contract price of $100,000, he can immediately sell it and make a large profit. He therefore sues Wilson for specific performance of the contract (a lawsuit to make Wilson sell him the house according to the terms of the agreement). The statute of limitations on a written contract might be four years. Technically, the complaint would be filed in a timely fashion. However, in fairness and equity, Jensen waited too long to file his action. Thus, laches could prevent him from prevailing in his action.

Remember that laches applies only in equitable cases. If Jensen sued Wilson for money damages for breach of the contract, and the appropriate statute of limitations was four years, time limitations would not be a bar. (However, under contract law,

CLAIM FOR DAMAGE, INJURY, OR DEATH	INSTRUCTIONS: Please read carefully the instructions on the reverse side and supply information requested on both sides of this form. Use additional sheet(s) if necessary. See reverse side for additional instructions.	FORM APPROROVED OMB NO. 1105-0008 EXPIRES 5-31-05
1. Submit To Appropriate Federal Agency:		2. Name, Address of claimant and claimant's personal representative, if any. *(See instructions on reverse.) (Number, street, city, State and Zip Code)*

3. TYPE OF EMPLOYMENT MILITARY CIVILIAN	4. DATE OF BIRTH	5. MARITAL STATUS	6. DATE AND DAY OF ACCIDENT	7. TIME *(A.M. OR P.M)*

8. Basis of Claim *(State in detail the known facts and circumstances attending the damage, injury, or death, identifying persons and property involved, th place of occurrence and the cause thereof) (Use additional pages if necessary.)*

9.   **PROPERTY DAMAGE**
NAME AND ADDRESS OF OWNER, IF OTHER THAN CLAIMANT*(Number, street, city, State, and Zip Code)*

BRIEFLY DESCRIBE THE PROPERTY, NATURE AND EXTENT OF DAMAGE AND THE LOCATION WHERE PROPERTY MAY BE INSPECTI   *(See instructions on reverse side)*

10.   **PERSONAL INJURY/WRONGFUL DEATH**
STATE NATURE AND EXTENT OF EACH INJURY OR CAUSE OF DEATH, WHICH FORMS THE BASIS OF THE CLAIM. IF OTHER THAN C NAME OF INJURED PERSON OR DECEDENT

11.   **WITNESSES**

NAME	ADDRESS*(Number, street, city, State, and Zip Code)*

12. *(See instructions on reverse)*   **AMOUNT OF CLAIM***(in dollars)*

12a. PROPERTY DAMAGE	12b. PERSONAL INJURY	12c. WRONGFUL DEATH	12d. TOTAL *(Failure to specify may cause forfeiture of your rights.)*

I CERTIFY THAT THE AMOUNT OF CLAIM COVERS ONLY DAMAGES AND INJURIES CAUSED BY THE ACCIDENT ABOVE AND A ACCEPT SAID AMOUNT IN FULL SATISFACTION AND FINAL SETTLEMENT OF THIS CLAIM

13a. SIGNATURE OF CLAIMANT *(See instructions on reverse side.)*	13b. Phone number of signatory	14. DATE OF CLAIM

CIVIL PENALTY FOR PRESENTING FRAUDULENT CLAIM	CRIMINAL PENALTY FOR PRESENTING FRAUDULENT CLAIM OR MAKING FALSE STATEMENTS
The claimant shall forfeit and pay to the United States the sum of not less than $5,000 and not more than $10,000, plus 3 times the amount of damages sustained by the United States. *(See 31 U.S.C. 3729.)*	Imprisonment for not more than five years and shall be subject to a fine of not less than $5,000 and not more than $10,000, plus 3 times the amount of damages sustained by the United States. *(See 18 U.S.C.A. 287.)*

95-108
Previous editions not usable

NSN 7540-00-634-4046

STANDARD FORM 95
PRESCRIBED BY DEI
28 CFR 14.2

EXHIBIT 3–5(a)   Claim form (front)

Jensen's damages would be the difference between the contract price and the fair market value of the house at the time the contract was to be performed, not the date that the action was filed.)

Tickler Systems

Missing a statute of limitations or a claim statute can result in a malpractice claim against the law firm. Therefore, all litigation firms have calendar or tracking systems to remind them of these and other important dates. These calendaring systems are known

PRIVACY ACT NOTICE

This Notice is provided in accordance with the Privacy Act, 5 U.S.C 552a(e)(3), and concerns the information requested in the letter to which this Notice is attached.

A. *Authority:* The requested information is solicited pursuant to one or more of the following: 5 U.S.C. 301, 28 U.S.C. 501 et seq., 28 U.S.C. 2671 et seq., 28 C.F.R. Part 14.

B. *Principal Purpose:* The information requested is to be used in evaluating claims.

C. *Routine Use:* See the Notices of Systems of Records for the agency to whom you are submitting this form for this information.

D. *Effect of Failure to Respond:* Disclosure is voluntary. However, failure to supply the requested information or to execute the form may render your claim "invalid".

INSTRUCTIONS

Complete all items – Insert the word NONE where applicable

A CLAIM SHALL BE DEEMED TO HAVE BEEN PRESENTED WHEN A FEDERAL AGENCY RECEIVES FROM A CLAIMANT, HIS DULY AUTHORIZED AGENT, OR LEGAL REPRESENTATIVE AN EXECUTED STANDARD FORM 95 OR OTHER WRITTEN NOTIFICATION OF AN INCIDENT, ACCOMPANIED BY A CLAIM FOR MONEY DAMAGES IN A **SUM CERTAIN** FOR INJURY TO OR LOSS OF

Any instructions or information necessary in the preparation of your claim will be furnished, upon request, by the office indicated in item #1 on the reverse side. Complete regulations pertaining to claims asserted under the Federal Tort Claims Act can be found in Title 28, Code of Federal Regulations, Part 14. Many agencies have published supplemental regulations also. If more than one agency is involved, please state each agency.

The claim may be filed by a duly authorized agent or other legal representative, provided evidence satisfactory to the Government is submitted with said claim establishing express authority to act for the claimant. A claim presented by an agent or legal representative must be presented in the name of the claimant. If the claim is signed by the agent or legal representative, it must show the title or legal capacity of the person signing and be accompanied by evidence of his/her authority to present a claim on behalf of the claimant as agent, executor, administrator, parent, guardian or other representative.

If claimant intends to file claim for both personal injury and property damage, claim for both must be shown in item #12 of this form.

The amount claimed should be substantiated by competent evidence as follows:

(a) In support of the claim for personal injury or death, the claimant should submit a written report by the attending physician, showing the nature and extent of injury, the nature and extent of treatment, the degree of permanent disability, if any, the prognosis, and the period of hospitalization, or incapacitation, attaching itemized bills for medical, hospital, or burial expenses actually incurred.

PROPERTY, PERSONAL INJURY, OR DEATH ALLEGED TO HAVE OCCURRED REASON OF THE INCIDENT, THE CLAIM MUST BE PRESENTED TO APPROPRIATE FEDERAL AGENCY WITHIN **TWO YEARS** AFTER THE CLAIM ACCRUES.

(b) In support of claims for damage to property which has been or can be economically repaired, the claimant should submit at least two itemized signed statements or estimates by reliable, disinterested concerns, or, if payment has been made, the itemized signed receipts evidencing payment.

(c) In support of claims for damage to property which is not economically repairable, or if the property is lost or destroyed, the claimant should submit statements as to the original cost of the property, the date of purchase, and the value of the property, both before and after the accident. Such statements should be by disinterested competent persons, preferably reputable dealers or officials familiar with the type of property damaged, or by two or more competitive bidders, and should be certified as being just and correct.

(d) Failure to completely execute this form or to supply the requested material within two years from the date the allegations accrued may render your claim "invalid". A claim is deemed presented when it is received by the appropriate agency, not when it is mailed.

Failure to specify a sum certain will result in invalid presentation of your claim And may result in forfeiture of your rights.

Public reporting burden for this collection of information is estimated to average 15 minutes per response, including the time for reviewing instructions, data sources, gathering and maintaining the data needed, and completing and reviewing the collection of information. Send comments regarding this burden other aspect of this collection of information, including suggestions for reducing this burden,

to Director, Torts Branch
Civil Division
U.S. Department of Justice
Washington, DC 20530

and to the
Office of Management and Budget
Paperwork Reduction Project (1105-0008)
Washington, DC 20503

INSURANCE COVERAGE

In order that subrogation claims be adjudicated, it is essential that the claimant provide the following information regarding the insurance coverage of his vehicle or property.

15. Do you carry accident insurance?   Yes, if yes give name and address of insurance company (*Number, street, city, State, and Zip Code*) and policy number.   No

16. Have you filed claim on your insurance carrier in this instance, and if so, is it full coverage or deductible? | 17. If deductible, state amount

18. If claim has been filed with your carrier, what action has your insurer taken or proposes to take with reference to your claim? (*It is necessary that you ascertain these facts*)

19. Do you carry public liability and property damage insurance?   Yes, If yes, give name and address of insurance carrier (*Number, street, city, State, and Zip Code*)   No

SF 95 (Rev. 7-85) BACK

* **U.S. GOVERNMENT PRINTING OFFICE: 1989--241-175**

EXHIBIT 3–5(b)   Claim form (back)

tickler system

A calendaring system.

as **tickler systems.** Before the advent of computers in the law firm, reminders were kept by hand. A firm might have used a special calendar or a small file box organized by dates. Today, numerous software packages exist that help firms keep track of important dates.

Even though a firm uses a computer, certain precautions should always be followed. First, when a case is tickled for the statute of limitations, it should be calendared early enough to allow for preparation of the complaint and for obtaining any necessary signatures. Second, the file should be re-calendared for a date near the statute of limitations, at which time it should be checked to verify that the complaint has in fact been filed. Third, if calendaring the case is not your responsibility as a litigation paralegal, you should still check cases assigned to you to make sure that proper calendaring has occurred. You might even wish to keep your own calendar, in addition to the firm's calendar, for cases assigned to you.

Feasibility of the Lawsuit

Even though an attorney may determine that a case has merit, that is, a cause of action exists, he may nevertheless decide that the lawsuit is not practical. Litigation takes a great deal of time and can cost a great deal of money, not only in attorney fees but in costs. For example, it may be necessary to hire expert witnesses to establish certain facts. Experts charge substantial fees for their services. Or there may be numerous witnesses who have to be questioned and deposed. This also is costly. Before an attorney accepts a case, he should always review it to see if it is practical. This involves reviewing the damages suffered by the plaintiff so that the value of the case can be determined. It also might involve some preliminary research into the defendant's ability to pay a judgment. You might be asked to assist in doing this.

Turning Down a Case

If an attorney decides not to accept a case, she must clearly communicate this to the concerned individual. This should be done in writing so that there is a record of the fact. Many attorneys have been sued for malpractice by individuals who claim that the attorney led them to believe that their cases were being handled and learned only after the statute of limitations had expired that the attorney had not in fact accepted the case.

In turning down a case, an attorney must exercise care in stating an opinion regarding the merits of the case to the prospective client. An attorney can be sued for malpractice for advising a person that he has no case if another attorney feels otherwise. It is also advisable to warn the person about any possible statute of limitations. See Exhibit 3–6 for a sample letter.

Ethical Considerations in Accepting a Case

All attorneys are subject to a certain code of conduct, usually defined by state law and referred to as *Canons of Ethics* or **Rules of Professional Conduct.** Although these rules apply to attorneys rather than paralegals, you must still be aware of them. The attorney's compliance with these rules often depends on factual and legal research done by the paralegal. Moreover, if a paralegal is working under the direction or supervision of an attorney, and the paralegal violates any of the rules, the attorney may nevertheless be held responsible. Ethical considerations enter into two aspects of the litigation

Rules of Professional Conduct
American Bar Association rules stating and explaining what lawyers must do, must not do, should do, and should not do. They cover the field of legal ethics.

OKIMURA & RESNICK
ATTORNEYS AT LAW

| Robert Okimura | 17 Plaza Square | Area Code 208 |
| Leslie Resnick | Boise, Idaho 83707 | Telephone 555-1212 |

Mr. Mark Jones
20 Birch Place
Boise, ID 83707

Dear Mr. Jones,

Thank you for contacting us regarding your dispute with ABC Corporation. As I explained to you on the telephone, our law firm is presently unable to represent you in this matter. Please note that our inability to accept your case is not a reflection or comment on the merits of your case. If you wish to pursue this matter you should consult other legal advice. If you decide to do so, you should act as soon as possible. As we have previously explained to you, the statute of limitations in these kinds of cases is _____ years from the date of your injury. If you have not filed a lawsuit within that time you will be prevented from doing so.

Very truly yours,

Robert Okimura,
Attorney at Law

EXHIBIT 3–6 Letter turning down case

process. First, certain ethical standards determine if the attorney can take a particular case. Second, other ethical standards govern the attorney's and the paralegal's conduct during the course of litigation.

Competency to Handle the Case

Obviously, an attorney should not accept a case if he does not possess the ability, knowledge, or time to handle it. This decision is up to the attorney, and the paralegal has little, if any, input into it. However, competency means more than simply having the ability to handle a case. It also means that attorneys are prohibited from neglecting cases that they have accepted. This can concern a paralegal. When you are assigned to a case, you should make sure that the case is not ignored. Some tickling or calendaring system should be established to remind the attorney or paralegal to regularly review all cases.

THE COMPUTERIZED LAW FIRM
Calendar Control

SCENARIO

Your attorney has accepted the Kelsey case and has made you part of the litigation team that will be handling the case. Part of your responsibilities will be monitoring the file and keeping track of important dates, including time requirements for filing a claim and the lawsuit itself. The attorney also expects that there will be several pretrial court hearings. Rules adopted by your local court impose strict time limits on all aspects of litigation and severe penalties for not complying with these limits. Along with the Kelsey case, you are working on several other cases in the office and have similar responsibilities in each of them. You will be responsible for monitoring not only your calendar, but also the calendars of the attorneys working on the cases.

PROBLEM

In a busy law firm, you may be working on several cases simultaneously. In each case there will be numerous time limitations on work, as well as several court appearances and appointments for the attorney. How do you keep track of all the dates?

SOLUTION

Numerous software products can assure that reminders of filing and other deadlines and dates are timely generated. With a computer reminder system, there is no chance that a paralegal will fail to turn a desk calendar page or neglect to pull a manual reminder from an index card file. To use a computer calendaring system you type in the dates you want to remember. When the program was ini-tially loaded onto the computer, the correct date was set. The computer has a clock and always knows the date. (Although, if you have a computer problem, you should check that the date is correct.) Each day, when you access the program, it displays any reminders for that date that were previously entered.

Software programs that contain calendaring features are generally referred to as personal information managers (PIMs) or case management software. Three popular examples of calendaring software are Abacus Law, Microsoft Outlook, and WordPerfect's CoreCentral. Today most calendaring programs not only contain a calendar, but also contain a to-do list or memo pad, and an address book. Some even allow you to set an alarm that will alert you to meeting or appointment times.

Another important development in computer-ized calendaring systems is the increasingly popular use of PDAs (personal data assistants) by lawyers and paralegals. A PDA such as the well-known Palm Pilot, is a small portable handheld computer that has taken the place of the pocket calendar. Attorneys can record dates wherever they are (in court or in another attorney's office). PDAs also contain address books and note pads. The PDA can be connected to the office's main computer and, with proper software, dates from the PDA can be downloaded to the main office calendar and vice versa. This greatly reduces the chance of dates not being calendared. Today, Palm Pilots have limited Internet access, allowing the user to receive and send e-mail.

Frivolous Claims

Lawsuits that have no merit should not be pursued. Again, this is usually determined by the attorney, but the attorney may rely on your research in making this decision. If an attorney handles a frivolous case, he risks being sued himself by the defendant in the action, in addition to subjecting himself to disciplinary proceedings by the state bar association. Furthermore, pursuing any claim or defense that has no evidentiary support is also a violation of Rule 11 of the Federal Rules of Civil Procedure. Any attorney violat-ing this rule is subject to sanctions or penalties imposed by the court.

Conflict of Interest

conflict of interest

Being in a position where your own needs and desires could possibly lead you to violate your duty to a person who has a right to depend on you, or being in a position where you try to serve two competing masters or clients.

A law firm cannot accept a case if a **conflict of interest** exists. A conflict of interest usually arises when a firm is asked to sue a party whom it currently represents or previously represented in another case. Although prior representation does not always result in a conflict, the potential for a conflict exists and must be closely examined before accepting the case.

A conflict is determined by whom the firm represents, rather than by whom any particular attorney in the firm represents. For example, in the case described in this chapter's commentary, your firm would have to consider suing Allied Auto Repair. Suppose, however, that one of the corporate attorneys in the firm had prepared and filed incorporation documents for that business on a previous occasion. Could a litigation attorney now sue the company? Probably not.

Before accepting a case, a firm must determine that no conflict exists. The larger the law firm, the more likely it is that some conflict may exist. As a litigation paralegal, you may be responsible for checking for conflicts. All law firms need to keep some centralized list of all clients. Without such a list, a conflict check could only be made by questioning each attorney in the firm. This is not only time consuming, but also unreliable. Most law firms, especially larger ones, now have centralized computerized lists of all clients. This makes the conflict check simple and more accurate.

Conflict problems can also arise when an attorney or a paralegal has changed jobs, and the prior law firm represented a party who is now a potential defendant. The prior relationship might result in a conflict of interest in the current litigation. Should you find yourself in such a situation, you should immediately inform the attorney handling the case. Steps can then be taken to isolate you from the case.

Even if a conflict does exist, the firm can still handle the case if the prior client agrees in writing to waive the problem. In the event that a conflict is not waived, the firm cannot accept employment in the new case.

Ethical Considerations after Accepting a Case

Communication with the Client

Lawyers owe a duty to their clients to keep them advised about the status of their cases. Failure of lawyers to do this is the basis of one of the most common complaints against attorneys. Litigation can sometimes take years, and much of the litigation process does not personally involve the client. If a lawyer fails to communicate with his client on some sort of regular basis, the client may think the attorney is doing nothing on the case. You can be a real asset to the attorney in maintaining communication with the client. In fact, parties often feel more comfortable dealing with the paralegal. In any event, if you have been assigned to a case, you should establish some procedure for regularly advising the client about the status of his action. And the most important rule to remember is to *always return phone calls promptly.*

Communication with the Opposing Party

It is unethical for an attorney or a paralegal working with an attorney to personally contact an opposing party who is represented by his own attorney. Contact must always be made with the attorney. If the opposing party is not represented by counsel, communication is allowed. If you are required to contact an opposing party, you should first verify that the opposing party is not represented. Naturally, an opposing party can be contacted to ascertain whether he is represented and who is representing him. However, once that information is disclosed, all further communication should cease.

Confidentiality

Communication between a client and an attorney is confidential. The attorney is prohibited from disclosing any information revealed to him by his client. Even mentioning the client's name, without discussing the facts of the case, may be a violation of this ethical requirement. As part of the litigation team, the paralegal is bound by the same rules. Whether you are present during conferences between the client and the attorney, whether the client directly communicates with you, or whether information is relayed to you by the attorney, you must honor the confidentiality. You should not discuss the case with anyone not directly involved in the case. Today, attorneys and paralegals must also consider confidentiality problems whenever they use technology tools such as a cellular phone or the Internet. Neither cellular phones nor the Internet provide a secure method for confidential communications. Communications over cellular phones and the Internet can be intercepted (either intentionally or accidentally).

Honesty

An attorney must never knowingly make a false representation about a case to a court or other tribunal. Although paralegals do not usually appear in court, you may frequently assist in the preparation of documents that are filed in court. You must be careful that factual and legal information is true and accurate.

In addition to honesty with the court, attorneys and paralegals should always be honest in their dealings with other attorneys and other paralegals. Aside from basic ethical considerations, a firm's reputation will be destroyed if its attorneys and paralegals cannot be trusted by other firms.

Attorney Fees

In setting fees in a case, an attorney is concerned with at least two ethical standards. First, the fee should not be unreasonable or unconscionable. Second, the fee arrangement, including any additional expenses, should be clearly explained to the client.

A fee in a litigation case can be set in a number of different ways. At the outset of the case the attorney could simply set a **flat fee,** or fixed sum, to handle the case. For example, an attorney and client might agree that the attorney will handle the client's contract dispute for $10,000. Because the amount of time needed to properly litigate a case is hard to predict, it is rare to see a fee set in this manner. However, if the fee is set this way, the attorney must make a reasonable, good-faith effort to make the fee commensurate with the expected work in the case.

flat fee

A legal fee based on a fixed sum rather than on an hourly rate or a percentage of a recovery.

hourly billing

A legal fee based on a fixed amount for each hour the law firm spends on the case.

More commonly, the attorney and client will agree to an hourly billing. In an **hourly billing,** the client is charged a fixed amount for each hour the law firm spends on the case. The hourly rate cannot be excessive, but there are substantial differences in fees charged by lawyers, often depending on the attorney's experience. It is also becoming common for firms to bill for paralegal time. For example, a firm handling some complicated business litigation might charge the client as follows: Senior Litigation Attorney—$350/hr; Junior Litigation Attorney—$225/hr; Paralegal—$125/hr. It is, of course, unethical to bill the client for time not spent on the case.

contingent fee

Payment to a lawyer of a percentage of the "winnings," if any, from a lawsuit rather than payment of a flat amount of money or payment according to the number of hours worked.

An alternative way of setting a fee in litigation is the **contingent fee,** a common arrangement in personal injury cases. In the contingent fee agreement the attorney takes a percentage of whatever recovery is obtained. If no recovery is made, the attorney receives no fee. In this type of fee arrangement, there are times when an attorney receives a large fee for little time spent. Such a result, however, does not make the arrangement unreasonable. Contingent fees have been allowed on the theory that they permit people to pursue cases they could not afford otherwise.

A *fee* is the compensation that an attorney receives for his time and efforts in a case. However, it is not the only expense incurred during the litigation process. Courts require filing fees to process documents. Investigators and experts are often needed to help prove the case, and process servers have to be paid to serve papers. Out-of-pocket expenses such as these are known as **costs.** Most attorneys expect that the client will pay the costs of suit in addition to the fee that is charged. Even if the case is handled on a contingent fee basis, the attorney may request that the client put up funds to cover expected costs. Sometimes the attorney will advance or pay for these costs himself, expecting reimbursement (in addition to his fee) when the case is settled. It is important for the attorney to make this clear to the client.

costs

Expenses of one side in lawsuit that the judge orders the other side to pay or reimburse.

Only the attorney may set fees. The paralegal is not permitted under professional guidelines to be involved in establishing fees in a case. However, you should be aware of the fee structure in case a question arises about a billing entry during the course of litigation.

Written Fee Agreements

The fee arrangement between the client and the attorney should always be in writing and signed by the client. In some jurisdictions, this is now required by law. However, even if not required, common sense dictates that the agreement should be clearly set forth in writing to avoid any dispute. The fee arrangement is usually included in a document referred to as a **retainer** agreement. See Exhibit 3–7 for a sample retainer agreement.

retainer

1. Employment of a lawyer by a client. 2. The specific agreement in no. 1.

Fee Sharing

In addition to ethical standards regarding the amount of fee a lawyer may charge, there are also standards regarding fee sharing. Generally, an attorney cannot share a fee in a case with a nonlawyer. This includes a paralegal.

THIS AGREEMENT IS BETWEEN JANET KELSEY, hereafter referred to as "Client" and OKIMURA AND RESNICK hereafter referred to as "Attorney". This agreement shall govern the respective rights and responsibilities of Client and Attorney, unless a subsequent agreement is made in writing.

1. **Claims Covered by Agreement.** Client retains Attorney to represent her in connection with a claim for damages for injuries suffered by Client while riding on a bus owned and operated by the City of Boise on or about April 4, ____. This Agreement does not cover any other possible related claims that may arise and may require legal services (for example, workers' compensation claims or disputes with Client's insurance company).

2. **Services to Be Performed by Attorney.** Attorney agrees to perform the following legal services, if necessary, with respect to the claim described above:
   * investigation of claim
   * preparing and filing lawsuit
   * negotiation
   * trial
   * if judgment is obtained, opposing motion for new trial Attorney is authorized to associate or employ, at Attorney's expense, other counsel to assist in performing the services required by this Agreement.

3. **Services Not Covered by This Agreement.** The following services are not covered by this Agreement and if any are required to be done, additional fee arrangements shall be made between Attorney and Client:
   * defending any cross-complaint against Client in connection with above matter
   * any appeal in the above matter, regardless of who prevails at trial
   * any retrial ordered after post trial motion or as a result of a mistrial, or after reversal on appeal
   * proceedings in connection with enforcing any judgment

4. **No Guarantee as to Result.** Client acknowledges that Attorney has made no guarantee as to the outcome or the amounts recoverable in the above matter.

5. **Contingency Fee to Attorney.** Client acknowledges that she has been advised by Attorney and is aware that any contingency fee arrangements are not set by law and that such a fee is negotiable between Attorney and Client. Client agrees that Attorney shall be paid thirty-three and one-third percent (33⅓ %) of any recovery, whether such recovery is by way of settlement, judgment or compromise and Client agrees this is reasonable. Client further understands and agrees that costs and expenses incurred by Attorney shall be reimbursed before the contingency fee is computed.

6. **Litigation Costs and Expenses.** Attorney is authorized to incur reasonable costs and expenses in performing legal services under this Agreement. Client agrees to pay for such costs and expenses in addition to the contingency fee listed in paragraph 5.
   (a) **Particular costs and expenses:** The costs and expenses necessary in this case may include any or all of the following;
      * court filing fees
      * process serving fees

(continued)

EXHIBIT 3–7 Retainer agreement

- private investigator fees
- photographic/graphic artist t fees
- fees to experts for consultation and/or appearance at deposition or trial jury fees
- court reporter fees
- mail, facsimile transmission, messenger and other delivery charges
- transportation, meals, lodging and all other costs of necessary out-of-town travel
- long distance telephone charges
- photocopying (in office) at $.20/page

(b) **Client's responsibility to costs** Attorney may advance such costs and expenses on Client's behalf but is not obligated to do so. Client agrees to reimburse Attorney upon demand for any such advances. Client is responsible for such reimbursement regardless of the status or outcome of the litigation.

7. **Effect of Discharge by Client.** Client shall have the right to discharge Attorney at any time upon written notice to Attorney. Such discharge shall not affect Client's obligation to reimburse Attorney for costs incurred prior to the discharge. Attorney shall be entitled to the reasonable value of legal services performed prior to such discharge to be paid by Client from any subsequent recovery on the claim covered by this Agreement.

8. **Attorney's Lien.** To secure payment to Attorney of all sums due under this Agreement for legal services, Client hereby grants Attorney a lien on Client's claim and on any recovery Client may obtain, whether by judgment or otherwise.

9. **Arbitration of Dispute.** Any dispute arising between Attorney and Client regarding fees charged or services rendered under this Agreement, including any claim for breach of contract, negligence or breach of fiduciary duty, shall be resolved by binding arbitration, conducted in accordance with the rules of the American Arbitration Association.

Dated:

Attorney: Client

_____   _____

EXHIBIT 3-7 Retainer agreement *(continued)*

Property of Client—Trust Accounts

An attorney cannot commingle his own assets or property with property belonging to a client. To handle this kind of a situation, attorneys have special bank accounts, known as **trust accounts,** into which they deposit all money belonging to their clients. It is allowable to have one trust account for many clients, as long as accurate records are kept.

In litigation, trust accounts are utilized for two main purposes—advances by the client and settlement or satisfaction of judgments. First, if the client gives the attorney money that is specifically designated for costs, then the money should be deposited in a trust account until the cost is actually incurred. The attorney should not deposit the funds into his general account. Likewise, if the client gives the attorney a fee advance, that should also be deposited into the trust account until the fee is actually earned. Second, when a case is settled, the attorney must exercise care regarding any money he

trust account (trust deposit)
Money or property put in a bank account to be kept separate (often for ethical or legal reasons) or used for a special purpose.

FINDING IT ON THE INTERNET

The Internet provides numerous sources for paralegals in the initial stages of litigation. There are several good Web sites dealing with legal ethics. One site that will give you current news, as well as links to the rules of professional conduct for the various states, is **</http://www.legalethics.com/>**. Another site that will provide links to state ethical rules is **</http://www. findlaw.com/>**. On the home page search for "state bar." This leads you to links to the state bar associations for all states. Ethical rules can generally be accessed through the state bar home page. The ethical rules for NALA and NFPA can be found on their Web sites, **</http://www.nala.org/>** and **</http://www.paralegals.org/>**.

Numerous Web sites also provide free sample legal forms. To find sample client interview forms, retainer agreements, and various letters, go to **</http://www.lectlaw.com/>** and look for the "Forms Room." For additional federal and state litigation forms check **</http://findlaw.com/>**. On the home page search for "court forms." Many federal court forms can be found at **</http://www.uscourts.gov/>**. Link to the "Library" and you will find "forms."

a. Access the sites for the ethical rules for NALA and NFPA. Write a memo briefly summarizing each of the guidelines that would apply to the litigation paralegal working on the Kelsey case that has been discussed in this chapter.

b. Access the **lectlaw** and **findlaw** form sites. Locate and download at least three forms from each site that might be appropriate for the *Kelsey* case. On the **findlaw** site, choose forms from your state.

receives. A settlement check is primarily the property of the client. However, the attorney does want to be certain that he receives his fee and costs. In fact, the attorney may have a lien against the settlement if so provided in the retainer agreement. Because of the client's interest in the check, however, the attorney cannot deposit it into his personal account. The attorney must deposit the check into the trust account. After he makes certain that the settlement check has cleared, he can make proper disbursements from the trust account, paying the client his share and reimbursing himself for his costs and fee. If the trust account contains money for more than one client, the attorney should always make sure that the check has cleared before making any disbursements. Failure to do so could result in the property of one client being used for the benefit of another.

The importance of proper control and management of trust accounts cannot be overemphasized. Intentional misuse of clients' funds is theft and is punishable criminally. Negligent misuse of client funds often results in disciplinary proceedings against the erring attorney. This is one area where bar associations are especially strict.

Special Ethical Concerns for Paralegals

Although paralegals should be careful to follow all ethical standards imposed on attorneys, other concerns also affect legal assistants. Both the National Association of Legal Assistants (NALA) and the National Federation of Paralegal Associations have adopted ethical standards or guidelines for the paralegal profession. Included in those guidelines are the following:

1. Paralegals or legal assistants should disclose their status as a legal assistant at the beginning of any professional relationship.
2. Paralegals should protect or preserve all confidential information obtained by them.
3. Paralegals should not engage in any activity involving the unauthorized practice of law, including giving legal advice.
4. Paralegals should not establish the attorney-client relationship nor set fees.
5. Paralegals should be honest and accurate in all timekeeping and billing records.

Summary

- Before filing any lawsuit, it must be determined that a cause of action, or legally recognized right to sue, exists. This may involve researching the law and analyzing the evidence in the case. The paralegal must understand the legal and factual basis for the cause of action to properly assist the attorney in preparing for trial.

- All lawsuits must be filed in a timely manner. Time limitations for filing lawsuits are known as statutes of limitations and claim statutes. The equitable concept of laches also limits the time in which to file suit. Time limits vary depending on the type of case and the jurisdiction. All firms maintain some type of tickler system to keep track of time requirements.

- In addition to reviewing the legal basis of the lawsuit and the ethical restraints in accepting a case, an attorney should consider the practicalities of the lawsuit. In particular, the damages and the ability of the defendant to pay a judgment must justify the cost of litigation.

- An attorney must clearly notify a prospective client if he decides not to take a case. He should also warn the individual of time limitations in pursuing the case. The attorney must also be careful in making any representations regarding the merits of the case.

- In deciding to accept a case, an attorney is bound by certain ethical standards. She cannot accept a case if she is not competent to handle it, if the case is without merit or frivolous, or if there is a conflict of interest.

- After accepting a case, the members of the law firm, especially the attorney and the paralegal, are bound by other ethical standards. They should keep the client advised about the status of the case. They must never communicate personally with an opposing party once they know that party is represented by his own attorney. They must honor the confidentiality of their client and not discuss the case with third parties. They must be honest in their dealings with the court and other law firms. Attorney fees should be reasonable and clearly explained to the client. In some cases written fee agreements are necessary. Any monies belonging to the client must be kept in a trust fund and not commingled with the attorney's personal property. Paralegals must be careful not to give legal advice and to properly identify themselves to clients.

Key Terms

cause of action	flat fee	statute of limitations
claim statute	hourly billing	tickler system
conflict of interest	laches	trust account
contingent fee	retainer	
costs	Rules of Professional Conduct	

Review Questions

1. What is a cause of action?
2. What is the importance of a cause of action to the litigation process?
3. What are the various types of time limitations on filing a lawsuit?
4. What is a tickler system and why is it important in a litigation law firm?
5. What practical considerations must be reviewed prior to accepting a case?
6. What is the proper procedure for turning down a case?
7. What are the various ethical standards that control an attorney's decision to accept a case?
8. How can a litigation paralegal assist the attorney in reviewing ethical standards that are considered prior to accepting a case?
9. What are the ethical responsibilities governing law firms that handle litigation?
10. What are the special ethical concerns of litigation paralegals?

Chapter Exercises

Where necessary, check with your instructor prior to starting any of these exercises.

1. Review the commentary at the beginning of the chapter. Research the potential causes of action that may exist against Allied Auto Repair, the city, the bus driver, and the driver of the other vehicle involved in the collision. Prepare an interoffice memorandum explaining your conclusions.

2. Research the laws of your state. Find the statutes of limitations for the following types of cases: an action for personal injuries based on negligence; an action for personal injuries based on strict liability; an action for personal injuries based on medical malpractice; an action for legal malpractice; an action for property damage based on negligence; an action based on a written contract; an action based on an oral contract; an action for fraud.

3. Review your state rules of professional conduct. You can probably find these rules on line or obtain a copy from your state bar association. Summarize rules that might affect a litigation paralegal.

4. During your client interview with Janet Kelsey, assume that she asks you the following questions. How should you respond?
   a. Do you think I have a good case?
   b. Should I take photos of the scene of the accident?
   c. How long will this case take if it has to go to trial?
   d. If the attorney files a lawsuit, what will court costs be?
   e. Based on your experience, what is my case worth?

5. Refer to Exhibit 3–1, Elements of a Cause of Action. Analyze the following factual situations and determine which, if any, cause of action exists.

   a. Connors and Loewe enter into a written agreement whereby Connors agrees to purchase Loewe's house. Prior to signing the agreement, Connors asked Loewe about the condition of the roof. Loewe tells Connors that the roof is in good repair. In fact, Loewe recently had a roof inspection done and was told that the roof was in terrible condition and should be replaced immediately. Shortly after Connors moves into the premises, a storm occurs and the roof leaks in several places.

   b. Engels buys a preassembled student desk for her grammar school son. When an overhead light goes out in her son's room, Engels stands on the desk to reach the light. The desk collapses and Engels is injured.

6. Refer to the various statutes of limitations set out in this chapter (see Exhibit 3–2). Consider the following cases. What would be the last date on which the complaint could be filed?

   a. On February 15, 2004 Jeffers and Holmes, both California residents, enter into an oral agreement whereby Holmes agrees to loan Jeffers money, which is due and payable on February 15, 2005. On February 15, 2005, Jeffers does not repay the money. Holmes wants to sue.

   b. Ruiz hires Baines and Baines, Attorneys at Law, to represent him in a lawsuit for personal injuries resulting from an automobile accident. Unfortunately, the attorneys miss the statute of limitations for the action and Ruiz's claim is barred. The complaint should have been filed March 1, 2004. On March 10, 2004 Ruiz calls the attorneys and asks about his case. They tell him that everything is going along and that he should be patient because lawsuits take a long time. After hearing nothing for four months, on July 12, 2004, Ruiz again calls the attorneys. This time he talks to a paralegal in the firm, who checks the file and tells him that she does not see any record of a complaint being filed. On July 20, 2004 Ruiz contacts another lawyer, who calls Baines and Baines. Finally, on July 30, 2004, Gerald Baines, one of the partners of Baines and Baines, admits that a complaint was never filed. Ruiz wants to sue Baines and Baines for malpractice. Apply California law (Exhibit 3–3).

   c. Assume that in the hypothetical situation of (b), the plaintiff is Jaime Ruiz who was born on December 28, 1992. Assume also that for this type of action, California law tolls the statute of limitations during a child's minority.

   d. Pedersen and her 12-year-old daughter are injured in a motor vehicle accident with a United States postal truck on March 15, 2004. They wish to sue the United States government for their injuries. By what date must a claim be filed? (See Exhibit 3–4.)

7. Assume that you are a litigation paralegal responsible for tickling or calendaring statutes of limitations for new cases. What date or dates would you calendar to make sure your office did not miss the statute of limitations for the cases mentioned in the previous question?

Chapter Project

Review the commentary at the beginning of the chapter. Research the following questions and present your findings in an interoffice memorandum:

1. What is the appropriate statute of limitations in your state for this case?

2. Do the laws of your state allow you to sue the city? If so, do any special claim statutes apply? If so, does Kelsey still have time to file a claim?

3. Are there other types of cases in your state that require a claim to be submitted prior to filing a lawsuit?

The *Bennett* Case
Assignment 3: Preliminary Claim

You have been given a copy of the Bennett research file along with a copy of the initial client interview form (see Appendix B). This file contains copies of relevant federal codes and regulations regarding discrimination claims under Title VII. The attorney handling the case is anxious to pursue a claim under Title VII. Your supervisor tells you that before filing this type of lawsuit a claim with either the state or the EEOC must be submitted. Your supervisor tells you that the next step is to file a claim with the EEOC. The requirements for this claim are found in the Code of Federal Regulations. You are to read this rule (29 C.F.R. 1601), a copy of which is in the Bennett research file, and draft a claim. The needed factual information should be located in the client interview form. You should also review the Web site for the Equal Employment Opportunity Commission (http://www.eeoc.gov/) for information on filing a charge of discrimination with the agency.

Chapter 4

Investigation and Evidence

CHAPTER OUTLINE

COMMENTARY—THE MORRISON CASE

Oscar Morrison has contacted your firm to represent him in a personal injury lawsuit against Acme, Inc. for asbestosis allegedly contracted on the job. Acme, Inc. is a manufacturer of products containing asbestos. The products were purchased and used by Morrison's employer, a tire manufacturer. Your attorney has asked that you handle the preliminary arrangements for the interview, help determine whether the firm should accept the case, locate the necessary forms to gather information during and after the interview, and coordinate the interview. Your attorney has explained that she would like for you to participate in the interview so that the client will be comfortable communicating with you throughout the expected lengthy litigation. You are to function as a member of the litigation team, which may consist of a senior attorney, several junior associates, and one or more paralegals.

OBJECTIVES

Chapter 3 discussed important preliminary considerations affecting the filing of a lawsuit. Interviewing and investigation are also important steps in beginning the litigation process. After reading this chapter, you should be able to:

- Outline the paralegal's responsibilities in preparing for the client interview.
- Describe how to set up a client interview.
- Describe an ideal client interview questionnaire.
- List forms or documents that might be needed during the client interview.
- Explain the paralegal's role during the client interview.
- Identify potential sources for locating fact witnesses or elusive defendants.
- Discuss the techniques for interviewing fact witnesses.
- Identify rules that control the admissibility of different forms of evidence.
- Describe methods for locating and preserving evidence.
- Explain the functions of an expert witness.
- Explain the paralegal's role in procuring an expert witness.

The Client Interview

Successful litigation begins with proper preparation and investigation of both the facts and the law. This preparation and investigation often starts with the client interview. In most cases, the client is the most knowledgeable about the facts of the case.

During a client interview, these facts are communicated to the attorney handling the case. The attorney is then able to determine what aspects of the case need further investigation or research. Not only is the client interview an essential step in the fact-gathering process, but it also establishes the foundation for the long-term relationship between the client and the firm. The interview establishes the tone for the representation. If the interview goes smoothly, the client's impression of the firm will be favorable. However, if the paralegal and attorney are not prepared for the interview, have not researched the issues, and are not familiar with the basic facts of the potential representation, the client will have good cause to question his or her choice of counsel.

The client interview affords the paralegal the opportunity to become an integral part of the litigation team. Although the attorney normally conducts an initial interview, a paralegal often plays an important role in the process. You may be asked to take various levels of responsibility for the interview, including:

1. researching potential causes of action or defenses,
2. scheduling the interview,
3. developing an interview questionnaire or form to fit the particular case,
4. gathering forms and documents the client will have to sign,
5. taking notes during the interview, and
6. producing a summary of the interview.

Preparation for Initial Client Interview

Researching Potential Causes of Action or Defenses   Preparation is essential to a successful interview. Once you are assigned a case such as the Morrison case discussed in the commentary of this chapter, you should take the opportunity to review all information available on the subject matter of the potential litigation and the causes of action or defenses. In the last chapter, various sources for researching the elements of a cause of action were described. In addition, however, you should find out as much as you can about the factual subject matter of the lawsuit. Your firm's library, the local library, and the Internet will offer an abundance of articles on recent asbestos cases, including who has been sued, the outcome of jury trials, and reports on damage awards. You should also refer to medical journals covering the causes and effects of asbestosis. Only by understanding the factual basis of the lawsuit will you be able to ask relevant and pertinent questions during an interview.

Scheduling the Interview   Once it is determined that a potential cause of action exists, the initial client interview can be scheduled. Before scheduling the interview, however, remember to check the firm's client lists to rule out any conflict with any of the potential defendants. In scheduling the interview, the attorney's calendar should be checked for acceptable dates. You may contact the client by telephone to discuss available dates or suggest a tentative date by letter and request confirmation that the date is acceptable. If contact is made by telephone, a confirming letter should be sent. The date for the initial interview should be set as early as possible. When setting up the initial interview, the client should be instructed to bring along all necessary information for preparing the case. This information will vary depending on the nature of the case.

However, it may include such items as names and addresses of opposing parties and all witnesses, copies of any correspondence between the client and the opposing party, and written verification of damages (medical bills, wage statements, etc.). Exhibit 4–1 is an example of an appointment-setting letter that requests the client to bring pertinent information to the interview.

The location of the interview is important. If the client is critically ill, has difficulty walking, or expresses reluctance to talk in the formal environment of the law firm, the interview may have to be held at the client's home, office, or hospital room. Most interviews in the law firm are conducted in either the attorney's office or a conference room. If a conference room is required, you may be asked to schedule the conference room and prepare it for the interview.

Enter the location and time of the interview on the attorney's calendar and on your calendar or reminder system. A follow-up telephone call to the client the day before the interview ensures that the attorney's time is not wasted because of a last-minute cancellation.

Developing Interview Questionnaires or Forms

It is important to have some idea of the questions to be asked during a client interview. During any client interview, the attorney or paralegal will first need to elicit general background information, such as address, telephone number, employer, and so on. The heart of the interview will, however, consist of questions specifically related to the case. Forms for client interviews containing sample questions can be found in many form books and practice manuals in the law firm's library. However, interview forms are useful only if they are tailored to the specific case. An interview form that your attorney utilized in a construction contract case would be worthless in an asbestosis case. If you cannot find a form specifically tailored to your situation, you will have to develop your own. To do this, you should follow the pattern set by a form that involves a similar case. You will then need to refer to your own factual and legal research into the case. Once you understand what the attorney has to prove at trial, you should be able to formulate questions geared toward gathering that information. Exhibit 4–2 is an example of an interview questionnaire.

Gathering Forms and Documents for Client Signature

Prior to the actual interview, you should set up the file and locate copies of all forms that the client will need to sign. The first form to be filled out is the **representation letter** or **retainer agreement** that establishes the ground rules of the litigation, including fees, billing rates, retainer, and work to be performed by the law firm. A sample retainer agreement was shown in Chapter 3 (Exhibit 3–3).

In Mr. Morrison's case, the client's medical history and related expenses must be documented. Information concerning Mr. Morrison's medical treatment by a hospital, doctor, physical therapist, or laboratory can only be obtained through a written release or authorization signed by Mr. Morrison. A **release** or **authorization** is a signed statement by the client that authorizes someone (such as a doctor or employer) to give the attorney information regarding the client, information that otherwise might be treated as confidential. Exhibit 4–3 shows a standard medical release form.

To further establish damages as a result of the alleged asbestosis, Mr. Morrison's employment records, tax returns, and/or earnings statements must also be obtained. The social security earnings record, which offers a complete history of the client's employment

---

representation letter

A letter from an attorney to a new client establishing the ground rules of the litigation, including fees, billing rates, retainer, and work to be performed by the law firm.

retainer agreement

An agreement between an attorney and a client setting forth the fee arrangement.

release

A document by which a claim or right is relinquished.

authorization

A signed statement empowering someone (such as a doctor or employer) to give out information that might otherwise be treated as confidential.

Schneider & Fenton
Attorneys at Law
45 North Main St.
San Antonio, Texas 78265
(512) 555-1312

Allyson Schneider   Anthony Fenton
Glen Bardwell   K.W. Post

Oscar Morrison
189 Montalban Dr.
San Antonio, Texas 78265

Dear Mr. Morrison,
An appointment has been scheduled for you with attorney Allyson
Schneider of our firm at 10 A.M. on Monday, June 15, at our offices to
discuss your case. This interview should require approximately one hour.
Please bring with you to the interview the following items checked on the
list below:

(X) Social Security number
( ) Copy of insurance policy
(X) Information relating to the opposing party, such as insurance
    carrier, etc.
(X) Accident or incident reports
(X) Photographs and/or diagrams of injury site
(X) Newspaper clippings relating to accident or injury
(X) Witness statements
( ) Description of automobiles involved in accident, including license
    tags, owner, and amount of damage
(X) Medical bills and information relating to treating physicians and
    hospitals
(X) Employment information concerning time lost because of accident
(X) Any other relative information or documents.

Producing the information requested at the time of the interview will
enable us to expedite the handling of your claim. Please call me if you
have any questions about the items requested.

Sincerely,

Alan Berkshire
Paralegal

EXHIBIT 4–1   Letter advising client of initial interview appointment

PERSONAL DATA:
Name: _____
Home Address: _____
Address for Billing: _____
Home Telephone: _____
Work Telephone: _____
Cellular Phone: _____
Fax Number: _____
E-mail: _____
Date of Birth: _____
Social Security No.: _____
Driver's License No.: _____
Spouse's Name: _____
Spouse's Work Phone: _____
Employer: _____
Address: _____

INFORMATION RELATING TO CLAIM:
Type of claim (EEOC, med. malpractice, etc.): _____
Date of incident leading to claim: _____
Brief statement of incident (or attach statement): _____
_____
_____
Itemize damages incurred to date: _____
_____
Do you anticipate additional damages? If so, describe: _____
_____
Name and address of any doctors you have seen: _____
_____
Identity, address, and phone of any potential witnesses: ____
_____
Description and location of any documents or correspondence pertinent
to litigation: _____
_____
_____
Have you made any statements to anyone (orally or in writing) regarding
this case? If so, describe. _____
_____
Do you have any insurance which covers this claim? If so, please describe.
_____
_____
Have you been served with any papers relating to this case? _____
Have you heard from any lawyers concerning this case? _____

PRIOR LITIGATION:
Type of litigation: _____
Date and place of litigation: _____
Outcome of litigation: _____
Attorney representing you: _____

EXHIBIT 4–2   Client interview form

> I, OSCAR MORRISON, hereby authorize and permit you to furnish to the law firm of SCHNEIDER & FENTON, or its representative, orally or in writing, all documents they request pertaining to my medical treatment as a result of or related to exposure to asbestos, including, but not limited to, all X rays, medical records, nurses' notes, medical charts, diagnostic studies, and medical opinions relating to my past, present, or future physical condition, treatment, care, or hospitalization.
>
> A copy of this authorization shall have the same effect and force as an original.
>
> _____
> OSCAR MORRISON

EXHIBIT 4–3   Medical authorization

> I, OSCAR MORRISON, hereby authorize and permit the law firm of SCHNEIDER & FENTON, or its representative, to inspect, review, and make copies of any and all employment and/or earnings records regarding myself, including, but not limited to, employment application, vacation leave, sick or medical leave, W-2 forms, termination, and any other documents relating to my employment with _____. The release of this information is to be used for litigation purposes.
>
> A copy of this authorization shall have the same effect and force as an original.
>
> _____
> OSCAR MORRISON

EXHIBIT 4–4   Authorization for release of information relating to employment and earnings

and earnings, should be requested early in the investigative process of this case. Exhibit 4–4 shows a release for that employment information.

These form releases should be signed, but not dated until they are used, to ensure that they are current. An employer or hospital might refuse to honor a release if the date is too old.

The Paralegal's Role in the Interview

You have completed the research assignments and prepared all the necessary forms. The day of the interview has arrived. Your attorney should introduce you to the client and explain your role in the case. Giving clients a copy of your business card will assist them in contacting you should the need arise. This will facilitate information exchange between the firm and its clients.

Your attorney may ask that you take notes during the interview and have them transcribed for the file. If you have prepared a questionnaire for the interview, you should give a copy to the attorney and keep a copy for yourself. You can then take notes on your copy of the questionnaire. This technique will make your note-taking easier. If you do not understand an answer to a question, or are unsure of a name or word, ask questions. Sometimes it is necessary to ask that the client spell proper names that may appear later in pleadings filed with the court. Always make sure that you have the correct spelling of your client's name. Your notes should be complete and accurate.

During the interview, particular note should be made of the statute of limitations. As soon as the interview concludes, you should make sure that a reminder, or tickler, is placed in the firm's litigation tracking system.

Prior to concluding the interview, review the checklist of information that the client was asked to furnish. If any information is missing, make a written list of it and give it to the client. Be sure that you calendar the file to check that you receive everything requested. In a personal injury case like the Morrison case, the client might also be asked to keep a **medical diary,** a document in which the client keeps track of medical treatment, daily health complaints, type and amount of medication, mileage to physicians' offices, and other related medical expenses. The client will be more receptive to keeping the journal up-to-date if he or she realizes that it will be used in calculating damages and evaluating the case for settlement. As the case progresses, the paralegal might periodically review the journal. Exhibit 4–5 shows a sample medical diary.

medical diary

A document in which the client keeps track of medical treatment, daily health complaints, type and amount of medication, mileage to physicians' offices, and other related medical expenses.

Interview Summary

Promptly upon completion of the interview, you should have interview notes typed for the attorney's review and a copy placed in the client's file. The interview summary may reveal areas that need further development, either from a legal issue or factual standpoint. You may utilize the form to develop a "to-do" list for additional investigation.

Locating Fact Witnesses or Elusive Defendants

Prior to filing a lawsuit, all available facts should be accumulated and organized. These facts are normally derived from the client, other witnesses, or documents. Mr. Morrison's interview may yield many of the facts necessary to pursue the filing of a lawsuit on his behalf. However, more information may be needed to substantiate his claims. For example, other employees at the tire company may have additional insight into the working conditions, chemicals to which he may have been exposed, and safety policies of the company. However, over the 10-year period of his employment, many of these coworkers may no longer be employed by the tire company. Steps must be taken to locate and interview these important fact witnesses.

In addition to locating fact witnesses, the defendant should be located prior to filing suit. Sometimes, pending litigation causes potential defendants to become elusive. You may be asked to research the opposing party's address for service of process. This effort should be made early in the investigation so that it does not hamper prompt serv-

DATE: _____

MEDICAL TREATMENT:

VISIT TO DR. _____ (NAME)

REASON FOR VISIT: _____
DIAGNOSIS: _____
MEDICATION PRESCRIBED: _____

VISIT TO HOSPITAL OR OTHER MEDICAL SERVICE:

NAME: _____
REASON FOR VISIT: _____
DIAGNOSIS: _____
TYPE OF TREATMENT: _____

HEALTH COMPLAINTS:

TIME OF COMPLAINT: _____
DESCRIPTION OF HEALTH COMPLAINT: _____

MEDICATION:

NAME OF MEDICATION: _____
PRESCRIBED BY: _____
CONDITION FOR WHICH PRESCRIBED: _____
_____
AMOUNT OF MEDICATION TAKEN: _____

ADDITIONAL NOTES RELATIVE TO HEALTH:

_____
_____
_____

EXHIBIT 4–5   Medical diary

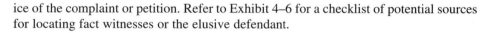

ice of the complaint or petition. Refer to Exhibit 4–6 for a checklist of potential sources for locating fact witnesses or the elusive defendant.

Steps for Locating the Agent of Corporations or Partnerships

The opposing party in the Morrison case is a corporation. Your client may know the physical address of the defendant. However, additional information is needed before the lawsuit can be filed. You will need the legal name of the company and the name and address of the individual who should be served with the suit. This individual is known as the **agent for service of process.** If the defendant is a corporation, this information is available from the secretary of state's office and may be obtained by telephone or use of a research database, such as LEXIS or WESTLAW. Other services on the Internet can also provide this information. In many jurisdictions, the secretary of

agent
A person authorized (requested or permitted) by another person to act for him or her; a person entrusted with another's business.

service of process
The delivery (or its legal equivalent, such as publication in a newspaper in some cases) of a legal paper, such as a writ, by an authorized person in a way that meets certain formal requirements. It is the way to notify a person of a lawsuit.

agent for service of process
Individual designated by a corporation who is authorized to be served with a lawsuit against the corporation.

❒ Client
❒ Client's competitors
❒ Accident report
❒ Court records of prior litigation
❒ Department of Motor vehicles
❒ Friends and/or neighbors
❒ Employer and/or coworkers
❒ Professional organizations or unions
❒ Telephone book
❒ County assessor or recorder
❒ Relatives
❒ Hospital and medical service providers
❒ Physicians
❒ Ambulance company
❒ The Internet

EXHIBIT 4–6   Checklist of sources for locating fact witnesses or elusive defendants

state has its own on-line home page, making this information readily available. In some states, if a defendant is a partnership or limited partnership, this information may also be available from the secretary of state's office. However, in other states, if a defendant is a partnership or limited partnership, this information may be filed in the county recorder's office in the county where the partnership has its principal place of business. This information should be obtained early in the investigative stage of the lawsuit.

Techniques for Interviewing Fact Witnesses

Once you have located a potential fact witness, make a telephone call to determine what information the witness has and whether the witness is willing to be interviewed. You should identify yourself as a paralegal working with the attorney representing Mr. Morrison. The witness should clearly understand who the potential parties in litigation are and what claims are being made on behalf of Mr. Morrison. If the witness has information that may be relevant to the case, a personal visit should be arranged to take his or her statement.

An interview form similar to the client interview form discussed earlier will expedite the interview and help elicit all pertinent facts from the witness. This form, a tape recorder, and a writing pad are necessary tools for the witness interview. A verbatim tape recording of the interview is preferable, but if the witness is reluctant to have his or her statement taped, you should be prepared. You will have to take written notes of the interview. In such a case, if possible, write out a statement and have the witness sign it before the interview concludes. Even if the statement is tape-recorded, you should probably take written notes in case the tape player malfunctions. Once the interview has

THE COMPUTERIZED LAW FIRM
Nonlegal Databases

SCENARIO

The Morrison case is set for trial in one week. One of your key witnesses is Jared Hill, who worked with your client. You phoned Mr. Hill to advise him of the trial date and discovered that the number was disconnected. You attempted to personally contact him at the home address you have in your file, but found that he has moved. You made an attempt to reach him at his last known place of employment, but were told that he no longer works there.

PROBLEM

Your attorney wants you to locate this witness and subpoena him for trial. You have checked the local telephone directory and contacted the post office, but have found no referral phone number or address. Your time is limited. How can you locate this witness?

SOLUTION

Numerous nonlegal databases available on the Internet provide information concerning the location of individuals and companies. National tele-phone directories, reverse directories, and other public resources are readily accessible and search-able by anyone for free. Addresses, telephone numbers, and sometimes e-mail addresses can be easily located. Some Web sites that provide this information are:

<http://www.four11.com>
<http://www.whowhere.lycos.com/>
<http://www.anywho.com>
<http://www.switchboard.com/>

People located outside the United States can be located through international directories located at <http://www.worldpages.com/>

Individuals who have unlisted telephone numbers can be more difficult to locate. However, several databases exist that contain public records that can help locate a person. Such records include real estate records, lien filings, business filings, lawsuit information and court dockets, and birth and death records. Often, sites that provide access to these databases charge a fee. One Web site to check is <http://www.knowx.com>.

been completed, a typed witness statement should be prepared, either from the recorded interview or from your written notes or statement. This typewritten statement can then be transmitted to the witness for review and signing. Never tape record a witness's statement, in person or over the phone, without the witness's knowledge and permission. In some jurisdictions this is a crime.

Selecting the location for the interview is critical. Remember that this witness's statement is voluntary. You should exercise extreme courtesy and cooperation in sched-uling the interview. The witness may prefer that the interview be in the evening so that it will not interfere with a job. Perhaps the witness does not want to travel downtown to the law firm, but would rather have the interview at his or her home in a suburb. Flexibility is essential. You should make all arrangements for the interview to suit the witness's preferences.

The attorney may participate in the interview or request that you conduct the inter-view alone. Good planning will ensure that the interview goes quickly and smoothly. Preparation may include a review of the information on the interview form and facts about the witness from the earlier client interview.

leading question

A question that shows a witness how to answer it or suggests the preferred answer.

Good interview techniques include listening attentively, taking detailed notes, and asking questions to clarify confusing or incomplete information. When asking questions, avoid **leading questions.** A leading question is a question that suggests the answer. For example, the question, "Isn't it true that the rubber company has a reputation for not caring about the welfare of its employees?" is a leading question. The witness feels that "yes" is the anticipated answer, and will tend to respond accordingly. A better way to phrase the question is, "Could you tell me what the rubber company's reputation is regarding the welfare of its employees?" This type of question calls for the witness's own feelings and is not suggestive. A witness should be encouraged to tell a story in his or her own words. Avoid the appearance of rushing the narrative or reacting to the story as it unfolds.

At times, more information may be derived from the client's body language than from the witness's own words. You should learn to evaluate the body language as well as the testimony of a witness and make note of any discrepancies. You should also make notes regarding the **demeanor,** or appearance, of the witness. Would she make a good witness in court? Is he articulate or does he ramble on? Is she hostile? Your evaluation of a witness can be very helpful to an attorney.

demeanor

Physical appearance and behavior. The demeanor of a witness is not what the witness says, but how the witness says it.

Thoroughness is critical in a witness interview. Failure to be thorough can result in a witness changing or adding to his or her testimony at the time of trial or deposition. You should endeavor to obtain the most complete information about the client's claim as possible. Also, keep in mind that the rules of evidence generally do not allow an attorney to introduce a written witness statement at trial unless the witness is present in court and testifies in person. If a witness is unavailable at the time of trial, there is, however, a way of presenting that testimony to the court. A formal deposition (as described in Chapter 8 and Chapter 9) can be taken. At the time of the interview, therefore, you should determine if the interviewee would be willing to testify at trial. You should also ask if the witness plans to leave the area or might be unavailable at the time of trial for some other reason. The attorney can then take steps to legally preserve his or her testimony for trial.

When the interview concludes, prepare a narrative summary of the interview. This summary is then presented to the witness to read and sign, verifying its accuracy. Though a signed statement is not admissible as evidence at trial, even if it is signed under penalty of perjury, it can be used to attack a witness's credibility if the witness changes his or her testimony.

Evidence

Proper investigation of any case requires a basic understanding of certain rules of evidence (either state or federal rules, depending on the court in which the matter is filed). These rules ultimately determine what information can be used at trial. Investigation of a case requires the paralegal to obtain information that will be admissible at trial. This does not mean, however, that an investigator should ignore inadmissible evidence. Such evidence might lead to other important and admissible evidence.

Evidence is defined in *Oran's Dictionary of the Law* as "all types of information (observations, recollections, documents, concrete objects, etc.) presented at a trial or other hearing." At the trial of the Morrison case, the finder of fact (judge or jury) will listen to the testimony of the witnesses and consider the documents admitted as exhibits in an effort to determine the true facts.

Types of Evidence

Evidence may be either direct or circumstantial. **Direct evidence** is evidence that a witness personally observed, and which, if believed, directly establishes a fact. For example, a fact witness might testify that he worked beside Mr. Morrison and personally saw him cough repeatedly as asbestos dust covered his body and clothing. This is direct evidence of the fact that Morrison was exposed to asbestos. **Circumstantial evidence** is evidence that is not based on personal observation, and thus does not directly establish a disputed fact. This type of evidence, however, often leads a judge or jury to infer a particular conclusion about the disputed facts. For example, evidence might be introduced that six of Morrison's coworkers also contracted asbestosis. A jury could draw an inference that something at work contributed to the condition. Both direct and circumstantial evidence are important in proving your client's case.

> **direct evidence**
> Proof of a fact without the need for other facts leading up to it. For example, direct evidence that dodos are not extinct would be a live dodo.

> **circumstantial evidence**
> Facts that indirectly prove a main fact in question.

Forms of Evidence

In any trial, attorneys use different forms of evidence to prove the elements of their case. For example, if the Morrison case were to go to trial, the attorneys would have witnesses testify. They would present medical and employment records. They might also have photographs of the workplace. The different forms of evidence would thus be testimony, documents, and photographs. Testimony is the most common form of evidence and consists of statements made under penalty of perjury by witnesses in response to questions by the attorneys. Documentary evidence is also common.

Other forms of evidence include physical objects (sometimes referred to as **demonstrative evidence**), presumptions, and judicial notice. Physical objects are items that have something to do with the case. In the Morrison case, that might be a sample of asbestos taken from the building where Morrison worked. Another type of demonstrative evidence is created for trial to help illustrate matters that are included in testimony or documents, such as charts or diagrams. For example, instead of photographs of the workplace, Morrison's attorneys might have a scale model of the building made. A recent trend in the use of demonstrative evidence is the production of animated, three-dimensional videos. Presentation software, such as PowerPoint, is also used frequently by trial lawyers to help illustrate various points.

> **demonstrative evidence**
> All evidence other than testimony.

Presumptions and judicial notice are referred to as forms of evidence because they are ways that attorneys have of proving a point. However, they are very different from the forms of evidence that we see or hear. In a sense, these are legal ways of proving points without testimony or physical evidence. A **presumption** is a rule of law that allows the trier of fact to draw an inference—because one fact has been established by traditional evidence another fact also exists. For example, in many jurisdictions, if a party can prove that a letter was mailed, the jury can draw an inference (presume) that

> **presumption**
> A conclusion or inference drawn. A presumption of law is an automatic assumption required by law that whenever a certain set of facts shows up, a court must automatically draw certain legal conclusions.

judicial notice

The act of a judge in recognizing the existence or truth of certain facts without bothering to make one side in a lawsuit prove them. This is done when the facts are either common knowledge and undisputed, or are easily found and cannot be disputed.

it was received. It is important to remember, however, that many presumptions can be rebutted or disproved by other evidence. **Judicial notice** allows a court to find that certain facts are true without the parties presenting evidence of the fact. Courts take judicial notice of facts that are commonly known or accepted. According to Federal Rules of Evidence, Rule 201, a court can take judicial notice of a fact not subject to reasonable dispute in that it is either (1) generally known within the territorial jurisdiction of the trial court or (2) capable of accurate and ready determination by resort to sources whose accuracy cannot reasonably be questioned.

Your role as a paralegal in the sample commentary case would be to actively seek and maintain all of the evidence, whether in the form of fact or expert witness testimony. This might involve locating a copy of the client's employment records or finding an elusive coworker who has knowledge of the existence of asbestos in Mr. Morrison's workplace. The issue of whether evidence, once obtained, is admissible is an important one. To determine whether a particular piece of evidence, verbal or written, is admissible requires knowledge of the appropriate rules of evidence.

Federal Rules of Evidence

The Federal Rules of Evidence were established pursuant to Title 28 of the United States Code. The purposes of the Federal Rules of Evidence are set out in Rule 102: "These rules shall be construed to secure fairness in administration, elimination of unjustifiable expense and delay, and promotion of growth and development of the law of evidence to the end that the truth may be ascertained and proceedings justly determined." A complete discussion of the rules of evidence and exceptions is impossible within this chapter or even this book. You will be introduced only to the general principles of the rules of evidence, including an overview of some specific rules of evidence that commonly affect litigation.

Relevancy Requirement (Rule 401 and Rule 402)

relevant evidence

Evidence that tends to prove or disprove a fact that is important to a claim, charge, or defense in a court case.

To be admissible, evidence must be **relevant.** Rule 401 defines this as "evidence having any tendency to make the existence of any fact that is of consequence to the determination of the action more probable or less probable than it would be without the evidence." No one piece of evidence need be sufficient in itself to persuade the judge or jury that a particular fact is true. It must only support the existence of the particular fact. In determining relevancy, a question often arises regarding background facts that may be necessary or helpful in understanding the ultimate disputed fact. For example, in the Morrison case, the defense attorney might have evidence that Mr. Morrison frequents gambling establishments on a regular basis. Obviously this has nothing to do with the facts of the case and, standing alone, would not be admissible. However, if the attorney can show that the gambling establishment has posted a warning about the presence of asbestos in the building's ceiling, then the fact that Mr. Morrison gambles frequently can be introduced as evidence that he has been exposed to asbestos outside the workplace.

The following are examples of facts that are generally found to be irrelevant and inadmissible:

1. Subsequent remedial measures: Where an injury occurs because of some defective or dangerous property, the fact that the condition has been repaired is not generally admissible.
2. Offer to compromise the claim: A party's offer to settle or compromise a claim is not admissible.
3. Promise to pay medical or other expenses: This is similar to a party's offer to settle and is not admissible as evidence of liability.
4. Existence of liability insurance: Whether one has insurance or not is not relevant to the issue of liability or damages.

Exclusion of Relevant Evidence (Rules 403–406)

Not all relevant evidence is admissible evidence. Rule 403 permits exclusion of relevant evidence if "its probative value is substantially outweighed by the danger of unfair prejudice, confusion of the issues or misleading the jury, or by considerations of undue delay, waste of time, or needless presentation of cumulative evidence." The court determines whether the negative aspects of the evidence outweigh its probative value.

Rules 404 and 405 deal with the exclusion of another type of evidence that many consider relevant—**character evidence.** Character evidence includes testimony about a person's reputation in the community or whether the person is felt by friends and coworkers to be honest or dishonest. Character evidence is not admissible if its purpose is to prove that an individual "acted in conformity" with his or her normal character traits on a particular occasion. However, character evidence is admissible when a person's character is in issue (Rule 405[b]). Under Rule 406, evidence to establish **habit**—how a person responds to a particular situation—may be admissible if it develops sufficient evidence of a repeated pattern of behavior to the extent that it is an automatic response (for example, unplugging the coffee maker after pouring the last cup of coffee).

character evidence
Testimony about a person's personal traits and habits that is drawn from the opinions of close associates, from the person's reputation in the community, or from the person's past actions.

habit
The way a person usually responds to a particular situation.

Documentary Evidence

Two basic rules relating to documentary evidence are the requirements for authentication and the best evidence rule. However, the fact that documents meet the requirements for authentication and the best evidence rule does not necessarily mean that the documents are admissible. They must still be relevant and comply with all the rules of admissibility, including the hearsay rule.

Authentication   Rule 901(a) of the Federal Rules of Evidence lists the requirement of authentication (or identification) of a document. The person presenting the document as evidence must establish that the document is what it purports to be—a contract, warranty, deed, and so forth. This is called *authenticating* the document. In the Morrison case, the human resources director for Mr. Morrison's employer might be asked to authenticate the company's written policy that guarantees that the workplace is a safe place, free of any health department or OSHA violations.

Many examples of methods of authentication are found in Rule 901(b), including testimony of witnesses with knowledge of the genuineness of the document, nonexpert opinion regarding handwriting, voice identification, telephone conversation, and public records or reports. For example, an individual who knew a decedent and often corresponded with him might be able to identify and authenticate a hand-written will. The witness would not have to be a handwriting expert. She would only need a basis for being able to identify the handwriting. Public records may be authenticated through testimony of an employee of the public office that the document indeed came from that office.

Self-Authentication

Rule 902 of the Federal Rules of Evidence permits self-authentication of certain documents without the required testimony of a witness to establish that authenticity. The following types of documents can usually be introduced without any testimony or other evidence showing authenticity:

- public documents,
- certified copies of public records,
- official (government) publications,
- newspapers and periodicals,
- trade inscriptions,
- acknowledged (notarized) documents, and
- commercial paper and related documents.

Best Evidence Rule

In the event of a dispute regarding the contents of a document, Rule 1002 of the Federal Rules of Evidence (often called the best evidence rule) requires that the original document be utilized, unless the original is unavailable or some other rule of evidence or state or federal statute permits the use of a copy. Additionally, if the authenticity of the original document is not is dispute, then a copy is admissible.

An example of a situation where the original document might be required is in a contract or will dispute. If the original document is not available, it will be necessary for the witness who testifies about its contents to cite sufficient reasons for failing to produce the original. (Rule 1004 lists other occasions when an original might not be required.) As a litigation paralegal, you should take particular care to obtain and safeguard original documents.

Hearsay Rule

hearsay
A statement about what someone else said (or wrote or otherwise communicated). Hearsay evidence is evidence, concerning what someone said outside of a court proceeding, that is offered in the proceeding to prove the truth of what was said.

One of the most involved rules of evidence is the hearsay rule. **Hearsay** is generally defined as an out-of-court statement introduced in court and offered to prove the truth of the statement made. It is generally a statement made by someone other than the person actually testifying in court. Hearsay includes documents as well as oral statements. For example, if the attorney in the Morrison case tried to introduce a written statement from a witness obtained through the investigative process, that written statement would be hearsay (and in this case probably inadmissible).

The hearsay rules are complex, but basically provide that a hearsay statement is not admissible as evidence unless it meets one of the stated exceptions to the rule. The hearsay rule and its numerous exceptions are found in Rules 801–806 of the Federal Rules of Evidence.

The underlying principle in attempting to exclude hearsay is to further the underlying role of evidence—to ensure truthful testimony at trial. In the courtroom, the attorneys for all parties have the opportunity to examine and cross-examine. Hearsay testimony does not afford that opportunity, and creates an atmosphere of unfairness. On the other hand, the various exceptions to the hearsay rule include situations where truthfulness is likely to be present.

Exceptions to Hearsay

Rules 803 and 804 of the Federal Rules of Evidence list the exceptions to the hearsay rule. You should be careful not to assume that a statement is automatically admissible because it fits an exception to the hearsay rule. Testimony must still comply with the other rules of evidence discussed earlier in this chapter, including relevance. Some of the more frequently encountered exceptions to hearsay include:

1. Excited utterance—Rule 803(2). Because of the excitement, the person making the statement is presumed to have had no time to fabricate the statement. Consider the following example. A police officer is called to a domestic disturbance. Upon arriving at the residence, the officer hears a gunshot and rushes into the residence, where he sees Harry lying on the ground, bleeding profusely. When Harry sees the officer, he exclaims, "Wanda tried to kill me!" If Wanda is prosecuted for attempted murder, the police officer can testify as to what Harry told him because, even though it is hearsay, it is an excited utterance.

2. Existing mental, emotional or physical condition (state of mind)—Rule 803(3). Statements that show the declarant's state of mind, emotion, or physical condition are admissible. This includes statements that show intent, plan, motive, mental feeling, or pain.

3. Statements made for the purpose of medical diagnosis or treatment—Rule 803(4). Patients seeking treatment from a doctor are presumed to be more likely to tell the doctor the truth to obtain appropriate treatment.

4. Business records—Rule 803(6). Records kept in the course of regular business activity generally fall within this exception, under the theory that businesses require accurate records for their operations.

5. Unavailability of person who made statement—Rule 804. Under some circumstances, certain types of hearsay are admissible if the person who made the statements is unavailable for trial. A witness is considered unavailable for trial only for the following reasons: death or illness, assertion of a privilege and refusal to testify, or inability of the court to secure the presence of that person at trial. Under these circumstances, if the witness had given prior testimony either at a hearing or a deposition, that prior testimony is admissible if the party against whom the testimony is offered had the opportunity to question the witness. As a paralegal, you should be aware that the attorney cannot unilaterally decide to use a witness's deposition in lieu of subpoenaing the witness to testify. The deposition is hearsay and therefore not admissible unless the witness is unavailable or all parties agree that it may be used.

6. Statements against interest—Rule 804(b)(3). When a person has made a statement against his or her legal, business, or financial interests, that statement is presumed to be true, because it is assumed that the person would have no reason to make up detrimental statements against himself or herself.

One of the important elements of the definition of hearsay is that the out-of-court statement is used to prove the truth of the statement made. Therefore, if the out-of-court statement is used for another purpose, it may be admissible. The most common example of this is a written statement of a witness. If introduced to prove the truth of the statement, it is hearsay. However, if the witness testifies at trial and gives testimony that conflicts with the written statement, the out-of-court statement can be used to impeach the credibility of the witness.

Privileged Communications

Rule 501 of the Federal Rules of Evidence delegates to the courts and state legislatures the responsibility of developing rules for evidence protected by privilege. The paralegal is charged with the responsibility of helping the attorney ensure that protected information or evidence is not disclosed during litigation. Chapters 8 through 13 discuss at length the types of privileges which may be asserted, including attorney-client, husband-wife, and physician-patient.

State Rules of Evidence

In the Morrison case, you would need to look at your state's statutes to determine the pertinent rules of evidence. Often the state will publish a compilation of all of its rules, including rules of civil procedure, appellate procedure, and so on.

Additional Resources Relating to Evidence

There are several excellent commentaries and treatises on the subject of evidence, including *Wigmore on Evidence* and *McCormick on Evidence*. Check a law library to locate additional information on evidence.

Methods for Locating and Preserving Evidence

Coworkers and other fact witnesses are essential to Mr. Morrison's case. However, testimony from witnesses is only one kind of evidence that can be used to prove a case. Written documents, photographs, and items of personal property are often introduced as evidence at trial to prove the facts of the case. In the situation described in the commentary, evidence such as photographs of the scene, medical records of Mr. Morrison, Environmental Protection Agency citations, time cards indicating days absent because of illness, and plant-safety programs are all critical. Your attorney may ask that you take responsibility for locating and organizing all available evidence.

Documents relating to your client, such as his medical bills or records and his employment records, are usually easy to obtain. If you have an authorization for the

---

Police Reports—Local, county, or state police and Department of Motor Vehicles

Automobile Ownership—Department of Motor Vehicles

Insurance Coverage—State Department of Insurance and Department of Motor Vehicles

Weather Reports—United States Weather Bureau

Fire Reports—Fire marshal

Aviation Records (on accidents or safety standards)—Federal Aviation Administration

Property Ownership or Taxes—Local tax assessor's office and State Department of Revenue

Birth and Death Records—Bureau of Vital Statistics and local coroner's office

Medical Treatment—Doctor, hospital, ambulance company, X ray firm, and physical therapist

Personal Data—Registrar of Voters, criss-cross directories, U.S. Post Office, Social Security Office, county court records (including judgments and/or liens, criminal, marriage and divorce), and the Internet

Newspaper or Publicity—Local newspapers and television stations, archives of local libray, and the Internet

---

EXHIBIT 4–7 Types and sources of evidence in a personal injury case

release of this information signed by the client, you can obtain these documents by sending a copy of that release to the appropriate person or business. For other types of evidence, a telephone call or letter may suffice; if it does not, a subpoena and deposition may be required. Moreover, any evidence in the possession or control of a defendant will have to be obtained through the proper discovery process. These last two methods are discussed in detail in subsequent chapters.

See Exhibit 4–7 for a checklist of types and sources of evidence in a personal injury case such as the Morrison case.

Evidence Control and Retrieval

You have assembled evidence to help substantiate Mr. Morrison's claim. This evidence includes photographs of the plant, labels from products used by workers in the plant, and copies of Mr. Morrison's X rays. In order to avoid charges by the opposition that the evidence has been tampered with or replaced, each piece of evidence should be tracked from its receipt by your law firm until its final introduction as a trial exhibit. Evidence should be marked to indicate its source, date of acquisition, and storage location. An **evidence log** will enable you to maintain an accurate record of the evidence, including any transfer of custody. Each time the evidence is removed from its storage location, the removal should be documented on the exhibit log. Exhibit 4-8 shows a suggested form for an evidence log.

evidence log
A document attached to an item of physical evidence recording the chain of possession (chain of custody) of that piece of evidence.

```
STYLE OF CASE: _____

EVIDENCE: _____

DATE ACQUIRED: _____ ACQUIRED BY: _____

MANNER BY WHICH ACQUIRED: _____
_____

PARTICULAR IDENTIFYING MARKS: _____

LOCATIONS OF EVIDENCE: _____

EVIDENCE CUSTODIAN: _____

CHAIN OF EVIDENCE CUSTODY:

RELEASED TO                 DATE              PURPOSE OF RELEASE


_____
_____
_____
_____
```

EXHIBIT 4–8 Evidence log

Complex litigation sometimes presents extra challenges for evidence control and production. Cases often involve hundreds or thousands of documents and may have many attorneys, located in different cities, working on the same case. A paralegal coordinating such a case must be concerned with how to store the documents, where to store the documents, and how to make them available to multiple attorneys who may be geographically separated. One solution is to convert all of the documents to electronic format and store them on a secure Internet site.

Preservation of Evidence

The method for preserving evidence varies, depending on the nature of the evidence. Photographs tend to fade or be damaged by handling. X rays require a special folder for preservation. An original $300,000 note may be maintained in the firm's vault, with a copy of the note retained in an envelope labeled with the location of the original.

Some forms of evidence do not lend themselves to storage in the law firm during lengthy litigation because of their size or daily use on a job site. Photographs of these exhibits may be taken and retained in the client's file for use in preparing the case for trial, at which time the original piece of evidence may be introduced.

Ensuring that evidence is preserved in its original form may be one of your responsibilities. Because of the varied nature of the evidence in Mr. Morrison's case, in-depth research on preserving the evidence could be required.

Expert Witnesses

In a case involving technical or medical issues, **expert witnesses** are often necessary. Experts can perform several functions in a case. They can be hired in an advisory capacity, to explain the technical aspects of the case to the attorney. More often, they are hired to be witnesses during the trial. Before individuals are allowed to testify as experts, they must be qualified by the court to do so. In qualifying experts, the court looks at their education, skill, and experience in that field. If an individual is qualified as an expert, at trial this individual can explain and simplify complicated technical issues for the judge or jury. For example, a jury might have difficulty understanding the mechanical functions of a tire manufacturing plant or the significance of a lung X ray. Expert witnesses may translate the technical language to easily understood language through photographs, charts, or models. Also, expert witnesses, unlike lay witnesses, are allowed to testify about their expert opinions regarding matters within their expertise. For example, in the Morrison case, a proper expert could testify that in his opinion materials to which Mr. Morrison was exposed at work caused the asbestosis.

The decision to hire an expert witness is made by the supervising attorney. However, you may be asked to locate an expert. Suggested sources for locating potential experts include:

- professional organizations,
- published court records of experts,
- other attorneys in your office,
- colleges or universities,
- professional journals,
- attorneys who have handled similar litigation, and
- the Internet.

If the expert has testified in prior cases, you might wish to talk to the attorney who tried the case to get an evaluation of the expert's ability as a witness. The demeanor of an expert witness can be even more important than that of a lay witness. Although the expert's professional credentials are important, his or her ability to explain matters to a judge or jury in a simple and clear manner, without appearing condescending, is just as important.

Once you have located an expert, you must keep certain practical considerations in mind. An expert's time is very valuable, and use of that time by your law firm can be expensive. Most experts charge the firm not only for the time they spend testifying in court, but also for any time spent in talking to the attorneys (or paralegals). Any interview of an expert must be carefully orchestrated to maximize the expert's time. Preparation in advance of the interview will obviate the need for a lengthy interview process. Know ahead of time what areas should be covered and make notes. Also, if the expert is local, arranging the interview to take place at the expert's place of business can save time and therefore expense.

expert witness
A person possessing special knowledge or experience who is allowed to testify at a trial not only about facts (like an ordinary witness) but also about the professional conclusions he or she draws from these facts.

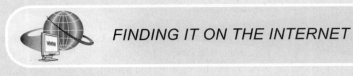

FINDING IT ON THE INTERNET

The Internet provides numerous sources to help litigation paralegals with the matters discussed in this chapter. The Federal Rules of Evidence can be found at **<http://www.law.cornell.edu>** (click on "Constitution and Codes"). They can also be found through **<http://www.uscourts.gov>** (click on "Federal Rulemaking," then on "Rules and Forms in Effect"). When accessing the federal rules through the Internet, make certain that you have accessed the current version. Older versions are posted in PDF format.

Experts can be located through numerous sources, including: **<http://www.expert4law.org>** and **<http://www.nocall.org>** (click on "Internet Resources" and look for "Expert Witnesses").

a. Access the Web site for the National Library of Medicine. Locate information about asbestos and write a memo summarizing findings that would be relevant to the Morrison case described at the beginning of this chapter.

b. Using any of the above sites, locate experts who might be helpful to the Morrison case. Make a list of experts and their areas of expertise.

c. Using the site **<http://www.statelocal.gov>,** locate information on the Environmental Protection Agency (EPA). (At the Web site click on "Search" and then on "Federal Web Locator.") Using the search feature on the EPA page, find information about asbestos. Write a brief memo summarizing information that might be helpful to the Morrison case.

One pitfall to avoid in securing an expert witness is the "professional testifying expert." An excessive number of court appearances can have a negative impact on the jury, especially if that expert has always testified for the plaintiff or for the defendant. An expert whose testimony has been balanced will be more effective.

Before deciding to use a particular expert, you should review the expert's resumé and determine if she has testified in prior cases. If she has qualified as an expert in prior cases, she is likely to be qualified by the court in your case. You should also review all prior cases to make sure that she has not given testimony that would contradict the testimony she expects to give in your case.

Your responsibilities in the area of expert witnesses may include locating an expert, coordinating the interview of the expert witness with the attorney, taking notes during an interview, reviewing the qualifications of the expert, reviewing prior testimony of the expert, and, if the expert is located some distance away, handling hotel and air travel reservations.

Summary

- A client interview establishes the foundation for the relationship between the client and the law firm. The paralegal is often involved in several different aspects of this procedure. Paralegal responsibilities might include researching potential causes of action or defenses prior to the interview, scheduling the interview, developing an interview questionnaire, gathering forms and documents for client signature, taking notes during the interview, and producing a summary of the interview.

- Locating witnesses who have knowledge of the facts of the case is an essential part of the litigation process and is often a paralegal function. Likewise, locating the defendant in the action is a task often assigned to paralegals. Various sources exist to help the paralegal find witnesses or elusive defendants. Some of those sources include the client, accident reports, official records, and computerized services.

- When interviewing fact witnesses, a paralegal should always be properly identified. The paralegal should always be courteous and consider the convenience of the witness. Tape-recorded interviews are preferred, but if the witness objects, a written statement or notes can be used. A questionnaire should be prepared before the interview, and care should be taken during the interview itself to avoid leading questions. After the interview, the paralegal should prepare a typewritten statement for signature by the witness. During the interview, the paralegal should observe and make note of the witness's demeanor.

- Rules of evidence dictate what facts, documents, and other evidence will be allowed at trial. In federal court, these rules are found in the Federal Rules of Evidence. To be admissible, evidence must be relevant, that is, tending to prove a fact that is important to the case, and not otherwise objectionable. Evidence is objectionable if its probative value is outweighed by undue prejudice or consumption of time; if it is documentary evidence and has not been properly authenticated; if it violates the best evidence rule; if it violates the hearsay rule and is not subject to one of the many exceptions; or if it is a privileged communication.

- Paralegals are often involved in locating and preserving evidence in a civil case. Evidence includes documents or other items that tend to prove the facts of the case. Items of evidence relating to the client can often be obtained by a simple request accompanied by a signed release from the client. In other situations, formal discovery methods must be utilized. After evidence is obtained, proper care must be taken to control and preserve the evidence for trial. To avoid charges that evidence has been altered, the chain of possession of the evidence must be verified.

- Expert witnesses are often essential in a case. They are able to explain technical matters to a judge or jury and can offer their professional opinions regarding issues in the case. Paralegals are sometimes asked to locate experts, coordinate interviews between the expert and the attorney, take notes during the interview, review the qualifications and prior testimony of the expert, and handle hotel and air travel reservations.

Key Terms

agent	direct evidence	medical diary
agent for service of process	evidence log	presumption
authorization	expert witness	release
character evidence	habit	relevant evidence
circumstantial evidence	hearsay	representation letter
demeanor	judicial notice	retainer agreement
demonstrative evidence	leading question	service of process

Review Questions

1. What are the paralegal's responsibilities in preparing for the client interview?
2. What are the steps in setting up a client interview?
3. What types of questions should be included in a client interview questionnaire?
4. What forms might be needed during the client interview for client signature?
5. What is the function of a paralegal during the client interview?
6. What are some possible sources for locating fact witnesses or elusive defendants?
7. Describe the various objections to admissibility of evidence.
8. What are the methods for locating, controlling, and preserving evidence?
9. What is the importance of the expert witness?
10. What is the paralegal's role in retaining an expert witness?

Chapter Exercises

Where necessary, check with your instructor prior to starting any of these exercises.

1. Review the commentary at the opening of this chapter and draft questions for your attorney to ask at the initial interview.
2. Assume that you are to interview one of Oscar Morrison's friends and coworkers. Draft a questionnaire to be used during the interview.
3. You have been asked to assist the attorney in finding an expert witness to help establish that Morrison's work environment contributed to the asbestosis. Identify and locate places in your general area where you might find such an expert.
4. When you review the Morrison file (case commentary) you find the following items. Discuss whether they are admissible pieces of evidence and if so, how they could be authenticated. If there are any hearsay problems be sure to include that in your analysis.
   a. photographs of the workplace
   b. a letter from Peter Wayans, president of Acme Inc., apologizing to Morrison for his company's involvement in his illness
   c. a letter from Acme Inc.'s insurance company stating that they were handling the claim
   d. a recorded statement from Joseph Polizo, a coworker of Morrison
   e. a deposition of Joseph Polizo
   f. copies of Morrison's medical bills
   g. copies of Morrison's medical records
   h. a report from the EPA detailing the hazards of exposure to asbestos.

Chapter Project

For this project you need to work with another student in the class. One of you should assume the role of a friend and coworker of Oscar Morrison, while the other assumes the role of a paralegal working in the firm representing Mr. Morrison. The "paralegal" is to conduct a tape-recorded interview of the coworker. After the interview is recorded, both students should prepare a typewritten statement of the interview.

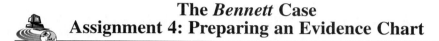

The *Bennett* Case
Assignment 4: Preparing an Evidence Chart

Prepare a list and description of the types and sources of evidence you might expect to find in the *Bennett* case. (Review Exhibit 4–7 for an example.)

Chapter 5

The Initial Pleadings

CHAPTER OUTLINE

COMMENTARY—THE HENDRICKS CASE

Your attorney has just given you a file containing the preliminary investigative reports and notes concerning new clients Margaret and Paul Hendricks. After reviewing the various documents in the file, and after discussing the matter with your attorney, you learn the following facts. While vacationing in Nevada, the Hendrickses, residents of the state of California, attended a sales presentation regarding vacation property located in Idaho. During the sales presentation, which was conducted by May Forrester, a real estate agent with Hearth & Home Real Estate Company, the Hendrickses were shown numerous color slides of the vacation property, all depicting large, level lots surrounding a manmade lake. The lots were owned by Paradise Found, Inc., an Idaho corporation. They were told during the presentation that the lots were ready for building. The lots were being offered for the price of $100,000. However, only two lots remained unsold, and the realtor expected these to go quickly. Swayed by the sales presentation, the Hendrickses purchased a lot without personally visiting the site. They paid cash and were given a deed. Shortly thereafter they visited the property in Idaho, only to find that the lot they owned was nothing like the photos they had seen. The lake was completely dry, no lots had been built on, and in fact a great deal of preparation would have to be done before any building. There were no utilities, sewers, or roads. They immediately contacted the realtor, May Forrester, the company she works for, Hearth & Home Real Estate Company, and the seller of the property, Paradise Found, Inc. The sellers have refused to return the Hendrickses' money and say that nothing can be done. Incidentally, the file also indicates that Hearth & Home Real Estate Company is really a partnership owned by Harry and Harvey Rice. Your attorney is anxious to initiate a lawsuit in this matter and has asked you to prepare a complaint for his review, naming all proper parties and containing all possible causes of action.

OBJECTIVES

Chapter 4 introduced the methods for obtaining information necessary to pursue a lawsuit. After that information is obtained, the next step in the litigation process is the preparation and filing of the initial pleadings. After reading this chapter, you should be able to:

- Define the term *pleadings.*
- Describe, in general, the contents of a complaint or petition.
- Discuss the various considerations in determining and identifying parties to the lawsuit.
- Analyze the various allegations found in a complaint.
- Explain the types of relief that can be requested in a complaint.
- Outline the steps in drafting a complaint.

- Explain the process of filing the complaint.
- Define a summons.
- List the different methods of serving a complaint.
- Describe the procedure for amending the complaint.

Initial Pleadings

Pleadings in General

After completing preliminary investigation, interviews, and research, the attorney determines whether to pursue the case. If the decision is made to proceed, the litigation process formally begins with the preparation and filing of appropriate pleadings. **Pleadings** are the various documents filed in a court proceeding that define the nature of the dispute between the parties. Not all documents filed with the court are pleadings. The term *pleading* technically refers only to papers that contain statements, or **allegations,** describing the contentions and defenses of the parties to the lawsuit. The pleadings set the framework for all of the steps and proceedings that follow. If an issue is not raised in the pleadings, the parties may be prevented from bringing it up at trial. Although pleadings relate to contentions of the parties, these documents are always prepared by the law firm representing the party. As a paralegal in a litigation firm, one of your duties might include the drafting of these documents. You might also be asked to review pleadings prepared by the opposing side.

The content and format of the various pleadings are largely controlled by the appropriate statutory law. Cases filed in federal court are governed primarily by the Federal Rules of Civil Procedure. Cases filed in a state court would be governed by the laws of the state. In addition to state rules, many county or area courts have their own individual rules, known as local rules of court. Within the federal court system, various district courts may also have their own local rules. Local rules can differ from one court to another, even if the courts are located in the same state. Before preparing or filing any pleading, therefore, you must check all local rules. In spite of the numerous technical rules that may govern pleadings, most courts take a fairly liberal attitude in reviewing or judging the sufficiency of the documents. The courts today are concerned that the parties resolve their disputes based on the merits of the case, rather than on some technical rule regarding the format of a document.

pleadings
Formal, written statements of each side of a civil case.

allegation
A statement in a pleading that sets out a fact that the side filing the pleading expects to prove.

The Complaint in General

Assuming that your law firm represents the plaintiff in an action, the initial pleading that you prepare and file, and that starts the court process, is generally known as a complaint, or in some cases a petition. The complaint is the pleading in which the plaintiff states the basis for the lawsuit. Generally the complaint does the following:

1. identifies the plaintiffs and defendants in the lawsuit, and describes their status and capacity to sue and be sued,

---

**UNITED STATES DISTRICT COURT
FOR THE DISTRICT OF NEVADA**

MARGARET HENDRICKS and)
PAUL HENDRICKS,)
)
      Plaintiffs)
)
   vs.   )
)
MAY FORRESTER,)
      Defendant)
	No.
	
	COMPLAINT FOR FRAUD

EXHIBIT 5–1 Designation of parties in caption

2. contains a statement showing that the court in which it is filed has proper jurisdiction and venue,
3. describes the factual basis for the lawsuit, and
4. makes a request or demand for some relief from the court.

The complaint itself usually follows a set format, with various parts known as:

1. The **caption**—the part of the complaint that identifies the court in which the complaint is filed, the names of the plaintiffs and defendants, and the title of the document (see Exhibit 5–1).
2. The allegations (or cause of action)—a description of the parties, statements showing proper jurisdiction and venue, the factual basis for the lawsuit, and a description of the loss or damages incurred.
3. The **prayer**—a request for some relief or remedy from the court.
4. The **subscription** and **verification**—the signature of the attorney filing the document, the date, and the plaintiff's statement, under penalty of perjury, that the contents of the complaint are true.

Before you begin to draft any complaint you should analyze your case, determine the purpose of your pleading, and outline the general content of your document. Specifically you should know:

- who will be named as parties and how they will be named,
- how you will show that jurisdiction and venue are proper,
- the type of claims or causes of action that will be included in the complaint, and
- the type of relief you are demanding.

Only after you have done this preliminary analysis should you begin to actually draft the complaint.

caption

The heading or introductory section of a legal paper. The caption of a court paper usually contains the names of the parties, the court, and the case number.

prayer

Request. That part of a legal pleading (such as a complaint) that asks for relief (help, money, specific court action, an action from the other side, etc.).

subscription (subscribe)

Sign a document.

verification (verify)

Swear in writing to the truth or accuracy of a document.

Parties to the Lawsuit

The parties to the lawsuit are known as the *plaintiff,* the one who files the action, and the *defendant,* the one who is sued. They are identified in the caption by their names, indicating whether they are named as plaintiff or defendant. For example, in the situation described in the commentary to this chapter, if the Hendrickses wished to sue the realtor, the names of the parties would appear in the caption as shown in Exhibit 5–1. In the body of the complaint, the parties are then described in more detail.

Normally the question of who is named as a plaintiff and who is named as a defendant is relatively simple. At times, however, problems can arise. As a paralegal involved in preparing or drafting a complaint, you should be aware of some of these problem areas.

Real Party in Interest

The plaintiff in any lawsuit should be the one who is entitled to the relief sought in the complaint. This is known as the **real party in interest.** In most cases, parties do not file lawsuits unless they have personally suffered some loss. However, at times a special relationship exists that creates a different situation. For example, an executor may wish to sue on behalf of an estate, or a trustee may sue on behalf of a trust, or a collection agency may wish to sue on a debt assigned to it for collection. In such cases, is the plaintiff the executor or the estate, the trustee or the trust, the collection agency or the creditor? Under Rule 17a of the Federal Rules of Civil Procedure, the executor, the trustee, and even the collection agency could be named as plaintiffs in the lawsuit, even though they are not suing on their own behalf. However, if the action is in state court, appropriate state laws should always be checked.

real party in interest
The person who will ultimately benefit from winning a lawsuit, whether or not that person brought it initially.

Status

The *status* of a party refers to the type of entity that describes the party. Most commonly a party to a lawsuit will be an individual, a corporation, a partnership or other unincorporated business, or a governmental agency. Unless a party is simply an individual, the status of the party will usually be described both in the caption and in a separate allegation within the body of the complaint. For example, if the Hendrickses were to sue the seller of the property, it would be identified in the caption as follows:

Example

```
                                        )
                                        )
vs.                                     )
                                        )
PARADISE FOUND, INC., an Idaho          )
Corporation,                            )
        Defendant                       )
                                        )
```

THE COMPUTERIZED LAW FIRM
Word Processing and Electronic Filing

SCENARIO

Your attorney is ready to file suit on behalf of the Henrickses and asks you to prepare a draft of the complaint for fraud and negligent misrepresentation for his review. The attorney gives you the office file containing his detailed notes from interviews with the Henrickses. He reminds you to look at the rules of court and make sure that your complaint meets all of the requirements. You have never prepared this type of complaint before. The statute of limitations is running and you have only a few days to file the complaint. To make matters worse, the court in which you are filing the complaint is 150 miles away from your office.

PROBLEM

You have a great deal to do and very little time in which to do it. You must look in form books to find a form for a complaint for fraud and negligent misrepresentation. Using that form and the facts of your case, you must then prepare a written complaint suitable for filing in court. Checking your rules of court, you find that every document filed in court must have a caption set in a certain format and each page of any document filed in court must contain a footer describing the document. Finally, you must arrange to have the complaint filed before the statute of limitations runs out. How can you do this?

SOLUTION

Lawyers have always relied on form books to provide them with samples to follow in preparing legal documents. Until recently, a form would usually be located in a book and then retyped with the specific facts of the case. Today, shortcuts exist.

Most traditional form books are now available on CD-ROM. A form from the CD can be copied directly into your word processor, eliminating the need for retyping.

Furthermore, two major word processing programs, Microsoft Word and Corel's WordPerfect, have many specially designed features for the legal environment, including easy ways to set up pleadings. Captions can be automatically and easily generated as well. The program asks specific questions, such as the name of the plaintiff and the name of the defendant, then automatically formats the caption. You will also find that you can automatically generate a footer on each page. (In addition to providing legally specific word processors, both Microsoft and Corel provide complete software packages, including calendaring software, databases, spreadsheets, and presentation software.)

Filing a complaint in a court some distance away when a statute of limitations is about to expire can be an ordeal. Regular mail is too uncertain, and hand delivery takes many hours. Today many courts accept both fax and electronic filing (e-mail) of documents, including complaints. In order to take advantage of filing electronically, you will probably be required to convert your complaint to a portable document format (PDF) file. To do this you need special software such as Adobe Acrobat. Transmitting a document as a PDF file provides an exact duplicate of the document in electronic form as well as more security against anyone changing the document. This software also has the ability to supply a digital signature to the document. In the Henrickses case, electronic filing could save hours of travel time and would be more reliable than the mail.

In addition, within the body of the complaint you would include a paragraph describing that status, such as the following:

Example

---

1. Defendant, PARADISE FOUND, INC., is and was at all times herein mentioned a corporation duly organized and existing under the laws of the state of Idaho.

Capacity

Minors and Incompetents   You also need to make certain that the parties named in the complaint have **capacity,** or the legal right, to sue or be sued. Competent, adult individuals generally have the right to sue or be sued. However, children or incompetent adults do not have the capacity to pursue their own lawsuits. Unless a general guardian or conservator has already been appointed, the court will appoint a special person, referred to as a **guardian ad litem,** to pursue the case on behalf of the minor or incompetent. Even the parents of a child cannot file a lawsuit on their child's behalf unless they have been appointed as guardians by the court. A guardian ad litem is usually appointed at the request of the parent or guardian. The person wishing to be appointed files a motion or a petition with the court prior to filing any lawsuit, asking to be named as guardian ad litem. The complaint in such a case would have the same caption as the petition or motion for the appointment of the guardian. The following is an example of how the parties would be designated in such a case.

capacity
Legal ability to do something.

guardian ad litem
A guardian who is appointed by a court to take care of the interests of a person who cannot legally take care of himself or herself in a lawsuit involving that person.

Example

MARY SMITH, a minor, by GEORGE SMITH, her guardian ad litem,	)
Plaintiff	)
	)
vs.	)
	)
DEF CORPORATION, a California Corporation,	)
Defendant	)
	)

Although children or incompetents cannot sue in their own names, they can generally be named as defendants in the complaint. However, after they are served with the complaint they may be entitled to have a guardian appointed to represent their interests. Again, local law should be reviewed to determine if the appointment of a guardian ad litem for a defendant is necessary and, if so, how is it accomplished.

Corporations and Other Business Entities   A corporation is a "person" for legal purposes, including lawsuits. As such it has capacity to sue or be sued in the corporate name. In fact, if a corporation is a plaintiff or a defendant in a lawsuit, it must be identified by the corporate name, rather than the name of the directors, officers, or share-holders. Exceptions do occur, however, in the case of corporate defendants. If the corporation fails to act like a corporation—not keeping corporate minutes, not holding meetings, failing to keep corporate assets separate from personal assets, and so on—then the individuals behind the corporation can be sued individually. This is known as *piercing the corporate veil.* The directors, officers, or shareholders of a corporation will also be named individually as defendants if they have personally done something wrong.

Business entities other than corporations may be treated differently. An unincorporated association, such as a partnership, does not have legal existence separate and apart from the partners. It is proper, therefore, for such an organization to sue and be sued in the name of its members. Whether or not such a business must be sued in the name of its members is a question of local law. For example, some jurisdictions allow a partnership to be sued in the partnership name. Before doing this, however, you should check the law regarding collection of a judgment when the individual partners have not been named. Limitations may be placed on which assets can be seized to satisfy the judgment. When suing a partnership or other unincorporated business entity, it is common to list both the partners' names and the business name, as in the following example:

Example

	)
	)
vs.	)
HARRY RICE and HARVEY RICE,	)
A partnership, doing business as	)
Hearth & Home Real Estate Co.,	)
Defendants	)
	)

Governmental Agencies   There is no question about the right of a governmental entity to sue on a claim. However, because of the common law doctrine of sovereign immunity (the king could not be sued), many jurisdictions have laws that limit and regulate the circumstances under which a governmental entity can be sued. Appropriate statutes must be checked to see if the claim is one for which the offending governmental agency can be sued. Even when a statute permits the government to be sued, many laws require that claims be filed with the governmental agency before actually filing a lawsuit. (See Chapter 3.) In such a case, it may be necessary to allege in the body of the complaint that this has been done.

Special Problems with Parties

Parties Using Fictitious Names   Many businesses do not use their true names in the operation of their businesses. Individuals, either operating alone or with others, often choose to do business under a name that has more business appeal than their real names. At times, even corporations will do business under a name other than the real corporate name. If a plaintiff uses a fictitious name in his business, a lawsuit that he files related to that business should identify the plaintiff by his proper name. If he wishes, the plaintiff may indicate that he is doing business under another name. The plaintiff would then be identified as follows:

Example

MARTIN REDSHAW, doing business as)
Marty's Diner,)
            Plaintiff)
)
    vs.)
)
)
)

If the plaintiff is doing business under a fictitious name, before the lawsuit is filed you should verify that the plaintiff has complied with all local laws regarding such usage. Some states, for example, require that fictitious name statements be filed, and failure to do so can affect the right of a party to sue in some cases.

When the defendant is doing business under a fictitious name, the true name of the party may be unknown to you when you are preparing the complaint. Your state may have various records that can be checked, but these are not always complete or accurate. It is therefore necessary to identify the defendant in the complaint by the fictitious name. In such a case, when the true name of the defendant or defendants is determined, the complaint can generally be amended.

Fictitious Defendants   Not to be confused with parties who use a fictitious name in business is a concept known as **fictitiously named defendants,** a procedure that is allowed in some jurisdictions. This term usually refers to defendants whose very identity is unknown. They are usually identified as "Does." In jurisdictions that allow their use, "Does" are commonly named as defendants in complaints to cover a situation in which a new defendant is discovered after the statute of limitations has run. In such a case the attorney argues that the complaint was filed against the newly discovered defendant within the statute of limitations; he was just referred to by an incorrect name. The attorney then tries to amend the complaint to "correct" the name. "Does" are not used in federal court. Instead, Rule 15 of the Federal Rules of Civil Procedure allows plaintiffs to name a newly discovered defendant even after the statute of limitations has run, as long as the new party received notice that the lawsuit had been filed within the time allowed for service, would not be unduly prejudiced, and knew that but for a mistake, he or she would have been named as a party in the original lawsuit. In such a case, the date of filing against the new party "relates back" to the original filing date.

fictitiously named defendants

Defendants in a lawsuit who are not identified by their correct names; usually refers to the practice in some state courts of including several "does" as defendants to provide for discovery of additional defendants after the statute of limitations has run.

Joining Multiple Parties

Many lawsuits involve disputes with multiple plaintiffs and/or defendants. The rules concerning joinder of multiple parties can be extremely involved and confusing.

permissive joinder

A concept allowing multiple parties to be joined in one lawsuit as plaintiffs or defendants as long as there is some common question of fact or law.

compulsory joinder (joinder)

A party or issue that must be included in a case.

However, joinder of parties usually falls into two categories: joinder that is allowed but not required, known as **permissive joinder;** and joinder that is required, or **compulsory joinder.** Before drafting any complaint with multiple parties, you may need to review these rules. For example, in the Hendricks case described in the commentary, you may need to know whether the Hendrickses can sue the realtor, the company for which she works, and the seller all in the same lawsuit. This is determined by the rules of joinder, which are usually found in the appropriate state laws (or Rules 19–21 of the Federal Rules of Civil Procedure, if the case is in federal court).

The rules regarding permissive joinder, joinder of parties that is allowed but not required, are usually very liberal. Parties are permitted to be joined together in a complaint as plaintiffs or defendants as long as there is some common question of law or fact and the claim arises out of the same occurrence or series of occurrences. Of course, you would not name someone as a plaintiff in a complaint unless your law firm represented that party. Whether certain parties *must* be joined in the same complaint is a more difficult issue. Generally, if the court cannot resolve the matter without the presence of a party, then joinder of the party is required. For example, suppose that title to a certain piece of real property is in question, and four different individuals are claiming ownership. If one of those parties files a lawsuit to determine ownership (known as a *quiet title action*), he would have to name the other three claimants as defendants. The court could not determine ownership unless all four parties appeared before the court. When parties are required to be joined in the lawsuit, they are sometimes referred to as **indispensable parties.**

indispensable party

A person who has such a stake in the outcome of a lawsuit that the judge will not make a final decision unless that person is formally joined as a party to the lawsuit.

Even when it seems that joinder of certain parties is essential to the case, if jurisdiction over one of the parties is impossible to obtain, the court may allow the matter to proceed without that party being named. These cases obviously present complicated legal issues that must be thoroughly researched before you prepare the complaint.

Class Actions

class action

A lawsuit brought for yourself and other persons in the situation.

At times the number of potential plaintiffs in an action becomes too numerous to be practical. When this happens, a class action can result. A **class action** occurs when one or more parties who share a claim with a multitude of others file a lawsuit in their own names and also claim to represent numerous others in a similar situation. To maintain a class action, the party filing the lawsuit must usually get permission from the court to proceed with the action. If the court grants permission, it will also direct that all members of the class get notice of the action. Generally the court also orders that all class members who can be identified should get individual notice. This can be an overwhelming and expensive task. If your firm is involved in a class action, as a litigation paralegal you may be asked to take responsibility for this part of the litigation. Included in the notice to all potential members of the class is usually an explanation that any potential class member can request in writing that he or she be excluded from the class. If a member does not request exclusion, that class member will be bound by any judgment in the case.

Class actions permit cases to be brought when the amount of damages suffered by each plaintiff is minimal but the total damages suffered by all is substantial. In such a case it is not practical for parties to maintain their own individual lawsuits. The cost of litigation would outweigh any benefit. By joining together, the class of injured parties is able to minimize expenses and justify the litigation.

Every jurisdiction has its own rules, found in statutes and cases, regarding class action lawsuits. These rules usually deal with such matters as who can file, who is entitled to notice of the action, how that notice is to be given, and who must bear the cost of notice. Rule 23 of the Federal Rules of Civil Procedure governs class actions in federal court.

Interpleader

A special type of action or complaint, known as **interpleader,** also involves questions of joinder of parties. *Interpleader* refers to a type of action in which several different parties claim ownership to a fund or property that is in the control of another. For example, an insurance company provides liability coverage to an airline with a policy limit of $1 billion. A plane crashes, and the heirs of the victims file claims with the airline and the insurance company in excess of $10 billion. If liability is clear, the insurance company might determine at the outset that it is going to have to pay the policy limits. However, the question of how this money is to be appropriated remains. The insurance company does not want to unilaterally make this decision, because it would probably be sued if the claimants did not agree with the distribution. The appropriate action, therefore, is for the insurance company to ask the court to decide how the funds should be disbursed. This is accomplished by filing an action in interpleader with the court, naming all of the claimants as defendants. The insurance company can then deposit the policy limits with the court and withdraw from the action, leaving the claimants to fight over the money.

interpleader
A procedure in which persons having conflicting claims against a third person may be forced to resolve the conflict before seeking relief from the third person.

Jurisdiction and Venue

The complaint in any action must contain some allegation showing that the lawsuit is being filed in the proper court. This involves questions of both jurisdiction and venue. In a complaint filed in federal court, these allegations are usually very specific. In showing jurisdiction, the plaintiff usually states why the action is being filed in federal court, giving a citation to the appropriate United States Code section. The Federal Rules of Civil Procedure contain sample allegations regarding federal jurisdiction (see Exhibit 5–2).

In state courts, jurisdiction is determined by state law. Normally it is not necessary to make any express statement that jurisdiction belongs in state court rather than federal court. Such a conclusion will usually follow from all of the facts alleged in the complaint. In many states, however, there are different kinds of trial courts with different kinds of jurisdiction. For example, some state trial courts are empowered to hear civil cases only when the amount in dispute is less than a set amount of money. Within the complaint and in the prayer, or demand for relief, it should be shown that the amount claimed is within the jurisdiction of the court in which the case is filed.

Jurisdiction founded on diversity of citizenship and amount.

Plaintiff is a [citizen of the State of Connecticut] [corporation incorporated under the laws of the State of Connecticut having its principal place of business in the State of Connecticut] and defendant is a corporation incorporated under the laws of the State of New York having its principal place of business in a State other than the State of Connecticut. The matter in controversy exceeds, exclusive of interest and costs, the sum specified by 28 U.S.C. §1332.

Jurisdiction founded on the existence of a Federal question.

The action arises under [the Constitution of the United States, Article _____, Section _____]; [the _____ Amendment to the Constitution of the United States, Section _____]; [the Act of _____, _____ Stat. _____; U.S.C., Title _____, § _____]; [the Treaty of the United States (here describe the treaty)] as hereinafter more fully appears.

Jurisdiction founded on the existence of a question arising under particular statutes.

The action arises under the Act of _____, _____ Stat. _____; U.S.C., Title _____, Sec. _____, as hereinafter more fully appears.

Jurisdiction founded on the admiralty or maritime character of the claim.

This is a case of admiralty and maritime jurisdiction, as hereinafter more fully appears. [If the pleader wishes to invoke the distinctively maritime procedures referred to in *Rule 9(h),* add the following or its substantial equivalent: This is an admiralty or maritime claim within the meaning of *Rule 9(h).*]

EXHIBIT 5–2 Sample allegations regarding federal jurisdiction

In federal or state courts, venue can be determined by a number of factors. The most common factor is the residence of the defendant. Proper venue can be shown in the complaint by an allegation that one of the defendants resides in the district in which the action is filed. Venue is also proper in the place where the cause of action arose. Therefore, another common way of establishing venue is by alleging that the cause of action arose in the district in which the action is filed. However, there are many different ways to establish venue, depending on the nature of the case (review Chapter 2.) See Exhibit 5–3 for examples of allegations showing venue.

At all times herein mentioned, defendant was and now is a resident of the County of _____, State of _____.

or

The County of _____ is the proper county in which to bring and maintain this action by virtue of the fact that defendant, ABC Corporation, has its principal executive offices located therein.

or

The County of _____ is the proper county in which to bring and maintain this action by virtue of the fact that the real property, which is the subject of this action, is located in said county.

EXHIBIT 5–3 Sample venue allegations

The Claim or Cause of Action

Although the complaint or petition usually follows certain legal technicalities, it is primarily a document that shows the factual basis for the lawsuit. It does not contain any discussion or analysis of legal theories. However, when reviewing the facts that are alleged in the complaint, the defendant's attorney and the court should be able to tell that there is a legal basis for the lawsuit, even though the legal basis need not be expressly stated in the complaint. How detailed this factual description must be depends on the jurisdiction in which the lawsuit is filed. If you recall the discussion in Chapter 3, you remember that before deciding to file any lawsuit, an attorney must determine that a party has a cause of action. That is, a kind of dispute exists in which one party is entitled to some kind of legal remedy. In some jurisdictions the complaint must contain factual allegations or statements that support each element of the cause of action. Because this method of pleading is based on a New York law known as the "Field Code," these jurisdictions are sometimes known as *code pleading* jurisdictions. Other jurisdictions, including the federal courts, have a less stringent requirement. For most types of cases, the complaint must contain sufficient facts to put the defendant on notice as to why he is being sued, but it is not essential that each element of the cause of action be supported by factual allegations. This method of pleading is known as *notice pleading*.

Even in notice pleading jurisdictions, some types of cases demand more detailed facts within the complaint. Rule 9 of the Federal Rules of Civil Procedure, for example, requires that allegations of fraud or mistake be stated with particularity. Furthermore, even though the federal rules allow fairly general and nonspecific pleading, more particular allegations are allowed. The use of more detailed allegations in a complaint may have an effect on later discovery and disclosure rights and obligations (discussed in Chapter 8) and should be carefully considered.

Although differences exist in the technical requirements between code pleading jurisdictions and notice pleading jurisdictions, any complaint that is sufficient under code pleading rules would also be sufficient under notice pleading rules. The important thing to remember is that both types of pleading require that facts, and not legal theories, be alleged. The Federal Rules of Civil Procedure contain an Appendix of Forms, including several that can be used as a basis for various types of lawsuits. These sample forms contain suggested language for stating a variety of claims or causes of action (see Exhibit 5–4). Remember, however, that these forms would only be a part of a complaint. For a complete document you would add a caption, the proper language showing jurisdiction, appropriate paragraphs showing status and capacity of the parties, as well as venue and any other relevant allegations. (Although the federal rules do not require that status and capacity be specifically stated, they often are.)

Complaint on a Promissory Note

1. Allegation of jurisdiction.
2. Defendant on or about June 1, 1935, executed and delivered to plaintiff a promissory note (in the following words and figures: [here set out the note verbatim]; [a copy of which is hereto annexed as Exhibit A]; [whereby defendant promised to pay to plaintiff or order on June 1, 1936 the sum of _____ dollars with interest thereon at the rate of six percent per annum].
3. Defendant owes to plaintiff the amount of said note and interest.

Wherefore plaintiff demands judgment against defendant for the sum of _____ dollars, interest, and costs.

Complaint for Negligence

1. Allegation of jurisdiction.
2. On June 1, 1936, in a public highway called Boylston Street in Boston, Massachusetts, defendant negligently drove a motor vehicle against plaintiff who was then crossing said highway.
3. As a result plaintiff was thrown down and had his leg broken and was otherwise injured, was prevented from transacting this business, suffered great pain of body and mind, and incurred expenses for medical attention and hospitalization in the sum of one thousand dollars.

Wherefore plaintiff demands judgment against defendant in the sum of _____ dollars and costs.

Complaint for Specific Performance of Contract to Convey Land

1. Allegation of jurisdiction.
2. On or about December 1, 1936, plaintiff and defendant entered into an agreement in writing a copy of which is hereto annexed as Exhibit A.
3. In accord with the provisions of said agreement plaintiff tendered to defendant the purchase price and requested a conveyance of the land, but defendant refused to accept the tender and refused to make the conveyance.
4. Plaintiff now offers to pay the purchase price.

EXHIBIT 5–4   Allegations describing claims

Wherefore plaintiff demands (1) that defendant be required specifically to perform said agreement, (2) damages in the sum of one thousand dollars, and (3) that if specific performance is not granted plaintiff have judgment against defendant in the sum of _____ dollars.

Complaint for Infringement of Patent

1. Allegation of jurisdiction.
2. On May 16, 1934, United States Letters Patent No. _____ were duly and legally issued to plaintiff for an invention in an electric motor; and since that date plaintiff has been and still is the owner of those Letters Patent.
3. Defendant has for a long time past been and still is infringing those Letters Patent by making, selling, and using electric motors embodying the patented invention, and will continue to do so unless enjoined by this court.
4. Plaintiff has placed the required statutory notice on all electric motors manufactured and sold by him under said Letters Patent, and has given written notice to defendant of his said infringement.

Wherefore plaintiff demands a preliminary and final injunction against continued infringement, an accounting for damages, and an assessment of interest and costs against defendant.

Complaint for Infringement of Copyright and Unfair Competition

1. Allegation of jurisdiction.
2. Prior to March, 1936, plaintiff, who then was and ever since has been a citizen of the United States, created and wrote an original book, entitled _____.
3. This book contains a large amount of material wholly original with plaintiff and is copyrightable subject matter under the laws of the United States.
4. Between March 2, 1936, and March 10, 1936, plaintiff complied in all respects with the Act of [give citation] and all other law governing copyright, and secured the exclusive rights and privileges in and to the copyright of said book, and received from the Register of Copyrights a certificate of registration, dated and identified as follows: "March 10, 1936, Class _____, No. ___."
5. Since March 10, 1936, said book has been published by plaintiff and all copies of it made by plaintiff or under his authority or license have been printed, bound, and published in strict conformity with the provisions of the Act of _____ and all other laws governing copyright.
6. Since March 10, 1936, plaintiff has been and still is the sole proprietor of all rights, title, and interest in and to the copyright in said book.
7. After March 10, 1936, defendant infringed said copyright by publishing and placing upon the market a book entitled _____, which was copied largely from plaintiff's copyrighted book, entitled _____.
8. A copy of plaintiff's copyrighted book is hereto attached as "Exhibit 1"; and a copy of defendant's infringing book is hereto attached as "Exhibit 2."
9. Plaintiff has notified defendant that defendant has infringed the copyright of plaintiff, and defendant has continued to infringe the copyright.
10. After March 10, 1936, and continuously since about _____, defendant has been publishing, selling and otherwise marketing the book entitled _____, and has thereby been engaging in unfair trade practice and unfair competition against plaintiff to plaintiff's irreparable damage.

EXHIBIT 5–4   *(continued)*

Wherefore plaintiff demands:

(1) That defendant, his agents, and servants be enjoined during the pendency of this action and permanently from infringing said copyright of said plaintiff in any manner, and from publishing, selling, marketing or otherwise disposing of any copy of the book entitled _____.

(2) That defendant be required to pay to plaintiff such damages as plaintiff has sustained in consequence of defendant's infringement of said copyright and said unfair trade practices and unfair competition and to account for

    (a) all gains, profits and advantages derived by defendant by said trade practices and unfair competition and

    (b) all gains, profits, and advantages derived by defendant by his infringement of plaintiff's copyright or such damages as to the court shall appear proper within the provisions of the copyright statutes, but not less than two hundred and fifty dollars.

(3) That defendant be required to deliver up to be impounded during the pendency of this action all copies of said book entitled _____ in his possession or under his control and to deliver up for destruction all infringing copies and all plates, molds, and other matter for making such infringing copies.

(4) That defendant pay to plaintiff the costs of this action and reasonable attorney's fees to be allowed to the plaintiff by the court.

(5) That plaintiff has such other and further relief as is just.

Complaint for Interpleader and Declaratory Relief

1. Allegation of jurisdiction.

2. On or about June 1, 1935, plaintiff issued to G. H. a policy of life insurance whereby plaintiff promised to pay to K. L. as beneficiary the sum of _____ dollars upon the death of G. H. The policy required the payment by G. H. of a stipulated premium on June 1, 1936, and annually thereafter as a condition precedent to its continuance in force.

3. No part of the premium due June 1, 1936, was ever paid and the policy ceased to have any force or effect on July 1, 1936.

4. Thereafter, on September 1, 1936, G. H. and K. L. died as the result of a collision between a locomotive and the automobile in which G. H. and K. L. were riding.

5. Defendant C. D. is the duly appointed and acting executor of the will of G. H.; defendant E. F. is the duly appointed and acting executor of the will of K. L.; defendant X. Y. claims to have been duly designated as beneficiary of said policy in place of K. L.

6. Each of defendants, C. D., E. F., and X. Y. is claiming that the above-mentioned policy was in full force and effect at the time of the death of G. H.; each of them is claiming to be the only person entitled to receive payment of the amount of the policy and has made demand for payment thereof.

7. By reason of these conflicting claims of the defendants, plaintiff is in great doubt as to which defendant is entitled to be paid the amount of the policy, if it was in force at the death of G. H.

Wherefore plaintiff demands that the court adjudge:

(1) That none of the defendants is entitled to recover from plaintiff the amount of said policy or any part thereof.

EXHIBIT 5–4 *(continued)*

(2) That each of the defendants be restrained from instituting any action against plaintiff for the recovery of the amount of said policy or any part thereof.

(3) That, if the court shall determine that said policy was in force at the death of G. H., the defendants be required to interplead and settle between themselves their rights to the money due under said policy, and that plaintiff be discharged from all liability in the premises except to the person whom the court shall adjudge entitled to the amount of said policy.

(4) That plaintiff recover its costs.

EXHIBIT 5–4   *(continued)*

Handling Multiple Claims

Often a plaintiff has more than one potential claim against the defendant. Again, consider the Hendricks case described in the opening commentary. If the plaintiffs can prove that their realtor knew that the slides of the property were forgeries and that the property was not suitable for building and lied to them about it, they have a claim for fraud or intentional misrepresentation. Such a claim, if proven, would entitle the plaintiffs to punitive damages in addition to their out-of-pocket losses. However, proving that a misrepresentation was intentional is sometimes difficult, and the plaintiff's attorney may wish to have a claim for negligent misrepresentation as well, in the event that the defendant's intent cannot be adequately shown. Certainly, in the case described, the realtor should have been more certain about her facts before making representations to prospective buyers. Proving negligent misrepresentation would entitle the plaintiffs to their actual losses but would not allow an award of punitive damages. This is an alternative claim, which can be stated in the complaint. Normally, this claim would be set out in a second cause of action, sometimes referred to as a **count,** separate from the first cause of action or first count for fraud. In the Hendricks case, other causes of action may also be possible. For example, the Hendrickses might simply wish to disaffirm the contract (rescind it) and get their money back (restitution). Additionally, because the Hendrickses did not have their own real estate agent, the facts might indicate that May Forrester was acting in a dual capacity, representing both Paradise Found, Inc. and the Hendrickses. As such, May Forrester would be in a special fiduciary relationship with the Hendrickses, a relationship that she abused. This could result in another claim.

A complaint may contain any number of causes of action or counts. Whenever a cause of action arises out of the same general factual situation, the rules of pleading usually allow them to be joined in the same complaint.

Determining whether the defendant's conduct toward the plaintiff results in more than one claim or cause of action can be very difficult. As a general rule, if the claims provide different remedies or are proven by different facts or evidence in the case, they should probably be separated into distinct causes of action. However, because the rules for interpreting pleadings are so liberal, if two or more claims are combined into one

count
Each separate part of a complaint or an indictment.

cause of action, the court could either allow the pleading to stand as written or allow it to be amended.

A question sometimes arises when a complaint contains two inconsistent causes of action. For example, consider the following situation. Bryant signs a contract with Yates to buy a house for $200,000. Before the time for the deal to close, Yates informs Bryant that he has changed his mind and will not sell. As of the date of sale, the value of the house had increased to $220,000. Bryant now has a choice. Does he want the house, or should he make Yates pay for any damages that he incurred because he did not get the house (the damages being the difference between the purchase price and the fair market value at the time and place of sale)? If he gets the house at the original contract price, he will not have incurred the loss of profit in the house. Therefore, asking both for specific performance of the contract and for damages because it was not performed are inconsistent. The rules of pleading usually allow the plaintiff to allege causes of action that are inconsistent. However, the plaintiff will not get a judgment on both of them.

Handling Multiple Parties

We have already seen that a complaint may contain multiple plaintiffs or defendants. When this occurs, questions always arise about whether the parties should be joined within the same cause of action, or whether separate causes of action are required. No absolute rules govern this situation, and the rules of pleading in most jurisdictions are liberal enough to allow almost any method of handling this situation. However, some guidelines are commonly followed.

Multiple Plaintiffs Multiple plaintiffs should be joined within the same cause of action if they have a joint claim or if they are suing for the same thing. For example, in the factual situation described in the commentary, both Margaret and Paul Hendricks are suing for the same thing—the damages that they sustained in buying the lot. Note that they are not each suing for one-half of the damages. They are suing together for the total damages. Therefore, they should be joined in the same cause of action.

When the plaintiffs are suing for something different, however, their claims should be in separate causes of action. For example, suppose that Herbert and Wanda Sepulveda, husband and wife, are both injured in the same automobile accident and wish to sue the driver of the other vehicle. In such a case they are suing for different things. He is suing for his injuries, and she is suing for her injuries. They would, therefore, have two separate causes of action. However, the two causes of action would be in one complaint. When there are multiple plaintiffs and defendants, it is not necessary that they all be parties to each of the causes of action. Again, when there is some common factual or legal basis among the various causes of action, they can be joined in one complaint.

Demand for Relief

Every complaint or petition filed in an action contains a demand for relief from the court, often called a *prayer*. Courts have the power to grant two different types of relief, money damages and equitable relief. Money damages usually means the award of money to the plaintiff as compensation for some loss. Equitable relief, in contrast, involves the court ordering the defendant to do something or to stop doing something other than simply paying money damages. In some state jurisdictions, only certain courts have the power to grant equitable relief. Before preparing and filing any complaint requesting this type of relief, be sure to check jurisdictional power of the court.

Money Damages

Probably the most common relief sought in a civil lawsuit is money damages. The primary purpose of damages in a civil suit is to compensate plaintiffs for a loss they have sustained. These damages are known as **compensatory damages.** In certain kinds of cases, compensatory damages may be referred to by other names. For example, in personal injury cases compensatory damages are categorized as either special damages or general damages. *Special damages* are actual out-of-pocket expenses incurred by the plaintiff, such as doctor bills and lost earnings. *General damages* are not out-of-pocket expenses, but include such things as pain and suffering, loss of use of a limb, or disfigurement caused by a scar. Even though general damages do not reimburse the plaintiff for an economic expense, they do compensate the plaintiff for some loss.

compensatory damages
Damages awarded for the actual loss suffered by a plaintiff.

Although money damages in most civil cases are compensatory in nature, sometimes a plaintiff is entitled to recover **punitive,** or **exemplary, damages.** These are meant to punish the defendant and are awarded only when the defendant has committed some extremely offensive act. Such damages are not favored by the courts and come under careful scrutiny by the appellate courts. Nevertheless, they are allowed in some cases.

punitive or exemplary damages (damages)
Extra money given to punish the defendant and to help keep a particularly bad act from happening again.

In the course of any lawsuit, the parties will inevitably incur substantial expenses, or costs. These can include such items as filing fees, process server fees, deposition fees, and expert witness fees. Costs are not included in computing the plaintiff's damages. However, if the plaintiff wins her lawsuit, she will generally be awarded certain costs in addition to the actual damages. However, should the defendant win the case, he will generally be awarded his costs from the plaintiff. Items included in these recoverable costs are usually determined by a specific statute. One element that is usually not included in the list of recoverable costs is the attorney fee in the case. Unless the lawsuit is based on a contract that specifically provides for the payment of attorney fees in the event of a legal dispute, or unless there is some special law governing the situation, parties are expected to pay their own attorney fees.

Equitable Relief

Some legal disputes cannot be settled by an award of money damages. For example, suppose Friedman sells Brockland his business. As part of the sales agreement, Friedman agrees not to open a competing business within a 50-mile radius for a period of two years. However, two months after the sale, Friedman opens a competing business across the street from Brockland. As a result, Brockland's business income substantially decreases. Although money damages might compensate Brockland for his past loss, if Friedman continues in business Brockland will continue to lose money, the exact amount of which would be difficult to calculate. Brockland would therefore prefer that the court order Friedman to close down his competing business. Such an order

equitable relief (equitable)
Just, fair, and right for a particular situation.

specific performance (performance)
Being required to do exactly what was agreed to.

rescission
The annulment of a contract.

restitution
Giving something back; making good for something.

declaratory relief
A court order defining or explaining the rights and obligations of parties under some contract or other document.

quiet title action
A way of establishing clear ownership of land.

injunction
A judge's order to a person to do or to refrain from doing a particular thing.

temporary restraining order (TRO)
A judge's order to a person to not take a certain action during the period prior to a full hearing on the rightfulness of the action.

preliminary injunction
A court order made prior to final judgment in the case, directing that a party take some action or refrain from taking some action until the trial in the case takes place.

would be a kind of relief known as **equitable relief.** (Lawsuits in which equitable relief is sought are known as *actions in equity,* whereas lawsuits in which money damages are sought are known as *actions at law.*) A complaint may combine a request for equitable relief and money damages.

The types of equitable relief that can be ordered by a court of equitable jurisdiction are varied. Some of the more common types of equitable relief are:

specific performance—An order requiring a party to perform a contract.

rescission—An order rescinding or voiding a contract.

restitution—An order to return money or property, usually paid in connection with a contract that was subsequently rescinded.

declaratory relief—A court order defining or explaining the rights and obligations of parties under some contract or other document.

quiet title—An order clarifying ownership of real property.

injunction—An order requiring a party to stop doing something.

Refer to Exhibit 5–4 for examples of complaints based on some of these types of equitable relief. Along with the award of equitable relief, the court will also probably award the prevailing party her costs of suit, just as it would in a case with an award of money damages.

Provisional Remedies

In most courts, a substantial time elapses between the filing of a complaint and the actual trial in that case. Therefore, when injunctive relief is the primary object of a lawsuit, the plaintiff often requests some immediate provisional remedy from the court as soon as a complaint is filed. Provisional remedies usually include a temporary restraining order and a preliminary injunction. A **temporary restraining order** usually compels the defendant to stop certain conduct immediately. These are granted without any formal hearing, based primarily on affidavits or declarations (written statements under penalty of perjury) submitted to the court. Because the courts are hesitant to grant any orders without giving all sides the opportunity for a full hearing, temporary restraining orders (TROs) remain in effect for a very short time, usually until a hearing can be scheduled in court. As soon as possible, then, a hearing is scheduled at which both sides have the opportunity to argue for or against the restraining order remaining in effect until the time of trial. This hearing is not a full trial of all the issues. Should the court decide to keep the restraining order in effect, it will issue a **preliminary injunction,** an order that remains in effect until the trial, at which time the injunction would become permanent if the plaintiff proves his case. In federal courts, temporary restraining orders and preliminary injunctions are governed by Rule 65 of the Federal Rules of Civil Procedure. The procedures that a party must follow to obtain these provisional remedies are similar to the procedures followed in motion practice and are discussed in more detail in Chapter 7.

Drafting the Complaint

Once you have identified the parties to the lawsuit, determined what causes of action the plaintiff has, and decided what relief is to be requested, you are prepared to start drafting the complaint for your attorney's review. Before actually writing the document, however, be sure to check any local court rules regarding technical requirements for the pleading. Is a certain type or size of paper required? Does the size of print matter? Is there a special format that must be followed? Many courts have special rules regarding these kinds of matters. Also, in order to save a great deal of time, you should check various form books in your law library (or a form file, if one is kept in the office) for a sample complaint that deals with a similar factual situation. Even the most experienced litigation attorneys and paralegals follow forms whenever possible. If a case is to be filed in federal court, *American Jurisprudence Pleading and Practice Forms Annotated,* published by the West Group, can be helpful, as are the forms found in the Appendix of Forms to the Federal Rules of Civil Procedure.

In some jurisdictions, a complaint is prepared on numbered paper known as *pleading paper.* However, many jurisdictions have discontinued this practice. As mentioned, the first part of any complaint or petition is known as the *caption.* The caption contains the name of the court in which the action is being filed, the names of the plaintiffs and defendants, and the title of the document. In some jurisdictions, it also contains the name, address, and telephone number of the attorney and the client being represented. In other jurisdictions, the caption also contains the addresses of the plaintiff and defendant (see Exhibit 5–5).

Below the caption is the body of the complaint, containing various jurisdictional and factual allegations that constitute the plaintiff's cause of action. These allegations are broken down into short, numbered paragraphs. As there is no absolute method for paragraphing, the use of form books or other sample complaints is very helpful in setting up this part of the complaint. In the absence of a form to follow, you can use normal paragraphing rules.

Even though there is no mandatory order in which paragraphing must be done, there are typically employed conventions:

1. In most cases you will see paragraphs on jurisdiction and venue first.

2. If any of the parties are businesses, either corporate or otherwise, allegations concerning their status or capacity then follow.

3. If there is more than one defendant in the lawsuit, it is standard to include an agency allegation. An *agency allegation* claims that one or more of the defendants were agents or employees of one or more of the other defendants. Such an allegation refers to the substantive legal principle of vicarious liability or respondent superior, a concept that imposes liability on an employer for certain acts of its employees.

Title of court ——————

**UNITED STATES DISTRICT COURT
FOR THE DISTRICT OF NEVADA**

Caption ——————

MARGARET HENDRICKS and)
PAUL HENDRICKS,)
    Plaintiffs,)   No.
)
) COMPLAINT FOR FRAUD,
    vs.) NEGLIGENT MISREPRESENTATION
) And BREACH OF FIDUCIARY DUTY
)
MAY FORRESTER, an individual,)
HARRY RICE & HARVEY RICE,)
a partnership, doing business as)
HEARTH & HOME REAL ESTATE CO.,) JURY TRIAL DEMANDED
PARADISE FOUND, INC., a)
corporation)

Plaintiffs allege against each and every defendant:

Allegations of first
cause of action ——————

FIRST CAUSE OF ACTION
(Fraud)

Jurisdiction

Diversity of
citizenship
establishes
jurisdiction ——————

1. Plaintiffs are; and were at all times herein mentioned, domiciled in and citizens of the state of California. Defendants, MAY FORRESTER, HARRY RICE and HARVEY RICE are and were at all times herein mentioned, domiciled in and citizens of the state of Nevada. Defendant, PARADISE FOUND, INC., was and is now a corporation duly organized and existing under the laws of the state of Idaho, with its offices and principal place of business in the state of Idaho. This is a civil action involving, exclusive of interest and costs, a sum in excess of $75,000. Every issue of law and fact in this action is wholly between citizens of different states.

2. Plaintiffs are informed and believe and thereupon allege that Defendants, HARRY RICE AND HARVEY RICE, are a partnership doing business as HEARTH & HOME REAL ESTATE CO.

3. Plaintiffs are informed and believe and thereupon allege that Defendant, PARADISE FOUND, INC., is a corporation duly organized and existing under the laws of the state of Idaho.

4. Plaintiffs are now, and at all times mentioned in this complaint have been residents of San Francisco County, California.

5. Plaintiffs are informed and believe and thereupon allege that at all times herein mentioned, each of the defendants was the agent and employee of each of the remaining defendants and in doing the things hereinafter alleged, was acting within the scope of said agency.

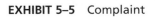

EXHIBIT 5–5 Complaint

6. On or about June 1, _____, in the City of Reno, State of Nevada, defendant, MAY FORRESTER, made the following false and fraudulent representations to plaintiffs: Defendant represented that certain real property was ideal vacation property, that said property had been approved for and was suitable for building, that said property abutted a manmade lake and that said property was worth at least $100,000.

7. The representations made by the defendant were false in that said real property has not been approved nor is it suitable for building, it is not adjacent to any body of water, and was and is valued at less than $5,000.

8. Defendant, at the time she made said representations, knew them to be false and made the statements with the intent to defraud and deceive plaintiffs and to induce them to purchase that certain real property described above.

9. Plaintiffs at the time the representations were made believed them to be true and had no reasons to believe that said representations were untrue. In reliance upon said representations, plaintiffs were induced to, and did purchase the above described real property. Had plaintiffs known the true facts they would not have taken such action.

10. By reason of the facts alleged, plaintiffs have been damaged in the sum of $100,000.

SECOND CAUSE OF ACTION

(Negligent Misrepresentation)

11. Plaintiffs reallege and incorporate by reference the allegations of paragraphs 1 through 7 above in their entirety.

12. At the time defendant, MAY FORESTER, made said representations, she had no sufficient or reasonable ground for believing said representations to be true in that she, the defendant, did not have information and data sufficient to enable her to make a determination whether the representations were true. At the time of making the representations, defendant concealed from plaintiff her lack of information and data that prevented them from making a true evaluation of the facts.

13. At the time said representations were made, plaintiffs had no knowledge of their falsity, but in fact, believed them to be true. Because of the fiduciary and confidential relationship which existed between defendant and plaintiffs, plaintiffs justifiably relied upon said representations.

14. Plaintiffs at the time the representations were made believed them to be true and had no reasons to believe that said representations were untrue. In reliance upon said representations, plaintiffs were induced to and did purchase the above described real property. Had plaintiffs known the true facts they would not have taken such action.

Allegations of second cause of action

Start by incorporating relevant paragraphs from first cause of action

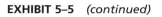

EXHIBIT 5–5 *(continued)*

Restate damages — 15. By reasons of the facts alleged, plaintiffs have been damaged in the sum of $100,000.

Allegations of third cause of action —

THIRD CAUSE OF ACTION

(Breach of Fiduciary Duty)

Plaintiffs allege against defendant MAY FORRESTER:

16. Plaintiffs reallege and incorporate by reference the allegations of paragraphs 1 through 15 above in their entirety.
17. Defendant, MAY FORRESTER, owed a fiduciary duty of loyalty, honesty, and confidentiality to plaintiffs by virtue of her status as their real estate broker.
18. The acts and omissions of defendant, MAY FORRESTER, as alleged above, constitute intentional breaches of their fiduciary duties to plaintiffs.

Restate damages — 19. As a direct and proximate result of defendant's breach of her fiduciary duties, plaintiffs have been damaged in the amount of $100,000.

20. Defedant's breach of fiduciary duties were willful, malicious, oppressive, and in conscious disregard of plaintiffs's rights. Accordingly, plaintiffs request punitive damages in the amount of $100,000.

WHEREFORE, plaintiffs pray for judgment against defendants as follows:

On the first cause of action:

Prayer or demand —
1. For judgment in the sum of $100,000.
2. For costs of suit.
3. For such other relief as the court deems just.

On the second cause of action:
1. For judgment in the sum of $100,000.
2. For costs of suit.
3. For such other relief as the court deems just.

On the third cause of action (against defendant, MAY FORRESTER, only):
1. For compensatory damages in the sum of $100,000.
2. For punitive damages in the sum of $100,000.
3. For costs of suit.
4. For such other relief as the court deems just.

Subscription (In some states attorney information goes on first page of complaint) —

Dated: September 1, _____

By _____

Glenda Yee
Attorney at Law
246 Marshall Ave.
San Francisco, CA 96730

EXHIBIT 5–5 *(continued)*

4. Following these standard allegations are various allegations describing the factual basis for the lawsuit and a description of the damages suffered.

All statements contained in a complaint, or any pleading, should be true. However, at times a plaintiff is not certain about some facts that must be alleged in the complaint. For example, the plaintiff may not know for sure if the defendant business is a corporation or some other business entity, although the plaintiff believes that it is incorporated. In such cases, the proper way to plead the facts is "on information and belief." See Exhibit 5–5 for an example of a complaint that might be filed by the Hendrickses. Paragraphs 2, 3, and 5 of the first cause of action illustrate allegations made on information and belief.

Many complaints contain more than one cause of action. In such a case, it is important to remember that each cause of action should be sufficient in itself to constitute a legally sufficient complaint. Because of this, it is often necessary to restate many of the same allegations that were alleged in prior causes of action. It is not necessary, however, to *expressly* restate those allegations. If something is being repeated, it can be referred to and incorporated by reference. Exhibit 5–5 contains three causes of action; see paragraph 11 for an illustration of a paragraph incorporation of prior allegations.

Remember that not all parties to the complaint must be parties to all causes of action. However, each of those named in the caption must be a party to at least one cause of action within the complaint, and this includes "Doe" defendants when such defendants are allowed.

After the allegations in the complaint you will find the prayer. The prayer is normally located at the end of all of the allegations. Following the prayer is the date, signature, and address of the attorney filing the complaint. Some jurisdictions also require that the attorney include a bar number. This signature is sometimes referred to as the *subscription.* In some jurisdictions the name, address, and telephone number of the attorney appear on the first page above the caption rather than at the end of the complaint. A signature or subscription is still required at the end of the prayer. Under Rule 11 of the Federal Rules of Civil Procedure, when an attorney signs a pleading in federal court, that attorney is making certain representations to the court. She is representing that the pleading is not being used for any improper purpose, that the contentions are warranted by law, and that the allegations have evidentiary support. If the court finds these representations to be false, it has the power to sanction the attorney. The prayer and signature are shown in Exhibit 5–5.

In the Hendricks case described in the commentary, if the attorney for the Hendrickses decided to sue all of the parties for fraud and negligent misrepresentation, and May Forrester for breach of a fiduciary duty, the entire complaint would look as shown in Exhibit 5–5.

In some jurisdictions, including federal court, if the plaintiff is requesting a jury trial in the case, that request is often included in the complaint. In federal courts, under Rule 38(b) of the Federal Rules of Civil Procedure, such a demand must be made no later than 10 days after service of the last pleading.

Also, in some jurisdictions certain kinds of complaints, such as those seeking injunctive relief or punitive damages, often are required to be verified, or sworn to under penalty of perjury. This is usually done by the plaintiff rather than the attorney. See Exhibit 5–6 for a sample verification.

I, Margaret Hendricks, am one of the plaintiffs in the above entitled action. I have read the foregoing complaint. The facts stated therein are within my knowledge and are true and correct, except those matters stated on information and belief, and, as to those, I believe them to be true and correct.

I declare under penalty of perjury under the laws of the State of Nevada that the foregoing is true and correct.

Executed this _____ day of September, _____, at San Francisco, California.

_____

EXHIBIT 5–6 Verification

Along with the complaint itself, many courts have a form cover sheet that must be filled out and accompany the complaint. See Exhibit 5–7 for a sample cover sheet from a federal court.

Also, if any plaintiff is a nongovernmental corporation, it must file a special disclosure statement required by Rule 7.1 of the Federal Rules of Civil Procedure. This statement identifies any parent corporation and any publicly held corporation that owns 10 percent or more of its stock or states that there is no such corporation. This disclosure statement is required to be filed by all nongovernmental parties at the time they file their first documents in court. Thus, if the defendant is a corporation, it must file a disclosure statement with its answer.

Filing the Complaint

filing (file)

Giving a paper to the court clerk for inclusion in the case record.

docket number

A number assigned to a lawsuit by the court; each pleading or document filed in the action must bear this number.

After the complaint has been prepared, reviewed by the attorney, and properly signed, it can be filed in the proper court (see Exhibit 5–8). **Filing** of a complaint means that the original of the document is given to the court. The court, in turn, assigns a number, known as a **docket number,** to the case and starts a file that will contain all subsequent pleadings and other documents dealing with the case. All subsequent pleadings and papers filed in connection with the case must contain the docket number to ensure proper filing. In order to file a complaint, the court usually requires a filing fee, which must be paid before the court will accept the document. Filing fees will be waived if the plaintiff can show financial hardship. Whenever you file a complaint with the court, you should have copies of the complaint on which the docket number and date of filing can be noted (usually two or three copies).

Many courts allow attorneys to file documents, including complaints, via fax and electronically. Usually an additional fee is imposed. Each court must be contacted for its own rules regarding fax and electronic filings.

The federal courts are now implementing a Case Management/Electronic Case Files (CM/ECF) system. CM/ECF allows courts to maintain case file documents in

JS 44 (Rev. 3/99)

CIVIL COVER SHEET

The JS-44 civil cover sheet and the information contained herein neither replace nor supplement the filing and service of pleadings or other papers as required by law, except as provided by local rules of court. This form, approved by the Judicial Conference of the United States in September 1974, is required for the use of the Clerk of Court for the purpose of initiating the civil docket sheet. (SEE INSTRUCTIONS ON THE REVERSE OF THE FORM.)

I. (a) PLAINTIFFS

DEFENDANTS

(b) County of Residence of First Listed Plaintiff _____
(EXCEPT IN U.S. PLAINTIFF CASES)

County of Residence of First Listed _____
(IN U.S. PLAINTIFF CASES ONLY)
NOTE: IN LAND CONDEMNATION CASES, USE THE LOCATION OF THE LAND INVOLVED.

(c) Attorney's (Firm Name, Address, and Telephone Number)

Attorneys (If Known)

II. BASIS OF JURISDICTION (Place an "X" in One Box Only)

☐ 1 U.S. Government Plaintiff
☐ 2 U.S. Government Defendant
☐ 3 Federal Question (U.S. Government Not a Party)
☐ 4 Diversity (Indicate Citizenship of Parties in Item III)

III. CITIZENSHIP OF PRINCIPAL PARTIES (Place an "X" in One Box for and One Box for Defendant)
(For Diversity Cases Only)

	PTF	DEF		PTF	DEF
Citizen of This State	☐1	☐1	Incorporated or Principal Place of Business In This State	☐4	☐4
Citizen of Another State	☐2	☐2	Incorporated and Principal of Business In Another State	☐5	☐5
Citizen or Subject of a Foreign Country	☐3	☐3	Foreign Nation	☐6	☐6

IV. NATURE OF SUIT (Place an "X" in One Box Only)

CONTRACT	TORTS		FORFEITURE/PENALTY	BANKRUPTCY	OTHER STATUTES
☐ 110 Insurance ☐ 120 Marine ☐ 130 Miller Act ☐ 140 Negotiable Instrument ☐ 150 Recovery of Overpayment & Enforcement of Judgment ☐ 151 Medicare Act ☐ 152 Recovery of Defaulted Student Loans (Excl. Veterans) ☐ 153 Recovery of Overpayment of Veteran's Benefits ☐ 160 Stockholders' Suits ☐ 190 Other Contract ☐ 195 Contract Product Liability	**PERSONAL INJURY** ☐ 310 Airplane ☐ 315 Airplane Product Liability ☐ 320 Assault, Libel & Slander ☐ 330 Federal Employers' Liability ☐ 340 Marine ☐ 345 Marine Product Liability ☐ 350 Motor Vehicle ☐ 355 Motor Vehicle Product Liability ☐ 360 Other Personal Injury	**PERSONAL INJURY** ☐ 362 Personal Injury— Med. Malpractice ☐ 365 Personal Injury — Product Liability ☐ 368 Asbestos Personal Injury Product Liability **PERSONAL PROPERTY** ☐ 370 Other Fraud ☐ 371 Truth in Lending ☐ 380 Other Personal Property Damage ☐ 385 Property Damage Product Liability	☐ 610 Agriculture ☐ 620 Other Food & Drug ☐ 625 Drug Related Seizure of Property 21 USC 881 ☐ 630 Liquor Laws ☐ 640 R.R. & Truck ☐ 650 Airline Regs. ☐ 660 Occupational Safety/Health ☐ 690 Other	☐ 422 Appeal 28 USC 158 ☐ 423 Withdrawal 28 USC 157 **PROPERTY RIGHTS** ☐ 820 Copyrights ☐ 830 Patent ☐ 840 Trademark	☐ 400 State Reapportionment ☐ 410 Antitrust ☐ 430 Banks and Banking ☐ 450 Commerce/ICC Rates/etc. ☐ 460 Deportation ☐ 470 Racketeer Influenced and Corrupt Organizations ☐ 810 Selective Service ☐ 850 Securities/Commodities/ Exchange ☐ 875 Customer Challenge 12 USC 3410 ☐ 891 Agricultural Acts

REAL PROPERTY	CIVIL RIGHTS	PRISONER PETITIONS	LABOR	SOCIAL SECURITY	
☐ 210 Land Condemnation ☐ 220 Foreclosure ☐ 230 Rent Lease & Ejectment ☐ 240 Torts to Land ☐ 245 Tort Product Liability ☐ 290 All Other Real Property	☐ 441 Voting ☐ 442 Employment ☐ 443 Housing/ Accommodations ☐ 444 Welfare ☐ 440 Other Civil Rights	☐ 510 Motions to Vacate Sentence **Habeas Corpus:** ☐ 530 General ☐ 535 Death Penalty ☐ 540 Mandamus & Other ☐ 550 Civil Rights ☐ 555 Prison Condition	☐ 710 Fair Labor Standards Act ☐ 720 Labor/Mgmt. Relations ☐ 730 Labor/Mgmt.Reporting & Disclosure Act ☐ 740 Railway Labor Act ☐ 790 Other Labor Litigation ☐ 791 Empl. Ret. Inc. Security Act	☐ 861 HIA (1395ff) ☐ 862 Black Lung (923) ☐ 863 DIWC/DIWW (405(g)) ☐ 864 SSID Title XVI ☐ 865 RSI (405(g)) **FEDERAL TAX SUITS** ☐ 870 Taxes (U.S. Plaintiff or Defendant) ☐ 871 IRS—Third Party 26 USC 7609	☐ 892 Economic Stabilization Act ☐ 893 Environmental Matters ☐ 894 Energy Allocation Act ☐ 895 Freedom of Information Act ☐ 900 Appeal of Fee Determination Under Equal Access to Justice ☐ 950 Constitutionality of State Statutes ☐ 890 Other Statutory Actions

V. ORIGIN (PLACE AN "X" IN ONE BOX ONLY)

☐ 1 Original Proceeding
☐ 2 Removed from State Court
☐ 3 Remanded from Appellate Court
☐ 4 Reinstated or Reopened
☐ 5 Transferred from another district (specify)
☐ 6 Multidistrict Litigation
☐ 7 Appeal to District Judge from Magistrate Judgment

VI. CAUSE OF ACTION (Cite the U.S. Civil Statute under which you are filing and write brief statement of cause. Do not cite jurisdictional statutes unless diversity.)

VII. REQUESTED IN COMPLAINT:
☐ CHECK IF THIS IS A **CLASS ACTION** DEMAND
UNDER F.R.C.P. 23

CHECK YES only if demanded in complaint:
JURY DEMAND: ☐ Yes ☐ No

VIII. RELATED CASE(S) IF ANY (See instructions):
JUDGE _____
DOCKET NUMBER _____

DATE _____
SIGNATURE OF ATTORNEY OF RECORD _____

FOR OFFICE USE ONLY

RECEIPT # _____ AMOUNT _____ APPLYING IFP _____ JUDGE _____ MAG. JUDGE _____

EXHIBIT 5–7 Cover sheet

JS 44 Reverse (Rev. 3/99)

INSTRUCTIONS FOR ATTORNEYS COMPLETING CIVIL COVER SHEET FORM JS-44

Authority For Civil Cover Sheet

The JS-44 civil cover sheet and the information contained herein neither replaces nor supplements the filings and service of pleading or other papers as required by law, except as provided by local rules of court. This form, approved by the Judicial Conference of the United States in September 1974, is required for the use of the Clerk of Court for the purpose of initiating the civil docket sheet. Consequently, a civil cover sheet is submitted to the Clerk of Court for each civil complaint filed. The attorney filing a case should complete the form as follows:

I.   **(a) Plaintiffs-Defendants.** Enter names (last, first, middle initial) of plaintiff and defendant. If the plaintiff or defendant is a government agency, use only the full name or standard abbreviations. If the plaintiff or defendant is an official within a government agency, identify first the agency and then the official, giving both name and title.

(b.) County of Residence. For each civil case filed, except U.S. plaintiff cases, enter the name of the county where the first listed plaintiff resides at the time of filing. In U.S. plaintiff cases, enter the name of the county in which the first listed defendant resides at the time of filing. (NOTE: In land condemnation cases, the county of residence of the "defendant" is the location of the tract of land involved.)

(c) Attorneys. Enter the firm name, address, telephone number, and attorney of record. If there are several attorneys, list them on an attachment, noting in this section "(see attachment)".

II.   **Jurisdiction.** The basis of jurisdiction is set forth under Rule 8(a), F.R.C.P., which requires that jurisdictions be shown in pleadings. Place an "X" in one of the boxes. If there is more than one basis of jurisdiction, precedence is given in the order shown below.

United States plaintiff. (1) Jurisdiction based on 28 U.S.C. 1345 and 1348. Suits by agencies and officers of the United States, are included here.

United States defendant. (2) When the plaintiff is suing the United States, its officers or agencies, place an "X" in this box.

Federal question. (3) This refers to suits under 28 U.S.C. 1331, where jurisdiction arises under the Constitution of the United States, an amendment to the Constitution, an act of Congress or a treaty of the United States. In cases where the U.S. is a party, the U.S. plaintiff or defendant code takes precedence, and box 1 or 2 should be marked.

Diversity of citizenship. (4) This refers to suits under 28 U.S.C. 1332, where parties are citizens of different states. When Box 4 is checked, the citizenship of the different parties must be checked. (See Section III below; federal question actions take precedence over diversity cases.)

III.   **Residence (citizenship) of Principal Parties.** This section of the JS-44 is to be completed if diversity of citizenship was indicated above. Mark this section for each principal party.

IV.   **Nature of Suit.** Place an "X" in the appropriate box. If the nature of suit cannot be determined, be sure the cause of action, in Section IV below, is sufficient to enable the deputy clerk or the statistical clerks in the Administrative Office to determine the nature of suit. If the cause fits more than one nature of suit, select the most definitive.

V.   **Origin.** Place an "X" in one of the seven boxes.

Original Proceedings. (1) Cases which originate in the United States district courts.

Removed from State Court. (2) Proceedings initiated in state courts may be removed to the district courts under Title 28 U.S.C., Section 1441. When the petition for removal is granted, check this box.

Remanded from Appellate Court. (3) Check this box for cases remanded to the district court for further action. Use the date of remand as the filing date.

Reinstated or Reopened. (4) Check this box for cases reinstated or reopened in the district court. Use the reopening date as the filing date.

Transferred from Another District. (5) For cases transferred under Title 28 U.S.C. Section 1404(a) Do not use this for within district transfers or multidistrict litigation transfers.

Multidistrict Litigation. (6) Check this box when a multidistrict case is transferred into the district under authority of Title 28 U.S.C. Section 1407. When this box is checked, do not check (5) above.

Appeal to District Judge from Magistrate Judgment. (7) Check this box for an appeal from a magistrate judge's decision.

VI.   **Cause of Action.** Report the civil statute directly related to the cause of action and give a brief description of the cause.

VII.   **Requested in Complaint.** Class Action. Place an "X" in this box if you are filing a class action under Rule 23, F.R.Cv.P.

Demand. In this space enter the dollar amount (in thousands of dollars) being demanded or indicate other demand such as a preliminary injunction.

Jury Demand. Check the appropriate box to indicate whether or not a jury is being demanded.

VIII.   **Related Cases.** This section of the JS-44 is used to reference related pending cases if any. If there are related pending cases, insert the docket numbers and the corresponding judge names for such cases.

Date and Attorney Signature. Date and sign the civil cover sheet.

EXHIBIT 5–7   *(continued)*

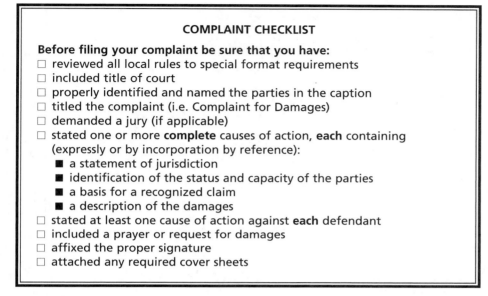

COMPLAINT CHECKLIST

Before filing your complaint be sure that you have:
☐ reviewed all local rules to special format requirements
☐ included title of court
☐ properly identified and named the parties in the caption
☐ titled the complaint (i.e. Complaint for Damages)
☐ demanded a jury (if applicable)
☐ stated one or more **complete** causes of action, **each** containing (expressly or by incorporation by reference):
   ■ a statement of jurisdiction
   ■ identification of the status and capacity of the parties
   ■ a basis for a recognized claim
   ■ a description of the damages
☐ stated at least one cause of action against **each** defendant
☐ included a prayer or request for damages
☐ affixed the proper signature
☐ attached any required cover sheets

EXHIBIT 5–8   Complaint checklist

electronic format, and to accept filings over the Internet. The CM/ECF system accepts PDF documents. A pleading can be prepared using conventional word processing software, then saved as a PDF file. After logging onto the court's Web site with a court-issued password, the filer enters basic information relating to the case and document being filed, attaches the document, and submits it to the court. A notice verifying court receipt of the filing is generated automatically. Other parties in the case then automatically receive e-mail notification of the filing. Regardless of how you file a complaint, always be sure that the document is filed within the statute of limitations. Not filing it on time will result in the lawsuit being dismissed.

The Summons

At the time the complaint is filed, the court will issue a summons. A **summons** is a form explaining that the defendant has been sued and should answer the complaint by a certain date. Issuance of the summons simply involves the clerk of the court affixing his or her signature to the form. It is expected that the attorney for the plaintiff will have the form filled out and will submit it to the clerk when the complaint is filed. The original summons is not filed with the court at this time. The plaintiff retains it until after the defendants have been served. At that time the original summons can be returned to the court for filing, along with evidence that the defendants have been served. In some courts, if the summons is not returned to the court within a certain time, the case can be dismissed. See Exhibit 5–9 for an example of a summons used in federal court.

summons
A notice delivered by a sheriff or other authorized person informing a person of a lawsuit against him or her.

✎AO 440 (Rev. 8/01) Summons in a Civil Action

UNITED STATES DISTRICT COURT

District of _____

_____

SUMMONS IN A CIVIL ACTION

V.

CASE NUMBER:

TO: (Name and address of Defendant)

YOU ARE HEREBY SUMMONED and required to serve on PLAINTIFF'S ATTORNEY (name and address)

an answer to the complaint which is served on you with this summons, within _____ days after service of this summons on you, exclusive of the day of service. If you fail to do so, judgment by default will be taken against you for the relief demanded in the complaint. Any answer that you serve on the parties to this action must be filed with the Clerk of this Court within a reasonable period of time after service.

_____   _____
CLERK   DATE

_____
(By) DEPUTY CLERK

EXHIBIT 5–9   Summons

Service of the Complaint

The defendant in any lawsuit is entitled to receive notice of the action. This is accomplished by service of process. A copy of the summons and a copy of the complaint must be delivered to the defendant. It is the plaintiff's responsibility, rather than the court's, to see that the defendant is properly served. As a litigation paralegal, one of your duties may be to arrange for service after the complaint has been filed.

All jurisdictions have rules regarding who can serve the papers, how they can be served, and time limits for service. For federal court, these rules are found in Rule 4 of the Federal Rules of Civil Procedure (see Exhibit 5–10). Although there may be some differences from one jurisdiction to another, there are some similar concepts. Generally, plaintiffs cannot serve the papers themselves. Someone must do it for them. Various law enforcement agencies and personnel, such as the United States Marshal or a local sheriff, sometimes take responsibility for serving civil complaints. They may, however, charge the plaintiff a fee for doing this. In other instances, the complaint is served by a licensed process server, an individual licensed by the state to serve papers. In some cases, the complaint is served by any adult who is not a party to the action.

You must be concerned not only about who serves the complaint, but also with how it is served. A common method of service is **personal service of process.** In personal service, a copy of the summons and complaint are personally delivered to the defendant. Sometimes this is difficult, if not impossible. Some laws, such as Rule 4 of the Federal Rules of Civil Procedure, allow a copy of the summons and complaint to be left with a competent adult at the defendant's residence. Some states also allow the papers to be served by mail or in some cases by publication. When personal service cannot be accomplished, appropriate laws must be reviewed to determine alternatives.

If the defendant in the lawsuit is a corporation, service is usually accomplished by serving an officer of the corporation or by serving an individual whom the corporation has designated to accept service. As previously noted, this individual is known as the agent for service of process. The names and addresses of corporate officers or agents for service can usually be obtained from the secretary of state where the corporation is incorporated or does business.

In addition to the manner of service, you also need to be concerned about any time limits that may affect service. For example, in federal court the copy of the complaint and summons should be served within 120 days of the filing of the complaint. Failure to do so, without justification, can result in dismissal of the action. (See Rule 4[m] of the Federal Rules of Civil Procedure.) It is a good idea, therefore, to tickle or calendar the file to check for timely service. After service has been completed, the person serving the complaint must certify in writing when, where, and how service was accomplished. This is done in a document called a **proof of service.** A form for the proof of service will probably be found on the reverse side of the summons. See Exhibit 5–11 for a copy of the form used in a federal court.

The proof of service should then be filed with the court.

personal service of process
Notice of a lawsuit or other proceeding that is given to a party by personally delivering a copy of the papers to that party.

proof of service
Written verification that papers have been delivered to a party, detailing when, where, and how the papers were delivered.

SERVICE UNDER RULE 4 OF THE FEDERAL RULES OF CIVIL PROCEDURE

Under Rule 4 of the Federal Rules of Civil Procedure, the complaint and summons can be served by any of the following methods:

To serve an individual within the United States

1. Any manner authorized by the state in which the defendant is served.
2. Personal delivery of a copy to the defendant.
3. Leaving the papers with a person of suitable age at the defendant's dwelling.
4. Waiver of service by the defendant.

To serve an individual in a foreign country

1. Internationally agreed method (i.e., Hague Convention).
2. Manner prescribed by law of foreign country, provided service is reasonably calculated to give notice.
3. Unless prohibited by foreign country, either personal delivery of the papers to defendant or any form of mail requiring signed receipt.
4. As directed by court.
5. Waiver of service by defendant.

To serve a minor or incompetent

1. If the defendant is within the United States, in a like manner to that prescribed by the law of the state in which service is made.
2. If the defendant is outside the United States, as prescribed by the law of the foreign country.

To serve a corporation or association

1. Delivery of a copy to an officer, managing agent, or agent authorized by statute and mailing of a copy to the defendant if that statute so requires.
2. Waiver of service.

To serve the United States Government and its agencies or officers

1. Delivery of a copy of the summons and complaint to the U.S. attorney, assistant U.S. attorney, or designated agent for the district in which the action is brought *and*
2. Mailing of a copy by registered or certified mail to the civil process clerk at the office of the U.S. attorney and sending of a copy to the Attorney General in Washington *and*
3. If the validity of any order of any federal officer or agency is involved, also by mailing of the papers to that officer or agency.
4. If a U.S. agency or officer is a named defendant, also sending of a copy of the papers to the agency or officer by registered or certified mail.

To serve a foreign government

1. Manner pursuant to 28 U.S.C. § 1608.

To serve a state or local government

1. Delivery of a copy to the chief executive officer or in any manner prescribed by the law of the state.

EXHIBIT 5–10   Service under Rule 4 of the Federal Rules of Civil Procedure

AO 440 (Rev. 8/01) Summons in a Civil Action

RETURN OF SERVICE

Service of the Summons and complaint was made by me[1]	DATE
NAME OF SERVER *(PRINT)*	TITLE

Check one box below to indicate appropriate method of service

☐ Served personally upon the defendant. Place where served:

☐ Left copies thereof at the defendant's dwelling house or usual place of abode with a person of suitable age and discretion then residing therein.

    Name of person with whom the summons and complaint were left:

☐ Returned unexecuted:

☐ Other (specify):

STATEMENT OF SERVICE FEES

TRAVEL	SERVICES	TOTAL $0.00

DECLARATION OF SERVER

    I declare under penalty of perjury under the laws of the United States of America that the foregoing information contained in the Return of Service and Statement of Service Fees is true and correct.

Executed on _____   _____
              Date   *Signature of Server*

                                         _____
                                         Address of Server

(1) As to who may serve a summons see Rule 4 of the Federal Rules of Civil Procedure.

EXHIBIT 5–11   Proof of service

Waiver of Service

Under Rule 4 of the Federal Rules of Civil Procedure, a defendant is encouraged to waive formal service of process. The rule sets out a procedure to be followed to accomplish this. The plaintiff sends by first-class mail the following documents: the complaint, a notice explaining the process of waiver and the consequences of failing to waive service, and a waiver form for the defendant to sign. The defendant then signs and returns the waiver-of-service form to the plaintiff's attorney within 30 days (or 60 days if the defendant is outside the country). Waiver of service is dependent on the defendant's agreement. If he fails to sign and return the written waiver form, then service must be accomplished in one of the more traditional methods. However, if the defendant refuses to waive service, the court can impose on that defendant the cost of subsequent service (see Exhibit 5–12 and Exhibit 5–13).

Amending the Complaint

Regardless of how careful you are when you draft a complaint, at times additions, deletions, or changes must be made. To do this you need to amend the complaint. Most jurisdictions view the rules of pleading very liberally. No court is interested in seeing a party lose a case because of some technical deficiency in the pleadings that could be easily corrected. As long as an amendment does not drastically alter the nature of the case, or cause any undue hardship to the defendant or delay in the case, it will probably be allowed. Rule 15 of the Federal Rules of Civil Procedure allows the plaintiff to amend the complaint once, as a matter of right, before an answer is filed. After that, the plaintiff generally needs either a stipulation from the other parties agreeing to the amendment or an order from the court. A **stipulation** *to amend the complaint* is a written agreement among all parties (signed by their attorneys) allowing the plaintiff to make certain changes in the complaint. It is generally filed in court along with the amended complaint. See Exhibit 5–14 for a sample stipulation to amend the complaint.

stipulation

An agreement between lawyers on opposite sides of a lawsuit.

If the plaintiff cannot obtain a stipulation, he must make a motion in court asking the court to allow the filing of the amended complaint. When a complaint is amended, the statute of limitations usually relates back to the original date of filing. In other words, a complaint can usually be amended even after the statute of limitations has expired. A major exception to this rule is when the amendment seeks to add a new defendant, one who was not named in the original complaint. As mentioned, in jurisdictions that allow their usage, the use of fictitiously named defendants, Does, avoids this problem. In such a case, when the complaint is amended, it is not to bring in a new defendant, but rather to correct the name of that defendant. In federal court, under Rule 15 of the Federal Rules of Civil Procedure, the amendment relates back to the original filing date only when the newly named party has received notice of the action within 120 days of its being filed, will not be prejudiced, and knew or should have known that but for a mistake he would have been sued in the original complaint.

AO 398   (Rev. 12/93)

NOTICE OF LAWSUIT AND REQUEST FOR
WAIVER OF SERVICE OF SUMMONS

TO: (A) _____

as   (B) _____ of (C) _____

    A lawsuit has been commenced against you (or the entity on whose behalf you are addressed). A copy of the complaint is attached to this notice. It has been filed in the United States District Court for the
(D) _____ District of _____
and has been assigned docket number (E) _____ .

    This is not a formal summons or notification from the court, but rather my request that you sign and return the enclosed waiver of service in order to save the cost of serving you with a judicial summons and an additional copy of the complaint. The cost of service will be avoided if I receive a signed copy of the waiver
within (F) _____ days after the date designated below as the date on which this Notice and Request
is sent. I enclose a stamped and addressed envelope (or other means of cost-free return) for your use. An extra copy of the waiver is also attached for your records.

    If you comply with this request and return the signed waiver, it will be filed with the court and no summons will be served on you. The action will then proceed as if you had been served on the date the waiver is filed, except that you will not be obligated to answer the complaint before 60 days from the date designated below as the date on which this notice is sent (or before 90 days from that date if your address is not in any judicial district of the United States).

    If you do not return the signed waiver within the time indicated, I will take appropriate steps to effect formal service in a manner authorized by the Federal Rules of Civil Procedure and will then, to the extent authorized by those Rules, ask the court to require you (or the party on whose behalf you are addressed) to pay the full costs of such service. In that connection, please read the statement concerning the duty of parties to waive the service of the summons, which is set forth at the foot of the waiver form.

    I affirm that this request is being sent to you on behalf of the plaintiff, this _____ day of
_____ , _____ .

_____
Signature of Plaintiff's Attorney
or Unrepresented Plaintiff

A—Name of individual defendant (or name of officer or agent of corporate defendant)
B—Title, or other relationship of individual to corporate defendant
C—Name of corporate defendant, if any
D—District
E—Docket number of action
F—Addressee must be given at least 30 days (60 days if located in foreign country) in which to return waiver

EXHIBIT 5–12   Notice of lawsuit and request for waiver of service of summons

AO 399 (Rev. 10/95)

WAIVER OF SERVICE OF SUMMONS

TO: _____
(NAME OF PLAINTIFF'S ATTORNEY OR UNREPRESENTED PLAINTIFF)

I, _____ , acknowledge receipt of your request
(DEFENDANT NAME)

that I waive service of summons in the action of _____ ,
(CAPTION OF ACTION)

which is case number _____ in the United States District Court
(DOCKET NUMBER)

for the _____ District of _____ .

I have also received a copy of the complaint in the action, two copies of this instrument, and a means by which I can return the signed waiver to you without cost to me.

I agree to save the cost of service of a summons and an additional copy of the complaint in this lawsuit by not requiring that I (or the entity on whose behalf I am acting) be served with judicial process in the manner provided by Rule 4.

I (or the entity on whose behalf I am acting) will retain all defenses or objections to the lawsuit or to the jurisdiction or venue of the court except for objections based on a defect in the summons or in the service of the summons.

I understand that a judgment may be entered against me (or the party on whose behalf I am acting) if an

answer or motion under Rule 12 is not served upon you within 60 days after _____ ,
(DATE REQUEST WAS SENT)

or within 90 days after that date if the request was sent outside the United States.

_____   _____
(DATE)   (SIGNATURE)

Printed/Typed Name: _____

As _____ of _____
(TITLE)   (CORPORATE DEFENDANT)

Duty to Avoid Unnecessary Costs of Service of Summons

Rule 4 of the Federal Rules of Civil Procedure requires certain parties to cooperate in saving unnecessary costs of service of the summons and complaint. A defendant located in the United States who, after being notified of an action and asked by a plaintiff located in the United States to waive service of summons, fails to do so will be required to bear the cost of such service unless good cause be shown for its failure to sign and return the waiver.

It is not good cause for a failure to waive service that a party believes that the complaint is unfounded, or that the action has been brought in an improper place or in a court that lacks jurisdiction over the subject matter of the action or over its person or property. A party who waives service of the summons retains all defenses and objections (except any relating to the summons or to the service of the summons), and may later object to the jurisdiction of the court or to the place where the action has been brought.

A defendant who waives service must within the time specified on the waiver form serve on the plaintiff's attorney (or unrepresented plaintiff) a response to the complaint and must also file a signed copy of the response with the court. If the answer or motion is not served within this time, a default judgment may be taken against that defendant. By waiving service, a defendant is allowed more time to answer than if the summons had been actually served when the request for waive of service was received.

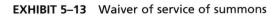

EXHIBIT 5–13 Waiver of service of summons

(CAPTION)

)   NO.
)   STIPULATION FOR FILING
)   OF FIRST
)   AMENDMENT COMPLAINT
)

The undersigned hereby stipulate that plaintiff may file the attached First Amended Complaint in this action, and further acknowledge service of a copy.

Attorney for Defendant

EXHIBIT 5–14   Stipulation for filing amended complaint

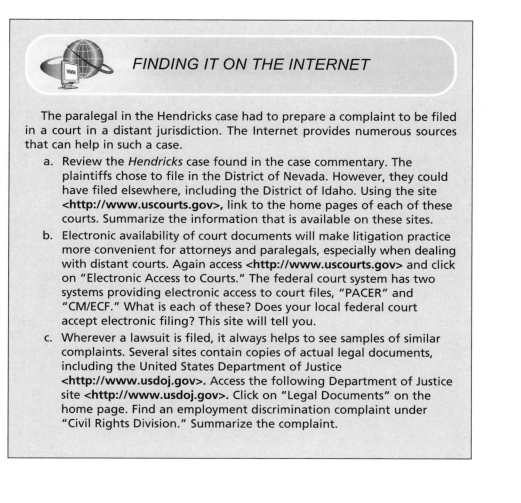

FINDING IT ON THE INTERNET

The paralegal in the Hendricks case had to prepare a complaint to be filed in a court in a distant jurisdiction. The Internet provides numerous sources that can help in such a case.

a. Review the *Hendricks* case found in the case commentary. The plaintiffs chose to file in the District of Nevada. However, they could have filed elsewhere, including the District of Idaho. Using the site **<http://www.uscourts.gov>,** link to the home pages of each of these courts. Summarize the information that is available on these sites.

b. Electronic availability of court documents will make litigation practice more convenient for attorneys and paralegals, especially when dealing with distant courts. Again access **<http://www.uscourts.gov>** and click on "Electronic Access to Courts." The federal court system has two systems providing electronic access to court files, "PACER" and "CM/ECF." What is each of these? Does your local federal court accept electronic filing? This site will tell you.

c. Wherever a lawsuit is filed, it always helps to see samples of similar complaints. Several sites contain copies of actual legal documents, including the United States Department of Justice **<http://www.usdoj.gov>**. Access the following Department of Justice site **<http://www.usdoj.gov>**. Click on "Legal Documents" on the home page. Find an employment discrimination complaint under "Civil Rights Division." Summarize the complaint.

After an amended complaint is filed with the court, it must be served. However, if the defendants have obtained an attorney to represent them, service can be accomplished by mailing a copy of the amended complaint to the attorney.

Summary

- Pleadings are the documents filed in a court that define the nature of the dispute between the parties. The initial pleading filed in a lawsuit by the plaintiff is known as the complaint, or in some instances the petition. The complaint or petition sets out the factual basis for the lawsuit. It is made up of a caption, which identifies the parties and the court; the body, which contains the factual allegations describing the dispute; the prayer, which is a request for relief; and the subscription, which consists of the signature and address of the plaintiff's attorney and the date. Sometimes complaints are verified, that is, they contain the plaintiff's statement that the contents of the complaint are true under penalty of perjury.

- Before naming the various parties to the lawsuit, you must determine that the plaintiff is the real party in interest, identify and describe the status of the plaintiff and the defendant, and determine that the plaintiff and the defendant have the capacity to sue and be sued. A plaintiff is the real party in interest when he is the one entitled to the relief requested in the complaint. Status refers to the type of entity that describes the party, such as individual, corporate, or other business entity or governmental agency. Most competent adult individuals, corporations, and unincorporated associations have capacity to sue or be sued in their own names. However, minors and incompetent adults cannot sue on their own behalf, and a guardian ad litem must be appointed to represent their interests. A governmental entity can be sued only when allowed by law. Some jurisdictions allow the plaintiff to name fictitious defendants, or Doe defendants, in a lawsuit to provide for later-discovered defendants. All jurisdictions allow multiple plaintiffs and defendants to be joined in one lawsuit, as long as there is some common factual or legal question among them. When the number of potential plaintiffs in a lawsuit is too numerous to be practical, a class action may be filed. In a class action, certain named plaintiffs represent members of a class in a similar situation.

- The complaint must contain some allegation showing that the court in which the action is pending has proper jurisdiction and venue in the case.

- The body of the complaint, referred to as the cause of action or sometimes a count, contains allegations that describe the factual basis for the lawsuit. Some jurisdictions, known as code pleading jurisdictions, require that each element of the cause of action be supported by factual allegations. Other jurisdictions, known as notice pleading jurisdictions, only require that there be sufficient facts to put the defendant on notice as to why she is being sued. A complaint may contain multiple counts or causes of action, as well as multiple parties, as long as some common question exists.

- Every complaint or petition contains a prayer, which is a request for relief from the court. Courts can grant either money damages or equitable relief. Money damages are usually compensatory, that is, compensating the plaintiff for a loss that he has sustained. In some cases, punitive damages are awarded. Punitive damages usually require some sort of extremely bad conduct on the part of the defendant. Equitable relief is varied, but includes orders such as specific performance, rescission, restitution, declaratory relief, and injunctions. Courts also have the power to grant provisional remedies such as a temporary restraining order or preliminary injunction pending the trial.

- Before drafting a complaint, you should check form books or form files for complaints with similar factual situations. The physical appearance of the complaint is usually determined by the laws of the jurisdiction in which the complaint is filed. Local rules of courts may also apply.

■ After the complaint has been reviewed by the attorney and signed by the appropriate parties, it is filed in court. Filing involves giving the document to the court clerk with an appropriate filing fee. The court then assigns a docket number to the case. All subsequent papers filed in the case must bear this number. A complaint must be filed within the statute of limitations.

■ A summons is a form that explains to the defendant that he has been sued. It is issued by the court clerk at the time the complaint is filed. After the defendant is served, the summons is returned to the court.

■ A copy of the complaint and a copy of the summons must be served on the defendant. Depending on the law of jurisdiction, these documents are usually served by a U.S. Marshal, local sheriff, licensed process server, or any adult who is not a party to the action. Service can be accomplished in different ways. Personal service (delivering a copy of the documents personally to the defendant) is preferred. Under some circumstances, substituted service (leaving a copy of the documents at the defendant's home or business with another adult) is allowed. Some jurisdictions also permit service by mail or by publication. After the papers are served, the individual serving the papers fills out a proof of service that is later filed with the court. The federal rules also encourage the defendant to waive service.

■ Additions, deletions, or changes to a complaint can be accomplished by amending the pleading. Amendments are liberally allowed, but after an answer has been filed, amendment requires either a stipulation from all parties or a court order. Unless an amendment adds new parties to the complaint, the statute of limitations relates back to the original date of filing the complaint.

Key Terms

allegation	guardian ad litem	quiet title action
capacity	indispensable party	real party in interest
caption	injunction	rescission
class action	interpleader	restitution
compensatory damages	permissive joinder	specific performance
compulsory joinder	personal service of process	stipulation
count	pleadings	subscription
declaratory relief	prayer	summons
docket number	preliminary injunction	temporary restraining order (TRO)
equitable relief	proof of service	verification
fictitiously named defendants	punitive or exemplary damages	
filing		

Review Questions

1. What is the purpose of pleadings?
2. What matters are generally contained in a complaint or petition?
3. What factors should be reviewed before determining who will be named as parties to a lawsuit?

4. What is the difference between notice pleading and code pleading?
5. What are the types of remedies that may be requested from a court?
6. What are the steps in drafting a complaint?
7. What is involved in filing a complaint?
8. What is a summons?
9. How is service of process accomplished?
10. What is the procedure for amending the complaint?

Chapter Exercises

Where necessary, check with your instructor prior to starting any of these exercises.

1. Review the laws of your state and find all state laws dealing with the initial pleadings in a lawsuit. Check with your local courts to see if any local rules of court in your area regulate any aspect of the initial pleading. Local rules of court are often found on the Internet homepage for the court.

2. Review the sample complaint found in this chapter. Does it meet the legal requirements in your state? If not, what would you have to change?

3. Find a set of form books in your law library that provide sample forms for use in the courts of your state. Find a form for a complaint or petition for fraud and negligent misrepresentation. How does it compare with the sample complaint in this chapter?

4. Review the complaint found in Exhibit 5–5. Identify by number the paragraphs that show
   a. venue
   b. damages
   c. the existence of the doctrine of respondeat superior

5. Review the case commentary, the complaint in Exhibit 5–5, and Rule 4 of the Federal Rules of Civil Procedure outlined in Exhibit 5–10. How could Paradise Found, Inc. be served?

6. Assume that you are ready to file the complaint found in Exhibit 5–5. Because the court is located some distance away you will be mailing the complaint and the summons to the court for filing. Draft a cover letter to the clerk of the court telling the clerk what documents are enclosed and what you want the court to do with the documents.

Chapter Project

Consider the following factual situation: Lowell Orloff, while shopping in a local department store, "The Wear House," tripped and fell on a piece of torn carpeting. Lowell suffered severe injuries, including a broken leg. Lowell incurred medical bills in excess of $5,000 and was off work for three weeks, losing earnings in the amount of $6,000. Lowell is married to Barbara Orloff. "The Wear House" is a corporation incorporated under the laws of your state. The correct corporate name is A & B Corporation. Using form books from your state, prepare a complaint on behalf of Lowell Orloff against The Wear House based on their negligent maintenance of their premises.

The *Bennett* Case
Assignment 5: Drafting a Complaint

Your supervising attorney is now ready to file a lawsuit on behalf of Bennett. You are to prepare a draft of the complaint. Check the Bennett research file (Appendix B) for a form to use in your preparation. The facts of the *Bennett* case will require you to make additions and changes to this form, however. Also, because this form was designed for a state action, you will have to add a paragraph establishing federal court jurisdiction. For further examples of employment discrimination complaints, review the Web site for the Civil Rights Division of the United States Department of Justice at <http://www.usdoj.gov/crt/casebrief.html>.

Chapter 6

Responses to the Initial Pleading

CHAPTER OUTLINE

COMMENTARY—THE GRANGER CASE

Your supervising attorney has given you the file of a new client who was recently named as a defendant in a lawsuit for personal injury damages. Included in the file are the attorney's notes and copies of a summons and complaint. (See Exhibit 6–1 for a copy of the complaint.) After reading the file and discussing the case with the attorney, you learn that the client, Linda Granger, owns a flower shop and had employed Wesley Linstrom to make deliveries. Deliveries were made in a van owned by Granger. According to your client, last year Linstrom was involved in an automobile accident that is the subject of this lawsuit. The morning of the accident, Linstrom took the van without Granger's knowledge and drove several hundred miles to visit his girlfriend. In the past your client had allowed Linstrom to use the van for some personal errands. However, these always involved very short distances, and he always asked ahead of time. The client also stated that Linstrom told her that the accident happened when the driver of the other vehicle stopped suddenly for no reason and he, Linstrom, was unable to stop because the brakes on the van failed. The file indicates that your client was served with a copy of the summons and complaint 15 days ago. Your attorney has requested that, after reviewing the file, you prepare responsive pleadings for review.

OBJECTIVES

Chapter 5 introduced the procedures for preparing, filing, and serving the initial pleading. The next step in the litigation process involves the response to a pleading. After completing this chapter, you should be able to:

- List the possible responses to the initial pleading.
- Describe the time limitations for these responses, along with methods for changing these limitations.
- Distinguish a general denial from a specific denial.
- Explain the importance of pleading affirmative defenses.
- Describe the general format of an answer.
- Explain the procedure for serving and filing an answer.
- Explain the process for amending responsive pleading.
- Define a counterclaim, cross-claim, and third-party complaint.
- Describe methods of raising legal challenges to the initial pleading.
- Describe results of a failure to file any response to the initial pleading.

**UNITED STATES DISTRICT COURT
FOR THE NORTHERN DISTRICT OF CALIFORNIA**

GORDON SHEFFIELD and AMY SHEFFIELD, Plaintiffs,	)))))	Civil No. 12345 COMPLAINT FOR NEGLIGENCE
vs.	))	
WESLEY LINSTROM and LINDA GRANGER, Defendants.	)))	

Plaintiff GORDON SHEFFIELD alleges:

JURISDICTION

1. Plaintiff is, and was at all times herein mentioned, domiciled in and a citizen of the state of California. Defendants and each of them are, and were at all times herein mentioned, domiciled in and a citizen of the state of Oregon. This is a civil action involving, exclusive of interest and costs, a sum in excess of $75,000. Every issue of law and fact in this action is wholly between citizens of different states.

FIRST COUNT

2. At all times herein mentioned, plaintiff was and now is a resident of the judicial district in which this action is filed.

3. At all times herein mentioned, defendant, LINDA GRANGER, was the owner of a certain motor vehicle, Oregon license number 123 XYZ.

4. At all times herein mentioned, defendant, WESLEY LINSTROM, was operating said motor vehicle with the permission and consent of defendant, LINDA GRANGER.

5. At all times herein mentioned defendant, WESLEY LINSTROM, was the agent, employee, and servant of defendant LINDA GRANGER, and at all times was acting within the course and scope of said agency and employment.

6. On May 1, _____, on a public highway called Market Street in San Francisco, California, defendant WESLEY LINSTROM negligently and carelessly drove the above-mentioned motor vehicle, Oregon license 123 XYZ, causing it to collide with another vehicle driven by plaintiff, who was also traveling on said highway.

7. As a result plaintiff was severely injured, having had his leg and arm broken and having suffered other bruises, contusions, and muscle strain. Also as a result plaintiff was prevented from transacting his business,

EXHIBIT 6–1   Complaint

suffered and continues to suffer great pain of body and mind, and incurred expenses for medical attention and hospitalization in the sum of ten thousand dollars ($10,000.00) and will continue to incur such expenses in an amount yet undetermined.

<u>SECOND COUNT</u>

Plaintiff, AMY SHEFFIELD, alleges against defendants and each of them as follows:

8. Plaintiff realleges and incorporates by reference the allegations of paragraphs 1 through 5 above in their entirety.

9. On May 1, _____, plaintiff was a passenger in a vehicle being driven by co-plaintiff, Gordon Sheffield, on a public highway called Market Street in San Francisco, California. At said time and place, defendant, WESLEY LINSTROM, negligently and carelessly drove a motor vehicle, Oregon license 123 XYZ, causing it to collide with the vehicle in which plaintiff, AMY SHEFFIELD, was a passenger.

10. As a result plaintiff was severely injured, having had her back broken and having suffered other bruises, contusions, and muscle strain. Also as a result plaintiff was prevented from transacting her business, suffered and continues to suffer great pain of body and mind, and incurred expenses for medical attention and hospitalization in the sum of fifteen thousand dollars ($15,000.00) and will continue to incur such expenses in an amount yet undetermined.

Wherefore plaintiff, GORDON SHEFFIELD, demands judgment against defendants and each of them in the sum of $100,000.00 and costs.

Wherefore plaintiff, AMY SHEFFIELD, demands judgment against defendants and each of them in the sum of $150,000.00 and costs.

Dated: April 30, _____

_____
TERRY ALVAREZ
ALVAREZ & COE
100 Market Street
San Francisco, California 94101
Attorney for Plaintiffs

EXHIBIT 6–1 *(continued)*

Responding to the Initial Pleading

After the initial pleading has been filed and served, the next step in the litigation process is up to the defendants. At this point they have various options. The defendants can contest the lawsuit, negotiate a settlement with the plaintiff, or do nothing at all. If the defendants challenge the lawsuit, they can do so on two bases. They can either contest the facts of the case or they can challenge the action on some legal basis. For example, in

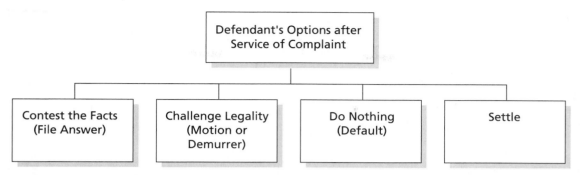

EXHIBIT 6–2   Defendant's options

the factual situation described in the opening commentary, defendant Granger might deny that at the time of the accident Linstrom was acting as her employee, or she might deny that his negligence caused the accident. In such a case she would be contesting the facts of the case. Alternatively, she might claim that she was not properly served with the complaint and summons and that therefore the action should be dismissed. This would be a legal challenge to the action (see Exhibit 6–2).

Time Limits

If the defendants choose to contest the action, they must act within certain time limitations. The time limit is normally fixed by the statutory laws of the jurisdiction in which the action is pending and can vary from one jurisdiction to another. In federal court the limit is normally 20 days, although there are some exceptions. For example, if the defendant is located out of the state, the time can be enlarged, or if the defendant is the United States government the time to answer is 60 days. Furthermore, if the defendant waived service under Rule 4, the defendant has 60 days in which to respond to the complaint and 90 days if the defendant is outside the United States.

Frequently, as in the *Granger* case, a substantial part of this time has elapsed before the defendant locates and retains an attorney. As a result, once an attorney is retained, only a few days may remain for the attorney to evaluate the case, consider the possibility of an early settlement, or prepare a proper response to the complaint or petition. In most cases, the time in which to respond can be extended or enlarged, either by obtaining a stipulation from the plaintiff's attorney (which may have to be approved by the court, depending on the laws of the jurisdiction) or by making a motion, or formal request from the court, for such an order.

Stipulations Enlarging Time

A stipulation *enlarging time* in which to respond is an agreement between the attorneys in an action that the defendant's attorney may have additional time in which to respond. In federal court this agreement or stipulation must be approved by the court, although in some state courts it need not be. If the stipulation is subject to court approval, it should follow the same formalities required of the pleadings and bear the caption and docket number of the case. See Exhibit 6–3 for an example of such a stipulation.

UNITED STATES DISTRICT COURT
FOR THE NORTHERN DISTRICT OF CALIFORNIA

GORDON SHEFFIELD and AMY SHEFFIELD,	)	Civil No. 12345
Plaintiffs,	)	STIPULATION AND ORDER
	)	FOR ENLARGEMENT
	)	OF TIME
	)	
vs.	)	
	)	
WESLEY LINSTROM and LINDA GRANGER,	)	
Defendants.	)	

IT IS STIPULATED by plaintiffs and defendant, LINDA GRANGER, through their respective counsel, that the time within which defendant, LINDA GRANGER, may have to respond to the complaint shall be, subject to approval by the court, extended to and including _____, _____ or such other date as the court may order.

There have been no previous stipulations or orders.

Dated _____, _____

_____
TERRY ALVAREZ
100 Market Street
San Francisco, California 94101
Attorney for Plaintiffs

_____
TAYLOR MARTIN
15 Plaza de Oro
Sacramento, California 94813
Attorney for Defendant

ORDER

Pursuant to the above stipulation filed herein, and good cause appearing, IT IS SO ORDERED.

Dated _____, ____

_____
Judge, District Court

EXHIBIT 6–3 Stipulation and order enlarging time to respond

If the stipulation does not require court approval, a letter between the attorneys confirming their agreement will suffice. The letter need not be filed in court, so it does not require a caption or docket number. Because you might be asked to write such a letter or prepare a formal stipulation for court approval, you should be aware of some possible problems which can arise. When preparing the stipulation, you should not state that the agreement is for an extension of time in which to "answer." Rather, you should state that the agreement is for an extension of time in which to "answer or otherwise respond." Plaintiff's attorneys have been known to complain or object when, having given a defendant an extension of time in which to "answer," they were served with a motion to dismiss or some other kind of legal challenge to the complaint. Although most courts refuse to sanction this type of narrow interpretation of the term "answer," you can avoid any problem by making the agreement clear.

Another problem arises when the attorneys agree to an **open stipulation.** Most agreements for extensions or enlargements of time are for a definite amount of time. Sometimes, however, especially if attorneys are seriously discussing settlement, the extension of time will be open-ended. In such a case, the parties stipulate that the defendant need not answer until she is given notice by the plaintiff. This is referred to as an open stipulation. If such an agreement exists in any case on which you are working, be careful to tickle or calendar the case for review so that it is not forgotten. This is particularly important if your firm represents the plaintiff.

open stimulation
An agreement between parties or their attorneys that a defendant need not answer a complaint within the time directed by law and need not answer until specifically notified by the plaintiff to do so.

Motions to Extend or Enlarge Time

If the defendant's attorney feels that more time is needed to prepare a response, and the plaintiff's attorney is unwilling to agree, an extension of time can be requested from the court. This is done by making a motion with the court. As mentioned, a *motion* is a formal request of the court for some kind of order. The details of motion practice are discussed in Chapter 7, but a motion to extend or enlarge time is usually made by filing papers with the court explaining the request and the reasons for it, serving these papers on the other attorneys in the action, and then possibly appearing in court for a short hearing on the motion.

Types of Answers

An answer is a pleading that challenges the plaintiff's right to the relief requested in the initial pleading. Normally this is done by contesting all or some of the facts alleged in the complaint or petition. Answers are prepared using one of three main formats: the general denial, the specific denial, or the qualified denial.

General Denial

The substance of a **general denial** is only one paragraph or allegation, in which the defendant denies all of the allegations contained in the complaint. In federal court, general denials are proper when the defendant is denying all of the factual contentions of the complaint, including the allegations of subject matter jurisdiction, personal jurisdiction, and venue. However, an alternative method of challenging jurisdiction or venue does exist. These matters, along with certain other defenses, can be raised by a motion to dismiss the action. This method is discussed later in this chapter.

Although many state jurisdictions follow the same procedures that apply in federal court, some states have different rules and procedures. Some state courts severely limit the use of general denials. In some courts general denials cannot be used if the

general denial
A type of answer in which all of the allegations of the complaint are denied.

complaint has been verified. Furthermore, the use of a general denial is insufficient to raise certain legal defenses, such as lack of personal jurisdiction. Such a defense must be raised by motion. In fact, filing an answer of any kind might constitute a waiver of this defense.

Specific Denial

specific denial

A type of answer in which the defendant specifically replies to each of the contentions alleged in the complaint.

A **specific denial** is an answer in which the defendant specifically replies to each of the contentions alleged in the complaint. The defendant replies to the various contentions by admitting them, denying them, or denying them on information and belief.

Most complaints or petitions contain some allegations that are uncontested. For example, a defendant in a lawsuit might agree that the court has jurisdiction to hear the case even though that defendant is challenging the plaintiff's right to recover any damages. Allegations or contentions to which the defendant agrees are admitted in the answer. An admission of an allegation can be explicit in the answer or it can be implied by silence. If an allegation is not specifically denied, it is deemed to be admitted. Therefore, in drafting an answer, you must always use care not to ignore any allegation, unless you want to admit it.

Occasionally, a defendant may not be absolutely certain about a certain allegation, or may not have sufficient knowledge of the facts. Just as the plaintiff is allowed to plead facts on information and belief, so also is the defendant allowed to deny allegations in the same manner. Denials based on information and belief should be used only when the pleader honestly does not have firsthand knowledge of the true facts. If the truth or falsity of acts is within the knowledge of the defendant, the defendant has an obligation to the court to express this knowledge. Likewise, if the information regarding the truth or falsity of an allegation can be easily obtained by the defendant, he has an obligation to do so.

Qualified Denial

qualified denial

A type of answer denying all of the allegations of the complaint except those that are specifically admitted.

A **qualified denial** is a combination of specific and general responses. In a qualified denial, the answering defendant expressly admits or denies certain allegations, then generally denies everything else.

Affirmative Defenses

affirmative defense

The part of a defendant's answer to a complaint that goes beyond denying the facts and arguments of the complaint. It sets out new facts and arguments that might win for the defendant even if everything in the complaint is true.

An **affirmative defense** is a fact or circumstance that will defeat the plaintiff's claim, even if the plaintiff can prove every contention alleged in the complaint. For example, suppose that the plaintiff has filed a lawsuit for breach of contract, alleging that the plaintiff loaned the defendant $75,000, and that when the loan was due the defendant refused to pay, and that the defendant continues to refuse to pay. Normally, if the plaintiff could prove these allegations at trial, the plaintiff would prevail and obtain a judgment for the amount of the unpaid loan. However, if the defendant alleges and proves that she filed bankruptcy and that this debt was discharged in bankruptcy, the plaintiff will lose the case. The fact that the debt was discharged in bankruptcy is an affirmative defense and operates to defeat the plaintiff's claim.

True affirmative defenses must be alleged in the answer or they will generally be deemed waived. Thus, in the situation just described, the defendant must specifically

THE COMPUTERIZED LAW FIRM
E-mail and Document Preparation

SCENARIO

Your firm has been retained to represent Linda Granger who was sued for damages. She was served with a copy of the complaint and summons a few weeks prior. Your attorney gave you a copy of the complaint and asked you to prepare an answer, including several affirmative defenses. She tells you that there is not much time left before the answer is due and asks you to give priority to this project. She will review your work as soon as you are finished. Unfortunately, before you finish, the attorney is unexpectedly required to go out of town to attend depositions. The depositions are expected to take at least seven days to complete. The answer must be filed in four days. No one else in the office is familiar with the case.

PROBLEM

You have three problems. First, you need to have your work reviewed by an attorney who may be several hundred miles away. Second, necessary corrections must be made to the document so that it can be filed. Third, the attorney must sign the pleading. Is there a way to do this in the limited time you have?

SOLUTION

One of the most important developments made possible through the Internet is e-mail. With a laptop computer, modem (usually installed in the laptop), and any telephone line, an attorney can remain in constant communication with his or her office, even if that attorney is hundreds of miles away. Today, an attorney can access the Internet and thus remain in contact with his or her office, even without a telephone line. A wireless connection to the Internet is possible through the use of technology known as "Wi-Fi."

Regardless of how the attorney connects to the Internet, the e-mail capabilities are the same. A document prepared in Microsoft Word or in Corel's WordPerfect can be easily attached to the e-mail message. Assuming that the recipient of the message also has the appropriate word processing software on his or her computer, the document is then downloaded and can be edited.

Word processing itself makes changing documents very simple. You can copy or move information in a document with a few simple keystrokes. Automatic paragraph numbering ensures the correct numbering of paragraphs following changes. Spell checks and grammar checks are used to avoid errors. Completely retyping documents to make changes or corrections has been eliminated entirely in law offices. With only a few days to file the answer, however, you still have the problem of getting a signed copy of the answer to the court. Many courts today accept electronic filing of documents. To do this, either you or the attorney will probably have to convert the word-processed document into a PDF format. When a document is in this type of format, it cannot be edited or changed, whereas a word-processed document can be manipulated. Special software, such as Adobe Acrobat, simplifies the conversion of a document into a PDF file. Courts that accept electronic filing also accept a digital signature. A digital signature is a special code that verifies the authenticity of the document. The answer in a PDF file with a digital signature, can then be e-mailed to the court for electronic filing. All of this can be accomplished even though the attorney is hundreds of miles away from his or her office and the court.

allege in the answer that the debt was discharged in bankruptcy. If the defendant simply denies that the money is owed, this is insufficient, and the plaintiff would still get a judgment.

Whether or not a matter is an affirmative defense is a question of substantive law. Some matters, such as expiration of the statute of limitations, operate as affirmative defenses in all kinds of cases. However, other affirmative defenses vary depending on the area of substantive law involved. In other words, what constitutes affirmative defenses in contract cases may be very different from what constitutes affirmative defenses in tort cases. Researching the substantive law of the case may be necessary to determine what affirmative defenses exist in a particular situation.

A partial list of affirmative defenses is found in Rule 8(c) of the Federal Rules of Civil Procedure. This list includes:

Affirmative Defenses Applicable to Contract Disputes
> accord and satisfaction
> duress
> estoppel
> failure of consideration
> fraud
> illegality
> payment
> release
> statute of frauds
> waiver

Affirmative Defenses Applicable to Tort Cases
> assumption of the risk
> contributory negligence
> injury by fellow servant

Affirmative Defenses Applicable to All Cases
> arbitration and award
> discharge in bankruptcy
> laches
> res judicata
> statute of limitations

If any of these defenses are claimed in an action in federal court, they must be specifically alleged in the answer as an affirmative defense. Failure to do so could result in the defense being waived. This list, however, is not all-inclusive. Other affirmative defenses do exist under different areas of substantive laws.

Drafting the Answer

An answer is a pleading that will be filed in court. As such, it follows the same general format as the complaint or petition. It contains a caption, body or allegations, prayer or "wherefore" clause, and signature. In some jurisdictions, it is prepared on pleading paper (paper that is numbered along the left side). Before drafting an answer, you might want to consult a form book, just as you do in drafting a complaint. Also,

---

UNITED STATES DISTRICT COURT
FOR THE NORTHERN DISTRICT OF CALIFORNIA

GORDON SHEFFIELD and AMY   )   Civil No. 12345
SHEFFIELD,   )   ANSWER
    Plaintiffs,   )
)
)
    vs.   )
)
WESLEY LINSTROM and LINDA   )
GRANGER,   )
    Defendants.   )

EXHIBIT 6–4   Caption for answer

before actually beginning to draft the answer, you should review the entire complaint. It is often helpful to make a copy of the complaint and next to each paragraph make a note as to how you plan to respond to the allegations in the paragraph. This will help ensure that you do not inadvertently neglect to respond to an important allegation.

Caption

The caption on an answer is similar to the caption on the complaint. The names of the plaintiff and defendant are listed just as they are on the complaint. The document is titled ("answer") and the docket number, which appears on the complaint, is included. The caption for an answer that would be prepared by your law firm on behalf of Granger would look as shown in Exhibit 6–4.

If the plaintiff has demanded a jury, that demand will generally appear in the caption of the complaint. It is not necessary that the defendant repeat this. However, if the plaintiff has not requested a jury, and the defense wants one, a jury demand should appear in the caption of the answer.

Body

The content of the body of the answer depends on whether it is a specific, general, or qualified denial. A general denial contains only one paragraph, as described previously. See Exhibit 6–5 for an example of a general denial.

A specific denial is more detailed. However, there are only a few different paragraphs or allegations that are generally used in an answer. If the defendant is denying all of the facts alleged in a paragraph of the complaint, the following paragraph could appear in the answer:

Caption has same party names and docket number as complaint

**UNITED STATES DISTRICT COURT
FOR THE NORTHERN DISTRICT OF CALIFORNIA**

| GORDON SHEFFIELD and AMY SHEFFIELD,
     Plaintiffs,

 vs.

 WESLEY LINSTROM and LINDA GRANGER,
     Defendants. |)
)
)
)
)
)
)
)
)
)
) | Civil No. 12345
 ANSWER |

Introductory paragraph names answering defendant

Defendant, LINDA GRANGER, answers as follows:

Defendant denies each and every allegation of plaintiffs' complaint.

Wherefore defendant prays:
1. That the court enter judgment dismissing the complaint;
2. That defendant be awarded costs incurred herein; and
3. That defendant be awarded such other and further relief as the court may deem just.

Dated: _____

Identify the specific answering defendant

TAYLOR MARTIN
15 Plaza de Oro
Sacramento, California
(916) 555-1212
Attorney for Defendant, Linda Granger

EXHIBIT 6–5   General denial

Example: Denial allegation

1. Defendant denies each and every allegation of Paragraphs 1, 2, and 3 of the complaint.

When a defendant is denying an allegation on information or belief, the following paragraph could be used:

Example: Denial on information and belief

2. Defendant denies having sufficient knowledge or information to form a belief as to the allegations contained in Paragraph 4 of the complaint.

Note that this paragraph does not contain an express denial of the allegations of the complaint. The federal rules provide that when a defendant states that she lacks information and belief about an allegation, this will be deemed to be a denial. Some attorneys, however, prefer to expressly deny the allegations, and some jurisdictions require it. In such a case, the following paragraph could be used:

Example: Denial on information and belief

3. Defendant denies having sufficient knowledge or information to form a belief as to the allegations contained in Paragraph 4 of the complaint, and thereupon denies said allegations.

For allegations in the complaint that the defendant admits, the following paragraph applies:

Example: Admission allegation

4. Defendant admits the allegations contained in Paragraph 5 of the complaint.

If the defendant wishes to admit part of a paragraph and deny part of it, the following paragraph could be used:

Example: Admission in part; denial in part

5. Answering Paragraph 6 of the complaint, defendant admits that an automobile collision occurred between plaintiff and defendant but denies each and every other allegation contained in said paragraph.

In a qualified denial, the following paragraph might appear in the body of the answer:

Example: Qualified denial

6. Defendant admits the allegations of Paragraphs 1, 2, and 3 of the complaint and denies each and every other allegation of plaintiff's complaint.

Answering a Multicount Complaint   In a complaint containing more than one count or cause of action, it is common to find a paragraph incorporating paragraphs from previous counts. (See Exhibit 6–1, Paragraph 8.) Responding to this paragraph sometimes presents difficulties, especially when some of the incorporated paragraphs have been admitted and some denied. The following is an example of a response that can be used:

Example: Incorporating by reference

7. In answer to Paragraph 8 of Count Two of the complaint, wherein plaintiff incorporates by reference certain paragraphs of Count One of the complaint, defendant admits, denies, and alleges to the same effect and in the same manner as she admitted, denied, and alleged to those specific paragraphs previously in this answer.

In answering a complaint with more than one count or cause of action, questions sometimes arise regarding the format of the answer. Should each cause of action or count be answered separately in the answer, or can an allegation in the answer contain replies to allegations in the various counts? It is purely a matter of preference and can be done either way. For example, in the *Granger* case, if Granger were to deny Paragraphs 4, 5, 6, 7, 9, and 10 of the complaint, the body of the answer could be set up in one of two ways:

Example: Multicount answer

Answer to Count 1

1. Defendant denies each and every allegation contained in Paragraphs 4, 5, 6, and 7 of plaintiffs' complaint.

Answer to Count 2

2. Defendant denies each and every allegation contained in Paragraphs 9 and 10 of plaintiffs' complaint.

Alternatively, the denial in the answer could be as follows:

Example: Multicount answer

---

1. Defendant denies each and every allegation contained in Paragraphs 4, 5, 6, 7, 9, and 10 of plaintiffs' complaint.

Affirmative Defenses Whether a defendant files a general denial or a specific denial, affirmative defenses might apply. In drafting an answer, it is necessary to review the substantive law of the case as well as the facts to determine if an affirmative defense exists. For example, suppose that in the factual situation described in the *Granger* case your client's records indicate that the accident occurred on April 29 instead of May 1. Because personal injury actions of this sort have a two-year statute of limitations in California, she would want to assert the expiration of the statute of limitations as an affirmative defense. The defendant might also want to assert the negligence of plaintiff, Gordon Sheffield, as an affirmative defense. In drafting the answer, affirmative defenses appear in the body following the paragraphs denying or admitting the allegations in the complaint. In an answer to a multicount complaint, affirmative defenses can be placed at the end of the answers to each count or at the end of answers to all of the counts (as is shown in Exhibit 6–6).

Prayer and Signature

The body of the answer is followed by a simple prayer, or "wherefore," clause, the date, and the signature of the attorney. In some courts, including federal court, the signature of the attorney is followed by the attorney's address. The prayer usually requests that the plaintiffs be allowed no recovery. The date, signature, and address follow the same format as the complaint.

UNITED STATES DISTRICT COURT
FOR THE NORTHERN DISTRICT OF CALIFORNIA

GORDON SHEFFIELD and AMY SHEFFIELD, Plaintiffs,)))))	Civil No. 12345 ANSWER
vs.))	
WESLEY LINSTROM and LINDA GRANGER, Defendants.)))	

Answer to First Count

Defendant, LINDA GRANGER, answers as follows:

1. Defendant admits the allegations of Paragraphs 1, 2, and 3 of the complaint.

2. Defendant denies each and every allegation of Paragraphs 4, 5, 6, and 7 of the complaint.

Answer to Second Count

3. In answer to Paragraph 8 of Count Two of the complaint, wherein plaintiff incorporates by reference certain paragraphs of Count One of the complaint, defendant admits, denies, and alleges to the same effect and in the same manner as she admitted, denied, and alleged to those specific paragraphs previously in this answer.

4. In answer to Paragraph 9 of Count Two of the complaint, defendant admits that plaintiff, AMY SHEFFIELD, was a passenger in a vehicle being driven by co-plaintiff, GORDON SHEFFIELD, but denies each and every other allegation contained in said paragraph.

5. Defendant denies each and every allegation contained in Paragraph 10 of the complaint.

First Affirmative Defense

As and for an affirmative defense, defendant alleges that plaintiffs' right to maintain this action is barred by the statute of limitations in that more than two years have now elapsed between the date plaintiffs' alleged cause of action arose and the date plaintiffs filed their complaint.

Second Affirmative Defense

As and for a separate affirmative defense, defendant alleges that plaintiffs were themselves negligent, in that plaintiff Gordon Sheffield

EXHIBIT 6–6 Answer

failed to use ordinary care in the operation of his motor vehicle and failed to keep a proper lookout for other vehicles, and that both plaintiffs Gordon Sheffield and Amy Sheffield failed to exercise ordinary care, in that neither wore a seat belt. Defendant further alleges that said negligence contributed in whole or in part to any injuries which may have resulted.

Wherefore defendant prays:

1. That the court enter judgment dismissing the complaint;

2. That defendant be awarded costs incurred herein; and

3. That defendant be awarded such other and further relief as the court may deem just.

Dated:_____, _____

_____
TAYLOR MARTIN
15 Plaza de Oro
Sacramento, California 94813
(916) 555-1212
Attorney for Defendant, Linda Granger

EXHIBIT 6–6 *(continued)*

In its entirety, an answer prepared on behalf of Linda Granger to the complaint described in the commentary would look as shown in Exhibit 6–6.

Verification

In federal court, complaints are not generally verified. In some state jurisdictions, however, plaintiffs are permitted to verify a complaint at any time. If the complaint has been verified, usually the defendant cannot use a general denial and, furthermore, must verify the answer.

Service and Filing

After the answer is prepared it must be served on the plaintiff or the plaintiff's attorney, and it must be filed in court. Normally, a copy of the answer is served before it is filed with the court. Not only must defense counsel serve the answer on the plaintiff, but if any codefendants have filed answers, they also must be served. The federal rules require that documents be served on all parties to the action (or their attorneys). The procedures for serving an answer are usually very simple. If a party is represented by an attorney, service can be made on the attorney rather than the party. The answer can be served on the attorney in any of the following ways:

1. by mail,

2. electronically (fax or e-mail), or

3. personally.

I, Taylor Martin, Attorney for defendant Linda Granger, do certify that a copy of the attached Answer was served on Terry Alvarez, Attorney for plaintiffs, by enclosing a true and correct copy in an envelope addressed to Terry Alvarez, 100 Market Street, San Francisco, California 94101, postage prepaid, and depositing the same in the United States mail at Sacramento, California on _____.

Taylor Martin
15 Plaza de Oro
Sacramento, California
(916) 555-1212
Attorney for Defendant, Linda Granger

EXHIBIT 6–7   Certificate of mailing

ANSWER CHECKLIST

Before filing the answer be sure that you have:

☐ Reviewed local rules for special format requirements
☐ Reviewed the complaint and determined how each paragraph will be answered
☐ Copied the caption, especially the docket number, correctly
☐ Included a demand for jury if plaintiff has not and you want a jury
☐ Included responses to each paragraph in the complaint unless they are admitted
☐ Included relevant affirmative defenses
☐ Affixed a proper signature
☐ Mailed a copy to plantiff's attorney
☐ Mailed a copy to plaintiff's attorney
☐ Attached a copy of a certificate of service to the answer

EXHIBIT 6–8   Answer checklist

Under the federal rules, before an attorney can be served electronically, the attorney must consent in writing. In state court, state or local rules should be consulted regarding this type of service. Regardless of how the answer is served, a certificate of service showing how the document was served and by whom it was served must be prepared. The original certificate of service should be affixed to the original answer and sent to the court for filing. See Exhibit 6–7 for an example of a certificate of service by mail.

As soon as the answer has been served, it should be filed in court. Courts may also require that a filing fee accompany the answer (see Exhibit 6–8).

Amending

Most courts have liberal rules regarding the amendment of any pleading, including an answer. Under federal rules, as long as the case has not been placed on the trial calendar, a party may amend an answer any time within 20 days after it is served. If more than 20 days has elapsed, or if the case has been placed on the trial calendar, the answer can be amended only with permission of the court or by written consent of the adverse party.

Counterclaims, Cross-Claims, and Third-Party Complaints

counterclaim
A claim made by a defendant in a civil lawsuit that, in effect, "sues" the plaintiff.

cross-claim
A claim brought by one defendant against another, that is based on the same subject matter as the plaintiff's lawsuit.

third-party complaint
A complaint brought by a defendant in a lawsuit against someone not in the lawsuit.

At times, defendants themselves have a claim and are entitled to some relief from the court. They may be asserting this claim against the plaintiff, a codefendant, or a third party (someone who is not a party to the original action). In federal court, when defendants assert a claim against a plaintiff, it is known as a **counterclaim.** When the claim is asserted against a codefendant, it is known as a **cross-claim.** Finally, when the claim is against a new party, it is known as a **third-party complaint.** Counterclaims and cross-claims are included with the answer. Third-party complaints are pleadings that are separate from the answer. See Table 6–1 for an outline of how defendant Linda Granger would handle various claims she might have.

Regardless of which form the defendant's claim takes, the content of the claim is the same. The content of the defendant's claim for relief is similar to the content of the plaintiff's claim in a complaint. Usually the defendant states the jurisdictional basis for the court's hearing the matter, unless the basis for the court's jurisdiction is the same as in the complaint. This is followed by numbered paragraphs describing the factual basis for the claim.

In some state jurisdictions, although defendants have the same rights to assert claims, the format and the names of the pleading differ. For example, in some states, if defendants assert a claim, they do so in a pleading called a cross-complaint. This pleading, which is separate from the answer, is used against a plaintiff, codefendant, or third party.

Counterclaims

In most instances, if a defendant has a claim against the plaintiff that arises out of the same transaction as the claim described in the complaint, that claim must be asserted

TABLE 6–1 *Sheffield v. Lindstrom and Granger,* Claims by Granger

Granger v. Sheffield	Defendant asserts claim against plaintiff	Counterclaim
Granger v. Linstrom	Defendant asserts claim against codefendant	Cross-Claim
Granger v. Brakefast	Defendant asserts claim against a new party	Third-Party Action

in a counterclaim, or the right to make a claim is lost. Moreover, because such a claim must be asserted or be deemed waived, it is not necessary that the counterclaim satisfy the court's jurisdictional requirements. The fact that the court has jurisdiction over the plaintiff's claim is sufficient. Counterclaims that must be asserted or lost are known as **compulsory counterclaims.** A compulsory counterclaim that is not included as part of the answer is thereafter barred. Exceptions occur when the assertion of the claim involves bringing in third parties over whom the court cannot acquire jurisdiction, or when the defendant's claim has already been asserted in another action. Of course, if a defendant fails to assert a compulsory counterclaim in the answer, under proper circumstances the responsive pleading can be amended to add the counterclaim. (Amendment of answers is discussed later in this chapter.)

Because it saves a great deal of court time, the courts encourage the parties to resolve all of their disputes in one action. Consequently, if a defendant has a claim against the plaintiff that did not arise out of the factual situation described in the complaint, she can still assert that claim in the answer as a counterclaim. Such a counterclaim is a **permissive counterclaim.** Unlike compulsory counterclaims, permissive counterclaims must satisfy the court's jurisdictional requirements. As a rule, claims forming the basis for a permissive counterclaim are not lost if they are not made as part of the answer.

In the *Granger* case, if Sheffield was negligent in operating his vehicle and that negligence was a cause of the accident, Granger could file a counterclaim against him for the damage to her vehicle. The factual situation might also provide the basis for a counterclaim for **contribution.** *Contribution* is a claim for partial reimbursement from a person whose wrongdoing contributed to the injuries claimed in the complaint. In this instance, if Linstrom and Gordon Sheffield were both negligent, they both contributed to Amy Sheffield's injuries. If Granger is found liable to Amy Sheffield (either as Linstrom's employer or as the owner of the van), she might be entitled to contribution from Gordon Sheffield. Although claims for contribution do relate to the claim of the complaint, they do not always have to be asserted with the answer. They can be raised after the liability of the defendant has been established. Exhibit 6–9 shows an example of an answer and counterclaim.

Because all counterclaims are part of the answer, they are served in the same manner as the answer.

Cross-Claims

A cross-claim, a claim by one defendant against another, is allowed whenever the claim arises out of the same transaction or occurrence that is the subject matter of the complaint. For example, again in the factual situation described in the commentary, if Granger believes that the accident was Linstrom's fault, she could file a cross-claim against him. Her claim might be twofold, just as the counterclaim was against Gordon Sheffield. First, she might be claiming damages for any destruction to her van caused by his negligence. Second, she might be claiming total reimbursement or **indemnification** for any judgment against her in the complaint. (Under the substantive law of torts, an employer is liable to third parties for injuries caused by the negligence of its employees while they are in the course and scope of their employment. However, the employer has

---

compulsory counterclaim (counterclaim)
A counterclaim based on the same subject or transaction as the original claim.

permissive counterclaim (counterclaim)
A claim made by a defendant in a civil lawsuit that, in effect, "sues" the plaintiff, based on entirely different things from the plaintiff's complaint.

contribution
The right of a person who has paid an entire debt (or judgment) to get back a fair share of the payment from another person who is also responsible for the debt.

indemnification
A concept allowing one defendant, who has paid a judgment, to seek reimbursement from another defendant.

UNITED STATES DISTRICT COURT
FOR THE NORTHERN DISTRICT OF CALIFORNIA

GORDON SHEFFIELD and AMY SHEFFIELD, Plaintiffs,	)))))	Civil No. 12345 ANSWER AND COUNTERCLAIM
vs.	))	
WESLEY LINSTROM and LINDA GRANGER, Defendants.	)))	

Answer to First Count

Defendant, LINDA GRANGER, answers as follows:

1. Defendant admits the allegations of Paragraphs 1, 2, and 3 of the complaint.
2. Defendant denies each and every allegation of Paragraphs 4, 5, 6, and 7 of the complaint.

Answer to Second Count

3. In answer to Paragraph 8 of Count Two of the complaint, wherein plaintiff incorporates by reference certain paragraphs of Count One of the complaint, defendant admits, denies, and alleges to the same effect and in the same manner as she admitted, denied, and alleged to those specific paragraphs previously in this answer.

4. In answer to Paragraph 9 of Count Two of the complaint, defendant admits that plaintiff, AMY SHEFFIELD, was a passenger in a vehicle being driven by co-plaintiff, GORDON SHEFFIELD, but denies each and every other allegation contained in said paragraph.

5. Defendant denies each and every allegation contained in Paragraph 10 of the complaint.

First Affirmative Defense

As and for an affirmative defense, defendant alleges that plaintiffs' right to maintain this action is barred by the statute of limitations, in that more than one year has now elapsed between the date plaintiff's alleged cause of action arose and the date plaintiffs filed their complaint.

Second Affirmative Defense

As and for a separate affirmative defense, defendant alleges that plaintiffs were themselves negligent, in that plaintiff Gordon Sheffield failed to use ordinary care in the operation of his motor vehicle, and failed to keep a proper lookout for other vehicles, and that both plaintiffs Gordon Sheffield and Amy Sheffield failed to exercise ordinary care, in that neither wore a seat belt. Defendant further alleges that said negligence contributed in whole or in part to any injuries which may have resulted.

Counterclaim

As a counterclaim against plaintiff, Gordon Sheffield, defendant alleges:

EXHIBIT 6–9   Answer and counterclaim

1. On or about April 29, _____, in a public highway called Market Street in San Francisco, California, plaintiff, Gordon Sheffield, negligently drove a motor vehicle, causing it to collide with another motor vehicle, owned by defendant Linda Granger.

2. That the motor vehicle driven by Gordon Sheffield was owned jointly by plaintiffs Gordon Sheffield and Amy Sheffield and that at all times herein mentioned was driven and operated by Gordon Sheffield with the knowledge and consent of plaintiff Amy Sheffield.

3. As a result of plaintiff's negligence, defendant's motor vehicle was damaged, and defendant has incurred expenses in the amount of $5,000 to repair said vehicle.

4. Also as a result of said motor vehicle collision, co-plaintiff, AMY SHEFFIELD, has commenced a tort action against defendant for the recovery of $150,000.00, her alleged damages resulting from the collision. Defendant alleges that should judgment be assessed against defendant in favor of plaintiff Amy Sheffield, that defendant Linda Granger is entitled to recover from plaintiff Gordon Sheffield all or part of said judgment.

Wherefore defendant prays:

1. That the court enter judgment dismissing the complaint;
2. That defendant have judgment against plaintiff Gordon Sheffield in the amount of $5,000.00;
3. That defendant have judgment against plaintiff Gordon Sheffield in an amount equal to any judgment in favor of plaintiff Amy Sheffield;
4. That defendant be awarded costs incurred herein;
5. That defendant be awarded such other and further relief as the court may deem just.

Dated: _____, _____

TAYLOR MARTIN
15 Plaza de Oro
Sacramento, California 94813
(916) 555-1212
Attorney for Defendant, Linda Granger

EXHIBIT 6–9 *(continued)*

a claim against the employee for reimbursement or indemnification.) Cross-claims often involve claims for indemnification. If Linda Granger were to file such a cross-claim, it would look as shown in Exhibit 6–10.

Because cross-claims are part of the answer, they are served in the same manner as the answer.

Third-Party Complaints

A defendant in a lawsuit may feel that some third party—that is, someone not named in the original complaint—is responsible, in whole or in part, for the damages claimed in the complaint. In the Granger case, facts suggest that the accident occurred because the brakes failed and Linstrom was unable to stop. Suppose that Granger had taken the van in to have the brakes checked two days before the accident and was told

**UNITED STATES DISTRICT COURT
FOR THE NORTHERN DISTRICT OF CALIFORNIA**

GORDON SHEFFIELD and AMY SHEFFIELD, Plaintiffs, vs. WESLEY LINSTROM and LINDA GRANGER, Defendants.	))))))))))) Civil No. 12345 ANSWER AND CROSS-CLAIM

Answer to First Count

Defendant, LINDA GRANGER, answers as follows:

1. Defendant admits the allegations of Paragraphs 1, 2, and 3 of the complaint.
2. Defendant denies each and every allegation of Paragraphs 4, 5, 6, and 7 of the complaint.

Answer to Second Count

3. In answer to Paragraph 8 of Count Two of the complaint, wherein plaintiff incorporates by reference certain paragraphs of Count One of the complaint, defendant admits, denies, and alleges to the same effect and in the same manner as she admitted, denied, and alleged to those specific paragraphs previously in this answer.

4. In answer to Paragraph 9 of Count Two of the complaint, defendant admits that plaintiff, AMY SHEFFIELD, was a passenger in a vehicle being driven by co-plaintiff, GORDON SHEFFIELD, but denies each and every other allegation contained in said paragraph.

5. Defendant denies each and every allegation contained in Paragraph 10 of the complaint.

First Affirmative Defense

As and for an affirmative defense, defendant alleges that plaintiffs' right to maintain this action is barred by the statute of limitations, in that more than one year has now elapsed between the date of plaintiffs' alleged cause of action arose and the date plaintiffs filed their complaint.

Second Affirmative Defense

As and for a separate affirmative defense, defendant alleges that plaintiffs were themselves negligent, in that plaintiff Gordon Sheffield failed to use ordinary care in the operation of his motor vehicle, and failed to keep a proper lookout for other vehicles, and that both plaintiff Gordon Sheffield and Amy Sheffield failed to exercise ordinary care, in that neither wore a seat belt. Defendant further alleges that said negligence contributed in whole or in part to any injuries that may have resulted.

Cross-Claim

As a cross-claim against defendant, Wesley Linstrom, hereinafter referred to as cross-defendant, defendant and cross-claimant, hereinafter referred to as cross-claimant, alleges:

EXHIBIT 6–10 Answer and cross-claim

1. One or about April 29, _____, on a public highway called Market Street in San Francisco, California, cross-defendant, Wesley Linstrom, without the knowledge or permission of cross-claimant, Linda Granger, negligently drove a motor vehicle, owned by cross-claimant Linda Granger, causing it to collide with another motor vehicle.

2. As a result of cross-defendant's negligence, cross-claimant's motor vehicle was damaged, and defendant has incurred expenses in the amount of $5,000 to repair said vehicle.

3. Also as a result of said motor vehicle collision, plaintiffs, GORDON SHEFFIELD and AMY SHEFFIELD, have commenced a tort action against cross-claimant for the recovery of $250,000.00, their alleged damages resulting from the collision. Cross-claimant alleges that should judgment be assessed against her in favor of plaintiff Amy Sheffield, that cross-claimant Linda Granger is entitled to recover from cross-defendant the amount of said judgment.

Wherefore defendant and cross-claimant prays:
1. That the court enter judgment dismissing the complaint;
2. The cross-claimant have judgment against cross-defendant Wesley Linstrom in the amount of $5,000.00;
3. That defendant have judgment against cross-defendant in an amount equal to any judgment in favor of plaintiff Amy Sheffield;
4. That defendant be awarded costs incurred herein;
5. That defendant be awarded such other and further relief as the court may deem just.

Dated: _____, _____

TAYLOR MARTIN
15 Plaza de Oro
Sacramento, California 94813
(916) 555-1212
Attorney for Defendant, Linda Granger

EXHIBIT 6–10   *(continued)*

that the brakes were in perfect condition. Under such circumstances, she might feel that the auto repair service should be responsible for any damages. She could, therefore, bring the auto repair service into the action by filing and serving it with a third-party complaint.

A third-party complaint, unlike the cross-claim and counterclaim, is a separate pleading. Because it is a claim for relief, it resembles the complaint. The main difference is in the caption, which changes to reflect the fact that a third-party complaint is being filed. The defendant filing the third-party complaint is now known as the defendant and third-party plaintiff. The person against whom the claim is asserted is known as the third-party defendant. A third-party complaint against the auto repair service would look as shown in Exhibit 6–11.

Under the Federal Rules of Civil Procedure, a defendant has the right to file a third-party complaint within 10 days of filing the answer. If the third-party complaint is filed within this time, no permission of the court is required. If a defendant decides to file a

UNITED STATES DISTRICT COURT
FOR THE NORTHERN DISTRICT OF CALIFORNIA

GORDON SHEFFIELD and AMY SHEFFIELD, Plaintiffs,	)))))	Civil No. 12345 Third-Party Complaint
vs.	)))	

WESLEY LINSTROM,
    Defendants
LINDA GRANGER,
    Defendant and
    Third-Party Plaintiff,
	))))))	

v.	))	
BRAKEFAST, Inc. Third-Party Defendant,	))	

Linda Granger, Third-Party Plaintiff, alleges:

1. Plaintiffs, GORDON SHEFFIELD and AMY SHEFFIELD, have filed against defendant LINDA GRANGER a complaint, a copy of which is hereto attached as "Exhibit A."

2. At all times herein mentioned, third-party defendant was an automotive garage engaged in the business of servicing and repairing automobiles including brake systems.

3. On or about April 25, _____, third-party plaintiff took her automobile, Oregon license XYZ 123, to third-party defendant's automotive garage for the specific purpose of having the brakes checked and serviced.

4. On or about April 25, _____, third-party defendant negligently and carelessly checked, serviced, and inspected said brakes and negligently and carelessly advised third-party plaintiff that said brakes were in good condition.

5. On or about April 29, _____, the brakes on said automobile failed, causing the vehicle to collide with another motor vehicle driven by plaintiff, Gordon Sheffield.

6. As a result of said collision, plaintiffs have filed the complaint attached as Exhibit A claiming damages from third-party plaintiff.

7. Any damages claimed by plaintiff are a direct and proximate result of the negligence of third-party defendant, and should any damages be

EXHIBIT 6–11 Third-party complaint

assessed against third-party plaintiff, she is entitled to judgment against third-party defendant in the same amount.

   Wherefore third-party plaintiff demands judgment against third-party defendant for all sums that may be adjudged against defendant, LINDA GRANGER, in favor of plaintiffs Gordon Sheffield and Amy Sheffield.

Dated: _____

                                        _____
                                        TAYLOR MARTIN
                                        15 Plaza de Oro
                                        Sacramento, California 94813
                                        (916) 555-1212
                                        Attorney for Defendant and
                                             Third-Party Plaintiff,
                                        Linda Granger

EXHIBIT 6–11   *(continued)*

third-party action after that time, permission from the court is required. This would be obtained by making a motion in court. At the time the third-party complaint is filed, it will be necessary to have a new summons issued, directed to the third-party defendant. See Exhibit 6–12 for a sample of such a summons.

   A third-party complaint and summons must be served in the same way as a complaint is served.

Replies and Answers

   Responses must be made to allegations contained in counterclaims, cross-claims, and third-party complaints. The response to a counterclaim is called a **reply.** Except for the title of the document, it resembles an answer in all respects. The responses to cross-claims and third-party complaints are called answers and do not differ from an answer to the complaint. Under the Federal Rules of Civil Procedure, all responses are due 20 days after service of the pleading containing the claim.

reply
In federal pleading, the plaintiff's response to the defendant's answer or counterclaim.

Amending

   Counterclaims, cross-claims, and third-party complaints can be amended once as long as a response to them has not been filed and served. Otherwise, court permission or the agreement of adverse parties is needed.

AO 441 (Rev. 8/01) Third Party Summons in a Civil Action

UNITED STATES DISTRICT COURT

District of _____

PLAINTIFF

V. DEFENDANT AND THIRD PARTY PLAINTIFF

THIRD PARTY SUMMONS IN A CIVIL ACTION

Case Number:

V. THIRD PARTY DEFENDANT

To: Name and address of Third Party Defendant

YOU ARE HEREBY SUMMONED and required to serve on

PLAINTIFF'S ATTORNEY (name and address)	DEFENDANT AND THIRD-PARTY PLAINTIFF'S ATTORNEY (name and address)

an answer to the third-party complaint which is served on you with this summons, within _____ days after the service of this summons on you, exclusive of the day of service. If you fail to do so, judgment by default may be taken against you for the relief demanded in the third-party complaint. There is also served on you with this summons a copy of the complaint of the plaintiff. You have the option of answering or not answering the plaintiff's complaint, *unless* (1) this is a case within Rule 9(h) Federal Rules of Civil Procedure, *and* (2) the third-party plaintiff is demanding judgment against you in favor of the original plaintiff under the circumstances described in Rule 14(c) Federal Rules of Civil Procedure, in which situation you are required to make your defenses, if any, to the claim of plaintiff as well as to the claim of the third-party plaintiff. Any answer that you serve on the parties to this action must be filed with the Clerk of this Court within a reasonable period of time after service.

CLERK

DATE

(By) DEPUTY CLERK

EXHIBIT 6–12 Third-party summons

AO 441 (Rev. 8/01) Third Party Summons in a Civil Action

RETURN OF SERVICE

Service of the Summons and complaint was made by me[1]	DATE
NAME OF SERVER	TITLE

Check one box below to indicate appropriate method of service

☐ Served personally upon the third-party defendant. Place where served:

☐ Left copies thereof at the third-party defendant's dwelling house or usual place of abode with a person of suitable age and discretion then residing therein.

Name of person with whom the summons and complaint were left:

☐ Returned unexecuted:

☐ Other (specify):

STATEMENT OF SERVICE FEES

TRAVEL	SERVICES	TOTAL $0.00

DECLARATION OF SERVER

I declare under penalty of perjury under the laws of the United States of America that the foregoing information contained in the Return of Service and Statement of Service Fees is true and correct.

Executed on _____   _____
                    Date   *Signature of Server*

                                        _____
                                        Address of Server

(1) As to who may serve a summons see Rule 4 of the Federal Rules of Civil Procedure.

EXHIBIT 6–12 *(continued)*

Legal Challenges to the Complaint

The primary purpose of an answer is to challenge the factual basis for the plaintiff's claim. However, not all defenses or challenges to a complaint deal with the truth or falsity of the factual allegations. Sometimes defendants wish to challenge the action on a more technical, legal basis. For example, the defendant might be challenging the court's authority to hear the case (jurisdiction), or the defendant might be claiming that she was not properly served with the complaint. Some jurisdictions, including federal court, allow this type of defense to be raised either in the answer or in a motion. Other jurisdictions require that certain defenses be raised in a special pleading, sometimes known as a **demurrer.**

In federal court, many legal challenges to the action are raised by the defendant in a motion to dismiss the case. A **motion to dismiss** is a request that the court immediately terminate the action without granting the plaintiff any of the relief that was requested in the complaint. Legal challenges or defenses that can be raised in a motion to dismiss under Rule 12 of the Federal Rules of Civil Procedure include:

1. lack of jurisdiction over the subject matter,
2. lack of jurisdiction over the person,
3. improper venue,
4. insufficiency of process,
5. insufficiency of service of process,
6. failure to state a claim upon which relief can be granted, and
7. failure to join a party under Rule 19 (an indispensable party).

The defenses of lack of subject matter jurisdiction, failure to state a claim, or failure to join a party can be brought up by the defendant at any time, even after all the pleadings have been filed. The other defenses must be raised in an answer or motion or they are waived.

If the defendant makes a motion to dismiss, she must do so before filing an answer and within the time permitted to answer (20 days after service of the complaint). Whether these defenses are raised by motion or by the answer, if a party so requests the court will usually hold a hearing prior to trial to determine the validity of the defense. If the motion to dismiss is denied, the court will generally require that the defendant file an answer within 10 days. An alternative method of challenging service of the complaint or personal jurisdiction is the motion to quash service of summons.

Another response to a complaint that is allowed in federal court is the *motion for a* **more definite statement.** If the complaint (or cross-claim, counterclaim, or third-party complaint) is so vague or ambiguous that the opposing party cannot reasonably be required to frame a responsive pleading, that party may petition the court to order the claimant to revise the pleading.

demurrer

A legal pleading that says, in effect, "even if, for the sake of argument, the facts presented by the other side are correct, those facts do not give the other side a legal argument that can possibly stand up in court." The demurrer has been replaced in many courts by a motion to dismiss.

motion to dismiss

A request that the court dismiss or strike the case.

more definite statement (motion)

A request that the judge require an opponent in a lawsuit to file a less vague or less ambiguous pleading.

In some state jurisdictions another type of pleading, known as a *demurrer,* is used to challenge the legal sufficiency of the complaint. The grounds for a demurrer are similar to those for a motion to dismiss the case. When a demurrer is filed, the court usually holds a hearing to determine the issues that have been raised. If the demurrer is sustained, either the case is dismissed or the plaintiff is given the opportunity to amend the complaint. If the demurrer is overruled, the defendant is given a short time in which to file an answer.

Failure to Answer

If a party fails to answer a pleading to which a response is required (that is, the defendant fails to answer the complaint, or the plaintiff fails to reply to a counterclaim), then a judgment by default may follow. In most jurisdictions, including federal court, obtaining a judgment is a two-step process. First, the plaintiff or the plaintiff's attorney files with the court an **affidavit**—a statement under penalty of perjury, sworn to before a notary—verifying that the opposing party has defaulted (not responded) and requesting that the clerk enter that party's default. Entry of default is not the same as a default judgment. **Entry of default** means that the failure to respond had been noted in the court's file. See Exhibit 6–13 for an example of the request to enter default and accompanying affidavit. After the default has been entered, then the claimant can apply for a default judgment.

To obtain a default judgment, the plaintiff must prove the claim. This can be done at a brief court hearing where evidence is presented to a judge. In lieu of a court hearing, many jurisdictions allow the plaintiff to submit affidavits to substantiate the claim. The laws of the jurisdiction determine the exact procedure that is followed, although generally a default judgment cannot be obtained if the defendant is a minor, incompetent, or in the military service. In federal court, the plaintiff may also request a hearing before a jury to determine the amount of damages.

affidavit
A written statement sworn to before a person officially permitted by law to administer an oath.

entry of default
Action by a court clerk noting that the defendant has failed to file a proper response to the complaint.

Setting Aside Defaults

Courts usually permit parties against whom a default judgment was entered to petition the court to set it aside by making a motion to set aside the default judgment. The most common grounds for making and granting such a motion are that the judgment was entered through mistake, inadvertence, surprise, or excusable neglect. This type of motion must usually be made within certain time limits after the judgment was obtained. For example, Rule 60 of the Federal Rules of Civil Procedure provides that the motion must be made within a reasonable time of the judgment having been rendered (but not to exceed one year). Default judgments can also be set aside, without a motion, if the plaintiff will stipulate or agree to do so.

**UNITED STATES DISTRICT COURT
FOR THE NORTHERN DISTRICT OF CALIFORNIA**

GORDON SHEFFIELD and AMY SHEFFIELD,) Plaintiffs,)	Civil No. 12345
)	AFFIDAVIT AND REQUEST
)	
)	TO ENTER DEFAULT
vs.)	
)	
WESLEY LINSTROM and LINDA GRANGER,) Defendants.)	

State of California

County of San Francisco

I, Terry Alvarez, being duly sworn say:

1. I am the attorney for plaintiffs in the above action.

2. A copy of the summons and complaint was served on defendant on May 15, _____, and the return of service of John Smith, United States Marshal, is on file in this action.

3. Defendant, Wesley Linstrom, has not answered or otherwise appeared in this action, and the time within which defendant may appear has expired.

TERRY ALVAREZ
ALVAREZ & COE
100 Market Street
San Francisco, California 94101
(415) 555-1212
Attorney for Plaintiffs

Subscribed and sworn to before me on June 20, _____

Request to Clerk to enter Default

To: Clerk

    Defendant, Wesley Linstrom, having failed to answer or otherwise appear in the above-entitled action, and the time for appearance having expired, you are requested to center his default pursuant to Rule 55(a) of the Federal Rules of Civil Procedures.

Dated June 20, _____

TERRY ALVAREZ
Attorney for Plaintiffs
100 Market Street
San Francisco, California 94101

EXHIBIT 6–13   Affidavit in support of entry of default

FINDING IT ON THE INTERNET

The *Granger* case described in the case commentary at the beginning of this chapter deals with an area of litigation known as personal injury litigation. To find out more about personal injury law, read information on the following sites: **<http://www.personal-injury-law.com/>**, and **<http://www. law.com/>**.

a. Read and summarize one article on personal injury litigation found on each of the sites listed above.

b. In the *Granger* case, one area of concern might be the value of the Granger van, especially if it suffered extensive damage. The popular Kelley Blue Book for determining vehicle value is on line at **<http://www.kbb.com>**. Assume that the Granger van is a 2002 Dodge Van (Ram Van 2500) with a V8, 5.2-liter engine, automatic transmission, power steering, AM-FM stereo, and dual air bags. The van has 50,000 miles. Access the Kelley Blue Book site and determine the retail and wholesale values of the van in your zip code area.

Summary

■ Defendants must respond to the initial pleading within certain time limitations. These time limitations are controlled by the laws of the jurisdiction in which the matter is pending. In federal court, the defendant generally has 20 days from the date of service of the complaint in which to respond. Time limitations in which to respond can be enlarged or extended, either by stipulation or agreement of the parties or by obtaining a court order. In some jurisdictions a stipulation to extend the time must be approved by the court.

■ An answer is a pleading that challenges the plaintiff's claim for relief. An answer can consist of either a general denial, a qualified denial, or a specific denial. A general denial contests all of the allegations contained in the complaint. In some jurisdictions a general denial cannot be used if the complaint has been verified. A qualified denial specifically admits or denies certain allegations, then denies everything else. A specific denial contains specific responses to each allegation contained in the complaint. An answer might also contain affirmative defenses. Affirmative defenses are facts or circumstances that operate to defeat the plaintiff's claim even if all of the contentions of the complaint are proven. Affirmative defenses are often matters of substantive law and therefore vary according to the nature of the case.

■ An answer is a pleading and as such follows the same general format as the complaint or petition in the case. It contains a caption that states the name and address of the attorney for the defendant, the title of the court and the case, the docket number, and the title of the document (answer). The body of the answer contains numbered paragraphs in which the defendant responds to the allegations of the complaint, followed by affirmative defenses, if they exist. The answer concludes with a prayer and the signature and address of the attorney filing the document. The answer is served on the plaintiff or her attorney and filed in court. Service can be accomplished by mailing a copy of the answer to the attorney, or to the plaintiff if unrepresented. An answer can usually be amended. In federal court a party may amend an answer any time within 20 days after it is served, as long as the case has not been placed on the trial calendar. After 20 days (or if the case is set for trial), court permission or a stipulation is required.

■ The defendant in any action has the right to make a claim for relief. In general she may make any claim that she has against the plaintiff whether it is related to the claim stated in the complaint or not. She may make a claim against a codefendant or a third person (not a party to the original action) if the claim stems from the circumstance or transaction described in the complaint. The names of the documents in which defendants assert their claim may differ from one jurisdiction to another. In federal court, a claim against the plaintiff is known as a counterclaim. A claim against a codefendant is known as a cross-claim, and a claim against a third person is known as a third-party complaint.

■ In addition to being contested on the factual allegations, lawsuits can be challenged on technical legal grounds (such as lack of jurisdiction, expiration of the statute of limitations, or insufficiency of service of process). Legal challenges are often raised in some manner other than the answer. In federal court, even though legal challenges can be asserted in an answer, a motion to dismiss the action or a motion to quash service of summons can be an alternative. A motion for a more definite statement is also a possible response when the complaint is so vague or ambiguous that the opposing party cannot reasonably respond. Some jurisdictions have a pleading known as a demurrer that also operates to challenge the complaint on technical legal grounds.

■ If a party fails to answer the complaint, the plaintiff can request that the defendant's default be entered in the court record and that a default judgment be granted in the plaintiff's favor. A court hearing may be required before the court will grant a judgment.

Key Terms

affidavit	demurrer	open stipulation
affirmative defense	entry of default	permissive counterclaim
compulsory counterclaim	general denial	qualified denial
contribution	indemnification	reply
counterclaim	more definite statement	specific denial
cross-claim	motion to dismiss	third-party complaint

Review Questions

1. What kinds of responses can the defendant make to the initial pleading?
2. What time limitations apply to these responses? Can these time limitations be changed? If so, how?
3. What is the difference between a general denial, a qualified denial, and a specific denial?
4. What is an affirmative defense, and why is it important?
5. What is the general format of an answer?
6. What is the procedure for serving and filing an answer?
7. How are responsive pleadings amended?
8. What are counterclaims, cross-claims, and third-party complaints?

9. What are the different ways in which a defendant can challenge legal deficiencies with the initial pleading or process?

10. What happens if the defendant fails to file a timely response to the initial pleading?

Chapter Exercises

Where necessary, check with your instructor prior to starting any of these exercises.

1. Review the laws of your state. How much time does a defendant have to respond to the initial pleading? Must a stipulation to enlarge or extend that time be approved by the court?

2. Review the laws of your state that deal with responses to the initial pleading. What responsive pleadings are allowed? What responsive motions are permitted?

3. Review the commentary at the beginning of this chapter. If the action were filed in your state court, and Granger were to file a claim against Linstrom, the Sheffields, and Brakefast, Inc., how would she do so?

4. Use a legal dictionary to define and/or explain the various affirmative defenses listed in this chapter.

5. Review the case commentary and the Complaint for Fraud, Negligent Misrepresentation, and Breach of Fiduciary Duty found in Chapter 5. Which, if any, of the affirmative defenses mentioned in Chapter 6 might apply? Explain your answer. Do the same for the case commentaries found at the beginning of Chapter 3 and Chapter 4.

6. Make a copy of the summons found in Exhibit 6–12. Fill out the summons based on the complaint found in Exhibit 6–11.

Chapter Project

Review the complaint found in Chapter 5 (Exhibit 5–5). Assume that your law firm represents May Forrester and that you have been requested to draft an answer and cross-claim on her behalf. You have been given the following facts: May Forrester was indeed a real estate agent working for Hearth & Home and did make a sales presentation to the Hendricktses. Prior to the sales presentation, she was given facts and photos regarding the property by one of her employers, Harry Rice. Rice told her that he had visited the property and had taken the photographs himself. During the sales presentation, she only repeated what she had been told. Furthermore, she had worked for Home & Hearth Real Estate for three years and had no reason to doubt her employer. Draft an appropriate answer and cross-claim.

The *Bennett* Case
Assignment 6: Responding to Defense Requests

Assume that your office was contacted by the counsel who was recently retained to represent defendant Rikards-Hayley. The answer is due to be filed in four days and they need more time to prepare their response. They would also like to enter into an agreement that all further papers can be served either by e-mail or by fax. Your supervising attorney has agreed to give the defense a 20-day extension for the answer. The attorney is also agreeable to electronic service of documents so long as the defense also agrees to that. You are to draft a proposed stipulation addressing these two matters.

Chapter 7

Motion Practice

CHAPTER OUTLINE

Motions Generally
Preparing, Serving, and Responding
Court Procedures Involving Motions
Specific Motions
Preliminary Injunctions and Temporary Restraining Orders

COMMENTARY—THE OVERLAND CASE

Your firm has just been retained by Overland Corporation, a farm machinery manufacturer, to represent it in a lawsuit. A complaint, naming Overland Corporation as defendant, was filed in federal court in the state of Nebraska. The complaint bases federal court jurisdiction on diversity of citizenship, alleging that plaintiff is a citizen of Nebraska and that defendant, Overland Corporation, is a resident of Delaware. The president of Overland Corporation, however, states that although Overland is incorporated in Delaware, it has its headquarters and conducts most of its business in Nebraska. Your supervising attorney has told you that because a corporation is a citizen both of the state of incorporation and the state where the principal place of business is located, she believes that diversity does not exist and that, therefore, the federal court does not have subject matter jurisdiction. She has asked you to draft a motion to dismiss the action on that basis.

OBJECTIVES

Chapter 6 introduced the various responses to initial pleadings. Some of those responses are presented to the court in the form of a motion. After completing this chapter, you should be able to:

- Define a motion.
- Explain the procedure for making a motion.
- Explain the procedure for opposing a motion.
- Define the term *affidavit*.
- Explain the role of the paralegal in setting motions for hearing.
- Explain the method for obtaining orders after hearings on the motion.
- Define the term *sanctions* and explain their use in motion practice.
- Identify some common pretrial motions.
- Explain the procedure for making motions during trial.
- Identify some common posttrial motions.
- Explain the procedures for obtaining preliminary injunctions and temporary restraining orders.

Motions Generally

During the course of litigation, questions or problems regarding the case inevitably arise. Sometimes these questions or problems involve practical, procedural issues. For example, in the case mentioned in the commentary to this chapter, the attorney representing Overland might not be able to adequately research the law and prepare responsive documents within 20 days of serving the client. As explained in Chapter 6, this problem is easy to solve. The attorney asks for and usually receives more time than the law normally allows. Other times these problems involve more complicated and substantial legal issues. For example, in the *Overland* case, the defense attorney believes that diversity of jurisdiction is lacking and that, therefore, the federal court is not the proper forum for the case. This issue is more complicated, and the parties may have a substantial disagreement regarding the facts and the law. Consequently, the defense attorney is less likely to get the plaintiff's attorney to agree to dismiss the case. If the attorneys cannot resolve the problems by themselves, a court order is required to settle the issue. The application for such a court order is a motion. Motions can relate to procedural problems with a case, such as motions for an extension of time in which to respond to a complaint. However, motions can also relate to more substantial evidentiary issues in the case, such as motions for summary judgment (described later in the chapter). The court orders that result from these motions may actually dispose of the entire case. For example, if a motion for summary judgment is granted, judgment is entered in favor of one party without further court proceedings, and the action in the trial court will end.

Except for motions made during the trial, motions are required to be written, filed in court, and served on the opposing attorneys (or parties, if not represented). If the motion is contested, the opposing attorneys will also file papers opposing the motion. Often the written documents are followed by a brief court hearing before the judge rules on the motion. Although they are not considered to be pleadings, in appearance motions do resemble pleadings. The documents filed in a motion follow the same formalities required of pleadings, and contain the same caption as the pleadings. As a paralegal, you might be asked to research the law governing the particular motion involved or prepare the written documents that are filed in court. You might also be requested to contact the court to set the motion for a hearing.

Preparing, Serving, and Responding

Many different types of motions are possible. Some motions are individually described by statute. These statutes explain the specific procedures and time limits for making such motions. Other motions may be only briefly described, if at all. Regardless of any special procedures that may apply to some motions, certain procedures are common to all motions.

Preparation of the Written Papers

The party making the motion, known as the **movant** or *moving party,* begins by preparing written papers for service and filing. These papers follow the same general format as pleadings. The written papers filed in making a motion usually include different documents: the motion, the notice of hearing on the motion, affidavits in support of the motion, and a memorandum of points and authorities in support of the motion. In motion practice, the term *motion* is used in two different contexts. On one hand, it

movant
Person who makes a motion.

UNITED STATES DISTRICT COURT
DISTRICT OF NEBRASKA

JOHN JONES,   )
    Plaintiff,   )
)   Civil No. 12356
)
    vs.   )   Motion to Dismiss
)
)
OVERLAND CORPORATION,   )
    Defendant.   )
)

    OVERLAND CORPORATION, by PAT RIVAS, Its attorney, moves the court to dismiss the complaint on file on the following grounds: the complaint in this action alleges that this action is filled in federal court because it involves a dispute between citizens of different states; however, the court lacks subject matter jurisdiction as alleged in the complaint, in that plaintiff and defendant are citizens of the same state, as is more clearly stated in the affidavit of Owen Young, hereto annexed as Exhibit A.

A Memorandum of Points and Authorities in support of this motion is served and filed with this motion.

Dated August 1, _____

                                      _____
                                      PAT RIVAS
                                      Attorney for Defendant
                                      769 Maine Street
                                      Omaha, Nebraska 68101
                                      (402) 555-1212

EXHIBIT 7–1   Motion to dismiss

---

refers to the whole process of making a request for an order from the court. On the other hand, it is used to refer to one of the documents filed in support of that request.

    The document entitled "motion" describes the nature of the motion, the grounds for the motion, and the relief requested. The content of the motion will obviously depend on the type of motion being made and will be specifically drafted for that purpose. A motion made on behalf of Overland Corporation to dismiss the complaint filed against it might look as shown in Exhibit 7–1.

    The **notice of hearing on the motion** is a simple paper stating when and where the court hearing on the motion will take place. It might look as shown in Exhibit 7–2.

    In many courts the motion and the notice of hearing on the motion can be combined into one document.

notice of hearing on the motion

The part of a written motion that describes the nature of the motion being made and tells when and where a hearing on the motion will occur.

UNITED STATES DISTRICT COURT
DISTRICT OF NEBRASKA

JOHN JONES,   )
    Plaintiff,   )
)   Civil No. 12356
)
   vs.   )   Notice of Motion
)
)
OVERLAND CORPORATION,)
    Defendant.   )
)

To: Lane Borman, Attorney for Plaintiff,

Please take notice, that the undersigned will bring the above motion on for hearing before this Court at Room _____, United States Court House, _____, City of Omaha on the _____ day of _____, at 10 o'clock A.M. of that day or as soon thereafter as counsel can be heard.

                         _____

                         PAT RIVAS
                         Attorney for Defendant
                         769 Maine Street
                         Omaha, Nebraska 68101
                         (402) 555-1212

EXHIBIT 7–2 Notice of motion

Although not always required, motions are commonly supported by affidavits. An affidavit is a statement, under penalty of perjury, sworn to before a notary or other person authorized to administer an oath. An affidavit usually describes the factual basis for making the motion and is made by the person having personal knowledge of those facts. It can be the statement of the attorney, a party, or a third person. Even though it may be the statement of a party or a witness, the attorney or paralegal will normally prepare the document based on what the individual has told them. An affidavit serves the same purpose as testimony from a party or witness and is used in lieu of that testimony. As such, an affidavit should be written in the first person and should contain detailed facts. An affidavit in support of the motion described in the commentary might look as shown in Exhibit 7–3.

In some courts, a **declaration** is used in lieu of an affidavit. Like the affidavit, a declaration is a statement under penalty of perjury, but it is not sworn to before a notary.

In drafting an affidavit or declaration, the following general format should be followed:

declaration

A statement under penalty of perjury that certain facts are true or believed to be true.

UNITED STATES DISTRICT COURT
DISTRICT OF NEBRASKA

JOHN JONES, Plaintiff,	))) Civil No. 12356)
vs.	)) Affidavit of Owen) Young in Support of) Motion to Dismiss
OVERLAND CORPORATION, Defendant.	)))

I, Owen Young, being first duly sworn, depose and say:

1. I am the president of OVERLAND CORPORATION, the defendant in this action, and am acquainted with the facts in this case, and have personal knowledge of the matter set forth in this affidavit.

2. I make this affidavit in support of the motion to dismiss the action.

3. I held the office of president of OVERLAND CORPORATION at all times mentioned in the complaint filed in this action.

4. At all times mentioned in the complaint, OVERLAND CORPORATION has been incorporated under the laws of the state of Delaware:

5. At all times mentioned in the complaint, OVERLAND CORPORATION has had its principal place of business in the state of Nebraska. The corporation maintains four sales offices throughout the state of Nebraska, maintain its primary bank account in the the state of Nebraska, and keeps copies of all corporate records within the state of Nebraska. Business conducted within the state of Nebraska accounts for more than 75% of the total income of said corporation.

_____
Owen Young

Subscribed and sworn to before me on _____, _____

_____

EXHIBIT 7–3 Affidavit in support of motion

1. The affidavit or declaration is usually, although not always, written in the first person. Even though it may be signed by a party or a witness it is written by the attorney or paralegal.

2. The first paragraphs should describe the affiant (person making the affidavit) or declarant and describe the person's relationship to the case. For example, is the

affiant the plaintiff, an employee of the plaintiff, or does the affiant have some other relationship to the case?

3. The affiant should state whether the affidavit is made in support of or in opposition to the motion and describe the general nature of the motion.

4. The affiant then states the facts supporting of or opposing the motion. This may be done in several short paragraphs. If not obvious from the facts, the affiant should include a brief statement that he or she knows the facts to be true based on his or her own knowledge.

Along with a supporting affidavit, most attorneys also support a motion with a **memorandum of points and authorities.** In some courts this is required. A memorandum of points and authorities is a legal argument in the form of a discussion or analysis of the law (statutes, cases, or constitutional provisions) that applies to the case. If you are asked to help prepare a memorandum of points and authorities, you will have to research the law that governs the case. Some courts also require that the moving party submit a proposed order for the court to sign at the hearing.

Although the general requirements for motion practice are found in the Federal Rules of Civil Procedure or appropriate state laws, the area of motion practice is often the subject of local rules of court, in both federal and state courts. Before preparing any motion, it is imperative that you review all of the laws regulating motion practice in the particular court in which the action is filed.

Service and Filing

The motion and supporting papers must be filed with the court and copies served on the other parties to the action. Service of motions is similar to service of an answer (by mail, electronically if consented to, or personally). Some jurisdictions also require that a separate copy of all papers be sent directly to the judge hearing the motion. This is referred to as a "chambers copy." All jurisdictions impose time limitations on the service of motions. Under the Federal Rules of Civil Procedure, unless changed by a specific statute or court order, the written motion and notice of hearing must be served not later than five days before the time set for the hearing. Rule 6 provides that whenever a time proscribed is less than 11 days, Saturdays, Sundays, and holidays are not counted in computing the time. This time period can be changed by court order or by local court rule. In fact, the five-day time requirement has been extended by many courts. You must be careful to check local rules of court regarding this time limit. State courts may have different time requirements, and even some federal courts have local rules that have changed this notice requirement. The most common method of serving motions is by mail. When service is by mail, by fax, or by e-mail, Rule 6(e) requires that you add three days to the time limit if any response is required. In other words, if the five-day time applied, you would have to mail the moving papers at least eight days before the hearing. (This is because the responding party will be filing responsive papers to the motion.)

Should a situation arise making it impossible or impractical to comply with the time requirement imposed by statute or local rule, the courts allow the moving party to request that the time be shortened. In a sense, this request is in itself a motion. Courts generally treat this as an **ex parte** motion, meaning that no prior notice need be given

memorandum of points and authorities

A legal argument in the form of a discussion or analysis of the law that applies to the case.

ex parte

With only one side present.

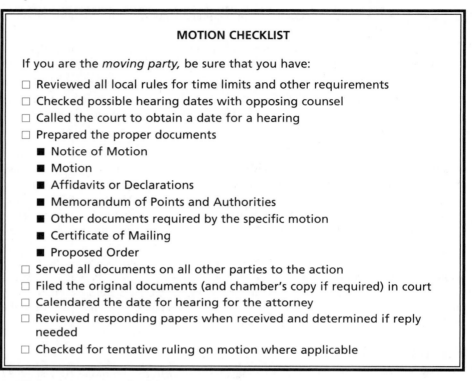

MOTION CHECKLIST

If you are the *moving party,* be sure that you have:

☐ Reviewed all local rules for time limits and other requirements
☐ Checked possible hearing dates with opposing counsel
☐ Called the court to obtain a date for a hearing
☐ Prepared the proper documents
  ■ Notice of Motion
  ■ Motion
  ■ Affidavits or Declarations
  ■ Memorandum of Points and Authorities
  ■ Other documents required by the specific motion
  ■ Certificate of Mailing
  ■ Proposed Order
☐ Served all documents on all other parties to the action
☐ Filed the original documents (and chamber's copy if required) in court
☐ Calendared the date for hearing for the attorney
☐ Reviewed responding papers when received and determined if reply needed
☐ Checked for tentative ruling on motion where applicable

EXHIBIT 7–4 Motion checklist: moving party

order shortening time

A ruling from the court, often in connection with motions, allowing a moving party to give less notice of a hearing on a motion than is required by statute.

proof of service by mail (certificate of mailing)

Verification that a pleading, motion, or other document has been served by mailing a copy of the document to another party or attorney.

nor any court hearing scheduled. If the court grants this request, it is often referred to as an **order shortening time.** The order shortening time is then served on the opposing party with the notice of hearing on the motion and the other moving papers. Service of a motion is usually accomplished by mailing copies of the moving papers to the opposing attorneys. Proof of service of the moving papers is in the form of an affidavit or declaration by the person mailing the papers and is sometimes known as a **proof of service by mail** or **certificate of mailing.** If electronic service is made, the certificate should indicate how service was conducted. See the checklist in Exhibit 7–4.

Responding to Motions

To oppose a motion, an attorney commonly serves and files papers in opposition. These usually consist of affidavits in opposition to the motion and a memorandum of points and authorities in opposition to the motion. These affidavits and the memorandum have the same technical requirements as do the moving papers. For most motions in federal court, opposing affidavits must be served not later than one day before the hearing. You must also consult local rules to determine how many copies should be filed and if a proposed order is required. Refer to the checklist in Exhibit 7–5. Again, the time limit will vary depending on the state or local rules. As a litigation paralegal, you might be involved in drafting these documents for the attorney's review. In some courts, the moving party is given the opportunity to reply in writing to the opposing papers.

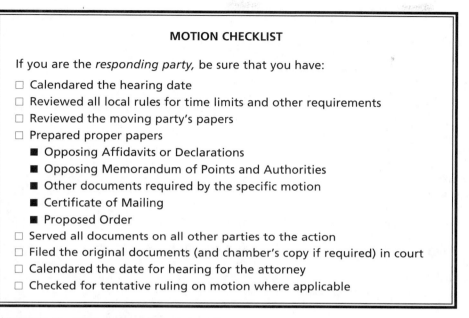

MOTION CHECKLIST

If you are the *responding party,* be sure that you have:

☐ Calendared the hearing date
☐ Reviewed all local rules for time limits and other requirements
☐ Reviewed the moving party's papers
☐ Prepared proper papers
  ■ Opposing Affidavits or Declarations
  ■ Opposing Memorandum of Points and Authorities
  ■ Other documents required by the specific motion
  ■ Certificate of Mailing
  ■ Proposed Order
☐ Served all documents on all other parties to the action
☐ Filed the original documents (and chamber's copy if required) in court
☐ Calendared the date for hearing for the attorney
☐ Checked for tentative ruling on motion where applicable

EXHIBIT 7–5 Motion checklist: responding party

Court Procedures Involving Motions

In addition to written documents, motions often involve court hearings. The attorneys for the moving and responding parties appear before a judge and present oral arguments in support of or in opposition to the motion. The judge considers the written documents and the oral arguments and then makes a decision. After the judge rules on the motion, a written order, reflecting that ruling, must be submitted to the judge for signature.

Hearings

Because a hearing on the motion is a court appearance, it must be handled by the attorney. However, as a litigation paralegal, you might have some responsibilities in scheduling the hearing. Different courts have different methods of scheduling motion hearings. In some courts motions are heard at set times and in set departments (sometimes referred to as "law and motion"). In other courts you might have to specifically arrange a time with the judge hearing the motion. This is done through the judge's clerk. In any event, scheduling the motion will probably require that you call the court, talk to the clerk handling the motion calendar, and arrange for a convenient date. Be sure to check your attorney's calendar for conflicts. It is also advisable to call the opposing attorneys prior to doing this to schedule the hearing at a time that is convenient for all parties. This eliminates the need for continuing the hearing date. When setting a motion for hearing, be sure that you allow sufficient time for service of the moving papers. In state courts you may have to give more than five days notice. Be sure

THE COMPUTERIZED LAW FIRM
Intranet and Form Files

SCENARIO

You are in the process of preparing a draft of a motion to dismiss in the Overland case, as requested by your attorney. In talking to another paralegal in the firm, you are told that she prepared and filed a similar motion in another case just recently. She looks at your case, and tells you that except for the names, case number, and dates your motion will be identical. Unfortunately, she does not have a hard copy of the papers. Furthermore, you work in a large law firm that has offices in several cities across the United States and, when she prepared the motion, the other paralegal was not working in your local office, although she was working for the same law firm.

PROBLEM

The documents you must draft are substantially similar to documents previously drafted in connection with other cases. Unfortunately, these documents were prepared by paralegals or attorneys working in different branch offices of your law firm. How can you minimize needless repetition?

SOLUTION

Motions often are little more than repetitive forms. Both Word and WordPerfect, the word processing programs described earlier, are excellent form-creation and management tools. With these programs, you can create forms for a new case from existing forms without having to retype everything.

For example, suppose your office filed a motion to dismiss in the case of *Nolan v. Ybara*. Except for the names, dates, and case number, the information contained in the motion is identical to the one you are preparing in the case of *Jones v. Overland Corporation*. If the motion in the *Nolan* case is saved to disk, it can be called up and revised. By using the "search" and "replace" functions, necessary changes can be easily made. (When you do change names, be careful that you also make any changes in pronouns or verb agreements affected by the change. For example, if you are changing "Mary Nolan" to "Overland Corporation," be sure to change "she" or "her" to "it" or "its" and always proofread the entire document!)

Today, you are not limited to looking for forms that you, personally, have prepared. Many law firms have created intranets for their firms. An intranet is a limited, highly secure type of internet, accessible only by certain users. An intranet can serve all members of a certain law firm, even those physically located in different regions of the country. If the firm has an intranet, a form file can be maintained on it. You can search the form file for the type of motion or other document you are preparing. Searching on an intranet is similar to searching the Internet. Thus, not only can you be saved from repeating work you have personally done, but you can also be saved from repeating work anyone in your firm has done.

you have checked this. Also be sure to check state rules regarding service by mail. State rules may require that time be added if the papers are served by mail, fax, or e-mail.

In lieu of court hearings on motions, some courts today are using telephone conference calls between the judge and the various attorneys. This can save substantial time. Local rules of court control this procedure.

Tentative Rulings

In many courts, all moving and responding papers must be filed several days before the scheduled hearing. This gives the judge the opportunity to review the papers and consider the merits of the motion. Many judges feel that the brief oral arguments that take place at the hearing are no more than a repetition of information already in the doc-

---

UNITED STATES DISTRICT COURT
DISTRICT OF NEBRASKA

JOHN JONES,   )
    Plaintiff,   )
)   Civil No. 12356
)
    vs.   )   Order
)
)
OVERLAND CORPORATION,   )
    Defendant.   )
)

    This action was heard on _____, on the motion of defendant, OVERLAND CORPORATION, for an order dismissing this action. Pat Rivas appeared as counsel for defendant, in support of the motion, and Lane Borman appeared as counsel for plaintiff in opposition thereto. It appears to the court that defendant is a citizen of the same state as plaintiff and that therefore this court lacks subject matter jurisdiction. Therefore,

    IT IS ORDERED that the complaint filed herein on _____, _____, be and it is hereby dismissed.

Dated _____

                                    _____
                                    Judge, District Court

EXHIBIT 7–6   Order after motion

uments. In an effort to save court time and avoid unnecessary hearings, some courts have adopted the practice of making a tentative ruling prior to the date of the hearing, usually a day or two prior to the hearing. Attorneys (or their paralegals) can then call the court and discover how the judge intends to rule on the motion. In some cases, this information is posted on the Internet. If the attorneys insist, they are still entitled to appear at the scheduled hearing.

Orders after Motions

After the motion is heard, the judge will make a ruling, which is called an **order.** Most courts require that the prevailing party prepare the written order for the judge's signature. As a litigation paralegal, you might be asked to do this. Some courts have local rules that require the moving party to submit a proposed order with the moving papers. Sometimes a judge's ruling on a case is not a simple grant or denial of the motion. At times orders become very involved. If you are asked to prepare an order after a hearing, be sure that you know exactly what must be included in the order. The attorney may give you her notes from the hearing, or may simply tell you what to include in the order. In either case, be sure that you understand the notes or directions before drafting the order. Exhibit 7–6 shows an example of an order.

order

A written command or direction given by a judge.

Sanctions

All courts expect that motions will be made or opposed in good faith. To prevent unnecessary or frivolous motions, courts generally have the power to punish an attorney who files such a motion. Courts also have the power to punish attorneys whose improper or unreasonable conduct causes the other side to make a motion. This punishment usually is in the form of an award of attorney fees to the opposing side. In some cases, if the court finds the behavior particularly unreasonable or unjustified, the court may find a party or attorney in contempt of court. Furthermore, if a party fails to comply with an order issued after a motion, the court may impose additional sanctions. In some extreme cases the court may even strike the pleadings of one who fails to comply with a court order, making it possible for the other side to win without trial. Should the court grant an order disposing of the case, that order would be immediately appealable.

Specific Motions

As mentioned earlier, there are many different kinds of motions, some of which are described in code sections, some of which are not. The more common motions mentioned in the Federal Rules of Civil Procedure and seen in many state jurisdictions are described here.

Pretrial Motions

Motions can be made at any time during the litigation process. Consequently, they deal with all aspects of litigation. Pretrial motions deal with issues or problems that arise before the trial occurs. Most often, these motions deal with requests that are ancillary to the primary relief requested in the complaint. These requests or motions often relate to the pleadings, the jurisdiction and venue of the court, and the discovery process. However, some pretrial motions deal with substantive issues that may affect the very right to trial.

Motion to Dismiss   A motion to dismiss the action is a request that the court terminate the lawsuit immediately, without a hearing on the merits of the plaintiff's claim. A motion to dismiss is often made in lieu of an answer, and if granted eliminates the need for an answer. Such a motion can be made for several reasons. In federal proceedings, a motion to dismiss the case is proper when the court lacks subject matter or personal jurisdiction, when venue is improper, when process (the summons) or service of process is insufficient, when the complaint fails to state a claim upon which relief can be granted, or when a necessary party has not been joined (Rule 12 of the federal rules).

motion for more definite statement

A motion made in response to a complaint in which the defendant challenges the clarity or specificity of the complaint.

Motion for a More Definite Statement   If a complaint (or other claim for relief) is so vague and ambiguous that it cannot be understood and responded to, the party required to respond may make a **motion for a more definite statement.** Such a motion is intended to require the claimant to clarify the allegations and make them more intelligible. The moving party is expected to point out the defects in the complaint and explain what details must be added to the claim. (Rule 12[e] of the federal rules).

Motion to Strike   A **motion to strike** is a request that the court delete portions of a pleading that are insufficient, redundant, immaterial, or scandalous (Rule 12[f] of the federal rules).

Motion to Amend   As discussed in previous chapters, all pleadings can be amended. Under some circumstances, pleadings can be amended as a matter of right without the necessity of a court order. If a court order is required, the party wishing to amend a pleading must make a **motion to amend.** The courts are very liberal in allowing parties to amend pleadings and will probably grant such a motion unless the amended pleading would unfairly prejudice the other party (Rule 15 of the federal rules).

Motion for Judgment on the Pleadings   After all pleadings have been filed in an action, any party may make a **motion for judgment on the pleadings.** The moving party in such a motion claims that the allegations in the pleadings are such that no controverted issues remain and judgment can be entered for only one party. For example, if the defendant were to admit all of the allegations in the complaint, no disputed issue would remain. The pleadings themselves indicate that the plaintiff is entitled to judgment (Rule 12[c] of the federal rules).

Motion for Change of Venue   If an action is commenced in the wrong judicial district, a party can request that the court transfer the case to a proper court by making a **motion for change of venue.** Furthermore, in cases where venue is proper in more than one district, a party can request a change of venue to another proper district for the convenience of parties and witnesses or in the interest of justice (28 U.S.C. § 1404).

Motion to Quash Return of Service   If the defendant claims that he was improperly served with the summons and complaint, he can make a **motion to quash the return of the service** (or motion to quash service of summons). A defendant is improperly served if the manner of service is not in accordance with the appropriate statute or if the defendant is not subject to the personal jurisdiction of the court. When such a motion is granted, service is negated. If the defect in service was in the manner of service, the defendant can be served again. However, if the court does not have personal jurisdiction over the defendant, the action cannot proceed in that court. If the plaintiff wants to pursue the case, he will have to begin the process again, this time in a court that does have personal jurisdiction over the defendant (Rules 4 and 12 of the federal rules).

Discovery Motions   An essential part of the litigation process is discovery, a legal process by which parties of the lawsuit are able to discover facts relevant to the case. Much of discovery involves requiring the opposing side to reveal relevant facts or provide pertinent documents. Problems often arise regarding exactly what has to be revealed or provided. If one party refuses to provide information to another, the party requesting the information can make a **motion to compel** the requested discovery. If the motion is granted, the court will order the party to comply with the discovery request and impose some sort of penalty or sanctions if the party refuses. If the court finds that the initial refusal to comply with discovery request was unreasonable, it can also impose sanctions for that initial refusal. Sanctions are usually in the form of attorney fees awarded to the moving party. Likewise, if the court finds that the motion to compel was not made in good faith, it can impose sanctions on the moving party. A second type

motion to strike

A request made to the court to delete part or all of a pleading; can also refer to a request made during trial to delete testimony.

motion to amend

A request by one party to the court to allow a change in the content of a pleading.

motion for judgment on the pleadings

A motion claiming that the allegations in the pleadings are such that no controversial issues remain and that judgment can be entered for only one party.

motion for change of venue

A request from a party that the court transfer the case to a proper court.

motion to quash the return of the service

Motion made by a defendant who claims that he was improperly served with the summons and complaint.

motion to compel

A request by one party to the court for an order requiring the other side to comply with a discovery request.

motion for a protective order

A motion made during discovery asking the court to limit a discovery request.

motion for summary judgment

A motion requesting that judgment be entered immediately because there are no disputed factual issues in the case.

of discovery motion is a **motion for a protective order,** which is a request that the court limit the other party's right to discovery (Rule 37 of the federal rules).

Motion for Summary Judgment One of the most important motions in litigation is the **motion for summary judgment.** In a motion for summary judgment, one party is asking the court to order that judgment be entered as a matter of law, without the necessity of trial, because there are no real disputes regarding material facts. When parties file pleadings they sometimes make allegations hoping, and even believing, that they will be able to prove them. However, as the parties prepare for trial, it sometimes becomes evident that problems exist. Before a case goes to trial, parties have the opportunity, either through investigation or formal discovery, to uncover and evaluate the evidence that will be introduced by both sides during trial. At this point, it may appear to one side that the opposition really has no valid admissible evidence to support their contentions. In other words, in spite of what the parties claimed in their pleadings, there is no evidence to support their facts. Since the purpose of trial is to resolve factual disputes, there is no need for trial.

Motions for summary judgment can be made either by plaintiffs or by defendants. For plaintiffs to prevail in such a motion, they must show that the facts supporting each element of their cause of action are undisputed. For defendants to defeat plaintiffs' motions, they must show the court that either there is a dispute regarding a material fact related to the cause of action, or that there are facts that support an affirmative defense. For defendants to make a successful motion for summary judgment, they only need to show that the plaintiff cannot prove any one of the elements of the cause of action, or that the existence of an affirmative defense is undisputed. For example, suppose that in the situation described in the case commentary, that Jones is a manufacturer and distributor of parts that Overland uses in its manufacture of farm machinery. Assume that Jones has sued Overland for $100,000 for parts that were shipped to Overland. Jones claims that no part of the $100,000 was paid. Jones makes a motion for summary judgment, supported by an affidavit and documents, establishing the following:

1. Jones and Overland entered into a written contract wherby Overland was to purchase parts from Jones at agreed prices.
2. Pursuant to a written purchase order, Jones delivered to Overland multiple parts at an agreed price of $100,000.
3. Overland received the parts and signed a receipt for the goods.
4. Overland failed to make any payment toward the $100,000 even though repeated requests have been made.

Jones has thus supported each element of a cause of action for breach of contract with factual evidence. Unless Overland can show that there is a dispute as to a material fact (or that an affirmative defense exists), a motion for summary judgment would be proper. However, suppose that Overland submitted an affidavit stating that it never received the goods. It claims that the signed receipt was for a different order. In such a case, a dispute regarding a material fact exists, and the court would deny the motion for summary judgment.

When making a motion for summary judgment, the parties often present their evidence to the court in the form of an affidavit. This can also be done by submitting depositions, answers to interrogatories, or answers to requests for admissions. (Depositions, interrogatories, and requests for admissions are methods of discovery and are discussed in subsequent chapters.) Along with these documents, the moving party will also submit a memorandum of points and authorities. In most cases, a party opposing a motion for summary judgment will present the court with opposing papers supported by affidavits, depositions, answers to interrogatories, or answers to request for admissions. The opposing party will also file a legal memorandum. All affidavits filed in support of or opposition to a motion for summary judgment must show that the persons making the affidavits are competent to testify to the matters stated within the affidavits, that the matters are within their personal knowledge, and that if they were testifying in court the statements would be admissible as evidence.

In addition to the normal moving papers (notice of motion, motion, affidavits, legal memorandum), many courts require the parties to submit a separate statement detailing the uncontested facts and showing how and where each fact is established (i.e., in an affidavit or in a deposition, including the page and line numbers). Responding parties must then submit a statement of contested facts, again showing their support for claiming that the facts are in dispute. In ruling on a motion for summary judgment, the court scrutinizes the various papers to see if a factual dispute does exist. At this point the court does not weigh the evidence or resolve a factual dispute. If a legitimate and genuine factual dispute exists, the motion must be denied, even if one side has overwhelming evidence.

A motion for summary judgment need not be directed to all of the issues in the case. A party can request a partial summary judgment or a summary judgment on certain issues in the case. For example, in a personal injury case there may be no factual dispute about liability, but a dispute may exist as to the amount of damages to which the plaintiff is entitled. If such a summary judgment is rendered, a trial is held to decide the remaining issues.

In making a motion for summary judgment, you must be careful to check the appropriate statute for time requirements. There are generally limits on how soon after commencement of the action that this type of motion can be made. Notice requirements for such a motion may differ from other motions. For example, under the Federal Rules of Civil Procedure, a motion for summary judgment must be served at least 10 days prior to the time fixed for hearing, rather than the five days required for other motions (Rules 56 of the federal rules). It is also very important to check local rules regarding summary judgment motions.

Motion for Sanctions The Federal Rules of Civil Procedure require attorneys to not file documents in court that are frivolous or that contain contentions or allegations that are not supported by the evidence. If an attorney violates this rule, the opposing side has a right to make a **motion for sanctions,** which is a request for penalties for violating the provisions of Rule 11 of the federal rules. The court can also act on its own initiative. The sanctions can include an order to pay a penalty to the court or an order to pay the other side's reasonable attorney fees and costs incurred because of the violation. The court can also impose nonmonetary sanctions, such as striking pleadings. Although similar sanctions can be imposed as a result of discovery violations, this section does not apply to discovery motions (Rule 11 of the federal rules).

motion for sanctions

A request to the court from one party that penalties be imposed on the other party for violating the provisions of Rule 11 of the Federal Rules of Civil Procedure.

Trial Motions

At the beginning of a trial, before any evidence is introduced, attorneys sometimes need to resolve questions or issues regarding matters of trial procedure. These often involve questions regarding the admissibility of certain kinds of evidence. For example, in a wrongful death case, the defendant may anticipate that the plaintiff's attorney will try to introduce photographs of the decedent that are graphic and inflammatory. The defendant might feel that these photos are too prejudicial and should be excluded from evidence. The defense attorney would therefore request that the court order that the evidence is inadmissible. This type of request or motion is made at the time of trial, but before evidence is actually presented. If it is a jury trial, it is important that these motions not be made in front of the jury. Motions such as this, made at the commencement of trial, are often referred to as **motions in limine.** Because all parties are present in court, no prior notice need be given, nor do the motions have to be in writing (although attorneys sometimes submit a memorandum of points and authorities in support of their position).

motion in limine

A motion or request made of the court, usually at the start of a trial and outside the presence of the jury.

Motions made during the course of the trial itself also differ from pretrial motions. Trial motions are often made in immediate response to testimony or other evidence that is offered in the trial. Obviously, there is no opportunity to prepare written papers. Because all sides are already present in court, no need for prior notice of the motion arises. Sometimes, however, the attorneys do know ahead of time that they are going to make a particular motion. One such motion is a **motion for judgment as a matter of law** under Rule 50 of the Federal Rules of Civil Procedure. This motion, which is made in jury trials, if granted results in the judge entering a judgment without allowing the jury to consider the evidence. The basis for this motion is that the party against whom judgment is entered has not introduced sufficient evidence for a reasonable jury to find in his favor. This motion can be made at any time during the trial as long as the party against whom judgment is sought has fully presented its evidence. In some state courts, a motion for a directed verdict, rather than a motion for judgment as a matter of law, is used. In a motion for a directed verdict, the moving party is asking the judge to tell the jury how it must decide a case. The basis for such a motion is the same as for a motion for judgment as a matter of law. Motions for directed verdicts are usually made at the end of the trial, after all the evidence has been introduced. Although the attorney can make these motions without a written motion or notice, the attorney may want to present the judge with a memorandum of points and authorities to support the motion. As a litigation paralegal, you might be asked to help research the law and prepare such a memorandum.

Posttrial Motions

Motions made after the trial has occurred often are directed at the judgment that the trial court has rendered. However, a posttrial motion may also relate to the assessment of costs against the party who lost the case.

Motion for Judgment as a Matter of Law   As described earlier, a motion for judgment as a matter of law can be made in a jury trial at any time before the case is submitted to the jury. Sometimes judges are reluctant to grant such motions because they feel that the jury should be given the opportunity to decide the case. If the judge does not grant such a motion, it can be renewed by the party after the jury decides the case, should it return an unfavorable verdict. In some state courts, when this motion is made after trial, a **motion for judgment notwithstanding the verdict** is used rather than the motion for judgment as a matter of law (Rule 50 of the federal rules).

Motion for a New Trial   The party who loses in a civil trial has the right to appeal that decision to a higher court. However, the appellate process is lengthy and costly. Prior to any appeal, that party also has the opportunity to request that the trial court itself set aside the verdict or judgment and grant a new trial by making a **motion for a new trial.** Such a request or motion is normally made before the judge who presided over the trial. This motion is proper in both jury trials and court trials (trials in front of a judge only). Grounds for such a motion might include jury impropriety, mistake in law, or newly discovered evidence.

Normally, very strict time limits control when this kind of motion can be made. The Federal Rules of Civil Procedure allows a party 10 days after entry of judgment to serve such a motion. If you are assisting an attorney in preparing this motion, pay close attention to statutory time restraints and be careful that all papers are promptly filed and served (Rule 59 of the federal rules).

Motion to Tax Costs   The prevailing party in a lawsuit is usually entitled to recover his costs in addition to the judgment. Costs include expenses such as filing fees and service fees incurred as part of litigation. The amount of the costs is usually presented to the court in written form when the trial is over (sometimes referred to as a *cost bill*). If the other party challenges any or all of these costs, that party does so by filing a motion with the court, known as a **motion to tax costs.** As in all posttrial motions, timing of the motion is critical (Rule 54 of the federal rules).

Motions for Relief from Judgment or Order   In Chapter 6 we discussed the fact that, under Rule 60 of the Federal Rules of Civil Procedure, a default judgment could be set aside by the court upon a showing that the judgment was entered due to the mistake, inadvertence, surprise, excusable neglect, or fraud of the party or the party's legal representative. Under Rule 60, the court has the power to set aside any judgment, order, or proceeding for the same reason. A request of the court by one party to do this is a **motion for relief from a judgment or order.** Depending on the law of the jurisdiction, additional grounds for the granting of relief may exist. For example, Rule 60 of the Federal Rules of Civil Procedure provides as follows:

> On motion and upon such terms as are just, the court may relieve a party or a party's legal representative from a final judgment, order, or proceeding for the following reasons: (1) mistake, inadvertence, surprise, or excusable neglect; (2) newly discovered evidence which by due diligence could not have been discovered in time to move for a new trial under Rule 59(b); (3) fraud (whether heretofore denominated intrinsic or extrinsic); (4) the judgment is void; (5) the judgment has been satisfied, released, or discharged, or a prior judgment upon which it is based has been reversed or otherwise vacated, or it is no longer equitable that the judgment should have prospective application; or (6) any other reason justifying relief from the operation of the judgment.

motion for judgment notwithstanding the verdict
In a jury trial, a request from one party that the judge decide the case in that party's favor on the basis that no facts have been proven that would support a jury's decision for the other party.

motion for a new trial
A motion made after a trial requesting that the judge set aside the verdict or judgment and grant a new trial to the parties.

motion to tax costs
A motion made after a trial challenging the costs of suit that are claimed by the prevailing party.

motion for relief from judgment or order
A request to the court by one party that the court set aside any judgment, order, or proceeding.

Motions for relief are generally required to be filed within a reasonable time, although the term *reasonable* is not defined. Usually, maximum time limits do exist for the filing of such motions.

In granting or denying a motion for relief, especially on the grounds of mistake or excusable neglect, the court has the right to exercise a great deal of discretion. If you are drafting affidavits for this type of motion, you should be as detailed as possible in explaining the reasons for making the motion.

Preliminary Injunctions and Temporary Restraining Orders

Chapter 5 described temporary restraining orders and preliminary injunctions. These provisional remedies are sometimes granted before trial and are ususally in conjunction with lawsuits that seek permanent injunctions. In federal court, the procedures for obtaining preliminary injunctions and temporary restraining orders are found in Rule 65 of the Federal Rules of Civil Procedure. Various local rules of court also control the procedures. Although these remedies are not normally considered to be motions, the method of obtaining these special equitable remedies is similar to motion practice.

A request for a preliminary injunction closely resembles a formal noticed motion. After a complaint is filed, the party requesting the preliminary injunction files papers in court requesting a preliminary injunction and setting the matter for a court hearing. This request is normally supported by affidavits setting forth the factual basis for the request. In lieu of affidavits, a verified complaint may be used. A memorandum of points and authorities is also usually filed. These papers must be served on the opposing party. A court hearing to determine whether to grant the preliminary injunction then takes place.

A temporary restraining order (TRO), which is granted only when a court finds that some immediate and irreparable harm will result without it, more closely resembles an ex parte motion and usually precedes a preliminary injunction. The request for a temporary restraining order resembles a motion, in that it asks the court for an order. Like a motion, it may also be supported by affidavits and a memorandum of points and authorities. This order may be requested and granted at the time that the complaint itself is filed. Furthermore, although the requesting party must appear before a judge, a full hearing, such as the one that takes place in a request for a preliminary injunction, rarely occurs. Although the courts strongly encourage the requesting party to give prior notice to the other side that a TRO is being requested, the court can issue a TRO without written or oral notice to the adverse party. When notice is given, it is usually done in an informal manner. It may even be a telephone call made a few hours prior to the request. Rule 65 of the Federal Rules of Civil Procedure allows the court to grant a TRO without any notice if facts show that the restraining order is needed to avoid immediate and irreparable injury and the applicant's attorney certifies to the court in writing what efforts (if any) have been made to notify the adverse party and the reasons supporting

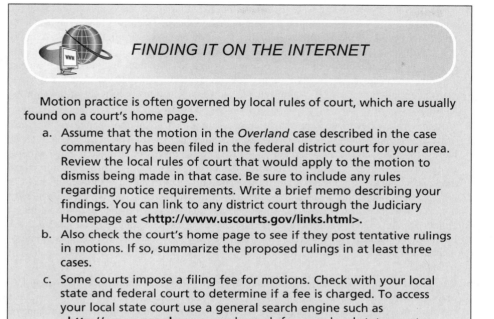

FINDING IT ON THE INTERNET

Motion practice is often governed by local rules of court, which are usually found on a court's home page.

a. Assume that the motion in the *Overland* case described in the case commentary has been filed in the federal district court for your area. Review the local rules of court that would apply to the motion to dismiss being made in that case. Be sure to include any rules regarding notice requirements. Write a brief memo describing your findings. You can link to any district court through the Judiciary Homepage at **<http://www.uscourts.gov/links.html>**.

b. Also check the court's home page to see if they post tentative rulings in motions. If so, summarize the proposed rulings in at least three cases.

c. Some courts impose a filing fee for motions. Check with your local state and federal court to determine if a fee is charged. To access your local state court use a general search engine such as **<http://www.google.com>** and search for your local state court.

the claim that notice should not be required. If a TRO is granted without notice, it must be followed as soon as possible by a hearing on a preliminary injunction, for which notice to the adverse party is required. The court will usually require that all of the moving papers for the preliminary injunction be filed prior to granting the temporary restraining order.

Summary

■ The application for a court order is known as a motion. Motions are a common occurrence during the course of any litigation and can take place before, during, or after trial. Except for motions made during the trial, motions are generally in writing, filed in court, and served on the opposing attorneys in the case. Even though motions are not pleadings, they are prepared in the same general format as pleadings.

■ The general procedure for making a motion involves filing and serving various documents with the court. These include the motion, which describes the nature of the request and the basis for it; the notice of motion, which states the date, time, and place of any hearing on the motion; affidavits in support of the motion; and a memorandum of points and authorities. Affidavits are statements made under oath before a notary. These statements are used in lieu of testimony. A memorandum of points and authorities is a discussion and analysis of the law controlling the case. A party wishing to oppose a motion does so by filing and serving affidavits and memoranda of points and authorities in opposition to the motion.

- Many motions involve court hearings. Scheduling the motion with the court is often a job for a paralegal. When setting a motion for hearing, care must be taken to allow enough time to give proper notice of the hearing to all parties. After the motion is heard, the judge's ruling is put in writing in a document known as an order. An order is normally prepared by the prevailing party. Some courts require that proposed orders be submitted with the moving papers. To prevent unnecessary or frivolous motions, courts have the power to punish attorneys who abuse the motion process. This punishment, known as sanctions, is usually in the form of attorney fees, but can also be a finding of contempt of court.

- Motions can be categorized as pretrial, trial, or posttrial. Pretrial motions include motions that are related to the pleadings, such as a motion to dismiss, motion for a more definite statement, motion to strike, motion for judgment on the pleadings, motion for change of venue, motion to quash return of service, and motion to amend. Pretrial motions also include discovery motions, motions for summary judgment, and motions for sanctions. Trial motions differ from other motions in that they usually do not have to be in writing. Because all parties are already in court, no prior notice is required. Nevertheless, attorneys sometimes like to present memoranda of points and authorities in support of trial motions. One common trial motion is the motion for judgment as a matter of law. Motions made after trial include motions for judgment as a matter of law, motion for new trial, motion to tax costs, and motion to set aside a judgment.

- Requests for preliminary injunctions and temporary restraining orders closely resemble motions. They are requests for court orders in a pending case. The requests for these orders are made in writing and are supported by affidavits or verified complaints and memoranda of points and authorities. Preliminary injunctions require formal notice to the opposing side and involve a court hearing. Like ex parte motions, temporary restraining orders do not always require notice, and a court hearing may involve the appearance of the moving party only.

Key Terms

declaration	motion for more definite statement	motion to strike
ex parte	motion for relief from judgment or order	motion to tax costs
memorandum of points and authorities	motion for sanctions	movant
motion for a new trial	motion for summary judgment	notice of hearing on the motion
motion for a protective order	motion in limine	order
motion for change of venue	motion to amend	order shortening time
motion for judgment notwithstanding the verdict	motion to compel	proof of service by mail (certificate of mailing)
motion for judgment on the pleadings	motion to quash the return of the service	

Review Questions

1. What is a motion?
2. What is the procedure for making a motion?

3. What is the procedure for opposing a motion?
4. What is an affidavit?
5. What role does the paralegal have in setting motions for hearing?
6. Describe the method for obtaining orders after a hearing on the motion.
7. What are sanctions and how are they used in motion practice?
8. What are some common pretrial motions?
9. How do trial motions differ from other motions?
10. What are some common posttrial motions?

Chapter Exercises

Where necessary, check with your instructor prior to starting any of these exercises.

1. Check your state laws regarding general motion practice. What forms must be filed to make a motion? What forms are generally filed in opposition to a motion? What are the time limits for giving notice of a motion? Are there any time limits for filing papers in opposition to a motion?

2. Determine whether the federal district court in your area has any local rules regarding motion practice. If so, review those rules. Are there any special procedures or time requirements that must be followed?

3. Determine whether the state court of general jurisdiction in your area has local rules regarding motion practice. If so, review those rules. Are there any special procedures or time requirements that must be followed?

4. Review the case commentary at the beginning of the chapter. Assume that Jones filed a complaint against Overland for $100,000 for parts that Jones sold and delivered to Overland, the amount becoming due on May 1, 2000. Analyze the following situations. What motion or motions would be appropriate? Explain your answers.

   a. Assume that Overland filed an answer admitting all of the allegations of the complaint but asserting as an affirmative defense the following: "In recent months defendant Overland Corporation has suffered severe financial setbacks and has been unable to meet its financial obligations. On or about May 1, 2000 defendants offered to pay plaintiff the sum of $1,000 per month toward the obligation described in the complaint, however plaintiff refused and continues to refuse such compromise." There is no dispute regarding Overland's financial situation or its offer to settle.

   b. Assume that Overland filed a general denial to Jones' complaint. During the discovery process, the deposition of the president of Overland Corporation was taken. During the deposition, the president admitted that Overland and Jones had a written agreement regarding the sale and purchase of parts; that Overland received the goods that were the subject of this lawsuit, and that payment was not made because of Overland's financial situation.

   c. Assume that Overland filed an answer to the complaint admitting all of the allegations of the complaint but asserting as a defense the fact that Overland has filed bankruptcy. Overland has in fact had its debts discharged in bankruptcy.

   d. Assume that Overland files an answer containing denials of all of the substantive allegations of the complaint. Overland adds a paragraph to the answer stating that "Jones should be precluded from maintaining any action in court because he is a dishonest, disreputable businessman who cheats everyone he deals with."

Chapter Project

Review the factual situation described in the opening commentary. Assume that the president of Overland, Owen Young, relates that the complaint and summons were handed to Barbara Dexter, a sales representative in the New York office of the company. Ms. Dexter has no position with the company other than as a salaried employee. This is the only copy of the summons and complaint that were served upon Overland. Your supervising attorney wants to challenge this service as not being in accordance with Rule 4 of the Federal Rules of Civil Procedure. Prepare the appropriate motion, notice of hearing, and affidavits for the attorney's review.

The *Bennett* Case
Assignment 7: Motion to Amend Complaint

The plaintiff's original complaint contained causes of action for discrimination and infliction of emotional distress. After interviewing several witnesses and reviewing various documents, the plaintiff's attorney has concluded that a cause of action for breach of contract also exists. The defendant will not stipulate to plaintiff amending the complaint. Therefore, you have been asked to prepare a motion to amend the complaint. Review Rules 7 and 15 of the Federal Rules of Civil Procedure, found in Appendix B, and then prepare a motion to amend the complaint.

PART III
DISCOVERY

Chapter 8

Overview of the Discovery Process

CHAPTER OUTLINE

COMMENTARY—THE JENKINS CASE

This morning you have a meeting with your attorney concerning a very important lawsuit. Your attorney has been retained by Dr. Theodore Jenkins to represent him in a lawsuit involving a tort case. Dr. Jenkins is CEO of Jenkins Enterprises, Ltd., headquartered in Pittsburgh, Pennsylvania, an aerospace company which has a contract with Clarke Aircraft, Inc. Under the terms of the contract, Jenkins Enterprises provided Clarke with the central control unit for Clarke's new single-stage space-plane, designated *Spaceliner I*. On its maiden flight, *Spaceliner I* suffered a systems malfunction that caused the spaceplane to crash land, injuring the pilot and causing extensive damage to a farm near the Clarke testing facility. After an extensive investigation, Clarke has determined that the cause of the accident was a total systems collapse caused by the failure of the Jenkins control unit. The current lawsuit was filed by Robert and Charlotte Henderson, the owners of the farm that was damaged by the crash. Both Robert and Charlotte were injured by flying debris from the crash, and their farmhouse and barn were damaged extensively. The Hendersons have sued both Clarke and Jenkins. Your firm represents Dr. Jenkins and Jenkins Enterprises in the suit. The complaint and the answer have been filed. The case will now proceed to the next step—discovery. This afternoon, you and your attorney will discuss the best discovery devices to use in this case and what steps can be taken to limit the discovery of the other party. You will find that the discovery process takes a lot of planning.

OBJECTIVES

In previous chapters, you had the opportunity to explore the steps involved in the litigation process. In this chapter you will be introduced to another critical part of the litigation process—discovery. After completing this chapter, you should be able to:

- Define discovery.
- Identify the five major methods of discovery.
- Outline the factors involved in choosing discovery methods.
- Describe the ethical considerations involved in the discovery process.
- Determine the scope of discovery.
- Differentiate among the attorney-client privilege, the work product privilege, the common interest privilege, and the Fifth Amendment privilege against self-incrimination.
- Explain how expert testimony is subject to discovery.
- Discuss the purpose of the confidentiality agreement and protective orders.
- Indicate the objectives of the federal Freedom of Information Act.

- Identify the obligations of attorneys to disclose relevant matter without the necessity of a formal discovery request.
- Discuss the need for voluntary cooperation in the discovery process.
- Explain how to obtain a discovery conference.
- Relate the process used to compel compliance with discovery and the sanctions that result from noncompliance.

The Nature of Discovery

Discovery is the legal process by which the parties to a lawsuit search for facts relevant to a particular case. Most people who have not been involved in litigation are surprised to learn that both sides in a lawsuit have the opportunity to gather all the facts relevant to that lawsuit. Accustomed as they are to the surprise witness produced at the last minute by a wide variety of television lawyers, most people believe that the attorney who wins a case is the one who manages to trap her opponent by concealing crucial evidence until the last possible second. The truth is exactly opposite to this fiction. Pretrial discovery is allowed because the law supports the principle that lawsuits should be decided on the facts and on the legal merits of the case, rather than on the ability of one attorney to conceal evidence or ambush the other attorney with surprise witnesses. In this part of the chapter, you will explore the objectives of discovery, some preliminary considerations in the discovery process, and some ethical considerations in discovery. The discovery stage is very important not only because it reveals the facts in a suit, but also because it helps shape the direction of the case. The results of an effectively conducted discovery process may encourage your attorney to proceed with the case. However, those results may also indicate that a settlement or a voluntary dismissal is in order.

discovery
The procedure that the parties to a lawsuit follow in order to uncover the facts that are involved in the suit. Generally, the system involves an exchange of information among the parties using certain established discovery techniques including depositions, interrogatories, requests for real evidence, requests for physical and mental examinations, and requests for admissions.

Developments Concerning Discovery

The courts have long encouraged parties to cooperate with one another in the discovery process in order to promote full disclosure of relevant facts before trial. In fact, however, too often attorneys have ignored the spirit of this law and engaged in behavior that, although not a technical violation of the letter of the law, has defeated the purpose of discovery. The Federal Rules of Civil Procedure are designed to facilitate discovery and discourage any attempts to circumvent its true purpose. Particularly, Rule 26 of the Federal Rules requires the parties to disclose certain information to the other party without the necessity of formal discovery requests. The rules also limit the formal discovery methods that are available.

Electronic Discovery

The discovery process has changed over the last decade as attorneys and paralegals adjust to advances in technology. For instance, it is now becoming a common practice to videotape depositions, whereas in the past attorneys were reluctant to use such an approach. Attorneys and paralegals are also taking advantage of the wealth of information available on the Internet to conduct informal discovery, to research the law, and to supplement traditional discovery techniques. For example, several new techniques, including Internet depositions, video conferencing, web conferencing, and Internet interrogatories, have become so popular that technical firms which specialize in providing such services are now being used by both large and small law firms, especially in big cities. Other advances in technology such as the use of mobile phones, personal digital assistants, fax machines, and e-mail have also made the discovery process more economical and more efficient.

The inevitable presence of computers in most places of business today has also changed the nature and the types of information and data that are discoverable. An enormous amount of diverse and vital information can be stored on computer files. This means that attorneys and paralegals must adjust traditional discovery techniques to include e-evidence. **E-evidence** includes computer-generated records such as those found in e-mail files, databases, calendering programs, and all other relevant data files created by spreadsheets, word processing, or any analogous program. It also means that clients, adversaries, and third parties must be prepared to preserve computer files and retrieve e-evidence in response to discovery requests. In addition, under Rule 26 of the federal rules, some forms of computer data must be disclosed automatically. The process has become so complicated that many law firms have found that it is necessary to employ **information technology (IT) experts** to guide them and their clients through preservation and retrieval procedures. Consequently, when your supervising attorney is determining who will be subject to discovery in a case, he must always remember to include those individuals responsible for the opposing party's computer system.

The Objectives of Discovery

As noted, one of the primary objectives of discovery is to prevent one of the parties from winning the lawsuit by surprise or trickery. However, this is not the only objective. Another goal is to determine the truth or falsity of the alleged facts that form the basis of the suit. A third objective of discovery is to examine the facts and weigh the advisability of proceeding with the case or settling early. Frequently a case that looks promising in the opening stages loses its viability as more and more facts come to light. For example, in the *Jenkins* case discussed in this chapter's commentary, if during discovery your supervising attorney uncovers evidence that several employees in the manufacturing department at Jenkins Enterprises had, unknown to the CEO, falsified inspection reports on the control unit which caused the accident, she may elect to settle the case with the Hendersons. In contrast, early discovery may reveal that your client's case is so strong that there is no need to proceed to trial. In such a situation, your attorney may decide to file a summary judgment motion. For instance, in this chapter's *Jenkins* case, your supervising attorney may discover that Clarke never actually used the Jenkins control unit or that several of Clarke's engineers severely altered the unit before installing it in the spaceplane. In such a situation, the law would clearly be on Jenkins' side and a summary judgment motion would be in order. A fourth objective of discovery is to preserve testimony that might be lost should a witness disappear

e-evidence

Computer-generated records such as those found in e-mail files, databases, calendering programs, and all other relevant data files created by spreadsheets, word processing, or any analogous program.

information technology (IT) experts

Individuals who are trained and experienced in the operation of computer systems and in preserving and retrieving computer-based data.

or become incapacitated or should records be lost or destroyed. Finally, some discovery methods can be used to impeach the credibility of a witness, should that witness offer testimony at trial that contradicts his or her earlier statements made during discovery.

Preliminary Decisions Regarding Discovery

Discovery can be an expensive and time-consuming process. Because of this, during the preliminary stages in a case an attorney must decide which discovery techniques are best suited to the lawsuit. In making this decision, the attorney must consider the cost and the amount of time involved.

Informal Discovery   The fact that formal discovery is an important part of the pretrial process does not mean that the informal process of uncovering information and evidence can be overlooked. Often a great deal of information can be gathered before the formal discovery process begins. In fact, the more information that can be collected at this time, the more efficient and economical the actual discovery process will become. For instance, it is often advisable for the attorney or the paralegal to visit any physical scene that is critical to the lawsuit. Thus, in the *Jenkins* case discussed in this chapter's commentary, the attorney may wish to visit the site of the accident so that she can take photographs and make measurements of the crash site. At that time the attorney or the paralegal may also want to call on neighbors in the vicinity to see if they can provide any information about the crash.

Web sites and databases can also be explored at this stage in the informal discovery process. For example, in the *Jenkins* case, the Web sites for Bristol Spaceplanes, Ltd., Boeing Aerospace, Britain in Space, and Starbase Industries, Ltd. would all be helpful for giving the attorney and the paralegal an introduction to some very basic facts about the type of vehicle involved in the crash. The paralegal's role can be very important during the informal stage of discovery because he or she can do much of the legwork involved in the process, thus saving time for the supervising attorney who can handle other matters that require her presence.

A Discovery Strategy   Many attorneys overlook the importance of drawing up an effective discovery strategy before launching into the actual discovery process. This is unfortunate because it often means that the attorney is placed on the defensive rather than the offensive side of the litigation process. Instead of moving forward at a measured and controlled pace, he is caught reacting to what the other side has already done. As a consequence, the attorney loses his grasp of the discovery process and spends far too much time patching up errors that could have been avoided had a strategic approach been arrived at during the earliest stages of the lawsuit. The key to success in developing a discovery strategy is not to reinvent the process for each situation, but to have a set routine that is followed in every case. Such a routine would involve a checklist of things that must be done before the discovery process begins. As we have already seen, a good portion of this can be done during the informal discovery process. However, some of it cannot be done until formal discovery begins. One of the first steps in the discovery strategy is to take the time to evaluate some of the new electronic discovery tools available to practitioners today. Another initial step involves identifying the type of e-data that is discoverable, as well as identifying those individuals who are responsible for the opponent's computer system. Your supervising attorney will most likely evaluate which of the traditional discovery methods would be best in each case.

Electronic Discovery Tools   **Electronic discovery, e-discovery,** and **digital discovery** are all terms that are used to designate discovery carried out with computers, generally using the Internet. No matter what it is called, however, there can be no doubt that e-discovery has become an important part of the routine in many law firms today. Personal computers, which are used to store data, create forms, and send e-mail, are as common in law firms today as the telephone and typewriter were in the past. Moreover, the use of audio- and videotaping as well as telephone, video, and web conferencing are becoming commonplace in many firms across the country. In addition, many law firms now take advantage of the convenient and economical resources available on the Internet. E-discovery involves the use of a wide variety of electronic resources to conduct discovery in an efficient and economical way. Consequently, the possible use of electronic discovery tools must be considered when your attorney draws up her discovery plan.

As we investigate each discovery technique in the chapters that follow, we will consider the available electronic versions of these techniques. So, for instance, in the chapter on depositions, we will examine the use of videotaped, telephone, and Internet depositions. Later, in the chapter on interrogatories, we will look at the use of interrogatories as an aid in structuring the discovery of electronic evidence. Nevertheless, at this stage in the discovery process your supervising attorney may want to consider the use of some electronic discovery devices to conduct informal discovery.

As noted, the advent of e-discovery also means that attorneys and paralegals must be attuned to the fact that a great deal of discoverable evidence is stored on computers. In many jurisdictions this means that traditional discovery rules must be interpreted in relation to data created by and stored in computers. In other jurisdictions it means keeping up with changes in the rules of discovery made to facilitate the preservation and retrieval of computer-generated records. Regardless of the rules, the attorney must also be prepared to deal with the actual discovery of computer records as well as the need to respond to e-discovery requests. All of this must be considered in the development of an effective discovery strategy.

Video and Web Conferences   One e-discovery tool that your supervising attorney might want to consider during informal discovery is the video conference. A **video conference** permits several individuals at widely separated geographical locations to discuss the planning of the case. The conference can involve preliminary discussions among attorneys and the client, and may include expert witnesses, thus reducing travel expenses. The video set-up generally requires the use of television cameras, microphones, monitors, and a speaker system at each location. Connections among various sites can be established using existing phone lines or a satellite transmission system. It is also possible to use personal computers to establish a web conference setup. A **web conference** permits individuals at separate locations to meet on line via the Internet using personal computers.

Choice of Discovery Methods   An attorney has five methods of discovery from which to choose: the deposition, interrogatories, a request for the production of documents and entry upon land for inspection, a request for physical or mental examinations, and a request for admission. In federal court, the discovery process is regulated by Rules 26 through 37 of the Federal Rules of Civil Procedure (see Exhibit 8–1).

---

e-discovery (also electronic discovery and digital discovery)
A series of techniques and tools that involve the use of a wide variety of electronic resources to conduct discovery in an efficient and economical way.

video conference
An electronic conference set-up which permits several individuals at widely separated geographical locations to discuss the planning of the case. The video set-up generally requires the use of television cameras, microphones, monitors, and a speaker system at each location.

web conference
An electronic conference set-up which permits individuals at separate locations to meet on line via the Internet using personal computers.

RULE 26   GENERAL PROVISIONS GOVERNING DISCOVERY; DUTY OF DISCLOSURE
Rule 26 covers general provisions of discovery, including the duty to disclose certain information. It sets out the scope of discovery as well as its limits. It also covers protective orders, timing and sequence of discovery, supplementation of discovery, planning for discovery, and the effect of signing discovery requests, responses, and objections.

RULE 27   DEPOSITIONS BEFORE ACTION OR PENDING APPEAL
Rule 27 allows the perpetuation of testimony even though an action cannot be presently brought to court, or when an appeal is pending.

RULE 28   PERSONS BEFORE WHOM DEPOSITIONS MAY BE TAKEN
Rule 28 specifies that a deposition must be taken before an officer authorized to administer oaths and take testimony. The rule also outlines the persons before whom a deposition can be taken in a foreign country. The rule eliminates persons who are related to or employees of the parties or the attorneys, as well as persons who have a financial interest in the action.

RULE 29   STIPULATIONS REGARDING DISCOVERY PROCEDURE
Rule 29 allows the parties to an action to modify in writing the discovery procedures outlined in the rules.

RULE 30   DEPOSITIONS UPON ORAL EXAMINATION
Rule 30 explains when depositions can be taken, notice requirements, examination and cross-examination, oath requirements, objections, motions to terminate or limit examination, failure to attend or failure to serve a subpoena, and exhibits, among other things.

RULE 31   DEPOSITIONS UPON WRITTEN QUESTIONS
Rule 31 discusses the service of depositions upon written questions, as well as the notice requirements, among other things.

RULE 32   USE OF DEPOSITIONS IN COURT PROCEEDINGS
Rule 32 outlines the circumstances under which a deposition can be used in court. For example, a deposition can be used to contradict or impeach the testimony of a witness. A deposition can also be used if the witness is dead, is located farther than 100 miles from the place of the trial or hearing, or is unable to testify because of age, illness, infirmity, or imprisonment. Also, the deposition will be allowed if the party who wants to introduce the deposition has been unable to make the witness attend by subpoena.

RULE 33   INTERROGATORIES TO PARTIES
Rule 33 explains the procedure for using interrogatories, the allowable scope of the interrogatories, and the use of interrogatories at trial. The rule also indicates when business records can be produced in lieu of answering interrogatories.

RULE 34   PRODUCTION OF DOCUMENTS AND THINGS AND ENTRY UPON LAND FOR INSPECTION OR OTHER PURPOSES
Rule 34 explains the scope of this discovery device as well as the process for its use. The rule specifies that this request can be made of nonparties.

RULE 35   PHYSICAL AND MENTAL EXAMINATIONS OF PERSONS
Rule 35 explains when a physical and/or mental examination can be ordered. It also explains the disposition of the report of the examining physician.

EXHIBIT 8–1   Federal Rules of Civil Procedure

RULE 36   REQUESTS FOR ADMISSION
Rule 36 outlines the procedure for requesting admissions. It also explains the effects of an admission.

RULE 37   FAILURE TO MAKE DISCLOSURE OR COOPERATE IN DISCOVERY; SANCTIONS
Rule 37 presents the procedure for filing a motion for an order compelling discovery. It also details the negative consequences of failing to comply with such an order, among other things.

EXHIBIT 8–1   *(continued)*

deposition
An out-of-court question and answer session under oath, conducted in advance of a lawsuit as a part of the discovery process. A deposition can be taken from a party to the lawsuit or from a witness who is not a party but who is believed to possess knowledge pertaining to the suit.

interrogatories
Written questions delivered, as part of the overall discovery process, by one party in a lawsuit to another party in the same lawsuit, requiring the second party to provide written responses to those interrogatories.

request for the production of documents and entry upon land for inspection
A request that a party or other individual involved in a lawsuit provide specific documents or other physical evidence to the party making the request for such documents or physical evidence. This discovery technique can also involve a request to enter land to inspect that land to gain facts in relation to the lawsuit.

Rule 26 sets out the general provisions concerning discovery. Rules 27 through 36 explain the various discovery techniques that can be used by litigants in federal court. The final rule, Rule 37, outlines the sanctions that are available when a party does not cooperate with discovery. A **deposition** is an out-of-court question and answer session under oath, conducted in advance of a lawsuit as a part of the discovery process. Depositions are regulated by Rules 27 through 32 of the Federal Rules of Civil Procedure. **Interrogatories** are written questions requiring written answers under oath and directed to a party, in which another party seeks information related to the litigation. Interrogatories are governed by Rule 33 of the federal rules. A **request for the production of documents and entry upon land for inspection,** which is covered by Rule 34, is a request that a party or other individual involved in a lawsuit provide specific documents or other physical evidence to the party making the request. As the name implies, this request may also involve a request to enter land to inspect that land to gain facts related to the lawsuit. A **request for a physical or mental examination** asks a party to undergo a physical or mental examination provided that the examination involves a condition that is at issue in the pending action. A **request for admission** asks a party to admit the truth of certain facts or the genuineness of a document so that these issues do not have to be proven at trial. An attorney must take into consideration both the expense and the time available when choosing from among these methods. Requests for examination and admission are regulated by Rule 35 and Rule 36, respectively.

Discovery and E-Data   During the initial discovery strategy, your attorney must make certain that she considers not only techniques for recovering e-evidence, but also the types of e-evidence that are discoverable and the individuals who are responsible for that e-data. Discoverable e-evidence falls into three categories: (1) types of e-evidence based on the configuration of the computer system; (2) types of e-evidence based on the nature of the evidence itself; (3) types of e-evidence based on its storage status. It is important for your supervising attorney to remember that her client may be called upon to furnish this information to the opposing party, and that she will want to create a discovery plan that includes all three categories of e-evidence, as well as the people responsible for managing that e-evidence.

The first type of e-evidence that should be included in a preliminary discovery plan is the configuration of the opposing party's computer system. This involves an understanding of the number and types of computers that are in operation in the party's ordinary business routine. During the planning stage it is important to remember that the term **computer** includes desktop PCs, laptops, mobile phones, personal digital assistants (PDAs), and home computers that are part of a network. It would also be helpful to know about any network systems that are a part of the party's operation, as well as the number and location of all work stations and all network servers.

The second type of e-evidence that must be included in the discovery plan is based on the nature of the evidence itself. For instance, e-evidence generally includes all relevant computer-generated records, including those found in e-mail files, databases, Internet records, intranet or portal records, calendering programs, and all other relevant data files created by spreadsheets, word processing, or any analogous program.

The third type of evidence is based on the storage status of the data. Data can be considered as either **active data, inactive data, back-up data, extant data,** or **paper data.** Data is considered active if it is in current use, and inactive if it is relatively up-to-date but is not used on a routine basis. In contrast, back-up data is information stored as a precautionary measure. Extant data is information which is hidden in the system, generally because it has been deleted. Paper data includes any e-data which has been reduced to a hard copy for filing purposes.

E-Evidence Personnel   It is also important for your supervising attorney to plan to uncover the identities of all of the individuals who are responsible for their own client's computer system, as well as those responsible for the opposing party's system. The individuals responsible for a company's or an institution's computer system will generally include not only top executives, but also middle-level managers and administrative assistants. It is also important to remember to include all in-house and independent information technology experts who have had a hand in shaping and maintaining the system. Your supervising attorney should consider using interrogatories to uncover both the identities of the relevant personnel and the types of e-evidence available. The interrogatories can then be used to guide the choice of those individuals who will undergo depositions. This information can also guide document-production requests.

Expense of Discovery   Discovery can be a very expensive proposition for both sides in a lawsuit. However, some techniques are less expensive than others. For instance, sending a set of interrogatories to a party is considerably less expensive than having that party sit for an oral deposition. The oral deposition would necessitate paying a court reporter to administer the oath and to transcribe the question and answer period. Oral depositions also involve more of an attorney's time, as the attorney must be physically present to interrogate the party. In contrast, the interrogatories would simply involve determining the questions to ask, typing or word processing those questions, mailing them to the party, and reviewing the answers when returned.

Amount of Time   If time is a more critical element than expense, the attorney might make an entirely different decision in choosing a method of discovery. Under the pressure of time, having the party sit for a deposition would be much more advantageous than sending interrogatories and waiting for written responses. In addition, the Federal Rules of Civil Procedure allow parties at least 30 days to respond to a set of interrogatories. Most states allow similar lengths of time. Moreover, although it is possible for courts to shorten this time limit, it is also possible for the court to extend that time,

request for a physical or mental examination

A request made by one party in a lawsuit to another party in that lawsuit to undergo a physical or mental examination provided that the examination involves a condition that is at issue in the pending action.

request for admission

A request made by a party in a lawsuit to another party in that lawsuit to admit to the truthfulness of a fact or the genuineness of a piece of evidence such as a written contract, a memo, or some other physical item.

computer

During the discovery process, the term *computer* includes desktop PCs, laptops, mobile phones, personal digital assistants (PDAs), and home computers that are part of a network.

active data

Computer-generated records within a computer system that are in current use.

inactive data

Computer-generated records within a computer system that are relatively up-to-date but are not used on a routine basis.

back-up data

Computer-generated records within a computer system that are stored as a precautionary measure.

extant data

Computer-generated records within a computer system that are hidden in the system, generally because they have been deleted.

paper data
Electronic data which has been reduced to a hard copy for filing purposes as a safeguard against the loss of that e-data due to the breakdown of the computer system.

causing further delay. The parties can also agree to extend or shorten the time as long as any agreement to do so is put in written form.

Ethical Considerations in Discovery

As noted earlier, the primary objective of discovery is to ensure that lawsuits are decided on the facts and the legal merits of the case, rather than on surprise or trickery. For such an objective to be met, however, all parties must treat the discovery process with the highest ethical regard. It is considered highly unethical for an attorney to stop the other party from obtaining evidence or to destroy evidence before the other party can see it. For example, in the *Jenkins* case from this chapter's commentary, it would be unethical for your attorney to destroy a letter, memo, voice-mail recording, computer printout, fax, or e-mail record that indicates that engineers at Jenkins Enterprises knew of a design flaw or a manufacturing defect in the control unit that caused the spaceplane to crash-land. Similarly, it is a violation of ethical principles to falsify evidence or to help someone else falsify evidence. It is also unethical for an attorney to make a discovery request that is unwarranted or to request much more information than is really necessary for the case. Naturally, because the paralegal's activities are actually an extension of the attorney's, she is also bound by these same ethical principles.

The Extent of Allowable Discovery

The Federal Rules of Civil Procedure limit discovery to information that will support the claims or defenses of the parties to the litigation. Most states impose similar limitations. Nevertheless, the extent of the discovery process is quite broad—broader, in fact, than the extent to which evidence can be introduced in a case once it has reached the trial stage. There are, however, several limits on the discovery process, including the attorney-client privilege, the work product privilege, the common interest privilege, the Fifth Amendment privilege against self-incrimination, controlled access to expert testimony, confidentiality agreements, and protective orders.

The Scope of Discovery

The amount and type of evidence that can be sought during the discovery process is vast compared to that which can be introduced at trial. Nevertheless, the evidence sought during discovery must be relevant to the claims or defenses in the case. Evidence is considered relevant if it tends to prove or to disprove facts that are necessary to determine the final outcome of the case. However, under Rule 26 of the Federal Rules of Civil Procedure, the evidence sought during discovery need not be admissible at the time of the trial, as long as it is reasonably calculated to lead to the discovery of evidence that can be introduced at trial. For example, most hearsay evidence is not admissible at trial. This ban against hearsay evidence means that in most situations a witness at trial cannot testify about the truth of what she heard someone else say. For example, in the *Jenkins* case introduced in this chapter, it would be hearsay to try to prove that Dr. Arthur DePuy, an employee of Clarke Aerospace, falsified a report concerning the failure of the Jenkins parts, by allowing Dr. Joanna Krauss to testify that Dr. Raymond Griffin told her of this. However, the statement by Dr. Krauss would be within the scope of discovery because it could lead to admissible evidence, namely the testimony of Dr. Griffin who actually saw Dr. DePuy falsify the data in the report.

Recent Amendments   In the year 2000, several amendments to Rule 26 of the Federal rules that relate to the scope and the nature of discovery were activated. One such amendment alters Rule 26(b)(1) so that the scope of discovery is limited to unprivileged matters that are "relevant to the claim or defense of any party." This wording represents a change over the phrasing of the old rule that permitted the discovery of evidence "relevant to the subject matter involved in the pending action." The intent of the committee charged with amending the rule was to eliminate the expense and time involved in overbroad discovery operations that were clearly authorized by the old rule. The committee, however, was careful to include a shelter provision, permitting the court to expand the scope of discovery if the party requesting the expansion successfully argues that it has good cause for expanding the search.

Limits on Discovery

Even though the scope of discovery is very extensive, it is not without limitations. Discovery, including matters that must be disclosed under Rule 26, is limited by several privileges. These include the attorney-client privilege, the work product privilege, the common interest privilege, the medical privilege, the confessor-penitent privilege, and the Fifth Amendment privilege against self-incrimination. Limits are also placed on access to expert testimony. In addition, the parties can initiate confidentiality agreements or ask the court to issue protective orders.

The Attorney-Client Privilege   The **attorney-client privilege** prevents the forced disclosure of written or oral communications between an attorney and a client or a prospective client. For a communication to be protected by the privilege, it must be made between the client and the attorney or the attorney's subordinate. This means that the privilege extends to communications made to the paralegal when the paralegal is acting as an agent of the attorney. The communication must also be made within the context of the attorney-client relationship. In other words, information revealed while seeking legal advice would be protected by the privilege, but statements made at a social gathering during polite conversation would not. The privilege belongs to the client, not the attorney. For example, in the *Jenkins* case discussed throughout this chapter, if Dr. Jenkins has no objection to the revelation of the contents of a discussion he had with your attorney, then the attorney could not assert the privilege herself. Certainly, she could advise Dr. Jenkins to assert the privilege. However, the client, Dr. Jenkins, has the final decision.

It is also important to know that the attorney-client privilege may be lost or waived by the client if the client does not intend the communication to be confidential, discloses the communication to others, or refuses to assert the privilege. Also, if a third party who is not related to the client is present during an attorney-client discussion, the privilege has been waived by the client. Naturally, such a waiver would not occur if the third party who is present is another attorney in the firm, a paralegal employed by the

attorney-client privilege
A privilege that belongs to the client in an attorney-client relationship that requires the attorney to treat all information revealed to him, or to anyone employed by the attorney, as confidential. Since the privilege belongs to the client rather than the attorney, only the client can give permission for the revelation of such confidential matters.

firm, or a legal secretary who works for the attorney. Thus, if you were asked to be present during a meeting between your attorney and Jenkins, he would not have waived his attorney-client privilege.

In a large and complex case, privileged documents may be disclosed inadvertently. Such disclosure could have serious results. To avoid this problem, it is possible to enter into an agreement with opposing counsel that the inadvertent production or disclosure of privileged information will not result in waiver of the privilege. This agreement may be incorporated in the protective order discussed later in this chapter. See Exhibit 8–2 for a sample protective order.

IN THE UNITED STATES DISTRICT COURT

Robert Henderson, et al.,	)))) Civil No. 05 C 2748) PROTECTIVE ORDER)
Plantiffs,	))
v.	))
JENKINS ENTERPRISES, LTD., et al.,	))))
Defendants.	)))

PURSUANT to Rule 26(c) of the Federal Rules of Civil Procedure, and stipulation of the parties, IT IS HEREBY ORDERED as follows:

1. This Protective Order (the "Order") shall govern all documents and other products of discovery obtained by the Plaintiff or Defendant, all information derived therefrom and all copies, excerpts, or summaries thereof, including but not limited to, documents produced pursuant to Rule 33(c) or Rule 34 of the Federal Rules of Civil Procedure, answers to requests for admissions, answers to interrogatories, documents subpoenaed in connection with depositions, and deposition transcripts (referred to collectively herein as Discovery Material). Any motions, briefs, or other filings incorporating Discovery Material are also governed by this Order.

2. All Discovery Material shall be treated as confidential, both during the pendency of and subsequent to the termination of this action. Discovery Material will be used solely for the purpose of this action and not for any other purpose. No Discovery Material will be disclosed to anyone except in accordance with the terms of this Order.

EXHIBIT 8–2 Sample protective order

3. Disclosure of Discovery Material shall be made only to attorneys of record for parties in the litigation; in-house counsel for the parties; persons employed by the law firms of the attorneys retained by the parties whose assistance is required by said attorneys in the preparation for trial of this case; expert witnesses and consultants who are retained by the parties in connection with this proceeding. Counsel for the party making disclosure to any of the aforementioned individuals shall first obtain the written agreement of any such individual to whom disclosure is made to be bound by the terms of this Order. This requirement may be satisfied by obtaining the signed acknowledgment on a copy of this Order that he or she has read the Order and understands its provisions.

4. Counsel for the parties making disclosure of Discovery Material to a party shall first obtain written agreement from the party producing said Discovery Material. Written agreement shall be obtained from any such party to whom Discovery Material is disclosed to be bound by the terms of the Order. This requirement may be satisfied by obtaining a signed acknowledgment on a copy of this Order that he or she has read the Order and understands its provisions.

5. Discovery Material shall be conspicuously marked by the producing party or witness "Confidential-Subject to Protective Order of the United States District Court."

6. In the event a party inadvertently produces for inspection privileged or potentially privileged documents, such production shall not constitute waiver of the attorney-client privilege, the work product privilege, or any other privilege with respect to the document or portion thereof, or with respect to any other document or testimony relating thereto. In the event that a document that is privileged, in whole or in part, is inadvertently produced, the party claiming privilege shall promptly identify each document being withheld as privileged, and the inspecting party shall forthwith return such document or documents.

7. Within thirty (30) days after the termination of this action, all confidential information, and copies thereof, including but not limited to any notes or other recording made hereof, shall be returned to counsel for the party who initially produced such documents.

8. Nothing in this Order shall prevent any party or nonparty from seeking a modification of this Order or from objecting to discovery which it believes to be otherwise improper.

DATED this _____ day of _____, 20____
SIGNED BY: U.S. MAGISTRATE

APPROVED AS TO FORM AND CONTENT BY:
(ALL COUNSEL OF RECORD)

EXHIBIT 8–2   *(continued)*

work product privilege
A privilege that protects any information prepared by an attorney in a lawsuit, if that information is prepared by the attorney or anyone employed by the attorney in anticipation of litigation or to present at trial.

Work Product Privilege
The **work product privilege** prevents the opposing party in a lawsuit from using the discovery process to obtain letters, memos, documents, records, and other tangible items that have been produced in anticipation of litigation or that have been prepared for the trial itself. If, for instance, in the *Jenkins* case, your attorney were to take notes during her interview with Dr. Jenkins, those notes would be considered work product and would, therefore, be protected by the privilege.

One problem with the work product privilege is determining which documents actually were prepared in anticipation of litigation. For example, in most hospitals it is common practice for health care professionals to make out "incident reports" when an error has been made. Thus, a nurse who accidentally gives a patient the wrong medication would have to fill out one of these reports. If the patient was hurt by the error and litigation resulted, the hospital attorney would argue that the incident report was prepared in anticipation of litigation, whereas the patient's attorney would maintain that it was not. The judge would determine whether the incident report is covered by the work product privilege.

Another problem with the work product privilege is that it is not an absolute privilege. Under Rule 26(b)(3) of the federal rules, disclosure may be compelled by showing that the party seeking discovery has a substantial need for the documents or materials for the preparation of her case and that she cannot, without undue hardship, obtain the equivalent of that material by any other means. Most courts continue to provide protection for the portion of work product that consists of "mental impressions, conclusions, opinions, or legal theories of an attorney or other representatives of a party concerning the litigation." Although the attorney is responsible for determining what confidential client material may be revealed, the paralegal should be constantly alert to protecting the attorney-client or work product privilege.

common interest privilege
The rule that protects any communication that takes place between attorneys for different clients when those clients share a common interest.

Common Interest Privilege
The **common interest privilege** is designed to protect any communication that takes place between attorneys for different clients when those clients share a common interest. The privilege actually preserves the attorney-client privilege and the work product privilege when information is exchanged among attorneys whose clients share such a common interest. The privilege protects oral statements, written notes, and printed memos that pass among such attorneys. The privilege can be invoked by attorneys representing either plaintiffs or defendants and can be asserted in both civil and criminal procedures. As a paralegal, your communication with another attorney or with the client of another attorney would also be protected if that client shared a common interest with the client represented by your attorney.

In order to succeed in raising the privilege of common interest, attorneys must demonstrate that the communication occurred because of an actual or a probable legal or other adversarial process. In addition, the attorney must show that his client does indeed share a common interest with the clients represented by the other attorneys involved in the action. For example, in the *Jenkins* case, if Jenkins Enterprises, Ltd. and Dr. Jenkins were to be represented by different attorneys, those attorneys could use the privilege to protect any communication made between them while planning a common defense for their clients. Finally, the communication must be made in a way that preserves the privileged nature of its content in relation to any adverse parties.

The Medical Privilege The **medical privilege** is designed to protect the patient rather than the medical practitioner. Although common law rules did not recognize the privilege, it is now a firmly established principle that is acknowledged in most jurisdictions. The medical privilege is designed to encourage patients to be candid with certain health care professionals, generally those who are charged with the primary care of the patient. Though the privilege is referred to as the *medical privilege,* it is broad enough to cover not only physicians but also psychiatrists, podiatrists, psychologists, and dentists. The privilege only applies if the relationship is a valid one for purposes of diagnosis, treatment, and/or care, and if the consultation in question was sought voluntarily. Thus, the privilege does not exist if the plaintiff in a lawsuit has been required to submit to a physical or mental examination as a part of the discovery process.

The Confessor-Penitent Privilege Any communication between a clergy member and an individual is protected by the **confessor-penitient privilege** when the relationship involves the spiritual support of the penitent. Although, strictly speaking, the privilege belongs to the penitent rather than the clergy member and thus the penitent can give up the privilege, the law protects a clergy member who has taken a religious oath not to reveal the content of such counseling sessions. It is clear that the privilege covers spiritual transgressions and concerns that the penitent has revealed to his or her confessor. However, some jurisdictions extend the privilege to cover matters associated with such a confession, whereas others expand it to include any confidential counseling session. Because of the differences among various courts, it would be wise for paralegals to check the status of this privilege in their jurisdiction.

Protection of Expert Testimony Expert testimony is frequently indispensable in a lawsuit. In a medical malpractice case, for example, it would be difficult for a jury to determine if a certain medical procedure was carried out properly without the use of expert testimony. Under Rule 26(a)(2) of the Federal Rules of Civil Procedure, parties are required to disclose the name of any expert who will testify at trial. Along with the name, information relating to the expert's opinion, report, and qualifications must also be provided. This information must be disclosed without the necessity of a formal discovery request. If the expert witness is to be compensated for his or her testimony or for a study undertaken for the case, that must also be revealed, as well as a list of other cases that the witness has served as an expert in either by deposition or at trial within the previous four years.

The Fifth Amendment Privilege against Self-Incrimination The Fifth Amendment to the United States Constitution states that "No person . . . shall be compelled in a criminal case to be a witness against himself." This is referred to as the Fifth Amendment **privilege against self-incrimination.** Because the privilege is specifically aimed at self-testimony in a criminal case, it is usually not available as a privilege in a civil lawsuit if the only object of the suit is to seek compensatory damages. Some courts have held, however, that if a civil lawsuit seeks to protect the public, the privilege may be successfully invoked. For example, if a civil suit is brought by a private party under federal antitrust law, the privilege may be successfully raised. This is because the purpose of antitrust law, like the purpose of criminal law, is to protect the public at large.

medical privilege
The medical privilege exists between a patient and a medical practitioner and is designed to protect the patient's confidential communication with the practitioner. The privilege covers communications made between the patient and physicians, psychiatrists, podiatrists, psychologists, and dentists.

confessor-penitent privilege
A privilege designed to protect the confidentiality of any communication between an individual and his or her confessor when the relationship involves the spiritual support of the penitent. The privilege belongs to the penitent rather than the confessor. However, the law also protects the confessor who has taken a religious oath not to reveal the content of such counseling sessions.

privilege against self-incrimination
A privilege granted by the Fifth Amendment to the United States Constitution that prevents a criminal defendant from being forced to testify against himself or herself.

Antitrust laws protect the public by imposing triple damages and thus discouraging antitrust activity. Furthermore, if a government agency is the plaintiff in the suit, it is also possible to invoke the Fifth Amendment privilege because such agencies are, by definition, designed to protect the public interests. This is also because a suit involving a government agency as the plaintiff is very similar in character to a criminal prosecution, which is also brought by the government. Similarly, if a witness could demonstrate that responding to a particular discovery request could expose her to a potential criminal prosecution, then the privilege may also be successfully invoked.

Confidentiality Agreements and Protective Orders   Often, a lawsuit will involve matters that one party wants to keep as secret as possible. For instance, in a trade secrets case, the owner of the trade secret would want to protect that secret by limiting the people who would have access to the secret, or the circumstances under which it is to be revealed. Such limitations can be imposed voluntarily through a **confidentiality agreement** or by court decree through a **protective order.** Confidentiality agreements and protective orders cover a wide spectrum. Some agreements and orders completely prevent all discovery of the secret material. Others designate a particular place and time for revelation of the protected information. Still others might indicate that only certain named parties can be present when the confidential matter is revealed. It is even possible for the agreement or order to stipulate that the information will be enclosed in sealed envelopes to be opened only at the judge's direction. Documents that fall into the category of "confidential" should be stamped with this designation prior to their production or disclosure to the other side. Protective orders are permitted under Rule 26(e) of the Federal Rules of Civil Procedure. It is also within the power of the court to cancel or alter a protective order should the need arise to do so. Exhibit 8–2 shows a sample protective order.

Federal Freedom of Information Act

Strictly speaking, the federal Freedom of Information Act is not solely a discovery tool. Rather, it was designed to help ensure that federal government offices will be accountable to the public they are supposed to serve. The act allows individuals to obtain copies of the documents and records produced and held by the offices, departments, and agencies of the federal government. However, because a wide variety of information is available through the provisions of this act, it can also be used during the discovery process. For instance, in the *Jenkins* case, several government agencies may have information on file that might be relevant to the lawsuit. Should the case call for gaining access to government records under the federal Freedom of Information Act, the job of soliciting that information may fall to the paralegal. In such a situation, the paralegal would draft a letter specifying the nature of the information and records sought. Exhibit 8–3 is an example of such a letter. Naturally, the paralegal should realize that the act does not allow access to all information held by the government. The act includes a list of items that cannot be obtained by the public. Included on that list are secret documents related to national security, internal personnel policies and practices, trade secrets and other confidential information, personnel records, and medical records, among others.

confidentiality agreement

An agreement that is designed to protect confidential information, trade secrets, and other secret data from being revealed during the discovery process in a lawsuit.

protective order

An order that is issued by the court in a lawsuit that protects a party in the suit from revealing information, documents, data, or other types of evidence to another party who has previously requested the production of that evidence.

**LAW OFFICES OF
PALENCIA, LAURITEG, BOTERUS, AND SELAN
PROFESSIONAL ASSOCIATION**

Holis Palencia	83924 Superior Avenue	Robert B. Boterus
Mary Lauriteg	Pittsburgh, Pennsylvania 23219	Hilda J. Selan
	(804) 555-3222	

September 9, 20____

U.S. Comptroller of the Currency
Department of the Treasury
Washington, D.C. 20219

Dear Sir:

Please send me copies of the following documents, records, and reports. I make this request under provisions of the Federal Freedom of Information Act.

[*To prevent delay, the list should be very precise.*]

Should you decide that you cannot send the documents I have requested, please explain the reason for your decision so that I can prepare an appropriate appeal.

Also, please let me know if any fees are involved in obtaining the documents, before you conduct the search. To allow me ample time to review these documents, I would like to receive them by September 19, 20____.

Thank you for your time and effort in this matter.

Cordially,

Stephanie J. Sherman
Paralegal

EXHIBIT 8–3   Sample request letter under the Freedom of Information Act

In the wake of the events of September 11, 2001, public access to many governmental records that were previously available was severely curtailed. For example, access to governmental records under the Freedom of Information Act, described previously, has been limited by governmental directives originating from the attorney general. One such directive reassures governmental agencies that their refusal to honor requests for the disclosure of governmental records will generally be upheld by the Department of Justice, indicating that the government intends to tighten its control over the dissemination of its own files. In addition, some agencies have removed information from their Web sites or have taken other measures to limit public access to federal records. For instance, the National Archives and Records Administration has removed some select information from its Web site, as has the NASA Glenn Research Center and the Federal Energy Regulatory Commission (FERC). In addition, the Internal Revenue Service has limited public access to its Freedom of Information Reading Room in Washington, D.C.

In contrast, while the public's access to governmental information has been curtailed, the government's power to gather information about the public has been greatly increased. For example, in response to a legislative plan submitted by the attorney general, the United States Congress recently enacted a new federal law—the Uniting and Strengthening America by Providing Appropriate Tools Required to Intercept and Obstruct Terrorism Act. Commonly known as the USA PATRIOT Act, or more simply as the Patriot Act, this law includes a number of provisions that extend the power of federal law enforcement agencies, such as the Federal Bureau of Investigation and the Secret Service, to conduct surveillance by intercepting wire, voice, and electronic communication transmissions. The act also amends such laws as the Federal Right to Financial Privacy Act, the Federal Fair Credit Reporting Act, and the Federal Deposit Insurance Act. For example, the new law has amended the Fair Credit Reporting Act so that consumer reporting agencies must now turn over to the federal government a consumer's records should a government agency deem those records relevant to a government intelligence operation involving terrorism. The Patriot Act also empowers the FBI to order libraries to surrender their records regarding library circulation reports, patron background information, and Internet-access records. Should the government become a party in any lawsuit being handled by its law firm, attorneys and paralegals must be aware of the government's increased power during discovery.

Duty of Mutual Disclosure under Rule 26

disclosure

The process of revealing some information that was previously unknown or difficult to comprehend.

Rule 26 of the Federal Rules of Civil Procedure now requires that the parties confer early in the proceeding. No discovery is to be conducted until after the parties confer. More importantly, the rule provides for mutual disclosure. **Disclosure** requires that the parties exchange certain information without the necessity of a formal discovery request. These disclosures occur at three different times in the course of litigation. Early in the case, the parties are required to exchange information identifying potential witnesses, documentary evidence, evidence of damages, and copies of insurance policies. Later in the case (no later than 90 days before trial), the parties must exchange information about expert witnesses who will testify at trial. Shortly before trial (no later than 30 days·before trial), the parties must exchange information about evidence they intend to use at trial.

The Discovery Conference under Rule 26

To facilitate the entire discovery process, Rule 26(f) of the Federal Rules of Civil Procedure mandates that the parties confer as soon as possible to accomplish a number of specified tasks, including the development of a discovery plan. The discovery plan ought to include the following:

1. any changes made in timing, form, or requirements for mutual disclosures;
2. subjects on which discovery is needed, a completion date for discovery, whether discovery should be conducted in phases, and whether discovery should be limited or focused upon particular issues;
3. what changes should be made in normal limitations on discovery; and
4. any orders that should be entered by the court.

Within 14 days of the Rule 26 conference, the parties are to file with the court a written report outlining their plan.

The Pretrial Conference under Rule 16   Rule 16 of the Federal Rules of Civil Procedure allows the court to direct the parties to come to the court to consider various pretrial matters, including the discovery process. Such a meeting is called a **pretrial conference.** Often such a conference takes place after the court has received a discovery plan from the parties. Under a year 2000 amendment to Rule 26(f)(4), the court may also be permitted to waive the written report required under Rule 26, provided the parties agree to file an oral report at the conference held under Rule 16. The court reviews the plan and discusses the matter with the attorneys, and then issues orders concerning any aspect of discovery or disclosure, including scheduling time limits in which to complete discovery.

pretrial conference
A conference that is designed to make the process of conducting a lawsuit as efficient, simple, economical, and fair as possible. The process may involve a simplification of the pleadings, a limitation on the witnesses to be called at trial, a narrowing of the issues to be considered at trial, a simplification of the discovery process, and so on.

Mutual Disclosures

Initial Disclosures   Except as otherwise stipulated or ordered by the court, within 10 days of their meeting, and without waiting for a discovery request, the parties should exchange the following information:

1. name and, if known, address and telephone number of anyone likely to have discoverable information relevant to the disputed facts of the case, identifying the nature of that information;
2. a copy of, or a description by category and location of, all documents, data compilations, and tangible things in the possession, custody, or control of the party;
3. a computation of damages claimed by the disclosing party, making available for copying or inspection any supporting documentation or other evidentiary material; and
4. any insurance agreement that may satisfy part or all of any judgment in the case must be available for copying and inspection.

Excluded Categories   A 2000 amendment to Rule 26 excludes certain types of proceedings from these initial discovery disclosure requirements. These exclusions are detailed in Rule 26(a)(1)(E) and include the following:

1. any action for review on an administrative record;
2. a petition for habeas corpus or other proceeding to challenge a criminal conviction or sentence;
3. an action brought without counsel by a person in custody of the United States, a state, or a state subdivision;
4. an action to enforce or quash an administrative summons or subpoena;
5. an action by the United States to recover benefit payments;
6. an action by the United States to collect on a student loan guaranteed by the United States;
7. a proceeding ancillary to proceedings in other courts; and
8. an action to enforce an arbitration award.

These proceedings have been explicitly excluded from the initial discovery disclosure requirements outlined in Rule 26, primarily because in many, perhaps most, situations these proceedings involve a minimum amount of discovery.

E-Evidence Disclosures   As noted, Rule 26(a)(1)(B) of the Federal Rules of Civil Procedure requires the initial disclosure of a wide variety of real evidence relevant to a lawsuit. Moreover, the rule specifically states that all "data compilations" must be part of this initial disclosure process. As a result, it is important to remember that this requirement clearly encompasses all significant computer-generated records, including those found in e-mail files, databases, calendering programs, and all other important data files created by spreadsheets, word processing, or any analogous program. This becomes a bit tricky when we remember that such compilations can be recorded on laptops, desktop PCs, personal digital assistants (PDAs), hard drives, floppy disks, mobile phones, computer tapes, and CDs. It is probably a good idea for your supervising attorney to make certain that any client involved in a lawsuit begins to immediately take stock of all computerized storage units and to make certain that all such data is preserved. Your supervising attorney must also remember that some employees still retain the habit of translating e-data into paper form for filing purposes. Consequently, paper copies of e-data must be included in any document search and retrieval effort.

Disclosure of Expert Testimony   Before trial, the parties must disclose to one another the identity of any person who may be called to testify at trial as an expert witness. This disclosure should be made at least 90 days before the trial date, unless the evidence is intended solely to contradict or rebut evidence of another expert. In such a situation, the disclosure should be made within 30 days after the disclosure made by the other party. Along with the identity of the expert, a copy of a written report prepared and signed by the witness should also be supplied. This report should contain the following information:

1. statement of all opinions to be expressed,
2. basis for all opinions,

3. data or other information considered by the witness in forming opinions,

4. any exhibits to be used as a summary of or support for opinions,

5. qualifications of the witness, including a list of all publications authored by the witness within the preceding 10 years,

6. compensation to be paid for study and testimony, and

7. a list of any other cases in which the witness has testified as an expert at trial or by deposition within the preceding four years.

E-Evidence and Information Technology Experts   As noted, Rule 26(a)(1)(A) of the Federal Rules of Civil Procedure requires the initial disclosure of the name, address, and telephone number of anyone likely to have discoverable information relevant to the claims and defenses in the case. In addition, Rule 26(a)(2)(A) requires the disclosure of expert witnesses that could be called in at trial to testify according to the provisions of Rules 702, 703, or 705 of the Federal Rules of Evidence. It would seem that both sections of Rule 26 cover information technology (IT) experts. This means that the names, addresses, and telephone numbers of all IT experts involved in preserving, storing, and retrieving computer data would have to be revealed as a part of the initial disclosure process. Of course, it could be argued that only those experts who actually evaluate the data are covered by the requirements of Rule 26. Nevertheless, good judgment would dictate that the revelation of all IT experts would be advisable. Also, while not explicitly referred to in the rules, it would also be a good idea to include the e-mail address, the mobile phone number, and the fax number of such witnesses. Certainly, it would also be advisable to ask the opposing party to include these additional numbers and addresses within their disclosure documents as well.

Pretrial Disclosures   Unless otherwise ordered by the court, various evidentiary matters must be disclosed at least 30 days before trial. These matters include the following:

1. name and, if not previously provided, address and telephone number of each witness, stating whether the party actually expects to call the person as a witness or whether the witness will be called only if needed;

2. designation of those witnesses whose testimony is expected to be presented by means of a deposition and a transcript of the pertinent portions of the deposition testimony; and

3. an identification of each document or other exhibit, separately identifying those which the party expects to offer and those which the party may offer if the need arises.

Any objection to the admissibility of deposition testimony or admissibility of documents or other exhibits must be made within 14 days of service of the pretrial disclosures by the other party. Any objections not made may be deemed waived.

Amendment to the Form Requirements   A year 2000 amendment to Rule 26 has slightly altered the form requirements for pretrial disclosures under Rule 26(a)(4). Previously, the rule required that all disclosures should be in writing, signed, served, and promptly filed with the court. The new rule eliminates the filing requirement but makes it mandatory that the disclosures be written, signed, and served. A disclosure must now be filed with the court only at the time it is used in the proceeding.

Duty to Supplement

All disclosures are required to be supplemented if the disclosing party later acquires information under the following circumstances:

1. if the party learns that in some material respect the information disclosed is incomplete or incorrect, and
2. if the additional or corrective information has not otherwise been made known to the other parties during the discovery process or in writing.

Cooperating with Discovery

It is to everyone's benefit for the discovery process to run as smoothly as possible. For this reason, most parties cooperate freely with discovery requests. However, there are times when parties refuse to cooperate. The rules of civil procedure provide methods for compelling discovery and sanctions for those who refuse to cooperate.

Voluntary Cooperation

Most of the time, attorneys involved in litigation will find that the other attorney and the other party cooperate with the discovery process. Parties cooperate generally for several reasons, all of which are based on enlightened self-interest. First, under the principle of reciprocity, each side knows that any attempt to disrupt the discovery process may result in a similar attempt by the other side. Second, each side knows that the court disapproves of any attempt to interfere with discovery. Finally, the rules of civil procedure provide severe sanctions for those parties who refuse to obey discovery orders made by the court. For these reasons, if one side resists the discovery process or any part of that process, the other side should make inquiries about the reason for such resistance. Often such problems can be resolved informally. For example, a party may resist sitting for a deposition because it is scheduled at an inconvenient time or place. A minor problem like this can be solved by explaining the importance of the discovery process to the party and rescheduling the deposition for a more acceptable time and place.

Involuntary Cooperation

Despite the inclination toward cooperation, there are times when parties may feel that they have legitimate reasons for resisting discovery. In such cases, the parties must turn to the court for a resolution of the differences.

Orders to Compel Discovery   If one of the parties in the litigation refuses to comply with a discovery request, the other party must move to force compliance. Under Rule 37 of the Federal Rules of Civil Procedure, the party seeking cooperation must file

THE COMPUTERIZED LAW FIRM
Litigation Support Software

SCENARIO

Your attorney has called you into her office to discuss the *Jenkins* case. She informs you that, in addition to calling several of the officers and other employees of Clarke Aircraft, Inc., in for depositions, she also intends to serve them with interrogatories and requests for the production of documents. Her preliminary investigation indicates that there will be hundreds of documents to be reviewed. She is concerned about keeping all of the information organized and accessible. She tells you about an old movie concerning a lawsuit where one party was inundated with box after box of documents so that one relevant piece of evidence could be easily hidden. While she does not suspect opposing counsel of those motives, she is worried that the amount of discovery will be overwhelming and unwieldy, especially if the case goes to trial.

PROBLEM

In a complex litigation matter where there is substantial discovery and a multitude of documents, how do you organize the material so that the attorney can properly review and compare information obtained from various methods of discovery, as well as information contained in hundreds, or even thousands, of documents? If the matter goes to trial, how can you easily identify and locate information and documents needed for the trial?

SOLUTION

All litigation firms today use computers and word processors. Many also use calendaring and billing software. Firms engaged in complex litigation, however, have special needs. In a case such as the *Jenkins* case, where there will be numerous depositions, interrogatories, and requests for documents, special software is required to organize these materials and to help make them accessible. Such software is often referred to as "litigation support" software. There are many of these specialized software packages on the market—Summation, Summation Blaze, Concordance, and Discovery Pro

are a few. Litigation support software products generally have similar capabilities (although not all programs do everything). These features include the following:

a database: This feature allows you to analyze and maintain records of all documents. Documents are identified and read by a person who extracts specified information from the document and enters that information into the appropriate database fields. The database can later be searched for all documents containing specified information in the fields. This allows the attorney to identify, compare, and analyze important documents.

imaging software: This feature allows you to scan in actual documents (rather than limited information from the document). With proper imaging software (optical character recognition software) you can annotate, index, and retrieve important documents. Of course, you also need a scanner to do this.

full-text searching: This feature allows documents in the program to be searched for key words or terms. If documents have been scanned in, the entire document can be easily retrieved and printed. If the document has not been scanned in, it is at least identified and can be easily located. This feature is used most commonly with transcripts of depositions that have been loaded into the program.

The proper litigation support software for any firm will depend on a number of factors. Several products should be compared before one is chosen. Most products have their own Web sites (usually the name of the product followed by **.com**), which often contain a live, on-line demo. The magazine *Law Office Computing* constantly reviews products and product updates. The magazine also has an on-line site, **<www.lawofficecomputing.com>**. Reviews and comparisons of several programs can be found here.

FINDING IT ON THE INTERNET

The Federal Rules of Civil Procedure can be accessed at the following address: **<http://www.law.cornell.edu/rules/frcp>**. Access the Web site, find the text of Rule 26, and check to see if there have been any recent updates of the provisions and requirements as stated under the rule.

The entire text of the Uniting and Strengthening America by Providing Appropriate Tools Required to Intercept and Obstruct Terrorism Act (The Patriot Act) can be accessed at **<http://www.epic.org/privacy/terrorism/ hr3162.html>**. Section 507 "Disclosure of Educational Records" increases the government's right to obtain a student's educational transcripts and financial records. Access the site, locate Section 507, and report on this increased level of governmental access.

An extensive article entitled "Access to Government Information Post-September 11th" can be found at **<http://www.ombwatch.org/article/ articleprint/213/-1/1/>**. Access the Web site and report on the contents of the article.

The Web site of the Administrative Office of the United States Courts can be accessed at **<http://www.uscourts.gov>**. The Web site contains a number of interesting features, including the most recent news releases from the federal courts and articles from *The Third Branch,* the court's newsletter.

 a. Access these press releases and find one that involves discovery, one that relates to an issue that interests you, or one that impacts upon paralegals. Write a report on that news release.

 b. Access *The Third Branch* and find an article that involves discovery, one that relates to an issue that interests you, or one that affects paralegals. Write a report on the issues in that article.

a motion with the court asking the judge to compel discovery. The judge will then decide whether to grant the motion. It is possible for the noncomplying party to have a legally sufficient reason for denying the discovery request. For example, in this chapter's *Jenkins* case, Jenkins Enterprises, Ltd., might argue that a request for a list of all customers that have had problems with their electronic control units falls outside the scope of discovery; that is, the list is not relevant to the claims or defenses of a party, and such a list could not lead to admissible evidence. If the objection is valid, the judge will deny the motion to compel discovery. If the objection is not valid, however, the judge will grant the motion and issue an order compelling cooperation with the discovery process. In the case of Jenkins' objection, the judge would likely see the objection as invalid and would, therefore, grant the motion to compel Jenkins' cooperation. Any motion to compel discovery, disclosure, or amend a previous response must be accompanied by a certification by the moving party that he has in good faith conferred or attempted to confer with the other party in an attempt to resolve the matter without court action.

Sanctions against Noncomplying Parties   If, after an order compelling cooperation is issued, a party still refuses to comply, the court can levy certain sanctions against the noncomplying party. Under Rule 37 of the Federal Rules of Civil Procedure, the sanctions include, but are not limited to, a dismissal of the action, the granting of a default judgment, the granting of reasonable expenses, including attorney fees, caused by the failure to cooperate, and a contempt-of-court ruling against the noncomplying party. Sanctions are permitted against either the attorney and the client, or both. This possibility should be considered when drafting a discovery plan. Discovery is an effective and necessary litigation tool. Abuse of discovery results in a protracted and complicated lawsuit.

Summary

- Discovery is the legal process by which the parties to a lawsuit search for facts relevant to a particular case. The primary objective of discovery is to prevent one of the parties from winning the lawsuit by surprise or trickery. An attorney has five methods of discovery from which to choose: the deposition, interrogatories, a request for the production of documents, a request for physical or mental examinations, and a request for admission. An attorney must take into consideration the expense involved and the time available in choosing from among these five methods. Ethical considerations also play a part in conducting discovery.

- The information sought during discovery must be relevant to the subject matter of the case and, at the very least, reasonably calculated to lead to evidence that can be introduced at trial. There are several limits to the discovery process, including the attorney-client privilege, the work product privilege, the common interest privilege, the medical privilege, the confessor-penitent privilege, limited access to expert testimony, the Fifth Amendment privilege against self-incrimination, confidentiality agreements, and protective orders. The federal Freedom of Information Act allows individuals to gain access to the documents and records produced and held by offices, departments, and agencies of the federal government. However, public access to such data has been severely limited by the attorney general in reaction to recent terrorist activities in the United States. In addition, the government's power to access information and to acquire data has been increased by the Patriot Act.

- Rule 26 of the Federal Rules of Civil Procedure requires parties to mutually disclose certain relevant information without the necessity of a formal discovery request. This information includes names, addresses, and telephone numbers of persons who have relevant information about disputed facts; a description and location of documents that are relevant to disputed facts; a list of all damages; and a copy of any insurance policies covering the claim. Before trial, parties must also disclose names, qualifications, opinions, and compensation of expert witnesses who will testify in the case. Additionally, before trial, each side must disclose the identity of persons who will or may be called as witnesses or whose depositions may be used, and a list of all exhibits to be introduced at trial. Furthermore, prior to conducting any discovery, the parties must meet and prepare a discovery plan.

- Most of the time, attorneys involved in litigation cooperate with one another during discovery. Those who do not may be compelled by the court to cooperate.

Key Terms

active data

attorney-client privilege

back-up data

common interest privilege

computer

confessor-penitent privilege

confidentiality agreement

deposition

disclosure

discovery

digital discovery

e-discovery

e-evidence

electronic discovery

extant data

inactive data

information technology (IT) expert

interrogatories

medical privilege

paper data

pretrial conference

privilege against self-incrimination

protective order

request for admission

request for a physical or mental examination

request for the production of documents and entry upon land for inspection

video conference

web conference

work product privilege

Review Questions

1. What is discovery?
2. List the five major methods of discovery.
3. What factors must be considered when choosing among discovery methods?
4. Name five unethical practices involved in the discovery process.
5. Explain what types of evidence can be legally obtained during the discovery process.
6. What are the differences among the attorney-client privilege, the work product privilege, the common interest privilege, and the Fifth Amendment privilege against self-incrimination?
7. Explain the purpose of confidentiality agreements and protective orders.
8. What is the purpose of the federal Freedom of Information Act?
9. What types of disclosures must be made by the parties under Rule 26 of the federal rules?
10. Describe the contents of a discovery plan as required under Rule 26 of the federal rules.
11. Why is voluntary cooperation necessary for the discovery process?
12. What consequences can result from a refusal to cooperate with an order compelling discovery?

Chapter Exercises

Where necessary, check with your instructor prior to starting any of these exercises.

1. Obtain a copy of the pertinent federal rules and a copy of the rules of your state governing discovery. Compare the two sets of rules and note any important differences.
2. Research your state's rules on the attorney-client privilege. Prepare a summary of those rules. Do the same for the rules governing the work product privilege and the common interest privilege.
3. Find a set of form books in your law library that provides sample forms for use in the courts of your state. Review the forms for a confidentiality agreement and a protective order. List and explain the different options that are available for drafting these documents.
4. Check the local rules of court for the federal district court in your area. Does Rule 26 apply?

5. Analyze the following situation and, using your understanding of the discovery rules as explained in this chapter, determine which of the following items in the *Jenkins* case would qualify as initial disclosures and which, under Rule 26 of the federal rules, would have to be provided to the Hendersons without waiting for a discovery request:

   a. a copy of a list of all of the components manufactured by Jenkins and delivered to Clarke over the last 12 months;

   b. a set of notes written by your supervising attorney during the initial interview with Dr. Jenkins;

   c. a memo detailing the problems that other companies have had with some of the component parts produced by Jenkins Enterprises;

   d. the names, addresses, and phone numbers of the officers of Jenkins Enterprises, Ltd.; and

   e. a video of a practice session during which Dr. Jenkins was questioned by an attorney in your law firm.

   In each situation, explain why the item in question should or should not be classified as an initial disclosure.

Chapter Project

Review the details of the *Jenkins* case. Draft a letter to Dr. Jenkins in which you explain the different types of privileges that may be available to limit Clarke Aircraft's discovery process as it relates to his case. Explain to Dr. Jenkins why each privilege would or would not be applicable in his case.

The *Bennett* Case
Assignment 8: Discovery Plan

Now that all the pleadings in the *Bennett* case have been filed, your supervising attorney will be meeting with the attorney for the defendants pursuant to Rule 26 of the federal rules to develop a mutual discovery plan. The federal rules require the parties to identify the subjects on which discovery is needed. You have been asked to review the file and make a list of specific subjects or topics on which discovery is needed. You have also been asked to identify which discovery methods (i.e., deposition, interrogatories, etc.) should be used to obtain the needed information.

Chapter 9

Depositions

CHAPTER OUTLINE

COMMENTARY—THE VELIKOVSKY CASE

Your supervising attorney has asked you to come into the conference room at your law firm to review the facts in a medical malpractice case that the firm will be handling. The client is a young woman named Elisha Velikovsky. Ms. Velikovsky was injured during what should have been a routine diagnostic X-ray procedure at Berea County Hospital (BCH). As a part of this diagnostic procedure, Dr. Arthur Langdon, one of the defendants in the case, was supposed to inject Ms. Velikovsky with a contrast medium. A contrast medium is a dye injected into a patient to help the radiologist visualize the patient's internal organs. Apparently, Ms. Velikovsky had an allergic reaction to the contrast medium and almost expired in the radiology department. At this point in the discovery process, a deposition has been planned for today. The person answering questions during the deposition will be David Cornwell, a radiologic technologist at BCH. Cornwell is not a party to the action. Instead, he is a witness who was working in the radiologic department at the time of the incident in question. Cornwell is expected to testify about certain irregularities in Dr. Langdon's procedures on the day of Ms. Velikovsky's test. Your supervising attorney asks you to organize the litigation file, summarize all previous discovery, and draft a deposition outline. The assignment is the beginning of your participation in taking an oral deposition.

OBJECTIVES

Chapter 8 introduced you to the discovery process. The deposition is an important discovery tool. After reading Chapter 9, you should be able to:

- Define deposition.
- Contrast the advantages and disadvantages of the oral deposition.
- Outline four trends in e-discovery.
- Explain the notice of intent to take an oral deposition.
- Identify the responsibilities of the paralegal in preparing for an oral deposition.
- Relate the duties a paralegal might perform during an oral deposition.
- Discuss the paralegal's role in making transcript arrangements.
- Explain the different types of deposition summaries.
- Determine the advantages and disadvantages of taking a deposition upon written questions.

The Deposition

A deposition is an out-of-court question and answer session under oath, conducted in advance of a lawsuit as a part of the discovery process. It is one of the most important and widely used pretrial discovery tools. As explained in Chapter 8, the use of depositions in federal court is regulated by Rules 27 through 32 of the Federal Rules of Civil Procedure. Under the 1993 amendment to Rule 26(d), depositions may not be taken prior to filing of the discovery plan, unless the deposition notice contains a certification, with supporting facts, that the person to be examined is expected to leave the United States and will subsequently be unavailable for examination in this country. The purpose of the deposition is to uncover and explore all facts known by a party to the lawsuit or by a nonparty witness involved in the lawsuit. A party or nonparty witness who is questioned during a deposition is called a **deponent.** As noted in Chapter 8, under Rule 26 of the federal rules, the scope of testimony during discovery is much broader than the scope of testimony during trial. During the taking of a deposition, an attorney is allowed to ask questions that could not be asked at trial because these questions seek evidence that is not admissible.

deponent
An individual who responds to questions during a deposition.

Moreover, according to Rule 26, during a deposition the attorney may ask the deponent not only any questions involving admissible evidence, but also any questions that could reasonably lead to the discovery of admissible evidence. The three types of depositions are the oral deposition, the deposition upon written questions, and the telephone deposition.

The Nature of the Oral Deposition

An **oral deposition** involves the actual presence of the deponent who responds aloud to the questions asked by an attorney. An oral deposition may be held in the attorney's office, at the courthouse, or at some other convenient location. Rule 30 of the Federal Rules of Civil Procedure regulates the use of oral depositions.

oral deposition
A deposition which involves the actual presence of the deponent who responds aloud to the questions asked by an attorney.

In the year 2000, several amendments to the Federal Rules of Civil Procedure that affect the taking of depositions went into effect. One key amendment slightly altered Rule 30 by explicitly limiting the amount of time that can be spent on a single deposition. Specifically, Rule 30(d)(2) now states that one deposition can take no more than a single day and a maximum of seven hours. The rule was written based on the assumption that the most cost-effective and time-efficient depositions are conducted at a single sitting—allowing, of course, for sensible, convenient breaks. The rule also permits the parties to make other arrangements on their own if, for whatever reason, that becomes preferable. Moreover, the rule also recognizes that certain unexpected situations, such as emergency health problems or sudden power failures, might interrupt a deposition, thus requiring that it be continued on another day. Nothing in the rule prevents the court from shortening the depositions of a particular case or for certain witnesses, if it feels such measures are warranted. The court can also make changes in the single-day requirement if such a change is appropriate in a given case.

Your supervising attorney may be involved in an oral deposition in one of two ways. First, he may ask questions of the opposing party or a nonparty witness. In this situation, your attorney is said to be *taking the deposition.* If, in contrast, your attorney's client is being questioned, then your attorney will be present at the deposition to protect the best interests of that client. In this role, your attorney is said to be *defending the deposition.*

Another individual who is sometimes present at a deposition is the **court reporter** or *certified shorthand reporter.* The court reporter will place the deponent under oath, will take a word-for-word account of the proceeding, and, if required, will produce a written copy of the deposition. This written copy of the deposition is known as the **transcript.**

Under Rule 30(b)(2) the party taking a deposition may specify the means by which the deposition will be taken. The options available for taking a deposition include audio recording, video recording, and stenographic recording. The party taking the deposition pays for the recording, regardless of the means used. Rule 30(b)(3) permits any party, without giving prior notice, to designate another method of recording the deponent's testimony other than the method specified by the party taking the deposition. The additional recording is made at the expense of the party arranging for that additional method. Under the amendment to Rule 26(c)(5), potential deponents may be excluded from a deposition by court order. To obtain such an order, the party or the person sitting for the deposition must file a motion with the court seeking the exclusion of the person in question and stating that the movant attempted to resolve the exclusion issue before seeking the court's intervention.

Advantages of the Oral Deposition

One major advantage of the oral deposition is that it gives the attorney taking the deposition the opportunity to see how well a witness or the opposing party will perform on the witness stand. This insight may help the attorney determine how best to handle the party or witness should he actually testify at trial. For example, should the deponent appear unsure about certain aspects of his testimony, the attorney could be prepared to convince the jury at trial that the witness should be considered unreliable. In contrast, an attorney defending a deposition can see how well the client reacts to questions under pressure. This knowledge will enable the attorney to help the client improve his performance when that client must testify in court.

For example, in the *Velikovsky* case, discussed in this chapter's commentary, your supervising attorney may elect to take the deposition of Dr. Langdon. In his initial deposition, the doctor may try to explain some of his actions by saying that he did not feel well at the time of Ms. Velikovsky's examination. If Dr. Langdon changes his testimony at trial, your attorney can use these alterations to demonstrate to the jury that Dr. Langdon's testimony is unreliable. Moreover, when the deponent is a party, a statement that he or she makes during the deposition can be taken as an admission, if the

court reporter
An individual who records word for word the testimony of sworn witnesses in court or at depositions and who may be required to compose a written transcript of that testimony.

transcript
A typed or word-processed copy of the testimony of a witness produced by a court reporter following the oral testimony of the witness at trial or at a deposition; an official record of the proceedings of a court.

statement contradicts what the deponent says during the trial. Also under Rule 801(d)(1)(A) of the Federal Rules of Evidence, prior statements made by a nonparty during a deposition can also be used to show the truth of the prior statement if that prior statement contradicts what the witness says at trial and as long as the witness can be cross-examined.

Another advantage of a deposition is that it can be used to preserve the testimony of a witness who might be unavailable to testify at trial. In fact, historically, the preservation of evidence for trial was the primary motivation for permitting depositions to be used in the first place. However, today, under Rule 32(a)(3), in order to use a deposition at trial, the court must be convinced that the witness is dead, ill, infirm, aged, imprisoned, out of the country, more than 100 miles away from the court, or has been unresponsive to a subpoena. As is often the case, there is an escape provision that permits the court to accept a deposition if an unusual situation makes the appearance of the witness at trial undesirable.

Disadvantages of the Oral Deposition

One primary disadvantage of the oral deposition is that it is inconvenient. Frequently the deposition must be taken at times and places that disrupt the regular office routine. Oral depositions are also expensive and time consuming. An oral deposition allows the defending attorney to gain insight into the other attorney's case and strategy. The oral deposition also allows deponents to rehearse their testimony before the trial. Such rehearsals often destroy the element of spontaneity.

E-Discovery and Oral Depositions

The cybernetic age has contributed an enormous amount to the procedure of taking depositions. A wide variety of electronic recording devices and procedures are now available to attorneys that were not available to their counterparts in days gone by. Perhaps the most widely used electronic recording device today is the video recorder. In addition, telephone depositions and Internet depositions are becoming more common.

Videotaped Depositions

Attorneys are currently becoming more acquainted with the advantages of videotaping depositions. For example, today attorneys can purchase videotaped depositions that show potential deponents how to be an effective witness. The instructions can help deponents to prepare for their own depositions by giving them tips and explaining how to act during a deposition. Attorneys defending depositions can also videotape their own clients during deposition rehearsals. The client can then watch the tape and make adjustments during the actual deposition.

Attorneys taking depositions can also use videotaping techniques as a part of their tactical package before trial. Certainly, it is advisable to make a video tape of a vital witness if that witness may be absent at the time of the trial because of severe illness, impending death, or the possibility of an extensive absence from the jurisdiction, as might occur, for example, in time of war when the deponent is a member of the armed forces or the news media. While a written copy of a deposition can also preserve the testimony of such witnesses, the videotape often has more dramatic appeal, provided that the taping is handled effectively.

An effective taping session generally involves the use of two cameras, one focused on the witness and the other on the questioning attorney. This multiple view prevents the type of boredom that can be provoked if the jury must watch a "talking head" on camera for any length of time. It is also advisable to use lavaliere microphones to insure a high-quality sound track for the recorded depositions. Lighting and background are also two important factors that must be taken into consideration when a videotaped deposition is planned.

The paralegal may have many responsibilities when a deposition is to be video-taped. For instance, she may be responsible for assembling and testing the equipment prior to the actual taping session. It may also be the job of the paralegal to make certain that the tapes are correctly labeled and properly stored. It is also important to remember that each new tape used during a deposition must begin with a statement of the date, time, and place of the deposition, the name of the deponent, and the name and address of the official who administered the oath to the deponent.

Telephone Depositions

The telephone deposition is an out-of-court question and answer session under oath conducted over the telephone. During such a deposition, the deponent and the questioning attorney are at separate locations. The court reporter who records the deposition is permitted to be with either the deponent or the attorney. Rule 30 of the Federal Rules of Civil Procedure permits the use of telephone depositions. The Rule 30 provision for telephone depositions also allows for "other remote electronic means." Rule 30 also indicates that a telephone or other remote electronic deposition is considered to have been taken in the district and at the place where the deponent is located and is actually answering the questions.

The telephone deposition is becoming more and more popular today. The cost saved by reducing expenses and the time saved by eliminating travel are attractive advantages. The downside of the telephone deposition is that it is often difficult to evaluate the appearance and effectiveness of the deponent on the telephone. Moreover, there is also the possibility of telephone communication difficulties. Nevertheless, the method is very useful to obtain an inexpensive deposition of a minor witness who lives far outside the jurisdiction. Your supervising attorney may request that you arrange the telephone deposition in the jurisdiction where the deponent is responding to the questions, arrange for the reporter and the electronic connection, and assist in the drafting of questions.

Electronic Depositions

One of the newest and most effective e-discovery tools uses the Internet for electronic deposition (e-deposition). Since Rule 30(b)(7) of the federal rules permits a deposition to be conducted by any "remote electronic means," some attorneys have attempted to conduct depositions via a live visual feed on the Internet. In fact, the practice has become so popular that several firms have been established across the country which specialize in conducting a wide variety of discovery techniques on the Internet.

One of the key advantages to an e-deposition is that it can be accessed anywhere, provided that an individual has an Internet connection, something which is almost as common as a television set in homes, schools, offices, and hotels today. Thus, the e-deposition can be viewed by all of the attorneys in a firm regardless of their location.

Often the video and audio appearance of the deponent during an e-deposition can be supplemented by an e-transcript that is synchronized with the video imagery. The e-deposition can also be augmented by a chatroom, permitting all those who are watching the deposition to "talk" in private to the attorney asking the questions. Moreover, the messages can be saved for later access. When the e-deposition has been completed, the e-transcript remains on-line and available to everyone involved in the case. Although e-depositions are now being used primarily by large law firms in major urban centers, the technique is the wave of the future and may soon be used in most law firms across the country. This is especially true as more computer-support firms are established to provide such services.

One of the primary advantages of an e-deposition is that it is cost effective. This is especially true if the e-deponent is located at a great distance or if it is necessary to e-depose experts because of the technical, scientific, or medical nature of the case. There are, of course, disadvantages to the e-deposition. One chief disadvantage is that, despite the real-time visual contact with the e-deponent, many subtle details can be lost due to the electronic nature of the communication. For example, it is often possible for an attorney to catch minor but significant signals from the deponent's speech and body language in a live deposition, which may not be possible in an e-deposition due to the poor quality of a video feed.

Video and Web Conference Depositions

As discussed in Chapter 8, another new e-discovery tool that your attorney might want to consider during discovery is the video conference. As mentioned, a video conference permits several individuals at widely separated geographical locations to discuss the planning of the case. A video conference site requires television cameras, microphones, monitors, and a speaker system at each location. Connections among sites can be arranged using phone lines or a satellite transmission network. A web conference, as noted, allows participants at several places to converse on line via the Internet using personal computers. It is possible to use either the video conference set up or the on-line web conference connection to conduct a deposition. As with the telephone and e-deposition, Rule 30(b)(7) of the federal rules authorizes the use of both video and web conference depositions. The difference between a web conference and an e-deposition simply involves the number of individuals who are connected on line during the actual deposition, and the two terms can be used interchangeably.

The Paralegal's Role before the Oral Deposition

You may be asked to assist the attorney in preparation of the deposition. Because you will be handling the procedural details of the deposition process, the attorney will be free to concentrate on developing the substantive legal issues to be explored during the deposition. In the preparation for a deposition, you may be asked to handle both the notice and subpoena requirements. You may also be asked to prepare questions.

Notice Requirement

Professional courtesy dictates that the attorney taking the deposition should contact the defending attorney to schedule mutually acceptable dates and times for taking the depositions of the defending attorney's clients. Sometimes, securing a mutually acceptable date is a difficult process. Because of their different strategic concerns in planning their cases, the two attorneys may have conflicting preferences as to who should take depositions first. Such conflicting strategic concerns are usually resolved by the attorneys themselves through friendly compromise. It is also possible that the party or witness will resist the prospect of having to sit for a deposition, either because he is apprehensive about the process itself or because he sees the deposition as providing assistance to the opposition. It is even possible for the potential deponent to feel that the deposition is an inconvenient and unnecessary burden that infringes on his work or leisure time. In such cases, it is the job of the defending attorney to allay the apprehensions of the client. Nevertheless, the attorney taking the deposition should make every effort to be flexible in scheduling a date and a time that is convenient for the party or witness.

The federal rules and the rules of most other jurisdictions require that formal notice of a deposition be given to the deponent and to each party. The length of time between the date that notice is required and the date of the deposition will be determined by the jurisdiction in which the case is being heard. Rule 32 of the Federal Rules of Civil Procedure prohibits the use of a deposition in a court proceeding against a party who received less than 11 days notice of the deposition, and who at the time of the deposition had a motion pending for a protective order requesting that the deposition either not be held or be held at a different time or place. Once an agreement on the deposition date has been reached, you may be asked to arrange for preparation and service of a **notice of intent to take oral deposition** (see Exhibit 9–1).

notice of intent to take oral deposition

A notice spelling out the date, time, and place of a planned deposition. The notice will also indicate the name and address of the intended deponent as well as the identity of the attorney who will ask the questions during the deposition.

This notice sets out the date, the time, the name and address of the person whose deposition is to be taken, and the means by which the testimony is to be recorded. Under Rule 30(b)(2) at the federal rules, the means of recording can include any of the electronic techniques previously mentioned. Thus, the notice must indicate if the deposition is to be videotaped or recorded electronically during an e-deposition. Rule 30(b)(2) also makes it clear that the party taking the e-deposition is responsible for bearing the cost of any e-discovery technique used.

Documents may also be obtained from a party to the litigation by serving a request for that party to bring those documents to the deposition. Rule 30(b)(5) of the Federal Rules of Civil Procedure allows for this process. However, the procedures of Rule 34, on production of documents, must also be followed whenever this is done. Thus, the specific documents or the categories of documents to be produced must be included in the deposition notice of attachment.

For example, in this chapter's *Velikovsky* case, your attorney will want to see Ms. Velikovsky's medical chart, her admission record, the pharmacy's record, any report filed by personnel in the radiology department, and all incident reports filed by

---

BEREA COUNTY COURT OF COMMON PLEAS

ELISHA VELIKOVSKY,	)
	) Civil Action No. 05-7507
Plaintiff,	)
	) NOTICE OF INTENT TO TAKE
	) ORAL DEPOSITION
v.	)
BEREA COUNTY HOSPITAL, et al.,	)
	)
Defendants.	)
	)
	)
	)
	)

To: Emma Archard, Attorney for Defendant,

PLEASE TAKE NOTICE that pursuant to Rule 30 of the Ohio Rules of Civil Procedure, Perry Matthews will take the oral deposition of David Cornwell before a notary public on January 9, 2006, at 4 P.M. and thereafter from day to day until completed, at the law offices of Bishop, Davidson, & Turner, 5477 East Ninth Street, London, Ohio 44124.

Testimony will be recorded by stenograph and videotape.

Respectfully submitted,

_____

Simon Bishop
Attorney for Plaintiff

CERTIFICATE OF SERVICE

I hereby certify that a true and correct copy of the foregoing Notice of Intent to take Oral Deposition has been furnished to counsel of record on this the twenty-first day of December, 2005.

_____

EXHIBIT 9–1   Notice of intent to take oral deposition

hospital personnel. In preparing a notice of deposition for Dr. Langdon, you might ask him to produce all documents related to the case to which he has access.

A request for records and documents at the time of a deposition is not, however, always the best way to handle discovery. If an attorney must wait to see the requested documents until the deposition, he may have to spend precious time reviewing the documents as the deposition proceeds. Moreover, subsequent examination of the documents often reveals information about which the deponent should have been questioned. This may necessitate the scheduling of another deposition.

No. **264**

Doc. **05-7507** Page **991**

COURT OF COMMON PLEAS

BEREA .... County, Ohio

ELISHA VELIKOVSKY

Plaintiff ....
vs.

BEREA COUNTY

HOSPITAL

et al. Defendant ....

SUBPOENA

Returned and Filed

RALPH KNOX

Clerk

By **HARRIET WILSHIRE**

Deputy Clerk

SHERIFF'S RETURN
Rev. Code. Secs. 2317.14; 2335.07, .31

.... Ohio, ... 20 ......

Received this writ .... 20 ...... at

.... o'clock .... M., and afterwards I served the same in the manner and at the time shown below, that is I read this writ to those witnesses whose names are marked R; I delivered a copy of it personally to those whose names are marked P; and I left a copy of it at the usual place of residence of those whose names are marked C. They are entitled to the number of miles set opposite their respective names. The others are not found.

NAMES OF WITNESSES	Miles	How Served	When Served 20 ......

FEES			
Service and return....... person, each			
Mileage, ... miles, at			
Total · · · · · · · · · · ·			

.... *Sheriff*
.... *County, Ohio*

By .... *Deputy*

EXHIBIT 9–2 Subpoena

Subpoena Requirement

subpoena

A written order issued by a court or an administrative agency commanding the presence of a person in order for that person to give testimony in an official proceeding. The word *subpoena* is an abbreviated form of the Latin term *subpoena ad testificandum.*

When the attorney taking the deposition is requesting a nonparty witness to testify, securing the deponent's presence will be necessary. The legal means for securing the presence of such a witness is a **subpoena** (see Exhibit 9–2). A subpoena is an official document issued by the clerk of court commanding a person to be present at a deposition.

To obtain a subpoena for a deponent in a federal lawsuit, you must provide a copy of the notice to take deposition to the clerk in the district where the deposition is to be taken. In state court, the state rules of civil procedures must be checked to determine who may serve a subpoena. In most states, a subpoena may be served by a sheriff, a bailiff, or any person who is not a party and who is 18 years of age or older. Your attorney may request that you serve the subpoena.

```
                                                          Form No.CB-1

              SUBPOENA—CIVIL CASE            CASE NO.  05-7507
                Rev. Code. Secs. 2317.11. .13. .13

To the Sheriff of  BEREA                    County, Ohio

        You are commanded to make due service and return of this Subpoena:
The State of Ohio,  BEREA              County, ss.    COURT OF COMMON PLEAS

To    DAVID CORNWELL
      9601 CONCORD AVENUE
      HAMPTON, OHIO

You Are Hereby Required to attend before the Court of Common Pleas at the Court House in
BEREA            County, on the   9th   day of  FEBRUARY          20 06 ,
at  1:00  o'clock P.M., to testify as witness.... in behalf of the   PLAINTIFF       in a
certain cause pending in said Court, wherein  ELISHA VELIKOVSKY
Plantiff , and     BEREA COUNTY HOSPITAL                    Defendant ,
and not depart the Court without leave.

      Herein fall not under penalty of the law.     WITNESS my signature and the seal of said Court,
                                                    this 30th day of JANUARY    20 06 ,
                                                    RALPH KNOX
                                                                              Clerk
ATTY.  Simon Bishop                                By HARRIET WILSHIRE
                                                                        Deputy Clerk
```

EXHIBIT 9–2 *(continued)*

In addition to the court costs incurred for a subpoena, it may also be necessary to reimburse the deponent for his appearance. For example, the witness may be entitled to reimbursement for mileage and meals. These costs would be in addition to the mandatory witness reimbursement fee provided by many states. Prior to obtaining the subpoena, check with the clerk of court to determine all of the fees involved in the process. Make certain that a check in the correct amount is furnished to the clerk issuing the subpoena.

A nonparty witness can be subpoenaed to produce documents at his deposition according to Rules 30 and 45 of the Federal Rules of Civil Procedure. This can be accomplished by serving the nonparty witness with a **subpoena duces tecum.** The subpoena duces tecum will contain a specific listing of the documents that the nonparty witness must produce at his deposition.

For example, in the *Velikovsky* case of this chapter's commentary, your supervising attorney may want Cornwell to produce all documents related to the case to which he has access. He might also ask him to produce a copy of the Berea County Hospital policy and procedure manual and any memos, notices, e-mails, or electronic attachments that outline procedures to be used in the radiology department. Records of any in-service training on the subject would also be helpful in this case.

subpoena duces tecum
A written order issued by a court or an administrative agency commanding the presence of a person in order for that person to give testimony and to surrender the evidence that is enumerated in the subpoena. Generally, such evidence takes the form of documents, records, letters, memos, and so on.

Preparation for the Deposition

Once the deposition has been scheduled and notice has been given to the potential deponent, preparation for the deposition begins. The nature of the preparation process depends on whether your attorney will be taking the deposition or defending it. If your attorney is taking the deposition, he will prepare to question the opposing party or a nonparty witness. If he is defending the deposition, he will prepare his own client to answer questions posed by the opposing attorney.

Preparation for Taking the Deposition   If your attorney is preparing to take a deposition, you have to do a variety of tasks designed not only to gather background information, but also to plan the actual deposition. In gathering background information, you will be required to review documents related to the deponent, to develop a history of events as they involve the deponent, and to summarize prior discovery pertaining to the deponent. In planning the deposition, you may be called upon to prepare a deposition outline and to plan the questions that your attorney will ask the deponent. During this step you may also be asked to prepare any exhibits that may be used during the deposition.

For example, in this chapter's *Velikovsky* case, you might be asked to compile Ms. Velikovsky's statements, medical bills, and medical history prior to Cornwell's deposition. You may also be asked to arrange for the hiring of a court reporter to place the deponent under oath, to record the question-and-answer session, and to provide the necessary transcripts. If the deposition is to be videotaped, you may be asked to set up and test the equipment before the taping session, to label the tapes, and to file the tapes properly. You may also be responsible for making certain that each new tape used during a deposition begins with a statement of the date, time, and place of the deposition, the name of the deponent, and the name and address of the official who administered the oath to the deponent. If the deposition is to be part of a video conference, the paralegal may assist in setting up the needed equipment. A video set-up for a video conference deposition requires the use of television cameras, microphones, monitors, and a speaker system.

The site of the deposition will also have to be arranged. In determining how far a deponent can be required to travel to a deposition, Rule 45 of the Federal Rules of Civil Procedure must be consulted. This rule states that, if a person who is not a party or an officer of a party has been issued a subpoena to appear for a deposition that is to be held more than 100 miles from the person's residence, place of employment, or place of transacting business, that person may file a motion with the court to quash or modify the subpoena. On the other hand, if the party who arranged the deposition can convince the court of the substantial need for the deponent's testimony or material cannot be otherwise obtained without undue hardship, the court may require the deponent to travel more than 100 miles provided that the deponent is reasonably compensated for the inconvenience. (See Chapter 2 for a discussion of the place of the district courts in the structure of the federal court system.) Residents of the district can be subpoenaed to appear at a deposition in the county where they reside, work, or transact business. The rule, however, does allow the court to choose another location that would be convenient to the deponent. A resident of another federal court district can be required to attend a deposition in the county where he or she is subpoenaed or within a 40-mile radius of that place. Again, the rule allows the court to set some other convenient location. As far as the actual physical setting of the deposition, there are no rules. The deposition may be held at the attorney's office, at the courthouse, or at some neutral site, such as a hotel meeting room.

Preparation for Defending the Deposition Should your client be asked to appear for a deposition, you may want to consult with your attorney to determine if any preliminary objections should be raised. For example, if your client has been asked to bring documents, records, letters, memos, or any other form of physical evidence to the deposition, your attorney may, depending on the circumstances, decide that certain objections are in order. As noted in Chapter 8, such objections can be based on the attorney-client privilege, the work product privilege, the common interest privilege, the Fifth Amendment privilege against self-incrimination, the medical privilege, or the confessor-penitent privilege.

A party or a nonparty witness who is asked to produce documents at the deposition may also object on the grounds that the request is **overbroad.** Such an objection claims that the request seeks more information than could ever be useful to the other party in the lawsuit. Another additional objection that can be raised is that the request is **duplicative.** This means that the other party has asked for the same information a number of different times in a number of different ways.

Once the preliminary discussion concerning objections is complete, you will need to prepare the client for the deposition. This will require an initial conference with the client. At the conference, your attorney explains the deposition process to the client and reviews anticipated areas of questioning. Usually such a conference should be scheduled prior to the day of the deposition. Such an early meeting will give the attorney time to react should the client be unable to produce a needed document, or should the client's planned testimony appear to contradict the testimony of another witness. If your attorney prefers extensive deposition planning, he may want to prepare an outline predicting the strategy of the opponent. You may be called upon to write a plan that anticipates the opposing attorney's questions. You may also be asked to organize any documents the witness has been asked to produce.

Often the preparation of the deponent must go beyond simply determining the subject matter of the question-answer period. Sometimes the witness must be coached on how to act during the deposition. For example, it may be necessary to help the deponent develop his technique by being encouraged to restate all questions, to answer questions carefully, and to ask for the clarification of ambiguous or puzzling questions. This advice should be heeded especially if the opposing attorney is asking deliberately misleading or intentionally confusing questions, or if that attorney is soliciting irrelevant or unnecessary information, which can often happen in such depositions. Deponents should also be cautioned never to volunteer any information not specifically sought by the interrogator. Sometimes it is also necessary to deal with an anxious or fearful deponent. Often, having the deponent view a videotape of another deposition will allay his anxiety, provided the tape depicts a fairly typical deposition. Such videos can reassure the deponent that the deposition procedure is an ordinary, uncomplicated process that happens on a routine basis in such lawsuits.

overbroad
A term that describes a request made during discovery that is so wide ranging and inclusive that it asks for more evidence than could ever be useful to the other party in the lawsuit.

duplicative
A term that describes a request made during discovery that replicates a request that was made at some previous time during the lawsuit.

1. Dress neatly but conservatively.
2. Listen to the question carefully. Take your time in answering.
3. Answer each question aloud. Avoid head nodding and shaking.
4. Answer the question asked, not the question you wish had been asked.
5. Do not volunteer information.
6. Be courteous, but not overly friendly.
7. Do not be argumentative. Do not lose your temper.
8. Do not interrupt the attorney's question.
9. If you do not understand the question, ask that it be repeated.
10. Listen carefully to any rephrasing of your answer. Correct any inaccurate rephrasing.
11. If you need to review a document to answer a question, request permission to do so.
12. If you do not know the answer to the question, say so. Do not guess or estimate. "I don't recall" is an acceptable answer.
13. Do not look at your attorney for help in answering a question.
14. Do not be distracted by objections made by your attorney.
15. If your attorney advises you not to answer a question, follow that advice.

EXHIBIT 9–3 Witness checklist for deposition testimony

mock deposition

A practice session that attempts to duplicate the question and answer period that will occur during a real deposition. The objective of a mock deposition is to help the party or witness rehearse for an upcoming deposition.

Many attorneys now conduct mock depositions. The purpose of the **mock deposition** is to help the party or witness prepare for an upcoming deposition. Such preparation will help the client know what to expect when her deposition is taken. This rehearsal not only relaxes the client, but also helps her recall the events about which she will be questioned. In the mock deposition, the client will be questioned by your attorney or another attorney in the firm. The format of the mock deposition should closely follow that of an actual deposition.

You may be asked to evaluate the effectiveness of the client during the mock deposition. In such an evaluation, the following questions should be considered: Is the client believable? Does the client answer questions completely? Does the client volunteer information not called for in the question? Many law firms provide a checklist for potential deponents that explains the procedure and outlines pitfalls to avoid. See the checklist in Exhibit 9–3.

The Paralegal's Role during the Oral Deposition

Notice of the deposition has been given, and preparation for the deposition is complete. Deposition time has arrived. Your job at the deposition will vary, based on your experience, the complexity of the case, and the attorney's division of responsibilities.

Your duties will also vary depending on whether your attorney is taking or defending the deposition. In either case, you will be asked to take notes and evaluate the witness. However, the focus of the notetaking and evaluating will depend on whether your attorney is taking or defending the deposition. You may also be called upon to control or produce documents and exhibits, depending upon your attorney's role in the deposition.

Notetaking

One of the most critical functions at the deposition is taking notes. Your notetaking will free your attorney to concentrate on the questions and the topics covered. If your attorney is taking the deposition, follow the deposition outline to make certain all questions are asked. Also, make certain the deponent answers each question. Use your notes to call incomplete or inconsistent answers to your attorney's attention. If your attorney is defending the deposition, note what facts the other attorney tends to focus upon as he questions your client. Moreover, try to determine whether the attorney's questioning pattern reveals his legal strategy in the case. Also, remember that your attorney is allowed to object to any question that he feels violates one of the privileges or principles discussed earlier in this chapter and in Chapter 8. Make certain that you accurately record these objections.

Witness Evaluation

You may be asked to assist in evaluating the effectiveness of a witness. If your attorney is taking the deposition, look for weaknesses in the deponent's testimony. The following questions should be addressed:

1. Has the deponent contradicted himself?
2. Does the deponent seem hesitant about certain aspects of his testimony?
3. How often does the deponent need to refer to notes or documents in order to answer your attorney's questions?
4. Is the deponent intimidated by your attorney?
5. How often does the deponent say that he does not remember certain facts?

Your evaluation will help your attorney determine how to use the deponent's testimony and how to treat the deponent should he be called on to testify at trial.

For example, in the *Velikovsky* case, your observations might reveal that Mr. Cornwell's description of the events surrounding Ms. Velikovsky's examination differs from the account given by Dr. Langdon. This information will help your attorney prepare for the examination of both Mr. Cornwell and Dr. Langdon at trial.

If your attorney is defending the deposition, your evaluation will be aimed at helping the witness improve his testimony. In this situation, the following questions should be addressed:

1. Does the deponent seem convincing?
2. Does he take his time in answering questions?
3. Does he volunteer information unnecessarily?
4. Is the deponent argumentative or overly friendly?

5. Does the deponent answer questions aloud, or does he rely on head nodding and shaking?

6. Is the deponent consistent in his testimony?

Your evaluation will help your attorney review his client's testimony as he plans his strategy leading to trial.

In this chapter's Velikovsky case, for instance, your evaluation of Ms. Velikovsky's deposition might help your attorney decide that he should have his client review the deposition before the trial to prevent any contradictions on the witness stand.

The Paralegal's Role after the Oral Deposition

Your responsibilities in the deposition process do not end with the final question. Postdeposition tasks may include assuming responsibility for the transcript and preparation of a deposition summary. This will require you to be familiar with the various types of deposition summaries that are available. If problems arise, the paralegal may also be involved in drafting and defending motions.

Transcript Arrangements

Both the attorney taking the deposition and the attorney defending the deposition may need to see a transcript. To obtain copies of the transcript, you must contact the court reporter to find out when the transcript will be ready. Many reporters will provide a copy of the deposition on a disk that facilitates summaries or even allows for the use of deposition summary software. Naturally, whether the reporter provides you with a disk or a paper copy of the deposition, you will be charged for the service. Moreover, if your attorney needs to see a copy immediately, the court reporter will probably charge an additional fee for having to speed up the process. You must also arrange for the appropriate number of copies, handle billing for the court reporter's services, and secure an appropriate date and place for delivery.

When you receive the deposition from the court reporter, you should distribute a copy to your attorney. The deposition should be reviewed for errors or significant omissions before it is summarized. This process can be speeded up if you compare the transcript with your deposition notes. You should also check the spelling of all unusual legal and medical terms.

The procedure for review of the deposition and signature by the deponent has been simplified by an amendment to Rule 30 of the Federal Rules of Civil Procedure. Review and signature are required only if requested by the deponent or party before the deposition has been concluded. The deponent has 30 days to sign and make any changes to the transcript after notice that the transcript or recording is available.

It is important to recall that web conferences and e-depositions can be supplemented by an e-transcript that is synchronized with the video imagery on the computer screen. Moreover, after completion of the e-deposition, the e-transcript is preserved on line and is thus accessible to anyone authorized to read it. In addition, both types of e-depositions are also enhanced by a chatroom feature that authorizes those observing the

THE COMPUTERIZED LAW FIRM
Full Text Searching

SCENARIO

It is the day of the Velikovsky trial. Dr. Langdon has just been examined by Samuel Rohmer, the attorney for Berea County Hospital (BCH). Dr. Langdon has testified that on the day of the Velikovsky examination he had eight hours of sleep prior to the session and was in perfect health. Your supervising attorney recalls that at some time during Dr. Langdon's deposition, he said that he had just finished an eight-hour shift when he was called back to BCH to cover the second shift because the physician scheduled for that shift had been involved in an accident. Your attorney also recalls that at another point in the deposition, Dr. Langdon had tried to explain some of his behavior by saying that he felt "flu-like symptoms accompanied by some dizziness." Unfortunately, your supervising attorney cannot recall exactly where in the deposition these remarks were made. Your supervising attorney asks for and is granted a half-hour recess before beginning the cross-examination of Dr. Langdon.

PROBLEM

Your attorney wants you to locate the discrepancies in Dr. Langdon's deposition. You have less than 30 minutes to search through a 157-page deposition. Conventional techniques prove useless. Your chronological summary provides no help. Paging through the deposition is too time consuming. The clock is ticking. Precious seconds are being lost. What can you do to save your client's case?

SOLUTION

One of the features of litigation support software described in the prior chapter is the ability to conduct a full-text search of depositions and other documents. The program works like this: At the deposition, the court reporter transcribes verbatim the testimony of the witness. The court reporter gives the transcript to the attorneys on a disk. The disk is then loaded into the litigation software. Recent developments in software for court reporters allow the court reporter and attorney to link their computers so that the court reporter's transcript is immediately fed into the attorney's computer. The attorney has an instantaneous record of the oral proceedings. New enhancements to litigation support software incorporate this feature so that it is not even necessary to obtain a copy of the transcript on disk (assuming that the computers for the court reporter and attorney are adequately equipped).

Once the transcript is loaded into the litigation support software, you can search the deposition for key words or phrases and locate any references by Dr. Langdon as to his physical condition. This is only one way in which this software can be used in connection with depositions. Software, such as the popular Summation programs, allows you to annotate or make notes to the transcript (printing these notes allows you to summarize the deposition electronically), to create and search databases of evidentiary documents, to search transcripts and document databases simultaneously (if a document is referred to in a deposition, it can be called up immediately and viewed), to perform searches of transcripts and document databases by date or by issue to create a case profile, and to print numerous reports. There is also software that will allow you to integrate and search video depositions. The features of this type of software, as well as the number of different products, are continually developing. To get a better and current idea of what can be done, visit the Summation Web site at <http://www.summation.com>.

e-deposition to "speak" discreetly to the attorney asking the questions. Significantly, the chatroom messages, like the e-transcript, can be saved for later access. None of this necessarily eliminates the need for a paper transcript of the e-deposition. In fact, it is wise to remember that most people read and interpret the text of an e-document much more completely and much more accurately in paper form. Consequently, it is unwise to place too much faith in e-copies of e-depositions, at least to the exclusion of paper copies of such documents. Moreover, it may also be necessary to have paper copies of e-depositions available at the time of the trial.

A year 2000 amendment to Rule 30 has altered the filing requirements for depositions. Under the old rule, transcripts had to be filed with the court. The new rule, specifically Rule 30(f)(1), requires that depositions be sent to the attorney who set up the deposition in the first place but does not require a filing with the court. This change was made to parallel Rule 5(d) of the Federal Rules of Civil Procedure, which expressly forbids the filing of depositions until such time as the deposition is actually used in the proceeding or until the court orders that the filing take place.

The Deposition Summary

The **deposition summary** is a written abridgement of a deposition which condenses the question-and-answer period down to a concisely written, understandable account. A properly written deposition summary can organize selected topics or subject matter into an orderly arrangement. Once the testimony has been arranged in the deposition summary according to a particular plan, inconsistent testimony may become evident. A well-drawn summary could also point out missing pieces of evidence that might lead your attorney to conduct further discovery.

Presummary Considerations   Before writing your deposition summary, determine when your attorney needs it. Determine the format to be used, the amount of detail required, and the issues or testimony your attorney wants pinpointed. It may be necessary to find out whether your attorney prefers a completely paraphrased summary or one that includes direct quotes from the deponent. Also, make certain you know whether your attorney wants you to write in phrases or complete sentences. Finally, determine which type of deposition summary your attorney wants you to use.

Types of Deposition Summaries   Basically, you have three types of deposition summaries from which to choose: the **page-line deposition summary,** the **topical deposition summary,** and the **chronological deposition summary.** The page-line deposition summary will record the information in the order in which it was actually presented during the deposition process (see Exhibit 9–4). Such a summary is helpful when the attorney is uncertain about just how to use the deponent's testimony. The page-line summary allows the attorney to review the testimony quickly and focus on areas that he wants to explore further. The topical deposition summary records the information produced by the deposition according to certain designated topics (see Exhibit 9–5). Such a deposition is useful when the attorney knows what areas he needs to concentrate on in planning his legal strategy. Finally, the chronological deposition summary records the information produced by the deposition based upon a specified temporal sequence (see Exhibit 9–6). Such a summary is needed when the chronology of events is of critical importance to the case.

---

deposition summary
A written abridgement of a deposition which condenses the question and answer period down to a concisely written, understandable account.

page-line deposition summary
A written abridgement of a deposition which records the information produced by the deposition in the order in which it was actually presented during the deposition process.

topical deposition summary
A written abridgement of a deposition which records the information produced by the deposition according to certain designated topics.

chronological deposition summary
A written abridgement of a deposition which records the information produced by the deposition based upon a specified temporal sequence.

PAGE-LINE DEPOSITION SUMMARY

Page	Line	Topic	Summary
4	9	Test	Patient Velikovsky was scheduled for an intravenous polygram.
8	17	Antidote	The antidote had to be retrieved from the pharmacy.

EXHIBIT 9–4   Page-line deposition summary

TOPICAL DEPOSITION SUMMARY

Topic	Page	Summary
Education	1	He received an associate's degree from Berea County Community College.
Employment Experience	1	Cornwell was employed by Berea County Hospital 6/5/96 as a radiologic technologist.
Certification	2	He became a certified radiologic technologist in 1997.
Patient's Chart	6	Cornwell identifies contents of Velikovsky's chart.
Patient's Condition	8	Velikovsky suffered cardiac arrest.

EXHIBIT 9–5   Topical deposition summary

CHRONOLOGICAL DEPOSITION SUMMARY

Date	Event	Page
1996	Graduated from college	1
1996	Employed at Berea County	3
1997	Certified as R.T.	2

EXHIBIT 9–6   Chronological deposition summary

The type of summary that you use in a case will depend not only on the facts involved but also on the legal issues that your supervising attorney wants to emphasize. For instance, in this chapter's *Velikovsky* case, your attorney may be primarily interested in demonstrating that Dr. Langdon was negligent in the procedure that he followed in administering the contrast medium. Therefore, your supervising attorney would be interested in tracing the steps followed by Dr. Langdon. In such a case, the chronological summary would be most helpful.

deposition upon written questions

A deposition before a court reporter that consists of oral responses by the deponent to written questions.

The Deposition upon Written Questions

A **deposition upon written questions** is a deposition before a court reporter that consists of oral responses by the deponent to written questions. Although the deponent is physically present at this type of deposition, the attorney who prepared the questions is not. Instead, he has submitted the written questions prior to the deposition. Rule 31 of the Federal Rules of Civil Procedure regulates the use of this type of deposition. Rule 31 incorporates the Rule 30 amendment limit on number of depositions, deposing the same witness twice, or taking a deposition before the time set by Rule 26(d). The time for serving written questions was also shortened under a 1993 Rule 31 amendment:

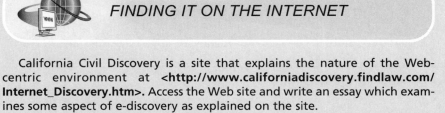

FINDING IT ON THE INTERNET

California Civil Discovery is a site that explains the nature of the Web-centric environment at **<http://www.californiadiscovery.findlaw.com/Internet_Discovery.htm>**. Access the Web site and write an essay which examines some aspect of e-discovery as explained on the site.

Federal Rules of Civil Procedure can be accessed at the following address: **<http://www.law.cornell.edu/rules/frcp>**. Access the Web site, find Rules 30, 31, and 32, and check to see if there have been any recent updates of the provisions and requirements as stated under these rules.

An extensive, detailed article entitled "Electronic Discovery: Making Your Opponent's Computer a Vital Part of Your Legal Team" can be found at **<http://cyber.law.harvard.edu/digitaldiscovery/library/cost/grenig.html>**. Access the Web site and report on the contents of the article.

A recent article on electronic depositions can be found on the Web site of the American Bar Association, which can be accessed at **<http://www.i-dep.com/news/abajournal_oct00.asp>**. Access the Web site and report on the contents of the article.

An article entitled "Electronic Discovery Is Here to Stay" can be found at **<http://cyber.lexisnexis.com/literature/pdfs/Arizona_Article_on_EDD.pdf>**. Access the Web site and report on the contents of the article.

cross-questions—14 days after notice and written questions are served

redirect questions—7 days after service of cross-questions

recross questions—7 days after service of redirect questions

Depositions upon written questions are easy and inexpensive. They are used primarily to obtain business records and testimony from a minor witness whose oral deposition could be very expensive because of the witness's distant location. Although this type of deposition is inexpensive, it does have certain disadvantages. For example, because the questions are written in advance, there is no way to ask follow-up questions based on the witness's answers. Similarly, there is no opportunity to observe the witness during the deposition.

Your attorney may request that you prepare the **notice of intent to take deposition upon written questions.** This notice is similar to the notice of intent to take oral deposition. It spells out the date, time, and place of a planned deposition upon written questions. The notice will also indicate the name and address of the intended deponent as well as the identity of the officer who will attend the deposition. A subpoena must accompany any such notice served upon a nonparty to the lawsuit.

An additional responsibility you may be asked to assume is the drafting of the written questions. To draft these questions, you should first review the pleadings and previous discovery. Determine the areas of examination to be included in the questions, draft the questions, and furnish them to your attorney for review and revisions. Once your attorney's changes have been made, incorporate those changes into your draft questions and arrange the written questions in final order.

notice of intent to take deposition upon written questions

A notice spelling out the date, time, and place of a planned deposition upon written questions. The notice will also indicate the name and address of the intended deponent as well as the identity of the officer who will attend the deposition. A subpoena must accompany any such notice served upon a nonparty to the lawsuit.

Summary

- A deposition is the written or oral testimony of a witness or party given under oath outside the courtroom. A person questioned during a deposition is a deponent. The scope of testimony during a deposition is much broader than the scope of testimony during trial.

- During an oral deposition, the deponent is actually present to answer the attorney's questions aloud. The attorney who asks the questions during the deposition is said to be taking the deposition. If the attorney's client is being questioned, the attorney is said to be defending the deposition. There are both advantages and disadvantages to oral depositions. One advantage of the oral deposition is that it gives the attorney taking the deposition the opportunity to see how well a witness or opposing party will perform on the witness stand. Another is that the oral deposition commits a deponent to one version of the facts. A third advantage is that the attorney defending the deposition can see how well his client reacts to questions under pressure. One disadvantage of a deposition is that it is inconvenient. Second, oral depositions are expensive and time consuming. Finally, the oral deposition allows a deponent to rehearse his testimony before trial. The use of videotaped depositions, as models, records, and rehearsals, is rapidly increasing.

- The cybernetic age has contributed a great deal to the procedure of taking depositions. Many electronic recording devices and procedures are available to attorneys today. One of the most-often used electronic recording devices is the video recorder. In addition, telephone depositions and e-depositions are common today. Another new e-discovery tool that is helpful is the video conference, which permits several individuals at widely separated locations to discuss the planning of the case. Another e-discovery tool is the web conference, which permits participants at different locations to have an on-line conversation via the Internet using personal computers. Both the video conference set-up and the on-line web conference connection can also be used to conduct depositions.

■ The role of the paralegal in the preparation for the deposition is quite broad. The paralegal may be asked to arrange for the preparation and service of a notice of intent to take an oral deposition. The paralegal may also be asked to obtain subpoenas for several deponents. Finally, the paralegal may be called upon to help prepare for the deposition. The exact nature of this preparation will depend upon whether the attorney is taking or defending the deposition.

■ During the actual deposition, the paralegal may be asked to take notes. The paralegal may also be asked to evaluate the effectiveness of the deponent.

■ After the deposition, the paralegal may have to obtain a transcript of the deponent's testimony. The paralegal may also have to write a deposition summary. There are three types of deposition summaries: the page-line deposition summary, the topical deposition summary, and the chronological deposition summary.

■ A deposition upon written questions is a discovery tool that requires the deponent to answer written questions orally in the presence of a court reporter. In the telephone deposition, the deponent and his attorney are present in one location, and the attorney taking the deposition is in another location asking the questions by telephone.

Key Terms

chronological deposition summary	mock deposition	overbroad
court reporter	notice of intent to take deposition upon written questions	page-line deposition summary
deponent		subpoena
deposition summary	notice of intent to take oral deposition	subpoena duces tecum
deposition upon written questions	oral deposition	topical deposition summary
duplicative		transcript

Review Questions

1. What is a deposition?
2. Name three advantages and three disadvantages of oral depositions.
3. Name four trends in e-discovery.
4. What is a notice of intent to take an oral deposition?
5. What responsibilities does a paralegal have in preparing for a deposition?
6. What responsibilities does a paralegal have during an oral deposition?
7. Explain the paralegal's role in arranging for a transcript.
8. Identify three types of deposition summaries.
9. What are the advantages and the disadvantages of taking a deposition upon written questions?

Chapter Exercises

Where necessary, check with your instructor prior to starting any of these exercises.

1. Review the laws of your state and find all state laws that deal with depositions. Check your local court rules to see if any local rules of court in your area regulate who may be present during the taking of a deposition. Also check local rules to see who may be present to record the questions and answers to a deposition.

2. Contact your local bar association. Try to find out how many local attorneys are using video equipment to instruct clients on how to conduct themselves during a deposition. Also find out if any local attorneys are using video equipment to help clients rehearse for their own depositions.

3. Analyze the following situation. David Cornwell, a certified radiologic technologist, was to be a witness in the case of *Elisha Velikovsky v. Berea County Hospital.* Attorney Simon Bishop was charged with the responsibility of conducting Cornwell's deposition. After the completion of Cornwell's deposition, a transcript was produced (see Appendix A). Read the transcript of the deposition and create one of the following: a chronological deposition summary, a page-line deposition summary, or a topical deposition summary. Use your own judgment in deciding which of the three types of depositions would best help your attorney's client in this case.

Chapter Project

Review the *Velikovsky* case in the opening commentary. Recall that your supervising attorney will be conducting the deposition of David Cornwell, the radiologic technologist. Draft a checklist for evaluating Cornwell.

The *Bennett* Case
Assignment 9: Setting Up a Deposition

Your supervisory attorney wants to take the deposition of Martha Yee, a former employee of defendant and coworker of Bennett. Prepare the notice of deposition for the defense attorney and subpoena for Ms. Yee.

Chapter 10

Interrogatories

CHAPTER OUTLINE

Interrogatories
Drafting Interrogatories
Drafting Answers to Interrogatories

COMMENTARY—THE WESTON MALL CASE

On December 3, 2005, Elizabeth Petrie was shopping for a birthday present for her sister, Georgette. After leaving her car in the parking garage, she crossed the connecting bridge to the mall. As she was descending the steps on the mall side of the bridge, the stairway collapsed and Ms. Petrie fell 12 feet to the ground. She broke her left leg, suffered a mild concussion, and sustained serious internal injuries. About three months later, Ms. Petrie decided to bring a lawsuit against the management of The Weston Mall Corporation, the owner and operator of Weston Mall. Your firm has been retained to represent Ms. Petrie. Your supervising attorney has asked you to draft interrogatories to be answered by The Weston Mall Corporation. The goal is to obtain additional information about the condition of the stairway as well as the general maintenance and repair procedures followed by the physical plant department of Weston Mall. You will also assist in preparing answers to interrogatories sent to your client by The Weston Mall Corporation's attorney.

OBJECTIVES

The preceding chapters gave you an overview of the discovery process and introduced you to the tools of discovery. Interrogatories are another effective discovery device. After reading this chapter, you should be able to:

- Define interrogatories.
- Explain the various purposes of interrogatories.
- List the advantages of using interrogatories.
- Outline the disadvantages of using interrogatories.
- Describe the specific types of interrogatories.
- Identify the types of topics covered in a set of interrogatories leading to a document production request for computer records.
- Explain the options available when a party refuses to answer an interrogatory.
- Outline the duty to supplement interrogatory answers.
- Describe when it would be appropriate to produce business records instead of a written interrogatory response.
- Explain the form of the interrogatory answer.
- Outline the objections that can be raised to interrogatories.

Interrogatories

Interrogatories are written questions submitted by one party in a lawsuit to another party in that suit. The responding party must answer these questions in writing and under oath. Rule 33 of the Federal Rules of Civil Procedure regulates the use of interrogatories in federal courts. As we have seen earlier in this text, many states have adopted the federal rules as their own. Still, you must always check for variations in state and local rules governing the use of interrogatories. The interrogatories must be answered by the party upon whom they are served. In the case of a partnership, a governmental agency, or a corporation, such as The Weston Mall Corporation, the answers are given by any officer or agent of that body. For example, in the *Weston Mall* case, a set of interrogatories might ask about the condition of the stairway prior to its collapse. An answer to these interrogatories could be given by any officer or agent of the corporation in a position to give a knowledgeable, informative, and honest response. Interrogatories should not be served until the parties have initially conferred as required under Rule 26 of the Federal rules. Once served, the answering party has 30 days to respond. Unlike depositions, interrogatories cannot be served on nonparty witnesses involved in the lawsuit.

Scope and Number of Interrogatories

You will recall from our earlier discussions on the scope of discovery that the type and the amount of evidence that can be sought by discovery is much broader than that which could be produced at the trial. A reference in Rule 33 of the federal rules to Rule 26(b)(1) makes it clear that this broad scope of discovery applies to interrogatories. The rule states that: "Interrogatories may relate to any matter which can be inquired into under Rule 26(b)(1), and the answers may be used to the extent permitted by the rules of evidence." All the interrogatories sent to a party at one time constitute a *set*. Multiple sets of interrogatories, however, can be served on the parties to a lawsuit. Within each set, each interrogatory is numbered for convenient reference. The federal rules require sequential numbering throughout all sets. For example, in this chapter's *Weston Mall* case, if the first set of interrogatories contained 20 interrogatories, the second set would begin with number 21. Because parties are automatically entitled to receive information through mutual disclosures under Rule 26, they are allowed to ask no more than 25 interrogatories (including discrete subparts). It is possible to increase the number of interrogatories by written agreement or with the court's permission. Some states also set such limits, although the allowable number of interrogatories varies from state to state.

Purposes of Interrogatories

The primary purpose of interrogatories is to obtain information about the basic facts in a case and to supplement the information required to be disclosed under Rule 26 of the Federal Rules of Civil Procedure. Interrogatories may also be used to determine the party's contentions and to identify specific individuals or documents that support those contentions. Not all state courts have rules comparable to Rule 26 or requiring automatic mutual disclosures. In such jurisdictions, interrogatories are commonly used to obtain the information that would otherwise be exchanged under Rule 26. That information might include the identity and location of both lay and expert witnesses that the other party intends to call to the stand at trial. It might also include the description and location of any relevant documents.

Properly drafted interrogatories can also help to narrow the issues and facts in preparation for trial. Also, like the deposition, interrogatories can be used to impeach a witness at the time of the trial. Finally, interrogatories may facilitate settlement of the case.

Advantages of Interrogatories

Interrogatories offer substantial advantages over other discovery methods. First of all, they are simple, inexpensive, and efficient. For instance, because a party answers interrogatories at her own pace, there is no need to schedule a special session convenient to all those involved. Interrogatories, therefore, avoid the logistical problems associated with depositions. Second, a set of interrogatories can be more thorough than a deposition. This is because interrogatories must be answered and verified by the party. The answering party has a duty to obtain the answer to an interrogatory if that information is in either the possession or the control of that party. The responding party also has the duty to provide the identity of the person who does have custody of a document if the party does not have it. A final advantage is the fact that interrogatories complement the other discovery techniques. For example, interrogatories may determine the identities of future deponents. They may also reveal documents that should be included in a subsequent request for production of documents.

Disadvantages of Interrogatories

Like the other discovery devices, interrogatories are not without their disadvantages. The first disadvantage is that they are limited to the parties to a lawsuit. Consequently, the use of interrogatories may not eliminate the need to take depositions at a later date. In fact, the use of interrogatories does not even eliminate the need to take the deposition of a party. Second, interrogatories lack spontaneity. Therefore, a party responding to a set of interrogatories has the time to draft self-serving answers. In addition, the answers are often edited by the attorney or the paralegal before they are sent out. Moreover, because the answers are written, they do not allow for immediate follow-up questions. Certainly, follow-up questions can be drafted and submitted, but this does not eliminate the possibility of further self-serving answers. Another disadvantage is that interrogatories may help the opposing attorney by motivating her to begin the preparation of her case earlier than she might ordinarily be inclined to proceed. In line with this, interrogatories can also alert the opposition to the direction of your case. In spite of these disadvantages, interrogatories are an effective discovery device.

Drafting Interrogatories

Paralegals are often asked to participate in drafting interrogatories. Your involvement in drafting the interrogatories will free your attorney's time so that she can concentrate on other matters. The drafting of interrogatories is one of the most important jobs that you may have during the litigation process, because properly drafted interrogatories not only provide information themselves, but also indicate the need to use other discovery devices. Your role in drafting interrogatories may later be expanded to include drafting a motion to compel the other party to respond to some of the interrogatories that have not been properly answered. You may also be responsible for reviewing the other party's response.

Preliminary Steps in Drafting Interrogatories

Before you can draft an effective set of interrogatories, you must take the time to familiarize yourself with the facts of the case. To do this properly, review the pleadings, the correspondence file, the attorney's notes, the research notebook, and the information provided in the initial and subsequent mutual discovery disclosures. Your review should be an active one. Take notes as you review the material and consider the types of questions you will want to ask the other party. In this chapter's *Weston Mall* case, for example, as a paralegal for the firm representing the plaintiff, Ms. Petrie, you would want to ask officials of The Weston Mall Corporation about the condition of the stairway at the time of the accident or about the maintenance and repair record associated with the collapsed stairway. Other questions may involve the circumstances surrounding the collapse of the stairway. Upon termination of the preliminary review, you will be ready to draft the interrogatories.

Form and Content of Interrogatories

The format that you use in drafting the interrogatories will be mandated by federal or state rules. Make certain to consult the appropriate court rules to determine the form required in your jurisdiction. In most jurisdictions, interrogatories contain a title, introductory paragraph, definitions, instructions, specific interrogatories, a signature, and a certificate of service.

Title of the Interrogatories and Introductory Paragraph   Discovery always involves the production of a wide variety of pleadings, motions, and requests. For this reason, all documents should carry an appropriate title. This procedure allows participants in the action to identify a document they have in their hands just by glancing at the title. The Federal Rules of Civil Procedure, as well as most state rules, also require the use of such titles. The title of the interrogatories should identify the party serving the interrogatories, the party receiving the interrogatories, and the number of the set of interrogatories:

Example

Defendant The Weston Mall Corporation's
First Set of Interrogatories
to Plaintiff Elizabeth Petrie

Pursuant to Rule _____, _____ Rules of Civil Procedure, you are to answer the interrogatories hereinafter set forth, separately, fully, in writing, and under oath. You should deliver a true copy of your answer to the undersigned attorney within 30 days after the date of service of these interrogatories.

EXHIBIT 10–1   Introductory paragraphs for interrogatories

The federal rules do not require an introductory paragraph. Nevertheless, tradition dictates including an introductory paragraph immediately after the caption of the case and the title of the interrogatories. Usually this paragraph identifies the recipient of the interrogatories. It also indicates that an answer is required within a specified period of time. The introductory paragraph should also state the appropriate federal or state rule under which the interrogatories are presented. Finally, the introduction may set forth the number of interrogatories permitted and the statutory requirements for supplemental answers. Exhibit 10–1 shows an example of the introductory paragraph.

Definitions   The definition section should be distinct so that the responding party can easily locate it. The heading "definitions" should be placed in the center of the page in bold-faced lettering. Definitions can be used to clear up discrepancies among words that have several meanings. They can also be used to establish the meaning of a word that is used frequently throughout the interrogatories. For example, in this chapter's *Weston Mall* case, the word "accident" may be repeated several dozen times. To avoid confusion, the definition section of the interrogatories might establish the definition in the following way, " 'accident' refers to the incident during which the plaintiff, Elizabeth Petrie, was injured on the premises of the Weston Mall, at 433 East 310th Street, Weston, Ohio." The definition section also conserves space and shortens the questions by eliminating the need to repeat the meaning of a word that appears throughout the interrogatories. Finally, properly drafted definitions can enlarge the number of questions asked by defining a word to include several subtopics. For example, as indicated in Exhibit 10–2, the words "identify" and "identity," when effectively defined, can result in an abundance of information about the people and the documents involved in a case.

Instructions   Instructions prevent confusion and help the party preparing the interrogatories to obtain the needed information. When drafting the instructions, be sure to include instructions for any desired action by the other party. Also make certain to offer the opposing party the opportunity to attach documents instead of answering an interrogatory. This will save time and avoid the need to file a request for production of documents.

It is also important, when drafting the instructions, to consider the time period that the interrogatories will cover. Your request should seek not only information about the incident that gave rise to the lawsuit, but also information about past conduct, conditions, and activities. For example, in the *Weston Mall* case, the accident took place on

1. To "identify" a document or state the "identity of" a document shall mean to state with respect thereto:
   a. The identity of the person who prepared it;
   b. The identity of the person who signed it or over whose signature it was or is issued;
   c. The identity of each person to whom it was addressed or distributed;
   d. The nature and substance of the document with sufficient particularity to enable it to be identified;
   e. The date, if any, which the document bears; and
   f. The present location of the document, including the identity of its custodian or custodians; or in lieu thereof, attach a copy of said document to your response to these interrogatories.
2. To "identify" or to state the "identity of" a person shall mean with respect thereto:
   a. The person's full name;
   b. The person's title and business or professional affiliation, if any, as of the time to which the answer relates; and
   c. The person's present title and business or professional and residence addresses.

EXHIBIT 10–2   Definitions

December 3, 2005. Your instructions may indicate that the applicable time period for the answers to the questions will extend from December 3, 2004 to the date the defendant actually answers the interrogatories. This will allow you to detect any preexisting problem with the stairway that might have contributed to the collapse of the structure. Drafting these instructions must be done with care, however. The inquiry must be comprehensive enough to discover relevant information, yet narrow enough to avoid an objection that the request is overbroad and burdensome.

Another topic often included in the instructions is the duty to supplement answers when additional information is received or there is a change in the content of any previous answer. However, it is important to note that not all states recognize this duty to supplement. Furthermore, the federal rules [Rule 26(e)] only require supplementation when ordered by the court or when a party learns that the response was materially incomplete or incorrect and the correct information has not otherwise been made known during the discovery process. The instructions should also explain how to deal with any objections that the responding party has to the interrogatories. For example, should the responding party object to part of a question, she should be instructed to answer any other part of that question that is not objectionable. A special instruction may also be used to inquire about any information withheld under a claim of the attorney-client privilege, the work product privilege, or the common interest privilege.

Because the instruction section of the interrogatories is a crucial part of this document, that heading should be centered and placed in bold-faced type. Some law firms

A. You are required by Rule _____ of the _____
   Rules of Civil Procedure to:
   1. Answer fully and factually each of the interrogatories hereinafter
      set out.
   2. Furnish all information called for by said interrogatory.
   3. Sign your response.
   4. Swear to your response.
   5. Serve same upon the undersigned attorney within thirty (30) days
      after the date of service of these interrogatories. You are further
      instructed:
B. Every interrogatory herein shall be deemed a continuing interrogatory,
   and you are to supplement your answers promptly if and when you
   obtain relevant information in addition to, or in any way inconsistent
   with, your initial answer to any interrogatory.
C. If you object to, or otherwise decline to answer, any portion of an
   interrogatory, provide all information called for in that portion of the
   interrogatory to which you do not object or which you do not decline
   to answer. If you object to an interrogatory on the grounds that to
   provide an answer would constitute an undue burden, provide such
   requested information as can be supplied without undertaking an
   undue burden. For those portions of any interrogatory to which you
   object or otherwise decline to answer, state the reason for such
   objection or declination.
D. The applicable period of time, unless otherwise provided, shall be from
   _____ to the date of answering these interrogatories.
E. If any answer is refused in whole or in part, on the basis of a claim of
   privilege or exemption, state the following:
   1. the nature of the privilege or exemption claimed;
   2. the general nature of the matter withheld (e.g., substance of
      conversation of the withheld information, name of originator);
   3. name(s) of person(s) to whom the information has been imparted;
      and
   4. the extent, if any, to which the information will be provided subject
      to the privilege or exemption.

EXHIBIT 10–3   Instructions

combine definitions and instructions, so check on the accepted procedure in your office. Exhibit 10–3 contains examples of the instructions that you might incorporate in the interrogatories directed to the plaintiff in the *Weston Mall* case.

Specific Interrogatories   Several types of interrogatories may be asked. Each of these is designed to elicit a different form of information related to the lawsuit. These special interrogatories include interrogatories that identify people, interrogatories that establish facts or lead to the discovery of facts, interrogatories that identify documents, and interrogatories that identify contentions. The number of specific questions allowed under the new federal rules is 25. Care must be taken in drafting questions, because "discrete" subparts are counted separately. Obviously this is so that attorneys do not defeat the 25-question limit by drafting compound questions with multiple subparts.

1. **Interrogatories that identify people.** The identities of the people who are involved in the lawsuit are very important. As part of the initial mutual discovery, you should receive names of persons who are likely to have discoverable knowledge relevant to the disputed facts that are stated with particularity in the pleadings. However, you may still wish to ask some specific questions about individuals. You may also be in a jurisdiction that does not provide for any mutual disclosure. For example, in the *Weston Mall* case of this chapter's commentary, you may need to determine the identities of any witnesses to the accident. You may also need to identify the maintenance workers who maintained or repaired the stairway that collapsed. It would also be helpful if you could uncover the identities of individuals who have direct knowledge of the condition of the entire physical plant of the mall to determine if there is a pattern of negligent behavior on the part of the mall employees charged with maintaining the condition of the premises.

Another area of questions about people concerns the identities of all persons who have given statements to the other party's attorney. For example, has the opposing attorney taken statements from witnesses, physicians, neighbors, safety experts, and so on? Once you receive this information, you will be able to schedule any depositions that your attorney decides are necessary. You will also be able to draft any document production requests that appear appropriate.

Finally, in some jurisdictions, interrogatories can be used to identify the expert witnesses that the opposition intends to call at trial as witnesses. Exhibit 10–4 gives an example of this type of interrogatory.

It is important to note that such an interrogatory can be asked only about an expert who will be called to testify at trial. If an expert will not be called to testify, this information is not discoverable. It is protected by the work product privilege.

2. **Interrogatories to establish facts.** Some of the questions in any set of interrogatories will seek to uncover facts surrounding the allegations in the pleadings. These questions should always be aimed at the most recent pleading filed by the opposition. Thus, if the plaintiff has filed an amended complaint, that amended complaint becomes the target of the fact-finding interrogatories, rather than the original complaint. Fact-finding interrogatories should cover the who, what, when, where, why, and how of the allegations. This is known as seeking the "five W's and an H."

3. **Interrogatories that identify documents.** Although mutual discovery may have revealed the existence of some documents, you may still wish to ask some specific questions regarding documents. Interrogatories directed at uncovering documents may seek information about medical reports, medical bills, earning statements, and income tax returns. Such questions may also seek to discover any statements received or given in connection with the accident. Pleadings and prior discovery are additional documents that interrogatories may ask about.

4. **Interrogatories that identify contentions.** Rule 33(c) of the Federal Rules of Civil Procedure states that an interrogatory need not be objectionable simply if it asks for "an opinion or contention that relates to fact or the application of law to fact." This

State the name, business address, title, and qualifications of each and every person whom you intend to or may call as an expert witness during the trial of this case. With respect to each such expert, state the following information:
  a. Describe in detail the subject matter about which the expert is expected to testify;
  b. Each and every mental impression and opinion held by the expert with respect to this lawsuit and all facts known by the expert (regardless of when the actual knowledge was acquired) that relate to or form the basis of such mental impressions and opinions;
  c. The style, case number, and court of each and every case in which such expert has previously provided expert testimony, whether by deposition or at trial;
  d. List and describe completely all facts provided to the expert witness for use in connection with the expert's analysis of all or any portion of the issues in this case. For any such facts that are in document form, you may instead attach a copy of such document to your response to these interrogatories; and
  e. If the expert has submitted a report, please recite verbatim all contents thereof or, if you prefer, a copy of same may be attached to your response to these interrogatories.

EXHIBIT 10–4   Expert witness interrogatory

is a crucial part of the interrogatories because it requires the disclosure of not only the contention, but also the basis for that contention. For example, in the *Weston Mall* case, the interrogatories sent to your client may seek the following contention.

Example

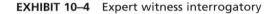

1. Do you contend that Defendant, The Weston Mall Corporation, was negligent by failing to maintain safe premises for its customers?
2. If so, please state all facts upon which you base your contention.
3. If your answer to question number 1 is yes, please identify every person who has knowledge or information relating to those facts.
4. If your answer to question number 1 is yes, please state whether any statements have been given by persons you identified in question number 3 above.
5. If your answer to question number 1 is yes, please identify any document or other evidence that you believe supports your contention.

The answers to these questions may not be obvious early in the lawsuit. Therefore, these types of questions are of greater value in a set of interrogatories filed toward the end of the discovery process. In fact, the court may order that this type of "interrogatory need not be answered until after designated discovery has been completed or until a pretrial conference or other later time."

E-Evidence and E-Interrogatories   One of the most effective ways for an attorney involved in a complicated lawsuit to obtain information about his opponent's computer records is by filing interrogatories aimed at determining the nature of those records. The most efficient way to gather e-evidence is to first send interrogatories, the answers to which can then guide the attorney's document-production requests. As is true of traditional interrogatories, the initial step in fashioning the e-interrogatories is to define all terms. The interrogatories that then follow should fall under several categories. First, the interrogatories should ask about the actual nature of the party's computer system. Such questions would attempt to determine the number and types of computers that are in operation as a part of the party's daily routine. This is not as simple as it seems on the surface. Sometimes certain computers may escape detection. This is why it would be helpful to make certain that the interrogatories specify that the term *computer* includes desktop PC's, laptops, mobile phones, personal digital assistants (PDAs), and home computers that are part of a network. It is also wise to remember that many employees retain the habit of filing paper copies of all e-documents, even those e-files that have been deleted from their computer system. In fact, some employers require the retention of paper copies as a precaution against a computer system failure.

Another set of questions attempts to determine the configuration of any network systems that are a part of the party's operation. Such questions should also identify the number and location of all work stations and all network servers. It is also important to ask about any upgrades that have occurred, any equipment changes, any reformatting, and any policies that involve the elimination of data. Closely related to these are the policies that mandate the preservation of certain records or any backup processes in use for the saving of data. Another set of questions should be specifically aimed at acquiring an understanding of the party's e-mail system. It is also important to obtain the names and a list of responsibilities of all individuals who are in any way involved in maintaining or servicing the party's computer system. This may include the identities of both in-house and outside information technology (IT) experts, as well as administrative assistants and interns who work with IT experts.

Summary Paragraph   No matter how careful you are in drafting interrogatories, you will not cover all the information you will need to help your client in the lawsuit. A summary paragraph can be used to request any information that may be relevant to the suit. Such a summary question might read, "Do you have any additional information relevant to the subject of the lawsuit which has not been previously covered in your foregoing answers to these interrogatories? If so, please state that information." There are problems, however, with using this type of summary question. Although there is no harm in asking such a question, the responding party may object on the grounds that it is either overbroad or vague.

Signature and Certificate of Service   At the end of the specific questions, a signature line for the attorney and the firm's address should be included. Following the signature block, a certificate of service sets out the date, type of service, and to whom service of the interrogatories was made. Interrogatories are not filed in the federal court. You should consult your state and local rules to determine if filing is necessary in your jurisdiction. Exhibit 10–5 is a checklist for the paralegal's use in drafting interrogatories.

1. Read the documents—correspondence, pleadings, statements, documents produced, and so on.
2. Understand what the attorney wishes to accomplish with this particular set of interrogatories.
3. Read the pertinent court rules to determine such items as format and number of interrogatories permitted.
4. Consult form interrogatories.
5. Draft preliminary portions of request: title of document, introductory paragraph, and definitions and instructions, including time covered, continuing nature of interrogatories, procedure to be followed for objections, and permission for the party to provide a document instead of describing same.
6. Draft interrogatories that are directed to your facts and issues. Remember to identify facts and expert witnesses and documents that form the basis for the party's allegations or defenses. Include interrogatories that ask for legal and factual contentions.
7. Keep the interrogatories simple.
8. Organize interrogatories into categories.
9. Make certain the interrogatories ask the who, what, when, why, where, and how questions.
10. Request all facts relied upon in the last pleading filed.
11. Interrogatories should not be excessive in length or number.
12. Read the interrogatories for possible objections. Revise to avoid objections, if possible.
13. Proofread carefully prior to submitting to attorney for review, signature, and execution of certificate of service.
14. Arrange for service and filing, if necessary.
15. Calendar the answer date and follow up for same.
16. Consult with the attorney regarding the possibility of filing a motion to compel.

EXHIBIT 10–5   Tips for drafting interrogatories

Motion to Compel

Usually the party responding to the interrogatories will cooperate fully. If there are objections to certain questions, such objections can frequently be resolved on a friendly basis. However, there are times when the other party does not cooperate. The motion to compel can help remedy this situation.

Once the opposing party's answers are received, you should promptly read each answer, review the objections, and note any answer that is incomplete, unclear, evasive, or nonresponsive. Your attorney will be required to communicate with the other attorney and make a good faith effort to resolve any problem (Rule 37 of the Federal Rules of Civil Procedure). However, if agreement cannot be reached between the parties, you may be asked to draft a motion to compel.

Rule 37 of the Federal Rules of Civil Procedure allows for the filing of a motion to compel the uncooperative party to respond to the interrogatories. The motion must contain a declaration from the attorney for the moving party stating that a good faith effort to resolve the matter was made. Sanctions are available under Rule 37 if the responding party fails to answer the interrogatories properly and completely. Normally the courts are reluctant to grant sanctions unless efforts have been made by the parties to resolve the problem.

Drafting Answers to Interrogatories

Like all other forms of discovery, responding to interrogatories requires patient and careful planning. Because your client is responsible for answering the questions, it is essential that she be contacted immediately upon the receipt of a set of interrogatories. Working with the client, you can then determine how much time is needed to respond, how each question should be answered, which questions must be supplemented, which questions are best answered with business records, and which questions require objections.

Determining Time Limits

As soon as your office receives a set of interrogatories, you should contact the client and forward a copy of those interrogatories to her. Remember that the deadline for responding is normally 30 days after the interrogatories were received. Most interrogatories cannot be answered quickly. Therefore, you will have to consult with the client to determine if the time allowed is realistic. If you and the client conclude that more time is required, your attorney will have to negotiate an extension of that time period. It is important to take care of this immediately, because in some jurisdictions the failure to respond on time may waive the right to object to any interrogatory for which a proper objection might have been made in a timely fashion. Exhibit 10–6 is a checklist for use in drafting interrogatory answers.

Answering the Interrogatories

Interrogatories directed to an individual must be answered by that individual in writing under oath. Interrogatories addressed to a corporation may be answered by any officer, agent, or employee who has the requested information. In the *Weston Mall* case, for instance, an employee who has information about the physical state of the stairway before it collapsed could answer interrogatories on that issue.

Form of the Answers   The client is responsible for answering the interrogatories. The client normally supplies the information to the attorney or the paralegal, who drafts the actual answers. Each interrogatory must be answered separately, in writing. In some jurisdictions, answers must be **engrossed** by restating the interrogatory to be answered. The form of the answer must duplicate the interrogatory. For example, if the interrogatory contains six subparts, the answer contains six subparts. Some states, notably

engrossment (or engrossing)
The process of creating the final form of a document just before that document is used in a formal setting.

1. Calendar deadline for answering interrogatories. Place several interim reminders into the system.
2. Send a copy of the interrogatories to the client and schedule a meeting to begin working on the answers.
3. Make another copy of interrogatories. Put one interrogatory on a page for drafting purposes. Place a copy of each interrogatory into a file. Any information or documents received that relate to that interrogatory should also be placed in the file.
4. Note on the individual interrogatories the names of individuals who might have the information to answer the interrogatory and the location of that information.
5. Review pleadings file for any previous answers to avoid contradictions.
6. Review possible objections to interrogatories.
7. Draft interrogatory answers after information is received from the client.
8. Review draft interrogatories with client and attorney. Arrange for signing, filing, if necessary, and service of interrogatories.
9. Remember to update interrogatory answers.

EXHIBIT 10–6   Checklist for drafting interrogatory answers

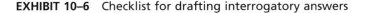

California, do not require that answers be engrossed. No rule requires answers to be complete sentences. Your attorney decides matters of writing style.

Content of the Answers   A party answering the interrogatories has a duty to make a reasonable investigation to obtain all information requested. Interrogatory answers must be straightforward and complete. On some occasions, however, you may need to qualify a response or indicate that the answer is unknown at the time. If the answer is unknown at the response time, you may state that fact and supplement the answers later if so required. If you do not answer a question because of lack of sufficient information, you must include the reason for failing to answer. If the answer to an interrogatory has been given in a previous response, you may refer to that prior response. All hearsay information should be designated accordingly. This can be done by beginning the answer with a qualifying statement such as, "I have no personal knowledge, but have been informed by . . ." A qualified response such as, "Upon information and belief . . ." should be adopted if you are not sure of your information or source.

You should disclose as little harmful information as possible. However, you must never deliberately conceal information that is requested in an interrogatory. Your attorney's role is to place the client in the best possible light in each answer without either distorting or misrepresenting the facts. One word of caution is appropriate here. Interrogatory answers are admissible only against the interest of the responding party. This means that you cannot use your client's answers to prove the facts in your case. However, because your client was under oath, the opposition may use them to impeach the testimony of your client. Naturally, not all interrogatories can be used in this fashion. Some interrogatories ask for relevant but inadmissible information.

Fulfilling the Duty to Supplement

Federal and state rules may vary on the duty of a party to supplement interrogatory answers. In federal court, the following situations require that interrogatory answers be supplemented:

1. If a party learns that the response given was in some material respect incomplete or incorrect and the additional or corrective information has not otherwise been made known; or
2. By order of the court or by agreement of the parties.

Because the duty to supplement interrogatory answers is a statutory requirement, your attorney will determine when updated answers are needed. However, you can assist in supplementing answers by maintaining a file on any interrogatories that might have to be updated.

Using Business Records Instead of a Written Response

Rule 33 of the Federal Rules of Civil Procedure provides for an alternative to answering an interrogatory in writing. A responding party may identify specific documents in which information might be found that would answer the question. The responding party must also pull the information together, identify the particular documents that answer the question, and give the other party the opportunity to review those documents.

Objecting to Interrogatories

Objections to interrogatories may be served with the answers or in a separate pleading. As might be expected, the same objections that are available in response to the other discovery devices are available in response to interrogatories. Rule 26(g)(2) and Rule 33 of the Federal Rules of Civil Procedure require that objections be signed by the attorney. As noted in previous chapters, the grounds for such objections include arguing that the answer to a particular question would provide information that is protected by the attorney-client privilege or the work product privilege. You may also argue that an interrogatory is irrelevant, overbroad, vague, or unintelligible. Another objection is that the interrogatories are unduly burdensome. If a question is objectionable in part only, it must be answered to the extent that it is not objectionable. You should not object to the whole question if part of it is proper.

The Attorney-Client Privilege, the Work Product Privilege, and the Common Interest Privilege   Recall that the attorney-client privilege seeks to protect any and all types of communication between the attorney and the client. In the same way, the work product privilege protects letters, notes, memos, documents, records, and other items that are prepared by an attorney in anticipation of a lawsuit. The common interest privilege protects any communication that takes place between attorneys for different clients when those clients share a common interest. Should an interrogatory ask for information that would violate these privileges, an objection can be raised. According to Rule 26(b)(5) of the Federal Rules of Civil Procedure, if an attorney objects to a question based on privilege, the objection must include a description of the nature of the documents, communications, or things not produced or disclosed in a manner that, without revealing the information, will enable the other party to assess the applicability of the privilege or protection.

The Medical Privilege and the Confessor-Penitent Privilege   Recall that the medical privilege that exists between a patient and a physician (psychiatrist, psychologist, dentist, podiatrist) is designed to protect the patient's confidential communication with medical professionals. Similarly, the confessor-penitent privilege protects the confidentiality of any communication between a person and confessor. While this privilege belongs to the penitent, the law also protects a confessor who has taken a religious oath not to reveal the content of such communications.

Inadmissible and Irrelevant Evidence   As we saw earlier in this chapter, the scope of discovery is much broader than the scope of evidence that can be presented at trial. Still, even the search for evidence during discovery has its limits. Any interrogatory must be reasonably calculated to lead to admissible evidence. If the answer to an interrogatory cannot be reasonably calculated to lead to admissible evidence, you may object to it. Also, should an interrogatory ask for information that is irrelevant to the subject matter of the lawsuit, you may object on that basis.

Overbroad, Vague, and Unintelligible Interrogatories   As mentioned, an *overbroad* interrogatory is one that is not narrowly defined and that is, therefore, difficult, if not impossible, to answer. A *vague* interrogatory is one that does not clarify exactly what information is sought. An *unintelligible* interrogatory is one that cannot be understood. All provide appropriate grounds for an objection.

unduly burdensome

A term that describes a set of interrogatories made during discovery that is so complex and detailed that it will require the party answering the interrogatories to spend excessive time, effort, and expense, and which will result in a burden on that party that far exceeds any benefit gained by the opposing party.

Unduly Burdensome Objections   The exact definition of an **unduly burdensome** set of interrogatories is elusive. Generally the courts ask the following questions to determine whether a set of interrogatories is unduly burdensome:

1. Will an inordinate amount of time be required to answer the questions?
2. Will the expense incurred in locating the answers be excessive?
3. Does the question seek information for which there is no compelling requirement?
4. Will the burden placed on the responding party exceed the benefit gained by the requesting party?
5. Has the information already been revealed during other steps in the discovery process?

The more of these questions to which the court can say yes, the more likely it is that the interrogatories will be found to be unduly burdensome.

Confidentiality Agreements and Protective Orders   As noted in previous chapters, often a lawsuit involves matters that one party wants to keep as secret as possible. For example, one party may have a trade secret that requires protection or a cus-

THE COMPUTERIZED LAW FIRM
Macros

SCENARIO

Your attorney has asked you to draft the interrogatories in the *Weston Mall* case. The attorney would like this set of interrogatories in the mail today. You are about to begin working on the project when she calls you into her office and tells you that one of the other paralegals in the firm has just called in sick. Your fellow paralegal was also working on several sets of interrogatories that your attorney needs by 1:00 P.M. She asks that you draft not only the interrogatories for The Weston Mall Corporation but also the ones on which the absent paralegal was working. You take a look at the preliminary work that was done on those interrogatories and you see that many of the parts of each are repeated in each set, even though the cases are very different. For example, you note that the caption of the case, several background questions, the certificate of service, and the law firm's signature block are all repeated, with only minor variations. You have also been told by your attorney that if you do a good job on this project, in the future you will be given several other similar projects.

PROBLEM

It will be very time consuming and quite repetitive to have to rekey all of these nearly identical parts. You could use a copy and paste command, however, you would like to have this information available in the future without having to call up any specific client file. Is there any shortcut you can take that will allow you to save this commonly used information and have it readily available in the future?

SOLUTION

Both Word and WordPerfect offer a time-saving device for the creation of repetitive text material. This time-saving device is known as a macro. A macro will store frequently used keystrokes that make up phrases or paragraphs. Once a macro is created it can be stored. You can assign the macro to a toolbar or you can create shortcut keys to run the macro. The "Help" feature on both Word and WordPerfect will lead you through the process of creating, storing, and calling up a macro. Additionally, both Word and WordPerfect have preinstalled macros to help with common tasks. To find out what these are, again use the Help menu. The use of macros allows you to avoid retyping common phrases or paragraphs without having to remember the names of prior files from which you could copy the material.

---

tomer list that it wants to keep as confidential as possible. Such limitations can be imposed voluntarily through a confidentiality agreement or by a court decree through a protective order. Interrogatories that seek information covered by a protective order or a confidentiality agreement should be answered in accordance with the terms of the order or agreement.

Burden of Proof   The party objecting to an interrogatory has the burden to prove the validity of the objection. Thus, the specific and particular grounds for the objection must be explained. The amount of detail required to sustain an objection in a hearing varies, depending on the nature of the objection. An objection based on privileged information or work product may be resolved by the judge's inspection of the documents **in camera,** a private viewing by the judge to determine the validity of the objection.

in camera

A term that describes a hearing or other proceeding that is held in the judge's private chambers out of the sight and hearing of any spectators; in private; in chambers.

FINDING IT ON THE INTERNET

The Federal Rules of Civil Procedure can be accessed at the following address: **<http://www.law.cornell.edu/rules/frcp>**. Access the Web site, find the text of Rule 33, and check to see if there have been any recent updates of the provisions and requirements as stated under the rule.

An article entitled "Document Discovery in the Electronic Age" can be found at **<http://www.thefederation.org/public/Quarterly/Spring01/seitz.htm>**. Access the Web site, read the article, and write a report on what the author says about the use of e-interrogatories.

An article entitled "Managing Electronic Discovery in Your Litigation System" can be found at **<http://www.abanet.org/1pm2/newsletters/litapps/s98cwiklo.html>**. Access the Web site, read the article, and write a report on the difference between the high-tech and low-tech approaches to e-evidence.

An article entitled "Electronic Discovery—Or, the Byte That Bit" can be found at **<http://www.llrx.com/features/byte.htm>**. Access the Web site, read the article, and write a report on how to find "hidden" data in a computer system.

Summary

- Interrogatories are written questions submitted by one party to another party. The responding party must answer these questions in writing and under oath. Rule 33 of the Federal Rules of Civil Procedure regulates the use of interrogatories in federal courts. Answers sought by interrogatories must be relevant to the pending lawsuit. However, those answers need not be admissible at the time of the trial, as long as they are reasonably calculated to lead to the discovery of evidence that can be submitted at trial. The primary purpose of interrogatories is to obtain information on the basic facts in a case, including any other people who may be involved in the lawsuit. Interrogatories may also be used to determine the party's contentions and to locate relevant documents. A set of interrogatories may also disclose the identities of both lay and expert witnesses that the other party intends to call to the stand at trial. Interrogatories offer substantial advantages over other discovery methods. However, they also have distinct disadvantages.

- One of the primary methods for an attorney to obtain information about the opposing party's computer records is by filing interrogatories designed to uncover the nature and extent of those records. The most proficient way to compile e-evidence is to send interrogatories, the answers to which will determine the attorney's document-production requests. The interrogatories should include several topics: (1) the actual nature of the party's computer system; (2) the configuration of any networks; (3) information on any upgrades, equipment changes, and reformatting; (4) the details of any policies that mandate the preservation or elimination of certain records; (5) information concerning any backup processes in use to save data; (6) a description of the the party's e-mail system; and (7) the names and responsibilities of all IT experts, their assistants, and interns involved in maintaining or servicing the party's computer system.

■ Most jurisdictions require a title, introductory paragraph, definitions, instructions, specific interrogatories, a signature, and a certificate of service for interrogatories. Several types of interrogatories may be asked. Each of these is designed to elicit a different form of information related to the lawsuit. These special interrogatories include interrogatories that identify people, interrogatories that establish facts or lead to the discovery of facts, interrogatories that identify documents, and interrogatories that identify contentions.

■ Because the client is responsible for answering the questions, it is essential that she be contacted immediately upon the receipt of a set of interrogatories. Working with the client, the paralegal can then determine how much time is needed to respond, how each question should be answered, which questions must be supplemented, and which questions are best answered with business records.

Key Terms

engrossment	in camera	unduly burdensome

Review Questions

1. What are interrogatories?
2. What are the purposes of filing interrogatories on the opposing party?
3. What are the advantages of using interrogatories?
4. What are the disadvantages of using interrogatories?
5. What are the specific types of interrogatories that can be asked?
6. What types of topics would have to be covered in any set of interrogatories designed to pave the way for a document-production request in relation to computer records?
7. What options are available to the requesting party should the responding party refuse to answer an interrogatory?
8. When is it necessary for the responding party to supplement an answer to an interrogatory?
9. When would the responding party substitute a business record instead of filing a written answer to an interrogatory?
10. What objections to interrogatories can be raised by the responding party?

Chapter Exercises

Where necessary, check with your instructor prior to starting any of these exercises.

1. Review your state's rules relating to interrogatories. Check local court rules to see if there are any restrictions on the number of interrogatories and/or the number of sets of interrogatories that can be filed in a lawsuit.
2. Prepare a chart of the objections to interrogatories that are permitted in the federal and state courts in your area.

3. Analyze the following situation and determine the proper response:

   a. Suppose that in the *Weston Mall* case, your supervising attorney has asked you to draft a set of interrogatories to be sent to The Weston Mall Corporation, the object of which is to lay the foundation for a later document-production request related to all e-evidence stored in the corporation's computer system. One set of interrogatories would have to attempt to determine the number and types of computers that are in operation as a part of the corporation's daily routine. How would you phrase the interrogatories to ensure that no computers escape consideration?

   b. Another set of questions would attempt to determine the configuration of the corporation's e-mail system. What questions would you consider asking about the e-mail system?

   c. Another set of questions would aim to obtain the names and a list of responsibilities of all individuals who are in any way involved in maintaining or servicing the corporation's computer system and any network systems that are a part of the corporation's operation. List the types of individuals who would have to be included in this question.

   d. Another set of questions would have to deal with the computer records themselves. What types of questions would you have to ask about these records?

Chapter Project

In your state's form book, locate a sample set of interrogatories for a case involving the type of accident that occurred in the *Weston Mall* case. Draft a set of interrogatories to the defendant corporation, in which you request all information relating to the accident. Also, if appropriate in your state, request information relating to the identity of all experts who will be called to testify at trial. Include questions on the subject matter about which each expert will testify, all opinions that each expert has on the matter, the case number and court of each case in which each expert has testified, and all facts provided to each expert witness for use in analysis of the case. Also, request a copy of any reports the expert witnesses have prepared in connection with the case.

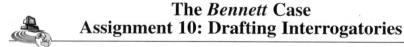

The *Bennett* Case
Assignment 10: Drafting Interrogatories

Your supervising attorney is interested in identifying all parties who worked for Bennett while she was acting manager as well as all parties who were involved in the hiring process of the permanent training manager. Your attorney is also interested in identifying all documents, including all e-evidence, that might contain relevant information. Prepare a set of interrogatories to be sent to the defendant requesting this information, as well as other relevant information.

Chapter 11

Physical and Mental Examinations

CHAPTER OUTLINE

COMMENTARY—THE RUSSELL CASE

Your attorney has decided to take a personal injury case. She has called you into the office to explain the details of the case. Her client, Charles Russell, was struck and injured by an SUV driven by the defendant, Emily Pitt. Ms. Pitt's attorney has asked your client to submit to a medical examination. Your attorney suspects that the opposing attorney in the case, Nigel Watson, is going to try to demonstrate that your client's injuries are not as serious as he contends. Your attorney has also asked Ms. Pitt to undergo an eye examination. This decision was made because Ms. Pitt is very nearsighted and was not wearing glasses or contacts on the night of the accident. Ms. Pitt has repeatedly asserted that her vision, especially her night vision, is adequate. Your supervising attorney has asked you to cooperate with Mr. Watson in scheduling Mr. Russell's examination. She also asked you to arrange for Ms. Pitt's eye examination.

OBJECTIVES

Chapters 8, 9, and 10 introduced two specialized types of discovery, depositions and interrogatories. The request for physical or mental examination is another effective tool in the discovery process. After reading this chapter, you should be able to:

- Define physical and mental examination.
- Outline four types of cases in which the physical and mental examination may be used.
- Explain the purposes for requesting a physical or mental examination.
- Outline the procedure for obtaining a physical or mental examination if the parties cannot agree to the examination.
- Define the concepts of "good cause" and "in controversy."
- Relate the responsibilities a paralegal might perform in the physical and mental examination process.
- Determine the possible consequences of a party's refusal to submit to a physical or mental examination.

physical or mental examination

An examination that a party to a lawsuit must undergo concerning a physical or mental condition that is at issue in a pending legal action.

The Physical or Mental Examination

A **physical or mental examination** is the examination that a party must undergo concerning a physical or mental condition that is at issue in a pending legal action. Such an examination is used when that physical or mental condition is an important factor in a lawsuit. One party to a lawsuit can request that the other party undergo a physical or mental examination. The request can be made even if the party who is to undergo the examination is a minor, in the custody of a parent, or a legally incapacitated person under the legal control of a guardian. Physical and mental examinations will, by their very nature, invade the privacy of the person undergoing the examination. For this reason, among others, this discovery tool is used only in certain types of cases.

Types of Cases Using Physical or Mental Examinations

Physical and mental examinations are often used in personal injury cases. In such cases, the physical or mental condition of a party can be very important in establishing the personal liability of the defendant or in determining the extent of the injuries suffered by the plaintiff. For example, in this chapter's *Russell* case, your supervising attorney has requested a physical examination to determine if Ms. Pitt is nearsighted and whether she has difficulty seeing after dark. Because your attorney has alleged that Ms. Pitt's failure to wear her glasses contributed to the accident, and because Ms. Pitt has stated that her eyesight is quite good, an eye examination would be in order here. Moreover, Mr. Watson, Ms. Pitt's attorney, has asked Mr. Russell to undergo a physical examination to determine whether his injuries are as serious as he contends.

Physical or mental examinations are not limited to personal injury cases, however. A physical exam might be requested to confirm the extent of the injuries in an industrial accident case. Such an examination may also be requested to determine the identity of the father of a child in a paternity suit or to establish whether a plaintiff is eligible for payments under the terms of a disability insurance policy. Whether or not an examination is requested often depends upon the purpose that the attorneys have in mind when they are planning the legal strategy in a lawsuit.

Reasons for Allowing Physical and Mental Examinations

One reason the law allows physical and mental examinations is to establish the truth about the plaintiff's allegation of physical or mental injuries. For example, in the *Russell* case, if Mr. Russell claims to have a pinched nerve as a result of the car accident, a physical examination could help determine whether he is telling the truth. Another reason for permitting physical and mental examinations is to discourage plaintiffs who have filed false or exaggerated claims. When plaintiffs are told that they must undergo a physical or a mental exam, they may decide to drop the suit rather than risk exposure as a fraud. In fact, the very existence of a rule allowing such examinations may deter the initial filing of fraudulent or exaggerated lawsuits. If a potential plaintiff finds out that the court may order a physical examination, that potential plaintiff may decide not to file that fictitious or exaggerated claim. One final reason for allowing such examinations is to uncover inconsistencies between a plaintiff's subjective complaints and the objective nature of the injury. In the *Russell* case, for instance, Mr. Russell may complain of severe back pain. A physical examination could determine whether there is an objective medical condition causing the pain.

Filing a Motion for Compulsory Examination

compulsory examination

An examination that a party to a lawsuit has been ordered by the court to undergo concerning a physical or mental condition.

notice

A formal notification of intent; the knowledge of a particular set of facts; the formal acquisition of the knowledge of a fact or set of facts.

Most physical and mental examinations are scheduled by mutual agreement of the attorneys for the parties. In such cases this mutual agreement should be set out in a letter or formal stipulation filed with the court. If agreement cannot be reached, however, a formal motion for **compulsory examination** will be necessary. Such a motion must establish good cause for the requested physical or mental examination. Exhibit 11–1 is an example of a motion for compulsory examination.

Rule 35(a) of the Federal Rules of Civil Procedure details the prerequisites for the content of a motion requesting an order for a physical or a mental examination. The party requesting the examination is responsible for giving notice to the person to be examined as well as to all the other parties or their attorneys. **Notice** is a formal written notification to the person to be examined and to the other parties. The moving papers, which are filed with the court and which give notice to the other party and the examiner, must specify the time, place, manner, conditions, scope of the examination, and the name of the person conducting the examination.

The motion must be specific. In the *Russell* case, for example, a broad request for Ms. Pitt to undergo a physical examination would be too vague and probably would not be ordered by the court. For instance, instead of simply asking for a physical examination, the motion could ask for an eye test to determine whether Ms. Pitt is nearsighted and has difficulty seeing after dark, which has more relevance to the case.

Requirements for Granting the Motion for Compulsory Examination

Rule 35 of the Federal Rules of Civil Procedure sets down the conditions under which a motion for a physical or mental examination will be granted by the trial judge. The rule gives the trial judge total discretion in determining whether the request for a physical or mental examination meets two essential requirements. These requirements are that there be "good cause" for the examination and that the nature of the condition be "in controversy."

Evidence of Good Cause

good cause

A legally acceptable reason for doing something or for refusing to do something.

As noted earlier, both a physical and a mental examination will, by necessity, invade the privacy of the person submitting to the examination. For this reason, the courts tend to define **good cause** very strictly. In general, the court will decide that good cause exists to order such an examination only if the same information cannot be found in any other way. Still, good cause is a flexible concept that varies from one case to another and from one type of examination to another. For example, in the *Russell* case, because the physical condition of Mr. Russell is an important aspect of the case, the need for an examination is obvious. This may not be true in other lawsuits, such as one involving the question of whether a person was mentally competent to enter a contract.

RAYFIELD COUNTY COURT

CHARLES RUSSELL,)
) Civil Action No. 05-61491

    Plaintiff,)
) MOTION FOR PHYSICAL
) EXAMINATION

    v.)
)

EMILY PITT,)
)

    Defendant.)
)
)

TO THE HONORABLE JUDGE OF SAID COURT:

    COMES NOW Emily Pitt, the Defendant in the above cause, and files this Motion under Rule 35 of the State Rules of Civil Procedure, to require Charles Russell, the Plaintiff in the above cause, to submit to a physical examination by Andrew Altick, M.D., at 9785 Lorain Avenue, in the city of Sparta, and respectfully show the Court as follows:

I.

    This is a case in which the Plaintiff alleges that he suffered permanent and disabling injuries as a result of an automobile accident on May 20, 2004 in the city of Athens in this state. The Plaintiff alleges that said accident was directly and proximately caused by the negligence of the Defendant.

II.

    Defendant denies the allegations made by the Plaintiff concerning his injuries and disabilities. Accordingly, the physical condition of the Plaintiff is in controversy.

III.

    Defendant has heretofore requested the Plaintiff to submit to a voluntary examination, and that request has been denied.

IV.

    Defendant requests that the Plaintiff be ordered by the Court to submit to an independent medical examination at the offices of Andrew Altick, M.D., 9785 Lorain Avenue, in the city of Sparta in this state, on March 25, 2005, at 2 P.M.

    WHEREFORE, the Defendant herein prays that the court grant this Motion in all respects and award all other and further relief to which Defendant is justly entitled.

Respectfully submitted,

_____

Nigel Watson
Attorney for Defendant

EXHIBIT 11–1 Motion for a physical examination

<u>Certificate of Service</u>

I hereby certify that a true and correct copy of the foregoing Motion for Physical Examination has been furnished to counsel of record on this the twentieth day of February, 2005.

_____

EXHIBIT 11–1 *(continued)*

Condition in Controversy

in controversy

In the case of a physical or mental examination, the prerequisite that the condition to be examined must be at issue in the lawsuit.

Rule 35 of the Federal Rules of Civil Procedure also requires that the physical or mental condition to be examined by the medical professional must be in controversy. To be **in controversy,** the condition to be examined must be at issue in the lawsuit. For example, a request for an order compelling a plaintiff to submit to a blood test would have nothing to do with a claim that his or her injuries prevent the performance of certain types of work. Such a request would not be ordered. In contrast, a request for an order to compel a defendant in a paternity suit to undergo a blood test to determine whether he could be the father of a child would be at the heart of the dispute; such a request would be granted. Similarly, a request for a mental examination would not be granted if neither mental nor emotional injuries have been alleged. However, if a plaintiff claims to be the victim of intentionally caused emotional distress, a mental examination would be appropriate. In the *Russell* case, because your attorney intends to prove that Ms. Pitt's poor eyesight contributed to the accident, and because Ms. Pitt has denied having eye problems, the matter is in controversy. Similarly, the extent of Mr. Russell's injuries is also in controversy.

Granting a Motion for Compulsory Examination

As noted earlier, Rule 35 gives the trial judge total discretion to decide if the party seeking a physical or mental examination has good cause for the request and whether the examination involves a condition in controversy. This discretion, however, does not mean that the moving party must prove his case on the merits as he would have to do at a trial. Nor does this discretion automatically mean that a hearing will be held prior to entry of an order for the examination. In some cases a hearing may be required. In others, the judge may decide that these requirements have been met on the basis of an affidavit filed by the attorney or a physician who believes that the examination is vital to establishing the claims or defenses of the case.

If the court decides to grant the motion for compulsory examination, it will issue an order compelling the party to submit to the examination. Usually the party seeking the order includes a proposed order when filing the original motion.

THE COMPUTERIZED LAW FIRM
The Administrative Database

SCENARIO

You have just been given a last-minute assignment in the *Russell* case by your supervising attorney. She has just met with Dr. David Weinstein of the Euclid Clinic. Dr. Weinstein has turned over to your attorney a photocopy of a complete set of Mr. Russell's medical records. Your supervising attorney has asked you to organize the material so that she can dig into the file and quickly retrieve information by date, by the name of the attending physician, by injury, or by the name of various medications.

PROBLEM

The file your attorney hands you is at least an inch thick. You are at a loss as to where to begin organizing the records. As you glance through the file, you realize that Mr. Russell has been treated by six different physicians, has been a patient in four different hospitals for a total of 10 weeks, and has been given eight different medications. Sorting all this out in the time allotted seems to be an impossible task. How will you solve the problem?

SOLUTION

Both Word and WordPerfect come bundled with several other software applications, including a database. The database associated with Microsoft is known as Access. The one associated with WordPerfect is known as Paradox. You can use either of these, or one of the many other database programs on the market, to prepare for Mr. Shirer's physical examination. Information that should be captured for future litigation purposes includes the dates of all visits to the doctor, the name of each doctor, the names and quantities of all medications taken, the medical problem for which each medication was prescribed, the doctor prescribing the medications, the dates and places of all hospitalizations, the attending physicians and nurses, the medication and the treatment received in the hospital, the patient's discharge date, and the nurses' and doctors' notes relating to the patient. Inputting all this data into the computer will assist your attorney in preparing for the medical examination. It may also indicate any problem areas, such as potential drug addictions or the failure to follow a doctor's orders for future therapy and exercise. Once the data is in the computer, your attorney will be able to quickly retrieve information by date, by the name of the attending physician, by injury, or by the name of various medications.

Exhibit 11–2 is a sample form of a proposed order for entry by the trial judge. The judge may or may not enter the proposed order as submitted. In fact, the judge could even change the number or type of examinations asked for in the motion. For example, in the *Russell* case, the judge might order several examinations of Mr. Russell to determine the nature and the extent of his injuries. The court also has the authority to order subsequent examinations if it feels the facts require further validation. In the *Russell* case, for example, part of Ms. Pitt's defense may be that Mr. Russell's problems stem from a previous industrial accident and not from his collision with her automobile. In such a case, the judge might order several examinations to help validate or invalidate that defense.

RAYFIELD COUNTY COURT

CHARLES RUSSELL,)
) Civil Action No. 05-61491
    Plaintiff,)
) ORDER
    v.)
)
EMILY PITT,)
)
    Defendant.)
)

This matter being heard on Defendant's Motion to compel the physical examination of Plaintiff, all parties having been given notice, and the court having heard arguments, it is hereby ordered that:

1. Plaintiff Charles Russell be examined by Andrew Altick, M.D., at 9785 Lorain Avenue, in the city of Sparta in this state, on March 25, 2005, at 2 P.M. unless the Plaintiff and Dr. Altick mutually agree to an earlier date and time.

2. Plaintiff shall submit to such neurological examinations and tests as are necessary to diagnose and evaluate Plaintiff's back and legs, so that Dr. Altick can reach opinions and conclusions about the extent of any injuries, their origin, and prognosis.

3. Dr. Altick shall prepare a written report detailing his findings, test results, diagnosis, prognosis, and opinions along with any similar reports on the same conditions, and deliver it to Defendant's attorneys on or before March 25, 2005.

Signed this 28th day of February, 2005.

_____
JUDGE

EXHIBIT 11–2 Sample order

The Paralegal's Role in Physical and Mental Examinations

Your role as the paralegal in the request for a physical or mental examination will depend upon whether your attorney or the opposing attorney has requested such an examination.

Arranging for the Examination of an Opposing Party

If your attorney has requested an examination of an opposing party, you may be asked to schedule the actual examination. In such a situation, you should contact the opposing counsel to see if there are any objections to the examination. If the other party is not agreeable, you may be asked to draft the motion for compulsory physical exam and a proposed order, as shown in Exhibit 11–2.

Fortunately, however, most physical and mental examinations are conducted by voluntary arrangement. If your attorney has requested the examination, it will normally be conducted by a physician of her choice, unless the party to be examined has a valid objection to that selection. This selection is not an absolute right, however. If the parties cannot agree on a physician, the court will make the selection. Check your local court rules to determine if they include an approved list of impartial experts from which the examining physician must be selected. In any event, Rule 35 of the Federal Rules of Civil Procedure requires that the examiner be "suitably licensed or certified."

Convenience should be a major criterion in the selection. If the party to be examined lives in Albany, New York, and the party requesting the examination selects a physician in New York City, the court could refuse to approve the physician selected. Parties may, however, be required to come to the city where the suit is filed for the physical or mental examination, even though they reside in another city.

Assuming that everyone involved is agreeable up to this point, your next job would be to contact the physician or laboratory to discuss the purpose of the examination and the nature of the case. Arrangements for payment of the physician or laboratory should also be discussed at the time of the initial contact.

Following the examination, you should contact the physician or laboratory and request a copy of the report. Once you have received the report, review it with the attorney and, when the report has been approved, pay the physician or the laboratory. Remember also to add that amount to the client's ledger for billing. Your attorney will direct when and where a copy of the medical report should be sent. Your attorney may also ask you to review the medical report and prepare a summary by chronology of events or category of injury. The fact that you have received a written report from the physician who examined the opposing party does not affect your attorney's ability to depose the examining physician. The independent examination under Rule 35 is not a substitute for discovery through a deposition or other available discovery tool.

Preparing the Client for an Examination

If your client has been requested to undergo a physical or mental examination, you should notify the client immediately. Your attorney will have explained to the client in the initial interview that such an examination is possible. However, the client may have some apprehension about the actual examination. Explaining the purpose and procedure to be utilized may give the client some comfort. This explanation can take the form of a letter to the client setting out the details concerning the examination. Exhibit 11–3 is an example of such a letter to the client.

You may be asked to meet with the client prior to the examination and review the types of information he can expect to be asked by the physician. Caution your client to refrain from telling the examiner anything he has discussed with your attorney. It is also

LAUREY, POPOVICH, MONTGOMERY, AND HUDSON
2785 Middleton Avenue
Sparta, New Jersey 07503

March 4, 2005

Mr. Charles Russell
P.O. Box 200
Athens, New Jersey 07506

Dear Mr. Russell:

You may recall that attorney Easton mentioned in your initial visit to our office that the other side may request an examination by a physician of their choosing to confirm the existence and the extent of your injuries. Mr. Nigel Watson, attorney for defendant Emily Pitt, has requested such an examination.

The examination is tentatively scheduled for March 25, 2005, at 2:00 P.M. The examining physician is Dr. Andrew Altick. His office is located at 9785 Lorain Avenue, Sparta, New Jersey. Please be at his office several minutes prior to that time so that the examination can begin on schedule.

This examination will consist of an examination of your neck and back injuries as well as several diagnostic X rays. The examination should last no longer than one hour.

Before the examination, you should review the medical recap sheet that you have prepared so that you may respond quickly and correctly to the physician's questions about prior illnesses, injuries, medication, etc.

Please cooperate with the physician, but do not volunteer any information not specifically requested. Do not exaggerate or minimize any medical problem about which you are asked.

Attorney Easton believes this examination will be beneficial in establishing the damages you have suffered to this date. If you have any questions about the examination, please let me know.

Thanks for your time.

Sincerely,

Paula K. Pepperton
Paralegal

EXHIBIT 11–3   Sample letter to client concerning physical examination

a sound practice to warn your client not to discuss the facts of the case with the examining physician. However, the client should be reminded to review all facets of his medical history, including the names of all doctors and hospitals who have treated him, the nature of the illness or injury, the names of medications, and the dates of all illnesses, injuries, or hospitalizations. For example, in the *Russell* case, Mr. Russell should not discuss with the physician anything he has talked over with you or your supervising attorney about the suit he has filed against Ms. Pitt. Nor should he discuss the accident itself. He should, however, be prepared to discuss intelligently his own medical history.

If you furnish the client with a medical summary sheet such as the one in Exhibit 11–4, it will help the client recall information that will probably be covered

MEDICAL RECAP

PHYSICIANS:

Name	Date of Visit	Diagnosis/Treatment
Sergei Gagarin Athens General Hospital 24771 Eastway Drive Athens, New Jersey (609) 555–5656	May 27, 2004	Broken leg Sprained neck Concussion
Donald O'Brien Athens General Hospital	May 28, 2004 to June 14, 2004	Treatment for above noted injuries
Donald O'Brien 7786 Broadway Avenue Sparta, New Jersey (609) 555-9988	June 27, 2004	Cast removed
Karla Bonfiglio 1524 East 310 Street Sparta, New Jersey (609) 555-7689	June 30, 2004 to September 9, 2004	Physical therapy

PRESCRIPTIONS:

Name	Date	Drug Prescribed/Reason
Sergei Gagarin Athens General Hospital 24771 Eastway Drive Athens, New Jersey (609) 555-5656	May 27, 2004	Tylenol w/Codeine Pain
Donald O'Brien 7786 Broadway Avenue Sparta, New Jersey (609) 555-9988	June 27, 2004	Vasotec/Hypertension

HOSPITALS/CLINICS:

Name	Date	Reason for Visit
Athens General Hospital 24771 Eastway Drive Athens, New Jersey (609) 555-5656	May 28, 2004 to June 14, 2004	Treatment for injuries noted above
Medtech Clinic 4444 Flowers Road Athens, New Jersey (609) 555-6714	June 30, 2004 to September 9, 2004	Physical therapy

EXHIBIT 11–4   Medical recap form

LABORATORIES/DIAGNOSTIC SERVICES:

Name/Referring Physician	Date	Service/Reason
Sergei Gagarin Athens General Hospital 24771 Eastway Drive Athens, New Jersey (609) 555-5656	May 28, 2004	Diagnostic X rays

---

EXHIBIT 11–4   *(continued)*

in the physical examination. However, the client probably should not take this summary into the examination room. Using such a written record to answer questions in the presence of the examiner may cast some doubt on your client's ability to independently recall his own medical history. Such a revelation may hurt your client's credibility, should it somehow come to the jury's attention at trial.

Your client may request that his own physician be present during the examination. That request must be made through the opposing attorney. Permission for the examining physician to attend is solely at the discretion of the trial judge, under the provisions of Rule 35 of the Federal Rules of Civil Procedure. Some states—California, for example—also allow a paralegal to accompany the client.

Sanctions   It is to be hoped that your client will submit without resistance to the requested examination. However, if your client does indicate that he intends to refuse to submit to the examination, then you should point out that such a refusal carries with it very severe sanctions or penalties.

Permitted sanctions include an order striking all or parts of pleadings, staying the proceedings until the order for the examination is obeyed, entry of a judgment by default against a defendant who refuses to submit to the examination, or the dismissal of a plaintiff's case if the plaintiff refuses to submit to the examination. Your client may also be ordered to pay the physician's fee if the client fails to appear for an appointment and it must be rescheduled.

Distributing the Medical Records   You must be very cautious when asking for a copy of the physician's report or the laboratory test results after the examination of your client has been conducted. This caution is necessary because the discovery provisions of Rule 35 of the Federal Rules of Civil Procedure are reciprocal. This means that if you request a copy of the report on your client's examination, then the other side can request copies of all reports in your possession that deal with the same condition, regardless of when those reports were made. Because of this, you should consult with your attorney before you request a copy of the medical report on your client. Although the reports in your possession do not automatically have to be produced, your request allows the opposing counsel to gain access to them as requested. Your attorney may not want to open that window of opportunity to the opposition. Because of this, you should consult with your attorney before you request a copy of the medical report on your client's examination.

FINDING IT ON THE INTERNET

The Federal Rules of Civil Procedure can be accessed at the following address: **<http://www.law.cornell.edu/rules/frcp>**. Access the Web site, find the text of Rule 35, and check to see if there have been any recent updates of the provisions and requirements as stated under the rule.

An extensive article involving Rule 35 of the federal rules, entitled "Emotional Distress Discovery in Employment Discrimination Cases," can be found at **<http://www.alolaw.com/CurrentDevelopments/cdemodistress.htm>**. Access the Web site, read the article, and write a report on what the author says about the use of Rule 35 exams for discrimination cases involving emotional distress.

An article entitled "Successful Medical Malpractice Litigation" can be found at **<http://www.paralegals.org/Reporter/Winter96/MedMal.html>**. Access the Web site, read the article, and write a report on the section entitled "Helpful Hints for Paralegals When Reviewing Medical Records."

An article entitled "Psychiatric and Psychological Examinations of Employment Discrimination Complaints: Fundamental Fairness or Unwarranted Invasion of Privacy?" at **<http://www.nysba2.org/media/barjournal/peebles.html>** discusses the question of privacy in relation to mental examinations. Access the Web site, read the article, and write a report on whether you see such examinations as the vindication of a fundamental right or as an invasion of privacy.

However, the rules of your state may allow opposing counsel access to your client's medical records regardless of any request on your part. This is especially true if your client is the plaintiff in a personal injury case. In such a situation you would want to request a copy of the report. Again, you should consult with your attorney and check the rules of your particular state before making such a request.

Summary

- A physical and mental examination is the examination of a party to a lawsuit to determine factual information about the physical or mental condition of that party. The request can be made even if the party is a minor, in the custody of a parent, or a legally incapacitated person under the control of a guardian. The examination is a tool used to establish the validity of allegations of mental or physical injuries.

- Most physical and mental examinations are scheduled by mutual agreement. If an agreement cannot be reached, however, a formal motion for a compulsory examination must be filed with the court.

- Rule 35 of the Federal Rules of Civil Procedure sets forth the conditions under which a motion for a physical or mental examination will be granted by the trial court. These requirements are that there be good cause for the examination and that the nature of the condition be in controversy.

■ The trial judge has total discretion as to whether the party seeking a physical or mental examination has good cause for the request and whether the examination involves a condition in controversy. If the court decides to grant the motion for the examination, it will issue an order compelling the party to submit to the examination.

■ The paralegal's role in the request for a physical or mental examination depends on whether the paralegal's attorney or the opposing attorney has requested the examination. The paralegal's role will also depend on whether the examination is proceeding by agreement or by a motion filed with the court.

Key Terms

compulsory examination	in controversy	physical or mental examination
good cause	notice	

Review Questions

1. Define physical and mental examination.
2. Name four types of cases in which a physical or mental examination might be requested.
3. Identify four reasons why the law allows one party to compel another party to submit to a physical or mental examination.
4. Give an example of a party "in the custody of" or "under the legal control" of another person.
5. Explain the concepts of good cause and in controversy as they relate to the physical and mental examination.
6. What is the procedure for obtaining a physical or mental examination if the parties cannot agree to the examination?
7. Explain the paralegal's role in arranging for the physical or mental examination of an opposing party.
8. Explain the paralegal's role in preparing the client to undergo a physical or mental examination.
9. What are the considerations to be evaluated prior to requesting a copy of the examinee's medical report?
10. What are the possible consequences of a party's refusal to submit to a physical or mental examination ordered by the court?

Chapter Exercises

Where necessary, check with your instructor prior to starting any of these exercises.

1. Review the laws of your state and find all laws that deal with requests for physical and mental examinations. Check your local court rules to see if any local rules of court in your area regulate any aspect of the request for a physical or mental examination.
2. Find the form books in your law library that provide sample forms for use in the drafting of legal documents in your state. Find a sample motion for a physical examination and a sample proposed order compelling such an examination. How do they compare to the samples found in this chapter?

3. Analyze the following situation and decide on the proper response. Suppose in the *Russell* case that your supervising attorney's client, Mr. Russell, has announced that he intends to refuse to show up for his scheduled appointment with Dr. Altick.

   a. What are the possible sanctions under the Federal Rules of Civil Procedure that Mr. Russell risks if he follows through on his threat? Explain.

   b. How would you dissuade Mr. Russell from going through with his threat to refuse to see Dr. Altick?

   c. Mr. Russell insists that his own physician be allowed to be present for his physical examination. Explain to Mr. Russell the circumstances that would allow this to occur.

   d. Mr. Russell also insists that you be allowed to be present for his physical examination. Does your state permit a paralegal to attend a physical examination such as the one ordered for Mr. Russell?

Chapter Project

Review the *Russell* case in the opening commentary. Draft a checklist of duties that you might expect to assume in preparing Mr. Russell for his physical examination. Also draft an e-mail message to your supervising attorney exploring the issue of whether you should request a copy of Mr. Russell's examination results, in light of the laws of your state.

The *Bennett* Case
Assignment 11: Stipulation for Medical Exam

Because Bennett claimed in her complaint that she suffered both physically and mentally as a result of defendant's action, the defendant has requested that she submit to both a physical and mental exam. Your supervising attorney has agreed to one examination to be conducted by Dr. Peter Ebert, a board-certified psychiatrist. The attorneys have also agreed that the doctor will not inquire into any events that occurred more than five years ago. The examination is scheduled for the 25th of next month. You have been asked to prepare a written stipulation reflecting this agreement. (See Chapter 8, Exhibit 8–2 for a general form for a stipulation.)

Chapter 12

Request for Documents

CHAPTER OUTLINE

COMMENTARY—THE MANNHEIM CASE

Viking Industries, Ltd. mounted a hostile takeover bid in an attempt to purchase Seigel Pharmaceuticals, Inc. The board of directors of Seigel invited Mannheim Laboratories, Ltd. to become the "white knight" in an attempt to outbid Viking. In accepting the challenge as Seigel's white knight, Mannheim relied on financial statements filed by the accounting firm of Shuster, Kane, Moulton, and Associates, Inc. After winning the takeover battle for Seigel, Mannheim found out that the unqualified opinion issued by the accounting firm grossly overvalued Seigel. This misinformation has led to a series of costly financial reversals for Mannheim. Mannheim Laboratories has retained your firm to bring suit against the accounting firm. Your attorney requests that you assist with all discovery matters including drafting a request to be served on Shuster, Kane, Moulton, and Associates, Inc. for the production of documents.

OBJECTIVES

Chapters 8, 9, 10, and 11 introduced you to depositions, interrogatories, and requests for physical and mental examinations. The next discovery technique is the request for documents. After reading this chapter, you should be able to:

- Define a request for production of documents.
- Differentiate among the alternative methods of obtaining documents.
- Determine when a request for production of documents should be served.
- Identify the different approaches to document requests.
- Explain the attorney-client privilege, the work product privilege, and the common interest privilege.
- Determine when confidentiality agreements or protective orders should be sought.
- Explain what objections are available to prevent the production of documents.
- Identify the duties of the paralegal in requesting the production of documents.
- Relate a paralegal's duties in responding to a request for production of documents.
- Explain the duties of the paralegal in organizing the documents from both sides.
- Explain when a party can request an inspection of property.

The Request for Documents

A **request for documents** is a request that a party or other individual involved in a lawsuit provide specific documents or other physical evidence to the party making the request for such documents or other physical evidence. Prior to the mutual disclosure amendments to Rule 26 of the Federal Rules of Civil Procedure, the majority of documents produced in a litigation were produced through this formal request for documents. Because of this significant change in production methods, we will examine the process of document production through mutual disclosure.

request for documents
A request that a party or other individual involved in a lawsuit provide specific documents or other physical evidence to the party making the request for such documents or physical evidence.

Recent Developments Concerning Mutual Disclosure of Documents

Rule 26(a)(1)(B) of the Federal Rules of Civil Procedure requires the initial disclosure of the following within 14 days after the initial conference of the parties: "a copy of, or a description by category and location of, all documents, data compilations, and tangible things in the possession, custody, or control of the party and that the disclosing party may use to support its claims or defenses, unless solely for impeachment."

Mutual Disclosures and E-Evidence

As previously indicated, Federal Rule 26(a)(1)(B) mandates that all "data compilations" must be included within the early stages of disclosure. This requirement plainly encompasses all relevant items of e-evidence including those found in e-mail files, databases, calendering programs, and all other relevant data files created by spreadsheets, word processing, or any analogous program. It is also clear that all forms of e-evidence are discoverable including data stored in laptops, desktop PCs, personal digital assistants (PDAs), hard drives, mobile phones, fax recording devices, floppy disks, computer tapes, and CDs. Moreover, any and all paper copies retained as back-up files for such e-data would also be discoverable, even those copies retained only as a precaution against a computer system failure. As we've seen, it is a good idea for your supervising attorney to use the early stages of discovery, including initial disclosure process, to determine the types of e-evidence that will be involved in the document-request stage of discovery.

Alternative Methods of Requesting Documents

In federal court, as well as in many state courts, in addition to mutual disclosure and a Rule 34 request for production, the parties to a lawsuit can request documents at the deposition of a party, or they can use a subpoena duces tecum to compel a nonparty to produce documents at the time of a deposition. The use of interrogatories may also result in the production of documents.

Request for Documents at the Deposition of a Party   Documents may be obtained from a party by serving a request for that party to bring those documents to her deposition. Rule 30(b)(5) of the Federal Rules of Civil Procedure allows this alternative. The specific documents or the categories of documents to be produced must be included in the deposition notice of attachment. Exhibit 12–1 is an example of this.

COURT OF COMMON PLEAS
CUYAHOGA COUNTY
STATE OF OHIO

MANNHEIM LABORATORIES, LTD.,
     Plaintiff,
 	
          v.
 	
SHUSTER, KANE, MOULTON, AND
ASSOCIATES, INC.,
     Defendants.
	)
	)
	) Civil Action No. 05-77976
	) NOTICE OF TAKING
	) DEPOSITION UPON
	) ORAL EXAMINATION
	)
	)
	)
	)
	)
	)
	)

TO: Jeremy Wickard, Attorney of Record for Defendant, Shuster, Kane, Moulton, and Associates, Inc., in the above styled and numbered cause.

Please take notice that the deposition of Karl Shuster, President and Chief Executive Officer of Shuster, Kane, Moulton, and Associates, Inc., whose address is 2168 Gibson Road, Mayfield Heights, Ohio, will be taken upon oral examination on October 31, 2005, beginning at 9 A.M., and continuing from day to day until completed.

The witness is requested to bring with him to the deposition those items in his custody or subject to his custody, care, or control, identified in Exhibit "A" attached hereto.

You are hereby invited to attend and cross-examine.

Respectfully submitted,

_____

Giacomo Striuli
Striuli, Grazak, and Usalis
2233 Hamilton Avenue
Cleveland, Ohio 44119
Tel.: (123) 555-1212
Fax: (123) 555-2323
Attorneys for Plaintiff
Mannheim Laboratories, Ltd.

<u>CERTIFICATE OF SERVICE</u>

I hereby certify that a true and correct copy of the foregoing has been mailed by first class mail, postage prepaid to Jeremy Wickard, 54392 St. Clair Avenue, Cleveland, Ohio, 44118, on this 29th day of September, 2005.

_____

EXHIBIT 12–1   Request for production of documents at deposition of a party

A request for documents at the deposition of a party is not always the most efficient way to handle document discovery. If an attorney must wait to see the requested documents until the deposition, she may have to spend precious time reviewing the documents as the deposition is in progress. Moreover, subsequent examination of the documents often reveals information about which the deponent should have been questioned. This may necessitate scheduling another deposition, which may or may not be allowed by the court.

Subpoenas Duces Tecum for a Nonparty to Produce Documents at a Deposition A nonparty can be subpoenaed to produce documents at deposition, according to Rule 45 of the Federal Rules of Civil Procedure. The deposition notice served on the nonparty will contain a specific listing of the documents to be produced. That list is repeated in the deposition subpoena served on the nonparty. This method of document production is handicapped by the same shortcomings that plague the request for documents at the deposition of a party. If the attorney is viewing the documents for the first time, she will waste valuable time at the deposition. Moreover, a later review of the documents may suggest the need to schedule another deposition. Again, the court may or may not allow a second deposition.

Interrogatories and the Production of Documents Sometimes the use of a set of interrogatories results in the production of documents. This is because Rule 33(d) of the Federal Rules of Civil Procedure allows a party answering a set of interrogatories to produce business records if the examination of those records will provide the answer to an interrogatory.

Interrogatories and E-Evidence Interrogatories are best used at an early stage in the discovery process to help your attorney determine what documents are available for a later document-production request. This is especially true of e-evidence which is often difficult to identify, retrieve, and interpret. Thus, the interrogatories ought to include questions related to the nature of the party's computer system; the configuration of any network systems that are a part of the party's operation; the number and location of all work stations, and all network servers; information on upgrades, equipment changes, and reformatting; details on any policies on the elimination of data; policies that mandate the preservation of certain records or any backup processes in use; information on the party's e-mail system; and a list of all individuals who are responsible for maintaining, upgrading, repairing, or servicing the party's computer system, including in-house and independent information technology (IT) experts. Once your supervising attorney has this information in hand, she will have a more specific idea of how to frame document requests and on-site visits to retrieve e-evidence.

Request for Documents to Parties Despite these other techniques, the request for documents still remains the most efficient and effective way to obtain documents. A request for production should not be served until the parties have initially conferred as required under Rule 26. Once served, the answering party has 30 days in which to respond. The court, however, may shorten or lengthen this time period. The opposing attorney's response to the request must indicate that her client will comply with the request or should indicate the grounds for any objection to the request. Exhibit 12–2 is an example of the opening paragraph in a request for documents.

COURT OF COMMON PLEAS
CUYAHOGA COUNTY
STATE OF OHIO

MANNHEIM LABORATORIES, LTD.,
    Plaintiff,

       v.

SHUSTER, KANE, MOULTON, AND
ASSOCIATES, INC.
    Defendants.

)
)
)   Civil Action No. 05-77976
)   REQUEST FOR DOCUMENTS
)
)
)
)
)
)
)
)
)

TO: Jeremy Wickard, Attorney of Record for Defendant, Shuster, Kane, Moulton, and Associates, Inc., in the above styled and numbered cause.

    Pursuant to Rule 34 of the Ohio Rules of Civil Procedure, Mannheim Laboratories, Ltd., plaintiff in the above cause, requests that Shuster, Kane, Moulton, and Associates, Inc., defendant in the above cause, produce for inspection and copying by Mannheim, within thirty days of service hereof or at such other time as may be agreed upon by counsel for the parties, originals or legible copies of the documents requested herein. You are also requested to serve upon plaintiff within thirty (30) days after service of this request a written response in accordance with Rule 34 of the Ohio Rules of Civil Procedure.

EXHIBIT 12–2   Introductory paragraph for a request for documents

In order for the responding party to comply with the request as efficiently as possible, the request must specify with "reasonable particularity" the general categories of documents or the particular documents that the other party wishes to inspect. The request should also specify a reasonable time, place, and manner of production. Naturally, the attorneys may alter these arrangements to make the production more convenient to all those involved in the process. The manner of production is also determined by negotiation and agreement between the attorneys. Sometimes the original documents will be required, whereas at other times copies will be sufficient. The Federal Rules of Civil Procedure do not limit the number of requests for production. Several requests may be needed in a complicated lawsuit involving many parties located across the country.

As might be expected, the term *documents* has a wide variety of meanings. Rule 34(a) of the Federal Rules of Civil Procedure defines **documents** to include such diverse items as photographs, graphs, computer printouts, calendars, and accounting records, among others. The scope of the rule extends not only to documents in the

document
An artifact that contains written matter, such as words or figures, in the form of a message or record.

actual custody of the party, but also to those documents under the "control" of that party. This means that the requesting party has the right to obtain some documents that are actually in the possession of a third individual, such as the other party's tax consultant. The rule also allows the requesting party to inspect and copy those documents.

It is also clear that the scope of Rule 34(a) includes requests for all forms of e-evidence. As we've seen, this means that your supervising attorney must be alert and ready to respond to document requests and on-site visits by the opposing party to obtain e-evidence. It also means that your supervising attorney must be prepared to draft effective document requests for e-evidence and to fashion explicit on-site-visit requests to retrieve e-evidence from the opposing party.

Preliminary Decisions Regarding Requests for Documents

In the opening commentary, your client, Mannheim Laboratories Ltd., has elected to sue the accounting firm of Shuster, Kane, Moulton, and Associates, Inc., which issued an unqualified opinion about the accuracy of Seigel's financial records. In this case your attorney will have to make some preliminary decisions regarding any requests for documents to be served on the defendant. Two crucial considerations involve the timing of the request and the potential cost of production of the documents.

Timing of the Request   Rule 34 of the Federal Rules of Civil Procedure prohibits serving a formal request for document production before the parties have conferred as required under Rule 26.

However, your attorney will probably initiate a request for production of documents as soon as possible. Often this will mean drafting a request for production prior to scheduling the first deposition. This early production request will enable the use of documents produced in preparing deposition questions.

On the other hand, in some cases it may be better to delay filing a request for documents until after depositions and interrogatories have been conducted. This is especially true of interrogatories which may help determine how to draft effective document requests. As we've seen, in the case of e-evidence, interrogatories can help determine such things as the nature of the party's computer system, the type of data available, and the identities of all of the people who are responsible for managing, maintaining, or servicing the party's computer system. After your attorney has access to these facts, she will have a better idea about the nature of any document request or on-site visit that ought to be conducted to recover e-evidence.

Cost of the Production   Your attorney should also consider the cost of having the documents inspected and reproduced. It is possible that your client will have to pay any expenses involved in photocopying, reproducing video- or audiotapes, or having duplicate photographs made, so your attorney must consider this factor carefully.

Other additional cost factors may also be involved in the recovery of e-evidence. As we shall see later, in order to assure the opposing party that his or her computer data will not be damaged, lost, or compromised during an on-site visit, it is sometimes necessary to hire an outside IT expert to conduct the details of the on-site examination and retrieval process. This will, of course, add to the cost of document production.

Therefore, it is advisable to inform the client of the extra cost that may be involved in the entire document-production process including, especially, the cost of e-evidence production.

Approaches to Document Production

An attorney's approach to document production is based on two factors. When responding to a document request, the attorney must decide on the organizational approach that will best serve her purposes. Similarly, the attorney must frequently decide on the number of documents to be produced.

Organization and Formatting of Documents A party producing evidence has a choice of three organizational approaches. The documents may be produced as they are kept in the usual course of business, according to categories specified in the document request, or as electronic files (e-files).

Producing the documents as they are kept in the usual course of business requires less time and effort by the responding party. If an enormous amount of information is requested by the other party, this approach would be appropriate. However, do not make the mistake of thinking that the phrase *in the usual course of business* allows the responding party to shuffle the documents to hide pertinent information.

Producing the documents according to the categories in the request requires additional time and effort for the responding party. Still, such an organizational effort can be managed if relatively few documents are requested. Naturally, the party initiating the request usually prefers this approach because it reduces the time and effort required to organize and analyze the documents. Moreover, the party producing the documents may also prefer this technique because it forces a review of all the requested documents, lessening the chance of inadvertently revealing privileged documents.

The Formatting of E-Evidence The third option available is not so much an organizational technique as a formatting tool. Even when it is possible to obtain most or all of the documents necessary for discovery in paper format, your attorney may still wish to file a request for the electronic counterparts of those paper copies. This is because the members of your law firm will have an easier time accessing e-evidence than they would sorting through file folders, envelopes, and boxes of paper evidence. This approach, however, is not without its own pitfalls. In order to actually save time, your supervising attorney must be certain that the electronically produced e-evidence received from the opposing party is in a format that is compatible with the computer system used in your law office. If the e-evidence is in a format that your computer system cannot access, you might spend more time trying to translate the data into a usable form than you would have spent sorting through the paper files.

Another organizational issue related to e-evidence is the question of how to organize the search through the files supplied by the opposing party. A wide variety of flexible search processes are available to the members of your law firm as they approach the accumulated e-evidence. For example, a search can be organized based upon the person who originated the document or the person who received the document. The search can also be organized around the date that it was written, altered, sent, or received. This method is especially effective with e-mail and word-processed documents. Another technique is to organize the search around key words that are likely to appear in the lawsuit. Thus, in this chapter's *Mannheim* case, your search might be organized around key words such as "Mannheim," "Seigel," "audit," and "financial statement."

The Number of Documents   The party responding to the request has three options available in producing the documents. These three options are the warehouse approach, the broad production approach, and the limited approach. Each has its own particular advantages and disadvantages.

In the *warehouse approach,* all documents, both relevant and irrelevant, are produced without any type of organization. The advantage for the producing party here is savings in the time and effort involved in organizing the documents. However, this approach does not relieve the attorneys and paralegals of the need to review the documents before releasing them. Also, by releasing all of the documents available to the party, some documents that appear irrelevant early in the litigation may later be discovered to be highly relevant. These apparently innocent documents could disclose information to which the requesting party is not entitled. Such a disclosure might assist the opposing party in preparing the case for trial.

In a *broad production,* all documents even remotely relevant are produced, even those not directly requested. This approach is advantageous because it can save time and effort later. The underlying premise is that all of these documents will be requested later anyway. By releasing them now, one eliminates the need to repeat the process of combing through the files a second and possibly even a third time. The disadvantage is that the responding party may release documents that the other party would never have requested.

A *limited production* is one in which only the documents requested are produced. The advantage here is the protection of relevant documents that the other party has yet to request. An attorney might elect this approach if the request is very limited in scope or if it is poorly drafted. However, the disadvantage is that later document searches may be necessary as subsequent requests are received.

The Volume of E-Evidence   In most, perhaps all, cases, the amount of e-evidence available within a company, institution, or organization's computer system far exceeds the paper evidence available. This is often due to the fact that many documents that e-workers believe they have deleted still exist somewhere in the system either as inactive or extant data. For example, in the *Mannheim* case, Karl Shuster of Shuster, Kane, Moulton, and Associates, Inc., may believe that he has deleted all e-mail in his desktop PC, in his home computer, in his PDA, and in his laptop that involves the Seigel audit. However, if he did not tell the recipients of those e-mails to delete their versions or if he did not inform those who received copies of those e-mail documents to do the same, each of those e-mails will still be discoverable. In addition, even if all of the copies were deleted, extant copies may exist that a sufficiently clever IT expert will be able to retrieve.

Because of this, and many other secluded places that e-evidence can be inadvertently stored, the extent of the e-evidence concealed within a computer network is often a mystery even to the most well-versed member of a company or institution.

Consequently, the targets of an early document-production request should not be the type of data as much as the computers (PCs, laptops, home computers, personal digital assistants [PDAs], and mobile phones) of key individuals on the opposing side who might be privy to important evidentiary e-documents. Still, such requests should also seek to examine e-mail files, network files, floppy disks, computer tapes, back-up data, and extant data. Moreover, some employees religiously keep paper copies of all e-documents sent, received, worked on, or processed by their office. Consequently, it would also be wise to include in the request all paper copies of any e-data retained by certain select individuals and their assistants. Thus, in the *Mannheim* case, for example, it would be best for your supervising attorney to target the e-files (and paper copies of those e-files, if they exist) of Karl Shuster, one of the key accountants at Shuster, Kane, Moulton, and Associates, Inc.

E-Discovery and Document Requests

The age of cybernetics has contributed enormously to the process of requesting documents. A wide variety of electronic data-storage techniques is available through computers. An attorney who is well-versed in the many types of computer data that are available, who understands that the term *computer* covers a wide variety of systems, who can structure a document request to retrieve the e-evidence and e-data relevant to his case, and who can plan and conduct effective on-site visits for e-data will be able to take advantage of the wide variety of e-evidence available today. Unfortunately, very few attorneys have this type of expertise. In fact, the realm of e-evidence is so mysterious to most attorneys that they either approach it with great fear and trepidation, or, worse yet, completely ignore the issue. The issue is made more complex by the fact that most judges are unsure about both the nature of e-evidence and the way that the rules of procedure, the rules of evidence, and even the local rules created by their own court apply to e-evidence. Moreover, since the infrastructure of each computer network and the facts within each lawsuit are distinct from one another, drafting common principles that apply in all cases is neither wise nor practical. On the other hand, ignoring the situation can only make matters worse.

When your supervising attorney drafts a document-production request under Rule 34 of the Federal Rules of Civil Procedure, he must be aware of the different types of e-evidence that exist within computer systems today. As discussed earlier, discoverable e-evidence falls into three groups: (1) types of e-evidence based on the configuration of the computer system, (2) types of e-evidence based on the nature of the evidence itself, and (3) types of e-evidence based on its storage status. Your supervising attorney must be sure to consider all of these categories when preparing a Rule 34 document-production request for e-evidence. As noted earlier, it is also critical to include the people responsible for collecting, managing, storing, and communicating that e-evidence. It is also important to recall that paper copies of e-data may exist and should be included in a search for e-evidence. Remembering these points will make the search for e-evidence productive.

Document-Production Requests and Computer Systems

The first type of e-evidence that must be considered in structuring a document-production request would be evidence based upon the configuration of the computer system itself. Your supervising attorney must be aware of the fact that most companies, institutions, organizations, and individuals store their data in more than one place. This involves an assessment of the types of computers that may be in operation in the party's ordinary, everyday routine. At this step, it is vital to recall that the phrase "computer system" incorporates such things as desktop PCs, laptops, mobile phones, PDAs, and home computers that are part of a network or that may be used as word-processing work stations or as storage for documents worked on away from the office. It would also be helpful to know whether the opposing party has access to either the Internet or to an internal intranet or portal system. Internet searches, intranet communications, and portal records may hold documents of importance to the lawsuit. Because of this, it would be wise to make certain that the definition and instruction section of the document-production request specifies that any petition for computer data means data stored in any of the just-named computer options. It is also wise to make sure that the definition and instruction section specifies that such petitions are meant to include all paper copies on file of any e-evidence mentioned in the request, even those that have been deleted and exist only in a hard-copy format.

Document-Production Requests and the Nature of the E-Evidence

The second type of e-evidence that must be included in the discovery plan is based on the nature of the evidence itself. For instance, e-evidence generally includes all relevant computer-generated records including those found in e-mail files, databases, calendering programs, and all other relevant data files created by spreadsheets, word processing, or any analogous program. E-mail, for example, can be a very profitable source of information in a lawsuit. The ease and efficiency of e-mail has made it one of the most popular means of communicating in business today. Many individuals use e-mail almost without thought. Moreover, they often have no reservations about sending e-mail messages that are blunt, informal, and even, at times, sarcastic. Much of this is due to the fact that in many workplaces, e-mail has replaced the telephone, the office intercom, the public address system, and the paper memo, as the quickest way to reach coworkers. Much of it is also due, however, to the fact that many workers forget that their e-mail messages are not as impermanent or ephemeral as discussions by the water cooler or in the cafeteria. Often, for instance, the receiver of an e-mail message may retain a copy in his or her computer, even though the sender has deleted it. Messages may even be automatically preserved in the memory of the mainframe computer. Some employees also routinely make paper copies of all e-mail messages. This practice should not be overlooked in any document request for e-evidence.

E-Evidence and Key Players in the Lawsuit   For these just-mentioned reasons, it is best to include in a document-production request the e-mail records (and paper copies of those e-mail records) of any key player in the lawsuit. For example, in the

Mannheim case, suppose that Karl Shuster, a CPA who is a key member of the accounting firm of Shuster, Kane, Moulton, and Associates, sent an e-mail to Jennifer Kane, another key member of the firm, in which he casts doubt upon the competency of Hayden Thorton, the junior CPA who conducted the audit of Seigel. Even if Shuster has deleted the e-mail from his outbox, there may still be a copy in Kane's inbox or archived within the computer. It is also possible that Shuster sent a copy of the e-mail to another member of the firm or that Kane forwarded it to someone else in the association. Moreover, it is distinctly possible, perhaps even probable, that one of those two individuals created a paper copy of the e-mail for his or her files. It is also possible that the administrative assistant or filing clerk who works for a key player may retain both e-copies and paper copies of such e-mail records. Therefore, these individuals should not be overlooked in a document request. Whatever the case, the point here is that even though a record appears to have been expunged, it may still exist somewhere.

E-Evidence and IT Experts   As we've seen, computer systems within the workplace have become so complex, so intricate, and so extensive that many businesses, organizations, and institutions have found that it is in their best interest to hire IT experts to direct their employees through the process of using their computer system to its best advantage. As has already been pointed out, Rule 26(a)(1)(A) of the Federal Rules of Civil Procedure requires the initial disclosure of the name, address, and telephone number of anyone likely to have discoverable information relevant to the disputed facts in the case. Obviously, this includes the IT experts involved in maintaining the opposing party's computer system. At this time during the request for production of documents, it would be advisable for your supervising attorney to make certain that the IT expert or experts of the opposing party are part of the request process. Certainly, IT experts may send and receive their own e-mail that may be discoverable and that may have a bearing on the case. However, it is also likely that they can access the system and retrieve hidden e-mail messages that have been deleted by their senders and receivers or archived automatically by the system itself. In this capacity, they would qualify as agents of the opposing party who have "custody, control, or possession" of the documents that your supervising attorney seeks to obtain. It is also important to recall that the administrative assistants and interns who work with IT experts also routinely retain e-copies and paper copies of all such files. Therefore, it would be wise to include such personnel in your supervising attorney's document request.

E-Evidence and Associated Individuals   It may also be important to determine whether the opposing party's computer system is configured as an intranet system or as a portal network. Whether the opposing party has installed an intranet system or a portal network can be crucial to the document-request process. Both types of systems are networks that are free from connections to other networks. However, when a business or organization has installed an intranet system, only employees have access to the system. Thus, the persons who have "custody, control, or possession" of the documents in that organizations would be limited, for the most part, to employees. In contrast, an organization with a portal network has probably extended the access to people who are associated with the organization. In the case of a business, persons associated with the organization might include people outside of the organization, such as suppliers, customers, and independent contractors. This means that your supervising attorney might need to determine how to include people associated with, but actually outside, the organization in the document-production request.

Document-Production Requests and the Storage of E-Evidence

The final category of e-evidence that must be included in the document-production request is determined on the basis of its storage status within the opposing party's computer system. As we've seen, data is considered to be either active data, inactive data, back-up data, extant data, or paper data. Data is considered active if it is of ongoing importance in the day-to-day operation of the business, institution, or organization. Data is termed inactive if it was produced and used recently, but is no longer critical to the daily operation of the workplace. On the other hand, back-up data is information that has somehow been preserved in the memory of the computer due to the chance that it may be needed in the future, because the active files have been deleted or destroyed accidentally by an operator's error or as the result of a computer malfunction. Such data may be captured on disk, tape, CD, or the computer's hard drive. Again, extant data is information which is hidden in the system, generally because it has been deleted. It usually takes an IT expert to dig out extant data that is present only in a residual form. Finally, paper data includes any e-data which has been transferred to paper form and retained by an individual.

Because of the variety of storage techniques available, it is a good idea to make sure that the definition and instruction section of the request specifies that any petition for computer data includes information that has been stored as active, inactive, back-up, extant, or paper data. In a document-production request it is also important to remember that data may also be stored off site. Often workers will have home computers, laptops, and PDAs in which data may be kept regardless of its storage status. Workers may also transport data home or to other locations on back-up tapes, CDs, and so-called "floppy disks." Most often, an employee takes data home on a disk, CD, or tape for the sake of convenience. Sometimes, however, an employee may relocate a disk, CD, or tape off site because of its sensitive nature. This would make the data on that disk, CD, or tape very interesting to the opposing party. Therefore, it is wise to draft the document-production request so that such disks, CDs, and tapes are not inadvertently excluded from that petition. Your supervising attorney should also remember that e-data may also have been saved in paper form.

The Expense Involved in the Retrieval of E-Evidence

Since it is often necessary to hire experts to recover, reformat, and interpret e-evidence, and because such operations frequently involve using special programs to retrieve the data, the expense of gathering e-evidence may begin to escalate over the outlay that would be involved in the retrieval of paper documents. In addition, because of the possible need to hire extra IT help and to obtain additional programs, extra time must also be factored into this recovery process. Therefore, your supervisory attorney must be ready to justify such requests and may have to be prepared to carry the burden of the extra cost involved. Finally, the possible creation of paper copies of e-files means that the expense associated with the request for and the retrieval of e-files does not always eliminate the expense of looking for paper files. In fact, in those cases that involve extensive back-up paper files, the cost of the search may actually escalate.

Protection of Documents

As noted earlier, a party served with a request for documents has 30 days to respond to that request. The response must indicate either that the party will comply or that the party objects to the request or to part of the request. If an objection is made as to part of a request, inspection of the remaining parts must be permitted. Grounds for such objections include arguing that complying with the request will violate either the attorney-client privilege, the attorney work product privilege, or the common interest privilege. Other objections include that the request is overbroad, duplicative, or irrelevant. If none of these objections are suitable, the documents may still be kept private by using a confidentiality agreement or a protective order.

The Attorney-Client Privilege

As explained in Chapter 8, the attorney-client privilege prevents the forced disclosure of communication between an attorney and a client. Like the other forms of discovery, a request for documents is limited by the attorney-client privilege. This extends to communications to or from both inside and outside counsel.

At an early stage in the discovery process, the paralegal should draw up a list of all attorneys who represented the client in matters relevant to the lawsuit. The list will be used to identify documents that should be withheld from the other party on the basis of the attorney-client privilege. Recall that the attorney-client privilege is waived if a document is disclosed to a third party. Care should therefore be taken to limit access to these protected documents.

The Work Product Privilege

As pointed out in the Chapter 8 discovery overview, the work product privilege prevents the opposing party from obtaining through discovery letters, memos, documents, records, and other tangible items that have been produced in anticipation of litigation or that have been prepared for the trial itself. Because the work product privilege protects tangible evidence, it is especially applicable to a request for documents. Investigator's reports and materials prepared by expert consultants who will not testify at trial are examples of protected work product. Handwritten notes penned by the attorney during office visits or phone conversations with the client would also be considered work product. Similarly, lists made by the client in response to a request by the attorney would be protected.

Unlike the attorney-client privilege, the work product privilege is not an absolute privilege. Disclosure of some documents may be compelled if the party requesting production of the documents has a substantial need for the documents and cannot, without undue hardship, obtain the equivalent of the material by any other means. Calculating the time period when a document could be considered work product can be difficult. Is a document prepared by in-house counsel six months prior to the beginning of the lawsuit protected by the work product privilege? Probably, if the attorney gives any legal advice or discusses potential litigation. If, however, in-house counsel sends a memo on some general legal issue, that memo would probably not be protected by the privilege even if sent six weeks before the lawsuit is brought against the company.

The Common Interest Privilege

As noted in Chapter 8, the common interest privilege will protect any communication between attorneys for different clients when those clients share a common interest. In reality, the privilege is designed to protect the attorney-client privilege and the work product privilege when information is exchanged among attorneys representing different clients with a common interest. The privilege is especially important in relation to document requests because it protects not only oral statements but also written notes and printed memos that pass among such attorneys.

The Medical Privilege and the Confessor-Penitent Privilege

Other privileges that can be used to protect evidence include the medical privilege and the confessor-penitent privilege. Look back to the medical privilege and recall that the privilege was established between a patient and a medical practitioner to shield any sensitive information that passes between the patient and the practitioner. In like manner, the confessor-penitent privilege was formulated to guard the confidences disclosed by the penitent to a clergy person. The privilege does specify, however, that the relationship must somehow be intended to provide spiritual assistance to the penitent. Unlike the other privileges, the confessor-penitent privilege also protects a confessor who has taken a religious oath not to betray the content or nature of the confession.

Overbroad and Duplicative Requests

A party who is responding to a request for documents may also object on the grounds that the request is overbroad. Such an objection would claim that the request is so wide ranging and inclusive that it asks for more evidence than could ever be useful to the other party in the lawsuit. In the *Mannheim* case, for example, if Mannheim requested all of the corporate minute books of Shuster, Kane, and Moulton, the accounting firm's attorney would be justified in objecting on the grounds that the request is overbroad.

Usually, such an objection is accompanied by an alternative suggestion. Thus, Shuster's response to Mannheim's request would refuse to produce all of the corporate minute books, but would promise to produce any corporate minute books that expressly refer to the takeover bid made by Viking Industries for Seigel and the audit of Seigel by Shuster, Kane, Moulton, and Associates, Inc., all of which would be relevant to the lawsuit. Another objection to a request for production of documents is that the request is duplicative. This objection argues that the other party has already asked for that information in another part of the request.

Inadmissible and Irrelevant Evidence

As you learned in Chapter 8, the scope of discovery is much broader than the scope of evidence that can be introduced at trial. Documents that would be inadmissible at trial can still be requested if those documents are reasonably calculated to lead to admissible evidence. However, documents that cannot reasonably be expected to lead to admissible evidence are not subject to discovery. Thus, the producing party may object to a request on those grounds. The producing party may also object on the ground that the documents sought are irrelevant to the lawsuit. Thus, in the *Mannheim* case, Shuster, Kane, and Moulton might object to a request for its certificate of incorporation on the ground that the certificate is irrelevant to the lawsuit. In contrast, if the lawsuit involved allegations that Shuster, Kane, Moulton, and Associates, Inc. was improperly incorporated, then a copy of the certificate of incorporation would be relevant, and no objection should be made.

Confidentiality Agreements and Protective Orders

The secrecy of documents may be difficult to preserve during discovery. In the *Mannheim* case, for example, at least two law firms (one for Mannheim, and one for Shuster, Kane, Moulton, and Associates, Inc.) would be working on the case. Both law firms will probably have several attorneys and paralegals involved in the suit. In addition, legal secretaries, word-processing personnel, copy center personnel, and receptionists, among many others, will have access to the documents. How can the privacy and secrecy of documents be preserved in this atmosphere? One way to maintain privacy and secrecy is to have everyone who works on the case sign a confidentiality agreement. Another way is to seek a protective order from the court to limit the people who are allowed to see the document or the circumstances under which the contents of the document will be revealed.

Inadvertent Production

Despite the most stringent safeguards, privileged documents are sometimes sent to the other party inadvertently. In complex litigation, parties often provide for this eventuality by an agreement to notify the other party of the accidental production of documents and request a return of all copies of the documents. Unfortunately, the parties to a lawsuit are not always cooperative. If a party in possession of inadvertently released documents refuses to return those documents, your attorney will have to file a motion asking the court to compel the return of those documents. If, however, the documents were released as a result of your negligence, the court may not be sympathetic and might very well refuse to grant your attorney's motion.

Requesting the Production of Documents

As a paralegal, you will often be involved in the drafting of requests for documents. Naturally, before you begin drafting a request, you should develop a working knowledge of the case. You can gain this understanding of the case by reviewing the pleadings binder, the correspondence file, the attorney's notes, and the research note-book. As you review these files, you should take notes of the possible types of documents or particular documents that are relevant to the case. In the *Mannheim* case, for example, as a paralegal for the firm representing Mannheim Laboratories, Ltd., you might want to see Shuster, Kane, Moulton, and Associates, Inc.'s corporate minute books, any auditing procedure manuals followed by the firm's accountants, any correspondence between Shuster and Seigel, any internal memos involving the takeover bid of Viking for Seigel, and any internal memos referring to the firm's audit of Seigel.

Once you have done this initial research, you will be ready to draft the request. However, your responsibilities will not end with the drafting of the request. As we shall see later in this section, you may also need to draft a motion to compel the other party to produce the documents, and you may be responsible for reviewing the documents once they are received.

Form and Content of the Request

Before sitting down to draft the request, you might locate sample requests for documents in form books or in the firm's word-processing form file. Of course, as no two cases are exactly the same, you will have to modify any form or sample request to fit the particular facts and issues in the case. Still, forms and samples can often be utilized for the basic areas of the request, such as the introductory paragraph and the definitions of terms. You will also need to be familiar with the pertinent court rules involving discovery. Each court may have individual rules relating to the number of requests allowed, the time allowed for responding to requests, the manner of objecting to requests, and the availability of a motion to compel the production of the requested documents.

Title of the Document and Introductory Paragraph   Document production often involves many parties and several requests. Your draft request for the production of documents should identify the party making the request, the party receiving the request, and the number of the request:

Example

MANNHEIM LABORATORIES, LTD.'S
FIRST REQUEST FOR PRODUCTION OF DOCUMENTS
TO DEFENDANT SHUSTER, KANE, MOULTON, AND ASSOCIATES, INC.

Using this type of detailed title avoids confusion and eliminates the need to read the entire request to determine the parties involved. The introductory paragraph of your request should list the applicable federal or state authority and the time and place of the production.

Definitions   The definition section is a pivotal area of the request. The heading "definitions" should be placed in the center of the page in bold-faced lettering. This emphasis will direct the party answering the request to that section for clarification of any ambiguous terms. Having a separate section devoted solely to definitions avoids the need to include this information in the body of the request. Some of the terms that may be defined include *agreement, document,* and *report,* among others.

Instructions   Because the instruction section of the request is also crucial, its heading should be placed in the center of the page in bold-faced lettering. Some law firms combine the definition and instruction sections of the request, so make certain that you check on your firm's procedure. The instruction section specifies the time period in which the documents should be produced. For example, in the *Mannheim* case, if Shuster, Kane, and Moulton's final audit of Seigel was issued on September 9, 2005, the request should cover at least the period from January 1, 2005, to the date of the upcoming production of documents. This entire period should be included because the negotiations, correspondence, memos, and interim reports that preceded the final opinion may be critical in litigating your client's case.

The instructions may also indicate whether the requesting party wants to see originals or copies of the documents. It is also customary to ask for the identity of anyone who has any of the requested documents not in the custody, possession, or control of the party served with the request. The instructions should also remind the responding party of the duty to supplement the production of documents with any documents found or created after the first production takes place. This can usually be done by labeling the request as a "continuing request." It is also customary to remind the responding party to correct any errors uncovered after the original production of documents.

Documents Requested   Rule 34 of the Federal Rules of Civil Procedure states that a request for documents must specify with "reasonable particularity" the general categories of documents or the individual documents that the requesting party wishes to inspect. This is accomplished in the section headed "documents requested." Generally, this section consists of a list of numbered paragraphs, each one specifying a document or a category of documents. Because the preceding paragraphs have explained the definitions and instructions, the job of listing the documents in this section has been considerably simplified. Exhibit 12–3 is an example of a request for production of documents that might be filed in the *Mannheim* case.

Final Responsibility in Drafting the Request

Responsibility for the final review and signature of the request for documents rests with the attorney. Once the request has been signed, you will have to arrange for service on the other party or parties. Under the Federal Rules of Civil Procedure, a request for production of documents need not be filed with the court. However, some states do have this filing requirement, so you should check your state and local rules on this matter. After the other party has been served with the request, place a reminder of the response due-date in the firm's tickler or calendar system. If a timely response is not received, you might check with your attorney to determine if an extension of time has been granted. If an extension has not been granted, then it may be necessary to file a motion to compel.

Motion to Compel

Usually, all the parties in a lawsuit will be cooperative during the discovery process. Dates and times for the production of documents are negotiated and adhered to with great regularity. Even when a party objects to the production of a document on

COURT OF COMMON PLEAS
CUYAHOGA COUNTY
STATE OF OHIO

MANNHEIM LABORATORIES, LTD., Plaintiff,	))) Civil Action No. 05-77976))
v.	)))
SHUSTER, KANE, MOULTON, AND ASSOCIATES, INC., Defendants.	))))))

PLAINTIFF MANNHEIM LABORATORIES, LTD.'s FIRST REQUEST FOR
PRODUCTION OF DOCUMENTS TO DEFENDANT
SHUSTER, KANE, MOULTON, AND ASSOCIATES, INC.

TO: Jeremy Wickard, Attorney of Record for Defendant, Shuster, Kane, Moulton, and Associates, Inc., in the above styled and numbered cause.

Pursuant to Rule 34 of the Ohio Rules of Civil Procedure, Mannheim Laboratories, Ltd., plaintiff in the above cause, requests that Shuster, Kane, Moulton and Associates, Inc., defendant in the above cause, produce for inspection and copying by Mannheim, within thirty days of service hereof or at such other time as may be agreed upon by counsel for the parties, originals or legible copies of the documents requested herein. You are also requested to serve upon plaintiff within thirty (30) days after service of this request a written response in accordance with Rule 34 of the Ohio Rules of Civil Procedure.

DEFINITIONS AND INSTRUCTIONS

1. Unless specified otherwise, documents requested herein include all those which were dated, written, rewritten, modified, sent or received from January 1, 2005 to September 9, 2005.

2. The following definitions apply to this request:

a. The term "agreement" means any document or oral statements that constitute or purport to be in whole or in part a contract, lease, or license, and includes all changes, amendments, covenants, alterations, modifications, interpretations, and drafts thereof, whether or not carried out.

b. The term "document" means any written, recorded, taped, typed, or word processed, whether produced, reproduced, filed, or stored on paper, cards, disks, tapes, belts, charts, films, cassettes, or any other medium, and shall include books, booklets, pamphlets, brochures, statements, speeches, memos, notebooks, agreements, appointment calendars, working papers, contracts, notations, records, telegrams, journals, diaries, or summaries, cash ledger books, checkbooks, corporate minute books, bank statements, stock transfer books, monthly statements, city tax returns, state tax returns, federal tax returns, and annual reports, and shall also include all drafts, originals, and copies.

EXHIBIT 12–3 Sample request for documents

c. The term "report" means any written, recorded, taped, typed or word processed, whether produced, reproduced, filed, or stored on paper, cards, disks, tapes, belts, charts, films, cassettes, or any other medium, and shall include books, booklets, pamphlets, brochures, statements, speeches, memos, notebooks, agreements, appointment calendars, working papers, contracts, notations, records, telegrams, journals, diaries, or summaries, cash ledger books, checkbooks, corporate minute books, bank statements, stock transfer books, monthly statements, city tax returns, state tax returns, federal tax returns, and annual reports, and shall also include all drafts, originals, and copies.

d. The term "defendants" means Shuster, Kane, Moulton and Associates, Inc., including their directors, officers, employees, and agents.

e. The phrases "relate to" and "relating to" shall be construed to include "refer to," "summarize," "contain," "include," "mention," "explain," "discuss," "define," "describe," "point out," "comment on," or "remark."

f. The words "and" and "or" shall be interpreted in such a way as to bring within the scope of the specification all responses that otherwise might be interpreted as being outside its scope.

g. The term "each" shall be interpreted to include the word "every," and the word "every" shall be interpreted to include the word "each."

h. The word "any" shall be interpreted to include the word "all," and the word "all" shall be interpreted to include the word "any."

i. A plural noun will be interpreted to be a singular noun, and a singular noun will be interpreted as a plural noun, whenever needed to bring within the scope of the specification all responses that otherwise might be interpreted as being outside its scope.

3. Produce each and every document in its original file folder, cover, envelope, or jacket, and write on that folder, cover, envelope, or jacket the person or the corporate office, department, subdivision, or subsidiary for which, by which, and/or in which the file is maintained.

4. Should you be unable to produce any of the documents called for in this request, explain the reason that you cannot comply.

5. Should you be unable to produce any of the documents called for in this request, because such documents are no longer in your custody, control, or possession, please identify the document and the reason that you no longer have custody, control, or possession of said document or documents.

6. Should you be unable to produce any of the documents called for in this request, because such documents are no longer in your custody, control, or possession, please identify the document, and the person, department, subdivision, or subsidiary that does have custody, control, or possession of said document.

7. Should you wish to assert the attorney-client privilege, the work product privilege, or any other privilege as to any of the documents called for in this request, then as to each document subject to such privilege, please provide an identification of such document, including the name of the document, the date of the document, the type of document, the author of the document, the receiver of the document, the names of all people receiving copies of the document, the names of all people who saw the original document, and a summary of the subject of the document in sufficient detail to allow the Court to determine the validity of the assertion of the privilege, should a motion to compel be filed.

EXHIBIT 12–3   *(continued)*

8. Each paragraph in this request should be interpreted independently and not in relation to any other paragraph for the purpose of limiting the request.

9. This request is to be considered a continuing request requiring the defendant to supplement the production of document with any documents found or created after the first production takes place.

10. The defendant has the additional duty to correct any errors that are uncovered after the original production of documents takes place.

11. Any questions that may arise as to this request for documents may be directed by the counsel for the defendant to the undersigned representative of the plaintiff before the dates set for the production of the documents that are the subject matter of this request.

DOCUMENTS REQUESTED

1. All documents, reports, and agreements that relate to the corporate organization of Shuster, Kane, Moulton, and Associates, Inc.

2. All documents, reports, and agreements that Shuster, Kane, Moulton, and Associates, Inc. directed to or were received by Seigel Pharmaceuticals, Inc.

3. All documents, reports, and agreements that relate to contracts, proposed contracts, draft contracts, negotiated contracts, contemplated contracts, or offers of contracts that passed between Shuster, Kane, Moulton, and Associates, Inc. and Seigel Pharmaceuticals, Inc.

4. All documents, reports, and agreements that constitute or relate to any and all communication between Shuster, Kane, Moulton, and Associates, Inc. and Seigel Pharmaceuticals, Inc.

5. All documents, reports, and agreements that relate to the audit conducted by Shuster, Kane, Moulton, and Associates, Inc. on the financial condition of Seigel Pharmaceuticals, Inc.

6. All documents, reports, and agreements that constitute internal communication within Shuster, Kane, Moulton, and Associates, Inc. that relate to Seigel Pharmaceuticals, Inc.

7. All documents, reports, and agreements that constitute internal communication within Shuster, Kane, Moulton, and Associates, Inc., that relate to Mannheim Laboratories, Ltd.

8. All documents, reports, and agreements that constitute or relate to any and all communication between Shuster, Kane, Moulton, and Associates, Inc. and Seigel Pharmaceuticals, Inc. concerning the Mannheim Laboratories, Ltd.

9. All documents, reports, and agreements that relate to the audit conducted by Shuster, Kane, Moulton, and Associates, Inc. on the financial condition of Seigel Pharmaceuticals, Inc. and that specifically refer to the Mannheim Laboratories, Ltd.

10. All documents, reports, and agreements that relate to the unqualified opinion issued by Shuster, Kane, Moulton, and Associates, Inc. on the financial health of Seigel Pharmaceuticals, Inc.

11. All documents, reports, or agreements that relate to the audit conducted by Shuster, Kane, Moulton, and Associates, Inc. on Seigel Pharmaceuticals, Inc. and that refer to the Mannheim Laboratories, Ltd. that are not covered by the prior requests herein.

12. All documents, reports, or agreements that relate to the audit conducted by Shuster, Kane, Moulton, and Associates, Inc. on Seigel Pharmaceuticals, Inc. and that refer to any and all other potential investors in Seigel Pharmaceuticals, Inc. that are not covered by the prior requests herein.

EXHIBIT 12–3   *(continued)*

13. All documents, reports, and agreements that relate to the financial structure of Seigel Pharmaceuticals, Inc. that are not covered by the prior requests herein.

Giacomo Striuli
Striuli, Grazak, and Usalis
2233 Hamilton Avenue
Cleveland, Ohio 44119
Tel.: (123) 555-1212
Fax: (123) 555-2323
Attorneys for Plaintiff
Mannheim Laboratories, Ltd.

CERTIFICATE OF SERVICE

I hereby certify that a true and correct copy of the foregoing has been mailed by first class mail, postage prepaid to Jeremy Wickard, 54392 St. Clair Avenue, Cleveland, Ohio, 44118, on this 29th day of September, 2005.

EXHIBIT 12–3   *(continued)*

the grounds that it is irrelevant, the document is often produced anyway. Similarly, objections on the grounds that the request is overbroad will often be followed by a narrowed response. However, sometimes the other party refuses to cooperate or makes invalid objections to the request. For this situation, the law provides the motion to compel. Rule 37 of the Federal Rules of Civil Procedure allows a party to file a motion asking the court to compel the uncooperative party to produce the document requested for inspection.

As the paralegal, you may be asked to draft this motion. Again, in preparation for the drafting of this motion, review your firm's form books or document file. Generally, however, your attorney will avoid the motion to compel as much as possible. Such motions are not favored by the court and should be used only when your attorney feels there is no other way to obtain information that is vital to the successful outcome of the lawsuit.

Reviewing the Documents of the Opposing Party

Once the documents requested have been received in your office, you may be asked to review those documents, either alone or with an attorney. Naturally, a knowledge of the facts, issues, and parties in the case is essential to a successful document review. However, it is also important for you to have an understanding of what your attorney is looking for as you inspect and review the documents. Therefore, you should ask your attorney for guidance in reviewing the documents. For example, it would be helpful for you to know which of the files must be read in-depth and which can be merely scanned. You might also want to know if your attorney is interested in a particular category of documents or in the documents produced by a particular individual.

Because reviewing a large volume of documents is a time-consuming and tedious task, you will want to try various techniques for expediting the job. One technique is to dictate file labels and a brief summary of the contents of each file. This will help you review more documents over a shorter period of time. Another technique is to keep a record of the files that you have reviewed. This will help you recall the precise location of documents that you have seen and consider crucial to the case.

If you are dealing with original documents, your attorney may want to have copies made of the more important documents. Your attorney will set the parameters for the documents that she will want you to copy. However, if there is any doubt about the value of a document to your case, designate the document for copying.

Responding to a Request for Documents

A document production is only as successful as the planning that precedes it. The first action you should take, once you have been served with a document request, is to determine if the production date is realistic. Other important elements in the successful production process are categorizing the documents, involving the client, and organizing the documents.

Determining a Target Date

Whether or not the requested target date is feasible depends to a great extent on the number of the documents in your client's possession and the number of people in the law firm who will assist in the production. However, estimating the volume of documents in a document production can be difficult. Often the first estimate will be revised several times as you locate and review pertinent documents. Nevertheless, you must make some initial assessment of the feasibility of meeting the deadline indicated in the request. Consulting with other paralegals who have been through several document productions may help you evaluate the deadline date.

Categorizing the Documents

You can make the task of documentation production easier if you divide the request into several general categories. For example, you might divide the request into the following categories:

Request 1	Accounting Information
Request 2	Marketing Plans and Correspondence
Request 3	Corporate Minutes, Bylaws, and Articles of Incorporation
Request 4	Research and Development
Request 5	Sales Projections

THE COMPUTERIZED LAW FIRM
Document Summary

SCENARIO

You and your attorney are in the middle of a deposition. The deponent is Karl Shuster, a CPA who is a partner in the accounting firm of Shuster, Kane, Moulton, and Associates, Inc. Shuster has just indicated that he had no idea that the financial report that his firm issued on Seigel Pharmaceuticals, Inc. would be seen and relied upon by the Mannheim Laboratories, Ltd. Your attorney, however, recalls seeing a letter that was written by Shuster and addressed to Regina Seigel, the president of Seigel Pharmaceuticals, Inc. In the letter Shuster referred to a list of third parties who would probably receive copies of the report. Included on that list was Kurt Mannheim, the founder and president of Mannheim Laboratories, Ltd. Before continuing with the deposition, your attorney would like to see that letter. She instructs you to return to your office and bring her a copy of the correspondence. Unfortunately, your attorney cannot recall the exact date or the primary subject of the letter. Nevertheless, she expects you to return with the letter within the next 15 minutes.

PROBLEM

Document production in massive and complex litigation is time consuming and cumbersome. Organizing thousands of documents for fast and accurate retrieval presents a challenge for you and your attorney. When you return to your office you realize the immensity of the task you face. Literally thousands of documents are stacked in boxes in your office and piled on shelves in your attorney's office. How are you going to locate a single letter?

SOLUTION

Fortunately for you, your law firm recently introduced an automated litigation support program to help with the numerous litigation tasks. One feature of this program is a database that allows you to organize and manage thousands of documents. Consequently, document coders hired by your law firm have already analyzed and extracted the pertinent data from the documents produced by the parties in this case. This information has been entered into the program. Your computer now has stored valuable information about each document, such as the date, the author, the recipient, carbon copy recipients, subject matter, type of document, and attachments. The high-speed search capacity of the computer permits you to locate the letter from Karl Shuster to Regina Seigel, dated May 20, 2005, in which Kurt Mannheim is named on a list of probable recipients of the financial report. Searching a database of 10,000 documents, the computer identifies this critically important document in a matter of minutes.

Selecting the proper software for document management may depend on a number of factors, such as the type of hardware, the number of litigation matters handled by the law firm, and the personnel available to support computerized litigation. Your law firm's general database may be sufficient to handle the demands of a litigation support system. If that is not a viable choice, the law firm's computer programmer might adapt the specialized requirements of a document summary database. Integrated litigation support programs, such as Summation, also contain document management capabilities. However, any database program can be adapted for this purpose.

Once the general categories are developed, subcategories can be easily defined. These categories and subcategories will give your document search a controlling structure that will guide your work.

Involving the Client in Document Production

Although you have established categories of the documents that you believe are responsive to the request, you must remember that only the client knows what types and how many documents actually exist. Also remember that only the client can make the documents available to the law firm for production. Therefore, the client must be involved in the production process as early as possible. You might begin by sending the client a copy of the request as soon as you receive it. Make certain that you point out the date by which the production is to be made so that the client is aware that the process should not be delayed. Next, schedule a meeting with the client as soon as possible to plan the document production.

Making Document Production a Joint Effort with the Client   Sometimes clients suggest that they conduct the document search without the aid of someone from the law firm. There are several disadvantages to this approach. First, clients are often unaware of the attorney-client privilege, the work product privilege, and the common interest privilege and may, therefore, not recognize protected documents. Second, clients may also fail to recognize the documents they actually must produce. Third, clients often do not comprehend the amount of time and effort involved in a document production. Finally, the client probably does not realize that sanctions can result if all the documents requested are not produced. Pointing out these disadvantages to your clients should help convince them to make document production a joint effort with the law firm. Your client may also suggest hiring an independent contractor to conduct the document search. Although there are reputable firms that can conduct such a search, it is generally not a good idea for your firm to relinquish control over the process.

Selecting a Client's Representative for Document Production   The client should designate a representative to coordinate the document production with the legal team. Often it is advantageous if that representative is a member of the client's in-house legal department. Whatever the case, the person chosen should know about the client's business during the entire period of time covered by the document request. Because the client's representative must devote a significant amount of time to the document production project, there is a tendency for clients to appoint junior executives who are new to the corporation. Such a move can be a mistake, not only because the junior executive will not be familiar with the entire case, but also because the other employees may refuse to cooperate with the "outsider." If you find yourself in this uncomfortable situation, you may seek the help of the client's in-house legal department to find a replacement. The replacement should be someone who is more familiar with the case and who will command the respect needed in such a sensitive operation.

Organizing the Document Production

Organization is a key factor in conducting a successful document production. One effective way to organize is to gather all of the required documents in one central location. Exhibit 12–4 is a checklist you might follow to locate and gather in one location all the documents from your client's executive offices and branches.

1. Review request for production and determine time and personnel required.
2. Forward request for production to client and request that a client representative be named to assist with the production.
3. Determine if the originals or copies of the documents will be produced.
4. Determine if the documents will be produced as kept in the ordinary course of business or by document request number.
5. Determine if only relevant documents will be produced or if the production will be a "warehouse" production.
6. Meet with the client's representative to begin planning the collection and organization of the client's files for production. Request an organization chart to determine departments and employees where responsive documents may be located. Ask for a dedicated workroom for the production, including telephones, office furniture, and supplies.
7. Search all of the pertinent files in the client's offices. Draw a map of each office or department to indicate the location and titles of files and file cabinets.
8. List all files removed on the document production log, and indicate the employee from whom the files were received, in addition to the date the files were received.
9. Request a copy of the client's document-retention policy to determine the length of time various types of documents are retained and the document storage and destruction policies of the client.
10. Request an index to the archived files to determine files that might pertain to the litigation. Order those files brought from archives to the production site.
11. Number each box as it is brought into the work area. Place that number on the log and index all files within the box, including source and date received.
12. Review the contents of each box of documents. Create new file folders labeled "Produce," "Non-produce," "Privilege/Work Product." Place a colored sticker or flag on each document about which there is a question. Ask the supervising attorney to review those documents immediately to determine the appropriate folder. In the case of documents that require redaction, make a copy of the original before doing the redaction, note the redaction at the top of the document, make a copy of the document with the redaction and place it in the "Produce" file; place the original and the original redacted copy in the "Non-produce" or "Privilege/Work Product" folders, as applicable.
13. Remove the privileged document folders from the workroom. Once the attorney has reviewed the documents and determined that the privilege designation is correct, these documents may be numbered with a different numbering prefix from the documents to be produced. A notation should be made on the production log to indicate privileged documents, the original files from which they came, and their document numbers once they are assigned.
14. After the document review has been completed, all documents to be produced should be copied and numbered. The document number can indicate the source of the documents. For example, documents from defendant A begin with "1," from defendant B with "2," and from third-party defendant "X" with "3."
15. Prepare a privilege list to attach to the response to the request for production.
16. Prepare the response to the request for production.
17. Index produced documents.

EXHIBIT 12–4 Checklist for production of client documents

18. Produce documents to the opposing party. The paralegal should remain in the production room at all times. No copies should be removed by the opposing party or its counsel.

19. Copy documents the opposing party designates for copying. Review the documents and notify your attorney of the documents requested by the opposing party. Forward the copies and a statement for the copying costs to the counsel for the opposing party. Make a notation on the production log of all copies received by the opposing party.

20. Return original documents to the client's office. Place a notation in the file that no documents are to be added to or taken from this file because the matter is in litigation. Begin a new file with the same file label for all new correspondence and documents. In the event of a supplemental request for production, you may be able to avoid reviewing files previously reviewed.

21. Make additional copies of documents produced and organize in chronological, subject matter, or witness order for later deposition exhibit, trial exhibit, or general trial preparation use.

EXHIBIT 12–4   *(continued)*

Controlling the Documents   Control is also an important factor in effective document production. You must be able to determine the location of any document among the thousands of documents that you will compile. For example, when your attorney asks for a one-page opinion that is part of a closing binder, you will be expected to locate the pertinent document quickly. Or if the client's chief financial officer needs to review the minutes of the board meeting at which the directors discussed the Shuster audit of Seigel, before the next board meeting, you must know exactly where that file is and make certain that the CFO has it on time for that meeting. Exhibit 12–4 includes steps that will help in the organization of the document production process.

Copying the Documents   The decision of when to copy the documents must be made early in the document-production process. Usually, it is not advisable to release original documents, because the release of such documents can handicap the daily operation of the client's business. Also, when original documents are released there is always the possibility that they may be lost. Finally, government regulations may prohibit the removal of some documents from the principal place of business.

Unfortunately, copying thousands of documents can be expensive and time consuming. Therefore, the legal team should always be aware of ways to reduce this expense. For example, time and money can be saved by waiting until the opposing counsel designates the documents that are to be copied. A disadvantage to this approach is that you may miss some documents that could be helpful to your client's case. Opposing counsel will have little interest in copying documents that support your client's position.

Numbering the Documents   Numbering and control are synonymous. Without an identifying number, it is virtually impossible to organize and control a document production. A number assigned to a document during the production process should remain with the document throughout the lawsuit. One technique for numbering the documents is the Bates numbering system. The **Bates numbering** system involves the numbering

Bates numbering
The numbering of documents in a lawsuit using a machine.

document production log
A method of keeping track of documents in a lawsuit by categorizing those documents based on source and file location. The document production log should also indicate whether the documents have been excluded as privileged.

privilege log
A method of keeping track of documents that are shielded by the attorney-client privilege, the work product privilege, or the common interest privilege.

of documents in a lawsuit using a machine. The Bates system served as the primary means of numbering documents for many years. Recently, however, computer-generated numbers on peel-off labels have replaced the Bates numbering system. The new system is different, but the result is the same. Documents can be identified quickly and easily.

Alpha prefixes can be used to identify the source of a document. For instance, the plaintiff's documents might begin with "A," while the defendant's begin with "B." However, you should not act too quickly in the numbering of the documents. All privileged documents must be removed from the production before the numbering to avoid suspicious gaps in the numbering system. Exhibit 12–5 represents a sample **document production log** to assist you in organizing the documents for production.

It is also wise to make out a **privilege log,** indicating all documents that are shielded by the attorney-client privilege, the work product privilege, or the common interest privilege. Exhibit 12–6 will help you compile such a log.

| STYLE OF CASE: | REVIEWER: | REVIEW DATE: |
| BOX NO. | SOURCE | |

FILE NAME	SOURCE	PRODUCE	NON-PRODUCE	PRIVILEGE	BATES NO.	DATE PRODUCED	OPOSING PARTY TO WHOM PRODUCED

EXHIBIT 12–5 Document production log

BATES NO.	DATE	DOC. TYPE	AUTHOR	RECIPIENT	COPIES	SUMMARY	TYPE PRIVILEGE

EXHIBIT 12–6 Privilege log

Reviewing, Labeling, and Filing Documents before Removal   A paralegal and an attorney should review all documents before they are removed from the client's office. Sometimes one or more of the client's original files will contain documents that you must produce, other documents that you need not produce, and still others that are protected by privilege. The documents that you will have to produce are called **responsive documents;** the documents that you do not have to produce are called **nonresponsive documents.** The protected documents are called **privileged documents.**

To separate these documents, set up three duplicate files. Place copies of the documents to be produced in one of the folders and give it the same title as the client's original file. Place the nonresponsive documents in the second file and label it "nonresponsive" or "non-produce." The term *non-produce* is simply a synonym for nonresponsive. Place the privileged documents in the third file and label it "privileged." All privileged files should be removed from the area where the responsive documents are kept. This simple precaution will prevent them from being inadvertently sent to the other party.

Sometimes a single document will contain information that you must produce and information that you need not produce. The same document may also include information that is protected by privilege. In such a case, cover the irrelevant or the protected information before making a photocopy. Place the notation "deletion" on the covered portion. This deletion process is referred to as **redaction.** Make two copies of the redacted page. Place one of the redacted copies in the file that is marked as the client's original file is marked. Place the other redacted copy in the nonresponsive file or the privileged file, whichever is appropriate.

Organizing and Indexing the Documents after Production

As the paralegal, you will have several duties following the production of your client's documents and the review of the opposition's documents. Because there will often be thousands of documents involved in the litigation, control problems will be very serious. You can aid in establishing tight control over these documents by organizing and indexing them.

Organizing the Documents after Production

Before the mass of information in these documents can be used properly, the documents must be organized. Organizational plans vary from case to case. Some cases are hinged on chronological events. Documents in such cases are ordered by dates. Other cases may be broken down into several subject categories. The documents would therefore be organized by those subjects. In other cases you will be asked to organize the documents in anticipation of the upcoming depositions. In such a case, you will need to pull together all documents related to the testimony of each deponent to be called. The method of organization is less important than the fact that the documents are organized in a way that will help you instantly locate a document when asked to do so.

If the case is to be managed manually, without the aid of a computer, several copies of each document should be made. One set can be placed in chronological order, a

---

responsive documents
Documents that must be presented to a party in answer to a request from that party for the production of those documents.

nonresponsive documents
Documents that need not be presented to a party in answer to a request from that party for the production of those documents.

privileged documents
Documents that are shielded by the attorney-client privilege, the work product privilege, or the common interest privilege.

redaction
A procedure that involves removing information from a document before duplicating the document and turning the duplicate over to another party in a lawsuit in response to a request for production. The removal is justified because the information is immaterial or priviledged.

second set in subject order, and a third set in deponent order. Keep the copies separate from the original numbered set and limit access to that original set. A missing original that is incorrectly numbered may disappear forever. The absence of that crucial document could have a severe impact on the case. Remember, control and organization are the keys to effective document management in any successful litigation.

Indexing the Documents after Production

An index of the documents produced by all parties is critical to controlling the files throughout the lawsuit. This index can be limited to the document number, date, author, recipient, document type, and a brief summary of its content. If you place the document in word processing or on the firm's computer, a particular document can be located quickly by any of the identifying labels. The index is your final control measure. However, this does not mean that you should minimize its importance. It may be a difficult job at the outset of the lawsuit, but it is much less difficult than searching for a document by trial and error later in the case.

Inspection of Property

The request for documents is directed only to documents. However, often a case involves tangible property, such as a piece of equipment or a parcel of real estate. Rule 34 of the Federal Rules of Civil Procedure provides a procedure through which the parties or their representatives can inspect property for the purposes of measuring, photographing, or testing.

Obtaining an Inspection

Normally, the demand for inspection is made informally by letter. The letter will also designate a date and place of inspection. If the date and time specified in the letter are inconvenient for the other party, another time and place can be set. In some instances, the party who has custody or possession of the property in question is reluctant to allow the other parties access to the property. Rule 34 of the Federal Rules of Civil Procedure sets out the procedure by which a party may demand that the party with custody of the property relevant to the case shall produce the property for inspection. The court will usually grant the inspection if it determines that inspection is calculated to lead to the discovery of evidence that will be admissible at trial.

demand for inspection
A discovery technique that involves a request to enter property to inspect that property to gain facts in relation to the lawsuit.

The procedure for gaining access to property in the possession of another party is simple. A **demand for inspection** must be prepared and served upon all parties in the litigation, even if it is directed only to the party that has custody of the property at issue. The property must be identified with reasonable particularity, and the demand must not be overly broad or vague. A demand for inspection may be made only upon the parties to the litigation. As in the case of depositions, a subpoena duces tecum must be prepared to require nonparties to produce tangible items for inspection at the time of deposition or trial. The subpoena duces tecum cannot be used to obtain access to real property.

FINDING IT ON THE INTERNET

California Civil Discovery explains the nature of the Web-centric environment at **<http://www.californiadiscovery.findlaw.com/Internet_Discovery. htm>**. Access the Web site and write an essay which examines the production of documents in relation to e-discovery as explained on the site.

The Federal Rules of Civil Procedure can be accessed at the following address: **<http://www.law.cornell.edu/rules/frcp>**. Access the Web site, find Rule 34, and check to see if there have been any recent interpretations of the provisions and requirements as stated under this rule.

An article entitled "An Integrated Approach for Model Based Document Production and Management," available at **<http://www.itcon.org/1996/1/ yacine.htm>**, examines how a business can solve several problems associated with electronic document retention and production. Access the article and report on the suggested solutions.

An article entitled "Document Production and Organization in Delaware," available at **<http://www.bayardfirm.com/graphics/seminarmaterials. pdf>**, examines how Rule 34 of the federal rules is applied in Delaware courts. Access the article and write a report that compares the Delaware approach to document production with the approach used in your state.

Responding to a Demand for Inspection

Under Rule 34, the respondent has 30 days to respond to the **demand** for inspection. The respondent may agree to the inspection, limit or place conditions on the inspection, or serve formal objections to the requests. Normally, inspections of land, buildings, or equipment must be timed so as not to interfere with the other party's normal use. If a test to be used on the property might destroy that property, the test may be conducted by an expert agreeable to both parties. A video recording may be made of the test.

E-Evidence and On-Site Inspections

Sometimes, it is necessary for your supervising attorney to ask for and obtain an on-site visit to further examine the computer system of an opposing party. It is clear that the wording of Rule 34 of the Federal Rules of Civil Procedure authorizes such on-site inspections. Rule 34(a) reveals that such on-site inspections are permitted in order for a party to enter premises that are held or overseen by a party in order to inspect and/or record either an object located on the premises or an operation carried out therein.

Clearly, this would include the computer system itself, as well as workstations, data storage facilities, and paper files of such e-data. The rule also specifies that the information must be inspected as it is preserved in the "ordinary course of business." There is very little doubt that in many, perhaps most, businesses, organizations, and institutions, the ordinary course of business involves the storage of data within an individual computer or within a computer system, as well as the paper copies of such e-evidence. As we shall see, the operation of the rule is made even more problematic because such requests can also be made of nonparties.

Reasons for the On-Site Inspection of a Computer System

On-site inspections of a computer system ought not to be engaged in on a whim or to harass an opposing party or someone associated with that party. Such inspections, no matter how carefully they are carried out, are likely to be intrusive, disruptive, time consuming, expensive, dangerous (to the stored e-data), and objectionable. Therefore, if your supervising attorney intends to conduct such an inspection, he should have a legitimate reason for doing so. For example, often a party may have no idea how to retrieve computer data that was the subject of an initial document request. As strange as this may seem at first glance, we must remember that obtaining e-evidence is not always as simple as obtaining paper evidence that can easily be lifted from a briefcase, pulled out of a filing cabinet, taken off a table top, or removed from a desk drawer. This is especially true when the e-evidence requested is extant data that was deleted but is still hidden somewhere within the data stream of the computer system.

There are other problems and concerns with the e-evidence produced or with the data collection process that might motivate your supervising attorney to ask for an on-site inspection. For example, the issues in the lawsuit may not be associated with the actual data produced, but with the operation of the entire computer system. Therefore, your attorney may require an on-site inspection by your firm's IT expert in order to track the daily computer operation of a party. Such an inspection might examine the handling of e-data to determine whether it is secure, controlled, and, above all, authentic. Moreover, such an inspection might also reveal the routine procedure of making paper files of e-data, something that even the workers within the system may have overlooked, forgotten, or taken as a matter of course. Other questions may surface after an initial document request has been filed and responded to and your supervising attorney begins to suspect that not all of the e-evidence requested has been delivered, either because the request has not been properly honored, because some of the relevant e-evidence has been deleted, or because the routine paper storage of deleted e-documents has been forgotten or ignored.

Procedures for the On-Site Inspection of a Computer System

The federal courts are extremely sensitive to the problems associated with permitting a party to enter the premises of another party in order to inspect the operation of a party's computer system. Part of this sensitivity arises because the courts realize that any on-site inspection is intrusive, expensive, and often threatens the integrity of the computer system itself as well as the very existence of its e-files. For example, in at least one case, the on-site inspection of a computer system for e-evidence resulted in an enormous amount of lost e-data from that system. The loss of the e-data was eventually traced directly to the careless actions of an IT expert from the opposing party who failed to follow proper protocols in the extraction of certain pieces of e-evidence. In addition, the inspection of a computer system will often involve privacy issues associated not only with classified business and employment records, but also with trade secrets and professional confidences.

For these reasons, the federal courts have, in a series of cases, developed a protocol for the handling of on-site inspections for e-evidence, whether that inspection calls for an examination of the operation of the computer system itself, or for the actual extraction of e-data from the system. This protocol must be followed when the federal courts have mandated the on-site inspection of a computer system. As we review the elements of this protocol, remember that the courts have several objectives in mind. First, they are attempting to preserve e-evidence that is relevant to the case. Second, they are attempting to keep the inconvenience, the intrusiveness, the danger, and the expense of the on-site visit to a minimum. Third, the courts are mindful of the need to respect sensitive material by ensuring the confidentiality and privacy of the records themselves and of trade secrets and professional confidences associated with that part of the business that is involved in the on-site inspection.

The Goals of the On-Site Inspection Protocol for E-Evidence   Again, it is crucial to keep in mind the goals and objectives of the court's on-site, e-evidence inspection protocol. These goals and objectives include: (1) to retrieve and preserve all e-evidence relevant to the case; (2) to regulate the extent of the production process so that unnecessary or repetitious e-evidence is not revealed or compromised in any way; (3) to minimize the inconvenience, intrusiveness, and expense of an on-site visit; (4) to preserve the privacy of certain business records; (5) to protect the privileged nature of trade secrets and professional confidences, and, above all, (6) to prevent the unnecessary and costly loss of e-data stored in a computer system.

The Steps in the On-Site Inspection Protocol for E-Evidence   To be effective, the protocol ought to include the following steps:

(a)   Before the actual document production process is to begin, the individuals involved in the search will set procedural restrictions. These ought to include a list of the key players whose computer stations and records will be a part of the search and a list of the computer stations which will be subject to the search.

(b)   It would also be wise at this point to determine which party or parties will be responsible for covering the expense of the on-site production process.

(c)   The parties should also decide which party or parties will be accountable for the expense that might be involved in recovering any lost or destroyed e-data that results from the search.

(d)   The parties ought to specify the status (active, inactive, back-up, and/or extant data) of the e-evidence subject to the search.

(e)   The parties should also specify whether any back-up paper copies of the e-data will be included in the on-site search.

(f) The individuals involved in the search should also establish a time frame in which the e-evidence will be gathered.

(g) An independent, objective IT specialist will be retained to conduct the search for e-evidence. The independent IT specialist must be mutually agreeable to everyone involved in the search. Moreover, he or she will operate as an official court representative.

(h) Rather than handling the actual e-evidence, the IT specialist should make copies that are turned over to the owner of the e-evidence. The owner of the e-evidence will then examine the copy to preserve any confidential or private data.

(i) After all private and confidential data is expunged from the e-evidence, it is turned over to the party that filed the document request.

Preparing for an On-Site Inspection for E-Evidence   It is very important for the party producing the e-evidence to properly prepare for an on-site visit of its computer operation system. Much of the anxiety, concern, and inconvenience that results from an on-site visit can be lessened if certain steps are taken to minimize the impact of such a search. Unfortunately, once a production request has been filed, it is often too late to avoid many of the troublesome aspects of the visit. Therefore, it is best to prepare for such a search as a part of the everyday process of doing business. In order to lessen the impact of a document-production request for e-evidence at the time of a lawsuit, your supervising attorney might advise clients, in advance, to initiate some of the following suggestions:

1. Instruct workers, especially IT specialists, about the ever-present possibility of a lawsuit against the company, organization, or institution. This means making certain that they carefully store, catalog, and retain e-data so that it can be retrieved easily without damaging the system, losing data, or spending valuable downtime, should a document-production request and an on-site investigation be called for during litigation.

2. Implement a plan that can be activated automatically to halt any routine deletion of e-data. This will minimize the loss of any crucial e-evidence and eliminate any suspicion that e-evidence has been deliberately destroyed to escape discovery.

3. Make certain that all IT specialists and their supervisors and assistants are prepared to deal with the rigors of discovery, but especially with the intrusive nature of an on-site inspection of computer operations.

4. Once a document production request and/or an on-site inspection has been filed, hold sessions to educate the key players and IT specialists about the facts in the case and the types of e-data that could be considered discoverable e-evidence.

5. After an on-site inspection request has been filed, advise key players and IT specialists about the protocol established by the courts for dealing with an on-site inspection. Make certain that they are fully acquainted with their individual roles and responsibilities in the operation of the protocol.

Summary

■ Five ways that documents can be obtained during discovery include a request for documents, mutual disclosure, a request for documents at the deposition of a party, a subpoena duces tecum for a nonparty to produce documents at the time of a deposition, and the option of producing business records as an answer to an interrogatory. A request for documents is a request by one party in a lawsuit to allow the first party access to documents that are relevant to the subject matter of the lawsuit. Two crucial preliminary considerations in a production request are the timing of the request and the potential cost of the production. Documents can be produced either as they are kept in the usual course of business or according to the categories specified in the document request. The three ways to respond to a document request are the warehouse approach, the broad approach, and the limited approach.

■ When an attorney structures a Rule 34 document-production request, he must be knowledgeable of the types of e-evidence available within a computer system. Discoverable e-evidence can appear within three groups: (1) types of e-evidence based on the configuration of the computer system, (2) types of e-evidence based on the nature of the evidence itself, and (3) types of e-evidence based on its storage status. An attorney must consider all of these categories when preparing a document-production request. It is also essential to include the key players and IT specialists involved in collecting, managing, storing, and communicating that e-evidence. Because of the need to hire experts who frequently use special programs to retrieve e-data, the expense of e-evidence document production is often greater than the expense involved in retrieving paper records. Consequently, an attorney seeking e-evidence must be prepared to verify the need for such data.

■ Not all documents requested must be produced. Some are protected by the attorney-client privilege, the work product privilege, or the common interest privilege. Other objections are that the request is overbroad, duplicative, or irrelevant. If none of these objections are available, the documents can still be protected by using a confidentiality agreement or a protective order.

■ The paralegal will often be called upon to draft the request for production of documents. The parts of the request include the title, the definitions, the instructions, and a list of documents requested. The paralegal may also need to draft a motion to compel the other party to produce the documents requested. The paralegal may be required to review and organize the documents once they arrive.

■ The paralegal will also be involved in responding to a request for documents. The steps in this process include determining a realistic production date, categorizing the documents, involving the client, and organizing the documents.

■ After document production by all parties, the paralegal may be required to organize the documents by various categories.

■ The request for documents is directed only to documents. Often a case involves tangible property such as a piece of equipment or a parcel of real estate. The Federal Rules of Civil Procedure stipulate a procedure through which the parties or their representatives can inspect property for purposes of measuring, photographing, or testing.

■ Since on-site inspections for e-evidence covered by Rule 34 are generally intrusive and expensive, the courts have been very careful to outline a detailed protocol that must be followed by the parties to a lawsuit. This protocol applies whether that inspection calls for an examination of the operation of the computer system itself, or for the actual extraction of e-data from the system. The court has several objectives in mind supporting the establishment of this protocol. They include: (1) the preservation of e-evidence relevant to the case; (2) minimizing the inconvenience, the intrusiveness, and the expense of the on-site visit; (3) ensuring the confidentiality and privacy of records, trade secrets, and professional confidences; and (4) preventing the unnecessary loss of e-data from the inspected computer system.

Key Terms

Bates numbering	nonresponsive documents	redaction
demand for inspection	privilege log	request for documents
document	privileged documents	responsive documents
document production log		

Review Questions

1. Name three alternative methods for obtaining documents besides mutual disclosure and serving a request for documents.
2. What is a request for documents?
3. Explain the factors to be considered in deciding whether to serve the other party with a request for the production of documents.
4. What are the three basic approaches to document production?
5. What are the three categories of discoverable e-evidence?
6. Distinguish among the attorney-client privilege, the work product privilege, and the common interest privilege.
7. Distinguish between the medical privilege and the confessor-penitent privilege.
8. When should a confidentiality agreement or a protective order be sought?
9. What objections can be raised to a request for production of documents?
10. What procedures can be used to obtain an inspection of property?
11. What protocol has the court established for an on-site visit to obtain e-evidence?

Chapter Exercises

Where necessary, check with your instructor prior to starting any of these exercises.

1. Review the laws of your state and find all laws that deal with requests for the production of documents. Check your local court rules to see if any local rules supplement or alter the state laws.
2. Obtain the form books in your law library that provide sample forms for use in drafting the legal documents in your state. Find a sample request for production of documents and compare it with the sample found in this chapter.
3. Review the laws of your state and find out whether your state allows the same objections to the request for documents as are outlined in this chapter.

4. Carefully consider each of the following documents and determine whether they should be a part of the document request that goes from Mannheim Laboratories, Ltd. to Shuster, Kane, Moulton, and Associates, Inc.

   a. A series of internal memos that are on file in the offices of Shuster, Kane, Moulton, and Associates, Inc. detailing the negotiations between Seigel and Shuster, laying the foundation for Shuster's audit of Seigel.

   b. A series of letters from Seigel to Shuster, Kane, Moulton, and Associates, Inc. concerning several inaccuracies that occurred the last time that Shuster audited Seigel.

   c. A contract between Shuster, Kane, Moulton, and Associates, Inc. and Infantino Industries, Inc., another firm that Shuster audits on a regular basis.

   d. Shuster, Kane, Moulton, and Associates, Inc.'s certificate of incorporation along with its appointment of a statutory agent for service of process.

   e. A series of internal memos between the auditing team working at Seigel and Bruce Kane, the accountant who previously handled the Seigel audit.

Chapter Project

Review the commentary at the beginning of this chapter. Recall that your firm has been retained by the Mannheim Laboratories, Ltd. to bring suit against Shuster, Kane, Moulton, and Associates, Inc. for issuing an inaccurate qualified opinion after an audit of Seigel Pharmaceuticals, Inc. Review the sample request for production of documents in this chapter or the one that you located in your state's form book. Assume that the defendant, Shuster, Kane, Moulton, and Associates, Inc., has responded to the request for documents and has delivered the documents that you asked for. Now you and your staff face the unenviable task of organizing and indexing these documents. You cannot handle the task by yourself, but the only other paralegal available has never had the opportunity to be involved in document indexing. Draft a memorandum in which you explain in detail to the new paralegal the process that the two of you must follow in organizing and indexing the documents that your firm has received from Shuster, Kane, Moulton, and Associates, Inc. Assume that you are going to have to organize the documents manually, without the aid of a computer. Be sure to ask the paralegal for her input into the organizational principle that will best fit this case.

The *Bennett* Case
Assignment 12: Drafting a Request
for Production

The answers to interrogatories submitted by the defendant in the *Bennett* case indicated that the defendant has copies of e-mails between several parties relating to Ms. Bennett. These e-mails are archived on a tape backup. Your attorney would also like to inspect the hard drives of the computers used by Darren Blackwood and Martin Yardly. Draft a request for production and/or for an on-site inspection to obtain these.

Chapter 13

Request for Admissions

CHAPTER OUTLINE

COMMENTARY—THE CASTILLO CASE

Your law firm has been hired to represent Dr. Alicia Castillo, a cybernetic engineer, who is convinced that she was wrongly discharged by her employer, Wentworth-Armstrong Computer Technical Services, Inc. (DBA Compuquick), where she was the chief cybernetic design engineer for nine years. The case has been proceeding rather well for several months and, at this point in time, the discovery process is just about over. While your supervising attorney was reviewing the files in the case, she identified several documents that must be established as the genuine article. In addition, she is determined to establish that certain facts are accurate. After making these determinations, your supervising attorney calls you into her office and assigns you the task of drafting a request for admissions. This request is to be served on Edward Wentworth, CEO of Compuquick. Two days later your law firm also receives a request for admissions. This one comes from the law firm of Kowalski, Moldovan, and Zuer, which is representing the defendants. Your supervising attorney again calls you into her office. This time she asks that you contact Dr. Castillo and ask her to help prepare a response to the request. In order to do as your supervising attorney has asked, you must research the appropriate court rules, including all applicable local court rules. It will also be necessary to look over the pleadings, the important documents, and all prior discovery, including any relevant e-evidence.

OBJECTIVES

Now that the discovery process has been nearly completed, you may need to establish the truthfulness, accuracy, and genuineness of the evidence that you and your attorney have compiled. For that purpose, you may need to file a request for admissions. After reading this chapter, you should be able to:

- Define *request for admission*.
- Relate the purposes for filing a request for admissions.
- Explain the uses of the request for admissions.
- List the advantages of the request for admissions.
- Identify the procedures involved in drafting a request for admissions.
- Explain the content of each section of a request for admissions.
- Differentiate among the responses and the objections to a request for admissions.

The Request for Admissions

The request for admissions is a request filed by one party in a lawsuit on another party in that lawsuit asking the second party to admit to the truthfulness of some fact or opinion. The request may also ask the party to authenticate the genuineness of a document. According to Rule 36 of the Federal Rules of Civil Procedure, a request for admissions may be served on any party in a lawsuit. However, the request may not be served on a nonparty. Under Rule 26(d), admissions cannot be served until the parties have conferred as mandated by Rule 26(f). A party has 30 days to respond. The federal rules place no limit on the number of requests that can be filed. However, some states (California, for example) do limit the number of requests that can be filed.

The request for admissions differs from all of the other discovery tools that we have examined thus far. In fact, some legal scholars would argue that the request for admissions is not, strictly speaking, a discovery tool at all. This argument is based on the fact that the request for admissions seeks a commitment regarding information that has already been discovered. Thus, it does not, in itself, "discover" anything. Nevertheless, it is a very powerful tool that can be used to great advantage.

Purposes of the Request for Admissions

The primary purpose of the request for admissions is to simplify a lawsuit by reducing the number and nature of the points in controversy. The simplification of the points in controversy has a "ripple effect," simplifying many of the other matters involved in the suit. For example, if there are fewer points in controversy, fewer witnesses will be necessary should the case reach the trial stage. The fewer witnesses that are needed, the more money that can be saved. These savings can be especially lucrative if the need for a variety of expert witnesses is eliminated. Simplifying the points in controversy could also lead to early settlement of the case. This is because claims and defenses that have no legal merit evaporate quickly under the scrutiny of a well-drafted request for admissions. Finally, a carefully drafted request for admissions can emphasize important factual information that is buried in volumes of documents and testimony.

Uses of the Request for Admissions

A request for admissions can be used in three different ways. First, it might be used to authenticate the genuineness of certain important documents. Second, the request can authenticate the truthfulness of certain facts or opinions. Finally, it can be used to authenticate the application of the law to the facts. A single request for admissions can be used to fulfill all of these uses.

Authenticating the Genuineness of Documents   One of the most widely recognized purposes of the request for admissions is to authenticate the genuineness of a document. For example, in the *Castillo* case, it would be very helpful if Mr. Wentworth, the CEO of Compuquick, Inc., were to authenticate the genuineness of the letter of dismissal sent to Dr. Castillo, the company's progressive disciplinary policy, the list of offenses for which an employee could be terminated, and the evaluation records of Dr. Castillo. Naturally, such documents could be authenticated at trial, but only after overcoming a number of evidentiary hurdles. These hurdles can be reduced in a request for admissions. It is important to note, however, that an individual may admit to the genuineness of a document and still object to its admissibility. For example, in this chapter's *Castillo* case, Mr. Wentworth may authenticate the document outlining progressive disciplinary procedures and the list of dischargeable offenses, but may object to its relevance and admissibility in this case. It is also important to note that a party who admits to the genuineness of a document does not at the same time admit to the truthfulness of the contents of the document. For instance, in the *Castillo* case, Dr. Castillo might be asked to admit to the genuineness of a letter of dismissal for failing to follow company policies and procedures. In admitting to the genuineness of the letter, she is not admitting to any of the alleged rule violations stated in the letter.

Authenticating the Truthfulness of Facts and Opinions A second use for a request for admissions is to authenticate the truthfulness of certain facts or opinions. In the *Castillo* case, for example, your supervising attorney may ask the CEO to authenticate the fact that he signed every employment evaluation of Dr. Castillo and that each of those employment evaluations stated that she had done outstanding work for the company. These admissions, however, only authenticate the content of the evaluations and the fact that they were signed by Mr. Wentworth. They do not admit anything about the actual quality of Dr. Castillo's job performance. Thus, your supervising attorney might also ask Mr. Wentworth to admit that Dr. Castillo did outstanding work. Note the differences among these admissions. The admissions about the content and the signature authenticate facts, whereas the admission about the actual quality of Dr. Castillo's job performance authenticates Mr. Wentworth's opinion. Factual admissions are usually easier to obtain than those that state an opinion.

Admissions about the truthfulness of facts and opinions in response to a request for admissions carry much more weight than an admission made using some other form of discovery. Anything that is admitted in a deposition, for example, can be altered or denied when the party takes the witness stand. Although this may make the witness look a bit less credible in the eyes of the judge and the jurors, the finders of fact must still weigh the alterations and denials against the rest of the witness's testimony. Such is not the case with an admission made in response to a request. Such an admission is taken as proven. Court permission is required for a party to withdraw an admission. Thus, such admissions can be very effective for the party obtaining them and very damaging to the party giving them.

Authenticating the Application of the Law to Facts A request for admissions can also combine the authentication of the facts in a case with the law that applies to those facts. For example, in the *Castillo* case, your supervising attorney may request Mr. Wentworth to admit that Dr. Castillo was employed by Compuquick on a contractual basis, and was therefore subject to the provisions of the employee policy manual, including the provisions regarding the list of dischargeable offenses and the policy on progressive discipline. Such an admission would shorten the time necessary to demonstrate the legal status of Dr. Castillo's employment. However, such an admission would not prove that she was wrongfully terminated, because other issues, such as whether she was blameless of any dischargeable offense, whether the disciplinary procedure was followed properly, and whether, in this situation, she was actually entitled to the policy's protection, must still be proven.

Advantages of the Request for Admissions

The request for admissions offers several advantages over other discovery devices. One principal advantage is that a request for admissions cannot be ignored or overlooked. This is because of the **deemed admitted** rule. Under this rule, any undenied request for admission is treated as if it were admitted. Also, if the response to the request does not conform to the requirements of Rule 36 of the Federal Rules of Civil Procedure, the court may order that the fact has been admitted. For example, in the *Castillo* case, if Mr. Wentworth's denial of the request to authenticate Dr. Castillo's status as a contractual employee is not specific enough, the court may rule that he has admitted that she is a contractual employee. Similarly, if Mr. Wentworth were to claim that he is unable to admit or deny whether Dr. Castillo performed her job well, and that claim is not detailed enough, the court may order that the matter has been admitted. In both of these examples, the court could instead order Wentworth to file an amended response to the request. Some states have altered the deemed admitted rule. In California, for instance, nothing is deemed admitted unless the party requesting the admission makes a motion to that effect.

An advantage that the request for admissions shares with interrogatories is that parties cannot refuse to respond simply because they lack the information needed to make the response. Rather, they must make a reasonable attempt to obtain the missing information. Moreover, a party cannot refuse to cooperate merely because the other party could obtain the information another way. Furthermore, although a request for admissions is usually made toward the end of the discovery process, such requests can be made at any time, even with the service of the summons and complaint. Thus, because a total knowledge of the facts is not a prerequisite for the request, it can be used as a learning tool. Finally, as noted earlier, in federal court there is no limit to the number of requests that can be filed. Some states, however, do place limits on the permissible number of requests for admissions.

deemed admitted

A principle which holds that an undenied request for admission is treated as if it were admitted.

Drafting the Request for Admissions

As a paralegal, you may be called upon to draft a request for admissions. This responsibility is extremely important because, as we have seen previously, properly drafted requests can save time and money and can often lead to early settlement of the lawsuit. Consequently, great care must be taken in preparing for and actually drafting the request.

Preliminary Steps in Drafting the Request for Admissions

Before you sit down to draft the request, you should do some preliminary work. First, discuss the matter with your attorney so that you understand the goals and objectives of the request. Then make certain that you review all previous pleadings and important documents as you assemble the facts. Also, take some time to look over the applicable federal or state and local court rules so that you can accurately determine response deadlines and procedural details.

As a last stage before actually writing the request, list and organize the admissions that the other party ought to make. For example, in the *Castillo* case, if Mr. Wentworth admitted that Dr. Castillo was a contractual employee, it would be very helpful to her case. It would also be beneficial for him to admit that she was covered by the provisions in the company's employment manual and that her job performance was satisfactory. With these suggested admissions in hand, check with your supervising attorney to make sure that you have not missed something.

Form and Content of the Request for Admissions

With your preliminary list of desired admissions in hand, locate a sample request in a form book or in your firm's word processing file. Naturally, no two situations are exactly the same, so you will have to modify the form to fit the facts of your particular case. Nevertheless, we can make some general statements about the title, the introductory paragraph, the definitions and instructions, and the specific request.

Title of the Request and the Introductory Paragraph   The title of your request should reflect the party making the request, the party receiving the request, and the number of the request:

Example

PLAINTIFF CASTILLO'S FIRST REQUEST FOR ADMISSIONS
TO DEFENDANTS EDWARD WENTWORTH AND
WENTWORTH-ARMSTRONG COMPUTER TECHNICAL SERVICES, INC.

Make certain that you cite the appropriate court rules in the introductory paragraph. If you follow the actual language of the rule, you will avoid any possible misunderstanding. The introductory paragraph should also include a demand for written answers to the request within the applicable time limits. Exhibit 13–1 includes a typical introductory paragraph for the request.

Definitions   As in the request for production of documents covered in Chapter 12, the definition section of the request for admissions may have a separate heading placed in the center of the page in bold-faced lettering. Terms that may be defined include such words as *document, letter, memorandum,* and *report,* among others.

Instructions   The heading "instructions" may also be placed in the center of the page in bold-faced letters. The instructions specify any procedures that should be followed in responding to the request. Often the request for admissions is so complex that it is not possible to include a separate instructional paragraph at the beginning of the request. In such a case the instructions must be included with each category of documents examined and with the list of facts to be admitted. For instance, in the *Castillo* case, the introductory section leading to a request to authenticate the genuineness of certain documents may have to specify that Mr. Wentworth is to admit that the

UNITED STATES DISTRICT COURT

ALICIA CASTILLO,   )
)   Civil Action No. 05-12363
    Plaintiff,   )
)
    v.   )
)
EDWARD WENTWORTH AND   )
WENTWORTH-ARMSTRONG   )
COMPUTER TECHNICAL   )
SERVICES, INC.,   )
)
    Defendants.   )

PLAINTIFF, Alicia Castillo ("Alvarez"), requests that the DEFENDANTS, Edward Wentworth ("Wentworth") and Wentworth-Armstrong Computer Technical Services, Inc. ("Compuquick"), within thirty days after the service of this request separately admit in writing, pursuant to Rule 36 of the Federal Rules of Civil Procedure and for the purposes of this action only, the truth of the following statements;

A. That each of the following documents listed below, the best copies of which are attached as Appendix A

    1. is genuine and is a complete and accurate representation of the actual writing which the document purports to represent;

    2. was prepared or sent by an officer or employee of Compuquick during his or her employment with Compuquick;

    3. was directed to or concerned matters within the scope of the employment of said officer or employee of Compuquick;

    4. was written and sent on or about the date listed on the document;

    5. was written on the basis of the officer's or employee's firsthand knowledge of the matter contained therein;

    6. was written in the ordinary course of business of Compuquick;

    7. was kept as part of the routine employee evaluation process at Compuquick:

        a. Castillo employee evaluation of September 9, 2003.

        b. Castillo employee evaluation of October 31, 2003.

        c. Castillo employee evaluation of January 19, 2004.

        d. Castillo employee evaluation of February 7, 2004.

        e. Castillo employee evaluation of March 17, 2004.

        f. Castillo employee evaluation of April 23, 2004.

        g. Memo of February 21, 2004.

        h. Memo of February 28, 2004.

        i. Memo of March 27, 2004.

        j. Memo of April 1, 2004.

        k. Memo of August 19, 2004.

EXHIBIT 13–1   Request for admissions

B. That the best copy of each of the documents listed below and attached as Appendix B
  1. is genuine and is a complete and accurate representation of the actual writing which the document purports to represent;
  2. was prepared or sent by an officer or employee of Compuquick during his or her employment with Compuquick;
  3. was directed to or concerned matters within the scope of the employment of said officer or employee of Compuquick;
  4. was written and sent on or about the date listed on the document;
  5. was written on the basis of the officer's or employee's firsthand knowledge of the matter contained therein;
  6. was written in the ordinary course of business of Compuquick;
  7. was sent as part of the dismissal process involving Castillo:
    a. Letter of September 9, 2003.
    b. Letter of September 15, 2003.
    c. Letter of December 23, 2003.
    d. Letter of January 29, 2004.
    e. Letter of February 14, 2004.
    f. Letter of March 17, 2004.
    g. Letter of June 16, 2004.
    h. Letter of August 31, 2004.
C. That the document entitled WENTWORTH-ARMSTRONG, HANDBOOK, the best copy of which is attached as Appendix C
  1. is genuine and is a complete and accurate representation of the actual writing that the document purports to represent;
  2. was distributed to all employees at Compuquick between August 19, 2002 and September 19, 2002;
  3. was received by Castillo on August 19, 2002.
D. That each of the following documents listed below, the best copies of which are attached as Appendix D
  1. is genuine and is a complete and accurate representation of the actual writing that the document purports to represent;
  2. was prepared or sent by an officer or employee of Compuquick during his or her employment with Compuquick;
  3. was directed to or concerned matters within the scope of the employment of said officer or employee of Compuquick;
  4. was written and sent on or about the date listed on the document;
  5. was written on the basis of the officer's or employee's firsthand knowledge of the matter contained therein;

EXHIBIT 13–1 *(continued)*

6. was written in the ordinary course of business of Compuquick;
7. was kept as part of the routine employee evaluation process at Compuquick:
   a. Research report on Worldview Software dated September 23, 2002.
   b. Research report on Worldview Software dated October 19, 2002.
   c. Research report on Worldview Software dated November 30, 2002.
   d. Research report on Worldview Software dated March 28, 2003.
   e. Research report on Worldview Software dated August 19, 2003.
   f. Research report on Worldview Software dated December 2, 2003.
   g. Research report on Worldview Software dated December 15, 2003.
   h. Research report on Worldview Software dated December 31, 2003.
E. That each of the following documents listed below, the best copies of which are attached as Appendix E
   1. is genuine and is a complete and accurate representation of the actual writing which the document purports to represent;
   2. was received by an officer or employee of Wyandott during his or her employment with Wyandott;
   3. was received within the scope of the employment of said officer or employee of Wyandott;
   4. was received on or about the date listed on the document;
   5. was kept in the ordinary course of business of Compuquick;
   6. was kept as part of the routine employee evaluation process at Compuquick:
      a. Letter of September 12, 2002.
      b. Letter of September 20, 2002.
      c. Letter of December 27, 2002.
      d. Letter of January 1, 2003.
      e. Letter of February 18, 2003.
      f. Letter of March 27, 2003.
      g. Letter of June 19, 2003.
      h. Letter of September 2, 2003.
F. That each of the following statements is true:
   1. Compuquick is incorporated under the laws of the state of Delaware and has its principal place of business in Seattle, Washington.
   2. Castillo was discharged on or about September 9, 2003.
   3. Castillo received favorable employee evaluations from September of 2001 to September of 2003.

EXHIBIT 13–1   *(continued)*

4. Castillo received all scheduled pay increases between September of 2001 and September of 2003.

5. Castillo received all scheduled promotions between September of 2001 and September of 2003.

DATED: Portland, Oregon
           March 27, 2005

Kent, Freidman, Hedges, and Cole

BY_____
A member of the firm

Attorneys for the Plaintiff
Dr. Alicia Castillo
750 Maple Street
Portland, Oregon
Tel.: (123) 555-1212
Fax: (123) 555-2323

TO: Dirksen, Vannice, and Raeder
      Attorneys for Defendant
      Wentworth-Armstrong Computer Technical Services, Inc. and Edward Wentworth, CEO of
      Wentworth-Armstrong
      17810 Brinkerhoff Blvd.
      Seattle, Washington

EXHIBIT 13–1   *(continued)*

documents in question were written by Compuquick employees, that the documents were sent to the named recipients, that they were sent on the dates noted on the documents, and so on. In contrast, the instructions leading to the list of facts and opinions to be admitted may simply read that Mr. Wentworth is to admit "that each of the following statements is true." (See Exhibit 13–1.)

Specific Requests   The request itself should be as simple as possible. The part of the request that lists the documents should be very specific as to the identity of each of those documents. It is best to list each document separately. Combining documents can cause confusion and can also open the request to objections. If possible, include any identifying dates or numbers found on the documents. Copies of the documents in the list must be gathered together and attached to the request with an appropriate identifying heading. For example, in the *Castillo* case, if you request the authentication of certain internal memos that passed between Mr. Wentworth and the human resources director at Compuquick, and the authentification of certain letters that passed between Mr. Wentworth and Dr. Castillo, you would include two separate lists, each with its own instructional paragraph. In turn, copies of the memos and letters would be attached to the request and labeled as such. The memos might be labeled "Appendix A" and the letters "Appendix B."

The part of the request that lists the facts and opinions to be admitted should also be very carefully worded. Each fact and opinion should be listed separately. All facts that are undisputed should be included in this list. By identifying and including those facts in the request, you may avoid having to argue those facts at the time of the trial. Also include facts that you know are true, but that you might have a difficult time proving at trial. If you can get an admission now, you will save a lot of work later. However, you should be very careful to avoid topics that will elicit an appropriate objection from the other party.

Responding to the Request for Admissions

Make certain, when you receive a request for admissions, that you determine that the target date is reasonable. Once you have established that the target date is reasonable, place a reminder of the due date on the firm's calendar. If you have the responsibility of drafting the response, you should meet with the client to cover the alternatives available in responding to each request. You should also consider any objections that you might raise to the request.

Alternative Responses to the Request for Admissions

Your response to the request must be filed on time. This may mean that you must work quickly. However, because of the finality of an admission, you should never sacrifice care and accuracy for speed. Before beginning the drafting process, you should review the applicable court rules relating to the format and procedure. The alternatives available in a response are:

1. to admit;
2. to deny;
3. to refuse to either admit or deny; or
4. to object.

When you draft the response, first copy each statement to which you are responding, exactly as it appears on the original request. If a statement is true, you must respond by admitting that it is true. However, if reasonable doubt exists as to the truthfulness of a particular statement, you may deny it. A statement that has been admitted is called a judicial admission. A **judicial admission** is a statement or other piece of evidence that has been admitted and can, therefore, be introduced during the trial.

Any statement that is not truthful should be denied. However, you should resist the temptation to deny a statement on a technicality, such as a misspelled word or an obvious typographical error. However, if the error actually alters the substance of the statement, you may consider denying it. For example, in the *Castillo* case, if your client is mistakenly identified as Alice Castillo, you probably would not be justified in denying the statement. However, if a statement listed her as Ms. Castillo, rather than Dr. Castillo, you might be justified in denying the statement, provided that a legal question as to her professional expertise was at the center of the case. Such questions,

judicial admission
A statement or other piece of evidence that has been admitted and that can, therefore, be introduced during the trial.

however, are best discussed with your supervising attorney. Be careful in your denials, because the other party may ask the court to compel your client to pay the cost of proving a matter that should not have been denied in the first place. Interestingly, even the losing party can make this request of the court.

Sometimes, when the deadline for a response is approaching, you may deny all requests and later amend your response, admitting those requests that should have been admitted in the first place. This practice has its dangers, however. The chief danger is the deemed admitted rule. As we have seen, under this rule, unless a party delivers a written denial or a detailed reason why that party cannot admit or deny a statement, that statement is deemed admitted.

The third alternative is to refuse to either admit or deny a request. However, the Federal Rules of Civil Procedure do not allow you to do this unless you have made a reasonable inquiry into the subject. Moreover, a lack of personal knowledge is not a proper basis for refusing to respond, unless the party has reason to doubt the credibility of the source of the information. Your response to the request for admission does not require verification in federal court. However, because some state and local rules demand such verification, you should check on the proper procedure in your area.

Objections to the Request for Admissions

Basically, the same objections that are available in response to the other discovery techniques are available in response to a request for admissions. As we have seen in previous chapters, the grounds for such objections include stating that complying with the request would violate the attorney-client privilege, the work product privilege, the common interest privilege, the medical privilege, or the confessor-penitent privilege. Other objections are that the request is overbroad, irrelevant, or duplicative. You may also object on the grounds that the statement is a compound request.

The Attorney-Client Privilege, the Work Product Privilege, and the Common Interest Privilege   As we have seen previously, the attorney-client privilege prevents the forced disclosure of communication between an attorney and a client. Similarly, the work product privilege protects letters, memos, documents, records, and other tangible items that have been prepared in anticipation of litigation. In addition, the common interest privilege protects any communication that takes place between attorneys for different clients when those clients share a common interest. If a request for admissions would violate any of these privileges, you could lodge an appropriate objection on those grounds.

The Medical Privilege and the Confessor-Penitent Privilege   As noted earlier in the text, the medical privilege will protect all confidential communications between a medical practitioner and his or her patient. Similarly, the confessor-penitent privilege was designed to shield confidences that pass between a member of the clergy and a penitent. Unlike the medical privilege, however, the confessor-penitent privilege also safeguards a member of the clergy who has offered a religious oath not to reveal such disclosures.

Inadmissible and Irrelevant Evidence   You will recall that the scope of discovery is much broader than the scope of the evidence that can be introduced at trial.

THE COMPUTERIZED LAW FIRM
Integrated Litigation Support

SCENARIO

Your supervising attorney has called you into her office to discuss the *Castillo* case. She indicates that she is concerned about the admission requests that have come for Dr. Castillo. The defendants have asked Dr. Castillo to admit that, before she was terminated, she was warned several times, both orally and in writing, that her job performance was below par. Dr. Castillo has denied that this happened. Before responding to the request, your supervising attorney wants you to review all prior discovery in the matter relevant to this issue, including interrogatories and depositions of all parties and witnesses. She also wants you to review all documents in your possession written by Dr. Castillo and delivered to her by the defendants. You have hundreds, perhaps even thousands, of pages of depositions, and other documents filed away in this case. Your supervising attorney would like the information by noon tomorrow when Dr. Castillo has an appointment to go over the request for admissions.

PROBLEM

You need to review and analyze an overwhelming amount of information in a short amount of time. How can you do this without working all night?

SOLUTION

Integrated litigation support programs, discussed in previous chapters, allow you to input all discovery and all documents in a single program. This can be done by keying in information, by downloading information from a floppy disk, or by scanning in documents. With all discovery located in one program, you can then use the full-text searching capabilities of the program to search all discovery and documents for certain key words or phrases. Thus, you could search all interrogatories, depositions, and documents for "job performance" or similar terms. Once the search is complete, you can generate a report specifying each instance where the phrase appears. This is done in a matter of seconds.

The capabilities of automated litigation support programs have grown considerably in recent years, increasing their popularity in litigation law firms. Not only do these programs allow you to handle individual discovery tasks such as deposition summaries and document production, they also allow you to see the whole picture. All discovery responses can be analyzed and compared. In large cases, this type of support has become a neccessity.

Despite the broad scope, however, any discovery request must be reasonably calculated to lead to admissible evidence. Should a request for admissions ask your client to respond to the truthfulness of a matter that could not be reasonably calculated to lead to admissible evidence, you may object on those grounds. Similarly, a request for admissions must address a fact, opinion, or document that is relevant to the lawsuit. The request for admissions must further the discovery process. If it does not, you may object.

Overbroad and Duplicative Requests   As mentioned, an overbroad request is one that is not narrowly defined. For instance, in the *Castillo* case, the lawsuit involves her employment with Compuquick. If the opposing party sought admissions regarding every employment evaluation ever filed on Dr. Castillo, even those involving part-time jobs when she was in high school, college, and graduate school, an objection that the request is overboard would be in order. Another objection is that the request is duplicative or repetitious. This objection argues that the request includes one item for

FINDING IT ON THE INTERNET

The Federal Rules of Civil Procedure can be accessed at the following address: <http://www.law.cornell.edu/rules/frcp>. Access the Web site, find Rule 36, and check to see if there have been any recent interpretations of the provisions and requirements as stated under this rule.

An article outlining a revision of the Discovery Rules of the Texas Courts can be found at <http://www.hbafam.org/articles/1999rules.html>. Access the article, find the rules in relation to admissions requests, and write an essay which compares the revised Texas rule to the federal rule.

The request for admissions for Missouri Family Courts is defined and explained at: <http://www.missouridivorcelawyer.com/discovery/admit. htm>. Access the Web site and compare and contrast this definition and explanation to that given in this chapter for the federal rule.

A request for admissions can be found for the Court of Common Pleas of Franklin County, Ohio at <http://www.finsolve.com/images/RequestFor Admissions.pdf>. Access the site and use the request as a model to draft hypothetical requests for admissions in the *Castillo* case that serves as the commentary case for this chapter.

Excerpts from a response to a request for admissions can be found on the Internet at <http://www.kmf.org/maydak/double-recording.html>. Access the site and use the set of responses as a model to draft hypothetical responses in this chapter's *Castillo* case.

The Rules of Civil Procedure for the Alaska Court System can be accessed at the following address: <http://www.lstate.ak.us/courts/cov.htm>. Access the Web site, find the Alaska rule on requests for admissions, and compare and contrast that rule to the federal rule and to the rule in your own state courts (unless, of course, you live in Alaska.)

admission that is repeated over and over. Your duty extends to only one request. Often requests are varied slightly to elicit a different answer. You should object to every variation of the request.

compound request

A request made by a party in a lawsuit to another party in that lawsuit to admit in a single statement the truthfulness of two or more facts.

Compound Requests   The **compound request** asks a party to admit in a single statement the truthfulness of two or more facts. The compound request makes a response tricky, if not impossible. Your objection should address the compound nature of the request and explain the difficulty that it presents in framing an accurate response. This objection may not, however, prevent the ultimate need to respond to the subject matter of the statement, as the opposing party can file an amended request.

Summary

■ A request for admissions is a request filed by one party in a lawsuit on another party in that suit asking the second party to admit to the truthfulness of certain facts or opinions or to authenticate the genuineness of certain documents. The primary purpose of the request is to simplify the points in controversy. An admission made in response to a request for admissions cannot be withdrawn without the court's permission. Any request that is not denied is deemed admitted.

■ In preparing to draft a request for admissions, the paralegal should discuss the matter with the attorney, review all pleadings, and look over the applicable court rules. The actual request for admissions will include the title, the introductory paragraph, the definitions and instructions, and the specific request. Copies of any documents involved in the request must be attached to the request.

■ The alternatives available in responding to a request for admissions are to admit, to deny, to refuse to either admit or deny, or to object. Grounds for objection include arguing that compliance with the request would violate the attorney-client privilege, the work product privilege, the medical privilege or the confessor-penitent privilege. Other objections are that the request is overbroad, irrelevant, or duplicative. A final objection is that the statement is a compound request.

Key Terms

compound request	deemed admitted	judicial admission

Review Questions

1. What is a request for admissions?
2. On whom may a request for admissions be served?
3. What is the principal purpose for filing a request for admissions?
4. What advantages does the request for admissions have over other discovery tools?
5. What preliminary steps should be taken before drafting a request for admissions?
6. List the parts of a request for admissions.
7. Explain the content of each part of a request for admissions.
8. List the possible responses to a request for admissions.
9. Point out the danger of not responding to a request for admissions.
10. List the possible objections to a request for admissions.

Chapter Exercises

Where necessary, check with your instructor prior to starting any of these exercises.

1. Review your state's rules relating to requests for admissions. Prepare a summary of the differences between the federal rules and your state rules. Also check your local court rules and do the same.
2. Prepare a chart of the objections to requests for admissions that are permitted in the federal and state courts in your area.

3. In the *Castillo* case, your attorney has received several requests for admission. Carefully consider each of the following requests and determine if they should be admitted.

   a. A request for admission asking that Dr. Castillo authenticate a photocopy of her employment application showing her signature under a statement that reads, "I, the undersigned, understand that, should I be employed by Wentworth-Armstrong Computer Technical Services, Inc., my employment would be at-will, and that, in accordance with the laws of this state, I can be discharged at any time, for any reason, with or without notice. I further understand that no one, except the CEO of Wentworth-Armstrong Computer Technical Services, Inc., has the authority to alter this at-will situation."

   b. A request for admission asking that Dr. Castillo authenticate a photocopy of the last page of the Wentworth-Armstrong Computer Technical Services, Inc. policy and procedure manual showing her signature under a statement which reads, "I, the undersigned, state that I have read and understood the contents of this employment manual. Moreover, I further state that I agree to abide by all rules, regulations, and procedures in said manual."

   c. A request for admission asking that Dr. Castillo authenticate a letter that she sent to Mr. Wentworth, the CEO of Wentworth-Armstrong Computer Technical Services, Inc., complaining of her harsh treatment while employed at his firm.

Chapter Project

Review the commentary at the opening of this chapter. Recall that, in this case, your firm is representing Dr. Alicia Castillo in a wrongful discharge suit against her former employer, Wentworth-Armstrong Computer Technical Services, Inc. (DBA Compuquick). The other defendant is Mr. Edward Wentworth, the CEO of Compuquick. Locate a sample request for admissions in your state's form book. Draft a request for admissions in which you request that Mr. Wentworth admit that he signed all of Dr. Castillo's employee evaluation forms, that all of those forms indicated that she did outstanding work for the company, that Dr. Castillo was a contractual employee, and that he personally believed that her job performance was satisfactory. Also request that he authenticate the attached document purporting to be the company's list of dischargeable offenses and its progressive disciplinary procedure. Also request that he authenticate the letter that he sent to Dr. Castillo announcing her termination and the internal memo that he sent to the company's human resources director informing the director of Castillo's discharge.

The *Bennett* Case
Assignment 13: Answering a Request for Admissions

Ms. Bennett has been served with a set of request for admissions concerning the following questions:

1. Do you admit that prior to being hired by Rikards-Hayley you had seen a psychologist for marital problems?

2. Do you admit that any of your current medical or psychological problems are due exclusively to marital problems you presently experience?

3. Do you admit that any of your current medical or psychological problems are in part due to marital problems you presently experience?

4. Do you admit that you tendered an oral resignation of your position with defendant?

5. Do you admit that all of the medical bills claimed in this lawsuit have been covered by insurance?

You have been asked to prepare a response to these questions. When you discussed the matter with Ms. Bennett, she told you that she did in fact have marital problems and that her husband had filed for divorce last week. She admitted to seeing a marriage counselor prior to her employment with defendant. However, she does not believe that any of this is relevant to the case. She assures you that all of her medical problems were caused by the defendant's actions. She does acknowledge that her bills have been paid by insurance. She also tells you that when she was terminated she replied, "You can't fire me. I quit." Prepare a draft of appropriate answers to requests for admissions. Be sure to assert proper objections.

PART IV
PRETRIAL, TRIAL, AND POSTTRIAL

Chapter 14

Settlements, Dismissals, and Alternative Dispute Resolution

CHAPTER OUTLINE

COMMENTARY—THE KOWALSKI CASE

Clark Kowalski is a nuclear physicist who is employed by Americans for Environmental Safety (AES), an independent organization of individuals devoted to protecting the environment. The Cuyahoga Valley Nuclear Power Plant, located on the outskirts of Cleveland, Ohio, and owned and operated by the Everett-Stimson Power and Light Company, had wanted Dr. Kowalski to inspect the power plant. The objective of the inspection was to reassure AES and the public that the plant was safe. Unfortunately, during the inspection tour, Dr. Kowalski was severely injured in an explosion. Shortly after the accident, a reporter asked Dr. Kowalski for an interview, during which Kowalski revealed some very damaging information about the plant's safety procedures. Shortly after the news story appeared, Dr. Kowalski decided to bring a lawsuit against Everett-Stimson. Because Everett-Stimson has filed a counterclaim against Dr. Kowalski for libel, your attorney thinks it would be a good idea to explore the possibility of settling some of these claims out of court. Accordingly, she asks you to organize the litigation file in preparation for a possible settlement. Depending on the outcome of the preliminary investigation, you may also be called upon to prepare a settlement summary, a settlement letter, or a settlement brochure. If a settlement is actually reached, you may also be required to draft a settlement agreement. This chapter covers the details surrounding the settlement process.

OBJECTIVES

Part III introduced you to the discovery process. Like the discovery process, the settlement process is an integral part of any lawsuit. After reading this chapter, you should be able to:

- Define settlement.
- Identify the preliminary decisions regarding settlement.
- Discuss the work that must be done in a preliminary investigation in the settlement process.
- Differentiate between a settlement summary and a settlement letter.
- Relate the duties a paralegal might perform in compiling a settlement brochure.
- Outline the nature of a settlement agreement.
- Explain the differences among general releases, partial releases, and mutual releases.
- Discuss the nature of a stipulated dismissal.
- Define the voluntary dismissal on notice.
- Explain a court-ordered involuntary dismissal.
- Discuss the nature of a consent decree.

- Explain the need for a settlement proceeds statement.
- Describe methods of alternative dispute resolution.

The Settlement

A **settlement** is an agreement or a contract between parties that terminates their civil dispute. Many civil cases end in a settlement. Often settlement negotiations are conducted simultaneously with active preparation of the lawsuit. In fact, the preparation of the lawsuit may actually lead to the settlement. This is because, as the attorney gathers information about the suit, she may decide that a settlement is in the client's best interests. In such a case, the lawsuit is settled quickly. If, however, the attorney decides not to settle, no time has been lost in the litigation process. To be an effective paralegal, you must understand the factors to consider in making a settlement decision. It also will be very helpful for you to know how to conduct a preliminary investigation.

settlement

To come to an agreement about; disposition of a lawsuit.

Decisions Regarding Settlement

An attorney must consider a number of factors before deciding to settle a case. Perhaps the two most obvious factors are time and money. Because the legal system is overburdened with a heavy case load, it is not uncommon for a court's calendar to be backed up for months. Some courts in large metropolitan areas have dockets that are backed up for years. This type of overcrowding may mean that a trial date cannot be set for months or even years after the original complaint has been filed. If your client cannot afford to wait that long for a judgment, then your attorney may elect to settle the case without going to trial.

Also recall that a lengthy and involved discovery procedure may be needed to gather the facts required to prove your client's case at trial. The more involved the discovery process, the more expensive the lawsuit becomes. For example, in the *Kowalski* case, discovery may be necessary to uncover not only the facts surrounding the explosion itself, but also the circumstances leading to the explosion. In addition, discovery will be needed to uncover whether the defendants had any knowledge of similar incidents involving the type of pump that exploded and harmed Dr. Kowalski. This will mean taking multiple depositions and also serving interrogatories, requests for production of documents, requests for disclosure, and requests for admissions. Your client may have to undergo a physical examination, and your attorney will probably want to inspect the site of the explosion. All of this costs money, which will erode the value of any final judgment rendered by the court.

Another settlement factor may be the particular court's decisions in similar cases. In the *Kowalski* case, for example, you may find that the court recently rendered a judgment favorable to a utility company in a case with facts very similar to the facts in your case. In such a situation, it may be in your client's best interest to engage in settlement negotiations.

Finally, the subsequent tactics of the other party's attorney may motivate a client to seriously consider a settlement. Recall, for example, that the defendant, in responding to a lawsuit, may elect to file a counterclaim against the plaintiff. The legitimacy of the counterclaim and the degree to which the defendant may succeed in presenting that counterclaim would be critical factors to consider in making any settlement decision. In the *Kowalski* case, for instance, Everett-Stimson has filed a counterclaim for libel against Dr. Kowalski. Such an event may motivate your attorney to consider the possibility of settling the case without proceeding to trial.

Preliminary Investigative Work

Generally, an offer to settle originates with the plaintiff. This is because the plaintiff's attorney is in the best position to assess the injuries to the client and can therefore set a reasonable figure as the basis for the settlement. Naturally, this means that some preliminary assessment work is in order. Usually this preliminary investigative work is the responsibility of the paralegal. During this stage, you will have to obtain a personal history of the client, a preliminary assessment of the client's present health, and a medical history of the client. You may also be required to calculate the damages in the case. You may have to probe some collateral areas to get an accurate picture of the probability of your client prevailing should the case go to trial.

The Client's Personal History   One of the preliminary steps in the settlement investigation is to obtain an accurate personal and financial history of the client. This would include the client's family information, education, employment record, and religious, professional, and civic organization memberships. It might also be helpful to determine if your client has any hobbies or participates in sports. For example, in the *Kowalski* case, it might be helpful to know that Dr. Kowalski was an avid tennis player prior to sustaining the injuries caused by the explosion in the power plant. Such information may be helpful later in calculating the damages that your attorney will seek in this situation.

The Client's Present Health and Medical History   The client's medical history before and after the accident are key factors in the case. You will have to determine the nature and the extent of the injuries the client has suffered. You will also need to find out what treatment he has undergone and will be compelled to undergo in the future. It will also be helpful to know what diagnostic tests were performed on the client and what therapy, if any, was performed. Furthermore, your attorney will want to know if the client was disfigured and if he has suffered any temporary or permanent disability as a result of the accident. Do not overlook any psychiatric or psychological damage that may have resulted from the accident. It is often advisable to have the client keep a medical diary on a daily or a weekly basis. Instruct the client to record any symptoms related to the accident and any medical visits to physicians, chiropractors, psychologists, and physical therapists.

Calculating Damages   If, as the paralegal, you are asked to calculate the damages in the case, make sure to organize and review all checks, receipts, income tax returns, and paycheck stubs furnished by the client. This will ensure that you have presented a concise and accurate picture of the damages. Extreme care should be exercised in this calculation because damages are often a substantial part of any settlement agreement.

Investigating Collateral Matters   Before your attorney can make an informed decision, she must take into consideration certain collateral matters. *Collateral matters* are considerations that go beyond the facts and the merits of the case but that, nevertheless, have a very real impact on the decision to settle or to proceed with the suit. For example, the attitude of the trial judge assigned to the case may play an important part in the decision. If, in the *Kowalski* case, you learn that the trial judge tends to rule in favor of utility companies in tort suits of this nature, your attorney may decide that a settlement would be in your client's best interest.

Another collateral area to look at is the experience or inexperience of the opposing attorney. If, in the *Kowalski* case, you are dealing with an attorney who has a strong record representing utility companies in this type of suit, your attorney will approach her with a different strategy than the strategy that would be used if the attorney were inexperienced.

Recent statutes and court rulings involving this area of the law must also be researched to help your attorney determine if any recent trends in the law make it advisable to settle the suit. For example, in the *Kowalski* case, it would be essential for your attorney to know whether there have been any changes in the law of Ohio that would affect the outcome of your case. This information will be helpful to your attorney when she negotiates for a settlement with Everett-Stimson.

Settlement Offers

As a paralegal, your talents may be used in a number of ways as your attorney prepares a settlement offer. Often the paralegal will be asked to draft a settlement summary, a settlement letter, or a settlement brochure. The complexity of the lawsuit and the amount of money involved will be primary factors in determining which of the three will be used in a given case.

Settlement Summaries and Letters

Once the preliminary investigative work has been completed, the information must be pulled together into a useful report. This report must convince the defendant that a settlement would be in its best interests. Depending on the situation, you may be charged with writing a settlement summary or a settlement letter. The objective of each is to persuade your opponent to agree to your settlement terms. The choice of which format to use is based on the complexity of the case and the amount of money involved. Drafting settlement summaries and settlement letters is an important part of the paralegal's role in the overall settlement process. The law firm's form files and personal injury form books should be used to prepare the initial draft of a settlement summary or settlement letter.

Settlement Summaries   Simple cases involving relatively inexpensive claims may be settled early, primarily because the cost of such litigation outweighs the benefit of a long and expensive suit. In such a case a short settlement summary may be drafted by the paralegal. The **settlement summary** compiles all essential information outlining

settlement summary
A summary of all essential information outlining the benefits of settling the case at an early stage in the litigation.

the benefits of settling the case at an early stage in the litigation. Settlement summaries are usually not much longer than one page. Exhibit 14–1 is an example of a settlement summary for the *Kowalski* case.

settlement letter

A detailed account of the information needed to determine the benefit of settling a case.

Settlement Letters   Cases that involve complex issues and an extensive list of damages may require the writing of a settlement letter. The **settlement letter** is a much more detailed account of the essential information needed to determine the benefit of settling a case. Often it is several pages in length, because it must cover a variety of material with much more detail than that required by the settlement summary.

Kowalski v. Everett-Stimson Power and Light Company, et al.
Common Pleas Court
Cuyahoga County, Ohio
Case No. 03-GD-980

Settlement Summary
      On the morning of November 27, 2002, at approximately 11:45, the plaintiff, Dr. Clark Kowalski, acting as a representative of Americans for Environmental Safety, and plant technician Samuel Kirk were making an inspection of the cooling system at the Cuyahoga Valley Nuclear Power Plant. An incident report filed by Samuel Kirk indicates that Dr. Kowalski had followed all proper safety procedures as he conducted his inspection. The incident report filed by Mr. Kirk also indicates that at approximately 11:47 that morning, while he and Dr. Kowalski were preparing to complete their inspection, a nearby hydraulic pump malfunctioned, causing an explosion that threw both Dr. Kowalski and him to the floor. Dr. Kowalski had been facing Mr. Kirk, with his back to the pump, and thus took the full force of the explosion in the upper back. Dr. Kowalski has testified that at approximately 11:47 on the morning of November 27, 2002, he was struck in the back by an explosive force. Dr. Kowalski has stated that at no time was he in any way in contact with said pump.
      Dr. Kowalski may recover in tort law under two theories: (a.) The defendants knew about the dangerous condition of the pump and negligently failed to remedy the situation or to warn Dr. Kowalski; and (b.) the defendants should have known about the dangerous condition of the pump but did not because of a negligently conducted inspection.
      Dr. Kowalski suffered third-degree burns across the upper one-half of his back. He also received a broken arm and a broken wrist. Dr. Kowalski also suffered a minor concussion, a sprained neck, and received minor cuts and abrasions to his face and hands. He also lost three teeth and will require a series of corrective dental operations as well as restorative plastic surgery. The medical expenses incurred by Dr. Kowalski total $52,440. The plaintiff also intends to seek $235,000 in damages for pain and suffering, plus $500,000 in punitive damages under the theory that the defendants' conduct was intentional. The plaintiff has also incurred lost wages amounting to $8,000.
      The plaintiff is asking for a total of $795,440 in damages. Because of the climate of anti-utility, anti-nuclear sentiment prevalent in Ohio at the present time, it is anticipated that the jury will award the full amount. However, in the interest of a speedy and just end to the suit, the plaintiff is willing to settle for an award of $400,000. This represents just slightly more than one-half of the anticipated recovery should the matter go to trial. The plaintiff is also willing to negotiate a payment plan, provided that he can receive an immediate cash payment of the first $100,000.

EXHIBIT 14–1   Sample settlement summary

The settlement letter begins with a statement of the facts involved in the case. Naturally, this statement of the facts must be written from the perspective of the defendant's potential liability. The letter also includes a detailed assessment of your client's injuries, your client's medical history, present medical condition, and future medical prognosis. To be convincing, the letter should also reveal the plaintiff's legal theory or theories of recovery. The amount of money spent by your client because of his injuries should be included as well as the amount of any wages he has lost because of those injuries. Finally, the settlement letter should present to the defendant a statement of the amount that your client is prepared to ask as a reasonable settlement. Exhibit 14–2 is an example of a settlement letter sent by Dr. Kowalski's attorney to the Everett-Stimson Power and Light Company.

**LAW OFFICE OF
EDWARDS, BLAKE, FITZSIMMONS, AND MYLORIE**

31753 EAST CLOVER AVENUE
CLEVELAND, OHIO 44121

MARCH 17, 2004

Ms. Charlene Bannister
Andrews, Bannister, Vilnius, and Friedman
The Billings Building, Suite 81989
2748 West Lexington Blvd.
Cleveland, Ohio 44117

RE: *Kowalski v. Everett-Stimson Power and Light Company, et al.*
Common Pleas Court
Cuyahoga County, Ohio
Case No. 03-CD-980

Dear Ms. Bannister:

In the interests of bringing the case of *Kowalski v. Everett-Stimson Power and Light Company, et al.,* to a speedy and just conclusion, I have been authorized by my client, Dr. Clark Kowalski, to make the following settlement offer to your client. Please consult with your client, give this settlement offer all due consideration, and contact my office with your response within fourteen days from the receipt of this letter.

Plaintiff's Background—Clark Kowalski was born on February 9, 1948, the first of seven children born to Mr. and Mrs. Vytautus Kowalski. The plaintiff attended St. Mary Magdalene Grade School in Willowick, Ohio; St. Joseph High School in Cleveland; John Carroll University in Cleveland; and Case Western Reserve University, also in Cleveland. He received his doctorate in nuclear physics from Case Western Reserve University in June of 1974. Dr. Kowalski has taught at a number of universities and colleges over the course of the last twenty years. He is an acknowledged expert in the field of nuclear physics, having no fewer than thirty scholarly articles to his credit. Prior to his accepting employment as nuclear physicist with Americans for Environmental Safety (AES), he directed the research department at the prestigious North Central Institute of Technology (NCIT).

EXHIBIT 14–2 Sample settlement letter

<u>Medical History</u>—Dr. Kowalski's medical history is notable for its lack of incident. He suffered a knee injury while playing tennis at St. Joseph High School in 1966. Aside from that, he has a mild case of hypertension that is kept under control by the daily administration of the minimum dose of Vasotec. He has no previous history of head, back, or arm injuries. Before the accident he was, in fact, in good enough health to win the Cleveland-Akron-Toledo Tri-City Amateur Tennis Championship for three years in a row.

<u>The Facts Surrounding the Accident</u>—On the morning of November 27, 2002, at approximately 11:45, Dr. Kowalski was making an inspection of the cooling system at the Cuyahoga Valley Nuclear Power Plant. The inspection of the plant by an AES representative had been arranged by Everett-Stimson to reassure AES and the public that the plant was safe. The attached incident report filed by Samuel Kirk indicates that Dr. Kowalski had followed all proper safety procedures as he conducted his inspection. The incident report filed by Mr. Kirk also indicates that at approximately 11:47 that morning, while he and Dr. Kowalski were preparing to complete their inspection, a nearby hydraulic pump malfunctioned, causing an explosion that threw both Dr. Kowalski and him to the floor. Dr. Kowalski had been facing Mr. Kirk with his back to the pump and thus took the full force of the explosion in the upper back. Dr. Kowalski's position shielded Mr. Kirk from the force of the explosion.

Dr. Kowalski's deposition, a copy of which is attached, also indicates that at approximately 11:47 on the morning of November 27, 2002, he was struck in the back by an explosive force. Dr. Kowalski has stated that at no time was he in any contact with said pump. He has indicated that he was talking to Mr. Kirk as they were preparing to complete their inspection when he was suddenly thrown from his feet by a sudden hot blast. He was looking at Mr. Kirk at the time and had no warning that the pump was about to explode.

<u>Theories of Recovery</u>—Dr. Kowalski may recover in tort law under two theories:
a. The defendants knew about the dangerous condition of the pump and negligently failed to remedy the situation or to warn Dr. Kowalski.
b. The defendants should have known about the dangerous condition of the pump but did not because of a negligently conducted inspection.

The first theory will be proven by an examination of the accident records of the Everett-Stimson Power and Light Company, which will clearly indicate that identical explosions involving identical pumps taken from the same lot number occurred at two other nuclear power plants owned and operated by Everett-Stimson. Testimony from Dr. Kowalski, Mr. Kirk, and from Julius Angelitis, the director of the Cuyahoga Valley Nuclear Power Plant, will indicate that neither Dr. Kowalski nor Mr. Kirk was informed of the previous accidents, despite Mr. Angelitis's knowledge of the accidents and his knowledge that Dr. Kowalski and Mr. Kirk would be working in the vicinity of the suspect pump. Such a failure to warn of impending danger would amount to negligent conduct, making the company liable for Dr. Kowalski's resulting injuries.

The defendants may wish to argue that Mr. Angelitis did not inform Dr. Kowalski about the dangerous pump because a recent inspection had revealed that the pump was not flawed. The defendants may argue that because of this favorable inspection they did not know that harm to the plaintiff would occur. If this is the argument presented by the defendants, then the plaintiff will call upon his second theory. That theory suggests that the inspection performed by the defendants must necessarily have been conducted in a negligent manner. The plaintiff will submit evidence that will convince a jury that even a cursory examination of the pump would have revealed the same flaw in this pump which caused the other two pumps to explode. The plaintiff will submit further convincing

EXHIBIT 14–2   (continued)

evidence that will prove that this pump exploded in the same manner and as a result of the same flaw that caused the other two pumps to explode.

Injuries to the Plaintiff—The initial medical examination conducted by Dr. Wesley Forbes, the staff physician at Cuyahoga Valley, indicated that Dr. Kowalski suffered third-degree burns across the upper one-half of his back. Dr. Forbes's initial assessment also indicated that the plaintiff received a broken arm and a broken wrist. The plaintiff was air-lifted to the Burn Unit at Cleveland Metropolitan general Hospital, where the diagnosis of his burns and broken bones was confirmed. Dr. Michelle Gonzales also found that Dr. Kowalski had suffered a minor concussion, a sprained neck, and had received minor cuts and abrasions on his face and hands. He also lost three teeth and will require a series of corrective dental operations as well as restorative plastic surgery. The reports issued by Dr. Forbes, Dr. Gonzales, and the dentist, Dr. Herman Kleinhenz, are attached.

Medical Expenses—The medical expenses incurred by Dr. Kowalski have been itemized on the attached forms. However, a general summary of those expenses includes the following items:

a.	Medivac Transportation to Cleveland Metro	$ 1,000
b.	Emergency Room Treatment	$ 2,300
c.	One-Week Hospital Stay at Metro	$ 9,800
d.	Orthopedic Treatment	$ 7,900
e.	Burn Unit Treatment	$ 8,000
f.	Radiology Department	$ 1,000
g.	Dr. Kleinhenz's Examination	$ 1,500
h.	Anticipated Oral Surgery	$ 2,400
i.	Anticipated Cosmetic Surgery	$ 9,900
j.	Anticipated Treatment	$ 8,640
	TOTAL	$ 52,440

Further Damages—The plaintiff, Dr.Kowalski, also intends to seek $235,000 in damages for pain and suffering plus $500,000 in punitive damages. The plaintiff has also incurred lost wages amounting to $8,000.

Proposed Settlement—The plaintiff is asking for a total of $795,440 in damages. Because of the climate of anti-utility, anti-nuclear sentiment prevalent in Ohio at the present time, it is anticipated that the jury will award the full amount. However, in the interest of a speedy and just end to the suit, the plaintiff is willing to settle for an immediate cash award of $400,000. This represents just slightly more than one-half of the anticipated recovery should the matter go to trial.

As counsel for the plaintiff, I urge you to take this settlement offer to your client in the spirit in which it is offered. I will look forward to your affirmative response.

Very truly yours,

Terry A. Mylorie

TAM/skg
Enclosures
CC: Dr. Clark Kowalski with enclosures

EXHIBIT 14–2 *(continued)*

Settlement Brochures

settlement brochure

A summary of facts designed
to get the other side to settle
a case.

The **settlement brochure** is a summary of facts designed to get the other side to settle a case. Naturally, the objective and the basic content of a settlement summary, a settlement letter, and a settlement brochure are the same. They differ, however, in the amount of the material presented and in the format used. The settlement brochure tends to be more elaborate, in that it includes photographs, charts, graphs, newspaper articles, witness statements, medical reports, and the like. It is frequently made more striking by its use of multicolored graphs and charts. A settlement brochure can be a very persuasive settlement tool. However, it is also expensive and is thus used most effectively in lawsuits seeking fairly large settlements. The individual parts of a settlement brochure should include a statement of the facts, the client's personal history, the client's medical history and medical condition, the damages suffered by the client, and an evaluation of the case and statement of the settlement. Exhibit 14–3 is an example of a table of contents that might be used for a settlement brochure in the *Kowalski* case.

Statement of the Facts   Like the settlement letter, the settlement brochure begins with a *statement of the facts* involved in the case. Again, this statement of the facts must be written from the perspective of the defendant's potential liability. However, the settlement brochure can also include witness statements, medical reports, newspaper articles, and photographs. The use of newspaper articles and photographs can be an especially effective way of creating a vivid effect. Consider, for example, the dramatic impact in the *Kowalski* case of including in your settlement brochure a front-page news story of an accident at the Cuyahoga Valley Plant and color photographs of the accident site and the injuries to Dr. Kowalski. Such a package can be very sobering to the defendant, who realizes that these same photographs may be presented to jury members who live near the Cuyahoga Valley Plant.

Client's Personal History   The *client's personal history* should also be included in the settlement brochure. To complete this section of the settlement brochure, you should review the preliminary investigative work that you did in the case. The personal

---

    I. Description of the Accident
       Witness Statements
       Photos of the Accident Scene
       Photos of the Plaintiff before the Accident
       Photos of the Plaintiff after the Accident
   II. Statement of the Facts
  III. Plaintiff's Personal History
  IV. Medical History of the Plaintiff
   V. Medical Condition of the Plaintiff
  VI. Medical Expenses
 VII. Evaluation of the Claim

EXHIBIT 14–3   Table of contents of settlement brochure

history includes the client's family information, education, employment record, and religious, professional, and civic organization memberships. It might also be helpful to include information about your client's hobbies or participation in sports. As in the case of the facts, photographs can also be used here. Photographs may be helpful later in calculating the damages that your attorney will seek in this situation.

Client's Medical History and Medical Condition   Like the settlement letter, the settlement brochure also includes a detailed assessment of your client's *medical history and medical condition*. Again, this should include the injuries suffered by the client as well as any future medical prognosis. To be convincing, this section of the settlement brochure can include the hospital records and the reports filed by any physicians and therapists involved in the case, as well as the client's medical diary. Again, photographs of the plaintiff's injuries can be a very effective supplement in this section of the brochure.

Damages, Evaluation, and Settlement   In a separate section devoted to **damages,** the amount of money spent by your client because of his injuries should be included as well as the amount of any wages he has lost because of those injuries. All checks, receipts, income tax returns, and pay stubs furnished by the client must be organized and totaled to present a precise and accurate picture of the damages. Finally, the settlement brochure should include an *evaluation of the claim* and present to the defendant a *statement of the settlement* that your client believes is reasonable.

damages
Money that a court orders paid to a person who has suffered damage (a loss or harm) by the person who caused the injury (the violation of the person's rights).

Settlement Agreements and Releases

If the parties reach an agreement based on the settlement offer, then it will be necessary to put the details of that settlement into some permanent written form. The complexity of the case and the settlement arrangement will determine whether the parties will want to use a settlement agreement or a release.

Settlement Agreements

A **settlement agreement** is actually a contract between the parties. As such, it must meet all the legal requirements of a contract. This means that it must involve the voluntary, mutual assent of the parties. It must involve the give-and-take element of consideration. Also, the agreement must be legal and must be made by parties with the capacity to contract.

Voluntary, Mutual Assent   Because a settlement agreement is a contract, it must be made with the voluntary, mutual assent of both parties. If the client is against the settlement, the attorney cannot agree to it no matter how lucrative and beneficial it may appear to be. In fact, the rules of ethical conduct that guide attorneys also specify this limitation on the attorney's power to represent a client. Similarly, to be voluntary, the settlement agreement must not result from duress or undue influence. Threats of bodily harm or threats to property would constitute duress.

settlement agreement
A contract between two or more parties to settle a case; it involves the voluntary, mutual assent of the parties and the give-and-take element of consideration. The agreement must be legal and must be made by parties with the capacity to contract.

consideration

The reason or main cause for a person to make a contract; something of value received or promised to induce (convince) a person to make a deal. Without consideration a contract is not valid.

Consideration   Because the settlement agreement is a contract, it will not be valid unless each side gains something and each side gives up something. This exchange of values is called **consideration.** Money is the most common form of consideration. In the *Kowalski* case, for example, your attorney may decide to ask Everett-Stimson for a $400,000 settlement to compensate your client for the injuries he suffered as a result of the explosion of the hydraulic pump used in the Cuyahoga Valley Nuclear Power Plant. Money, however, is not the only form of consideration. A promise to act or not to act may also be consideration. In the *Kowalski* case, for example, the consideration offered by Dr. Kowalski is his agreement to drop the lawsuit. Once the settlement has been agreed to, it is binding even if Dr. Kowalski later finds out that he had no legal basis for bringing the suit against Everett-Stimson.

Capacity and Legality   In order for the settlement to be enforceable in court, it must be made by parties who have the legal capacity to enter into a contract. If one of the parties is a minor, the parent or the guardian enters into the settlement agreement and obtains the court's approval on behalf of the minor. Naturally, the terms of the settlement must not require either party to do something that is illegal.

Form of the Settlement Agreement   The settlement should specify the identities of the parties, the action that gave rise to the claim, the type and extent of the injuries caused, the consideration given for the settlement, the time and circumstances under which any and all payments will be made, and any special conditions that have been agreed to by the parties. If a dispute arises over any part of the agreement, a court will interpret its provisions. If the court finds that a term of the agreement is vague or ambiguous, it may seek additional testimony or evidence to determine the intent of the parties at the time they entered into the agreement. Exhibit 14–4 presents an example of a settlement agreement in the *Kowalski* case.

Releases

If the facts and the legal issues involved in the lawsuit are not overly complex, the parties may be satisfied to settle the case by using a release, rather than a settlement agreement. Although a release is also a contract and, as such, accomplishes essentially the same thing as a settlement agreement, the release is much simpler and much shorter than the settlement agreement and, therefore, much more efficient. The two most common releases are the general release and the partial release. If both parties have agreed to release each other from any and all claims, then a mutual release is appropriate.

general release

A document by which a claim or right is relinquished.

General Release   A **general release** is used for full and final settlements. In a general release, all possible claims against all possible persons who might be liable for the plaintiff's injuries are settled. This type of release is advantageous for the defendant because the defendant can rest assured that no further action will be taken by the plaintiff in relation to the subject matter of the lawsuit. In the *Kowalski* case, for example, a general release would cancel all claims that Dr. Kowalski has or may have relating to the explosion at the Cuyahoga Valley Nuclear Power Plant. Exhibit 14–5 is an example of a general release form that might be used in the *Kowalski* case.

COURT OF COMMON PLEAS
CUYAHOGA COUNTY
STATE OF OHIO

CLARK KOWALSKI   )
    Plaintiff,   )
)   Civil Action No. 03-GD-980
)   SETTLEMENT AGREEMENT
    vs.   )
)
EVERETT-STIMSON POWER AND   )
LIGHT COMPANY, et al.   )
    Defendants.   )
)
)

THIS ACTION, Kowalski v. Everett-Stimson Power and Light Company, et al., Case No. 03-GD-980, was brought in the Common Pleas Court of Cuyahoga County, Ohio by Clark Kowalski, hereinafter called "plaintiff," against Everett-Stimson Power and Light Company and Cuyahoga Valley Nuclear Power Plant, hereinafter called "defendants." The plaintiff brought this action to recover damages for injuries received in an explosion at the Cuyahoga Valley Nuclear Power plant, a facility owned and operated by the defendant Subsequent to the filing of this action, the defendant in its answer filed a counterclaim against the plaintiff for libel relating to certain remarks made to a reporter for the *Cleveland Daily News,* and which appeared in that paper in a story dated December 19, 2002.

THIS AGREEMENT has been made and entered into at Cleveland, Ohio this 15th day of November, 2004.

WITNESSETH

WHEREAS, the parties desire to settle and adjust all matters relating to this action, all property rights, all payments in the nature of damages, or other allowances that each might be entitled to, and

WHEREAS, each of the parties is fully advised as to the extent of the injuries, the value of the property, and the prospects of the other,

NOW, THEREFORE, in consideration of the mutual covenants and agreements herein contained, the parties hereby acknowledge and agree as follows:

a. The plaintiff agrees to accept the sum of the Four Hundred Thousand Dollars ($400,000) in full satisfaction of all claims in the complaint filed against the defendant in Case No. 03-GD-980 in the Common Pleas Court of Cuyahoga County, Ohio.

b. The defendants agree to pay the plaintiff the sum of Four Hundred Thousand Dollars ($400,000) payable as follows: the sum of $100,000 payable in cash when the settlement agreement is final and signed, the sum of $300,000 payable over a seven-year period with 10 percent interest per annum, with the first payment of $4,000 beginning on the first day of the month following the signing and finalizing of this agreement and continuing at a rate of $4,000 per month on the first day of every month thereafter until paid in full.

c. The plaintiff agrees that there will be no prepayment penalty should the defendants decide to pay the balance early.

EXHIBIT 14–4 Sample settlement agreement

d. Contemporaneous with the signing of this agreement, the defendants shall execute a note payable to the order of the plaintiff, providing for the payment of the $400,000 as indicated above.

e. The parties agree that with the signing and execution of this agreement and of the aforementioned note, the parties shall cause the complaint in the action to be dismissed with prejudice.

f. The parties agree that with the signing and execution of this agreement and the aforementioned note, the parties shall cause the defendant's counterclaim in this action for libel to be dismissed with prejudice.

g. The plaintiff agrees that the payment of the sum of $400,000 is also in full satisfaction for all wrongful discharge claims that the plaintiff may have against the defendants.

h. The plaintiff shall sign and execute all releases prepared by the attorney for the defendants, provided that those releases are consistent with the provisions of this agreement.

i. The defendants are to pay court costs of the action.

It is further agreed that the forthgoing provisions are in full settlement of all claims that either party might assert against the other.

IN WITNESS WHEREOF, the parties hereto have executed this agreement on the day and the year first above written.

SIGNED AND ACKNOWLEDGED
IN THE PRESENCE OF

_____

_____   Clark Kowalski, Plaintiff

     _____

     President and CEO
     Everett-Stimson Power and Light Company

_____   _____

     Cuyahoga Valley Nuclear Power Plant

EXHIBIT 14–4 *(continued)*

partial release

The relinquishment of some claims and the retention of others by a party.

Partial Release In a complex lawsuit involving multiple claims, a party may elect to relinquish some claims while retaining others. In such a situation a **partial release** would be appropriate. This type of release is advantageous to the plaintiff because it preserves some of the grounds that he has for bringing a subsequent lawsuit against the defendant. However, the defendant also benefits because at least a portion of its potential liability has been eliminated. For example, in the *Kowalski* case, in addition to the negligence suit for the injuries suffered as a result of the explosion at the power plant, your client may have also filed an invasion of privacy suit against Everett-Stimson for making illegal tapes of his private phone conversations. Should Dr. Kowalski decide to settle the negligence suit against Everett-Stimson while maintaining the invasion of privacy suit, he would use a partial release.

COURT OF COMMON PLEAS
CUYAHOGA COUNTY
STATE OF OHIO

CLARK KOWALSKI　　　　　　　　　)
　　Plaintiff,　　　　　　　　　　　)
　　　　　　　　　　　　　　　　　)　Civil Action No. 03-GD-980
　　vs.　　　　　　　　　　　　　　)　GENERAL RELEASE
　　　　　　　　　　　　　　　　　)
EVERETT-STIMSON POWER AND　　　)
LIGHT COMPANY, et al.　　　　　　)
　　Defendants.　　　　　　　　　　)
　　　　　　　　　　　　　　　　　)
　　　　　　　　　　　　　　　　　)

　　Clark Kowalski, Plaintiff, in the above case, hereby releases the Defendants and all other persons, known or unknown, who may have contributed to the incident which forms the basis of this lawsuit, from all claims and demands for any act or matter whatsoever which may have arisen or may arise in the future.
　　Signed and sealed this 15th day of November, 2004, at Cleveland, Ohio.

EXHIBIT 14–5　Sample general release

Mutual Release　If the defendant in a lawsuit has filed a counterclaim against the plaintiff, then both parties in the case may find themselves in the position of relinquishing part or all of their claims in the suit. If this is the case, then a mutual release would be used. In a **mutual release,** each party relinquishes its claims against the other party. This type of release benefits both parties, because each of them can be assured that all potential liability in regard to this particular lawsuit has been eliminated. For example, in the *Kowalski* case, Everett-Stimson filed a counterclaim against Dr. Kowalski for libel, claiming that he made false statements to a newspaper reporter about certain inadequate safety procedures followed at the plant. If both Dr. Kowalski and Everett-Stimson agree to release each other, they would use a mutual release.

mutual release
An agreement by which each party relinquishes its claims against the other.

Form of the Release　Regardless of the type of release needed in a given case, it should include the identities of the parties, the action that gave rise to the claim, the consideration given for the release, and a specifically worded explanation of the claim that has been relinquished. Naturally, the release should also be signed by the parties. As in the case of the settlement agreement, if the court finds that a term of the release is vague or ambiguous, it may seek additional testimony or evidence to determine the intent of the parties at the time that they negotiated the release.

Dismissals, Consent Decrees, and Distribution of Funds

Once a lawsuit has been settled, an order for dismissal is drawn up. As an alternative to a dismissal, the parties may prefer to file a consent decree with the court. Finally, a statement outlining how the settlement funds will be distributed should be drawn up and delivered to the client.

Dismissals

There are three major types of dismissals: a stipulated dismissal, a voluntary dismissal on notice, and a court-ordered involuntary dismissal.

Stipulated Dismissals   The parties to a lawsuit may stipulate to a dismissal at any time and on any terms. A stipulated dismissal may be either with prejudice or without prejudice. A stipulated **dismissal with prejudice** means that the claim cannot be brought to court again at any time in the future. In contrast, a stipulated **dismissal without prejudice** means that the lawsuit can be brought at another time in any court that has jurisdiction to hear the case. If the parties fail to stipulate the form of the dismissal, the court presumes that the dismissal is without prejudice. In a stipulated dismissal, it is not necessary to state the terms and the conditions of the settlement. This type of dismissal avoids having to disclose, in public records, the amount of the settlement. It also preserves the confidentiality of the terms surrounding the settlement. Exhibit 14–6 is a stipulated dismissal.

Voluntary Dismissal on Notice   Rule 41 of the Federal Rules of Civil Procedure permits a plaintiff to voluntarily dismiss a claim without order of the court by filing a motion of dismissal "at any time before service by the adverse party of an answer or of a motion for summary judgment, whichever comes first." Although not required under the terms of Rule 41, the plaintiff should serve a copy of the dismissal upon the defendant. As in the case of the stipulated dismissal, this dismissal can be with prejudice or without prejudice. The presumption is that the dismissal is without prejudice unless the court order of dismissal specifically states that it is with prejudice. Exhibit 14–7 reflects a dismissal without prejudice.

Court-Ordered Involuntary Dismissal   The court has the authority to dismiss an action if a party has failed to proceed with an action or if the party has failed to comply with a court order. For example, in the *Kowalski* case, if your client fails to comply with a court order compelling him to respond to repeated discovery requests from Everett-Stimson, the case may be dismissed by the court. In addition, the court may dismiss if the plaintiff's evidence is insufficient to establish liability against the defendant. A dismissal marks the end of the case. Normally, it does not result in the court's entry of a judgment. Exhibit 14–8 gives an example of a court-ordered involuntary dismissal.

Consent Decrees

As an alternative to a dismissal, the parties may elect to use a consent decree. A **consent decree** outlines the details of the settlement agreed upon by the parties. The parties file the decree with the court, requesting that the judge examine the agreement

dismissal with prejudice

A court order or judgment that ends a lawsuit. No further lawsuit may be brought by the same persons on the same subject.

dismissal without prejudice

A court order or judgment that ends a lawsuit. A further lawsuit may be brought by the same persons on the same subject.

consent decree

A settlement of a lawsuit or prosecution in which a person or company agrees to take certain actions without admitting fault or guilt for the situation causing the lawsuit

COURT OF COMMON PLEAS
CUYAHOGA COUNTY
STATE OF OHIO

CLARK KOWALSKI   )
   Plaintiff,   )
)   Civil Action No. 03-GD-980
   vs.   )   STIPULATED ORDER OF
)   DISMISSAL
)
EVERETT-STIMSON POWER   )
AND LIGHT COMPANY, et al.)
   Defendants.   )
)

    On this 15th of November, 2004, it is stipulated between counsel for the Plaintiff, and counsel for the Defendants that this action be dismissed without prejudice regarding all claims and counterclaims of the parties.

_____
Attorney for Plaintiff

_____
Attorney for Defendant
Everett-Stimson Power and Light Company

_____
Attorney for Defendant
Cuyahoga Valley Nuclear Power Plant

EXHIBIT 14–6   Stipulated order of dismissal

and either approve or disapprove the terms that they have set forth. Most of the time the judge will have no hesitation in rendering approval. Once it has been approved by the court, the consent decree is just as effective as a judgment would have been, had the case gone to trial. Unlike the terms of a stipulated dismissal, the settlement terms of a consent decree become a public record. Because of the official nature of the consent decree, should one of the parties violate the terms of a decree, that party may be held in contempt of court.

Distribution of Settlement Funds

Distribution of funds is often made when the stipulated dismissal is signed or when the court has approved of the consent decree. A settlement proceeds statement should be prepared, similar to a closing statement in a real estate transaction, to account for the receipt of all proceeds. Such an accounting avoids later problems or questions by a party as to the payment of any expense involved in the settlement.

COURT OF COMMON PLEAS
CUYAHOGA COUNTY
STATE OF OHIO

CLARK KOWALSKI)
  Plaintiff,)
) Civil Action No. 03-GD-980
    vs.) VOLUNTARY DISMISSAL
) WITHOUT PREJUDICE
)
EVERETT-STIMSON POWER)
AND LIGHT COMPANY, et al.)
  Defendants.)
)

    Having reviewed the Plaintiff's Motion for Voluntary Dismissal Without Prejudice in this action, it is hereby
    ORDERED this 15TH day of November, 2004, that this action be dismissed without prejudice regarding all claims of the parties.

                                         _____

EXHIBIT 14–7 Voluntary dismissal without prejudice

COURT OF COMMON PLEAS
CUYAHOGA COUNTY
STATE OF OHIO

CLARK KOWALSKI)
  Plaintiff,)
) Civil Action No. 03-GD-980
    vs.) COURT-ORDERED
) INVOLUNTARY DISMISSAL
)
EVERETT-STIMSON POWER)
AND LIGHT COMPANY, et al.)
  Defendants.)
)

    Upon consideration of the failure of the Plaintiff to timely prosecute this action, it is hereby
    ORDERED this 15th day of November, 2004, that the complaint filed in this action against the Defendants is hereby dismissed.

                                         _____

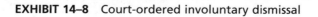

EXHIBIT 14–8 Court-ordered involuntary dismissal

Alternative Dispute Resolution

Although negotiated settlements are obviously the most desirable way of resolving civil disputes, parties often lack the objectivity needed to reach reasonable compromises. In the past few years the legal community has adopted a number of different methods to help parties properly evaluate their cases for settlement purposes. Usually these procedures utilize the services of a neutral person or group of people who try to bring the parties to an agreement or who give the parties their independent evaluation of the case. These methods or procedures are collectively referred to as alternative dispute resolution (ADR).

The various methods of alternative dispute resolution have proven to be an effective means of resolving civil disputes. This has benefited not only the parties to a civil dispute but also the court system. The benefit is such that most courts now require many litigants to submit to at least one form of alternative dispute resolution before the court will set the case for trial. Alternative dispute resolution occurring during the course of litigation and required by the courts is referred to as court-related alternative dispute resolution. If court-related ADR does not produce a mutually agreeable result, the parties resume litigation.

In some instances, the parties, rather than the court, initiate alternative dispute resolution. They can do this prior to filing a lawsuit or even during the course of litigation. Furthermore, the parties can agree to be bound by any result, giving up their right to litigate. Of course, they can also agree that the alternative dispute resolution procedure will not be binding. Alternative dispute resolution voluntarily undertaken by the parties is sometimes referred to as *private* or *voluntary alternative dispute resolution.*

Court-Related ADR

In 1990, Congress passed the Civil Justice Reform Act of 1990 (28 U.S.C. § 1). This statute required every federal district court to develop a plan to resolve civil disputes more smoothly and swiftly. To accomplish this goal, federal trial courts either require or encourage most litigants to attempt some method of alternative dispute resolution before the case can be tried. Unless the parties agree otherwise, these alternative dispute resolution procedures are not binding on the parties. If either side is not satisfied with the suggested method of resolving the case, that party has the right to proceed to trial. The various methods of court-related ADR include early neutral evaluation, mediation, nonbinding arbitration, summary jury trials, and summary bench trials.

Early Neutral Evaluation   In an early neutral evaluation, litigants meet with an outside neutral person who is an expert in the subject matter of the case. This expert is also likely to be an attorney. During this procedure, the parties and their counsel exchange information and position statements. They can then make brief oral presentations to the evaluator. The evaluator provides a nonbinding evaluation of the merits and value of the case. The purpose is to facilitate settlement. All written and oral communication in connection with this type of proceeding is confidential, and the parties and their attorneys might be asked to sign a confidentiality agreement.

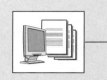

THE COMPUTERIZED LAW FIRM
Document Assembly

SCENARIO

At 1:00 P.M. on Friday, your attorney calls you into her office. She has just received a call from Charlene Bannister, the attorney for Everett-Stimson Power and Light. Apparently, Everett-Stimson has decided to settle the case for $400,000. Your attorney has already talked to Dr. Kowalski, who has given his permission to accept. Your attorney is anxious to conclude the settlement before Ms. Bannister leaves for the Middle East on Monday morning.

PROBLEM

Your attorney is scheduled to return to the county courthouse on another matter at 1:30 P.M. She asks that you draft all settlement documents and deliver them to the courthouse during an anticipated recess at 3:00 P.M. so that she can review them. You will need to fax the documents to Ms. Bannister for approval and put them in final form for execution of the settlement documents on Saturday morning. Drafting the lengthy, complicated settlement documents is time consuming. The time to complete the project is limited. How can you accomplish this mammoth undertaking in less than two hours?

SOLUTION

Software available to law firms today includes programs that simplify drafting long, standardized legal documents. These programs work with word processors (particularly Word and WordPerfect), and are known as "document assembly" or document generator programs. This type of software is often a questionnaire-predicated software package that asks targeted questions in order to assemble a document incorporating those answers into otherwise standard paragraphs. A document generator is similar to a building block. One answer determines the next question. The word processing part of the program then takes all the applicable paragraphs to build the settlement agreement. The speed, accuracy, and completeness that can be obtained by using the document generator cannot be obtained with standard word-processing programs. Some popular assembly programs include Hot Docs, CAPS, and WinDraft. You can read more about Hot Docs and CAPS on their Web sites at <http://www.capsoft.com/index.html> and WinDraft at <http://www.lawtech.com/windraft>.

Mediation   Like early neutral evaluation, mediation is a nonbinding, confidential process. In mediation, a neutral mediator (usually an attorney selected by the court) tries to facilitate settlement negotiations between the parties. Unlike an early neutral evaluator, the mediator does not give an opinion regarding the case, but rather tries to strengthen the communication between the parties. The mediator also tries to get the parties to examine the strengths and weaknesses of their sides of the case. Again, the sessions are confidential.

Nonbinding Arbitration   Nonbinding arbitration is an adversarial hearing before a neutral party or arbitrator who listens to each side and then makes a decision (an *award*) regarding the dispute. The arbitrator is selected by the parties from a list of candidates provided by the court. Most cases have one arbitrator, but sometimes a case is heard by a three-person panel. Prior to the hearing, each party may submit written statements summarizing its case, identifying significant factual and legal issues, and listing proposed witnesses. At the arbitration hearing, each side puts on evidence. Based on the evidence, the arbitrator or arbitration panel makes an award or judgment. Either party can then reject the award and demand a trial in court. If neither party rejects the award, it becomes a final judgment in the case.

Summary Jury Trial   In a summary jury trial, the parties put their evidence before a six-person jury, which renders a nonbinding decision. The evidence may be presented in summary fashion so that it does not take as long as an actual jury trial would. The jury is also given a limited time in which to deliberate. Its members are encouraged to come to a consensus, but if they cannot, their opinions and findings are relayed to the attorneys trying the case. A summary jury trial requires more time and expense than the other methods of ADR and thus is not favored, except in extraordinary cases.

Summary Bench Trial   A summary bench trial resembles a summary jury trial except that the case is tried before a judge rather than a jury. Again, evidence is often introduced in a condensed manner so as to avoid the lengthy process of an actual trial.

Early neutral evaluation, mediation, and nonbinding arbitration are the most favored forms of ADR.

Private ADR

Parties often wish to avoid the court process in its entirety. They therefore look to ADR as a means to accomplish this. In many instances, the parties agree to be bound by alternative dispute resolution, although in some cases they do not. Methods of private ADR include negotiation, mediation, binding arbitration, minitrials and private judging. Two of these methods of private ADR, mediation and arbitration, are becoming increasingly popular with litigators, as evidenced by a report on the American Arbitration Association's Web site which indicates that in the 2002 timeframe it administered over 230,000 cases, with the assistance of more than 8,000 arbitrators and mediators worldwide.

Negotiation   Probably the most common method of resolving disputes is negotiation. Negotiation involves the disputing parties discussing their problems with one another. If an agreement is reached, then the negotiation results in a settlement. In most cases, negotiation starts before the parties file any lawsuit in court. If the parties are able to reach an agreement at an early stage in the negotiations, then a lawsuit may never be filed. However, if the parties are unable to reach an early settlement, they often continue their informal negotiations even though one party has filed a lawsuit.

Mediation   Mediation voluntarily undertaken by the parties resembles mediation proceedings that are ordered by the court as part of its ADR procedures. The only difference is in the selection of the mediator. In private mediation, the mediator is selected without the assistance of the court. Parties generally tend to use mediation in a case where they believe they can reach an agreement with the assistance of a neutral third party, or when there will be a relationship between the parties that continues after resolution of the conflict. Another positive factor in the choice of mediation to resolve a dispute is that it is available earlier than traditional litigation, in which a trial setting may be several years after the filing of a lawsuit. Inherent with the potential time saved by choosing mediation over litigation is the resulting money saved by the potentially shorter time period required to resolve a dispute.

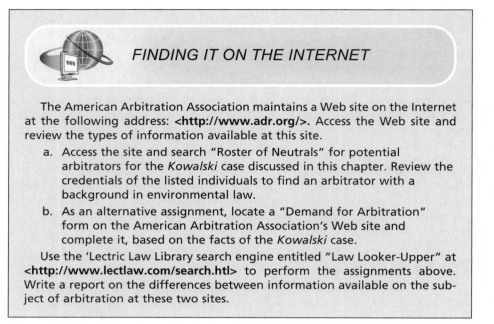

FINDING IT ON THE INTERNET

The American Arbitration Association maintains a Web site on the Internet at the following address: **<http://www.adr.org/>**. Access the Web site and review the types of information available at this site.

a. Access the site and search "Roster of Neutrals" for potential arbitrators for the *Kowalski* case discussed in this chapter. Review the credentials of the listed individuals to find an arbitrator with a background in environmental law.

b. As an alternative assignment, locate a "Demand for Arbitration" form on the American Arbitration Association's Web site and complete it, based on the facts of the *Kowalski* case.

Use the 'Lectric Law Library search engine entitled "Law Looker-Upper" at **<http://www.lectlaw.com/search.htl>** to perform the assignments above. Write a report on the differences between information available on the subject of arbitration at these two sites.

Binding Arbitration   A binding arbitration hearing resembles a nonbinding arbitration hearing. However, in addition to the binding nature of the decision, the preliminary steps in this procedure are substantially different. First, the parties must agree to binding arbitration. That is, the parties must agree to give up their right to sue and agree to accept the arbitrator's decision. This is often done before any dispute has arisen, and is usually found in a written contract in a clause providing that "in the event of a dispute, the parties agree that it shall be resolved through arbitration." Such provisions are becoming common in business and commercial transactions. Arbitration clauses are also frequently found in automobile insurance policies under the uninsured motorist provisions. Also, many health care providers are asking their patients to sign such agreements.

A second difference between binding and nonbinding arbitration appears in the way the hearing is set up. In binding arbitration, one of the disputing parties usually requests in writing that the dispute be arbitrated. Such a writing may loosely resemble a complaint. Because the court is not a party to binding arbitration, the parties must formulate the details of the arbitration hearing, including selection of the arbitrator, on their own. For parties who are already disputing, this can be a major problem. Various organizations exist that can help the parties with this. One of the most popular is the American Arbitration Association, which has adopted a set of rules to be followed for maintaining the arbitration if the parties agree. Those rules are available at the American Arbitration Association's Web site, <http://www.adr.org/>. Once a binding arbitration award is made, it is usually final.

Minitrial   Minitrials are proceedings in which high-level executives of all the parties are brought together to hear each other's case as presented by its lawyers and presided over by a neutral (often a retired judge) party. After hearing the evidence, the executives are encouraged to engage in settlement discussion. This is a nonbinding type of proceeding.

Private Judging   In recent years, especially in areas where the courts are very congested, parties have resorted to hiring their own private judge to try the case. A trial occurs in much the same way as it does in formal litigation. The major advantage to the parties is that they are not restricted by the court calendar. Trial can be scheduled at a time convenient for the parties and the judge. In most instances, these private judges are retired trial and appellate court judges. Decisions from these proceedings are usually binding.

Summary

- A settlement is an agreement or a contract between parties that terminates their civil dispute. Most civil cases end in a settlement. The preliminary investigative work in the settlement process is often the responsibility of the paralegal. The paralegal will have to obtain a personal history of the client, a preliminary assessment of the client's present health, and a medical history of the client. In addition, the paralegal may be required to calculate the damages in the case. There are also some collateral areas that the paralegal may have to probe to get an accurate picture of the probability of the client prevailing should the case go all the way to trial.

- Once the preliminary investigative work has been completed, the information must be pulled together into a settlement report. This report must convince the defendant that a settlement would be in its best interests. Depending on the situation, you may be charged with writing a settlement summary, a settlement letter, or a settlement brochure.

- A settlement agreement is actually a contract between two or more parties. As such, it must meet all the legal requirements of a contract, including the voluntary mutual assent of the parties, the element of consideration, legality, and capacity. If the facts and the legal issues involved in the lawsuit are not overly complex, the parties to the suit may be satisfied to settle the case by using a release rather than a settlement agreement. The two most common releases are the general release and the partial release. If both parties have agreed to release each other from any and all claims, a mutual release is appropriate.

- There are three major types of dismissals: a stipulated dismissal, a voluntary dismissal on notice, and a court-ordered involuntary dismissal. The parties to a lawsuit may stipulate to a dismissal at any time and on any terms. A stipulated dismissal may be either with prejudice or without prejudice. Rule 41 of the Federal Rules of Civil Procedure permits a plaintiff to voluntarily dismiss a claim without order of the court by filing a motion of dismissal. The court has the authority to dismiss an action if a party has failed to proceed with an action, if the party has failed to comply with a court order, or if the plaintiff's evidence is insufficient to establish liability against the defendant. As an alternative to a dismissal, the parties may elect to use a consent decree. A consent decree outlines the details of the settlement agreed upon by the parties. The parties file the decree with the court, requesting that the judge examine the agreement and either approve or disapprove the terms that they have set forth. When the stipulated dismissal is signed or when the court has approved the consent decree, a settlement proceeds statement should be prepared to account for the receipt of all proceeds.

- Alternative dispute resolution involves several different procedures used by parties to a civil dispute as a means of resolving their dispute without the necessity of trial. Such procedures can occur prior to or subsequent to any lawsuit being filed. Sometimes these procedures provide an exclusive remedy for the parties. Other times the procedures are only an attempt to avoid trial. ADR in connection with a pending case is often referred to as court-related ADR. ADR voluntarily undertaken by the parties is sometimes referred to as private or voluntary ADR. The various methods of court-related ADR include early neutral evaluation, mediation, nonbinding arbitration, summary jury trial, and summary bench trial. The methods of voluntary ADR include negotiation, mediation, arbitration, minitrials, and private judging.

Key Terms

consent decree	general release	settlement agreement
consideration	mutual release	settlement brochure
damages	partial release	settlement letter
dismissal with prejudice	settlement	settlement summary
dismissal without prejudice		

Review Questions

1. What is a settlement?
2. What are some of the preliminary decisions surrounding settlement?
3. What areas must be investigated before a settlement offer is made?
4. What is the difference between a settlement summary and a settlement letter?
5. How does a settlement brochure differ from a settlement summary and a settlement letter?
6. What is a settlement agreement?
7. What is a release? What types of releases are available?
8. What are the advantages of a stipulated dismissal?
9. When is a voluntary dismissal on notice allowed?
10. Under what circumstances can a court order an involuntary dismissal?
11. How does a consent decree differ from a stipulated dismissal?
12. What is a settlement proceeds statement?
13. Describe the various methods of court-related ADR.
14. Describe the various methods of private or voluntary ADR.

Chapter Exercises

Where necessary, check with your instructor prior to starting any of these exercises.

1. Review the laws of your state and find all laws that deal with settlements. Check your local court rules to see if there are any specific rules of court in your area regulating settlements.
2. Prepare an interoffice memorandum in which you explain the preliminary investigative work that you would have to do in the *Kowalski* case.
3. Check with your local bar association to see if any ADR services exist in your area. If so, contact them and see exactly what services they provide.

4. Assume that Dr. Kowalski has decided to settle the negligence suit against Everett-Stimson while maintaining the invasion of privacy suit. Prepare a partial release to facilitate that partial settlement.

5. Assume that both Dr. Kowalski and Everett-Stimson agree to release each other from all claims in the *Kowalski* litigation. Prepare a mutual releae to accomplish that settlement.

Chapter Project

Review the *Kowalski* case in the opening commentary. Recall that Dr. Kowalski has elected to sue the Cuyahoga Valley Nuclear Power Plant and its owner and operator, the Everett-Stimson Power and Light Company, for the injuries he sustained in the explosion of a hydraulic pump. Also recall that he is considering an additional lawsuit for invasion of privacy against Everett-Stimson. Note also that Everett-Stimson has brought a counterclaim against him for libel. Draft a memo in which you explore the factors to be taken into consideration in a decision regarding the possibility of offering to settle.

The *Bennett* Case
Assignment 14: Drafting a Settlement Letter

Substantial evidence exists supporting Alice Bennett's claims. Your attorney now has copies of several employment evaluations which are all excellent. Several of her prior coworkers, including Martha Yee, confirm that she was a competent and efficient acting manager. None of them could understand why she was not hired permanently for the position. Her physician, Dr. Susan Bell, a board-certified psychiatrist, has written a report detailing the various physical and mental symptoms experienced by the plaintiff. The doctor attributes these to her work experience. To date her medical bills total $10,000. Bennett has been unemployed since she was terminated approximately 18 months ago. The doctor feels that she may be able to return to work in 6 months. In the meantime, she has no income. You have been asked to draft a letter to the defendant requesting settlement in the amount of $1 million. Before drafting the letter, review 42 U.S.C. § 2000e regarding Title VII claims as well as the complaint filed on Ms. Bennett's behalf.

Chapter 15

Trial Techniques

CHAPTER OUTLINE

COMMENTARY—THE LERMENTOV CASE

You have been called into a meeting with your attorney to discuss the details of an upcoming trial. The trial involves your client, a certified public accountant named Mikhail Lermentov, who was injured in a fire last year while he was conducting an audit at the laboratories and main offices of Billicheck-Kendall Pharmaceuticals, Inc. The company has attempted to deny liability for Lermentov's injuries by claiming that all maintenance and security work done in their building is performed by two independent companies, Sergi Selinkov Security, Inc., and the Kolata Maintenance Corporation. Although the trial date is three months away, your attorney is concerned about the heavy workload that she has in several other cases. Therefore, she requests that you immediately begin to assist in preparing the *Lermentov* case for trial. Your responsibilities will include handling the file organization, preparing a trial notebook, coordinating witness preparation, selecting and organizing trial exhibits, and assisting in obtaining jury information.

OBJECTIVES

In the first two parts of this book you explored the litigation process, the beginning of a lawsuit, the pleadings, and motion practice. In Part III you were introduced to the details of the discovery process. As you can well imagine, this preliminary work and the discovery process can produce volumes of documents as well as significant information about the facts in the case. Before trial, this diverse information and these volumes of documents must be organized. Other pretrial matters must also be taken care of. This chapter introduces the preparations that must be made before the trial. After reading this chapter, you will be able to:

- Explain the paralegal's role in organizing the file and amending pleadings.
- Describe the purpose and content of the trial notebook.
- Outline the paralegal's role in preparing witnesses for trial.
- List the standards by which a trial exhibit should be tested.
- Explain the paralegal's participation in preparing trial briefs.
- Determine the paralegal's logistical duties in preparing for trial.
- Outline the paralegal's role in preparation for a focus group or mock trial.
- Describe the paralegal's role in the jury process.
- Discuss the paralegal's function at trial.

Preliminary Preparation for Trial

The preparation for trial actually begins at the initial client interview. It is at this point that the attorney begins to assess the merits of the case to determine what course of action to take. Each of the processes and tasks that we have examined thus far in the text advances the prosecution or the defense of the case. Although most cases are settled or dismissed before reaching the trial stage, you must proceed on the assumption that eventually the case will reach trial. Some preparation tasks may be performed several months in advance of trial, whereas others must be handled at the last minute.

Whatever the case, your client will prevail only if you and your attorney are thoroughly prepared for all eventualities. One task that you can perform to aid in this preparation is to prepare a trial checklist. The checklist should include all the tasks that must be performed before the trial and the timeframe for completion of those tasks. If you monitor this checklist faithfully and regularly, you will ensure that the case is truly ready for the trial. Exhibit 15–1 is an example of a trial checklist.

1. Calendar trial date and dates trial preparation tasks must be completed.
2. Notify the client and witnesses of trial date and need for meeting to prepare for trial testimony.
3. Review litigation file and organize. Complete any action necessary on this file.
4. Prepare and serve trial subpoenas.
5. Review chronology and cast of characters, and update if necessary.
6. Complete trial notebook.
7. Designate and organize trial exhibits. Prepare trial exhibit log.
8. Research potential expert witnesses and prepare a binder of the results.
9. Prepare witness list.
10. Verify that all discovery responses include all fact and expert witnesses on the witness list. Supplement discovery responses, if necessary.
11. Assist with preparation for a focus group or mock trial.
12. Assist with trial brief.
13. Visit the courtroom and diagram location of trial exhibits, documents, briefcases, etc.
14. Locate a "war room" at a nearby hotel if the trial is out of town. Arrange for food to be delivered during the trial.
15. Arrange travel and hotel for client and witnesses.
16. Pull the documents to be introduced by a witness, according to the examination outline in the trial notebook. Assist with preparing the witness for testimony at trial.
17. Assist with collecting jury demographics data. Determine the type of juror desired, considering the facts, legal issues, and parties involved. Develop juror profile sheets for the trial notebook.

EXHIBIT 15–1   Trial preparation checklist

File Organization

One of the tasks in trial preparation that can be completed during the preliminary stages is the organization of the litigation files. Naturally, it is best if the files are kept current as the case develops. For example, each time a pleading is filed by either side it should immediately be placed in the pleadings binder. However, the hectic pace of most law firms will challenge even the most efficient paralegal. Consequently, not all litigation files are kept up to date. The setting of the trial date, however, signals the need to organize the litigation file. This will mean reviewing all the pleadings and motions that have been filed in the case. It will also necessitate locating all documents, records, deposition transcripts, and interrogatories produced during discovery. You may also have to transcribe all witness interview notes that you have not yet examined. Reviewing the litigation files at an early stage will probably add a number of items to the "to do" list on the trial preparation checklist (see Exhibit 15–1). This should not overly concern you, however. The only thing that you should be concerned about is the thorough preparation of your case.

Amending the Pleadings

One problem that might surface during organization of the file is the need to amend the pleadings in the case before the time to do so expires. According to Rule 15 of the Federal Rules of Civil Procedure, once a case has been placed on the trial calendar, the pleadings in that case can be amended only with permission of the court or with the written consent of the opposing party. Fortunately, most state courts do not have this strict requirement. However, it is best to check local court rules to determine the procedure that must be followed should you find that a pleading in your case must be amended after the trial date has been set.

The Trial Notebook

trial notebook

A binder that contains, in complete or summary form, everything necessary to prosecute or defend a case.

The trial notebook, a vital part of any trial preparation, is usually the paralegal's responsibility. The **trial notebook** is a binder that contains, in complete or summary form, everything necessary to prosecute or defend a case. Preparation of the trial notebook, like the preparation of the trial itself, begins with the initial client interview. The contents and the organization of the trial notebook are determined by the individual preferences of the attorney or the paralegal. The form of the notebook is dictated by the type of case, the number of pleadings, the complexity of the legal issues, the number of exhibits and witnesses, and the anticipated length of the trial. However, most trial notebooks include the following basic sections: (1) information regarding the parties and the attorneys; (2) the pleadings, motions, and discovery responses; (3) the witnesses; (4) the expert witnesses; (5) document indexes; (6) deposition summaries; (7) chronology; (8) the cast of characters; (9) legal research; (10) trial exhibits; (11) jury profiles and instructions; (12) the trial outline; (13) the attorney's notes; and (14) the "things to do" list.

The Parties and the Attorneys   The first entry in the trial notebook is a list of all the parties and attorneys involved in the lawsuit. This list can also function as a service list for pleadings. In addition to the names and addresses of the attorneys, the list should include the telephone numbers, fax numbers, and e-mail addresses of their law firms.

Updating this list is extremely important. Each time a pleading is received, you should check to determine that the attorney's name, firm, address, and client represented are correct on your list of parties and attorneys. If you do not take this simple precaution, you may mail a pleading to the wrong address or to an attorney who has withdrawn from a case. Such an error is not only embarrassing and costly, but also grounds for a potential malpractice action.

Pleadings, Motions, and Discovery Responses   In a simple case, a copy of all the pleadings, motions, and discovery responses would be filed in the trial notebook. However, in a complex case only pertinent pleadings, such as the complaint and the answer, would be placed in the notebook, because of space limitations.

Witnesses   This section should include a list of all witnesses, their telephone numbers, addresses, fax numbers, and e-mail addresses, and a copy of their trial subpoena, if one was issued. If possible, also include a summary of the factual areas that each witness is expected to cover in his testimony. Your attorney will also benefit from an outline of the questions that the witnesses will be asked at trial. Exhibit 15–2 is an example of a witness list that contains the type of information that will help you locate a witness rapidly, either before or during the trial.

Expert Witnesses   At the beginning of this section, place a list of all expert witnesses that each side intends to call at trial. As in the case of the factual witnesses, include their addresses, telephone numbers, fax numbers, and e-mail addresses. Copies of each expert's curriculum vitae should also be included. A **curriculum vitae** will list the expert's professional credentials. The list will include each witness's educational and professional credentials, as well as a summary of his publications and research projects. If the witness has written any reports regarding the present case, they should also be included in this section. You may also want to include a list of any other cases in which the expert has testified and a list of all documents or other materials that the expert has reviewed for the case. A major component of this section is the list of questions that each expert will be asked at trial.

curriculum vitae

A list of an expert's credentials, including each educational and professional credential, and a summary of publications and research projects.

Document Indexes   In a simple case, the trial notebook may contain all documents that are produced in the case. However, in the more complex cases, an index of all documents produced by each party should be sufficient. A comprehensive but clear *document index* will enable you to quickly yet unobtrusively locate a document during trial, when time and discretion are of the essence.

Deposition Summaries   A complex case may require a separate binder for the deposition summaries. You will recall from our discussion in Chapter 9 on depositions that a deposition summary is a written record that reduces many hours of testimony to a few concisely drawn, easily read, and quickly understood pages. The three types of deposition summaries are the page-line deposition summary, the topical deposition summary, and the chronological summary. The *page-line deposition summary* covers testimony as it occurred in the deposition itself. The *topical deposition summary* organizes the material into specific subject areas. Finally, the *chronological deposition summary* organizes the testimony according to a particular time sequence. A complex case involving numerous depositions would require an index of these summaries. The index

Name and Address	Tel#	Role	Subpoena Served/ Returned
Yuri Vilnius	542–4999	CEO of Sergi Selinkov, Inc. Finances and Organization of Sergi Selinkov	9/9/03 9/15/03
Maria Mendez	756–9989	Secretary at Billicheck-Kendall Witness to fire	9/15/03 9/17/03
Carl Loggia	756–9989	CPA at Billicheck-Kendall Finances of B-K	9/15/03 9/17/03
Lon Robertson	756–9989	Janitor at Sergi and Kolata Witness to fire	9/15/03 9/16/03
Julius Vilnius	756–9989	CEO of Billicheck-Kendall Organization Chart for B-K	9/15/03 9/25/03
Kay Vilnius	756–9989	Treasurer of Billicheck-Kendall Organization Chart for B-K Finances of B-K	9/15/03 9/25/03
Albert Vilnius	481–9997	CEO of Kolata Maintenance Organization Chart for Kolata Finances of Kolata Vice President of Billicheck-Kendall Organization Chart for B-K Finances of B-K	9/15/03 9/25/03
Vytautas Vilnius	481–9997	Treasurer Kolata Maintenance Organization Chart for Kolata Finances of Kolata Vice President of Billicheck-Kendall Organization Chart for B-K Finances of B-K	9/15/03 9/25/03
Rachel Friedman, M.D.	825–1409	Physician at Red Forest County Hospital	9/15/03 9/17/03
Jay Kellerman, M.D.	825–1409	Physician at Red Forest County Hospital	9/15/03 9/17/03
Abe Greenstein	825–3800	Professor Auburn University	9/16/03 9/18/03

EXHIBIT 15–2 Witness list

should be arranged in alphabetical order by the last name of each deponent. In simple cases involving only a few depositions, an index is not needed.

Chronology   Another important tool in the trial notebook is the *chronology*—the listing of what happened, when it happened, where it happened, and who was involved. A properly constructed chronology also includes source documents that indicate how each of these facts was learned. However, a chronology is more than a document index sorted by date. A chronology moves from the beginning of the case—the first client interview—and includes the most current information on the case up to the time of trial. Use database software, not word-processing software, to create your chronology. If your firm has a multi-user database, several trial team members can simultaneously enter, edit, or review the facts in the chronology. The most important benefit of a database-generated chronology is the ability to quickly make choices in what is to be printed from a voluminous chronology—perhaps facts dealing with a particular issue, witness, or timeframe. When reviewing documents, depositions, and so forth for preparation of a chronology, list facts, not documents. For each fact, begin by entering the information reflected in Exhibit 15–3. Include both prospective facts and disputed facts in your chronology. You may not have a document source at the time of the entry, but that can be added when a document is subsequently produced, or a deposition of a witness is taken. Certain facts in a chronology may not have an associated date. Use "N/A" in the date column. When the chronology is sorted, all facts for which a date is inappropriate will be sorted together.

Just as a good chronology is more than a document index, it is more than a diary of events in the case. The chronology is a knowledge base of facts. Some attorneys prefer to utilize a chronology rather than a deposition summary. Enter in the chronology the critical facts from each deposition and the source of the fact. The consistent entry of names, organizations, and document types is particularly important when developing the chronology. One solution to the possibility of inconsistent entry of data is to incorporate information from the cast of characters. In addition to some facts that have no associated date, many facts in your chronology may have an incomplete date. For example, the client has stated in his deposition that a meeting took place in March, 2003, or that the decision to sell the company was made in "the fall of 2003." The entry is critical, and should be entered into the computer as 03/00/03. Such an entry is a reminder that further research is needed to establish the exact date of the meeting. Each fact in the chronology should be flagged as being either disputed or undisputed. A separate column might be added to the chronology form to indicate the disputed status.

A chronology should include issues in addition to dates and facts. The majority of cases involve multiple and often complex issues. Develop a list of case issues and apply those issues to your chronology, perhaps through a column entitled "Related Issues." Creating a link between facts and issues in a chronology facilitates printing chronologies of facts relating only to a particular issue. From the issue list, develop the chronology to include facts currently known about an issue and a "wish list" of facts. This might include testimony that you "wish" you could obtain from a treating physician, accident witness, or other key players in a case. A chronology reflects important and trivial facts. An additional column in the chronology might be used to "rate" the significance of a fact to a case. As the trial approaches, you must review the chronology

DATE	EVENT	SOURCE	NOTES
4/25/02	Incorporation of Sergi Selinkov, Inc.	Secretary of State's Records/Delaware	Formed to provide security for B-K
4/26/02	Incorporation of Kolata Maintenance	Secretary of State's Records/Delaware	Formed to provide maintenance for B-K
4/29/02	Shareholders meetings for both Kolata and Sergi Selinkov canceled	Carl Loggia	Initial indication that the two new corporations will not become separate entities
5/5/02	Bank accounts opened for Kolata and Sergi Selinkov	Carl Loggia	Both accounts undercapitalized
2/7/03	Semi-annual safety inspection of B-K performed jointly by employees of Kolata and Sergi Selinkov	Kolata and Sergi Selinkov records Lon Robertson	Inspection not carried out properly indicates negligence
2/7/03	Repairs performed on heating unit in storeroom	Lon Robertson	Indicates that repairs were done negligently
2/28/03	Lermentov arrives at B-K for audit	Lermentov, et al.	Indicates lawful presence
3/4/03	Date of fire	Lermentov, et al.	Several people will testify as to the events surrounding the fire
3/4/03 to 5/11/03	Lermentov's hospital stay	Hospital records Several physicians	Extent of injuries must be explained

EXHIBIT 15–3 Chronology of the case

for completeness by checking key documents, pleadings, witness interviews, depositions, and exhibits to make certain that all dates have been taken from these sources and placed in the chronology.

The Cast of Characters The *cast of characters* is a roster of all key participants in the case. This list can be drawn from witness interviews, documents, depositions, exhibits, and pleadings. In a case with a crowded list of key persons, the cast of characters can provide valuable identification. As is true of the chronology, you must be careful to update the cast of characters as new information is received. The failure to include one name in the cast may be a critical omission that could cause serious problems at trial.

on point
A law or prior case that directly applies to the facts of the present case.

Legal Research This section of the trial notebook should contain copies of all cases that are on point with the legal issues involved in the present case. A case **on point** is one that has been decided in your jurisdiction and that involves both facts and legal principles that are so similar to the facts and principles in the present case that your attorney feels the court will be bound to follow the court's ruling in that earlier case. If the cases on point are numerous and lengthy, the paralegal should include a summary of each and a citation to the case and maintain the actual case in a separate, clearly marked binder.

Trial Exhibits   This section should include the list of plaintiff's and defendant's proposed trial exhibits, which are normally required in connection with the pretrial conference. In addition, the paralegal should place a copy of each exhibit that her attorney plans to introduce into the notebook. A form entitled "Trial Exhibits List" is included in this section of the trial notebook. As an exhibit is introduced, the paralegal notes on this form: the exhibit number; the party introducing the exhibit; the witness through whom the exhibit was introduced; whether there was any objection to the exhibit; and the court's ruling on the objection, either admitting or rejecting the exhibit. If an exhibit consists of an enlargement, photograph, or medical model, for example, a hard copy of the exhibit should be included in the notebook, or an entry should be made to indicate what the exhibit is, and its location.

Jury Profiles and Instructions   This section of the trial notebook consists of two parts. The first part is a jury profile. The *jury profile* gives a narrative description of the characteristics of the ideal jury that you would like to assemble in the case. For example, you might want the jury to include persons with a certain background or with a certain level of education. Exhibit 15–4 is a sample that you might use to develop a profile of your ideal juror.

The second part of this section is the jury instructions. **Jury instructions** explain the legal principles that the jury must apply to the facts in the case in reaching the verdict. Jury instructions also outline the procedures that the jury members must follow as they attempt to reach a verdict. Although these will change during the course of the trial, drafting a proposed set of jury instructions and placing them in the trial notebook will save a substantial amount of time during the trial. A disk containing the proposed set of jury instructions should be included with trial materials to enable changes while the trial is in process. The ultimate responsibility for giving the jury instructions lies with the judge. However, attorneys are permitted to suggest the substance of those instructions to the judge and may object when they feel the judge has not properly instructed the jury. Attorneys who fail to object to jury instructions cannot raise the inaccuracy of the instructions as an issue on appeal.

jury instructions
Directions given to the jury explaining the law that applies in the case and spelling out what must be proven and by whom. These instructions are given just before the jury is sent out to deliberate and return a verdict.

Trial Outline   A *trial outline* is a chronological listing of the tasks that must be performed just prior to and during the trial. Such a chronological outline is a vital part of the trial notebook, because it simplifies and organizes the tasks facing the paralegal and the attorney as the trial date approaches. For example, the paralegal may be asked to assist in drafting the questions to be used during voir dire. **Voir dire** is the process by which the jurors are questioned to determine any bias that they might have that would affect their ability to be fair and impartial in the case. The paralegal may also be asked to assist in drafting the opening statement, the questions to be used during the examination of friendly witnesses, the questions to be asked during the cross-examination of the opposing witnesses, and the closing argument. All of these tasks would be listed on the trial outline. Allow space on the trial outline for annotations and changes.

voir dire examination
The preliminary in-court questioning of a prospective witness (or juror) to determine competency (or suitability) to decide a case.

Case Name: _____

Case Number: _____

Juror Name: _____ Juror No. _____

Age: _____ Sex: _____ Marital Status: _____

Cultural Background: _____ Religion: _____

Nationality: _____

Education: _____ Economic Status: _____

Physical Appearance: _____ Dress: _____

Body Language/Facial Expressions: _____

Behavioral Information (drinking, law enforcement background, etc.):

_____

_____

_____

Personality Characteristics: _____

Prior Jury Experience: _____

Litigation (Plaintiff or Defendant): _____

_____

Other Information: _____

_____

_____

_____

_____

_____

_____

_____

_____

_____

_____

EXHIBIT 15–4 Juror profile

Attorney's Notes Blank pages should be inserted in this section of the trial notebook for the attorney's notes about witnesses, legal issues, or other general information to be used during the trial.

Things to Do List In addition to the trial preparation checklist, you will discover tasks that must be performed in the case. You should make notes of these items as they arise, then transfer them to the trial calendar specifically developed for the case.

Preparation of Witnesses

As a paralegal, you will be instrumental in preparing the witnesses for trial. One task that you may have to perform is arranging for the sending of subpoenas to certain witnesses. You may also be charged with communicating the details of the trial to the witnesses. Finally, you may be required to arrange and attend all witness preparation meetings.

Subpoena of Witnesses

You must consult with your attorney to determine if any witnesses will require a subpoena. In some instances, attorneys prefer to subpoena only witnesses who are not considered "friendly." However, a friendly witness may request a subpoena to present to an employer as evidence that she has been ordered to appear and testify.

Trial subpoenas require the same procedure as deposition subpoenas. You should review your state and local rules to determine if there are any unusual requirements for subpoenas. Generally, any person 18 years of age or older may serve subpoenas. In state courts, the sheriff, a sheriff's deputy, or a local constable may also perform this task.

In federal courts, the subpoena process is governed by Rule 45 of the Federal Rules of Civil Procedure. According to Rule 45, the clerk of court is responsible for issuing subpoenas. Exhibit 15–5 is an example of this type of subpoena.

In federal court under Rule 45, a federal marshal can serve a witness with a subpoena. However, the rule also states that any person who is 18 years of age or older can also serve a subpoena. A witness who has been subpoenaed and who has been requested to produce documents may object to the document request within 10 days of service. The objection must be in writing and must be served on the attorney who made the original document request.

A trial subpoena must be personally served on the witness. In addition, all mileage and witness fees required must be tendered to the witness. Finally, the return-of-service information on the subpoena must be completed and filed with the court for the subpoena to be considered valid. An important paralegal responsibility is checking for the filed return prior to the time the witness is to testify. Failure to do so may result in a "no-show" witness and a major hole in your trial schedule.

Communicating with Witnesses

The preparation of a witness for trial is much more involved and generally much more critical than the preparation of the witness for the deposition. For this reason it is usually advantageous for the paralegal to work with the witnesses in the case from the time of the initial interview. This early involvement will build a relationship that facilitates communication and helps put the witness at ease while working with the paralegal.

As the paralegal, you may be asked to communicate with witnesses early in the trial preparation period about the basic details of the trial, including the date, the location, and the anticipated length of the testimony. The witnesses should also be informed that they may have to meet with the attorney and the paralegal closer to the time of the

AO 89 (Rev. 5/85) Subpoena

United States District Court

DISTRICT OF _____

_____
V.

SUBPOENA

CASE NUMBER: _____

TYPE OF CASE		SUBPOENA FOR	
☐ CIVIL	☐ CRIMINAL	☐ PERSON	☐ DOCUMENT(S) or OBJECT(S)

TO:

YOU ARE HEREBY COMMANDED to appear in the United States District Court at the place, date, and time specified below to testify in the above case.

PLACE	COURTROOM
	DATE AND TIME

YOU ARE ALSO COMMANDED to bring with you the following document(s) or object(s): *

☐ *See additional information on reverse*

This subpoena shall remain in effect until you are granted leave to depart by the court or by an officer acting on behalf of the court.

U.S. MAGISTRATE OR CLERK OF COURT	DATE
(BY) DEPUTY CLERK	

This subpoena is issued upon application of the:

☐ Plaintiff ☐ Defendant ☐ U.S. Attorney

QUESTIONS MAY BE ADDRESSED TO:

ATTORNEY'S NAME, ADDRESS AND PHONE NUMBER

* If not applicable, enter "none".

EXHIBIT 15–5 Subpoena

AO 89 (Rev. 5/85) Subpoena

RETURN OF SERVICE(1)			
RECEIVED BY SERVER	DATE	PLACE	
SERVED	DATE	PLACE	

SERVED ON (NAME)	FEES AND MILEAGE TENDERED TO WITNESS(2)
	☐ YES ☐ NO AMOUNT $ _____

SERVED BY	TITLE

STATEMENT OF SERVICE FEES

TRAVEL	SERVICES	TOTAL

DECLARATION OF SERVER (2)

I declare under penalty of perjury under the laws of the United States of America that the foregoing information contained in the Return of Service and Statement of Service Fees is true and correct.

Executed on_____   _____
                 Date   *Signature of Server*

                                           _____
                                              Address of Server

ADDITIONAL INFORMATION

(1) As to who may serve a subpoena and the manner of its service see Rule 17(d), Federal Rules of Criminal Procedure, or Rule 45(c), Federal Rules of Civil Procedure.

(2) "Fees and mileage need not be tendered to the deponent upon service of a subpoena issued on behalf of the United States or an officer or agency thereof (Rule 45(c), Federal Rules of Civil Procedure; Rule 17(d), Federal Rules of Criminal Procedure) or on behalf of certain indigent parties and criminal defendants who are unable to pay such costs (28 USC 1825, Rule 17(b) Federal Rules of Criminal Procedure)".

EXHIBIT 15–5   *(continued)*

trial. Remind the witnesses to review their depositions and/or affidavit at least once before the meeting.

Exhibit 15–6 is an example of a letter that transmits to a witness basic information about the trial and his role in the case. By signing the letter and agreeing to remain in touch with you for availability at trial, the witness may feel committed to whatever length of time is required for his testimony.

It is essential that the paralegal be able to reach witnesses to advise them of changes in the trial schedule. The trial notebook should contain the address, telephone number, and email address of each witness. Also, the client and all the witnesses should be given a designated contact person at the law firm. Each morning and afternoon during the trial, the client and the witnesses should check with this person to make certain that there have been no changes in the schedule and order of witnesses.

POPSON, PIERCE, RUEBER, AND BURKE
5293 St. Clair Avenue
Red Forest, Alabama 36107
January 3, 2004

Mr. Carl Loggia
Certified Public Accountant
4226 Superior Avenue
Red Forest, Alabama 36107

RE: *Lermentov v. Billicheck-Kendall Pharmaceuticals, Inc.*

Dear Mr. Loggia:

The trial in the above-captioned case has been scheduled for January 19, 2004, at the Red Forest County Court House, in Courtroom Number 1, 96 Public Square, Red Forest, Alabama.

We would appreciate your keeping us informed of your location at all times because there may be a change in the trial starting date. If for any reason you will be unable to attend to testify during the period of January 19 to February 7, please let us know immediately.

By signing a copy of this letter at the space indicated below, you agree to comply with the terms of this letter.

Sincerely,

_____

Laura Burke
Attorney-at-Law

ACCEPTED AND AGREED TO
THIS _____ DAY OF _____, 20 _____:

_____

EXHIBIT 15–6   Letter to witness regarding trial

Witness Preparation Meeting

Shortly before trial, you should arrange a meeting between each witness and your attorney. Before the meeting, you may be asked to collect all documents that refer to the witness. You should review the witness's deposition and note any areas that gave the witness difficulty or that may require further clarification. You may be asked to assist the attorney with the preparation of or to prepare an outline or actual questions that your attorney anticipates asking each witness during the trial. Make sure that you also correlate the necessary trial exhibits with that outline. During the witness preparation meeting, your attorney will explain the trial process to each witness. She will also explain what is expected from each witness. Many attorneys conduct mock questioning sessions so that the witnesses will know exactly what questions will be asked during direct examination. Your attorney may request that you videotape this mock questioning session for evaluation of the witness's appearance and testimony prior to trial.

Preparation of Exhibits and Briefs

Often the paralegal is called upon to gather and organize the exhibits in a case. This responsibility may require obtaining enlarged exhibits or unusual graphics. The paralegal may also have to set up a chronology or organize a set of statistics. Whatever the case, it helps to know what to look for in the evaluation of those exhibits. It is also possible that the paralegal may be called upon to help conduct research for the trial brief.

Preparing Trial Exhibits

Many of the deposition exhibits will be used at trial. In some jurisdictions, court rules require that the parties exchange lists of all the trial exhibits before the trial. Once you have established the documents or the materials that your attorney will introduce at trial, you may begin to prepare a trial exhibit log that will trace the trial exhibit's progress throughout the trial. You will need this whether you are working with enlarged exhibits, unusual graphics, or a chronology of the case. It is also important for the paralegal to know how to determine the effectiveness of a document that may be used as a trial exhibit.

Enlarged Exhibits and Unusual Graphics   It may be necessary for you to obtain enlarged exhibits or unusual graphics. For example, in the *Lermentov* case, your attorney may request that you have Mr. Lermentov's X rays enlarged for the jurors to view during his testimony. In addition, many litigation support services offer models of various parts of the human anatomy, created to show the effects of certain types of injuries to various parts of the body. You should also obtain printed copies of any charts or diagrams that will be used as exhibits. For instance, if you use a large chart to portray the extent of Mr. Lermentov's medical expenses in this case, you should prepare a printed copy for the jury to take into the jury room when deliberations begin. Photographs should also be reproduced by a photocopy machine. All of these exhibits must be secured several weeks in advance of the trial. Once your attorney has selected the exhibits that she plans to use, you should immediately locate companies that can produce effective trial exhibits.

Preparing a Chronology of the Case   A chronology of the case, especially in a tort suit like the *Lermentov* case, is an effective trial exhibit. You should review the litigation files and documents and construct the critical events in the case. The chronology should include the date of the accident, the days that Mr. Lermentov was unable to work, the dates of all doctor visits and periods of hospitalization, the dates of all physical therapy treatments, and the date that he finally returned to work. A color-coded, large trial board may be an effective way to present the chronology of the *Lermentov* case. Removable color magnets might also be utilized with this type of trial exhibit to focus on a particular type or length of treatment. Jurors can more easily assimilate a large amount of data if it is presented in an enlarged, color-coded, well-organized exhibit.

Evaluating Documents as Trial Exhibits   In most lawsuits the discovery process produces a mountain of documents. Not all of these documents, however, make effective trial exhibits. Consequently, it is crucial that the paralegal ask the following questions to evaluate how effective a document will be as a trial exhibit:

1. Is the document relevant?
2. Is the document admissible?
3. Is the document necessary?
4. Does the document support the cause of action?
5. Is the document confusing?
6. Does the document contain repetitive information?
7. Will the document detract from the witness's testimony?
8. Does the document increase the effectiveness of the witness's testimony?
9. Is the document easy to read from the jury box and counsel table?
10. Is the document accurate?
11. Does the document have an attractive appearance?
12. Is the document clear?
13. Can a clear and readable copy of the document be made?
14. Can the procedural foundation be laid for introduction of the document at trial?

If the document meets these tests, it is marked as a trial exhibit and entered on the trial exhibit log. You should also make copies of the exhibit and place those copies in manila folders. Label the files by trial exhibit number and by the name of the witness through whom the exhibit will be produced. Make copies of each exhibit for all of the attorneys, a copy for the judge, a copy for the trial notebook, and at least two extra copies.

Researching for the Trial Brief

If your jurisdiction requires the filing of a trial brief, you may be asked to assist with its preparation. A **trial brief** explains the legal issues involved in the case and the law that demonstrates the validity of the position your attorney has taken in relation to

trial brief
A document prepared by a lawyer to use at trial. It usually contains lists of witnesses, evidence, and citations as well as arguments to be presented.

those issues. The purpose of the trial brief is to inform the trial judge of the legal arguments your attorney intends to make at trial. Exhibit 15–7 is an example of a trial brief.

Your role in preparation of the trial brief may consist of legal and factual research. For example, your attorney may request that you locate specific testimony from a particular witness's deposition. You may also be asked to determine the validity of the cases cited in the brief. This task is known as a **cite check.**

The paralegal is often responsible for coordinating the preparation and filing of the brief with the court. You should be familiar with your local court rules pertaining to the form of the brief, the number of copies needed, and the time for filing.

cite check

Looking at all the citations in a document to verify accuracy and proper form.

COUNTY COURT
RED FOREST COUNTY
STATE OF ALABAMA

MIKHAIL LERMENTOV	)	Civil Action
Plaintiff,	)	No. 03-71891
	)	
vs.	)	PLAINTIFF'S
	)	TRIAL BRIEF
BILLICHECK-KENDALL	)	
PHARMACEUTICALS, INC.	)	
Defendant,	)	
	)	
et al.	)	

BACKGROUND

    This is a personal injury action arising out of a fire that occurred on March 4, 2003, at the headquarters of Defendant Billicheck-Kendall Pharmaceuticals, Inc., in Red Forest, Alabama. The fire started in a storeroom when a portable heating unit that had been recently repaired by Lon Robertson, an employee of Defendant Kolata Maintenance Corporation, ignited. The fire rapidly spread to combustible chemicals that were left in the storeroom, causing a dangerous flame to envelop the fourth-floor offices. A safety inspection, conducted jointly on 2/7/03 by employees of Defendant Kolata Maintenance Corporation and Defendant Sergi Selinkov Security, Incorporated, failed to note the accumulation of dangerous, highly combustible chemicals in the storeroom.

    Plaintiff Mikhail Lermentov, a certified public accountant, hired as an independent contractor by Defendant Billicheck-Kendall Pharmaceuticals, Inc., was conducting an annual financial audit in an office adjacent to the storeroom at the time of the occurrence and was severely injured. Plaintiff sustained third-degree burns over his chest, hands, forearms, and legs, necessitating two full months of hospitalization and treatments.

Normally an employee cannot sue his or her employer.

An independent contractor has a different relationship with its employer and may bring a legal claim.

EXHIBIT 15–7 Trial brief

Plaintiff demonstrates reasons to the court for holding parent coporation liable.

The subsidiary corporations are virtually assetless, making any judgment against them worthless.

Defendant tries to escape blame by looking to other defendants.

"Piercing the corporate veil" is a term used when the court is willing to look beyond the name of a corporation to assess damages and liability against the individual directors and officers, or to treat one corporation as one and the same as another corporation, such as when a parent/subsidiary relationship exists, and one corporation serves as a mere agent for the other corporation.

Plaintiff could also have brought a claim against the individual officers and directors of defendant Billicheck-Kendall Pharmaceuticals, Inc. under the theory of piercing the coporate veil.

LIABILITY OF DEFENDANTS

Plaintiff contends that both Defendant Kolata Maintenance Corporation and Defendant Sergi Selinkov Security, Incorporated are subsidiaries that were formed, financed, and operated solely for the benefit of the parent corporation, Defendant Billicheck-Kendall Pharmaceuticals, Inc. Defendant Kolata Maintenance Corporation was incorporated and provides maintenance and janitorial services strictly for the parent corporation. Likewise, Defendant Sergi Selinkov Security, Incorporated, was created solely to provide security and protection services for the parent corporation and does no work for any other entity. Both subsidiaries were formed in a feeble attempt to shield the parent corporation from legal liability as a result of claims arising from the performance of faulty or negligent repair work and security services, as in the instant case.

The Defendant Billicheck-Kendall Pharmaceuticals, Inc. maintains that the inspection and repair work were carried out by employees of the security firm of Sergi Selinkov Security, Incorporated and the maintenance firm of Kolata Maintenance Corporation, who were hired as independent contractors, thereby exonerating Defendant Billicheck-Kendall Pharmaceuticals, Inc. from any and all liability. Plaintiff denies this claim and will prove at the time of trial that both subsidiaries acted as mere empty shells and that they are corporations in name only, entitling Plaintiff to "pierce the corporate veil" and hold Defendant Billicheck-Kendall Pharmaceuticals, Inc. completely responsible for Plaintiff's injuries.

The injuries sustained by Plaintiff on the morning of March 4, 2003, were the direct result of the fire that broke out at the corporate headquarters of Defendant Billicheck-Kendall Pharmaceuticals, Inc. Said fire was caused by the negligence and carelessness of the Defendants Billicheck-Kendall Pharmaceuticals, Inc., Sergi Selinkov Security, Incorporated, and Kolata Maintenance Corporation, and their agents, servants, and/or employees. Defendant Billicheck-Kendall Pharmaceuticals, Inc. knew or should have known of the dangerous and defective conditions existing on its premises and warned the Plaintiff. Defendant Billicheck-Kendall Pharmaceuticals, Inc. was further negligent in that Defendant, its agents, servants, and/or employees failed to perform or negligently and carelessly performed safety inspections of the premises, and failed to detect or correct safety hazards that might endanger persons lawfully on the premises. In addition, Defendant, its agents, servants, and/or employees failed to repair or negligently and carelessly repaired the defective heating unit, creating a dangerous and hazardous condition that seriously and permanently injured and damaged the Plaintiff.

As the evidence clearly shows, neither Sergi Selinkov Security, Incorporated nor Kolata Maintenance Corporation was an independent corporation. At all times from the date of their incorporation to the date

EXHIBIT 15–7 *(continued)*

of the fire that severely injured Plaintiff, both corporations were acting as a part of the overall operation of Billicheck-Kendall Pharmaceuticals, Inc. In fact, the sole purpose for incorporating the two entities was to protect the parent corporation from liability in two areas, maintenance and security. In the interests of justice, the court must pierce the corporate veil and reach Billicheck-Kendall Pharmaceuticals, Inc. as the parent corporation of both Sergi Selinkov Security, Incorporated and Kolata Maintenance Corporation.

In the alternative, counsel for Plaintiff will demonstrate that, even if the corporate veil is not pierced and the court concludes that both subsidiaries are independent contractors, Billicheck-Kendall Pharmaceuticals, Inc. should still be held liable for the injuries suffered by Plaintiff. The duty of a landowner to maintain his or her property in a reasonably safe condition, the duty of proprietors to protect third parties from injury caused by inherently dangerous activities or conditions, and the duty of employers and suppliers to comply with all safety provisions of the Labor Code are all nondelegable duties.

When Billicheck-Kendall Pharmaceuticals, Inc. gave the maintenance and security responsibilities to its subsidiaries, it was attempting to sidestep these duties. The law in this state is quite clear on this matter. Such duties cannot be delegated. Therefore, despite the independent contractor status of Sergi Selinkov Security, Incorporated and Kolata Maintenance Corporation, Billicheck-Kendall Pharmaceuticals, Inc. is still liable.

The facts will reveal at the time of trial that both Defendant Sergi Selinkov Security, Incorporated and Defendant Kolata Maintenance Corporation are "alter egos" of Defendant Billicheck-Kendall Pharmaceuticals, Inc. In support, Plaintiff will offer the following:

If the court applies the law to the facts of the case and draws a different conclusion, plaintiff is offering alternate theories of law for recovery.

a. The parent corporation incorporated both subsidiaries, neither of which has assets of its own.

b. The parent corporation shares common directors and officers with its subsidiaries.

c. The parent corporation, Defendant Billicheck-Kendall Pharmaceuticals, Inc., owns all stock and finances of both of its subsidiaries, which are grossly undercapitalized.

d. Neither subsidiary does business with any entity other than the parent corporation.

e. The directors and officers of both subsidiaries take all orders from the parent corporation and do not act in their corporations' own self-interests, nor do they follow any of the legal requirements for a corporation.

EXHIBIT 15–7   *(continued)*

PLAINTIFF'S WITNESSES	
WITNESSES	**TESTIMONY**
(not in order of appearance):	
a. Carl Loggia (CPA), former employee of Billicheck-Kendall Pharmaceuticals, Inc.	Neither Sergi Selinkov Security, Incorporated nor Kolata Maintenance Corporation were ever intended to be anything other than a front for Billicheck-Kendall Pharmaceuticals, Inc. in the event of a lawsuit against Billicheck-Kendall Pharmaceuticals, Inc. for any injuries occurring at Billicheck-Kendall Pharmaceuticals, Inc.
b. Maria Mendez, secretary, employee of Billicheck-Kendall Pharmaceuticals, Inc.	Neither Sergi Selinkov Security, Incorporated nor Kolata Maintenance Corporation were ever intended to be anything other than a front for Billicheck-Kendall Pharmaceuticals, Inc.
c. Lon Robertson, employee of Sergi Selinkov Security, Incorporated and Kolata Maintenance Corporation	Safety and security inspection procedures used by Sergi Selinkov Security, Incorporated and Kolata Maintenance Corporation; will also testify about the repairs.
d. Rachel Friedman, M.D., physician at County Hospital	Extent of Mr. Lermentov's injuries.
e. Jay Kellerman, M.D., physician at County Hospital	Extent of Mr. Lermentov's injuries.
f. Yuri Vilnius, CEO of Sergi Selinkov Security, Incorporated	Sergi Selinkov Security, Incorporated has always been treated as an extension of Billicheck-Kendall Pharmaceuticals, Inc.
g. Julius Vilnius, CEO of Billicheck-Kendall Pharmaceuticals, Inc.	Organization and operation of Billicheck-Kendall Pharmaceuticals, Inc.
h. Kay Vilnius, Treasurer of Billicheck-Kendall Pharmaceuticals, Inc.	Financial structure of Billicheck-Kendall Pharmaceuticals, Inc., Sergi Selinkov Security, Incorporated, and Kolata Maintenance Corporation.

EXHIBIT 15–7   *(continued)*

i. Albert Vilnius, CEO of Kolata Maintenance Corporation, Vice-President of Billicheck-Kendall Pharmaceuticals, Inc.

Relationship between Billicheck-Kendall Pharmaceuticals, Inc. and Kolata Maintenance Corporation.

j. Vytautas Vilnius, Treasurer of Kolata Maintenance Corporation, Vice-President of Billicheck-Kendall Pharmaceuticals, Inc.

Relationship between Billicheck-Kendall Pharmaceuticals, Inc. and Kolata Maintenance Corporation.

k. Abe Greenstein, Professor at Auburn University

Lost wages and reduction in future earnings potential.

PLAINTIFF'S DAMAGES

The devastating effects of the fire upon Plaintiff is readily apparent. Mikhail Lermentov, who was 35 years old at the time of the occurrence, suffered third-degree burns over 30% of his body. Tragically, his arms were most damaged and will probably always be disabled. Plaintiff had numerous painful operations and procedures during his initial two-month hospitalization and will require many such operations and procedures in the future. Plaintiff's arms are covered with motion-restricting scars. Plaintiff will always suffer from limitation of motion, altered sensation, itching, and skin sensitivity. It is hoped that with continued physical therapy, Plaintiff will be able to resume working in some capacity.

The injured Plaintiff sustained the following:

Hospitalizations

County Hospital	3/4/03–5/11/03
County Hospital	5/30/03–6/2/03
County Hospital	6/15/03
County Hospital	10/4/03–10/6/03

Medical Expenses

County Hospital	$281,112
County Hospital	$3,402
County Hospital	$800
County Hospital	$1,654
Prescriptions	$3,488
Dr. Friedman	$35,000
Dr. Kellerman	$20,008
County Radiologists	$4,213
Physical Therapy Associates	$6,000

EXHIBIT 15–7   *(continued)*

APPLICABLE LAW

The line of cases supporting Plaintiff's claim for piercing the corporate veil is as follows:

Kwick Set Components, Inc. v. Davidson Industries, Inc., 411 So. 2d 134 (Ala. 1982). In this case the Supreme Court of Alabama court pierced the corporate veil of Capital Components, Inc., a wholly owned subsidiary of Kwick Set Components, Inc. Davidson Industries, Inc. had sold goods to Capital Components, Inc., which then delivered them to Kwick Set Components, Inc. Kwick Set Components, Inc. used the goods. Kwick Set Components, Inc. never paid Capital Components, Inc., and Capital Components, Inc. never paid Davidson Industries, Inc. Subsequently, Capital Components, Inc. went out of business. When Davidson Industries, Inc. found out that Capital Components, Inc. had been a subsidiary of Kwick Set Components, Inc. and that all the goods sold to Capital Components, Inc. had gone directly to Kwick Set Components, Inc. without payment, Davidson Industries, Inc. asked the court to pierce the corporate veil and hold Kwick Set Components, Inc. liable. The court agreed for three reasons. First, Kwick Set Components, Inc. and Capital Components, Inc. had the same president and the same directors. Second, all goods used by Kwick Set Components, Inc. were purchased through Capital Components, Inc. Third, the entire purpose of Capital Components, Inc. had been to postpone or totally avoid payment for goods purchased through Capital Components, Inc. This demonstrates that Capital Components, Inc. had no corporate identity separate from Kwick Set Components, Inc. In conclusion, the court quoted an earlier case, *Forest Hill Corp. v. Latter & Blum Inc.,* 29 So. 2d 298 (Ala. 1947), in which the Supreme Court of Alabama said "the courts will not allow the corporate entity to successfully masquerade through its officers, stockholders, representatives, or associates so as to defeat the payment of its just obligations." *Id.* at 302.

Matrix-Churchill v. Springsteen, 461 So. 2d 782 (Ala. 1984). In this case the court restated and approved the standard it had established in the *Kwick Set* case.

Messick v. Moring, 514 So. 2d 892 (Ala. 1987). In this case the Supreme Court of Alabama outlined three elements that must be present in order to pierce the corporate veil. These elements are:

1. The dominant party must have complete control and domination of the subservient corporation's finances, policy, and business practices so that at the time of the attacked transaction, the subservient corporation had no separate mind, will, or existence of its own.

2. The control must have been misused by the dominant party. Although fraud or the violation of a statutory or other positive legal duty is misuse of control, when it is necessary to prevent injustice or inequitable circumstances, misuse of control will be presumed.

3. The misuse of control must proximately cause the harm complained of. *Id.* at 895.

EXHIBIT 15–7 *(continued)*

Simmins v. Clark Equipment Corp., 554 So. 2d 398 (Ala. 1989). In this case the Supreme Court of Alabama approved of the factors and elements presented in the *Messick* case.

Cohen v. Williams, 318 So. 2d 279 (Ala. 1975). In this case the court held that the plaintiff need not prove that the defendant corporation engaged in fraud to convince the court to pierce the corporate veil. Rather, the court concluded that the court can pierce the corporate veil if it is convinced that upholding the separateness of the entities will cause an injustice. The court stated, "actual fraud is not necessarily a predicate for discarding the theory of separate corporate existence. It may also be discarded to prevent injustice or inequitable consequences." *Id.* at 281.

Woods v. Commercial Contractors, Inc., 384 So. 2d 1076 (Ala. 1980). In this case the court reaffirmed its position in *Cohen v. Williams,* stating that "the theory of corporate existence can properly be discarded, even in the absence of fraud, to prevent injustice or inequitable consequences." *Woods,* 384 So. 2d at 1079.

Barrett v. Odum, May & DeBuys, 453 So. 2d 729 (Ala. 1984). In this case the Supreme Court of Alabama reaffirmed the principle that corporate existence can be disregarded to prevent injustice even in the absence of fraud.

Deupree v. Ruffino, 505 So. 2d 1218 (Ala. 1987). In this case the Supreme Court of Alabama again reasserted that fraud is not a necessary element in a case involving an attempt to pierce the corporate veil.

United Steelworkers v. Connors Steel, 847 F.2d 707 (11th Cir. 1988). In this case the United States Court of Appeals for the Eleventh Circuit, in interpreting Alabama law, upheld the position that the corporate veil can be pierced to prevent inequity even without a showing of fraud.

In support of the doctrine of nondelegable duties are the following:

Dixie Stage Lines v. Anderson, 134 So. 23 (Ala. 1981). In this case the Supreme Court of Alabama set down the nondelegable duty exception to the rule that the proprietor is not liable for the negligent acts of an independent contractor. The court said, "a person is responsible for the manner of the performance of his nondelegable duties, though done by an independent contractor, and therefore, that one who by his contract or by law is due certain obligations to another cannot divest himself of liability for a negligent performance by reason of the employment of such contractor." *Id.* at 24.

Arlington Realty v. Lawson, 153 So. 425 (Ala. 1934). In this case the court states that landlords have a nondelegable duty to see that proper care is used in making repairs to their property.

Alabama Power Co. v. Pierre, 183 So. 665 (Ala. 1938). This case reiterates and approves the nondelegable duty exception laid down by the Supreme Court of Alabama in the *Dixie Stage Lines* case.

Knight v. Burns, Kirkley & Williams Construction Co., 331 So. 2d 651 (Ala. 1976), In this case the Supreme Court of Alabama cites with approval the nondelegable duty exception established in the *Dixie Stage Lines* case.

EXHIBIT 15–7   *(continued)*

General Finance Corp. v. Smith, 505 So. 2d 1045 (Ala. 1987). In this case the court again upholds the nondelegable duty exception.

Boroughs v. Joiner, 337 So. 2d 340 (Ala. 1976), In this case the Supreme Court of Alabama specifically identifies the performance of inherently dangerous activities, such as the storing of combustible materials, as a nondelegable duty. In doing so the court quotes with favor the *Restatement (Second) of Torts* § 427 (1965), which states, "One who employs an independent contractor to do work involving a special danger to others which the employer knows or has reason to know to be inherent in or normal to the work, or which he contemplates or has reason to contemplate when making the contract, is subject to liability or physical harm caused to such others by the contractor's failure to take reasonable precautions against such danger." *Id.* at 342.

Laura Burke, Trial Attorney
Attorney for the Plaintiff
Popson, Pierce, Rueber, and Burke
Attorneys at Law
5293 St. Clair Avenue
Red Forest, Alabama 36107
(205) 725-8788
[facsimile number]

EXHIBIT 15–7 *(continued)*

Coordinating Trial Logistics

The paralegal is often responsible for coordinating the logistics of a trial. If the trial is held at the local court where your attorney usually works, coordinating the logistics will be a routine matter. However, when the trial is held in another district or another county, or when your client and many of the witnesses are from out of town, you will have to arrange for accommodations. Also, for both local and out-of-town trials you will have to examine the courthouse and contact local court personnel.

Arranging for Accommodations

When the trial is to be held in another district or county, or when your client and several of the witnesses are from out of town, you as the paralegal may be responsible for travel, hotel, and food arrangements. Often a suite of offices in a hotel near the courthouse is set up as a *war room*. The war room is an area containing additional trial documents and supplies. It also doubles as a conference room where the legal team, the client, and the witnesses may gather during trial recesses or at the end of the trial day to regroup and prepare for the next day of the trial.

You should locate hotels near the courthouse and determine if your firm has a corporate account with any of them. An actual review of the available hotel accommodations is necessary to ensure that the site contains the space and set-up required for your particular trial needs. Once the hotel has been selected and the necessary rooms reserved, make any travel arrangements that may be required for the client and out-of-town witnesses. Make certain to confirm the travel arrangements in writing. Write to the client and the witnesses informing them of the location of the hotel and the details of the travel plans. Remember to enclose the airline tickets, along with a map of the area around the courthouse and the hotel.

Once the trial is under way, the paralegal may be called upon to arrange for catered meals in the war room to avoid crowded, noisy restaurants around the courthouse. This arrangement also prevents the awkwardness of being seated in a restaurant next to the opposing counsel or several of the jurors. However, often these arrangements should be delegated to another member of the legal team. This delegation may be especially important at the relatively short lunch breaks that occur during the trial, because often the paralegal will be needed elsewhere. For example, the paralegal may have to use this valuable break time to locate a witness, secure another copy of an exhibit, or locate a case for inclusion in the trial brief.

Visiting the Courthouse

If the trial is to be held in another district or another county, or if you have never been to the courthouse where an upcoming trial is scheduled, you should visit that courthouse several weeks before the trial is to be held. Determine the location of telephones, photocopy machines, fax machines, restrooms, and vending machines. You may also need to locate a work area for meeting with the client or witnesses during the trial.

In many courthouses, all of the courtrooms are identical. Often, however, a courthouse will have several courtrooms, each of which is configured differently. Therefore, if possible, you should try to locate and examine the exact courtroom where the trial will be held. Determine the amount of space available for exhibits, briefcases, and supplies. Also check for the location of easels, charts, chalkboards, overhead projectors, slide projectors, video equipment, and audio equipment. This check is critical because you will have to bring any equipment that your attorney will need that is not provided by the court. Look around and note whether the courtroom is equipped with enough electrical outlets for the operation of a VCR or a laptop computer. If you think that the number or location of these outlets is inadequate for your needs, you will have to arrange for adapters or extension cords.

A *trial box,* consisting of all supplies needed during the trial, should be put together after the visit to the courthouse. Any special items noted during the courthouse tour should be included in the trial box. Exhibit 15–8 indicates items that you may want to consider placing in your trial box.

Contacting Court Personnel

The paralegal should also schedule a meeting with the court clerk and the court reporter before the trial. Determine if the courtroom will be available the evening before or early the morning of the trial for the delivery of exhibits and documents.

❏	Court rules (federal or state and local rules)	❏	Exhibit stickers
❏	Manila folders	❏	Roll of quarters (for copier, vending machines, etc.)
❏	Pencils		
❏	Pens	❏	Copy card (for law library or clerk's office copy machine)
❏	Stapler		
❏	Staple puller	❏	Bus pass
❏	Staples	❏	Aspirin
❏	Rubber bands	❏	Cough drops
❏	Paper clips	❏	Antacid
❏	Binder clips	❏	Kleenex
❏	Post-It notes	❏	Extension cord
❏	File labels	❏	Tape recorder
❏	Hole punch	❏	Blank tapes
❏	Yellow pads	❏	Batteries for tape recorder

EXHIBIT 15–8 Contents of a trial box

You may also need to arrange for security clearance and access to the courthouse elevators and the loading dock after hours. The paralegal should also ask the clerk whether trial exhibits and other trial material can be left in the courtroom throughout the trial, or if arrangements must be made to remove those items at the end of each trial day.

During the trial, the court clerk will receive many calls and inquiries concerning the case. If the paralegal furnishes the clerk with a list of the law firm personnel who will be present in the courtroom, the possibility of missing an important telephone call is diminished. The court reporter will make a transcript of the trial proceeding. You should meet with the court reporter prior to the trial and give him your business card just in case there are any problems in the transcription of trial testimony.

Preliminary Steps in the Trial Process

The *Lermentov* case, which served as the commentary case opening this chapter, has not settled, despite lengthy settlement discussions and mediation efforts. Consequently, the time for the trial has arrived.

Although most cases are settled or dismissed before reaching the trial stage, you must proceed on the assumption that eventually the case will reach trial. This means making a preliminary determination of whether a jury trial or a trial by a judge alone will be in the best interests of your client. If you are going to face a jury, one of the first steps in the trial will be to select the jurors. This selection process must be carried on with great care because the jurors play a key role in the success or failure of your case.

Decisions Regarding Jury Trials

The Seventh Amendment to the United States Constitution guarantees the right to a trial by jury in certain types of civil cases. The amendment states, "In Suits at common law, where the value in controversy shall exceed twenty dollars, the right of trial by jury shall be preserved, and no fact tried by a jury, shall be otherwise re-examined in any Court of the United States, than according to the rules of common law." The amendment clearly preserves the right to a jury trial in cases involving common law for those litigants who wish to take advantage of that right. It does not, however, give the litigants a right to a jury trial in cases tried in equity. This is why, for instance, jury trials are not allowed in divorce proceedings, in disputes involving custody rights, or in other equitable cases.

Factors in Choosing a Judge or a Jury Trial   Several factors should be considered by your attorney as she attempts to decide whether it would be in the best interests of the client to try the case before a judge or before a jury. The first factor to consider is the complexity of the case. If the case involves legal issues and concepts that may be difficult for the lay person to grasp, your attorney may prefer to present the case before a judge. The same might be true if the facts in the case are extremely complicated. Another factor to consider is available time. In general, the attorney can be relatively certain that a trial before a judge will take less time than a jury trial. This is because in a trial before a judge there is no need to select the members of the jury and no need to explain the law or the legal process to the judge—he will already be well versed in both.

Another factor to consider is the condition of the client. If the case is a personal injury case involving a client who has been disfigured or otherwise permanently disabled, the attorney representing the plaintiff would probably want to ask for a jury trial. In the *Lermentov* case, for example, your attorney would most likely decide to demand a trial by jury. Because the plaintiff has been badly burned through absolutely no fault of his own, your attorney would want to rely on eliciting the sympathy of the jury. In contrast, attorneys who represent large, impersonal corporate defendants, like Billicheck-Kendall in the commentary, might prefer to have a judge decide the case. Naturally, any party requesting a jury trial will have that request honored, because, as noted earlier, trial by jury is a constitutional right.

Even the location of the trial can be a factor in the decision to demand a jury trial. If your client is a local community member, and the opposition is someone from out of town, your attorney may elect to demand a jury trial. In the *Lermentov* case, for example, the plaintiff is a locally prominent CPA who was born and raised in the town of Red Forest, Alabama, whereas the defendant is a large corporation that was formed in Delaware. This would seem to indicate that your attorney would prefer a jury trial. However, she might also consider the fact that Billicheck-Kendall is the largest employer in town and is therefore an integral part of the local economy. Knowledge of the importance of Billicheck-Kendall to the economic health of Red Forest might cause her to reconsider the advisability of demanding a jury trial.

Requesting a Jury Trial   The fact that the Constitution guarantees the right to a jury trial does not prevent the courts from making the request for such a trial the responsibility of the litigants. For example, Rule 38(b) of the Federal Rules of Civil Procedure requires the litigants to demand a trial by jury. Such a demand must be made in writing at any time after the lawsuit has begun, but not later than 10 days after the last pleading in the case has been filed. If such a demand is not made by either party, the right has been voluntarily surrendered by the parties. This means that the trial will be conducted before a judge. In such a trial the judge acts as both the finder of fact and the determiner of law. In a jury trial the jury plays the role of factfinder.

The Jury Process

In the past, planning for, conducting, and winning a case before a jury were largely matters of chance. Today, however, attorneys have a wide variety of tools at their disposal to help them maximize the effectiveness of a jury trial. These techniques include the juror profile, the mock jury trial, and the shadow jury.

Preparing a Juror Profile

The purpose of the juror profile is to determine a composite profile of the ideal jurors for a particular case. Social psychologists and litigation specialists are equipped to provide law firms with valuable statistics and jury sampling information. These statistics and information are designed to create not only the image of the preferred jurors but also a profile of the jurors that your attorney will want to avoid. For example, in the *Lermentov* case the litigation specialist may conclude that well-educated, white-collar workers will be more sympathetic to your client. One reason for this may be that your client is a well-educated, white-collar professional. Another reason may be that well-educated jurors tend to be skeptical of the motives of large corporations like the defendants in this case. The social psychologists and litigation specialists may also indicate that lower-income, less-educated jurors may be swayed by the presence of the corporate defendants. Your attorney would therefore try to steer away from including such people on the jury as often as possible. It is also important to remember that the cost of this service may be prohibitive for smaller cases. If the expense results in a favorable decision or reduces the judgment against a client, though, the cost will certainly be justified.

Holding a Mock Jury Trial

Complex cases often require a jury trial of several months. To help facilitate a favorable jury decision, many firms stage a mock trial prior to the date of the actual trial. A **mock trial** is a practice trial. Again, social psychologists and litigation specialists can be retained to arrange the mock trial. Legal directories, litigation journals or newspapers, and Internet Web sites are excellent sources for locating companies that specialize in conducting mock trials.

The paralegal is often responsible for arranging the mock trial. The first step in the mock trial is to select the mock jury. A **mock jury** is a group of independent individuals chosen to reflect the probable makeup of the actual jury. Again, social psychologists and litigation specialists can interview and hire the persons to make up the mock jury. Once the mock jury panel is selected, your firm presents the mock trial. Key witnesses and principal exhibits are presented to the jury in the same way that they will be pre-

mock trial
A practice trial prior to the date of the actual trial, intended to reveal the strengths and weaknesses of a party's case.

mock jury
A group of independent individuals chosen to reflect the probable makeup of the actual jury.

sented at the actual trial. Part of your legal team also presents the case that you envision being presented by the opposition. For best results, the jurors should not know which side your law firm represents. This will ensure an impartial evaluation. The mock jury evaluates the testimony and exhibits and renders the verdict.

Following their decision, the jurors may be questioned about their perceptions of the strengths and weaknesses of the case. For example, in the *Lermentov* case you may discover that the medical model you intended to present at trial is far too complicated for the jury to understand. Or you may discover that your attorney's cross-examination of the opposing witnesses offended certain jury members. In contrast, you may find that some of the evidence presented by the corporate defendants was very convincing. You would then want to concentrate your forces on countering this evidence. The period between the mock trial and the actual trial should be devoted to correcting these and other weaknesses pointed out by the mock jury.

Using Shadow Juries

The increasing complexity of litigation has resulted in the introduction of a technique known as the shadow jury. A **shadow jury** is a secret jury selected by the law firm or the outside consulting firm. In choosing individuals to serve on the shadow jury, the law firm or the consulting firm attempts to match as closely as possible the individuals serving on the actual jury. The shadow jury then attends the trial. To assure fairness, these individuals are not told which side of the lawsuit has retained them. During each break and at the end of each day's court session, the shadow jury reports to another paralegal or legal team member on their impressions of the trial witnesses, the exhibits, and the attorneys. The shadow jury's reports are given considerable weight. Adjustments in the order of witnesses, changes in the trial exhibits, or alterations in the attorney's technique may result from the observations and the suggestions made by shadow jury members. A substantial amount of expense and time is involved in this exercise. If the shadow jury strengthens a case, however, both the expenses and the time are well-spent.

shadow jury
A group of persons (selected to be similar to the real jurors) paid by one side in a lawsuit to observe the trial and give their reactions.

Jury Selection

All cases involving a jury begin with the process of selecting or *seating* the jury. The jury members are selected from a jury pool that has been gathered from among the local citizenry. Most jury pools are taken from the ranks of registered voters. Once a jury pool has been assembled at the courthouse, members of the pool are asked to fill out preliminary information forms, copies of which are given to the attorneys in the case. These forms are used as part of the jury selection process. In federal court, a civil trial uses 12 jurors. However, the parties are allowed to stipulate that fewer than 12 jurors will hear the case. Many state courts require only eight jurors for a civil trial. Most states also allow parties to stipulate that fewer than eight jurors may hear their case. The federal court and most state courts also allow for the use of alternate jurors.

The Voir Dire Process

Literally, *voir dire* means "to speak the truth." In trial practice, *voir dire* is the process by which the jurors are questioned to determine any bias that they might have that would affect their ability to be fair and impartial in the case. For example, in the *Lermentov* case your attorney would want to determine if any potential jurors are related to or are friends of the officers and employees of Billicheck-Kendall, Sergi Selinkov Securities, Inc., or the Kolata Maintenance Corporation. She might also want to know if any of the potential jurors has any financial interest in the outcome of the trial. Such information would indicate bias on the part of the juror and would be grounds for a challenge. Each side in the suit has an unlimited number of these *challenges for cause.*

Peremptory Challenges

peremptory challenges

The automatic elimination of a potential juror by one side before trial without needing to state the reason for the elimination. Each side has the right to a certain number of peremptory challenges.

Each side also has a limited number of **peremptory challenges.** The federal courts and some states allow only three such challenges; other states allow as many as four. Additional peremptory challenges are allowed when alternate jurors are to be chosen. However, the number of peremptory challenges is always limited, because an attorney making a peremptory challenge does not have to give a reason for the challenge. He simply exercises the peremptory challenge, and the juror is dismissed. The objective of the peremptory challenge is to allow attorneys an opportunity to dismiss jurors for certain "intangible" reasons that cannot be logically explained to the court. For instance, your attorney may feel that there is a certain air of hostility about a certain juror, or she might feel that the "chemistry" is not right between them. Such an instinctive reaction, though genuine enough to cause concern, would be difficult to explain to the court. For these instinctive situations, the law has provided the peremptory challenge.

The Trial

Opening Statement

opening statement

The introductory statements made at the start of a trial by lawyers for each side. The lawyers typically explain the version of the facts best supporting their side of the case, how these facts will be proved, and how they think the law applies to the case.

The first step of the actual trial is the presentation of **opening statements.** The objectives and scope of these statements are not as precise and definitive as one might expect in a profession that prides itself on both accuracy and clarity. Still, the opening statement is one of the most important steps, if not the most important step, in a jury trial. Consequently, a skillful attorney will know that he should keep the opening statement brief, use ordinary language in the statement, make the statement interesting, and use appropriate body language in delivering that statement.

Definition and Limitations   Each side in a jury trial is allowed time to make an opening statement. An opening statement presents facts to the jury and introduces the evidence that the attorney intends to use to prove those facts. A general rule of trial procedure states that attorneys are not permitted to argue their cases during opening statements. The exact meaning of this rule is not clear. Consequently, the judge has an enormous amount of discretion in what the attorneys can and cannot say during opening statements. Some judges are strict in adhering to the general guideline that attorneys cannot argue their cases in the opening statement, whereas others are more lenient, allowing attorneys to introduce points that another judge would almost certainly label as argument. This means that, to be successful in an opening statement, an attorney must have an understanding of just how much "argument" a particular judge will allow.

Such an understanding comes from experience and from a willingness to ask questions about the processes when the attorney is unfamiliar with a court and its judges.

Importance of the Opening Statement   The imprecise nature of the opening statement is made even more critical because of its importance. Some legal scholars argue that the opening statement is the most important part of the trial. These scholars have several rather convincing reasons for placing such importance on the opening statement. First, because the opening statement occurs so early in the trial, the jurors are very attentive. This attentiveness heightens their awareness of what is being said and done during the opening stages. As the trial progresses, and they become more comfortable and secure in the courtroom, their attentiveness lessens. Also, although jurors are counseled to remain as objective as possible, they are, nevertheless, human beings who have a natural tendency to pick sides in any adversarial contest. After all, when they watch a television show or a movie, they know whose side they are supposed to be on. When they attend a sports event, people are quick to pick sides.

The jurors carry this tendency to choose sides with them into the courtroom, and as early as the end of the opening statements may have unconsciously decided who is the "good guy" and who is the "bad guy." This places a heavy burden on the attorney who has been labeled the "bad guy" and gives an edge to the one who has been labeled the "good guy." The advantage given to the good guy has been termed by some scholars as the "halo effect" and by others as the "white hat syndrome." Basically, the halo effect or the white hat syndrome means that everything said by the good guy and every piece of testimony and evidence that is introduced in support of the good guy's argument is interpreted favorably, while everything damaging to that side's case is somehow rationalized or explained away. Of course, this does not mean that a juror will never change her mind. It just means that attorneys who have been labeled bad guys have a much more difficult time getting jurors to believe them.

Characteristics of a Good Opening Statement   Because so much of the success of a jury trial seems to depend upon the opening statement, an attorney should take great care in fashioning it. A good opening statement should be brief, interesting, understandable, sincere, and tactful.

Delivering a Brief Opening Statement   Setting an absolute maximum length of time for an opening statement beyond which an attorney should never wander is difficult. Similarly, it is difficult to set a minimum length of time. It is, however, safe to say that an attorney should rarely, if ever, pass up the opportunity to make an opening statement, unless both parties waive that right. Waiving the opening statement, or even postponing it, gives an unnecessary psychological advantage to the other party. The opening statement should be long enough to capture the attention and imagination of the jurors, but not so long that it puts them to sleep. Most opening statements can be limited to 30 to 45 minutes. Occasionally, when the facts are extremely complex, more time will be needed. Conversely, when the facts are simple, less time will be needed.

Delivering an Interesting Opening Statement   At the beginning of this section, we noted that the jury's attention level is very high at the opening of the trial. The good attorney will take advantage of this attention level by delivering an interesting, even captivating, opening statement. This can be done by reducing the opening statement to a narrative. The opening statement involves facts, and nothing conveys facts in a more interesting or convincing fashion than a story. Cold, antiseptic facts, exhibits, and statistics should be avoided in favor of conveying a sense of the people and the action involved in the case. For instance, in presenting the case of Mr. Lermentov to the jury, your attorney might begin by stating that, "On the morning of March 4, 2003, Mr. Mikhail Lermentov awoke and prepared for a routine day conducting an audit at the offices of Billicheck-Kendall here in downtown Red Forest. At that time he had no idea that this day would be one of the worst of his entire life." From this point on, your attorney would follow the events of that day much as if she were telling a story. Such an opening statement is much more likely to capture the attention and sympathy of the jurors than one limited to a long procession of facts.

Delivering an Understandable Opening Statement   Your attorney will be more likely to gain the interest and sympathy of the jury members if she avoids legal jargon and speaks the language of the jurors. Opening statements that are full of legal terms and unintelligible Latin phrases are guaranteed to alienate jury members, who may already view all attorneys with a certain degree of distrust, if not downright hostility. If your attorney, for example, buries the *Lermentov* opening statement in references to *respondeat superior, vicarious liability, piercing the corporate veil,* and *alter egos,* she may bury her case along with it. In addition, depending upon the opinion of the judge in the case, the use of such terms may be considered arguing the case. Your attorney will do better to speak in ordinary, everyday language.

Delivering a Sympathetic Opening Statement   An attorney must always remember that he is the client's advocate. This means that the jury expects the attorney to be on the client's side. To make the opening statement as convincing and sympathetic as possible, the attorney must show the jury that he believes in the righteousness of the client's cause. If the jury members doubt the attorney's dedication to vindicating the client's rights, they will have little faith in anything that he says on behalf of that client. For these reasons an attorney should immediately identify himself with the client's cause. The jury will be much more convinced by the attorney who says, "We will prove that our case against the defendant is as solid as a rock," than one who says, "Don't believe everything the other side has to say about the plaintiff."

Delivering a Tactful Opening Statement   As noted earlier, the attorney should be brief, interesting, understandable, sympathetic, and sincere in the opening statement. However, this can go for naught if jurors are intimidated by the presence and actions of the attorney. For this reason, the delivery of the opening statement should be as tactful as possible. Attorneys should not be overly emotional, too loud, or excessively boastful in the opening statement. Rather, they should be soft-spoken, even-tempered, and genuine. It is also important for the attorney to keep her distance from the jury. Climbing on top of jurors may make a powerfully dramatic scene in a movie or television show, but in real life it invades the space of the jurors, intimidates them, and destroys their concentration on what the attorney is saying.

The Presentation of Evidence

As we saw earlier, the paralegal is instrumental in preparing witnesses for trial. During the presentation of evidence, this preparation pays off. The presentation of evidence can be divided into two stages: the case in chief and the rebuttal. During the case in chief, both sides present the testimony and evidence they hope will convince the jury of the validity of their case. The plaintiff presents his evidence by calling witnesses to testify and placing those witnesses under direct examination. The defendant then has the right to conduct a cross-examination of each witness. The roles are then reversed. The defendant places her witnesses on the stand for direct examination. The plaintiff then has the opportunity to engage in cross-examination.

The Plaintiff's Case in Chief   If the plaintiff's attorney feels that certain facts in the case are uncontested because they were admitted to in response to a request for admissions, were a part of the defendant's answer, or were admitted in some other pleading or discovery device, then those facts may be read into the record. This generally occurs before the plaintiff calls the first witness.

Direct Examination by the Plaintiff   The plaintiff's attorney calls each of the witnesses who will provide facts to verify the validity of the plaintiff's version of the case. The plaintiff's attorney subjects each of those witnesses to direct examination. This is a question-and-answer period conducted under oath and recorded by the court stenographer. In general, the plaintiff's attorney may not ask her own witnesses leading questions. A leading question is one containing the answer. For example, your attorney could not call Mr. Lermentov to the witness stand and ask him, "Isn't it true that the storeroom next to the room where you conducted the audit for Billicheck-Kendall contained combustible material?" Such a question would be considered leading and would not be permitted.

Leading Questions by the Plaintiff   There is an exception to the rule that prohibits asking leading questions. When an attorney is faced with an adverse or hostile witness, he is permitted to ask leading questions. For example, in the *Lermentov* case, your attorney has elected to call several adverse witnesses, including Yuri Vilnius, CEO of Sergi Selinkov; Julius Vilnius, CEO of Billicheck-Kendall; Kay Vilnius, treasurer of Billicheck-Kendall; Albert Vilnius, CEO of Kolata Maintenance and vice-president of Billicheck-Kendall; and Vytautas Vilnius, treasurer of Kolata Maintenance and vice-president of Billicheck-Kendall. Each of these witnesses is also an adverse party and could, therefore, be the legitimate target of leading questions by Lermentov's attorney. For instance, Lermentov's attorney would be permitted to ask Julius Vilnius the following question: "Isn't it true that the storeroom next to the room where the audit was conducted contained combustible chemicals?"

Rules Regarding the Plaintiff's Direct Examination   The process of asking precisely the right questions during a direct examination session is not as easy as it may appear. Preparing in advance is essential. All friendly witnesses should be properly and thoroughly prepared before the day of the trial. They should meet with the attorney and discuss the questions that will be asked, the answers that the witness intends to give, and the probable questions to expect on cross-examination. An attorney should never ask a question to which she does not already know the answer. The time for exploratory questions is during the discovery process, not at trial. An attorney also needs to know when to stop asking questions. Once the attorney has elicited the facts that she wants, questioning should stop. Continuing questions after that point can be very damaging.

Cross-Examination by the Defendant   When the plaintiff's attorney has completed the direct examination of each witness, the defendant's attorney has the opportunity to engage in cross-examination. In federal court and in most states, the scope of cross-examination is limited to facts covered in direct examination. If the defendant's attorney wants to explore new territory with a witness, he will have to call the witness during the defendant's direct examination session. The objective of cross-examination is to discredit the witness, to cast doubt on the accuracy of the witness's testimony, or to show that the witness is somehow biased in favor of the plaintiff. One way the defendant can do this is to show that the testimony delivered at trial by the witness contradicts the testimony presented during the discovery process. Another way is to use leading questions that require simple "yes" or "no" answers from the witness, thus limiting his ability to elaborate on those answers.

Redirect Examination by the Plaintiff   When the defendant has completed the cross-examination of a witness, the plaintiff's attorney has the opportunity to redirect questions to that witness. The objective of this part of the trial process is to allow the plaintiff's attorney the chance to reestablish the credibility of her witnesses and to clear up any factual disputes raised on cross-examination. To make redirect examination as efficient as possible, the plaintiff's attorney is limited to those matters addressed by the defendant's counsel during the cross-examination period.

The Defendant's Case in Chief   Once the plaintiff has completed her case in chief, the roles are switched, and the defendant has the same opportunity. The defendant's efforts are directed to discrediting the case that was presented by the plaintiff. The objective is to demonstrate that the plaintiff's version of the facts is not supported by the evidence. In addition, if the defendant raised any affirmative defenses, now is the time to present evidence that demonstrates the validity of these defenses.

Direct Examination by the Defendant   The defendant's attorney calls his witnesses and subjects them to direct examination. This is the same type of question-and-answer period that was conducted by the plaintiff. As was the case with the plaintiff's attorney, the defendant's counsel may not ask his own witnesses leading questions. For example, the defendant's attorney could not call Lon Anderson, an employee of both Sergi Selinkov and Kolata Maintenance, to the witness stand and ask him, "Isn't it true that Sergi Selinkov and Kolata Maintenance management decisions were made separately from any and all management decisions made for Billicheck-Kendall?" Such a question would be considered leading and would not be permitted.

Leading Questions by the Defendant   As is the case with the plaintiff's counsel, when the defendant's attorney is faced with an adverse or hostile witness, he is permitted to ask leading questions. For example, in the *Lermentov* case, if the defense attorney has elected to call Mr. Lermentov to testify, he would be the legitimate target of leading questions by Billicheck-Kendall's attorney. For instance, Billicheck-Kendall's attorney would be permitted to ask Mr. Lermentov the following question: "Isn't it true that you knew of the risk imposed by the combustible chemicals located in the store-room next to your office?"

Rules Regarding the Defendant's Direct Examination   The same rules governing the plaintiff's strategy on direct examination also apply to the defendant's plan for direct examination. Thus, the defendant's attorney should prepare in advance by meeting with friendly witnesses before trial. The defendant's attorney should never ask a question to which he does not already know the answer, and he should develop the discipline to know when to stop asking questions.

Cross-Examination by the Plaintiff   When the defendant's attorney has completed the direct examination of each witness, the plaintiff's attorney has the opportunity to engage in cross-examination. The scope of cross-examination allowed to the plaintiff is limited to facts covered in direct examination. Like the defendant, the plaintiff wants to discredit the defendant's witnesses, to cast doubt on the accuracy of their testimony, or to show that the witnesses are somehow biased in favor of the defendant.

Redirect Examination by the Defendant   When the plaintiff has completed the cross-examination of a witness, the defendant's attorney has a chance to redirect questions to that witness. This step allows the defendant the same chance that the plaintiff had to reestablish the credibility of his witnesses and to clear up any factual disputes raised on cross-examination.

The Presentation of Rebuttal Evidence   After each side has had the opportunity to see the entire case in chief presented by the other party, both have the chance to present rebuttal evidence. **Rebuttal evidence,** or evidence in rebuttal, is designed to discredit the other side's evidence and to reestablish the credibility of the side presenting the rebuttal. To make the rebuttal as efficient and as fair as possible, the scope of rebuttal is limited to the evidence presented during the case in chief. No new evidence is to be presented during the rebuttal. When the plaintiff has completed her rebuttal, the defendant has the same chance to call rebuttal witnesses. Some states use the term *surebuttal* to describe the defendant's rebuttal. Others use the phrase *evidence in rejoinder* or *rejoinder evidence*. Regardless of the terms used to describe it, the defendant's rebuttal is limited to the rebuttal evidence put forth by the plaintiff.

rebuttal evidence
Formal contradiction of statements made by an adversary.

Closing Argument

As the trial begins to wind down, one of the final steps is the presentation of the closing argument. The objective and scope of the closing argument are more precise and definitive than for the opening statements. The evidence has already been presented, so it is clear that the closing arguments must refer to that evidence and must attempt to convince the jury that the attorney's interpretation of that evidence is the correct one.

Definition and Limitations   Each side in a jury trial is allowed time at the end of the presentation of evidence to make a closing argument. The closing argument will help jurors review the evidence that the attorneys introduced during the trial. Unlike the procedure followed during the opening statements, which prevents the attorneys from arguing their case, during the closing arguments attorneys are permitted to do their best to persuade jurors of the validity of their case. Moreover, they are also permitted to attack the presentation of the other side's evidence.

The Strategy of the Closing Argument   During closing arguments, each attorney will explain her theory of the case and will demonstrate how the evidence presented at trial supports that theory. Each attorney will also do her best to destroy the jury's belief in the credibility of the other side's witnesses. Destroying the credibility of the opponent's witnesses can be accomplished in a number of ways. First, the attorney may demonstrate that the witness has contradicted himself on the stand. The attorney may also point out discrepancies between the witness's testimony in a deposition or interrogatories and his testimony during the actual trial. It may also be demonstrated that the witness lacks credibility because of bias or because of the inability of the witness to really know the facts that he testified to.

Characteristics of a Good Closing Argument   As noted earlier, the jury has a heightened awareness of the trial process at the beginning of the trial. The same is true, though to a lesser degree, at the end of the trial. This fact, plus the fact that this is the attorney's last chance to reach the jury, makes the closing argument very important. Because so much of the success of a jury trial depends upon the closing argument, an attorney should take great care in fashioning it. It is critical to know the characteristics of a good closing argument. To be effective, a closing argument must be well-planned and persuasive.

Delivering a Well-Planned Closing Argument   Planning is important because the closing statement must organize a mass of evidence and testimony into a coherent pattern that the jury can understand. The attorney begins the closing argument with his theory of the case and then moves to an explanation of the burden of proof and the evidence that strengthens his theory. The attorney also attempts to point out weaknesses in the evidence the other side has presented. As noted earlier, the attorney also tries to discredit the witnesses upon whom his adversary has relied.

Delivering a Persuasive Closing Argument   The closing argument must be persuasive. Persuasiveness is often difficult to manufacture, so it is extremely helpful if the attorney is convinced of the righteousness of her client's cause. If jury members doubt the attorney's dedication to vindicating the rights of the client, they will have little faith in anything that she says on behalf of that client. For these reasons, in the closing argument, as in the opening statement, an attorney should identify herself with the client's cause. In the *Lermentov* case, for instance, the jury will be much more easily convinced by your attorney if she concludes her argument by saying, "We have proven that the officers and directors of Billicheck-Kendall attempted to hide behind the facade of Sergi Selinkov and Kolata Maintenance in a feeble attempt to escape their legal obligation to protect all those who used their offices," than if she were to say, "The defendant's attorney did not prove that Sergi Selinkov and Kolata Maintenance were not the alter egos of the defendants."

Jury Deliberations

The responsibility of giving the jury instructions belongs to the judge. Once instructions have been given to the jury members, they retire to consider the case and to decide on a verdict. Once a verdict has been rendered, either party may request that jury members be polled. Jury members may also be required to answer interrogatories to determine if their verdict is in line with the answers to those interrogatories.

Jury Instructions   In both federal and state courts, the judge has the responsibility of delivering jury instructions. These instructions include an explanation of the law, the burden of proof, the weight that should be given to the evidence, the process to be followed during the deliberations, and the verdicts that can be rendered. Usually, such instructions are given to the jury after the closing arguments, immediately before the deliberation process begins. However, the judge may instruct the jury on some things, such as the law relating to the procedure at trial, the duties and the functions of the jury, the law that pertains to the case, and the use of evidence, before the trial begins and whenever needed during the actual course of the trial. Also, although the responsibility of final jury instructions belongs to the judge, the attorneys have, at the close of evidence, the opportunity to file a written request with the judge to deliver the instructions in a particular way. Before closing arguments the judge will inform the attorneys how she will instruct the jury. After closing arguments, the judge delivers the jury instructions. Before the jury retires to consider its verdict, the attorneys may, out of the hearing of the jury members, object to the instructions. The objection must specifically explain the grounds for the objection.

Actual Deliberations   Once the jury is behind closed doors, it considers the evidence in light of the instructions given by the judge and attempts to arrive at a verdict. If the jurors are confused about some point or unsure of the law, they can ask for clarification from the judge. The jury can also see any of the evidence presented at trial. In federal court, in a civil case, a unanimous verdict is required, unless the parties have agreed on some number less than a majority. In many state courts, a three-fourths majority is sufficient for a verdict in a civil case. Once a verdict has been reached, it is placed in writing, and the jurors return to the courtroom, where the verdict is read aloud.

Rendering a Verdict   After a verdict has been rendered, either party may request that jury members be polled. Jury members may also be required to answer interrogatories to determine if their verdict is in line with the answers to those interrogatories.

Polling the Jury   *Polling the jurors* involves asking each juror if the verdict announced was the verdict that he or she rendered. As long as the required number of jurors answer that the verdict announced is the verdict that they agreed to, there is no problem and the jury is dismissed. For example, suppose in the *Lermentov* case eight jurors were involved in the deliberations. Suppose further that three-fourths of those jurors were required for the rendering of a verdict. If six of the eight answer during the polling process that they agreed with the verdict, the jury members are discharged. If, however, fewer than six concur with the verdict, then the jurors are sent back to continue their deliberations.

Interrogatories and the Jury   Prior to deliberation, either side in the case can ask that the jury be required to answer interrogatories as part of the deliberation process. The purpose of the interrogatories is to ensure that the jury really understood the determinative issues of law and fact in the case. The party making such a request must also submit written copies of these interrogatories to the judge and to the opposing attorney.

If the judge approves the interrogatories, they are submitted to the jurors prior to their deliberations. During jury instructions, the judge explains the use of the interrogatories to the jurors. They are then required to answer them in writing and return the written answers with their verdict. As long as the answers are consistent with the verdict, the verdict will stand. Should even a single answer be inconsistent with the verdict, the judge may order the jury to conduct further deliberations. In some situations, the judge may even elect to order a new trial.

Motions During Trial

While a trial is still in progress, the litigants have the opportunity to end the dispute in a number of different ways. As discussed in Chapter 14, settlement may occur even after the trial has commenced. During the trial, a party may attempt to arrive at a speedy conclusion by asking the court to grant a motion for directed verdict. Also, throughout the trial, both parties have the opportunity to present a variety of motions to the court, including a motion for involuntary dismissal, a motion to strike, or a motion for mistrial.

motion for a directed verdict

A motion made during a jury trial, requesting that the judge tell the jury how they should decide the case.

Motion for a Directed Verdict   One of the options open to litigants during the trial is to file a **motion for a directed verdict,** which asks the judge to instruct the jury to render a verdict for the party filing the motion. The rule allows this motion to be raised after the opposing party has closed its presentation of evidence. If the motion is denied, it can be raised again at the conclusion of the party's own evidence, or after the closing arguments. Naturally, the motion must explain the grounds upon which it has been made.

motion for involuntary dismissal

A motion requesting dismissal of a lawsuit by the court, either prior to judgment or by virtue of a judgment against the plaintiff based upon the verdict of the jury or the decision of the court after trial.

Motion for Involuntary Dismissal   In a nonjury trial, a defendant might, upon completion of the presentation of plaintiff's evidence, move for dismissal upon facts and law, without waiving the right to offer evidence if the motion is not granted. This motion is similar to a motion for directed verdict in cases tried to a jury. The judge can rule on the motion at the time it is made, or wait until the close of the trial. Requirements for a **motion for involuntary dismissal** are discussed in Rule 41(b) of the Federal Rules of Civil Procedure.

If the court denies the motion or renders judgment on the merits against the plaintiff, the court must make findings of fact required by Rule 2(a) of the Federal Rules of Civil Procedure. In the event that the court denies the defendant's motion or reserves its decision until the conclusion of the presentation of evidence, the defendant may renew its motion after all of the evidence has been presented.

motion to strike

A request that immaterial statements or other things be removed from an opponent's pleading.

Motion to Strike   A party may move to strike evidence that has been improperly admitted. For example, if a witness blurts out an answer to opposing counsel's question quickly, before her counsel can object, the witness's counsel may move to strike that testimony. The **motion to strike** should include a request that the judge instruct the jurors, in a jury trial, to disregard the improper evidence during its deliberations.

motion for mistrial

A motion asking that the judge terminate a trial prior to its conclusion because the jury is unable to reach a verdict, because of prejudicial error that cannot be corrected or eliminated by any action the court might take, or because of the occurrence of some event that would make it pointless to continue.

Motion for Mistrial   In a **motion for mistrial,** a party asks the court to terminate the trial before judgment and set the case for trial at another time, on the basis of improprieties. This motion should be reserved for an impropriety so severe that a party cannot receive a fair trial before that particular jury. Usually, improprieties can be corrected by instructing the jury to disregard the impropriety. Possible improprieties might include improper and inflammatory argument, or improper contact between a party and a jury member or members.

Motions at the End of Trial

After the jury has rendered its verdict, and the court has entered its judgment, a dissatisfied party has the opportunity to file a motion for a judgment not withstanding the verdict and a motion for a new trial.

Motion for a Judgment Notwithstanding the Verdict   A **motion for a judgment notwithstanding the verdict** asks the court to have the verdict and its judgment set aside. To grant such a motion, the court must be convinced that a group of reasonable individuals would not have reached such a verdict and that the jury's decision is wrong as a matter of law. The judgment notwithstanding the verdict is also known as a *motion for judgment n.o.v.* or a *motion for a JNOV.* These abbreviations come from the Latin phrase *non obstante veredicto,* which means "notwithstanding the verdict."

In federal court, the counterpart motion is a motion for judgment as a matter of law.

Motion for Judgment as a Matter of Law   A **motion for judgment as a matter of law** is made in a jury trial. If granted, it results in the judge entering a judgment without allowing the jury to consider the evidence. The basis for this motion is that the party against whom judgment is entered has not introduced sufficient evidence for a reasonable jury to find in its favor. This motion can be made at any time in the trial as long as the party against whom judgment is sought has fully presented its evidence.

If the court denies a motion for judgment as a matter of law (or its state court counterpart, motion for a judgment notwithstanding the verdict), made at the close of evidence, the motion may be renewed by service and filing within 10 days after entry of judgment. A **motion for new trial** under Rule 59 of the Federal Rules of Civil Procedure may be combined with this renewal of the motion for judgment, or, in the alternative, only a motion for new trial may be filed. See Chapter 16 for more discussion of posttrial motions.

The Paralegal's Role at Trial

The paralegal's role at the trial involves the same general areas that the paralegal was involved in during the preparation stages. These areas of participation include witnesses, exhibits, notetaking, jury selection, and general trial coordination tasks.

Ensuring the Presence of Witnesses

The paralegal may be responsible for locating and having the witnesses present in the courtroom for their testimony. Your witness control log, discussed earlier, will assist you in coordinating the production of witnesses at the appropriate times. You may also be asked to provide for transportation of witnesses. This task may even

motion for a judgment notwithstanding the verdict
A motion asking the court to have the verdict and its judgment set aside because a group of reasonable individuals would not have reached such a verdict and the jury's decision is wrong as a matter of law.

motion for judgment as a matter of law
In a jury trial, a request from one party that the judge decide the case in that party's favor on the basis that no facts have been proven that would support a jury's decision for the other party.

motion for new trial
A motion asking the trial court to order a new trial when prejudicial error has occurred or when, for any other reason, a fair trial was prevented.

THE COMPUTERIZED LAW FIRM
Presentation Software

SCENARIO

You are the only paralegal on the trial team for the *Lermentov* case. Because you used litigation support software throughout the discovery phase of the trial, you feel confident that you will be able to retrieve documents, prior deposition testimony, answers to interrogatories, requests for disclosures, and admissions easily and readily. However, after a brief meeting with your attorney you find that you still have work to do. Your attorney wants to be sure that she has the full attention of the jurors during her opening statement and closing argument. She anticipates that these will both be lengthy and complex, and she wants to be sure that the jurors remember some important points. She has asked you to help her put together a visual presentation to emphasize the important aspects of her opening statement and closing argument.

PROBLEM

How do you create a visual presentation to meet the attorney's need and what equipment will be needed in court to effectively use the presentation?

SOLUTION

Professionals in all areas realize the importance of visual aids in any type of presentation. Trial attorneys also recognize this. Software, known as presentation software, helps a trial attorney or paralegal put together a visually appealing type of computer slide show. Using templates provided in the software, the user creates "slides" containing both colorful text and graphics to help emphasize points. Software, such as Microsoft PowerPoint or Corel's Presentation, also allow you to insert graphs and charts designed with the companion spreadsheet programs. Relevant photographs taken with digital cameras can also be inserted into the slide presentation. These slides are displayed to the jury on a screen or monitor with the use of a special projector connected to the computer running the program. In a trial situation, the attorney would use a laptop computer. This same laptop computer can also be used to run litigation support software, such as Summation, described in previous chapters.

If your attorney plans to use a laptop computer (or any specialized hardware) in court, you should check the courtroom ahead of time. You may need extension cords or plug adapters in order to use your equipment. Remember that some courtrooms are old and were not designed for today's technology. You should also check with the court clerk to make sure that the judge does not have any special limitations on the use of technology in his or her courtroom. With adequate preparation and planning, presentation software can greatly enhance a trial attorney's presentation to the jury.

include picking up out-of-town witnesses arriving at the airport. If possible, you should delegate this responsibility to another member of the legal team so that you are not away from the courtroom for any extended period of time. The paralegal may also be called upon to calm or reassure a nervous witness. It may even be your responsibility to work with hostile witnesses whom your attorney is forced to call to the stand. Your demeanor must be firm but relaxed when dealing with hostile witnesses. If a contact person for witnesses has been designated at the law firm, you should check with that person frequently to ensure that all witnesses will be present in court as scheduled.

Keeping Track of Exhibits

During the trial, you must keep track of exhibits introduced by both sides. The exhibit log must be maintained to keep track of which exhibits have been offered and admitted, which exhibits have incurred objections, and whether the exhibit was ultimately admitted into evidence. At each break in the trial, you should compare the court reporter's original exhibits against the exhibit log to be sure that all exhibits are accounted for. During the trial, you should confer with your attorney at the end of each day to determine which exhibits will be introduced the next day. Review your exhibit files to make certain that adequate copies of these exhibits are ready for the next trial session.

Participating in Jury Selection

As the paralegal assigned to the case, you may be asked to prepare a jury seating chart similar to the one depicted in Exhibit 15–9. The purpose of this chart is to track voir dire examination. While your attorney is conducting the jury examination, you should note the verbal and nonverbal communication of potential jurors, particularly with respect to factual issues or prejudices that are germane to the case.

Follow the voir dire examination outline from the trial notebook. Note the response of each potential juror. The paralegal and the attorney may confer to compare their observations about the jury panel before the final jury selection.

The paralegal must record the information learned through the voir dire process to assist the attorney with the decisions regarding which jurors to strike and which to retain. Unless you are fortunate enough to have a remarkable memory, it is very difficult to process and record all of the requisite information while your attorney is in the process of questioning the potential jurors.

Lermentov v. Billicheck-Kendall Pharmaceuticals
Civil Action NO. 03-71891
Jury Seating Chart

1. Pete Anderson	2. Nancy Rodriquez	3. Carole Peczniak	4. Joy Speigel	5. Gaspar Ortega	6. Christine Calderone

—Back Row—

7. Hubert Conaughton	8. Hedeki Seki	9. Andrew Glanzburgh	10. Monroe Szarkowski	11. Gustave Schoenborn	12. Chifton Wheeler

—Front Row—

EXHIBIT 15–9 Jury seating chart

The 'Lectric Law Library maintains a search engine entitled "Law Looker-Upper" at <http://www.lectlaw.com/search.html>.

a. Access the search engine and use the key word function to find articles relating to jury research. Use the information from that search to prepare a memo relating to the advisability of employing a jury consultant for the *Lermentov* case.

b. As an alternative assignment, research your state's pattern jury charge and draft jury instructions for the *Lermentov* case.

The use of a spreadsheet that lists the potential jurors in either alphabetical or seating order will make this process much less cumbersome. This spreadsheet enables you to enter on your laptop computer all personal and case-specific information that will go into your attorney's decision-making process for each potential juror. Additional information that should be entered includes notes of strikes, including who struck the individual, how many strikes each side has used, and potential jurors who have been excused for cause by the judge. This chart preserves critical and complete information on the jury selection process in the event that becomes an issue on a subsequent appeal of the final decision in the case.

Taking Notes During the Trial

Your attorney's full energy and concentration must be directed toward the witness on the stand, the objections raised by opposing counsel, and the court's rulings on particular motions. You should, therefore, assume the responsibility for taking full and accurate notes of the trial proceedings. A lined notebook with a wide left margin will assist you in noting inconsistencies in testimony, incomplete answers to questions, and exhibits that have not yet been admitted into evidence. You may want to use red ink to record "things to do" that arise during the trial. Note the beginning time of each session and all breaks. These notations will enable you to quickly locate a particular piece of information.

Summary

- One trial preparation task that can be completed during the preliminary stages is the organization of litigation files. It is best if files are kept current as the case develops. Each time a pleading is filed by either side, it should immediately be placed in the pleadings binder. One problem that might surface during organization of the file is the need to amend the pleadings in the case before the time to do so expires. The paralegal must check federal or local rules to determine the procedure to be followed if a pleading must be amended after the trial date has been set. The paralegal must also prepare a trial notebook. The form of the trial notebook is dictated by the type of case, the number of pleadings, the complexity of the legal issues, the number of exhibits and witnesses, and the anticipated length of the trial. However, most trial notebooks include the following basic sections: (1) the parties and attorneys; (2) the pleadings and motions; (3) the witnesses; (4) the expert witnesses; (5) document indexes; (6) deposition summaries; (7) chronology; (8) the cast of characters; (9) legal research; (10) trial exhibits; (11) jury profiles and instructions; (12) the trial outline; (13) the attorney's notes; and (14) the "things to do" list.

■ The paralegal must consult with the attorney to determine if any witnesses will require a subpoena. In some instances attorneys prefer to subpoena only witnesses who are not considered "friendly." However, a friendly witness may request a subpoena to present to an employer as evidence that he has been ordered to appear and testify. The paralegal may be asked to communicate with the witnesses early in the trial preparation period about the basic details of the trial, including the date, the location, and the anticipated length of the testimony. The witnesses should also be informed that they may have to meet with the attorney and the paralegal closer to the time of the trial. Shortly before trial, the paralegal should arrange a meeting between each witness and the attorney. During the witness preparation meeting, the attorney will explain the trial process to each witness.

■ Often the paralegal is called upon to gather and organize exhibits in a case. This responsibility may require obtaining enlarged exhibits or unusual graphics. The paralegal may also have to set up a chronology or organize a set of statistics. Whatever the case, it helps to know what to look for in the evaluation of those exhibits. It is also possible that the paralegal may be called upon to help conduct research for the trial brief.

■ The paralegal is often responsible for coordinating the logistics of a trial. Often logistics will be a matter of routine. However, when the trial is held in another district or another county, or when the client and many of the witnesses are from out-of-town, the paralegal will have to arrange for accommodations. Also, the paralegal will have to examine the courthouse and contact local court personnel.

■ The purpose of the jury profile is to determine a composite profile of the ideal jurors for a particular case. Social psychologists and litigation specialists can provide law firms with valuable statistics and jury sampling information to create not only the image of preferred jurors but also a profile of the jurors that your attorney will want to avoid.

■ The paralegal is often responsible for arranging a mock trial. The first step in the mock trial is to select the mock jury. Key witnesses and principal exhibits are presented to the jury in the same way that they will be presented at the actual trial. The mock jury evaluates the testimony and the exhibits and renders a verdict. Following their decision, the jurors may be questioned about their perceptions of the strengths and weaknesses of the case. The period between the mock trial and the actual trial should be devoted to correcting the weaknesses pointed out by the mock jury. The paralegal may also be asked to prepare a jury seating chart to track voir dire examination. While the attorney is conducting the jury examination, the paralegal notes the verbal and nonverbal communication of potential jurors.

■ The increasing complexity of litigation has resulted in the introduction of a technique known as the shadow jury, a secret jury selected by the law firm or an outside consulting firm. The shadow jury attends the trial and at breaks and the end of each session is questioned about the effectiveness of the trial procedures.

■ The paralegal may be responsible for locating and having witnesses present in the courtroom. During the trial the paralegal must keep track of exhibits. The exhibit log must be maintained to keep track of which exhibits have been offered and admitted, which have incurred objections from opposing counsel, and which were ultimately admitted into evidence. The paralegal must assume the responsibility for taking full and accurate notes of trial proceedings. A lined notebook with a wide left margin will assist the paralegal in noting inconsistencies in testimony, incomplete answers, and exhibits that have not yet been admitted into evidence. Paralegals often use red ink to record "things to do" that arise during the trial.

■ During the trial, both parties have the opportunity to present a variety of motions to the court, including a motion for involuntary dismissal, motion to strike, or motion for mistrial. Another option open to a party at the conclusion of the evidence is to file a motion for directed verdict, asking the judge to instruct the jury to render a verdict for the party filing the motion.

Key Terms

cite check	motion for involuntary dismissal	opening statement
curriculum vitae		peremptory challenges
jury instructions	motion for judgment as a matter of law	rebuttal evidence
mock jury		shadow jury
mock trial	motion for mistrial	trial brief
motion for a directed verdict	motion for new trial	trial notebook
motion for a judgment notwithstanding the verdict	motion to strike	voir dire examination
	on point	

Review Questions

1. What are the paralegal's duties in trial preparation?
2. What is the purpose of the trial notebook?
3. What are the contents of the trial notebook?
4. What responsibilities does the paralegal have in preparing witnesses for trial?
5. What are the standards by which a trial exhibit is evaluated?
6. What duties does the paralegal have in preparing the logistics of the trial?
7. What motions might be appropriate during a trial?
8. What are the paralegal's duties in preparing for the jury process?
9. What duties does the paralegal perform during the trial?
10. What are the major components of a trial?

Chapter Exercises

Where necessary, check with your instructor prior to starting any of these exercises.

1. Review your local court rules relating to jury selection. Check to see if these rules differ in any substantial way from the rules enumerated in the Federal Rules of Civil Procedure.
2. Prepare a memorandum describing what a paralegal should look for during a visit to an out-of-town courthouse.
3. Prepare a trial exhibit list for the *Lermentov* case for both parties.
4. Draft a memorandum to your attorney reflecting the trial tasks that you have completed for the *Lermentov* case and listing outstanding trial assignments. Utilize the information related to paralegal trial duties in this chapter.

Chapter Project

In this chapter, locate the detailed explanation of the contents of the trial notebook. Next, review the facts presented in the *Lermentov* case, which appears in the opening commentary to this chapter. Draft a memorandum to a new paralegal in your law firm instructing him on the contents of a trial notebook for the *Lermentov* case. Make certain to include instructions for each area of the notebook.

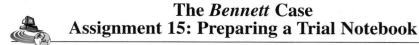

The *Bennett* Case
Assignment 15: Preparing a Trial Notebook

The *Bennett* case is going to trial. You have been asked to create a trial notebook. Organize all documents you have prepared in connection with the case and create sections in the notebook for information to be inserted prior to trial.

Chapter 16

Posttrial Practice

COMMENTARY—THE IMPERIAL CASE

A federal court jury recently awarded $10 million to Paragon Centre, a ten-story office building in downtown Houston. The decision stated that the Imperial Gasoline Company, a major national gasoline distributor incorporated in Delaware and headquartered in Pennsylvania, was negligent in permitting a leak from its abandoned gas station a block from Paragon Centre to spread through the elevator shaft of the office complex. The building was evacuated for less than two hours. Three employees in the building suffered nausea and dizziness from the fumes. They were treated and released from a local hospital. There was no structural damage to the building. However, the jury found that the future value of the building was diminished because of the stigma associated with the gasoline incident. The firm that represented Imperial at trial is unable to prosecute an appeal and has withdrawn from its representation of the client. Imperial has hired your local firm to appeal what it feels is an excessive jury award in light of the minimal injury to the building. Imperial also suspects that the large jury award was due in part to local prejudice in Houston against a large, out-of-town corporate entity that the jurors felt damaged a small, local, real estate developer. Your attorney has requested that you immediately obtain a copy of the testimony from the six-week-long trial. This testimony encompasses 20 volumes and more than 100 exhibits. Accordingly, your attorney asks that you summarize the transcript and draft the necessary posttrial documents. You may also be asked to participate in the preparation of an appellate brief. This chapter covers the details of the posttrial process.

OBJECTIVES

The posttrial process is the final stage in the litigation process. After reading this chapter, you should be able to:

- Identify posttrial motions.
- Define appeal.
- Identify the two major parties to an appeal.
- Explain the nature of a notice of appeal.
- Explain the purpose of a supersedeas bond.
- Determine the paralegal's duties in drafting an appellate brief.
- Describe the paralegal's role in the oral argument.
- Discuss the final procedures in an appeal.

Posttrial Motions

Motion for a New Trial

Rule 59 of the Federal Rules of Civil Procedure allows a dissatisfied party to file a motion asking for a new trial. A motion for a new trial must state the legal grounds on which a new trial should be granted. The court may grant such a new trial on the following grounds: (1) the verdict was contrary to law; (2) the verdict was totally defective; (3) irregularity in the court proceeding; (4) excessive or insufficient damage awards; (5) jury misconduct; or (6) newly discovered evidence. For example, in the *Imperial* case, your attorney may feel that some irregularity in the court proceedings may have resulted in the excessive damage award. She may, for instance, feel that the closing remarks of Paragon's attorney inflamed the jury, igniting a prejudicial passion against your client. Such a situation would call for the filing of a motion for a new trial.

Under Rule 59 of the Federal Rules of Civil Procedure, a motion for a new trial or a motion to alter or amend a judgment must be filed with the court within 10 days of the entry of judgment. Some state courts allow a longer period of time. Ohio courts, for instance, allow 14 days for the filing of a motion for a new trial. Whatever the case, it is important for the paralegal to realize that the actual entry of a judgment could be several weeks or even months after the decision itself has been rendered. You should therefore monitor the court's docket to determine the actual date of the entry of judgment. This date begins the official posttrial time clock.

The Preliminary Steps in the Appeal

As a paralegal, you will be instrumental in preparing the appeal. An **appeal** is filed by a party who has lost a case or who is dissatisfied with a judgment or a court order. The appeal asks that a higher court review the lower court's decision. A person bringing an appeal is referred to as the **appellant.** The person who opposes an appeal is the **appellee.** The appellee may also file a cross-appeal. A **cross-appeal** is an appeal filed by the appellee based on a different legal rationale than the appeal filed by the appellant. Only questions of law are subject to review. The appellate court has no authority to consider questions relating to the facts of a case. For example, in the *Imperial* case, no facts may be introduced concerning the safety record of Imperial over the 10 years it has operated in the Houston area. However, your attorney may argue that the judge erred in his instructions to the jury. This argument relates only to the law that should have been applied in the case. Appeals are expensive, time consuming, and often unsuccessful. However, the appeal is an essential element in the legal system. Without appeals there would be no check on the legal decision making of the trial courts.

appeal
Asking a higher court to review the actions of a lower court in order to correct mistakes or injustice.

appellant
The person who appeals a case to a higher court.

appellee
The person against whom an appeal is taken.

cross-appeal
An appeal by the appellee.

In recent years, the appellate process has been simplified in the federal courts. The clerk in the district court supervises the preparation of the court record—that is, all pleadings and transcripts in the case—for an appeal. The clerk also provides the attorneys with the appropriate forms and copies of the local rules. In contrast, involvement in the state appellate process generally requires more attention to the state court procedural rules.

You should be familiar with federal, state, and local rules for the appellate process. The preliminary steps in an appellate procedure generally include (1) notice of appeal; (2) bond for costs or a supersedeas bond; (3) transcript order and preparation of pertinent record sections; and (4) filing of briefs by both parties. Following these preliminary steps, oral arguments are presented to the court, and the court renders its decision. Exhibit 16–1 charts the stages of an appeal in the federal court up to and including the time for the filing of the briefs. The chart also notes the time limits for completing each stage, and the underlying federal appellate court rules.

Notice of Appeal

notice of appeal

A document filed with the appellate court and served on the opposing party, giving notice of an intention to appeal.

Only one document is required for the filing of an appeal. That document is the **notice of appeal,** which lists the party or parties taking the appeal, the judgment, the order or the portion of the judgment appealed (including the caption of the case in the trial court), and the court to which the appeal is taken. Exhibit 16–2 is an example of a notice of appeal.

According to Rule 4(a) of the Federal Rules of Appellate Procedure, the original of the notice of appeal must be filed with the clerk of the district court from which the appeal is taken within 30 days after the entry of the judgment or the order. Rule 4(a) also states, however, that if the United States or one of its agencies or officers is a party in the case, the notice of appeal must be filed within 60 days after entry of the judgment or the order. Rules 58 and 79(a) of the Federal Rules of Civil Procedure answer the controversy of the meaning of "entered" with regard to a judgment or order. These rules direct that a judgment or order is "entered" in a civil case when it is set forth in a separate document approved by the court, signed by the court or court clerk, and entered in the clerk's docket.

This requirement for a separate document is intended to clarify the beginning of the appeal period. Parties have argued in the past that the appeal time begins with the judge's announcement of the ruling from the bench or the judge's filing of a memorandum decision. Rule 12(b) of the Federal Rules of Appellate Procedure requires that the attorney who filed the notice of appeal must, within 10 days after filing the notice, file a statement with the circuit clerk naming the parties that the attorney represents on appeal. Another party may file a notice of appeal within fourteen days after the date the first notice was filed, or within the time period prescribed by Rule 4(a) of the Federal Rules of Appellate Procedure.

The appellant must pay two separate docketing fees to the clerk of the district court upon the filing of the notice of appeal. The district court clerk then forwards these fees to the clerk of the appellate court. These fees consist of the filing fee of $5 (under 28 U.S.C.A. § 1917) and the docketing fee of $100 (under 28 U.S.C.A § 1913). An appeal is valid even if these fees are not paid with the filing of the notice of appeal. The

ACTION	TIME DUE	FED. APP. RULE
Notice of Appeal	30 days after entry of judgment or order in a separate document.	4(a)(1)
	60 days in cases involving United States, its offices, agencies, or parties.	4(a)(1)
	If timely motion for new trial, judgment as a matter of law, JNOV, motion to amend or alter judgment, or motion to amend or make additional findings of fact, time for appeal for all parties runs from entry of order denying.	4(a)(1)
Supersedeas Bond	Supersedeas bond given at or after time of filing notice of appeal or order allowing appeal.	4(7)
Record and Transcript Appellant	Within 10 days after filing notice of appeal or entry of an order disposing of the last timely remaining motion of a type specified in Rule 4(a), whichever is later, appellant places written order for transcript or files a certificate stating that no transcript will be ordered. At or before time for perfecting appeal, appellant makes written request designating portion.	10(b)
Record and Transcript Appellee	Within 10 days after service of appellant's order for transcript, appellee designates additional parts of transcripts.	10(b)
Transcript-Reporter	If transcript cannot be completed within 30 days of receipt of order, reporter shall request extension of time from clerk of court of appeals.	11(b)
Briefs	Appellant must file a brief within 40 days after record is filed. Appellee must file brief within 30 days after service of appellant's brief. Reply brief must be filed within 14 days after appellee's brief, and at least 3 days before argument.	31(a)

Note—when a party is either required or permitted to act within a designated time period after service on that party, three calendar days are added to the response period, unless the paper is delivered on the date of service reflected in the proof of service. Rule 26(c) of the Federal Rules of Appellate Procedure states that a paper that is signed electronically is not treated as delivered on the date of service shown on the proof of service.

EXHIBIT 16–1   Appellate timetable and procedures—federal courts

clerk of the district court is required to serve notice of the filing of a notice of appeal by mailing a copy of the notice to counsel of record for each party other than the appellant, or to the last known address of a party not represented by counsel. A note is made in the court docket of the names of the parties to whom the clerk mailed copies of the notice of appeal and the date of the mailing. Docketing an appeal occurs when the notice of appeal and certified copies of docket entries are received by the clerk of the court of appeals.

**IN THE UNITED STATES DISTRICT COURT
FOR THE SOUTHERN DISTRICT OF TEXAS, HOUSTON DIVISION**

Paragon Centre,   )
)
    Plaintiff,   )   CIVIL ACTION NO. 02-81891
)
    vs.   )
)
Imperial Gasoline Co.,   )
)
    Defendant.   )
)
)

NOTICE OF APPEAL

Notice is hereby given that the Imperial Gasoline Company, Defendant herein, hereby appeals to the United States Court of Appeals for the Fifth Circuit from the final judgment entered in this action on July 18, 2003.

Respectfully submitted.

By: _____
Attorney for the Defendant
Kirchendorfer, Lehane, Zuer, and Musil
216264 Crestview Drive
Houston, Texas 75247
[Telephone number]
[Facsimile number]

EXHIBIT 16–2   Notice of appeal

Appeal Bond

supersedeas

A judge's order that temporarily holds up another court's proceedings or, more often, temporarily stays a lower court's judgment.

supersedeas bond

A bond put up by a person who appeals a judgment. The bond delays the person's obligation to pay the judgment until the appeal is lost.

An appeal does not automatically stay, or halt, the judgment or the execution of the judgment in the lower court. A party must apply to the district court for a stay. Therefore, an appellant in a civil case may be required to post a bond to cover the cost of the appeal and a supersedeas bond to stay the enforcement of the judgment. A **supersedeas bond** is a promise, supported by a form of surety, to secure suspension of a judgment and delay execution upon the judgment, pending the outcome of the appeal. The appellant and its surety, usually an insurance company, agree to pay to the appellee the amount of any damages sustained due to the delay caused by the appeal if the appellant loses the appeal. The court has the authority to set the amount of the supersedeas bond, based on a monetary value set to the risk taken in the appeal. For example, in the *Imperial* case, the court might establish a supersedeas bond of $2 million because of the amount of the verdict and because of the additional devaluation of the real estate as the appellate process continues.

Under Rule 7 of the Federal Rules of Appellate Procedure, the district court may require an appellant to file a bond or provide other security in such form and amount as the court finds necessary to ensure payment of costs on appeal. Security costs for the appeal include the cost of filing fees for docketing the appeal, the cost of the clerk's preparing and transmitting the record, and the cost attributed to the losing party for transcribing and printing the necessary copies of the briefs, appendixes, and records. Costs are eventually paid by the party losing the appeal.

Ordering the Transcript

Under Rule 10(b) of the Federal Rules of Appellate Procedure, within 10 days of the filing of the notice of appeal the appellant is responsible for making a written request, on a form supplied by the district court clerk, to the court reporter for the complete transcript, the official daily record of the court proceeding, or desired portions of the transcript. A copy of the request is filed with the clerk of the district court. If the appellant does not order a copy of the transcript, the appellant must file a certificate stating that no transcript will be ordered. The appellant must also notify the clerk of the appellate court that the transcript has been ordered. Exhibit 16–3 is an example of the Transcript Purchase Order form available on the various courts of appeals Web sites.

Responsibilities of Appellant and Appellee   According to Rule 10(b) of the Federal Rules of Appellate Procedure, if the entire transcript is not included in the appeal, the appellant, within 10 days of filing the notice of appeal, must file a statement of the issues that will be presented on appeal. This statement, along with a copy of the order for the transcript or a copy of the certificate stating that no transcript will be ordered, must then be served on the appellee. Under the provisions of Rule 10(b), the appellee then has 10 days to file and serve on the appellant a designation of any additional parts of the transcript that the appellee wants included. If the appellant does not order the additional parts, the appellee may order those parts or apply to the district court for an order requiring the appellant to do so.

Responsibilities of the Court Reporter   Under provisions of Rule 11(b) of the Federal Rules of Appellate Procedure, the court reporter must acknowledge receipt of the order for the transcript. According to Rule 11(b), the reporter must also note at the bottom of the order the date on which the reporter expects to complete the transcript. The reporter then transmits the order to the clerk of the court of appeals.

Rule 11(b) also provides that if the transcript cannot be completed within 30 days of receipt of the order, the court reporter must request an extension of time from the clerk of the court of appeals. The clerk then notes the extension of time granted on the docket and notifies the parties. The court reporter files the completed transcript with the clerk of the district court within 30 days after receipt of the transcript order form and notifies the clerk of the court of appeals of the filing. Under Rule 11(b), if the court reporter does not file the transcript within the allotted time, the clerk of the court of appeals notifies the district judge and takes such steps as may be directed by the court of appeals, including sanctions.

Responsibilities of the Paralegal   As the paralegal, you will have a variety of responsibilities in relation to the transcript. You should, first of all, maintain close contact with the court reporter to make sure of the timely filing of the transcript. Contact

⬥AO 148
(Rev. 6/88)

UNITED STATES COURT OF APPEALS
FOR THE FEDERAL CIRCUIT

) Appeal from ☐ U.S. District Court for _____
               ☐ Court of International Trade
               ☐ Claims Court

–VERSUS--

) TRIAL COURT NO. _____

) CIRCUIT COURT NO. _____

TRANSCRIPT PURCHASE ORDER
(See Rules 10(b) and 11(b) of the Federal Rules of Appellate Procedure)

PART 1 -   TO BE COMPLETED BY APPELLANT WITHIN 10 DAYS OF FILING OF NOTICE OF APPEAL.
         Copies to be distributed by appellant as follows: Copies 1, 2, and 3 to court reporter; Copy 4 to Trial Court;
         Copy 5 to appellee; Copy 6 retained by appellant.

    A. Complete one of the following:
        ☐ A transcript is not needed for the appeal
        ☐ A transcript is already on file
        ☐ Request is hereby made to the reporter for a transcript of the following proceedings (give particulars):
           Note: voir dire and closing arguments are not prepared unless specifically requested.

        Note: Unless the entire transcript is ordered, appellant must attach a statement of the issues to Copies 4 and 5.
    B. I certify that financial arrangements have been made with the reporter. Payment is by:
        ☐ Private funds
        ☐ Government expense (civil case). A motion for transcript has been submitted to the trial judge.

SIGNED _____ Date _____ COUNSEL FOR _____
ADDRESS _____
TELEPHONE _____

PART II - TO BE COMPLETED BY COURT REPORTER.
         Copy 1 and 3 retained by the reporter; Copy 2 to be transmitted to the Court of Appeals on same date transcript
         order is received.
         Date Purchase Order received: _____ .
         Estimated completion date: _____ .
         Estimated number of pages: _____ .

I certify that satisfactory financial arrangements ☐ have ☐ have not been completed with appellant for payment of the cost
of the transcript.

                  _____
                  Signature   Date

              Telephone: _____

PART III-NOTIFICATION THAT TRANSCRIPT HAS BEEN FILED IN THE TRIAL COURT.
         (To be completed by court reporter on date of filing transcript in Trial Court and this notification must be
         to Court of Appeals on same date.)

This is to certify that the transcript has been completed. _____ volumes of transcript have been filed with the Trial Court
today.

_____   _____
      Date   (Signature of Court Reporter)

DISTRIBUTION: COURT REPORTER (3 copies), TRIAL COURT, TRIAL, APPELLANT
(Two of Court Reporter's copies are for completion of Part II and Part III and transmittal to Clerk, U.S. Court of Appeals, Federal Circuit, 717 Madison Place, N.W.
Washington, D.C. 20439.)

EXHIBIT 16–3 Transcript Purchase Order form

the reporter periodically to determine the projected release time for the transcript. If the reporter is unable to complete the transcript within the designated timeframe, designate the order in which you would like to receive parts of the transcript. For example, in the *Imperial* case, if your attorney plans to base the appeal on the judge's erroneous instructions to the jury and on the opposing attorney's inflammatory closing arguments, you would want to request those portions of the transcript first. Once the transcript has been received, review it for accuracy, comparing the transcript with any notes taken by the attorney or the paralegal from the law firm that originally tried the case.

Transmitting the Record

The district court clerk is responsible for arranging in chronological order the original papers filed with the district court. The clerk must also number and index those documents. Once this has been accomplished, the clerk must transmit the record and a certified copy of the docket entries to the court of appeals. This must be done within 15 days of the filing of the notice of appeal, or 15 days after the filing of the transcript, whichever is later. If the deadline cannot be met, the district court clerk must notify the court of appeals of the reasons for the delay and request an extension.

The district clerk will not send to the court of appeals unusually bulky or heavy documents, physical exhibits other than documents, or other parts of the record designated for omission by the local rules of the court of appeals, unless directed to do so by either a party or the circuit clerk. In the case of unusually bulky or heavy exhibits, a party must make arrangements with the clerks of both courts in advance for their transportation and receipt.

The parties may stipulate, or in response to a motion, the district court may order that the district clerk retain the record temporarily for the parties' use in preparation of the appeal. In such an event, the district clerk must certify to the circuit clerk that the record on appeal is complete. Upon receipt of the appellee's brief (or earlier in the event the parties agree or the court orders), the appellant must request that the district clerk forward the record to the circuit court.

Enlargement of Time

If your attorney determines that the time permitted for the appeal is insufficient, you may be asked to draft a **motion for enlargement of time.** Such a motion is authorized by Rule 26 of the Federal Rules of Appellate Procedure. This motion should set forth the reasons that the additional time is needed and the number of additional days required. The court of appeals will generally grant additional time for a new firm taking over an appeal, especially if the case is lengthy and complex. The motion for enlargement of time must be served on all counsel of record. Exhibit 16–4 is an example of a motion for enlargement of time.

motion for enlargement of time

A motion requesting additional time for an appeal, including the reasons that the additional time is needed and the number of additional days required.

**IN THE UNITED STATES COURT OF APPEALS FOR
THE FIFTH CIRCUIT**

Paragon Centre,	)	
	)	
	)	APPEAL NO. 03-31753
Plaintiff-Appelle,	)	
	)	
vs.	)	
	)	
Imperial Gasoline Co.,	)	
	)	
Defendant-Appellant.	)	
	)	
	)	

Appeal from the United States District Court
For the Southern District of Texas
Houston Division, Civil Action No. 02-81891

MOTION FOR AN ENLARGEMENT OF TIME

Now comes Appellant, Imperial Gasoline Company, and files this motion to request that the time for filing its brief be enlarged by 30 days, to October 19, 2003 and, in support of this motion, Appellant shows the following:

I.

The judgment from which this appeal is taken was rendered in cause No. 02-81891 in the Federal District Court for the Southern District of Texas, Houston Division, on June 20, 2003. The appeal was perfected on July 18, 2003. The transcript was filed on August 1, 2003, and the statement of facts was filed on August 10, 2003. Appellant's brief is to be filed on or before September 19, 2003.

II.

The undersigned attorney is solely responsible for the preparation of the Appellant's brief.

III.

The undersigned is lead counsel for a medical malpractice action involving complex issues, Cause No. 03-31791, *Montgomery v. The Stepford-Carmichael Medical Institute,* which is set for trial in the Federal District Court, Southern District of Texas, Houston Division, beginning next week. The court has scheduled three weeks on its docket to hear the case.

WHEREFORE, PREMISES CONSIDERED, Appellant requests the court to enlarge the time for filing Appellant's brief to October 19, 2003.

EXHIBIT 16–4 Motion for an enlargement of time

Respectfully submitted,

By: _____

Attorney for the Defendant-Appellant
Kirchendorfer, Lethane, Zuer, and Musil
216264 Crestview Drive
Houston, Texas 75247
[Telephone number]
[Facsimile number]

CERTIFICATE OF SERVICE

I hereby certify that a true and correct copy of the foregoing has been mailed by first class mail, postage prepaid, to Simon Zuercher, 35713 Marion Road, Baytown, Texas, on this 9th day of September, 2003.

By: _____

Attorney for the Defendant-Appellant

EXHIBIT 16–4   *(continued)*

The Appellate Brief

Often the paralegal is called upon to participate in the drafting of the appellate brief. Your research, writing, organizational, and analytical skills must be employed in this vital part of the appellate process. The court of appeals will not hear witnesses nor see evidence. The brief must therefore be well researched and well written to have the necessary persuasive power.

Drafting the Appellate Brief

The appellate brief is an integral part of the appeal. This formal document consists of the legal issues, the important facts, the legal arguments, and the legal authorities. You may be called on to help draft several types of briefs. These are the appellant's brief, the appellee's brief, and the reply brief. It is also possible for your attorney to, at some time, write and file an amicus curiae or intervenor brief. An **amicus curiae** (literally, "friend of the court") or *intervenor brief* is one that is voluntarily filed by an attorney who is not a part of the case but who has been granted permission to present some legal argument before the court. Before beginning work on a brief, you should locate and review the format of the appellate briefs filed either in that particular case or in that appellate court. You may be asked to assume the responsibility for compiling and organizing the various sections of the brief.

amicus curiae (intervenor)

A person allowed to give argument or appear in a lawsuit (usually to file a brief, but sometimes to take an active part) who is not a party to the lawsuit.

Format of the Brief   In 1998, an amendment to Rule 32(a)(7) of the Federal Rules of Appellate Procedure dramatically changed the method for measuring the length of briefs. A principal brief that does not exceed 30 pages or a reply brief that does not exceed 15 pages is not limited as to the number of words or lines of text. Briefs over

THE COMPUTERIZED LAW FIRM
Submitting an Appellate Brief

SCENARIO

Your attorney calls you into her office and tells you that the *Imperial* case has been appealed. The appellate brief is due in three days. The attorney tells you that she has researched the case and written a draft of the opening brief. It has been some time since the attorney has handled an appeal and wants to be certain that the brief conforms to all the local rules of court. Also, before submitting the brief, your attorney would like you to cite check the document, making sure that all citations are current and verified. She also wants you to prepare a table of authorities for the brief.

Your office does not have a copy of the local rules of court for the appellate court in which you must file the brief. You can obtain a copy of the rules from the court, but the court is more than an hour drive from your office. Also, even though you took courses in legal research, you remember that manually checking citations was a nightmare, not to mention time consuming.

PROBLEM

You are under a time pressure. Not only are you working on this case, but also you are working on another case that is getting ready to go to trial. How do you get a copy of local appellate rules without making a lengthy trip? How can you cite check the brief quickly but accurately? How can you prepare a table of authorities without spending hours of time?

SOLUTION

Many courts, including federal appellate courts, maintain home pages on the Internet. On these Web sites they generally post the latest local rules of court and may even have downloadable forms.

Your local federal appellate court can be located through the following site: **<http://www. uscourts.gov>**. If you know the number of the circuit you can go directly to that home page by typing **<http://www.ca[#].uscourts.gov>** (i.e., Texas would be **<http://www.ca5.uscourts.gov>**. If for some reason you did not have a site address (URL), you could use any of a variety of search engines and look for the "United States Courts of Appeals."

Your second problem is also easily solved. *Shepards* is now available through the on-line Lexis service. Verifying authorities this way is simple and current. The citation to be checked is entered and the authority is instantly verified. There is no need to check multiple supplements nor try to read and interpret numerous abbreviations found in *Shepards* in print. Westlaw contains a similar product called KeyCite, which is similar to *Shepards* and also verifies cites. Additionally, Westlaw provides special software, known as WestCheck®, which is an automated citation-checking software product that verifies citations in a legal document or in a manually entered citations list. This software, used in conjunction with your Word or WordPerfect document, automatically reads and verifies the citations included in the document. Thus your appellate brief can be cite checked in only a few minutes and your results are up to date.

Generating a table of authorities is also easily done. Both Word and WordPerfect have features that will automatically generate a table of authorities. As the document is typed, authorities to be placed in a table of authorities are specially "marked." A table of authorities, in proper format, can be automatically generated when the brief is completed.

that length must contain no more than 14,000 words or 1,300 lines of single-spaced text. Footnotes, headings, and quotes count in these limits. However, Rule 32(a)(7)(B) provides that "the corporate disclosure statement, table of contents, table of citations, statement with respect to oral argument, any addendum containing statutes, rules or regulations, and any certificates of counsel do not count toward the limitation."

This new rule attempts to ensure that each party on appeal has the same amount of text in a brief regardless of the particular word processing technology utilized. In addition, the new rule eliminates a formerly common practice of using footnotes, margin adjustments, and font changes to increase the amount of permissible text in a brief.

Appellate Brief Colors   The color requirements for appellate brief covers include: (1) appellant—blue; (2) appellee—red; (3) amicus curiae or intervenor—green; (4) reply—gray, and any supplemental brief—tan. The appendix, if separate from the brief itself, must be in a white cover. Front covers of the brief and appendix must include: (1) the name of the court; (2) the number of the case; (3) the title of the case; (4) the nature of the proceedings; (5) the name of the lower court; (6) the title of the brief; and (7) names, office addresses, and telephone number of counsel representing the party on whose behalf the brief is filed.

Researching the Law   An experienced paralegal is often asked to assist in researching the law in preparing the appellate brief. Responsibilities in this regard may include researching potential legal theories, locating supporting authority, researching pertinent parts of the record, and verifying the correctness of both the citations and the brief format.

Drafting the Statement of Facts   Good writing skills and an analytical mind are requirements for drafting the statement of facts. Knowing where to find the pertinent facts to incorporate in the appellate brief is critical. It is also important to be able to figure out which facts should be included in the relatively short statement of facts. To accomplish these tasks, you may be required to summarize the transcript and index testimony for inclusion in the appellate brief. Familiarity with the transcript will enable you to effectively assist your attorney with the drafting of the brief. Indexed summaries of the transcript and exhibits should be incorporated into a three-ring binder and provided to each member of the legal team working on the brief. The binder might also include pertinent pleadings, trial exhibits, statutes, and cases that will be relied on in the brief.

Appellant, Appellee, and Reply Briefs

As noted previously, the three most important briefs that you may be required to work on are the appellant's brief, the appellee's brief, and the reply brief.

Appellant's Brief   The requirements for the **appellant's brief** vary slightly among the federal circuit courts of appeal, but generally include the following in the order indicated:

appellant's brief
Brief of the person bringing an appeal.

1. A corporate disclosure statement if required by Rule 26.1.
2. Table of contents, with page references.
3. Table of cases in alphabetical order, with page references and list of statutes, treatises, and law review articles, including the author's name where appropriate, with page references.
4. Statement of jurisdiction.
5. Statement of issues.
6. Statement of the case, the nature of the case, the course of the proceedings, and disposition in the court below.

7. The statement of facts that are relevant to the legal issues, including appropriate references to the record.

8. Summary of the argument.

9. The argument, including the reasons for the contentions regarding issues, as well as citations to authorities, statutes, and parts of the record relied upon, and so on.

10. A short conclusion listing the exact relief sought.

11. Certificate of compliance, if required by Rule 32(a)(7) of the Federal Rules of Appellate Procedure.

The appellant is also required to file an appendix to its brief, which includes the following parts:

1. Relevant docket entries in the lower court proceeding.

2. Relevant portions of the pleadings, charge, findings, or opinion.

3. Judgment, order, or decision in question.

4. Any other parts of the record to which the parties wish to direct the attention of the court.

Ten copies of the appendix must be filed with the clerk. One copy is served on each counsel of record. Rule 30(d) of the Federal Rules of Appellate Procedure specifies the arrangement of the appendix as follows:

1. Table of contents, with page references to the beginning of each part of the appendix.

2. Relevant docket entries.

3. Other parts of the record in chronological order.

Exhibits designated for inclusion in the appendix may be placed in a separate volume. The cover of a separately bound exhibit volume must be white. Four copies of this separate *exhibits volume* must be filed with the appendix, and a copy served on counsel for each party.

appellee's brief
Brief of the person who opposes an appeal.

Appellee's Brief   The **appellee's brief** should follow the requirements of the appellant's brief, with the exception that none of the following are required unless the appellee is dissatisfied with the appellant's statement: (a) the jurisdictional statement; (b) the statement of the issues; (c) the statement of the case; (d) the statement of the facts; or (e) the statement of the standard of review.

Reply Brief   Rule 28(c) of the Federal Rules of Appellate Procedure permits the appellant to file a brief in reply to the appellee's brief. The appellee may also file a cross-appeal. As noted earlier in this chapter, cross-appeal is an appeal filed by the appellee based on a different legal rationale than the appeal filed by the appellant. If the appellee files a cross-appeal, the appellant will file a brief in response to the issues presented in the cross-appeal. The appellee can then file a reply to the appellant's response. No further briefs are permitted, except by leave of the court. A reply brief must contain a table of contents, with page references, and a table of authorities that includes cases arranged alphabetically, and statutes and other authorities, complete with references to the pages of the reply brief on which the authorities are cited.

Filing and Service of Appellate Briefs

According to Rule 31 of the Federal Rules of Appellate Procedure, the appellant must file and serve its brief within 40 days after the date on which the record is filed. The appellee has 30 days after service of the appellant's brief to file and serve its brief, unless service upon the appellee was by mail. In this situation, the appellee is ,allowed three additional days for filing the brief. Under Rule 31(a), the appellant's reply brief is due 14 days after service of the appellee's brief. It must, however, be filed at least three days before the argument of the case, except for good cause. A brief is deemed timely filed if it is mailed within the time permitted by the pertinent court rule. It does not have to actually reach the clerk's office by that day.

Rule 31 of the Federal Rules of Appellate Procedure allows a court of appeals to require the filing of a greater, as well as a lesser, number of copies of briefs than the 25 copies noted in the rule. This rule also requires that two copies must be served on each unrepresented party and on counsel for each separately represented party. As the paralegal, you should refer to the local rules published by your particular circuit to determine the appropriate number of copies to be filed. If the appellant fails to file its brief within the time allowed, the appellee may move for a dismissal of the appeal. If the appellee fails to file a brief, it will not be heard at the oral argument, except by permission of the court.

Coordinating the Oral Argument

The **oral argument** is the presentation of the basis for the appeal before the court of appeals. Oral arguments are permitted in all appellate cases unless, pursuant to local rules, a three-judge panel, after examination of the briefs, unanimously decides that oral argument is not needed for any of the following reasons:

oral argument
The presentation of each side of a case before an appeals court. The presentation typically involves oral statements by a lawyer, interrupted by questions from the judge.

1. the appeal is frivolous;
2. the dispositive issues have been authoritatively decided; or
3. the briefs and records adequately present the facts and legal arguments, thereby reducing the possibility that the decision-making process would be significantly advanced by oral argument.

If such a local rule exists, the party desiring the oral argument may file a statement with the court listing the reasons that it should be granted the oral argument. The court notifies the parties of the date, time, and place of the oral argument. The court also notifies the parties of the amount of time allotted for each side's presentation. The appellant opens and closes the oral argument. Even though the parties do not request oral argument, the court may direct that the case be argued.

Preparing for the Oral Argument

The paralegal's duties related to oral argument may vary, depending on the complexity of the case, the economic constraints, or the paralegal's experience. As an experienced paralegal, you may be asked to prepare for and attend the oral argument.

Outline of the Argument You may be requested to assist your attorney in preparing the written outline for the oral argument. This outline is incorporated into the oral argument notebook, which may include copies of pertinent cases and pleadings. Capsule summaries of the trial transcripts may also be included in the oral argument notebook.

Research Notebook for Justices For the convenience of the court, you may be asked to prepare a notebook of research for each justice, consisting of cases that your attorney anticipates the court will need to consider in its decision. The cases may be indexed by the court rendering the decision or alphabetically by the parties. Additionally, the notebook may include summaries of the records that have been organized and indexed.

Delivery of the Exhibits to Court You may also be given the responsibility to deliver the exhibits to the court of appeals for the oral argument. You will also have to make arrangements for the prompt removal of these exhibits. This is especially important because Rule 34(g) of the Federal Rules of Appellate Procedure provides that any physical evidence not removed within a reasonable time after notice to the counsel by the clerk is to be destroyed or disposed of.

Assisting at Oral Argument

As in the deposition or the trial, you may be asked to attend the oral arguments and make complete notes for your attorney's use during her portion of the oral argument. Thus, your attorney will be free to concentrate on her argument, without the distraction of making notes during the opposition's argument.

Final Procedures

We are nearing the end of the litigation process. After the court of appeals has rendered a decision, a dissatisfied party may seek to continue the appellate process. However, should the defendant eventually lose the case, the plaintiff may use certain posttrial judgment procedures to secure payment of the award.

Further Appeal Procedures

Under provisions of Rule 40 of the Federal Rules of Appellate Procedure, if the losing party desires to appeal the decision of the court of appeals, a petition for rehearing should be filed. A **petition for rehearing** asks that a higher court's decision be reviewed. This petition must be filed within 14 days after the judgment is entered, unless the time is either shortened or enlarged by order of the court. The requirements for a petition for rehearing are the same as those for briefs, and, therefore, subject to Rule 32 of the Federal Rules of Appellate Procedures, unless the court permits or a local rule provides differently. A petition for rehearing must not exceed

petition for rehearing
A request to reconsider an action that may have been wrongfully taken or overlooked in a previous hearing.

rehearing
A new hearing to reconsider an action that may have been wrongfully taken or overlooked in a prior hearing.

petition for certiorari
A request to a higher court for review, but which the higher court is not required to take for decision.

certiorari
A writ from the higher court asking the lower court for the record of the case.

judgment creditor
A person who has proven a debt in court and is entitled to use court processes to collect it.

judgment debtor
A person who has yet to satisfy a judgment that has been rendered against him or her.

postjudgment interrogatories
Written questions that the judgment debtor must answer in writing about his or her assets.

15 pages. A petition for a rehearing is not a prerequisite to the filing of a petition for certiorari. A **petition for certiorari** is a request for a rehearing before the United States Supreme Court.

Posttrial Judgment Procedures

Statutory remedies allow for the execution of a judgment within 30 days after the entry of judgment. The party seeking to execute on the judgment is known as the **judgment creditor.** The party who must pay the judgment is known as the **judgment debtor.** Often it is helpful for the judgment creditor to uncover details about the financial condition of the judgment debtor. To facilitate this process, the law permits postjudgment discovery. Postjudgment discovery procedures offer the judgment creditor a relatively simple and inexpensive method of determining the amount and the location of a party's assets. **Postjudgment interrogatories,** for example, are written questions that the judgment debtor must answer in writing about his assets. A **postjudgment deposition** can also be taken after sending the opposing counsel a **notice of intent to take oral deposition by nonstenographic means.** This type of deposition is taken with only a dictating machine or a tape recorder, with no court reporter present. The judgment creditor could also use a postjudgment request for production of documents to obtain necessary financial information from the judgment debtor.

Without the filing of a supersedeas bond, a writ of execution may be issued 10 days after entry of a final judgment order. A **writ of execution** is a court order compelling the seizure of the judgment debtor's property to satisfy the judgment. Proper notice must be given to the public and to anyone who has an interest in that property before it can be sold at a public auction. In addition, the judgment debtor must be given the opportunity to pay the judgment creditor before the auction is held. The law also prescribes the order in which certain types of property can be seized and sold at auction. Usually, personal property is seized and sold before real property is subject to seizure. After the auction has been held and the debt satisfied, any remaining amount goes to the judgment debtor.

Another means by which the judgment creditor could collect is by using a posttrial garnishment. A **posttrial garnishment** is a separate but ancillary lawsuit, filed in the court that rendered the judgment. The **garnishment** is brought against a third-party **garnishee** that is holding assets belonging to the judgment debtor. The judgment creditor must obtain a writ of garnishment. (See Exhibit 16–5.) The garnishee is then served with the writ and a summons. The garnishee will be compelled to reveal how much of the judgment debtor's money or property is in its possession. Once this is known, the judgment creditor can seize the money or property or prevent the judgment creditor from receiving any of that money or property. Bank accounts and wages can be the targets of a posttrial garnishment. However, state and federal laws protect a certain percentage of the debtor's income so that she can still make a living, despite the garnishment.

postjudgment deposition
A deposition that can be taken after judgment, with only a dictating machine or a tape recorder, with no court reporter present.

notice of intent to take oral deposition by nonstenographic means
A notice sent to opposing counsel of an intent to take a deposition after the judgment by use of only a dictating machine or a tape recorder, with no court reporter present.

writ of execution
A document that orders a court official to take a debtor's property to pay a court decided debt.

execution
Carrying out or completion. An official carrying out of a court's order or judgment.

posttrial garnishment
A separate, but ancillary, lawsuit, filed in the court that rendered the judgment, to permit the judgment creditor to collect on a judgment.

garnishment
A legal process, taken by a creditor who has received a money judgment against a debtor, to get the debtor's money. This is done by attachment of a bank account or by taking a percentage of the debtor's regular income.

garnishee
A person who holds money or property belonging to a debtor and who is subject to a garnishment.

**IN THE UNITED STATES DISTRICT COURT
FOR THE SOUTHERN DISTRICT OF TEXAS, HOUSTON DIVISION**

Paragon Centre,   )
)
    Plaintiff,   )   CIVIL ACTION NO. 02-81891
)
vs.   )
)
Imperial Gasoline Co.,   )
)
    Defendant.   )
)
)

<u>WRIT OF GARNISHMENT</u>

TO: THE TEXAS LONGHORN BANK AND TRUST COMPANY, 444 Houston Plaza, Houston, Texas, 75429, Garnishee;

1. Paragon Centre is the plaintiff in the case of Paragon Centre v. Imperial Gasoline Company, in Civil Action No. 02-81891, in the Federal District Court for the Southern District of Texas, Houston Division. In this case the plaintiff has a valid, uncollected judgment against the defendant for the sum of $750,000 with interest charged at a rate of 10% per year and costs of the suit.

2. Plaintiff has applied for a writ of garnishment against The Texas Longhorn Bank and Trust Company.

3. You are hereby commanded to appear before this court at 9 A.M. on November 22, 2003. You will at that time be required to answer under oath what property belonging to the defendant you have in your possession or had in your possession when this writ was served upon you, and what money owing to or belonging to the defendant you have in your possession or had in your possession when this writ was served upon you. At that time you will also be required to answer under oath what other persons you know of who have property belonging to the defendant in their possession or had in their possession at the time this writ was served upon you, and what other persons you know of who owe the defendant money or have possession of money belonging to the defendant or had in their possession when this writ was served upon you money belonging to the defendant.

4. The official who served this writ upon you is also charged with serving the defendant, Imperial Gasoline Company, with a true copy of this writ.

Dated and Issued on October 22, 2003.

ATTESTED TO BY:

_____
Clerk of the Federal District Court,
Southern District of Texas,
Houston Division

_____
Presiding Judge

EXHIBIT 16–5   Writ of garnishment

FINDING IT ON THE INTERNET

The Federal Rules of Appellate Procedure, together with appellate rules for the Fifth Circuit, can be accessed at **<http://www.ca5.uscourts.gov/ docs/frap-iop.htm>**.

Access this site and determine the following information relating to an appeal of the *Imperial* case.

a. Review the appellate rules for the Fifth Circuit and determine the final date to file a Notice of Appeal, assuming an entry of judgment or Order date of July 18, 2003.

b. Determine the number of copies of the appellant's brief that must be forwarded to the Fifth Circuit.

c. Research the Fifth Circuit's Web site and report to your attorney the median length of time that an appeal takes in that circuit, based on the most recent statistics available.

A zip format of the Federal Rules of Appellate Procedure is available at **<http://www.afda.org/afda/key/rules.htm>**.

Appellate rules for the Supreme Court are located at the following site: **<http://www.law.cornell.edu/rules/supct/>**.

Summary

- If the court has denied a motion for judgment as a matter of law (or its state court counterpart, motion for a judgment notwithstanding the verdict), made at the close of evidence, the motion may be renewed by service and filing within 10 days after entry of judgment. A motion for new trial under Rule 59 of the Federal Rules of Civil Procedure may be combined with this renewal of the motion for judgment, or, in the alternative, only a motion for new trial may be filed. The motion for new trial will state the legal grounds for the new trial.

- An appeal is filed by a party who has lost a case or who is dissatisfied with a judgment or a court order. The appeal asks that a higher court review the lower court's decision. A person bringing an appeal is referred to as the appellant. The person who opposes an appeal is the appellee. Only questions of law are subject to review. The appellate court has no authority to consider questions relating to the facts of a case. The preliminary steps in an appellate procedure generally include (1) notice of appeal; (2) bond for costs or a supersedeas bond; (3) transcript order and preparation of pertinent record sections; (4) filing of briefs by both parties. Following these preliminary steps, oral arguments are presented to the court, and the court renders its decision.

- The appellate brief is an integral part of the appeal. This formal document consists of the legal issues, the important facts, the legal arguments, and the legal authorities. There are actually several types of briefs that you may be called on to help draft: the appellant's brief, the appellee's brief, and the reply brief. It is also possible for your attorney to write and file an amicus curiae or intervenor brief. An amicus curiae or intervenor brief is voluntarily filed by an attorney who has been granted permission to present some legal argument before the court. The appellee may also file a cross-appeal. A cross-appeal is an appeal filed by the appellee based on a different legal rationale than the appeal filed by the appellant. If the appellee files a cross-appeal, the appellant will file a brief in response to the issues presented in the cross-appeal. The appellee can then file a reply to the appellant's response.

■ Oral argument is the presentation of the basis for the appeal before the court of appeals. Oral arguments are permitted in all appellate cases unless, pursuant to local rules, a three-judge panel, after examination of the briefs, unanimously decides that oral argument is not needed. The paralegal may be requested to assist the attorney in preparing the written outline for the oral argument. This outline is incorporated into the oral argument notebook. For the convenience of the court, the paralegal may be asked to prepare a notebook of research for each justice, consisting of cases that your attorney anticipates the court will need to consider in its decision. The paralegal may also be given the responsibility to deliver the exhibits to the court of appeals for the oral argument. As in a deposition or trial, the paralegal may be asked to attend the oral argument and make complete notes for the attorney's use during her portion of the oral argument.

■ If the losing party desires to appeal the decision of the court of appeals to a higher court, a petition for rehearing should be filed. A petition for rehearing asks that a higher court's decision be reviewed. A petition for certiorari is a request for a rehearing before the United States Supreme Court. Statutory remedies allow for the execution of a judgment within 30 days after the entry of judgment, or sooner. The party seeking to execute the judgment is known as the judgment creditor. The party who must pay the judgment is known as the judgment debtor. Often it is helpful for the judgment creditor to uncover details about the financial condition of the judgment debtor. To facilitate this process, the law permits postjudgment discovery. Without the filing of a supersedeas bond, a writ of execution may be issued 10 days after entry of a final judgment order. A writ of execution is a court order compelling the sale of the judgment debtor's property to satisfy the judgment. Another means to collect a judgment is by using a postjudgment garnishment.

Key Terms

amicus curiae	garnishment	petition for certiorari
appeal	judgment creditor	petition for rehearing
appellant	judgment debtor	postjudgment deposition
appellant's brief	motion for enlargement of time	postjudgment interrogatiories
appellee	notice of appeal	posttrial garnishment
appellee's brief	notice of intent to take oral deposition by nonstenographic means	rehearing
certiorari		supersedeas
cross-appeal	oral argument	supersedeas bond
execution		writ of execution
garnishee		

Review Questions

1. What is a motion for a judgment notwithstanding the verdict?
2. What is a motion for judgment as a matter of law?

3. What is a motion for a new trial?
4. What is an appeal?
5. Who are the parties to an appeal?
6. What is a supersedeas bond? What is its purpose?
7. List and define four types of appellate briefs.
8. What duties does the paralegal have in relation to oral arguments?
9. What postjudgment discovery devices are available to a judgment creditor?
10. What posttrial judgment procedures are available to collect a judgment?

Chapter Exercises

Where necessary, check with your instructor prior to starting any of these exercises.
1. Review the laws of your state and find all state appellate court rules. Compare the state and federal court rules to determine the differences between the two.
2. Prepare a memorandum describing the duties of the paralegal during the appellate process in relation to the transcript.
3. Use the facts contained in the *Imperial* case to draft 10 postjudgment interrogatories to Paragon Centre.
4. Prepare a notice of intent to take oral deposition by stenographic means for Jackson R. Towery, Chief Financial Officer of Paragon Centre. Draft 10 questions for your attorney to include in her deposition of Mr. Towery to determine the actual damages sustained by Paragon Centre because of the loss of tenants following the gas leak.

Chapter Project

Review the *Imperial* case in the opening commentary. Recall that the case originated in Houston, Texas: the appeal must therefore be brought in the Fifth Circuit Court of Appeals. Remember also that each circuit has local rules that must be followed, in addition to the Federal Rules of Appellate Procedure. Draft a memo in which you tell a new paralegal in your firm about the requirements for the appellant's brief in the *Imperial* case.

The *Bennett* Case
Assignment 16: Filing an Appeal

The *Bennett* case went to trial. The plaintiff lost and now wants to appeal. Prepare the notice of appeal and request for reporter's transcript. Also, check with your local federal court and determine what the filing fee is for the notice of appeal.

APPENDIX A

SAMPLE DEPOSITION

```
 1   ELISHA VELIKOVSKY                        )
 2                                            )   Civil Action No. 05-7507
 3        Plaintiff,                          )
 4                                            )
 5                                            )
 6        v.                                  )
 7                                            )
 8   BEREA COUNTY                             )
 9   HOSPITAL, et al.                         )
10                                            )
11        Defendants.                         )
12   _____   )
13                                            )
14
15
16   APPEARANCES:
17
18   Bishop, Davidson & Turner
19   By: Simon Bishop
20   For the Plaintiff
21
22   Stephens, Wilcox, Brantley & Matlock
23   By: Emma Archard
24   For the Defendants
25
26   STIPULATIONS:
27
28
```

```
 1        It is hereby stipulated and agreed by and between counsel that all objections, except as to
 2   the form of the questions, be reserved until the time of the trial.
 3
 4                                            David Cornwell, R. T., sworn
 5
 6   BY MR. BISHOP:
 7
 8   Q.  Would you please state your full name for the record?
```

449

9
10   A. David Austin Cornwell.

11
12   Q. Where are you employed, Mr. Cornwell?

13
14   A. Berea County Hospital.

15
16   Q. At what address is Berea County Hospital located?

17
18   A. 17810 Glessner Avenue, in Berea.

19
20   Q. Mr. Cornwell, would you briefly list your educational background.

21
22   A. I attended Berea County Community College, where I earned an associate of applied science
23   degree in radiologic technology.

24
25   Q. Do you have any board certification?

26
27   A. Yes. I became a registered radiologic technologist in 1996 and a certified radiologic
28   technologist in 1997.

[Page 3 of 20]

1   Q. Would you explain the process required to become a certified radiologic
2   technologist?

3
4   A. At least an associate's degree is required, plus satisfactory performance on a state-
5   administered, nationally recognized examination.

6
7   Q. How many hours of clinical work were you required to perform as part of
8   your education?

9
10   A. I was required to perform 320 hours of supervised radiologic work at an
11   approved center.

12
13   Q. At what approved center did you perform your clinical work?

14
15   A. At BCH.

16
17   Q. And BCH is . . .

18
19   A. I'm sorry. BCH is Berea County Hospital.

20
21   Q. So, prior to being hired by BCH, you had 320 hours of clinical experience in their X-Ray
22   Department.

23
24   A. Radiology Department.

25
26   Q. I beg your pardon.

27
28

1   A. It's called the Radiology Department.

2

3   Q. So, prior to being hired by BCH, you had 320 hours of clinical experience in their Radiology

4   Department?

5

6   A. Actually, I had a lot more experience than that.

7

8   Q. Why is that?

9

10   A. Under state rules, once you're in your second year of an accredited radiologic

11   program, you can work in a department as long as you're under the

12   supervision of a CRT.

13

14   Q. What exactly is a CRT?

15

16   A. A Certified Radiologic Technologist.

17

18   Q. So, you were hired by BCH during your second year in the program at Berea County

19   Community College?

20

21   A. That's correct.

22

23   Q. How many hours per week did you work?

24

25   A. Well, it varied, but usually around 20.

26

27   Q. So, before being hired on a full-time basis, you had worked how long for BCH?

28

1

2   A. About six months.

3

4   Q. When were you hired on a full-time basis?

5

6   A. Right after graduation.

7

8   Q. Totaling all this time, how long have you worked for the X-Ray, that is, the Radiology

9   Department at BCH?

10

11   A. Two years.

12

13   Q. Are you familiar with the procedure manual at BCH?

14
15   A. Yes. Everyone is required to read it and sign a form that indicates that they
16   have done so.
17
18   Q. And did you read it and sign the appropriate form?
19
20   A. Yes I did.
21
22   (Deposition Exhibit 1 marked for identification)
23
24   Q. Mr. Cornwell, I'd like you to take a look at the document that I have marked Exhibit 1 and
25   tell me if that is the form that you signed.
26
27   A. Yes. That's it.
28

[Page 6 of 20]

1   Q. And is that your signature?
2
3   A. Yes, it is.
4
5   (Deposition Exhibit 2 marked for identification)
6
7   Q. Mr. Cornwell, I'd like you to take a look at the document that I've marked
8   Exhibit 2 and tell me if that is a copy of the policy and procedure manual used
9   at BCH.
10
11   A. Yes, it is.
12
13   Q. Mr. Cornwell, in a typical day at the hospital, how many patients do you see in the
14   Radiology Department?
15
16   A. Typical day—there's no such thing as a typical day. I probably see on an average of 30 to 40
17   patients a day.
18
19   Q. Since you see so many patients, it is unlikely that you'd remember any single patient.
20
21   A. That's true.
22
23   Q. Mr. Cornwell, do you remember a patient named Elisha Velikovsky?
24
25   A. I sure do.
26
27   Q. But you've just testified that you don't remember most of your patients.
28

1 A. She's the first one I ever saw come close to dying, so I'll always remember her.

3 Q. Do you remember why Ms. Velikovsky was taken to the Radiologic Department?

5 A. Yes. She was scheduled for an IVP.

7 Q. And what is an IVP?

9 A. An intravenous pyelogram.

11 Q. Is this procedure dangerous?

13 A. Not usually.

15 Q. But it can be.

17 A. Oh sure, if the patient is allergic to the contrast material.

19 Q. Mr. Cornwell, let's back up for a moment. Explain the procedure you performed on Ms.
20 Velikovsky.

22 A. Well, we inject the patient with a contrast material. The contrast material acts sort of like a
23 dye. That allows the radiologist to see things that he ordinarily wouldn't see absent the
24 contrast material.

26 Q. And you say that this is a dangerous procedure.

28 A. It can be if the patient has an allergic reaction to the contrast medium.

1 Q. Mr. Cornwell, did Ms. Velikovsky realize the dangers involved in this procedure?

3 A. I don't think so.

5 Q. And why do you say that?

7 A. Well, the radiologist never explained it to her.

9 Q. And who was the radiologist on March 17 of last year when Ms. Velikovsky underwent this
10 examination?

12 A. Dr. Arthur Langdon.

14 Q. How do you know that Dr. Langdon did not explain the procedure to Ms. Velikovsky?

16 A. Well, he gave me the informed consent form and told me to get her signature on it.

17
18   Q. And what is an informed consent form?
19
20   A. It's a form that explains the dangers of the procedure and tells the patient what alternatives
21   are available.
22
23   Q. And did you get her signature?
24
25   A. Yes.
26
27   Q. Did she ask you what the form was for?
28

[Page 9 of 20]

1   A. Yes.
2
3   Q. And did you tell her?
4
5   A. I never got the chance.
6
7   Q. Why not?
8
9   A. Dr. Langdon came into the room and told her it was just for insurance purposes.
10
11   Q. Is that standard procedure?
12
13   A. That depends.
14
15   Q. What does it depend on?
16
17   A. Well, it depends on the radiologist.
18
19   Q. What does the policy and procedure manual say?
20
21   A. Oh, the procedure manual is clear as a bell. It says the radiologist is required to explain the
22   dangers of the procedure to the patient and to get her signature.
23
24   Q. How often did Dr. Langdon violate this explicit procedure?
25
26   BY MS. ARCHARD:
27
28

[Page 10 of 20]

1   A. I object. Mr. Cornwell has not been present every time Dr. Langdon has
2   performed his job in the Radiology Department. Therefore, he is not qualified to
3   answer that question.

4

5   BY MR. BISHOP:

6

7   Q. How many times have you observed Dr. Langdon violating this procedure?

8

9   A. Every time I've worked with him.

10

11   Q. Mr. Cornwell, are there any procedures that should be followed to help prevent an allergic
12   reaction to a contrast material?

13

14   A. Well, you really should ask patients if they have any allergies.

15

16   Q. On the day in question, did Dr. Langdon ask Ms. Velikovsky about her allergies?

17

18   A. No.

19

20   Q. Do you remember why he did not ask her about her allergies?

21

22   A. I guess he thought we didn't have the time.

23

24   Q. Would the patient's chart include this information?

25

26   A. Yes.

27

28

[Page 11 of 20]

1   (Deposition Exhibit 3 marked for identification)

2

3   Q. Mr. Cornwell, I'd like you to look at the document that I've marked Exhibit 3 and tell me
4   what it is.

5

6   A. It's a copy of Ms. Velikovsky's chart.

7

8   Q. And what does it say about her allergies?

9

10   A. It just says that she answered "yes" when she was asked about her allergies.

11

12   Q. Is there any other information on her chart about her allergies?

13

14   A. No.

15

16   Q. Is that unusual?

17

18   A. No, not really.

19

20   Q. Why not?

21

22 A. Sometimes the patient doesn't know exactly what she's allergic to, and sometimes the
23   admitting nurse doesn't ask or gets busy with something else, things like that.
24
25 Q. I see. Now, to your knowledge, did Dr. Langdon check Ms. Velikovsky's chart?
26
27 A. No, he didn't.
28

[Page 12 of 20]

1   Q. You're certain?
2
3   A. Yes.
4
5   Q. How can you be so certain?
6
7   A. I asked him if he wanted to see the chart, and he said no.
8
9   Q. Why was that?
10
11 A. Well, like I said before, he thought we didn't have the time for petty details.
12
13 Q. Were those his words?
14
15 A. Which words?
16
17 Q. You said that Dr. Langdon didn't think you had time for "petty details." Did he use the
18   words "petty details"?
19
20 A. Yes. That was one of his favorite sayings.
21
22 Q. Now, since Ms. Velikovsky's chart indicated a long history of allergies, would the IVP have
23   been canceled?
24
25 A. Not necessarily.
26
27 Q. Why not?
28

[Page 13 of 20]

1   A. There are a few relatively new contrast materials that could be substituted for the one that
2   we usually use.
3
4   Q. Such as?
5
6   A. Well, let's see, there's Iopamidol and Iohexol.
7
8   Q. Why would these be preferable?

9
10   A. The risk of anaphylactic shock is much lower if you use them.
11
12   Q. Just what is anaphylactic shock?
13
14   A. That's what happened to Ms. Velikovsky.
15
16   BY MS. ARCHARD:
17
18   A. I object. The witness is not in a position to say exactly what happened to
19   Ms. Velikovsky.
20
21   BY MR. BISHOP:
22
23   Q. Mr. Eckerson, could you rephrase your answer without referring to Ms. Velikovsky?
24
25   A. I've forgotten the question.
26
27   Q. What is anaphylactic shock?
28

[Page 14 of 20]

1   A. That's the medical term for an allergic reaction.
2
3   Q. And is it life-threatening?
4
5   A. It can be, yes.
6
7   Q. If the risk of shock is much less with these materials, why didn't Dr. Langdon
8   use them?
9
10   A. He told me that he thought they were much too expensive.
11
12   Q. Are there any other precautions that can be taken to lessen the risks that go along
13   with an IVP?
14
15   A. Yes. You're supposed to have some intravenous epinephrine nearby and ready to
16   go just in case.
17
18   Q. And what is intravenous epinephrine?
19
20   A. It's sort of like an antidote.
21
22   Q. And was that antidote available?
23
24   A. Not exactly.
25

26 Q. Would you explain what you mean by that?

27

28 A. We had some in the hospital, but we didn't have it in the Radiology Department.

[Page 15 of 20]

1 Q. Was Dr. Langdon aware of this?

2

3 A. Yes.

4

5 Q. How can you be so certain?

6

7 A. Because I told him so.

8

9 Q. And how did he react?

10

11 A. Well, he got really angry. You see, we were really swamped that day and I think he just

12 didn't want to take the time.

13

14 Q. And what did you do?

15

16 A. Well, I told him again that we really shouldn't perform the test without the

17 epinephrine.

18

19 Q. What did he do then?

20

21 A. Well, he told me he was running the department and to mind my own business.

22

23 Q. What did you say to that?

24

25 A. I told him it was my business.

26

27 Q. How did he react?

28

[Page 16 of 20]

1 A. He told me to go to pharmacy and get the epinephrine.

2

3 Q. And did you?

4

5 A. Yes.

6

7 Q. What transpired next?

8

9 A. Apparently, Dr. Langdon went ahead with the test after I left. When I got back, the crash

10 cart was already there. Ms. Velikovsky had apparently suffered cardiac arrest.

11

12 Q. Is it standard procedure to begin such a test without the antidote present?

13
14   A. Absolutely not.
15
16   Q. You're certain of this?
17
18   A. Yes, I am. I was so shook up I double-checked the manual about 50 times. Without the
19   epinephrine you're not supposed to do anything.
20
21   Q. Yet Dr. Langdon went ahead with the test?
22
23   BY MS. ARCHARD:
24
25   A. I object. Mr. Cornwell was not present in the room when the alleged test took place. He
26   cannot possibly know whether Dr. Langdon administered the test.
27
28

[Page 17 of 20]

1   BY MR. BISHOP:
2
3   Q. Mr. Cornwell, what is hospital policy at BCH when something like this event
4   occurs?
5
6   A. You're supposed to fill out an incident report.
7
8   Q. And was one filled out in this case?
9
10   A. Not to my knowledge.
11
12   Q. Do you know why not?
13
14   A. Dr. Langdon said it wasn't necessary.
15
16   Q. Is that standard procedure?
17
18   A. No, like I said, the manual says to fill out an incident report.
19
20   BY MR. BISHOP:
21
22   A. I have no further questions.
23
24   BY MS. ARCHARD:
25
26   Q. Just for the record, Mr. Cornwell, you were not actually present in the X-Ray Department
27   when Ms. Velikovsky suffered her trauma, is that correct?
28

1   A. No, it's not correct.

2

3   Q. It's not correct? How so?

4

5   A. It's called the Radiology Department, not the X-Ray Department.

6

7   Q. Very well, then. You were not present in the Radiology Department when Ms. Velikovsky
8   suffered her trauma?

9

10 A. Yes. Like I said, I'd been sent to pharmacy.

11

12 Q. So you really don't know what happened in your absence?

13

14 A. No. I only know that when I came back to the department the crash cart was
15   already there.

16

17 Q. Mr. Cornwell, do you know in fact that an incident report was never filed?

18

19 A. No. I only know that Dr. Langdon told me that it wasn't necessary to fill out an incident
20   report in this case.

21

22 Q. How often have you seen that happen?

23

24 A. See what happen?

25

26 Q. How often have you witnessed events that you thought needed an incident report when
27   none was filed?

28

1   A. Practically every day.

2

3   Q. Mr. Cornwell, if Ms. Velikovsky's heart attack had not resulted from an allergic reaction to
4   the contrast medium, but had resulted from natural causes, would an incident report be
5   required?

6

7   A. No. An incident report is required only when someone has made a mistake.

8

9   Q. Mr. Cornwell, are you still employed at HGH?

10

11 A. Yes. But not in the Radiology Department

12

13 Q. Why not?

14

15 A. I left the department about six months ago.

16
17   Q. Why was that?
18
19   A. I decided I couldn't take the pressure.
20
21   Q. Pressure like the day Ms. Velikovsky suffered her alleged allergic reaction?
22
23   A. I guess so.
24
25   Q. Isn't it possible that you were the one who made the mistake on the day that Ms. Velikovsky
26   suffered her trauma?
27
28   A. I don't see how.

[Page 20 of 20]

1   Q. Well, you just said that you couldn't take the kind of pressure you said you were under that
2   day in the Radiology Department.
3
4   A. I didn't say that I couldn't take the pressure on that particular day.
5
6   Q. Admit it, Mr. Cornwell, you cracked under pressure that day and decided that you, and not
7   Dr. Langdon, a well-trained and highly respected radiologist, knew what was best for the
8   patient.
9
10   BY MR. BISHOP:
11
12   A. I object. You're badgering the witness. Move on with the examination.
13
14   BY MS. ARCHARD:
15
16   Q. Mr. Cornwell, between the radiologist and the radiologic technologist, who is presumed by
17   the medical profession to know what's best for the patient?
18
19   A. The radiologist, I guess, but . . .
20
21   Q. That's all. I have no further questions for this witness.
22
23
24
25
26
27
28

APPENDIX B

BENNETT RESEARCH FILE

Contents

Client Interview Summary

Relevant United States Code Sections on Employment Discrimination (42 U.S.C. §2000e et seq.)

Relevant Code of Federal Regulations Regarding Claim to EEOC (29 C.F.R. 1601)

Relevant provisions from Federal Rules of Civil Procedure (Rules 7 and 15)

Sample Complaint Form—Employment Discrimination

Client Interview Summary

Personal Data

Name	Alice Bennett
Home Address	2367 Meadow Ln., New York, New York
Address for Billing	Same
Home Telephone	212 555-1212
Work Telephone	None
Cell Phone	212 555-3987
Fax Number	None
E-mail	aben@yahoo.com
Date of Birth	09/15/1970
Social Security No.	215-90-1111
Spouse's Name	Robert Bennett
Employer	None

Information Relating to Claim

Client, Alice Bennett, provided the following information: Client believes that she was a recent victim of employment discrimination based on gender which occurred at Rikards-Hayley, an investment banking firm located at 121 Centre St., New York, New York. She began working for Rikards-Hayley four years ago (she started work on January 5). Her first job was in training and development, where she received nothing but superior evaluations from her supervisors. Approximately two years ago she was promoted to acting manager of the department. As acting manager she received superior evaluations.

Five months ago the company decided to fill the manager position permanently. Bennett applied for the position. She was told by her supervisor, Darren Blackwood, that management liked her work but that she did not quite fit the image they were seeking. She needed to lose weight as well as change her attitude toward male employees. She was perceived as being "too assertive." It would be better, she was told, if she could show more deference. Bennett was not hired as manager. Instead, the company hired Martina Yardly.

After Yardly was hired, Bennett states that her life was made miserable. Yardly criticized her work constantly. She also made comments about her appearance, stating that even though she was not hired as manager, she should still try to lose weight and "fix herself up." Two months ago, Bennett was fired.

When male employees in Bennett's position are terminated from Rikards-Hayley, they commonly receive a severance package consisting of one year's salary. Bennett received a severance package consisting of six months salary.

As a result of her treatment at work, Bennett claims that she suffered physically and emotionally. She is still seeing a doctor for physical and mental side effects of the stress. To date her medical bills total $2500. She has also been unable to find other work. In the year before she was terminated, Bennett earned $150,000.

Relevant United States Code Sections—Employment Discrimination
Title 42

§ 2000e. Definitions

For the purposes of this subchapter—

(a) The term "person" includes one or more individuals, governments, governmental agencies, political subdivisions, labor unions, partnerships, associations, corporations, legal representatives, mutual companies, joint-stock companies, trusts, unincorporated organizations, trustees, trustees in cases under Title 11, or receivers.

(b) The term "employer" means a person engaged in an industry affecting commerce who has fifteen or more employees for each working day in each of twenty or more calendar weeks in the current or preceding calendar year, and any agent of such a person, but such term does not include (1) the United States, a corporation wholly owned by the Government of the United States, an Indian tribe, or any department or agency of the District of Columbia subject by statute to procedures of the competitive service (as defined in section 2102 of Title 5), or (2) a bona fide private membership club (other than a labor organization) which is exempt from taxation under section 501(c) of Title 26, except that during the first year after March 24, 1972, persons having fewer than twenty-five employees (and their agents) shall not be considered employers.

§ 2000e-2. Unlawful employment practices

(a) Employer practices

It shall be an unlawful employment practice for an employer—

(1) to fail or refuse to hire or to discharge any individual, or otherwise to discriminate against any individual with respect to his compensation, terms, conditions, or privileges of employment, because of such individual's race, color, religion, sex, or national origin; or

(2) to limit, segregate, or classify his employees or applicants for employment in any way which would deprive or tend to deprive any individual of employment opportunities or otherwise adversely affect his status as an employee, because of such individual's race, color, religion, sex, or national origin.

§ 2000e-5. Enforcement provisions

(e) Time for filing charges; time for service of notice of charge on respondent; filing of charge by Commission with State or local agency; seniority system

(1) A charge under this section shall be filed within one hundred and eighty days after the alleged unlawful employment practice occurred and notice of the charge (including the date, place and circumstances of the alleged unlawful employment practice) shall be served upon the person against whom such charge is made within ten days thereafter, except that in a case of an unlawful employment practice with respect to which the person aggrieved has initially instituted proceedings with a State or local agency with authority to grant or seek relief from such practice or to institute criminal proceedings with respect thereto upon receiving notice thereof, such charge shall be filed by or on behalf of the person aggrieved within three hundred days after the alleged unlawful employment practice occurred, or within thirty days after receiving notice that the State or local agency has terminated the proceedings under the State or local

law, whichever is earlier, and a copy of such charge shall be filed by the Commission with the State or local agency.

(f) Civil action by Commission, Attorney General, or person aggrieved; preconditions; procedure; appointment of attorney; payment of fees, costs, or security; intervention; stay of Federal proceedings; action for appropriate temporary or preliminary relief pending final disposition of charge; jurisdiction and venue of United States courts; designation of judge to hear and determine case; assignment of case for hearing; expedition of case; appointment of master.

. . . .

(3) Each United States district court and each United States court of a place subject to the jurisdiction of the United States shall have jurisdiction of actions brought under this subchapter. Such an action may be brought in any judicial district in the State in which the unlawful employment practice is alleged to have been committed, in the judicial district in which the employment records relevant to such practice are maintained and administered, or in the judicial district in which the aggrieved person would have worked but for the alleged unlawful employment practice, but if the respondent is not found within any such district, such an action may be brought within the judicial district in which the respondent has his principal office. For purposes of sections 1404 and 1406 of Title 28, the judicial district in which the respondent has his principal office shall in all cases be considered a district in which the action might have been brought.

(g) Injunctions; appropriate affirmative action; equitable relief; accrual of back pay; reduction of back pay; limitations on judicial orders

(1) If the court finds that the respondent has intentionally engaged in or is intentionally engaging in an unlawful employment practice charged in the complaint, the court may enjoin the respondent from engaging in such unlawful employment practice, and order such affirmative action as may be appropriate, which may include, but is not limited to, reinstatement or hiring of employees, with or without back pay (payable by the employer, employment agency, or labor organization, as the case may be, responsible for the unlawful employment practice), or any other equitable relief as the court deems appropriate. Back pay liability shall not accrue from a date more than two years prior to the filing of a charge with the Commission. Interim earnings or amounts earnable with reasonable diligence by the person or persons discriminated against shall operate to reduce the back pay otherwise allowable.

(k) Attorney's fee; liability of Commission and United States for costs

In any action or proceeding under this subchapter the court, in its discretion, may allow the prevailing party, other than the Commission or the United States, a reasonable attorney's fee (including expert fees) as part of the costs, and the Commission and the United States shall be liable for costs the same as a private person.

Relevant Code of Federal Regulations—Claim to EEOC
Title 29 Part 1601

COMMISSION

PART 1601—PROCEDURAL REGULATIONS—Table of Contents

Subpart B—Procedure for the Prevention of Unlawful Employment Practices

Sec. 1601.12 Contents of charge; amendment of charge.

(a) Each charge should contain the following:

(1) The full name, address and telephone number of the person making the charge except as provided in Sec. 1601.7;

(2) The full name and address of the person against whom the charge is made, if known (hereinafter referred to as the respondent);

(3) A clear and concise statement of the facts, including pertinent dates, constituting the alleged unlawful employment practices: See Sec. 1601.15(b);

(4) If known, the approximate number of employees of the respondent employer or the approximate number of members of the respondent labor organization, as the case may be; and

(5) A statement disclosing whether proceedings involving the alleged unlawful employment practice have been commenced before a State or local agency charged with the enforcement of fair employment practice laws and, if so, the date of such commencement and the name of the agency.

(b) Notwithstanding the provisions of paragraph (a) of this section, a charge is sufficient when the Commission receives from the person making the charge a written statement sufficiently precise to identify the parties, and to describe generally the action or practices complained of. A charge may be amended to cure technical defects or omissions, including failure to verify the charge, or to clarify and amplify allegations made therein. Such amendments and amendments alleging additional acts which constitute unlawful employment practices related to or growing out of the subject matter of the original charge will relate back to the date the charge was first received. A charge that has been so amended shall not be required to be redeferred.

Rule 7. Pleadings Allowed; Form of Motions

(a) PLEADINGS. There shall be a complaint and an answer; a reply to a counterclaim denominated as such; an answer to a cross-claim, if the answer contains a cross-claim; a third-party complaint, if a person who was not an original party is summoned under the provisions of Rule 14; and a third-party answer, if a third-party complaint is served. No other pleading shall be allowed, except that the court may order a reply to an answer or a third-party answer.

(b) MOTIONS AND OTHER PAPERS.

(1) An application to the court for an order shall be by motion which, unless made during a hearing or trial, shall be made in writing, shall state with particularity the grounds therefor, and shall set forth the relief or order sought. The requirement of writing is fulfilled if the motion is stated in a written notice of the hearing of the motion.

(2) The rules applicable to captions and other matters of form of pleadings apply to all motions and other papers provided for by these rules.

(3) All motions shall be signed in accordance with Rule 11.

(c) DEMURRERS, PLEAS, ETC., ABOLISHED. Demurrers, pleas, and exceptions for insufficiency of a pleading shall not be used. (As amended Dec. 27, 1946, eff. Mar. 19, 1948; Jan. 21, 1963, eff. July 1, 1963; Apr. 28, 1983, eff. Aug. 1, 1983.)

Rule 15. Amended and Supplemental Pleadings

(a) AMENDMENTS. A party may amend the party's pleading once as a matter of course at any time before a responsive pleading is served or, if the pleading is one to which no responsive pleading is permitted and the action has not been placed upon the trial calendar, the party may so amend it at any time within 20 days after it is served. Otherwise a party may amend the party's pleading only by leave of court or by written consent of the adverse party; and leave shall be freely given when justice so requires. A party shall plead in response to an amended pleading within the time remaining for response to the original pleading or within 10 days after service of the amended pleading, whichever period may be the longer, unless the court otherwise orders.

Civil Rights
III. Discrimination in Particular Matters
E. Employment
4. Sexual Discrimination

§ 92. COMPLAINT, PETITION, OR DECLARATION—DISCRIMINATION IN EMPLOYMENT BASED ON SEX—DAMAGES FOR DISCRIMINATION, UNLAWFUL DISCHARGE, AND FRAUD

[Title of Court]

_____,	)
[Plaintiff, Petitioner],	)
v.	) No. _____
_____,	) [Designate name of document]
[Defendant, Respondent].	)

COMPLAINT

FIRST CAUSE OF ACTION

Discrimination

1. Plaintiff, _____ [name], is a resident of _____ County, _____ [state], residing at _____ [address], _____ [city], _____ [state].
2. Defendant, _____ [name of corporation], is a corporation duly organized and existing under the laws of _____ [state], engaged in the business of _____, with its principal place of business located at _____ [address], _____ [city], _____ County, _____ [state].
3. _____ [If applicable, set forth allegations regarding other defendants, and add that each defendant was the agent and employee of each of the other defendants and acted for all pertinent purposes within the scope and course of employment.]
4. The acts alleged took place primarily within _____ County, _____ [state], at _____ [specify location of where all or most of purported discriminatory acts took place].
5. On _____ [date], plaintiff filed a _____ [verified] complaint with _____ [specify pertinent state administrative agency], alleging that defendant had committed an unlawful employment practice against plaintiff in violation of _____ [cite statute] within the preceding _____ [period of time].
6. On _____ [date], _____ [administrative agency] issued plaintiff a right-to-sue letter informing plaintiff of the right to file suit against defendant within _____ [period of time]. On _____ [date], plaintiff informed _____ [administrative agency] that plaintiff had determined to file suit against defendant privately and requested that the accusation filed with _____ [administrative agency] be dismissed.

7. Plaintiff is a female, _____ years of age, born on _____ [date]. Plaintiff began working for defendant on _____ [date]. From plaintiff's hiring to _____ [date], she worked for defendant in numerous clerical positions. On _____ [date], plaintiff was promoted by defendant to _____ [specify position] at defendant's _____ [specify facility]. On _____ [date], plaintiff was again promoted by defendant to the position of _____ [specify] at _____ [location] and served in that position until _____ [date]. Plaintiff has worked competently and loyally for defendant throughout her _____ [number] years of employment.

8. As _____ [specify position], plaintiff was one of a group of _____ [specify job classification], _____ [number] men and _____ [number] women. On _____ [date], defendant decided to attempt a consolidation of _____ [specify job classifications] into a smaller number of offices. As the initial step in this process, defendant organized at _____ [location] a pilot program that would serve as a model for such consolidations.

9. To head the _____ [specify office] defendant promoted _____ [name of employee] from _____ [location]. _____ [Name of male employee], a man, is _____ [number] years of age and substantially less qualified for that position than plaintiff. _____ [Name of male employee] had _____ [number] years of experience with defendant. He started as a _____ [specify position], and was promoted to _____ [specify]. _____ [Set forth facts regarding any further promotions affecting employee.] By the time of _____ [male employee's] promotion to _____ [specify], plaintiff worked for defendant for _____ [number] years in _____ [specify] and had held the position of _____ [specify] for _____ [number] years. By _____ [date], plaintiff was not only substantially more experienced than _____ [name of male employee], but was more competent at _____ [specify managerial position].

10. In spite of this overwhelming difference in suitability for _____ [specify position], defendant entirely overlooked and rejected plaintiff for _____ [specify position]. _____ [Name of male employee] was placed in _____ [specify position], at a pay level and a benefit level substantially above plaintiff's.

11. _____ [If applicable, set forth any further facts supporting claim of defendant's promotion of other parties less qualified than plaintiff.]

12. _____ [If applicable, set forth any further facts supporting plaintiff's claim of promotion requests and defendant's refusal to promote and further facts supporting plaintiff's claim that promotion slots were filled with males with substantially less employment experience than plaintiff.]

13. Instead of a promotion to _____ [specify position], defendant offered plaintiff a position as a _____ [specify]. _____ [If applicable, add: At such time, defendant did offer plaintiff a _____% pay increase to accompany the move, but stated that her salary would be "red-circled," or frozen at the new level thereafter.]

14. _____ [If applicable, set forth any further facts supporting claim of defendant's general or systematic discriminatory pattern in favor of equivalently less

experienced and qualified males and against equivalently more experienced and qualified females.]

15. After plaintiff's service and qualifications were persistently ignored in favor of less able and qualified male employees, and after defendant informed plaintiff that she would not be considered for positions she was amply qualified for in favor of less qualified men, plaintiff found her position completely untenable and resigned on _____ [date].

16. The conduct of defendant, as set forth above, constitutes unlawful discrimination against plaintiff on the basis of sex, in violation of _____ [cite statute].

17. As a proximate result of defendant's conduct, plaintiff has suffered and continues to suffer substantial losses in earnings, job experience, retirement benefits, and other employee benefits that she would have received absent defendant's discrimination. Furthermore, plaintiff has incurred additional costs and expenses due to defendant's discrimination. Plaintiff does not know at this time the exact amount of her damages, but is informed and believes, and thereon alleges, that the amount of her loss will be $_____ or more. Plaintiff requests leave of the court to amend the _____ [complaint or petition or declaration] when these damages are more fully known.

18. As a further proximate result of the above-mentioned acts, plaintiff has suffered humiliation, mental pain and anguish, all to plaintiff's damage _____ [of $_____].

19. The above-mentioned acts of defendant were willful, wanton, malicious, and oppressive, and justify the awarding of exemplary and punitive damages _____ [of $_____].

SECOND CAUSE OF ACTION

Breach of Contract

20. Plaintiff refers to the allegations of Paragraphs 1 through 15 of the First Cause of Action, and by such reference repleads and incorporates them as though fully set forth here.

21. At all times relevant to this action, defendant has represented to employees in various writings, including but not limited to, personnel policies and procedure manuals, retirement and profit-sharing plan and employee guidelines, that their employment relationship with defendant would be based on good faith, that employees would be treated fairly and equitably, that employees would be judged on the basis of individual merit and ability, and that employees would receive just compensation for their services rendered to defendant. These provisions and representations form part of plaintiff's express employment contract with defendant.

22. Prior to plaintiff's constructive discharge by defendant on _____ [date], plaintiff had performed all conditions, covenants, promises, duties, and responsibilities required of her to be performed in accordance and in conformity with her employment contract.

23. On _____ [date], defendant breached plaintiff's contract and wrongfully failed to judge plaintiff on the basis of merit and ability, and wrongfully and without

cause forced plaintiff to resign by committing such deliberate actions that rendered plaintiff's working conditions intolerable.

24. As a result of defendant's breach of contract as mentioned above, plaintiff has suffered and will suffer damages in excess of the jurisdictional requirements of this court. Plaintiff requests leave to amend this _____ [complaint or petition or declaration] on learning the extent of the damages.

THIRD CAUSE OF ACTION

Breach of Implied Covenant of Good Faith and Fair Dealing

25. Plaintiff refers to the allegations of Paragraphs 1 through 15 of the First Cause of Action and Paragraphs 21 through 23 of the Second Cause of Action, and by reference repleads and incorporates them as though fully set forth here.

26. The above-described employment agreement has implied in law a covenant of good faith and fair dealing by which defendant promised to give full cooperation to plaintiff in her performance under the employment agreement and to refrain from any act that would prevent or impede plaintiff from performing all of the conditions of the agreement.

27. Beginning on approximately _____ [date], and culminating with defendant's constructive discharge of plaintiff on _____ [date], defendant breached its implied covenant of good faith and fair dealing with regard to plaintiff by:

(a) discriminatorily refusing to judge plaintiff on the basis of her ability and merit;

(b) refusing and failing to make available to her equal opportunity for promotion and advancement;

(c) failing and refusing to reconsider plaintiff's merit and ability for promotion or transfer;

(d) failing to give any consideration to plaintiff's long-term record of employment service;

(e) violating company procedures regarding job interviews for openings and transfers, including but not limited to, interviews of qualified candidates who have expressed a desire to be considered; and

(f) failing to consider fairly plaintiff for either _____ [specify position] or _____ [specify position] despite plaintiff's abundant qualifications and the impending elimination of plaintiff's present position by defendant, all with the object of denying plaintiff the opportunity to continue in _____ [specify position], forcing plaintiff to quit her employment, reducing salary costs, and avoiding its obligation to pay plaintiff employment and retirement benefits.

28. As a proximate cause of defendant's breach of the covenant of good faith and fair dealing, plaintiff has suffered and continues to suffer substantial losses in earnings, retirement benefits, and other employee benefits that she would have received had defendant not breached the agreement. _____ [If applicable, add: Plaintiff requests leave to amend this _____ (complaint or petition or declaration) on learning the extent of the damages.]

29. As a further proximate resulting of the above-mentioned acts, plaintiff has suffered humiliation, mental pain and anguish, all to plaintiff's damage _____ [of $_____].

30. The above-mentioned acts of defendant were willful, wanton, malicious, and oppressive, and justify the awarding of punitive and exemplary damages _____ [of $_____].

FOURTH CAUSE OF ACTION

Wrongful Discharge

31. Plaintiff realleges and incorporates by reference each allegation contained in Paragraphs 1 through 15 of the First Cause of Action, Paragraphs 21 and 23 of the Second Cause of Action, and Paragraphs 26 and 27 of the Third Cause of Action, and by reference repleads and incorporates them as though fully set forth here.

32. The above-described actions of defendant constitute a wrongful discharge entitling plaintiff to general, compensatory, and punitive damages.

FIFTH CAUSE OF ACTION

Intentional Infliction of Emotional Distress

33. Plaintiff realleges and incorporates by reference each allegation contained in Paragraphs 1 through 15 of the First Cause of Action, Paragraphs 21 and 23 of the Second Cause of Action, and Paragraphs 26 and 27 of the Third Cause of Action, and by reference repleads and incorporates them as though fully set forth here.

34. Defendant, in committing the above-described acts, intended to and did inflict severe emotional distress upon plaintiff. Defendant acted with a reckless disregard of the probability of causing emotional distress to plaintiff.

35. As a direct result of the outrageous acts and omissions, conduct, and discrimination, plaintiff became physically distraught and sustained shock to her nervous system and suffered severe emotional distress, all resulting in damages to her _____ [in excess of $_____].

SIXTH CAUSE OF ACTION

Fraud, Deceit, and Misrepresentation

36. Plaintiff realleges and incorporates by reference each allegation contained in Paragraphs 1 through 15 of the First Cause of Action, Paragraphs 21 and 23 of the Second Cause of Action, Paragraphs 26 and 27 of the Third Cause of Action, and Paragraph 34 of the Fifth Cause of Action, and by reference repleads and incorporates them as though fully set forth here.

37. Defendant made material misrepresentation of the fact that plaintiff be judged on the basis of merit and ability, and that plaintiff would be given an opportunity to inter-

view and be evaluated for all the positions opening up in the _____ [specify office].

38. Defendant concealed facts from plaintiff which defendant had an affirmative duty to disclose to the effect that defendant would not provide plaintiff with an opportunity to be evaluated on a nondiscriminatory basis for transfer or promotion.

39. Defendant held itself out as being situated so that plaintiff would reasonably rely on defendant. Defendant made the material misrepresentations and concealed facts with the knowledge of the falsity of the representations made, with the intent to induce plaintiff to rely on such representations. As a consequence, plaintiff reasonably relied on the fraudulent and material misrepresentations.

40. As a result of defendant's fraud, deceit, and misrepresentations as set forth above, plaintiff has suffered and will suffer damages in excess of the jurisdictional requirements of this court. _____ [If applicable, add: Plaintiff requests leave to amend this _____ (complaint or petition or declaration) on learning the extent of the damages.]

41. Defendant's fraudulent actions towards plaintiff were willful and intentional, and were made with the intent to vex, annoy, oppress, and injure plaintiff, and therefore plaintiff is entitled to punitive damages _____ [of $_____].

Wherefore, plaintiff requests judgment as follows:

On Second Cause of Action

1. Actual damages against defendant of $_____, with interest thereon from the date of judgment until paid.

On First, Third, Fourth, Fifth, and Sixth Causes of Action

1. Actual damages _____ [of $_____, or to be established at trial];

2. General and compensatory damages _____ [of $_____];

3. Punitive damages _____ [of $_____].

On all Causes of Action

1. Costs of suit;

2. Reasonable attorneys' fees; and

3. Such other and further relief as the court may deem just and equitable.

Dated: _____.

[Signature]

GLOSSARY

active date   Computer-generated records within a computer system that are in current use.

affidavit   A written statement sworn to before a person officially permitted by law to administer an oath.

affirm   1. Make firm; repeat agreement; confirm. 2. When a higher court declares that a lower court's action was valid and right, it *"affirms"* the decision.

affirmative defense   The part of a defendant's answer to a complaint that goes beyond denying the facts and arguments of the complaint. It sets out new facts and arguments that might win for the defendant even if everything in the complaint is true.

agent   A person authorized (requested or permitted) by another person to act for him or her; a person entrusted with another's business.

agent for service of process   Individual designated by a corporation who is authorized to be served with a lawsuit against the corporation.

allegation   A statement in a pleading that sets out a fact that the side filing the pleading expects to prove.

alternative dispute resolution (ADR)   Ways to resolve legal problems without a court decision; for example, arbitration, mediation, minitrial, rent-a-judge, summary jury trial, and so on.

amicus curiae (intervenor)   A person allowed to give argument or appear in a lawsuit (usually to file a brief, but sometimes to take an active part) who is not a party to the lawsuit.

answer   The first pleading by the defendant in a lawsuit. This pleading responds to the charges and demands of the plaintiff's complaint. The defendant may deny the plaintiff's charges, may present new facts to defeat them, or may show why the plaintiff's facts are legally invalid.

appeal   Asking a higher court to review the actions of a lower court in order to correct mistakes or injustice.

appellant   The person who appeals a case to a higher court.

appellant's brief   Brief of the person bringing an appeal.

appellate jurisdiction   The power and authority of a higher court to take up cases that have already been in a lower court and the power to make decisions about these cases. The process is called appellate review. Also, a trial court may have *appellate jurisdiction* over cases from an administrative agency.

appellee   The person against whom an appeal is taken.

appellee's brief   Brief of the person who opposes an appeal.

arbitration   Resolution of a dispute by a person (other than a judge) whose decision is binding. This person is called an *arbitrator*. Submission of the dispute for decision is often the result of an agreement (an *"arbitration clause"*) in a contract. If arbitration is required by law, it is called *"compulsory."*

arbitrator   The person who resolves a dispute in an arbitration hearing.

attachment   Formally seizing property (or a person) in order to bring it under the control of the court. This is usually done by getting a court order to have a law enforcement officer take control of the property.

attorney-client privilege   A privilege that belongs to the client in an attorney-client relationship that requires the attorney to treat all information revealed to him or her, or to anyone employed by the attorney, as confidential. Since the privilege belongs to the client rather than the attorney, only the client can give permission for the revelation of such confidential matters.

authorization   A signed statement empowering someone (such as a doctor or employer) to give out information that might otherwise be treated as confidential.

back-up data   Computer-generated records within computer system that are stored as a precautionary measure.

Bates numbering   The numbering of documents in a lawsuit using a machine.

brief   A written statement prepared by one side in a lawsuit to explain its case to the judge. It usually contains a fact summary, a law summary, and an argument about how the law applies to the facts. Most such "briefs" are not brief.

capacity   Legal ability to do something.

caption   The heading or introductory section of a legal paper. The caption of a court paper usually contains the names of the parties, the court, and the case number.

cause of action   1. Facts sufficient to support a valid lawsuit. 2. The legal theory upon which a lawsuit ("action") is based.

certiorari (Latin)   "To make sure." A request for certiorari (or "cert." for short) is like an appeal, but one which the higher court is not required to take for decision. It is literally a writ from the higher court asking the lower court for the record of the case. [pronounciation *sir*-sho-*rare*-ee]

character evidence   Testimony about a person's personal traits and habits that is drawn from the opinions of close associates, from the person's reputation in the community, or from the person's past actions.

chronological deposition summary   A written abridgement of a deposition which records the information produced by the deposition based upon specified temporal sequence.

circumstantial evidence   Facts that indirectly prove a main fact in question.

cite check   Looking at all the citations in a document to verify accuracy and proper form.

civil law   Laws dealing with private disputes between parties.

civil litigation   The process of resolving private disputes through the court system.

civil procedure   The laws and rules that govern how noncriminal lawsuits are handled by the individuals involved and by the court.

claim statute   A type of law that requires a written notice describing a claim to be presented to the defendant before a lawsuit can be filed.

class action   A lawsuit brought for yourself and other persons in the same situation.

common interest privilege   The rule that protects any communication that takes place between attorneys for different clients when those clients share a common interest.

compensatory damages   Damages awarded for the actual loss suffered by a plaintiff.

complaint   The first main paper filed in a civil lawsuit. It includes, among other things, a statement of the wrong or harm done to the plaintiff by the defendant, a request for specific help from the court, and an explanation why the court has the power to do what the plaintiff wants.

compound request   A request made by a party in a lawsuit to another party in that lawsuit to admit in a single statement the truthfulness of two or more facts.

compulsory counterclaim (counterclaim)   A counterclaim based on the same subject or transaction as the original claim.

compulsory examination   An examination that a party to a lawsuit has been ordered by the court to undergo concerning a physical or mental condition.

compulsory joinder (joinder)   A party or issue that must be included in a case.

computer   During the discovery process, the term *computer* includes desktop PCs, laptops, mobile phones, personal digital assistants (PDAs), and home computers that are part of a network.

concurrent jurisdiction (concurrent)   "Running together"; having the same authority; at the same time. For example, courts have concurrent jurisdiction when each one has the power to deal with the same case.

confessor-penitent privilege   A privilege designed to protect the confidentiality of any communication between an individual and his or her confessor when the relationship involves the spiritual support of the penitent. The privilege belongs to the penitent rather than the confessor. However, the law also protects the confessor who has taken a religious oath not to reveal the content of such counseling sessions.

confidentiality agreement   An agreement that is designed to protect confidential information, trade secrets, and other secret data from being revealed during the discovery process in a lawsuit.

conflict of interest   Being in a position where your own needs and desires could possibly lead you to violate your duty to a person who has a right to depend on you, or being in a position where you try to serve two competing masters or clients.

consent decree   A settlement of a lawsuit or prosecution in which a person or company agrees to take certain actions without admitting fault or guilt for the situation causing the lawsuit.

consideration   The reason or main cause for a person to make a contract; something of value received or promised to induce (convince) a person to make a deal. Without consideration a contract is not valid.

contingent fee   Payment to a lawyer of a percentage of the "winnings," if any, from a lawsuit rather than payment of a flat amount of money or payment according to the number of hours worked.

contribution   The right of a person who has paid an entire debt (or judgment) to get back a fair share of the payment from another person who is also responsible for the debt.

costs   Expenses of one side in a lawsuit that the judge orders the other side to pay or reimburse.

count   Each separate part of a complaint or an indictment.

counterclaim   A claim made by a defendant in a civil lawsuit that, in effect, "sues" the plaintiff.

court of appeals   A court that decides appeals from a trial court. In most states it is a middle-level court (similar to a United States Court of Appeals) but in some states it is the highest court.

court reporter   An individual who records word for word the testimony of sworn witnesses in court or at depositions and who may be required to compose a written transcript of that testimony.

criminal law   Having to do with the law of crimes and illegal conduct.

criminal procedure (criminal action)   The procedure by which a person accused of a crime is brought to trial and given punishment.

cross-appeal   An appeal by the appellee.

cross-claim   A claim brought by one defendant against another that is based on the same subject matter as the plaintiff's lawsuit.

curriculum vitae   A list of an expert's credentials, including each educational and professional credential, and a summary of publications and research projects.

damages   Money that a court orders paid to a person who has suffered damage (a loss or harm) by the person who caused the injury (the violation of the person's rights).

declaration   A statement under penalty of perjury that certain facts are true or believed to be true.

declaratory relief   A court order defining or explaining the rights and obligations of parties under some contract or other document.

deemed admitted   A principle which holds that an undenied request for admission is treated as if it were admitted.

default   Failure to take a required step in a lawsuit; for example, to file a paper on time. Such default can sometimes lead to a "*default* judgment" against the side failing to file the paper.

defendant   The person against whom a legal action is brought. This legal action may be civil or criminal.

demand for inspection   A discovery technique that involves a request to enter property to inspect that property to gain facts in relation to the lawsuit.

demeanor   Physical appearance and behavior. The demeanor of a witness is not what the witness says, but how the witness says it.

demonstrative evidence   All evidence other than testimony.

demurrer   A legal pleading that says, in effect, "even if, for the sake of argument, the facts presented by the other side are correct, those facts do not give the other side a legal argument that can possibly stand up in court." The demurrer has been replaced in many courts by a motion to dismiss.

deponent   An individual who responds to questions during a deposition.

deposition   An out-of-court question-and-answer session under oath, conducted in advance of a lawsuit, as a part of the discovery process. A deposition can be taken from a party to the lawsuit or from a witness who is not a party but who is believed to possess knowledge pertaining to the suit.

deposition summary   A written abridgement of a deposition which condenses the question-and-answer period down to a concisely written, understandable account.

deposition upon written questions   A deposition before a court reporter, which consists of oral responses by the deponent to written questions.

direct evidence   Proof of a fact without the need for other facts leading up to it. For example, direct evidence that dodos are not extinct would be a live dodo.

disclosure   The process of revealing some information that was previously unknown or difficult to comprehend.

discovery   The procedure that the parties to a lawsuit follow in order to uncover the facts that are involved in the suit. Generally, the system involves an exchange of information among the parties using certain established discovery techniques including depositions, interrogatories, requests for real evidence, requests for physical and mental examinations, and requests for admissions.

dismissal with prejudice   A court order or judgment that ends a lawsuit. No further lawsuit may be brought by the same persons on the same subject.

dismissal without prejudice   A court order or judgment that ends a lawsuit. A further lawsuit may be brought by the same persons on the same subject.

diversity of citizenship   The situation that occurs when persons on one side of a case in federal court come from a different state than persons on the other side. *Complete diversity* (all of the plaintiffs are from a different state than all the defendants) allows the court to accept and decide the case based on the court's diversity jurisdiction, provided that certain other criteria are met. Diversity of citizenship also applies to suits between citizens and foreign nationals.

docket number   A number assigned to a lawsuit by the court; each pleading or document filed in the action must bear this number.

document   An artifact that contains written matter, such as words or figures, in the form of a message or record.

document-production log   A method of keeping track of documents in a lawsuit by categorizing those documents based on source and file location. The document-production log should also indicate whether the documents have been excluded as privileged.

duplicative   A term that describes a request made during discovery that replicates a request that was made at some previous time during the lawsuit.

e-discovery (also electronic discovery and digital discovery)   A series of techniques and tools that involves the use of a wide variety of electronic resources to conduct discovery in an efficient and economical way.

e-evidence   Computer-generated records such as those found in e-mail files, databases, calendaring programs, and all other relevant data files created by spreadsheets, word processing, or any analogous program.

engrossment (or engrossing)   The process of creating the final form of a document just before that document is used in a formal setting.

entry of default   Action by a court clerk noting that the defendant has failed to file a proper response to the complaint.

equitable relief (equitable)   Just, fair, and right for a particular situation.

evidence log   A document attached to an item of physical evidence recording the chain of possession (chain of custody) of that piece of evidence.

ex parte   With only one side present.

exclusive jurisdiction (exclusive)   If a court has exclusive jurisdiction over a subject, no other court in the area can decide a lawsuit on that subject.

execution   An official carrying out of a court's order or judgment. For example, a writ of execution orders a court official to take a debtor's property to pay court-decided debt, usually by holding an execution sale.

expert witness   A person possessing special knowledge or experience who is allowed to testify at a trial not only about facts (like an ordinary witness) but also about the professional conclusions he or she draws from these facts.

extant data   Computer-generated records within a computer system that are hidden in the system, generally because they have been deleted.

fictitiously named defendants   Defendants in a lawsuit who are not identified by their correct names; usually refers to the practice in some state courts of including several "Does" as defendants to provide for discovery of additional defendants after the statute of limitations has run.

filing (file)   Giving a paper to the court clerk for inclusion in the case record.

flat fee   A legal fee based on a fixed sum rather than on an hourly rate or a percentage of a recovery.

form books   Books containing sample forms for legal professionals to follow in preparing pleadings and other documents.

garnishee   A person who holds money or property belonging to a debtor and who is subject to a garnishment.

garnishment   A legal process, taken by a creditor who has received a money judgment against a debtor, to get the debtor's money. This is done by attachment of a bank account or by taking a percentage of the debtor's regular income.

general appearance   Coming before a court and submitting to its jurisdiction in a case.

general denial   A type of answer in which all of the allegations of the complaint are denied.

general jurisdiction   The power of a court to hear and decide any of a wide range of cases that arise within its geographic area.

general release   A document by which a claim or right is relinquished.

good cause   A legally acceptable reason for doing something or for refusing to do something.

guardian ad litem   A guardian who is appointed by a court to take care of the interests of a person who cannot legally take care of himself or herself in a lawsuit involving that person.

habit   The way a person usually responds to a particular situation.

hearsay   A statement about what someone else said (or wrote or otherwise communicated). Hearsay evidence is evidence concerning what someone said outside of a court proceeding that is offered in the proceeding to prove the truth of what was said.

higher court   Court of appeals.

hourly billing   A legal fee based on a fixed amount for each hour the law firm spends on the case.

in camera   A term that describes a hearing or other proceeding that is held in the judge's private chambers out of the sight and hearing of any spectators; in private; in chambers.

in controversy   In the case of a physical or mental examination, the prerequisite that the condition to be examined must be at issue in the lawsuit.

in rem jurisdiction   The authority of a court to hear a case based on the fact that property, which is the subject of a lawsuit, is located within the state in which the court is situated.

indemnification   A concept allowing one defendant, who has paid a judgment, to seek reimbursement from another defendant.

indispensable party   A person who has such a stake in the outcome of a lawsuit that the judge will not make a final decision unless that person is formally joined as a party to the lawsuit.

inactive data   Computer-generated records within a computer system that are relatively up-to-date but are not used on a routine basis.

information technology (IT) experts   Individuals who are trained and experienced in the operation of computer systems and in preserving and retrieving computer-based data.

injunction   A judge's order to a person to do or to refrain from doing a particular thing.

interpleader   A procedure in which persons having conflicting claims against a third person may be forced to resolve the conflict before seeking relief from the third person.

interrogatories   Written questions delivered, as part of the overall discovery process, by one party in a lawsuit to another party in the same lawsuit, requiring the second party to provide written responses to those interrogatories.

judgment   The official decision of a court about the rights and claims of each side in a lawsuit. "*Judgment*" usually refers to a final decision that is based on the facts of the case and made at the end of a trial. It is called a *judgment on the merits.*

judgment creditor   A person who has proven a debt in court and is entitled to use court processes to collect it.

judgment debtor   A person who has yet to satisfy a judgment that has been rendered against him or her.

judicial admission   A statement or other piece of evidence that has been admitted and which can, therefore, be introduced during the trial.

judicial notice   The act of a judge in recognizing the existence or truth of certain facts without bothering to make one side in a lawsuit prove them. This is done when the facts are either common knowledge and undisputed or are easily found and cannot be disputed.

jurisdiction   1. The geographical area within which a court (or a public official) has the right and power to operate. 2. The persons about whom and the subject matters about which a court has the right and power to make decisions that are legally binding.

jury instructions   Directions given to the jury by the judge just before he or she sends the jurors out to deliberate and return a verdict, explaining the law that applies in the case and spelling out what must be proven and by whom.

laches   The legal doctrine that a delay (in pursuing or enforcing a claim or right) can be so long that the person against whom you are proceeding is unfairly hurt or prejudiced by the delay itself. Laches is an equitable defense, used when a plaintiff delays unfairly in starting a lawsuit.

leading question   A question that shows a witness how to answer it or suggests the preferred answer.

legal error   A mistake in the way the law is interpreted or applied to a situation.

limited jurisdiction   Authority to hear only certain kinds of cases.

local rules of court   Rules that are adopted by individual courts and apply only in those courts.

long-arm statutes   A state law that allows the courts of that state to claim jurisdiction over (decide cases directly involving) persons outside the state who have allegedly committed torts or other wrongs inside the state. Even with a long-arm statute, the court will not have jurisdiction unless the person sued has certain minimum contacts with the state.

lower court   Another term for a trial court.

mediation   Outside help in settling a dispute. The person who does this is called a *mediator*. This is different from arbitration in that a mediator can only persuade, not force, people into a settlement.

mediator   The person who helps settle a dispute through mediation.

medical diary   A document in which the client keeps track of medical treatment, daily health complaints, type and amount of medication, mileage to physicians' offices, and other related medical expenses.

medical privilege   The medical privilege exists between a patient and a medical practitioner and is designed to protect the patient's confidential communication with the practitioner. The privilege covers communication made between the patient and physicians, psychiatrists, podiatrists, psychologists, and dentists.

memorandum of points and authorities   A legal argument in the form of a discussion or analysis of the law that applies to the case.

mock deposition   A practice session that attempts to duplicate the question-and-answer period that will occur during a real deposition. The objective of a mock deposition is to help the party or witness rehearse for an upcoming deposition.

mock jury   A group of independent individuals chosen to reflect the probable makeup of the actual jury.

mock trial   A practice trial prior to the date of the actual trial, intended to reveal the strengths and weaknesses of a party's case.

more definite statement (motion)   A request that the judge require an opponent in a lawsuit to file a less-vague or less-ambiguous pleading.

motion   A request that a judge make a ruling or take some other action. Motions are either *granted* or *denied* by the judge.

motion for a directed verdict   A motion made during a jury trial, requesting that the judge tell the jury how they should decide the case.

motion for a judgment notwithstanding the verdict   A motion asking the court to have the verdict and its judgment set aside because a group of reasonable individuals would not have reached such a verdict and the jury's decision is wrong as a matter of law.

motion for a new trial   A motion made after a trial requesting that the judge set aside the verdict or judgment and grant a new trial to the parties.

motion for a protective order   A motion made during discovery asking the court to limit a discovery request.

motion for change of venue   A request from a party that the court transfer the case to a proper court.

motion for enlargement of time   A motion requesting additional time for an appeal, including the reasons that the additional time is needed and the number of additional days required.

motion for involuntary dismissal   A motion requesting dismissal of a lawsuit by the court, either prior to judgment or by virtue of a judgment against the plaintiff based upon the verdict of the jury or the decision of the court after trial.

motion for judgment on the pleadings   A motion claiming that the allegations in the pleadings are such that no controversial issues remain and that judgment can be entered for only one party.

motion for mistrial   A motion asking that the judge terminate a trial prior to its conclusion because the jury is unable to reach a verdict, because of prejudicial error that cannot be corrected or eliminated by any action the court might take, or because of the occurrence of some event that would make it pointless to continue.

motion for more definite statement   A motion made in response to a complaint in which the defendant challenges the clarity or specificity of the complaint.

motion for relief from judgment or order   A request to the court by one party that the court set aside any judgment, order, or proceeding.

motion for sanctions   A request to the court from one party that penalties be imposed on the other party for violating the provisions of Rule 11 of the Federal Rules of Civil Procedure.

motion for summary judgment   A motion requesting that judgment be entered immediately because there are no disputed factual issues in the case.

motion in limine   A motion or request made of the court, usually at the start of a trial and outside the presence of the jury.

motion to amend   A request by one party to the court to allow a change in the content of a pleading.

motion to compel   A request by one party to the court for an order requiring the other side to comply with a discovery request.

motion to dismiss   A request that the court dismiss or strike the case.

motion to quash service of summons   A request that the court declare that service of the complaint and summons is invalid, either because the court lacks jurisdiction over the defendant or because of some procedural problem with the service itself.

motion to quash the return of the service   Motion made by a defendant who claims that he was improperly served with the summons and complaint.

motion to strike   A request made to the court to delete part or all of a pleading; can also refer to a request made during trial to delete testimony.

motion to tax costs   A motion made after trial challenging the costs of suit that are claimed by the prevailing party.

movant   Person who makes a motion.

mutual release   An agreement by which each party relinquishes its claims against the other.

negotiation (negotiate)   1. Discuss, arrange, or bargain about a business deal. 2. Discuss a compromise to a situation.

nonresponsive documents   Documents that need not be presented to a party in answer to a request from that party for the production of those documents.

notice   A formal notification of intent; the knowledge of a particular set of facts; the formal acquisition of the knowledge of a fact or set of facts.

notice of appeal   The process by which appellate review is initiated; specifically, written notice to the appellee advising him or her of the appellant's intention to appeal.

notice of hearing on the motion   The part of a written motion that describes the nature of the motion being made and tells when and where a hearing on the motion will occur.

notice of intent to take deposition upon written questions   A notice spelling out the date, time, and place of a planned deposition upon written questions. The notice will also indicate the name and address of the intended deponent as well as the identity of the officer who will attend the deposition. A subpoena must accompany any such notice served upon a nonparty to the lawsuit.

notice of intent to take oral deposition   A notice spelling out the date, time, and place of a planned deposition. The notice will also indicate the name and address of the intended deponent as well as the identity of the attorney who will ask the questions during the deposition.

notice of intent to take oral deposition by nonstenographic means   A notice sent to opposing counsel of an intent to take a deposition after the judgment by use of only a dictating machine or a tape recorder, with no court reporter present.

on point   A law or prior case that directly applies to the facts of the present case.

open stipulation   An agreement between parties or their attorneys that a defendant need not answer a complaint within the time directed by law and need not answer until specifically notified by the plaintiff to do so.

opening statement   The introductory statements made at the start of a trial by lawyers for each side. The lawyers typically explain the version of the facts best supporting their side of the case, how these facts will be proved, and how they think the law applies to the case.

oral argument   The presentation of each side of a case before an appeals court. The presentation typically involves oral statements by a lawyer, interrupted by questions from the judge.

oral deposition   A deposition which involves the actual presence of the deponent who responds aloud to the questions asked by an attorney.

order   A written command or direction given by a judge.

order shortening time   A ruling from the court, often in connection with motions, allowing a moving party to give less notice of a hearing on a motion than is required by statute.

original jurisdiction   The power of a court to take a case, try it, and decide it (as opposed to *appellate jurisdiction,* the power of a court to hear and decide an appeal).

overbroad   A term that describes a request made during discovery that is so wide ranging and inclusive that it asks for more evidence than could ever be useful to the other party in the lawsuit.

page-line deposition summary   A written abridgement of a deposition which records the information produced by the deposition in the order in which it was actually presented during the deposition process.

paper data   Electronic data that has been reduced to a hard copy for filing purposes as a safeguard against the loss of that e-data due to the breakdown of the computer system.

partial release   The relinquishment of some claims and the retention of others by a party.

peremptory challenges   The automatic elimination of a potential juror by one side before trial without needing to state the reason for the elimination. Each side has the right to a certain number of peremptory challenges.

permissive counterclaim (counterclaim)   A claim made by a defendant in a civil lawsuit that, in effect, "sues" the plaintiff, based on entirely different things from the plaintiff's complaint.

permissive joinder   A concept allowing multiple parties to be joined in one lawsuit as plaintiffs or defendants as long as there is some common question of fact or law.

personal jurisdiction   The power or authority of the court to make a ruling affecting the parties before the court.

personal service of process   Notice of a lawsuit or other proceeding, which is given to a party by personally delivering a copy of the papers to that party.

petition   A written request to a court that it take a particular action. In some states the word is limited to written requests made when there is no other side in a case; and in some states, "*petition*" is used in place of "*complaint*" (the first pleading in a lawsuit).

petition for certiorari   A request to a higher court for review, but which the higher court is not required to take for decision.

petition for rehearing   A request to reconsider an action that may have been wrongly taken or overlooked in a previous hearing.

physical or mental examination   An examination that a party to a lawsuit must undergo concerning a physical or mental condition that is at issue in a pending legal action.

plaintiff   A person who brings (starts) a lawsuit against another person.

pleadings   Formal, written statements of each side of a civil case.

postjudgment deposition   A deposition that can be taken after judgment, with only a dictating machine or a tape recorder, with no court reporter present.

postjudgment interrogatories   Written questions that the judgment debtor must answer in writing about his or her assets.

posttrial garnishment   A separate, but ancillary, lawsuit, filed in the court that rendered the judgment, to permit the judgment creditor to collect on a judgment.

prayer   Request. That part of a legal pleading (such as a complaint) that asks for relief (help, money, specific court action, an action from the other side, etc.).

preliminary injunction   A court order made prior to final judgment in the case, directing that a party take some action or refrain from taking some action until the trial in the case takes place.

presumption   A conclusion or inference drawn. A presumption of law is an automatic assumption required by law that whenever a certain set of facts shows up, a court must automatically draw certain legal conclusions.

pretrial conference   A conference that is designed to make the process of conducting a lawsuit as efficient, simple, economical, and fair as possible. The process may involve a simplification of the pleadings, a limitation on the witnesses to be called at trial, a narrowing of the issues to be considered at trial, a simplification of the discovery process, and so on.

primary sources   Books that contain the actual law (e.g., case reporters, codes, constitutions).

privilege against self-incrimination   A privilege granted by the Fifth Amendment to the United States Constitution that prevents a criminal defendant from being forced to testify against himself or herself.

privilege log   A method of keeping track of documents that are shielded by the attorney-client privilege, the work product privilege, the medical privilege, the confessor/penitent privilege, or the common interest privilege.

privileged documents   Documents that are shielded by the attorney-client privilege, the work product privilege, the medical privilege, the confessor/penitent privilege, or the common interest privilege.

procedural law   The rules of carrying on a civil lawsuit or a criminal case (how to enforce rights in court) as opposed to substantive law (the law of the rights and duties themselves).

proof of service   Written verification that papers have been delivered to a party, detailing when, where, and how the papers were delivered.

proof of service by mail (certificate of mailing)   Verification that a pleading, motion, or other document has been served by mailing a copy of the document to another party or attorney.

protective order   An order that is issued by the court in a lawsuit that protects a party in the suit from revealing information, documents, data, or other types of evidence to another party who has previously requested the production of that evidence.

punitive or exemplary damages (damages)   Extra money given to punish the defendant and to help keep a particularly bad act from happening again.

qualified denial   A type of answer denying all of the allegations of the complaint except those that are specifically admitted.

quasi in rem jurisdiction   Authority of a court to hear a case based on the fact that the defendant owns property that is located within the state, even though that property is not the subject of the lawsuit.

quiet title action   A way of establishing clear ownership of land.

real party in interest   The person who will ultimately benefit from winning a lawsuit, whether or not that person brought it initially.

rebuttal evidence   Formal contradiction of statements made by an adversary.

redaction   A procedure that involves removing information from a document before duplicating the document and turning the duplicate over to another party in a lawsuit in response to a request for production. The removal is justified because the information is immaterial or privileged.

rehearing   A new hearing to reconsider an action that may have been wrongfully taken or overlooked in a prior hearing.

release   A document by which a claim or right is relinquished.

relevant evidence   Evidence that tends to prove or disprove a fact that is important to a claim, charge, or defense in a court case.

remand   Send back. For example, a higher court may remand (send back) a case to the lower court, directing the lower court to take some action.

removal   The transfer of a case from one court to another (most commonly, from a state to a federal court, often for civil rights reasons).

reply   In federal pleading, the plaintiff's response to the defendant's answer or counterclaim.

representation letter   A letter from an attorney to a new client establishing the ground rules of the litigation, including fees, billing rates, retainer, and work to be performed by the law firm.

request for a physical or mental examination   A request made by one party in a lawsuit to another party in that lawsuit to undergo a physical or mental examination provided that the examination in question involves a condition that is at issue in the pending action.

request for admission   A request made by a party in a lawsuit to another party in that lawsuit to admit to the truthfulness of a fact or the genuineness of a piece of evidence such as a written contract, a memo, or some other physical item.

request for documents   A request that a party or other individual involved in a lawsuit provide specific documents or other physical evidence to the party making the request for such documents or physical evidence.

request for the production of documents and entry upon land for inspection   A request that a party or other individual involved in a lawsuit provide specific documents or other physical evidence to the party making the request for such documents or physical evidence. This discovery technique can also involve a request to enter land to inspect that land to gain facts in relation to the lawsuit.

rescission   The annulment of a contract.

responsive documents   Documents that must be presented to a party in answer to a request from that party for the production of those documents.

restitution   Giving something back; making good for something.

retainer   1. Employment of a lawyer by a client. 2. The specific agreement in definition no. 1.

retainer agreement   An agreement between an attorney and a client setting forth the fee arrangement.

reverse   Set aside. For example, when a higher court reverses a lower court on appeal, it sets aside the judgment of the lower court and either substitutes its own judgment for it or sends the case back to the lower court with instructions on what to do with it.

Rules of Professional Conduct   American Bar Association rules stating and explaining what lawyers must do, must not do, should do, and should not do. They cover the field of legal ethics.

secondary sources   1. Persuasive authority. 2. Writings about the law, such as articles, treatises, and encyclopedias.

service of process   The delivery (or its legal equivalent, such as publication in a newspaper in some cases) of a legal paper, such as a writ, by an authorized person in a way that meets certain formal requirements. It is the way to notify a person of a lawsuit.

settlement (settle)   To come to an agreement about a price, debt, payment of a debt, or disposition of a lawsuit.

settlement agreement   A contract between two or more parties to settle a case; it involves the voluntary, mutual assent of the parties and the give-and-take element of consideration. The agreement must be legal and must be made by parties with the capacity to contract.

settlement brochure   A summary of facts designed to get the other side to settle a case.

settlement letter   A detailed account of the information needed to determine the benefit of settling a case.

settlement summary   A summary of all essential information outlining the benefits of settling the case at an early stage in the litigation.

shadow jury   A group of persons (selected to be similar to the real jurors) paid by one side in a lawsuit to observe the trial and give their reactions.

special appearance   Showing up in court for a limited purpose only, especially to argue that the court lacks jurisdiction over you or your client. *Special appearances* have been replaced in federal courts and many state courts by motions or pleadings for the same purpose.

specific denial   A type of answer in which the defendant specifically replies to each of the contentions alleged in the complaint.

specific performance (performance)   Being required to do exactly what was agreed to.

statute of limitations (limitation)   A time limit. For example, a statute of limitations is a law that sets a maximum amount of time after something happens for it to be taken to court.

stipulation   An agreement between lawyers on opposite sides of a lawsuit.

subject matter jurisdiction   The authority that a court has to hear a particular type of case.

subpoena   A written order issued by a court or an administrative agency commanding the presence of a person in order for that person to give testimony in an official proceeding. The word *subpoena* is an abbreviated form of the Latin term *subpoena ad testificandum*.

subpoena duces tecum   A written order issued by a court or an administrative agency commanding the presence of a person in order for that person to give testimony and to surrender the evidence that is enumerated in the subpoena. Generally, such evidence takes the form of documents, records, letters, memos, and so on.

subscription (subscribe)   Sign a document.

substantive law   The basic law of rights and duties (contract law, criminal law, accident law, law of wills, etc.) as opposed to procedural law (law of pleading, law of evidence, law of jurisdiction, etc.)

summons   A notice delivered by a sheriff or other authorized person informing a person of a lawsuit against him or her.

supersedeas   A judge's order that temporarily holds up another court's proceedings or, more often, temporarily stays a lower court's judgment.

supersedeas bond   A bond put up by a person who appeals a judgment. The bond delays the person's obligation to pay the judgment until the appeal is lost.

supplemental jurisdiction   A federal court's right to decide a claim based on a nonfederal issue if this claim depends on the same set of facts as does a federal claim in the case before the court.

supreme court   The highest of the United States courts and the highest court of most, but not all, of the states.

temporary restraining order (TRO)   A judge's order to a person to not take a certain action during the period prior to a full hearing on the rightfulness of the action.

third-party complaint   A complaint brought by a defendant in a lawsuit against someone not in the lawsuit.

tickler system   A calendaring system.

topical deposition summary   A written abridgement of a deposition which records the information produced by the deposition according to certain designated topics.

transcript   A typed or word-processed copy of the testimony of a witness produced by a court reporter following the oral testimony of the witness at trial or at a deposition; an official record of the proceedings of a court.

trial   The process of deciding a case (giving evidence, making arguments, deciding by a judge and jury, etc.). It occurs if the dispute is not resolved by pleadings, pretrial motions, or settlement. A trial usually takes place in open court, and may be followed by a judgment, an appeal, and so on.

trial brief   A document prepared by a lawyer to use at trial. It usually contains lists of witnesses, evidence, and citations as well as arguments to be presented.

trial court   A court where the parties to a lawsuit file their pleadings and present evidence to a judge or jury.

trial notebook   A binder that contains, in complete or summary form, everything necessary to prosecute or defend a case.

trust account (trust deposit)   Money or property put in a bank to be kept separate (often for ethical or legal reasons) or used for a special purpose.

unduly burdensome   A term that describes a set of interrogatories made during discovery that is so complex and detailed that it will require the party answering the interrogatories to spend excessive time, effort, and expense, and which will result in a burden on that party that far exceeds any benefit gained by the opposing party.

venue   The local area where a case may be tried. Court systems may have jurisdiction (power) to take a case in a wide geographic area, but the proper *venue* for the case may be one place within that area for the convenience of the parties or other reasons. Jurisdiction is the subject of fixed rules, but venue is often left up to the discretion (good judgment) of the judge.

verification (verify)   Swear in writing to the truth or accuracy of a document.

voir dire examination   The preliminary in-court questioning of a prospective witness (or juror) to determining competency (or suitability) to decide a case.

video conference   An electronic conference set-up that permits several individuals at widely separated geographical locations to discuss the planning of the case. The video set-up generally requires the use of television cameras, microphones, monitors, and a speaker system at each location.

Web conference   An electronic conference set-up that permits individuals at separate locations to meet on line via the Internet using personal computers.

work product privilege   A privilege that protects any information prepared by an attorney in a lawsuit, if that information is prepared by the attorney or anyone employed by the attorney, in anticipation of litigation or to present at trial.

writ   A judge's order requiring that something be done outside the courtroom or authorizing it to be done.

writ of execution   A document that orders a court official to take a debtor's property to pay a court-decided debt.

INDEX